201745584

A Moment in Time

Veronica Lucan

Copyright © 7th Countess of Lucan

Mango Books

WEST SUSSEX LIBRARY SERVICE	
201745584	
Askews & Holts	18-Dec-2017
B LUC	

First edition published 2017

Copyright © 7th Countess of Lucan, 2017

The right of Veronica, 7th Countess of Lucan to be identified as the author of this work has been asserted in accordance with the Copyright, Designs & Patents Act 1988.

All rights reserved. No part of this book may be reprinted or reproduced or utilised in any form or by any electronic, mechanical or other means, now known or hereafter invented, including photocopying and recording, or in any information storage or retrieval system, without the prior permission in writing of the publishers.

ISBN: 978-1-911273-24-0 (hardcover)
ISBN: 978-1-911273-26-4 (ebook)

All photographs from the private albums of
Veronica, 7th Countess of Lucan
Copyright © The Estate of 7th Countess of Lucan, 2017

Published by Mango Books
www.mangobooks.co.uk

18 Soho Square
London W1D 3QL

A Moment in Time

A Moment in Time

1   The Beginning 1
2   Early Life 30
3   Courtship 47
4   Introductions 55
5   Marriage 62
6   Frances 73
7   George 84
8   Otto 88
9   Horses 93
10   Fire Auto Marine 96
11   Greville 99
12   Doctors 102
13   Camilla 113
14   Dally Flood 117
15   Mews House 127
16   Jenkins Sacked 129
17   Christmas Gubbs 133
18   Flood Acapulco 136
19   After Kidnap 149
20   Jobbins 167
21   Dublin 172
22   Arthur Jones 177
23   Pierrette 189
24   Sandra 193
25   Attack 201
26   Inquest 208
27   Inquest Continued 226
28   Coroner 244
29   Imbroglio 250
30   Imbroglio Continued 258
31   Conspiracy 264
32   In Conclusion 276

Index 279

1
The Beginning

Major
The Lord Bingham M.C.
15 Montagu Square

BUCKINGHAM PALACE

19th December 1934

My dear Bingham,
   I am desired by The Queen to tell you how delighted Her Majesty is to hear of the birth of your son. The Queen earnestly trusts that all goes very well with Kaitilin and your boy, and hopes that he will ever be a great happiness to his mother and to you and to all to whom he will be so dear.

Yrs ever
Harry Verney

*

Her Majesty Queen Mary's hopes and good wishes could hardly have been more opposite to that which actually happened. Few sons starting, on the face of it, with so many advantages in life, could have become the cause of such great unhappiness to all to whom he was so dear and I will attempt to show how all this might have come about.

His father was George Charles Patrick, 6th Earl of Lucan M.C., born in 1898, a soldier by profession who succeeded in 1949 and died on 21st January 1964. His mother, born in 1900, was Kaitilin Elizabeth Anne Dawson, heiress and only daughter of Capt. The Hon Edward Dawson R.N., second son of 1st Earl Dartrey, who married in 1898 Lady Elizabeth Selina Meade (d. 1924), daughter of 4th Earl of Clanwilliam.

Kaitilin's grandfather was 1st Earl of Dartrey. The Clanwilliam's family name is Meade, and the Earl of Dartrey's family name was Dawson. The earldom became extinct in 1933 because of the lack of a male heir.

The 5th Earl of Lucan married Violet Sylvia Blanche Spender Clay OBE who described her own family as 'gentry'. "We were gentry," she used to say when my husband and I had luncheon with her after our marriage.

I don't think my mother-in-law doted on my husband - in fact I think she was pulling the rug from underneath his feet with her socialist views.

I did not know his father for very long, but I think he might have been rather a weak man - I have read of him being described as 'gentle shepherd', referring to his time as Chief Opposition Whip, House of Lords 1954-1964. I believe it was Lord Longford who said this. However, one evening I sat next to a man at dinner who regaled me the entire meal with his dislike of my father-in-law and how he had achieved undeserved preferment during his army career.

My husband was sent to America during the war to live with a fabulously rich family called Tucker, and Mrs Tucker was known as Aunt Marcia. He returned after the War to live at number 22 Eaton Square.

Violet Spender Clay was brought in as an 18-year-old heiress to shore up the finances of the future 5th Earl of Lucan (born in 1860), George Charles, Lord Bingham (GCVO, KBE etc), whose own father's extravagance was bringing the family to bankruptcy. His father, the 4th Earl (George KP), born in 1830, married in 1859 Lady Cecilia

The Beginning

Catherine Gordon-Lennox, daughter of the 5th Duke of Richmond. This alliance was not approved by the Duke, as he considered the then Lord Bingham's character and financial position were not satisfactory.

The marriage went ahead despite these objections and the Duke's fears were well founded. The 4th Earl's inability to live within his income was such that the grocer at Castlebar was demanding £400 for unpaid bills, and the Earl hadn't the funds with which to pay. Violet found to her great alarm that her money was being used to finance the rather objectionable old 4th Earl (whose own father - the 3rd Earl - was involved in the Charge of the Light Brigade) to prevent the disgrace of bankruptcy. It so alarmed the young Binghams that ever after they were too afraid to invest or speculate and put their money into "safe" things like gilt edged stock, and their money, too, dwindled, but in a less dramatic fashion. "If only we had been better advised," she used to say to us sadly. Violet thought that the estate was being handled in an incompetent manner, but she was too much in awe of an aristocratic husband twice her age to say so. Indeed, early on in their marriage he rattled his newspaper while she was playing the piano and she interpreted this as having annoyed him, and she never played again.

In 1829, Lady Anne Brudenell, sister of the future 7th Earl of Cardigan, married George Charles Lord Bingham, eldest son of the 2nd Earl of Lucan. Both these men were soldiers by profession. The 3rd Earl of Lucan was partially to blame for the loss of the Light Brigade because of his bad relationship with his brother-in-law Lord Cardigan.

The order for the Charge was given by Lord Raglan and was open to misinterpretation, but if the brothers-in-law had been on good terms and were able to discuss the order, the tragedy might have been avoided. Lord Lucan wrote a letter airing his grievance against a senior officer, Lord Raglan hoping it would be published with Lord Raglan's despatch. The letter would go to the Secretary for War, the Duke of Newcastle. The rules of the service laid down that such a letter must be transmitted through the Commander in Chief and Lord

Lucan addressed a letter to Lord Raglan. He stressed the ambiguous wording of Lord Raglan's last two orders, the impossibility of disobeying an order. He wrote: "I cannot remain silent. It is, I feel, incumbent on me to state those facts which I cannot doubt, must clear me from what, I respectfully submit, is altogether unmerited."

The Earl of Lucan was recalled. The Duke of Newcastle officially communicated to Lord Raglan the inevitable consequence of Lord Lucan's letter. Lord Lucan, by writing this letter, had placed himself in a position towards Lord Raglan rendering his withdrawal from the army in Lord Raglan's command in all respects advisable.

On 14th February, Lord Lucan left the Crimea. Lord Cardigan had preceded him some weeks earlier, but he came home a hero. On 1st March Lord Lucan arrived in England and at once sent his son, Lord Bingham, to the Commander in Chief, Lord Hardinge, to demand a court martial, which was refused. On 2nd March, Lord Lucan addressed the House of Lords on the subject of his recall, and again on the 6th and the 9th. On 5th March he sent another demand for a court martial. It, too, was refused.

On 19th March Lord Lucan once more addressed the House of Lords at great length on his recall and his being refused a court martial, and a debate followed. The House was against him. No motion was brought forward to support his application for a court martial. He had not succeeded. Lord Lucan's unpopularity was now great, and when he was made KCB (Knight Commander of the Bath) and, in November 1855, Colonel of the 8th Hussars, *The Times* wrote scathingly of the appointment. Again, he wrote angry letters which *The Times* willingly published.

Lord Lucan survived Lord Cardigan by 20 years. He had the consolation of military honours; he was promoted General, made Gold Stick and Colonel of the 1st Life Guards; in 1865, made GCB (Grand Cross of the Bath) in 1869, and finally promoted to Field-Marshal in 1887.[1] I have recently read that correspondence has come to light which shows that it was Captain Nolan who brought Lord

---

1 My husband always used to refer to him as The Field Marshal.

Raglan's order to Lord Lucan, at the same time saying untruthfully that Lord Raglan had said "Attack" when in fact he had said only that he should make a show of force. If Captain Nolan had not been killed shortly afterwards, he would have been court martialled.

His most important act in 1858 was to remove the disabilities of Jews in taking the Parliamentary Oath. Orthodox Jews were unable to sit as Members of Parliament, as their religion precluded them from taking the oath. Lord Lucan proposed the insertion of a clause empowering each House to modify the form of oath required of its members, and a bill on this principle was passed by both houses on 1st July 1858.

No one could have cared more for the survival of her family than Violet did. She was slight, delicately-made and shy. I did not know my grandmother-in-law until after she was widowed. She painstakingly noted all the family possessions, knew their history and worried constantly - but she was just a natural worrier. She was nothing like her grandson. She had four children: in 1898, my husband's father George Charles Patrick; my husband's Aunt Margaret, born in 1905, later to become Countess Alexander of Tunis; my husband's Aunt Barbara, who married Major John Bevan MC (Johnny Bevan); and my husband's Uncle John, born in 1904, who married Dorothea Chatfield (Aunt Dodo).

My mother-in-law's parents had been engaged to be married for several years, but the formality was such that they still called each other Lady Elizabeth and Captain Dawson until they married. This long wait for marriage may have caused there to be only one child, and regrettably not a boy. The earldom of Dartrey became extinct in 1933 because of the lack of a male heir.

My mother-in-law, as their only child, may have tried to compensate for this deficiency with much study and with her interest in the conditions of the poor (and there was a huge difference between rich and poor), which caused her relations to tie up her money so she could not give it all away. She had an ambition to be a doctor, especially with a view to helping Muslims and women. Her mother died in 1924 following an accident involving her shoes while she was in Queen Mary's service.

I don't think I had a particularly good relationship with my mother-in-law, and not only because I was a Conservative voter. My mother-in-law was an only child and never went to school, so she didn't have her corners rubbed off. From the letters which are available, it appears that she wanted to doctor the Muslim women because they lived rather far afield, and so doctors who had to earn their own living could not afford to go.

My father-in-law Pat was severely wounded in 1918 with gunshot wounds to the stomach. He won a Military Cross, and his mother wrote to him saying that she hoped he would put away all thoughts of inferiority now that he had proved himself by winning an MC.

I thought my husband's younger brother, Hugh, had more of an inferiority complex than my husband. I used to talk to him quite a lot when he came for supper at 46 Lower Belgrave Street on a Sunday evening (my mother-in-law came on alternate Sundays). He did not go to Eton, and was very much a younger son. He was sent to Charterhouse and went on to Hertford College Oxford, where he took a degree in Science and failed. He took it again and did get a degree, but his mother's influence showed. He might have been better advised to read English Literature.

Pat continued with his army career and met his future wife Kaitilin Dawson while he was ADC to the Governor General of the Union of South Africa (Earl of Athlone) and she Lady in Waiting to HRH Princess Alice, Countess of Athlone, between 1924 and 1926.

After this appointment, my father-in-law went to China with his Regiment and my mother-in-law started her training to qualify as a doctor and they corresponded.

7th July 1927, my mother-in-law wrote to my father-in-law:

> All your remarks about my doctoring plans are extremely sensible and all - but leave me entirely unconvinced! Of course there are thousands of doctors, but most of them have to earn their living - which bars most of the far-afield jobs for them - women doctors are really (I'm told) wanted in Moslem countries - I know it will be a long time - but that's my idea for the future. For a start if I get my degree

our Shoreditch M.U.H., says he can easily find me work.

And for most of my 8 years training I can live at home. You must forgive me for inflicting my plans and schemes on you like this - I'm so thrilled about it & of course I can't tell the family till the time comes - & there'll be no end of a row then!

(How shocked the aunts would be!)

1st January 1928:

2nd Bn Coldstream Guards

Kaitilin my dear, a happy New Year to you.

And what about your future? If you pass the exam! Where will you do your four year's course? - And will you be a fully qualified doctor? able to administer the appropriate pill for any known disease, & to bluff the patient when you don't know!

On 8th November 1929, she wrote to my father-in-law saying:

I do so dreadfully wish it could be yes!

He had been courting her for some time but she played 'hard to get', the dream of doctoring Arabs dying hard.

Aldershot: My father-in-law to my mother-in-law, November 1929:

Oh Kait, my dear - you were so nice to me last night and I was such a tongue-tied ass that I couldn't tell you what I felt. (And I took 55 minutes by the clock to screw myself up to ask you to marry me!)

He's a lucky fellow, "Someone Else" - but Kait, I can't bear to think of you all alone and unhappy. You said you couldn't put up with a makeshift, but - I don't mind being the makeshift! Perhaps it is my ideals are not high enough -

I've got a dreadful feeling of certainty that what you said last night was quite final but will you tell me whether anything may happen, some time, somewhere, to make you change your mind?

Sunday. November 1929:

My dear one. So it is final. I might have known that your mind was made up by the way you spoke.

One thing has been tormenting me - whether, if I'd asked you in 1926 before I went to China the answer would have been the same? Then I was only beginning to think of the possibility of asking you to marry me. I felt so very young then. But why I took so long when once I came back last year, heaven knows -

Kait dearest, are you being fair to yourself? I know I'm a selfish brute because I want you for myself - but why should you give away the whole of your precious life like this and why shouldn't some of the nice things come your way?

Don't ever worry about me but what hurts me is to think of your trouble and your loneliness - and now I see for certain, what I only suspected before that I could never come within a thousand miles of being good enough for you, so perhaps it is all for the best - though it seems pretty grim at first.

But thank heavens there's one thing you've given me - and that's something to try and live up to - if I only could. It's something to try for and keep before one and I'm grateful for that:-

Blessings on you dear Kait and all my love.

P.

Pat's diary, 23rd November 1929:

Thirty-one tomorrow! It rather horrifies me chiefly I suppose it is the effect of the rejection & the reaction from the hopes which I have (now I come to think of it) been building up for 3 years at least - & had come to look on as all but realised. That made it such a much worse shock.

This self-examination brings out so many more defects even than I had admitted before! I'm shown up, under the light of an example like I've got before me now, for an idle, pleasure-loving self-satisfied child. (Just as typical of the "idle rich" as some of the people I laugh at; my pleasures may be different from theirs, but they're there, and I pander to them.) Material-minded, weak as water, selfish, not independent.

Another cause for the state of mind is having left "home" (the 2nd Btn) and being about to venture on to the world outside. A leap in the dark, Going out from the pleasant warmth of friends one knows, & privilege to the bleak moor of competition (in an element which I know I'm actually at my worst - making my way among a lot of other people. Eton was not a happy time for me & I feel that I haven't altered much in my power of holding my own among equals - socially).

I feel rather lost, nowhere to go. This leave - I don't know what to do with it. I can't afford to go abroad - (& that wd mean one of two things; going by myself, to Switz. Or Morocco, or with Bar. to Madeira

The Beginning

> & lazing) I've got no "invit" - except Billy Joliffe to Tiree & I'm not sure that that wd really amuse me enough, - Then, it seems wrong to spend it enjoying myself when someone else is working. Should I go & do a job somewhere in the "East End ? or go and ship as a hand at sea? or do a course of something useful - like economics or First Aid? Or a walking tour? Or do an attachment after all, to French Army? If I let it slide, as I probably shall, & go to one or two Hunt Balls & to Tiree, shan't I be giving way to natural inertia?

However, there was a dramatic change between 23rd November 1929 and 1st December 1929, when he proposed and was accepted. He had low self-esteem and was quite prepared to be what my future mother-in-law described as a "makeshift". She, on the other hand, had high self-esteem. But like many a woman before her, she decided on the security of marriage to be the best option. They married on 23rd December 1929.

The pair shared a love of travelling - something only the rich could afford. I do not know where they travelled or how they travelled. They were not short of money.

There was a certain anxiety early in the marriage, as my mother-in-law failed to conceive but they kept on trying.

Mother-in-law and daughter-in-law were to disapprove of each other, and I quote from my mother-in-law's letter written while they were on holiday together early in the marriage, circa 1931, to Pat, my future father-in-law, from Cap Martin Hotel:

> She [Violet] gets herself worried to death over little things - and really one gets rather bored with her perpetual complaints about people: there may be some people she likes and admires, but if there are she never mentions them! They're either rich & vulgar, or mean, politically they're dangerous or untrustworthy: their daughter has married an impossible Jew or their son is completely irresponsible. So it's becoming rather trying!

By 16th September 1932 she was pregnant and complained of haemorrhoids, saying what an undignified ailment it was. In later life, my husband never failed to have paroxysms of laughter when the subject of haemorrhoids was brought up and it may have originated from conversations about this "undignified ailment".

Brownhill, 4th August 1932:

> Went to see Miss Hill this evening - a good bill of health & the head is down in the pelvis at last, as I thought - which is v. much to the good - my only complaint is one large distressing - and - almost universal! I've never had one before & I thought at first I must have scratched myself on a bramble!! It's an undignified ailment! tho' pleasantly reminiscent of the Ark of the Covenant!

Their first child, my husband's elder sister Jane, was born, and a nanny called Flora Coles was employed to look after her, plus an under nurse, on their return from the Sudan - where Jane had been taken as well.

26th September 1933, 68 Cheyne Walk, SW3. My mother-in-law to my father-in-law:

> Took Jane to the School Inaugural yesterday. She was very good, appeared to enjoy the red robes. She met a lot of the nobs of the profession! (I trust it may stand her in good stead!) All the school people were there, of course, Dr Garrett Anderson, Sir Farquar Buzzard & Aitken & a lot of people from hospital.
>
> Hay's first day of exams don't appear to have been too good. She boshed her forensic question - a nasty thing about the mental deficiency acts.

From this letter, we see that the medical mania was still with my mother-in-law, and her daughter Jane already 'programmed' to be a doctor, which indeed she became when she had grown up.

Hay was a woman friend of hers whom she later asked to become the children's guardian. "She boshed her forensic question - a nasty thing about the mental deficiency acts" is interesting, because my husband was continually quoting the Mental Health Acts to all and sundry before and after our custody case. Clearly my mother-in-law would have had some difficulty with this question too and she would have boshed it! She wrote in her affidavit: "In my view as a lay person my daughter-in-law is not normal and needs treatment!"

She did not write much about her second pregnancy with my husband, but described one of his "roaring evenings", a typical account of evening crying. She also mentioned that my husband had

The Beginning

a cold in his nose which was tiresome, as he was bound to pass it on. My husband was much given to catching colds all his life. She noted that my husband asked for his father a lot.

He did not appear to me to be very fond of his father in the very short time that I knew my father-in-law. However, he needed father figures and the first was Stephen Raphael. Charlie Sweeny also gave him help and advice, and he appeared to need it.

Sometime in early 1940, the four children set sail for the USA. Jane was aged 7, my husband aged 5, Sally aged 3 and Hugh was a babe in arms. In sole charge was Miss Flora Coles, their nanny. It was common practice at the time for those who could afford it to send their children abroad to safety, as nobody knew how long the War would last. Miss Coles was a superior nanny, and someone who could be trusted to take the four children across the Atlantic. I believe they headed for Halifax, Nova Scotia or Toronto to await negotiations for a permanent base. My husband never discussed anything about his separation during the War to me.

My father-in-law's elder sister Barbara Bevan was already in the USA with her three children, and arranged for the family to go to Mrs Carll Tucker, who was then aged about sixty. She was very rich indeed[2] and had two sons, Luther Tucker, who was an Episcopalian Minister, and Carll Tucker Jr, who was Editor of *The Patent Trader*, published in Connecticut. Her husband was still alive at this stage. She owned a mansion on Park Avenue and a house at Mount Kisco called Penwood, and a beach house at Hobe Sound, Florida. Her sons were young but grown up and married.

Lady Barbara Bevan wrote to my mother-in-law, beginning:

> Kaitilin darling, even John, the shyest one, was talking and laughing to us right from the start. They are so frightfully well and happy. They must have put on a little weight and they have grown as well.

She gave a description of Miss Harrison, the children's nursery governess: "5' 8" thin, greyish hair, dresses rather well."

---

[2] Apparently the Tuckers made their money in finance at the end of the 19th century.

> I can't tell you the improvement in John's shyness. Until now, I had never been able to get anything out of him, but this time he treated me like a long lost friend, and showed me all his toys and treasures, and told me about his school. And he no longer looked down as he used to but looks you straight in the eye, and never puts his finger in his mouth...

She continued:

> I also asked Miss Harrison if John has had any of those screaming fits since she had been there, and I am thankful to say that she said no. Sometimes he gets very angry and says "I hate you, I hate you" & gets rather rude and wild, but she remains quite calm & doesn't tell him it is rude to talk like that, but she changes the subject and in a very short time he has quite recovered and never sulks...

> They lead the life of all American children, which seems very upside down to our way of life. When they come in at about 5, they start their baths and have supper (which consists of a chicken or fish or meat dish with 2 or 3 vegetables, and a sweet) at 6. They then play or sing until just before 7, when John and Sally are put to bed.

I don't know how my husband's mother reacted to receiving letters. I would have thought that she might have regretted sending them away to the USA. She was probably very involved with her work in a pathology lab at the Royal Free Hospital.

During September 1941, nanny Flora Coles wrote a letter to my mother-in-law and said:

> She is writing to you, but everyone seems to think Halifax is out of the question, and Mrs Tucker suggests a day school here which all the children go to. She did not mention it to me, but to Lady Barbara. The children are all well but the double change has been rather upsetting and they have been rather difficult about the sleeping arrangements here. It is a very big house and I have a bedroom which was meant to sleep in for the hot weather, there are beds in both then I was offered a room for Jane a very long way off in another wing and a room for John not so far but down a long corridor. He did not like the idea of sleeping alone so we thought Jane should have that room, and John have one of the beds in my room but the first night Jane got very upset and said she did not like the other room so it ended in there both being with me. The next night Jane and John went to bed in Jane's room but at 1 am poor Jane came along and said John was screaming and she did not know what to do so I had to bring him in

with me, then Jane wanted to come so I had them all again. Tonight Jane and Sallie are in Jane's room and I trust they will stay there. Hugh is sleeping well again, but John has woke every night since it got so hot. He has complained of the pain in his knee again 2 or 3 times. The weather is cooler today.

I hope you are getting all our letters. I have written twice a week, and I see you have only received so far the ones from the ship. I believe letters can be sent quicker from here but costs more. By the way, there was a difficulty about bringing any money over the border, and it was only by a great concession through Mrs Bruce that I was allowed any money. However she got it changed into American dollars which however meant that it was worth less and then I had to pay 40 dollars head tax (8 dollars each) on entering the states that equals about £10 of our money so my funds are rather melting away. I think Mrs Bruce must have paid for the children's passports. I am sure you will write and thank her for the great trouble she took to get us through. Well we hope to hear soon from you only one letter so far to me but the children just got Lord Bingham's.

    Yours faithfully,
    F. Coles.

I don't know if the children had American passports, but I wouldn't have thought so.

On 29th August 1940, my mother-in-law wrote:

These photographs came in an envelope with no letter. Isn't it odd? I am writing to thank Mrs Tucker - (I suppose it was she that sent them?) perhaps that will extract a letter from her.

8th September 1940:

What do you think of enclosed from Nannie? I wish she sounded happier. Jane's letter is lovely. As to the church problem Nannie will by now have had a letter from me saying let her go if she wants to. All the same, I can't help faintly resenting Mrs T carrying her off like that!

The atheist beliefs rearing its ugly head - a recurring theme:

Mt. Kisko. N.Y.
Aug 23rd 1940

My dear Lady Bingham,
Your letter of August 8th came through with amazing speed. I am

sorry that it has not been more promptly answered. (But I did manage to get off by air mail some snaps of the three older children taken immediately upon their arrival by my husband). The reason of my delay in writing was that problems in my family necessitated time consuming adjustments in the household & also there were doctors examinations & interviews with the head master of the local day school, introductions to the staff, the sports class & endlessly listening to Nannie whose complaints ran the gamut of past glories to present differences & objections to my spoiling the children & to taking the children out without her. Up to the present moment not one thing has been favourably commented upon but the four children have prospered. They are dears - Sally & Hugh are completely at home. Sally beguilingly naughty, Hugh very good for such a wee boy. Jane mothers them all, feels responsible for their good behaviour. She is progressing with her riding & should become a good horse-woman because she is attentive to instruction & unafraid. John is good on a horse too although his legs are short for our fat ponies. We are looking about for two smaller ponies for the younger children.

John is mixing well now with the children's groups. He seems very fond of Mr Tucker & friendly with us all, although he was shyest upon arrival. Jane is actually the most aloof with us. With other children she is at once en rapport. I should have said this earlier but I was distracted by the fascinating subject of your children.

My husband & I have been endlessly pro ally since 1914. It is therefore a joy to us to have something concrete to do for England now - although it is only the care of four of her smaller citizens. He has entered the three children in the Ripporram Day School nearby where all the neighbouring children go. Sally stays a short time only, Halifax is 8 or 9 hours by air from us. We understand perfectly the impossibility of your sending any money out of England. We will see the children are suitably clad doctored and educated while with us as though they were our own grandchildren.

It is a very great comfort to us to have Lady Barbara to talk over our problems with. We hope that we will be able to ask her to visit us soon again but our guest rooms have been occupied this summer - as never before. She was understanding and helpful. I need not add how deeply I sympathise with you & Lord Bingham on this tragic separation. But England must win while we wait for her victory, we will care for your children.

  Sincerely yours
   Marcia Tucker.

Separation to a greater or lesser extent affected many children

The Beginning

during the War. Obviously my husband must have felt abandoned, but he did not discuss this with me.

Nanny Coles was sent back to England in October 1940 and the children were left without anyone they knew from England. Mrs Tucker preferred American ways. Nanny Coles would have annoyed Mrs Tucker with her perpetual complaints.

The four children continue to grow up in America, surrounded by everything that Marcia Tucker imagined such well-born children would have been surrounded by in England, but who, in fact, because of their mother's socialist ideas, would not have been. They were surrounded by all the trappings of wealth - servants to cater to their every whim, food plentiful and their own house to live in. My mother-in-law presumably believed in socialism!

Marcia Tucker was a Republican, used to getting her own way, who worshipped regularly at the Episcopalian church, a great admirer of English things and the English way of life. She owned a Rolls Royce (quite rare at that time) and her family in their heyday had owned a magnificent yacht called *White Migrant*. I have explained that her family made their money in finance during the latter part of the nineteenth century. She had been pro ally since 1914, which is quite some time.

My husband was later to call his two powerboats after that vision of opulence - *Migrant* and *White Migrant*.

His two mother figures were so opposite in ideas for the upbringing of children that I used to call the effect on my husband the Marcia/Kaitilin dichotomy. Mrs Tucker surrounded the children with wealth, comfort, opulence and Christian beliefs, while my mother-in-law would disapprove of this and was either an atheist or an agnostic, but probably an atheist.

During this time my husband was sent to The Harvey School or to Harvey in Connecticut - a school for the sons of well-heeled Americans, where I gather for some reason he was unhappy and attempted to burn it down - he set fire to it. He wrote to his parents at this time but there was no hint of unhappiness. We never discussed his unhappiness at the school.

Meanwhile, my mother-in-law had been publishing from her platform of Assistant in a Pathological Department at the Royal Free Hospital. She had been pursuing her doctoring dream. I wonder if she ever considered that she might have been better employed looking after her children in the USA.

In 1945 the War had ended and V.E. Day passed, and the children returned to England some time before V.J. Day. At Tilbury Docks, elder sister Jane had to point out their parents standing on the Quayside. It appears that the children did not recognise their parents. They were reunited and returned to 22 Eaton Square and Nanny Coles.

24th September 1945
44 Queen Anne Street, W.1.

Dear Colonel and Mrs Bingham,

I fear I have taken a very long time to make a new contact with you about John.

Assuming things to be as they were, I want to strongly advise you to try to get my colleague Dr Clifford Scott to treat John by psycho analysis. Dr Scott is back in civilian work and is establishing himself not very far from you at 49, Queen's Gate Gardens, SW7.

With good wishes,

   Yours sincerely,
     D.W. Winnicott

My husband wrote letters to his father, and I quote from one of them:

5th November 1945

Dear Daddy,

My dog is coming next weekend. I have got a collar and a leash & a blanket & comb for her. I am going to call her Lavercham - I saw the name in Singe's works - I hope Hughie will not think of calling her Lavatory.

Do you think you will be able to come back for Christmas? I hope so.

This letter is written by Mummy because I can only use my left hand.

Jane & Sally were here today -
We were not able to get any fireworks.

   Lots of love from John.

The Beginning

20th November 1945, from Pat to my mother-in-law:

> It's good that John's puppy is arriving: do you expect a lot from it? - I mean in helping John, mentally?

After learning that my husband had an accident with phosphates - playing with chemicals - Violet Lucan wrote to my father-in-law on 18th November 1945 saying:

> Thank goodness your John's explosion was no worse but are chemicals ever safe for children as young as he is? I can't think they are.

At the same time, my mother-in-law was corresponding with my father-in-law on the subject of my husband and the children, but particularly on his disturbed behaviour. We have no proof that my husband ever had psychoanalysis but he continued to see Dr Winnicott through 1946.

My father-in-law wrote that my husband did not like the look of Bryanston, so they had to take him to see Eton. My husband chose Eton and went to Coleridge's. He appears to have been about average on school work, but he was not confirmed as my mother-in-law wrote a letter saying that he must not be coerced into confirmation but it must be left to him to decide. This was tantamount to saying that he is not to be confirmed, as boys more or less have to be herded into doing this. This was later to prove our first common denominator.

22nd June 1946, from Pat to my mother-in-law:

> Nice to hear of John being so helpful to everyone. I hope he liked his Whitsun weekend. How does he behave to H [Hay] and E [Evans]?

13th August 1946:

> I got my first letter from John, with a second one enclosing a negative of a colour photograph he took. It's very neatly typed & beautifully expressed and spelt. He says he's got a movie-camera: how on earth? Some time exposures taken in school have mostly come out well, and "I have large lists from all my friends of the ones they want! There is no reason why they shouldn't pay me for them" - well, no, I suppose not, but... I hope he only charges out-of-pocket expenses for them, though I suspect he looks on it as a money-making affair. I must try

& gently indicate that one doesn't make money out of one's friends! But how? Do you think raising the scale of pocket money is indicated or alternatively paying his photographic expenses? I'm afraid the money-making notions he came back from America with are still there. Pat.

27th August 1946:

All you tell me about John is cheering. I suppose getting to know other boys has convinced him that school is an unpleasant thing that can't be avoided: that's my interpretation of his wish for a home as far from school as possible! I had been hoping that your Poole camp[3] would have given you opportunity to hike or motor a bit about Dorset & so taken away any nasty taste from Bryanston...

I think the pocket money idea an excellent one: the old basis was rather mean - for Jane & John anyway. Pat.

29th August 1946:

My dear, how disappointing that John had a relapse & how loathsome for you. You poor dear. How damnable it is that I can't be with you to share all this worry. Pat.

15th September 1946:

Yesterday also brought letters from John & Sal. John devoted most of his to the rearrangement of furniture at No. 22 - which is rather regrettable. He did mention some of your trips from Amroth & Deirdre, & his prowess on the billiard-table! but he gave a wealth of details (with plan) about every piece of furniture in the sitting room which he must remember very vividly. Pat.

22nd September 1946:

John wrote & sent me specimens of his indoor photography - some rather indifferent ones of Deirdre & Sally, which he seems very proud of. I think one should take him to an exhibition of amateur photographers, to give him a standard... You say he still hates the idea of Bryanston: it was probably a bad mistake to take him down there before one had time to find out his views - but there it is, Should we now - or next Spring. Say, take him & show him Eton?

---

[3] "Every moment spent away from London is a waste of time" - my husband's words.

The Beginning

One letter from my husband whilst at Eton:

F.J.R. Coleridge's Esq.,
Eton College
Windsor.

Dear Mummy and Daddy,

I went over to Hallgrove today and had lunch with Aunt Katie and a terrible old woman called "Sibbie Samuels" who claimed that she knew you and Daddy in the old days. You wouldn't believe the greasy things she said to Aunt Katie. She had been to a funeral in the morning but said that Aunt Katie worked like a tonic on her. Aunt Katie turned rain into sunshine. Aunt Katie was always a 'naughty gel' you know 'hopping' over to Paris. Aunt Katie was quite a pioneer with those aeroplanes and always an absolute 'dear'. She had the revolting habit of always taking hold of Aunt Katie's wrist when she said something. She claimed to be desperately hard up, but still managed to arrive in an enormous chauffeur-driven car (not hired).

I am glad you are coming to the School concert but it means evening clothes. On no account must you stay to Boy's Dinner on the Sunday. They don't know when you're leaving (some time on Sunday) but it might be a good thing to fix up lunch with the Alexanders' so you have a fairly genuine excuse.

It was fun having Uncle Johnny and Aunt Barbara on St. Andrews day. Unfortunately it was bitterly cold in the afternoon so we didn't go out.

School Cert is in full swing and Illingworth and Dewhurst are therefore in the process of failing. Dewhurst will pass in one subject and Illingworth in none. I expect Shane will be trying again at Harrow.

Aunt Katie said that John (the Turk) is coming home in February. Nunc, she says, is not all that well. Richard wants to go and farm in the West Country. Anne is much better and Robert might go out to Australia for Schweppes. I don't think she likes Meg. Love from John.

My husband's father succeeded in 1949 and caused a sensation by choosing to sit on the socialist benches. It was a dreadful blow to his mother Violet. Her sister-in-law, a daughter of the 4th Earl of Lucan and then Duchess of Abercorn, called my father-in-law "a traitor to his class." Violet remembered this right up to her death.

I think my husband took Modern Languages at Eton and got German and French at 'O' Level. His mother and father fancied themselves at languages and attempted to learn Russian and Arabic, but my husband did not appear to have been very good at this for when I knew him he couldn't speak French or German.[4]

He said he was not particularly good at games at school and felt this to be a cause of lack of popularity, and during our marriage he practiced any sport he was engaged in assiduously. He would take the car to a golf course and on the practice ground drive off a couple of hundred balls and continued to have indoor lessons with the golf professional Leslie King at intervals.

On the rare occasions that he was invited to shoot, he would beforehand go to a shooting school in North West London to practice and get his eye in. He learnt to water ski at Ruislip and worked hard at this. He had a natural talent for golf like his father, and could drive the ball a very long way and at home would practice with weights to strengthen his arm muscles, which were not as strong as he would have liked.

He did not appear to have made any close friends while at Eton. I met James Dunsmure, son of a Major Henry Dunsmure, but only once, and Tim Goad, who went into his father's fur business and who asked my husband to be best man at his wedding to a local squire's daughter, but they saw each other seldom and usually spoke over the telephone when Tim thought there was something good going on in the fur market.

Fred Coleridge,[5] later Provost of Eton, could have got him a place at the University - I don't know which University, but probably Oxbridge - but as he knew he could not afford a car, he decided against this and he told me that this had been a mistake. It suggested that he was OK academically, if a University education was a possibility for him. After Eton, he had to do his National Service and from his letters we can get a picture:

> Dear Daddy,
> There are masses of Etonians - 11 out of the 16 in my hut. I am very

---

[4] I also learnt German for a year before I left school, but if you cannot practice speaking German daily you soon lose it, although you can sometimes read it accurately.

[5] I don't know if he was a relation of Samuel J. Coleridge.

short of money so can you send me some quickly. My address is:

Sgt. O'Flynn
Brigade Squad
Guards Depot,
Caterham.

I am here for 8 weeks exactly, but we don't get leave for 4 weeks. The C.O. is a Lt. Col. PGI Reed of the Irish Guards. The Adj is a Maj. Ratcliffe. The officer in charge of the Brigade Squad is Captain Digby (Coldstream) who seems quite nice. And our Sergeant is O'Flynn of the Irish Guards. There is a v. nice Trained Soldier in charge of the hut. Love John.

P.S. Can you also send a pair of braces and forward any letters that come for me. John.

22853532 RCT. Bingham
Sgt. O'Flynn
Brigade Squad,
Guards Depot,
Caterham,
Surrey.

Dear Mummy and Daddy,

Can you send me as quickly as possible a knife, fork and spoon (any old ones) and some handkerchiefs and my electric razor and lots of rags.

Things are not going too badly but there is an awful lot of polishing to do.

The unfortunate thing is that only half of the Coldstream candidates will get a commission in the Coldstream and of the 12 candidates there are 5 who are more likely than myself to get in. The alternative is either to sign on for 3 and a half years in which case you are nearly certain to get in provided, of course, that you pass WOSBI and everything or to just get a commission as a NS man, be refused by the Coldstream and spend your NS in some mouldy regiment because there is no chance in the rest of the guards and a slight chance in the Household Cavalry. But Captain Digby said that when I had finished with Caterham he would be able to give me a pretty good idea as to whether I would be in the lucky half.

We get five days leave for Easter (Thurs to Mon. Midnight) which I think start from 4 weeks this Thursday. Love John.

PS I am nearly bald as a result of the attentions of the barber.

Can you also send me a tin enamel drinking mug and 2 prs of 'bungy' rubber things size 9 which I can fit inside my boots. They are a sort of false sole.

2nd November 1953
2nd Bn.
BAOR

Dear Daddy,

We arrived 5 hrs late because the boat was held up by fog at Harwich. Otherwise, we had a very pleasant journey.

I've discovered quite a lot about things. First we pay for mess bills out of our non-army accounts - i.e. I pay them out of Barclays. Shooting is rather expensive a game-licence costing £6.

We have arrived at rather an unfortunate time, as the Major-General is coming to inspect the Bn on the 9th Nov. Phillips and myself have both been given platoons in No 1 Coy. There only are two platoons in each Coy and three rifle Coys. So the Bn. is very much under strength. There is no drill course for young officers.

Jim Sawdon, the QM, asked to be remembered to you, as did the ORGMS who was in your Bn in 1941.

I'm afraid blues are going to be necessary as I'm told there is no chance of second hand as three ensigns have just been demobbed and anyway I don't think they were the right size. The trouble is that the picket officer has to wear them and we're all picket officers 3 times during November. Keenan Phillips said they couldn't make them without a 'half-time' fitting but you'll have to tell him to do the best he can as there is no chance of getting back until the end of February. You might also tell them to really hurry up about it as the sooner they arrive, the sooner things will become easier.

Some people went shooting this afternoon but I didn't see them go so I don't know what sort of things they were wearing. I have a suspicion it's rather grand because on the 'Lontin' side I met Capt. Wallis-King who was immaculately attired in white breeches, stock, and black riding jacket coming back from a 'hack'.

Don't forget the *Daily Express* competition. Some of the coupons I cut out have not been completed - i.e. A, B, or C. Also can you redirect any mail that comes as it might be the news that I have won a car. There will also be the letter from the Insurance and from the car Mart.

Have you applied to the Brit.Gen. Insurance for a refund as the car was insured till the 6th Jan.

The price of drink here is incredible. Gin, whisky, rum etc are 4d and all liquers 7d-9d. Love John

The Beginning

5th November 1953

Dear Mummy & Daddy,

I got the letters and *The Reason Why*[6] which promises to be quite good from the first few pages I read.

Everything is going quite smoothly so far. A lot of officers are away on courses and leave and they come and go every day.

My Coy Cmd is Capt. Wallis-King but he is going on a course and Andrew Mayes (son of C. Mayes, beak at Eton) takes over.

The adjutant is Victor Le Fanu who is very nice, but who is said to be drill-mad and that is all he is interested in.

Sup. Coy is commanded by Sir Ralph Anstruth who behaves like a man of 50 or 60. He is 39. He owns a 1923 Rolls Royce and spends a lot of his time under the bonnet. He is the only officer who sits for a long time over his port, or he is said to anyway.

The other ensigns are all v. Nice. Wall, Fitzherbert, Gage, Scott, Gibbs and us three. I am the leading pl cmd of No 1. Coy which means that for the Maj-Geb's parade on Monday my pl marches past first.

I think the shooting is off for this year as the season ends on Jan 1st and a licence cost 65 marks = £5.8.0. Apparently it's not worth while going shooting without, or on someone elses's licence. Someone gets shot nearly every time or someone's dog does and without a licence you are not insured.

There aren't many bridge players among the ensigns, 3 of us and the rather older people are said to play poker a bit too high and quite well. (I don't know is the answer to this.)

Can you ask Keenan Phillips to send with the blues some leather buttons (10 big 5 small) and a tunic cap star that goes on one's beret for manoeuvres.

The mess-bills are rather high out here. One ensign (non-smoker) got a bill for £15 and he was away for 10 days of the month. The trouble is that the mess left London £2,000 in debt and is now only £600 or it has been reduced by £600 since the Bn have been in Krefeld. It means that the glass of cointreau that costs 5d in the NAAFI costs 1/6 in the mess. I will probably be able to come back in February sometime but there is no hope for Christmas. I hope you haven't sent the photograph off to George or the Tuckers yet. I will send you a letter to accompany them. Can you try and find some reasonable frame for them to go in?

---

6   Cecil Woodham-Smith wrote *The Reason Why*, about the Charge of the Light Brigade, with the help of the Lucan papers which were given to him by Pat Lucan.

A Moment in Time

I rather think the officers don't like Jim Sawdon and will be rather pleased to see the back of him.

If I do win £4 or £500 in the *Daily Herald* car comp it will be easy enough to buy a car out here for sterling because there are lots of officers in BAOR who are going home and want to sell their cars.

The Bn is moving to Hubelrath where the Irish Guards were on the 6th Jan. The Scots Guards are there too. It is only 25 miles away from here.

Don't forget to pay my allowance into Barclays as I don't want to pass too many dud cheques around the mess.

We have each got a soldier servant which is nice. Love John.

2nd Bn.

Dear Mummy & Daddy,

My blue hat has arrived from Herbert Johnsons but the idiots sent a cap-star with it when I had twice reminded them not to. John Coddy's cap star is going to be difficult as the prongs that go into the hat aren't nearly long enough. I shall have to have them lengthened somehow.

A travelling salesman came from Garrards in London yesterday with a selection of watches, cigarette lighters etc. He had the most lovely Coldstream star I have ever seen. It was quite like Mummy's but rather nicer I think. It cost £150 in England and £105 out here.

I am slowly discovering what not to drink out here. I found out, rather too late, that sherry is the most expensive drink (1/6 a glass). Also it is more economical to have two glasses of cointreau at dinner than one of port.

The riding is going quite well. We have got on to jumping now which is great fun.

I have done a lot of pistol shooting recently and am getting deadly accurate. I could now almost take the part of any cowboy in a film. It is nice being able to go and draw as much ammunition as you want. I usually loose off 100 rounds in each session.

Has the result of the *Herald* car comp. come out yet? I refuse to believe I haven't won at least a share in the £1000.

I could come home for Christmas from the 22nd-28th Dec. But I'm not sure that it's worth it. I could catch the night boat from the Hook which gets in 9am the 23rd. I would have to start back morning of the 27th to arrive by 8.00 am the 28th. That gives me 4 clear days in England. Flying is too expensive - £16 return.

Can you send me. A (your plus fours.) B (the boating jacket) C (the two photographs for George & the Tuckers.

The Beginning

> What does everyone want for Christmas? Send me a list quickly. Love John.

My husband did not make lasting friendships, but he adapted well and boarding school experience helped, as well as did being sent away in his early years.

10th November 1953:

> Dear M & D,
>
> Havergal arrived on Friday and said he tried to ring up but there was no answer...

12th November 1953:

> Dear Mummy & Daddy,
>
> I got my copy of *The Reason Why* which I enjoyed very much - what was the literary lunch like?
>
> We are not now moving to Hubelrath as was planned for January. Instead we stay at Krefeld anyway until October.
>
> I think I probably will get a licence for the shooting. I think I should have to have some plus-fours as everyone who went out on Saturday was wearing them. Could you send your pair and I can wear them with my jacket.
>
> I went to a concert with Maud in Krefeld. Clifford Curzon was playing in the Emperor and there was a Mozart concert. It was quite good.
>
> The mark situation is going to become very bad apparently. After Christmas we will only be allowed to draw ¼ of our pay in marks which is £4½. The papers are being a very long time about announcing the winners in the car comp. I am getting impatient because a car would be a great asset out here. About 7 officers have cars.
>
> The RQMS and the ORGMS are called Penfold and Betts and I can't remember which said he knew you. I enclose a list of officers. The ones I have ticked are on leave or doing courses.
>
> There is quite a good cinema in barracks which has four different films a week.
>
> Don't forget the plus-fours as if poss I want them on Saturday.
>
>   Love John.
>
> AHG FORTESCUE MBE MC
> JL DARRLL MC
> JW YOUNGER MBE
> JW PROCTER

17th November 1953:

Dear M & D,

I was very disappointed to see in the *News Chronicle* that I had not won one of the 4 cars. You must tell me the minute the results in the *Herald* come out.

The Major-General inspection went off all right. He is a tiny, very scruffy little man and a tremendous meal was laid on for him, with caviar and everything...

30th December 1953:

2nd Bn

Dear M & D,

I've had a bit of luck and been appointed ski-ing officer of the Bn with Humphrey Maud who has done even less ski-ing than me. Can you get hold of Hay (who offered me her skis) and ask her to get them sent from Switzerland to Winterberg which is the army ski-ing school. We take about 5 guardsmen with us and there is some form of team race at the end. The dates are Jan 23rd - Feb 7th. If she sends them straight to Winterberg station I'll be able to collect them when I arrive.

I suppose there isn't anything in the line of ski-ing clothes that would fit me. Trousers are the main things and any large jersey. There won't be any ski boots but those I shall have exported free of purchase tax. Apparently there is only one type of boot that is any good made in England and I don't know the name yet. It sounds great fun, although Winterberg is not mountainous (it is on the outside of the Walberk) and full of service corps, captains and families.

We got to Sennelager on Monday the 4th so can you hurry up the Beret Cap star.

I have just seen the most marvellous film, called 'Lili' with Leslie Caron.

Apparently Christmas in the Bn was not much fun. It involved wallowing in beer in the Sgts mess most days which was all right for people like Havergal (with big bladder). Christmas is merely an excuse for being roaring drunk for 4 days on end and the same for the New Year, which, thank God, I am escaping.

I haven't discovered about leave yet because Victor Le Fanu is still on leave but it may be possible to have leave in April provided I am not carted for the Trooping.

We are missing Col. George's inspection because of the ski-ing which is a relief.

The boating jacket buttons polish up well and the OR overcoat is looking quite smart with K & P's buttons.

I shot quite straight in a small bore team competition (inter coy) I got 91/100 & 92/100 on my two targets.

There are 4 new officers coming in Jan. Two from Eaton Hall and a Major Kenneth Sweeting who is said to be ghastly. He is only just junior to Geoff Darrell so he must be getting on. The other one is a subaltern called Dick Cooper and as far as I can remember from the Depot is not very desirable. (He gave the Brigade Squad a lecture on regimental history.) Love, John.

From these letters we can see how concerned he was about the cost of everything, anxious about clothes and correct cap badges. He appeared to have enjoyed riding and have been quite good at shooting. He was so anxious to have a car (why didn't his parents buy him one?). He wrote about ski-ing, which he always tried hard at. He wrote about a concert and refers to a film and the fact that there was a cinema. He sounded like a perfectly normal young man who was rather short of money. His Eton letter sounded very 'on the ball' to me - good observation, interesting with suggestions.

He didn't find being a new recruit a daunting experience, and told me that boarding school experience told. Those who had never been found it hard to adjust, were homesick and incapable of covering up badly bulled kit. He passed WOSB (War Office Selection Board) and told me the following account of his interview.

He started with the usual feelings of trepidation and answered a few questions. He was then asked what games he played and he replied, "Tennis, golf and ping pong." The interviewer replied, "Ah, how good to hear you say 'ping pong' you've no idea how often I have to hear it called 'table tennis'." He was through and they chit chatted through the rest of the interview.

His tastes for the 'sweet life' showed early. He was to be seen at St Moritz, going down the Cresta and Bob Runs in 1957, 1958, 1959 and thereon. In the summer he was at Le Touquet for golf and at Cannes and Eden Roc. He did not have any real steady girlfriends. Closest came the daughter of a 2nd Baron, who did appear ski-ing at the same time and on some occasions in the summer.

My husband's father stood up to his wife and provided their daughter Sally with a marriage settlement in 1958, and also released some capital for their son, my husband. Very significant victory despite sobs from their mother, who objected to this because of her socialist views.

He was a 2nd Lieutenant in the 2nd Bn of his father's old regiment, the Coldstream. They played tennis in summer and shooting was preferred in winter, along with cards, especially poker. Apparently he was a past master in the art of bluff, and said to be the best poker player in the battalion and they played virtually every night.

His Uncle Johnny Bevan, a senior partner in a well known firm of stockbrokers, got him a job in a merchant bank in the investment department at a salary of £500 a year. In the evening he played poker in a tight school at Crockfords (an old established casino), where among others middle-aged women played. It was a great school for him. The women had to be watched every moment or they would scoop chips out of their bin, and they never missed a thing or an opportunity to cheat although the stakes were low.

He met Stephen Raphael, a stockbroker and gambler who was then aged about 54, who became his mentor. He had a dubious war record. At the outbreak of the Second World War he went to Canada. When he returned at the end of the War he was blackballed by every gentleman's club in London. People were very strict about war records in those days. Stephen Raphael had inherited a great deal of money when young. He was an orphan and had 'blown' large sums, but had learnt his lesson the hard way and learnt it well. Stephen Raphael introduced him to a poker game at the Hamilton Club just off Park Lane.

Sometime in 1960, thanks to money made available by his father, my husband retired from the Bank and went on a tour of America, staying with Aunt Marcia and playing golf for money, which he loved. When my husband returned from America he took up gambling professionally.

He now had enough money to have a flat of his own, and chose a modern flat behind the facade of the Nash Park Crescent on the top floor, number 50. He decorated it to his taste, mostly in green. I don't know how much the flat cost - I don't think he bought it outright. The flat was unfurnished when he took it on. His bedroom was small and contained a three-quarter size double bed. The sitting room contained his grand piano and a second hand sofa plus an armchair. He had bought a couple of reproduction Canalettos to hang on the walls, but the ceilings had no cornice. The bathroom was covered in black glass which was difficult to keep clean. There was one more small room, which could be used as an extra bedroom or a dining room.

He bought a new Aston Martin and a powerboat. Backgammon was beginning to become popular and he became rather good, with instruction from Stephen Raphael.

In the South of France he met Sir Gordon and Lady Vereker (Roxanna). She was very rich and American, much enamoured of titles. They owned a magnificent house called Domaine de Beaumont not far from Eden Roc, and he cultivated them as he met them both in St Moritz and the South of France, when they entertained him. I do not know where he met Manchester stockbroker John Wilbraham, but I do know that his father and Robin Hill's (later 8th Marquess of Downshire) father were both alcoholics. Robin Hill's sister is Caroline Hill, the piano teacher. He asked John Wilbraham to be his best man at our wedding.

My husband was not particularly good company - not witty or amusing, but generous. He didn't pay much attention to clothes when I first met him, and many people have described him as handsome in the manner of Marcello Mastroianni - but I have also heard him described unflatteringly as a Frenchman's idea of what an English lord looked like.

2
Early Life

I was born on May 3rd 1937 at Worsted Farm, Uckfield, Sussex. My father was forty at the time and it was his second marriage. My mother was twenty and I was her first child. My father was the son of a Regular Army officer who had spent most of his army career in India, and his mother had been a schoolmistress before her marriage and was called Mary Clementina Shaw. Her first husband had been killed when a cricket ball hit his temple, and she married my grandfather because he resembled her first husband with whom she had been very much in love.

She loved to bet on horses and became so heavily in debt during their marriage that my grandfather had to put a notice in a local newspaper saying that he would no longer be responsible for her debts.

He was very bad tempered and grew rather eccentric in his old age, and became a supporter of the Nazis, with only his advanced age preventing him from being interned during the Second World War. My grandmother had cataracts and when in a temper he would smash her glasses, and she was rather frightened of him. He commuted his pension but my grandmother unexpectedly predeceased him, and he paid dearly for this generosity in his old age. He was born in Banffshire and had had a strict Presbyterian upbringing, and was educated at Aberdeen Grammar School. My grandmother came from Yorkshire and painted watercolours of India.

My father was at the Military Academy at Woolwich at the outbreak of the First World War and was soon sent to the Western Front. He was a good officer and won a Military Cross and my grandfather was very proud of him, and had the following extract from Army Orders printed:

> June 8th 1918
>
> He went forward to a Gun Position which was under heavy barrage and extricated a man who had fallen under the burning camouflage and exploding ammunition. The ammunition exploding killed the man he was carrying. He then organised a party to put out the fire and by his gallantry and example enabled the Position to recommence fire.

After the War he was posted to Athlone, where he met the Hon. Violet Louisa Handcock (b. 1895), only daughter of the 6th Baron Castlemaine. He was said to be very good looking and they fell in love, being married on 12th February 1919.

He was posted to India after the War and their first child, Hazel Patricia, was born there in 1921. He then decided to resign his commission in common with many others, and they set off for South Africa with the intention of farming. Unfortunately, there was a drought for about four years. Their second child was born in 1927 and named Pamela Jean, but the financial position was such that his wife returned to her parents in Ireland, taking their children with her.

My father told stories of starving in Cape Town, but he had the good fortune to meet a woman called Veronica Judd (he was later to name me after her), who rescued him and they started a nightclub together. After a while, he returned to England and he was divorced.

He did a variety of jobs from juvenile leads with Jack Hulbert and Cicely Courtneidge to travelling for firms, and met my mother while she was working as a receptionist at the Hotel Metropole, which had once been managed by her late father in Bournemouth. She was 18 or 19 at the time. Her father, my grandfather, had been trained as a hotelier in France and was said to have been good at his job and his wife Muriel, my grandmother, very efficient.

They had four children, of which my mother was the youngest. Unfortunately, my grandfather died of diabetes when my mother was 13 and there followed a very anxious time for the whole family. They had to leave the Hotel Metropole. My Uncle Kenneth, their elder son, was articled to a firm of solicitors. My Aunt Elna, their next daughter, was taught to colour photographs. My Uncle Ronald, who came next, was still at his public school and my mother, who left school at 15 and looked much older than her age, took a job as a receptionist. She then fell ill with a goitre and thyroid trouble and had to have an enforced rest, as the doctors did not want to operate on the goitre as she was so young and hoped it would go down of its own accord, which happily it did. She was then able to return to her employment as a receptionist, where my father met her.

They married on 21st October 1936 and my father bought a farm in Sussex, where I was born. My mother hated market day, which was a Thursday, for my father would go in to the local town and stay drinking with his acquaintances, sometimes until late at night, and she complained a great deal about this. On 21st January 1939 (she was two months pregnant with my sister), my father was driving home at about 3pm in the afternoon when he swerved to avoid an oncoming car, crashing into a tree. He was taken to hospital but my mother was not allowed to see him as he was so badly injured.

He died before twelve that night, the day before his 43rd birthday. I was said to have cried all night and it was indeed paradise lost for me. I was only twenty months old and the concept of death was impossible to explain to me at that age. It was to have a profound effect on me. I had been very fond of him and was often thought to be looking for him.

He had called me, rather tactlessly, 'Veronica' after Veronica Judd and 'Mary' after his mother. I obviously had to cope uncomprehendingly with my mother's grief and the hard time that followed. His life was insured, but the insurance company contested the claim saying that he had had a motoring accident before and had damaged his hand, which he had. My mother got half the sum he was insured for.

My mother wrote to his commanding officer saying how much he had loved the army, asking if he could have a military funeral. The officer replied that he was happy to do what he could for a brother officer, and my father was taken through the streets on a gun carriage before his burial in East Grinstead.

He had been best man to my future stepfather's sister Joan on her marriage to Sidney Gascoigne-Smith in South Africa, although Jim Margrie (my future stepfather) was much younger than he was and married. My mother lived with them for a while after selling up during her pregnancy and confinement with my sister, whom she called Christina Muriel so that she would have the same initials as my father.

My mother was very proud of my sister and I, and treated us as though we were her little princesses. She used her own wartime clothing coupons for our benefit in order that we should be well dressed. When not at school, we would be changed into afternoon clothes by our nanny and taken for a walk in the Rhododendron-filled gardens or taken in summer to Bournemouth's beautiful pebbleless beach.

I had the most wonderful collection of children's books, some beautifully illustrated. I loved Just William and Rupert Bear. I can remember my mother reading to me at bedtime extracts from my favourite children's book, *The Wind in the Willows*, which was a great treat. I was a voracious reader and by the age of 9 I was even reading adult books, but whether I understood them is open to doubt. I read a banned book called *Forever Amber*, which my mother had been given and thought the descriptions of the plague were why the book was banned. That was not the reason it had been banned!

I had the usual games such as Ludo and Snakes and Ladders, and many puzzles. My mother insisted that my sister and I say our prayers (The Lord's Prayer) before we went to sleep, and we attended Sunday School. I used to listen to the wireless with my mother during the War for information. I have enjoyed listening to programmes on the radio ever since.

My mother used to cook the most delicious curry dishes, long before curry became as popular as it is now in this country. My mother was rather strict but I think she was nearly always fair, but sometimes made me eat food I didn't like, merely because she thought I was delicate and that it would build me up!

Eventually my mother bought a house in Bournemouth, and that was where we spent the War years. I was able at that age to experience the War and remember it. The air raid sirens, the blackout and the bombing are memories that still endure. I remember going to the Lansdowne, a central part of Bournemouth, and seeing how the Hotel Metropole and other buildings had taken a direct hit and been reduced to dust and rubble. I was sad to see such destruction of familiar buildings. We had an air raid shelter built in the garden, and when we heard the air raid siren go off we would go down into it amid the sandbags. I would be wearing my siren suit and carrying my gas mask. We waited for the All Clear siren to allow us to return safely to our house. The beach was protected by an iron structure in the sea, presumably to prevent any German boats coming up the beach.

My mother employed a Swiss nanny called Nanny Knecht, but she left and was replaced by a Roman Catholic named Miss Mangan, a delicate woman much given to migraine. She left and my mother employed a governess called Miss Sail. I was very fond indeed of Miss Sail, unlike the nannies. She taught me to read and write, together with a smattering of history, botany and geography. I liked Miss Sail because she stimulated my intellect - nannies don't do this as a rule.

I was then sent to Queensmount School when I was about six or seven. My sister started school when she was rather younger than when I started, and I was made responsible for taking her to school. We had to take two buses to get to the school, and my sister quite deliberately would delay things so that I would be late. I would get an order mark as I was in the First Form, but nothing would be said to her as she was in the Kindergarten. Obviously I resented her for making me late and eventually my mother employed someone to take her to school and bring her home again. It was not possible at that stage to see if we differed very much physically, although I was thought to be delicate.

I did a great deal of dancing as a child as well as riding, and as a result of this I became knock-kneed and had to stop for a year and had to sleep in splints covered in linseed oil.

I then had to have an operation for appendicitis and contracted meningitis at the nursing home, and nearly died. I then had another operation for removal of my tonsils and adenoids. I was permanently in poor health and regularly given aperients such as Lixen, syrup of figs and Milk of Magnesia, whether I needed them or not. I was an inveterate bed-wetter and was taken to see a child psychologist called Dr Doris Odlum who recommended that my mother should buy me a teddy, which she did and it was much loved for several years.

My teddy was called 'Pinky', but was left behind when we moved to South Africa. My mother did get rather cross when I wet my bed, although many children do this. She did try to do something about it, however, which is why I saw Dr Doris Odlum.

I made friends at school and we all enjoyed the radio serial *Dick Barton Special Agent*, which preceded *The Archers*. My particular friends pretended to be either Dick Barton or Snowy White, and I was Jock Anderson. I was aware that I was an orphan and that most children had both a father and a mother.

I was beaten as a child when I was disobedient, but it was considered quite a normal form of discipline in the 1940s and I have no feelings of resentment about it. What I hated was having to sit in front of a cold congealing mass of food and being made to stay there until I had eaten it and be lectured about "the starving children of Europe." I absolutely loathed puddings such as tapioca, honeycomb mould, junket and rice pudding, and as a result of being forced to eat them I have never been very fond of food. It was to do with my being delicate, and it was thought that milk-based food would counteract this.

My maternal grandmother lived with us during the War and I was very fond of her. She used to go to the Spiritualist Church, and from time to time would give us messages from the Spirit World, particularly involving my father. She used to take me to their annual Fete from which I always returned with something I treasured. She also took me to see *The Mikado* and *The Pirates of Penzance*, which I thoroughly enjoyed at the Bournemouth Pavilion. She was a Conservative voter and interested me in politics. Her MP in Kent was Pat Hornsby-Smith, whom she much admired. My grandmother always remembered my birthday with a much appreciated one pound note, and gave me the same for Christmas. The first purchase I remember was a fountain pen, which cost six shillings.

My mother remained friendly with Gwen Margrie, who was by then a grass widow as her husband (my future stepfather) was in a POW camp. He had been a RAF navigator and was shot down by enemy gunfire into the sea at the beginning of the War. He had been on the hunger marches and had jumped over the Wooden Horse, and was also in Stalag Luft III.

My future stepfather returned from the POW camp. He was very thin and had to take care not to eat too much until he had fully recovered. As a result of their continuing friendship with my mother, my future stepfather fell in love with her. I was not really aware of my mother's relationship with my future stepfather. My mother still employed nannies and I remember Nanny Shepherd looked after my sister and I whilst my mother spent time with our future stepfather. My mother told me that my future stepfather was not used to children, but nothing more than that.

Gwen was obviously devastated by this and refused to give him a divorce. As a result, my mother and future stepfather decided to emigrate to South Africa. My mother told me that we were going there to stay with our future stepfather's sister, Joan. I never saw Gwen again.

I believe we left from Heathrow in a Sabena airlines aircraft bound for South Africa. In those days (1947), such a journey took about three days because of the necessary landings and take-offs in order to refuel. Our first landing was Schiphol airport and we were given an enormous meal there. After this we landed to refuel at Tunis, Kano, Elizabethville and Leopoldville before the final leg of our journey to Johannesburg.

Sometimes we experienced turbulence which caused many passengers to be sick, and the gangway was lined with used sick bags which added to the horror of the flight for me. My future stepfather, as he had been in the RAF, was invited by the pilot to view the aircraft from his perspective, which must have pleased him and my mother.

We arrived in Johannesburg and spent the night in a hotel there. The next morning we were woken up by a black African waiter, who asked what we wanted for breakfast. He was the first black African I had ever seen.

We went to Grahamstown to stay with Jim Margrie's sister Joan and her husband Sidney Gascoigne-Smith, who had three daughters. He was a master at a boys' public school there called St Andrews. The Gascoigne-Smiths were very puritanical and gave my mother a hard time as she was not married to my stepfather, and my sister and myself did not escape indirect censure, and as a result we were always served last at meals and were not offered second helpings.

The Gascoigne-Smiths' eldest daughter had already left home and their second daughter Lindsay was fifteen so rather out of my age group, but Barry was eleven and I enjoyed playing with her. She had a beautiful dolls' house and never objected to the amount of time I spent playing with it. She introduced me to an ice cream parlour where we had an Ice Cream Special, which was ice cream in a fizzy drink taken with a straw, and also took me to the Bioscope (cinema), which showed a film in the morning, a different one in the afternoon and another one in the early evening. I cannot remember what the house was like, except that it had a stoep (a veranda) that surrounded the house.

Eventually, my mother could not put up with the Gascoigne-Smiths any longer and so we took to the road travelling about South Africa. I was about ten-years-old. My future stepfather had purchased a Buick 8 American automobile. They were very short of money, so they took a job as trainee manager and manageress of a hotel called The Pollock in Port Elizabeth. I learnt to swim there but had very little companionship from other children, but was very pleased to have learnt to swim. My sister and I were then left in Port Elizabeth as boarders in a school called The Collegiate School. The boarding department was run by a Scottish woman who thought of schools as being like *Tom Brown's School Days*, and the 'New Pots', as we were called, were ragged unmercifully. We had to sing a song dressed in a bathing costume, a beret and gym shoes. When we returned to our dormitory, we found our clothes strewn about the floor as our drawers had been vandalised. I was particularly unhappy as most of the girls were Afrikaans and had not been allowed to forget the Boer War.

I went into a decline and refused to get up out of bed or eat, so the school doctor decided that in spite of the detriment to our education, we must be reunited with our parents who were by then manager and manageress of The Carlton Hotel, Grahamstown, which was the leading hotel there.

I was then sent as a day girl to the Diocesan School for Girls DSG and it was much better. There were a higher proportion of English settlers at the school. I was quite happy there, but by then Gwen Margrie had given a divorce, being the only way to get alimony and so it was decided to return to England as my mother and future stepfather feared a bloodbath. Dr Malan and then Dr Verwoerd were in charge at about this time.

We came back to England on the last voyage of SS *Llandovery Castle*, which was rather like steerage on a great liner, but we wanted to see Zanzibar and Egypt and the pyramids, which we did. I was singularly unappreciative of the wonderful places I saw and have disliked travelling ever since. I enjoyed sunbathing on the upper deck and slept there in the very hot weather. The voyage took eight weeks, and all four of us shared a cabin which was cramped, hot and claustrophobic.

I loved the boat in the end and was sad to leave it. I cannot remember if there were many children on board, but I can remember playing deck quoits, which I thoroughly enjoyed. This is a game played with a circular ring made of rope or rubber and tossed to an opposing player with something like a tennis court net to throw it over.

We arrived back in England and went to Bournemouth, where my parents rented a flat as a base while they looked for work. Strong &

Co. of Romsey offered them the tenancy of the Wheatsheaf Hotel, North Waltham. They took it and we moved in on 4th January 1950. The Wheatsheaf was a 16th century country pub with a minstrel's gallery containing a grand piano which I used to practice on, as I had piano lessons at school. It was quite large and rambling, and in those days much traffic passed by, unlike today when it is bypassed. It also catered to the locals who lived nearby, although there were not many who came. The saloon bar was frequented by those who were travelling on to Salisbury or Winchester or even further afield.

My parents considered they were 'done' on the ingoing, which was the sum charged by the outgoing tenants for furniture, glasses etc., and never recovered financially from this. But for me, it was great fun. Attached were five acres of fields and the gardener/handyman took me bird-nesting and showed me the delights of the countryside. As a family group, we were all very fond of animals and my parents started a small-holding with heifers, pigs, geese, poultry, pullets and bantams, and also started to grow curly kale, potatoes, peas, runner beans, lettuce, strawberries and raspberries.

I sat the Common Entrance for St Swithun's School, Winchester, and I passed with the suggestion that I have private tuition in maths, as geometry and algebra were still a mystery to me. I started at St Swithun's on my thirteenth birthday and I had to be driven some four miles by car to catch a local bus to take me into Winchester and another bus to take me up the hill. I thoroughly enjoyed it to begin with as I had been away from school for so long and started making friends.

I cannot think that I benefitted or otherwise from my experience in South Africa. I just accepted the school uniform, neither liking it or disliking it, but I noted that I didn't grow very much and was pleased at the thought that I would not be costing my parents money because they wouldn't have to buy more school uniform for me.

I invited two girls to spend half-term with me and the visit went very well and was much enjoyed. I wanted to go up a form in the autumn and stay with my new friends, so I worked very hard to pass the exams at the end of the summer term. If I was not able to make up the work done in the school year during the previous autumn and spring terms, I would have to stay down and do another year in the same form.

I did very well indeed in the examinations and was not only put up a form but a division as well, and went into the 'brainy' division. I left my new friends behind and although I maintained my position in this form, I never did as well again.

My sister and I were given a pony called Rusty. I already had dogs, cats and rabbits as pets but the arrival of Rusty, which caused us to join the local pony club, made school take second place in my mind. Rusty was soon joined by Saudi, who kicked me in the head and I was concussed so he was sold and replaced by Firefly. I had a passion for Firefly. She was an ex pony racer who had run under the name of Severn Sisters II and was 14.3 hands high. Some people would describe her as a thoroughbred weed or a blood weed. Not quite a horse, but every appearance of a thoroughbred. I just loved animals so I was always happy to be with them whether riding them or cleaning out the stables, or putting saddle soap on their tack. I remember them today with a fondness as though it were yesterday.

Because of her racing past she pulled a great deal and especially out hunting, so I read books on how to cure this and took her out of a double bridle and put her in a softer vulcanite pelham. Stables were built for them so they could shelter from the cold at night, but we had great difficulty in getting our stepfather to pay for corn and I dreaded asking him to pay the blacksmith for shoeing. We went to gymkhanas and won prizes, but as we didn't have a box we always hacked everywhere, sometimes great distances. Firefly and I got to know each other very well indeed. As I felt she did not have enough corn to hunt all day, I would often walk home for miles beside her so she would not get too tired.

Soon after my parents bought her, I daydreamed the whole of the summer term of winning the showing class at the Oakley Show. I now had a pony that really looked something. The day arrived and we entered the ring and did our little piece, walking and trotting in front of the judges, but when it came to galloping she kept tossing her head and galloped recklessly round the ring, foaming at the mouth, and I had green slime from her tossing head on my face. We then stood in a line for the judges to look at each pony. One by one they were called out and suddenly I realised with sick misery that Firefly had been placed last. We must have had one of those judges who like children's ponies to have good manners as well as good looks. However, the head of our district Pony Club, Colonel Wiggin, did not agree or guessed at my misery and he went to the microphones and announced that Firefly had been awarded a special rosette. He was a very nice man and just the right sort of person to head a pony club.

My mother and stepfather did not take much interest in our Pony Club activities. They were always struggling to make ends meet and I understood this. It fostered in me independence - I didn't need parental approval.

There were lots of children, some with rich parents, belonging to the Vine Hunt. The Vine Hunt covered the Basingstoke and Newbury area. The hunt was to ride to hounds with a view to killing a fox. At Pony Club rallies a few parents arrived in smart cars with hampers in the boot, but myself and most of the other children had a nicely packed lunch wrapped in greaseproof paper plus an apple or an orange which we had crammed into our pockets.

The Pony Club and its activities filled all my free time and I am sure if I had boarded at St Swithun's I would have achieved more 'O' Levels than I did. There were too many distractions at home.

I left school in the summer of 1954 with no occupation in mind. I just stayed at home and hunted all that autumn. After much discussion, it was decided to send me to an Art School in Bournemouth, as I had Art at 'O' level. My step-grandfather and step-grandmother lived in Bournemouth and would be able to keep an eye on me. My step-grandfather had always been very fond of me, and he had been most concerned that I was still at home doing nothing and so he organised digs for me with a widow and her daughter. I went to the Art School in the January of 1955, and for the first time in my life I was very happy indeed and was reminded of this by a popular song of the time called *Stranger in Paradise*. I liked the work - I was working for my Intermediate Examination with the long-term view of becoming a graphic designer. There were male students at the college and I soon made firm friends with one of them and we were always going to parties at 'The College', as it was known, and going for walks around Bournemouth. In the summer we sunbathed, went to dances, took part in the local rag and generally enjoyed ourselves.

I went home for the summer holidays and my stepfather suggested that I might like to help him in the bar. I was good at adding up and it was fun meeting so many people and there was no doubt that I proved somewhat of an attraction to the place with my fair hair, brown back and arms. There I met one Friday evening a man about thirty, short, stocky and blonde. I was told later he was a stockbroker and we talked a little. On the Sunday evening he came with his father, who asked my stepfather if I could come and stay at their country house in Somerset the following weekend. My parents agreed and he came to collect me in his MGB the following Friday, and there began a relationship which proved to be unhappy, unfulfilling and frustrating as well.

He drove me down to Somerset and we stopped at several pubs on the way and we chatted, and he seemed to be very sophisticated. His parents were already in bed and he showed me upstairs to my room and I was given my first proper kiss, which was a great surprise.

I must explain that I had only three cotton dresses, and it was at a time when all girls wore crinkly nylon petticoats underneath their dresses to make them stick out. I had one navy blue one, one pillar box red one and one pale blue one. The next morning I put on my red dress and met his mother for the first time. I can still remember the gasp she gave on seeing me, even now. I looked very young for my age, with my fair hair made even fairer by the sun and wearing a red dress, and this was at a time when girls were expected to conform to a particular image. I enjoyed the weekend and he asked me for another and I realised that I was falling in love for the first time.

I now went reluctantly back to the Art School in Bournemouth and my thoughts were all with my new boyfriend called Tony. He invited me to stay during the Christmas holidays with his parents at their

London flat, but sadly I felt that he was losing his first enthusiasm.

I returned again to the Art School for the spring term but my interest had waned. It would be another four years before I achieved my NDD (National Diploma in Design), and also by that time I had discovered I wasn't nearly as talented as most of the students there.

That summer I left the Art School and started to help my stepfather in the bar, and some people suggested that I become a model. It was the 'thing' for girls to do at that time. As a result I went to a modelling school and completed a course. I had photographs taken and a composite made which I took round to photographers during the day and returned home at night. I had not forgotten my boyfriend Tony, and still saw him from time to time. I got a few freelance jobs modelling teenage fashions, doing catalogue work and hair design photographs, but it didn't begin to keep me and finally I went for an interview to a firm of coat and suit manufacturers for a job as a petite house model. The designer was gay and preferred his clothes to be shown by a model with slim hips, and I got the job. The collection was made on me - I had to go for endless fittings in gloomy workrooms in the rag trade area and, when not modelling, sewed labels into the coats and made up pattern books.

I was now working in London and decided to live away from home permanently. One of the house models introduced me to a friend who needed someone to share her flat and I moved in with her. Later on I went to an agency and found a room at the top of a house in Gloucester Place which was owned by an elderly woman who rented rooms to augment her income. She had a larger room which was rented to an actress, Judy Carne. We made friends and she used to let me use her room when she was out, as it had a long mirror and my room was so tiny and damp you could hardly call it a room at all.

My sister did a secretarial course and had found a flat and some girls from school with whom to share it, but they needed a fifth girl and so I was asked to join them as they had to give a month's rent in advance, and as I had the necessary down payment, I moved in.

Tony was not in love with me as I was with him, and so I told him that I didn't want to see him any more although that was a very difficult thing for me to do. I started to learn shorthand and typing in the evening with a view to getting a job with a more promising future. It was very tiring work being a house model. You arrive at a quarter to nine, put your make up on and the show can start as early as nine o'clock and you could have less than an hour for lunch and then go on working until six, even having to stay later if the buyer had not made up her mind.

I decided to give up modelling and went to work as a receptionist/typist, which meant that when I had nothing to do I could practise on a typewriter and improve my skill. I didn't earn much at the job, but when my shorthand had been perfected I went to work in a typing pool at the Iron and Steel Board. It was good experience as there was a lot of figure work and precision typing. Also, one had to take dictation from quite a number of different men on rather a technical subject, so that my shorthand had to be reasonable and I could not rely on memory and guesswork. Then I chose to do temporary work. I was quite good at this, the hours were shorter, people were more grateful if you were good at your work and didn't take one for granted, and above all I was free and there was variety.

I did not go out with men very often, although in the unprotected situation of a girl living in a flat, I was fair game. Then, one by one, the girls left the flat and we found replacements through agencies. These girls only stayed a short time and the original closeness of the flat was lost. I suggested to my sister that we buy an extra bed and put it in the smaller bedroom and have six girls, which would mean that my sister and I would have to pay only half a rent each, paid in cash anyway so the others didn't discover. The girls all seemed rather unhappy and stories of abortions and visits to VD clinics were commonplace. It surprised me how seldom these girls were rung up by their parents, and none came to see how their daughters were living. The spectre of getting older and still working at a humdrum job and never getting married hung over us all. We worked hard at our meagre wardrobes, lent each other clothes and I took to dressmaking for the others. The cold was frightful in winter, and the only warm place was in bed and in my case I had only blankets. Still we carried on trying and accepting all invitations to parties in the hope that 'he' would come along and release us from a difficult life.

My parents did not visit, but our relationship was rather more distant than for many people. Children are very unreasonable and I think I thought it was rather disloyal to my father to replace him. My mother and stepfather had a daughter in May 1957 who they called Tessa, but as I was twenty years older than she was, I did not see much of her.

I decided to give up temporary work and got a permanent job near the flat with some people who were putting on a West End musical. There was just one office and two men who ran it. I got to know them rather well, and when the show folded and they had to go into liquidation, we remained friends and discussed what we were going to do next. I said I was thinking of doing typing and duplicating on my own, and one of the men said "That's it, printing." He knew of a firm called Scripts Limited who printed scripts by the off-set litho method. He always thought 'big', and they rented offices above the Brompton Arcade in Basil Street, and I joined them. The business expanded and printed letterheads, indeed all sorts of things and it was interesting work. I asked the husband of one of the girls with whom I had shared the flat to put some money into the firm, and I was made a director of the company. Although I did many more hours than I would have done if I was an employee of the company, somehow I never felt it was a waste of life time or anything like that because there was a possible future in it and I was working for myself.

I had a great deal of companionship from my two fellow directors, and discussing the business was much more rewarding than the time I spent with the men I struggled through an evening with from time to time. I particularly enjoyed the company of one of my fellow directors, who was also an actor called John Atkinson. He owned a barkless dog, a Basenji called Koya, and I often went for walks with them in Hyde Park.

I didn't fall in love again and was beginning to despair of ever doing so but was still working at this eventuality. I had remained friendly with one of the girls even after she had left the flat and married a Dane, and I used to stay with them in their house near South Holmwood in Surrey. She introduced me to some friends of hers who lived in the North of England, and it was arranged that I should go to a weekend party there and they would drive me up.

Apparently, they were short of girls and I set about persuading my sister to go. She said she wanted to go to a twenty-first birthday party in London but I objected very forcefully, saying she would know all the men who would be there and here was a chance to break new ground. I persuaded her and through my friends who lived in South Holmwood, it was arranged that she would be driven up by Bill Shand Kydd and his girlfriend.

Bill Shand Kydd was the son of a talented wallpaper designer who had made a great deal of money, and I think he had also patented polyfiller. Shand Kydd arrived to collect her in something resembling a Maserati and she sat in the back while his girlfriend sat beside him in the front. During the weekend, my sister got on so well with him that on the way back she was sitting in the front and his girlfriend in the back. Bill took her out non-stop, and in a very short time they became engaged to be married. We were both very thrilled about this and soon afterwards she moved into his flat. I found another girl to replace her from an agency, and from thereon had no rent to pay.

3
Courtship

My sister got married to Bill Shand Kydd in January 1963 at Holy Trinity Brompton, and had a large reception at the Hyde Park Hotel. I was one of her three adult bridesmaids. She left for her honeymoon and married life, and I returned to the Melbury Road flat to live with five almost total strangers.

I decided I would like to live on my own and found a ground floor bedsitting room with a bathroom and kitchen at 34 Wilton Crescent and continued to work with the off-set litho printing company. Some time in March, I was invited to stay at the Shand Kydd's country house, Horton Hall, near Leighton Buzzard. On the Saturday, we all went to a drinks party before lunch following a golf match at the local golf course. I was introduced to among others John Bingham. I had heard of him as my sister had mentioned him, but we just shook hands and said "How do you do?" and there was no further exchange between us. In the afternoon there was a point-to-point and we went in a land rover. My sister and I and a hunting friend stayed in the land rover most of the afternoon as it was cold, talking and watching the racing from the finish.

I noticed my future husband, then Lord Bingham, standing against the rails with some other men betting or laying odds. I thought he seemed somewhat apart from the others - this may have been because he looked rather different - in that he looked a gentleman almost in caricature. This manifested itself in the way he was dressed, baggy cavalry twills, tweed cap, his height and his moustache on his youthful face added to that impression.

I did not see him again until the following August. I had been told by my sister that they had met him in the South of France. He had his boat with him, where he appeared short of people to have dinner with as he was always ringing them up and asking if he could join them.

As a result of these meetings, Bill Shand Kydd said to him that he must come and stay with them at their country house, and asked him what girl he would like invited along and he asked for me. My sister informed me that he had asked for me and that he had socialist parents who were a cause of some concern to him, and that he was a professional gambler. My sister also warned me by saying "He's only a gambler and he's said to be queer."

I was duly trotted up for the weekend and we met in the drive where he had just got out of his green Aston Martin. He smiled at me and I walked on ahead. Bill Shand Kydd dominated the mealtime conversation and we all laughed a great deal, but neither of us said very much. On the Saturday afternoon, the others went off to look at the horses, and we stayed behind and he offered to teach me to play backgammon. He patiently taught me the moves and I attempted to learn. I didn't feel any chemistry. I had no impression of him other than that I have already described.

Later that evening some girls with loud voices arrived with their mother to have drinks with the Shand Kydds. My immediate impression was very confident girls who would be good at drinks party conversation. I retreated to a sofa at the back of the room, and to my surprise he followed me and started to talk seemingly having no interest in the new arrivals, although they were good looking and most men would have joined in some sort of conversation with them. They left and we had dinner. By then I realised that he was rather interested in me. He said 'goodnight,' and smiled at me and asked if he could drive me home on the Sunday evening. I did not feel excited, but I was pleased and agreed to his suggestion. When we got into the car and started to talk I discovered that he had not been confirmed. Neither had I. It seemed a curious common denominator, but it was one that got us talking. He dropped me off at Wilton Crescent and asked me out the following Tuesday. He arrived to collect me in his London runabout, which was a grey Simca. As soon as we were both in the car, he switched on the radio and we drove in silence with the delicious smell of an expensive aftershave filling the car. We got out at Annabel's, the fashionable nightclub which had recently opened in Berkeley Square, and walked in after he had signed the register.

I believe that he had been to the club before, although it had opened only very recently. I later discovered he was a founder member.

We sat down and we talked - or rather he talked. He told me about his powerboat *White Migrant*, which he kept on the Hamble. He confided his hope of winning the *Daily Express* Powerboat Race that September. He then asked me if I would join him for a weekend at the Hamble Manor Hotel and go out on his boat. He told me that Bill Shand Kydd and other powerboat enthusiasts would also be staying there.

We drove down, and it seemed clear that he was very involved with his boat and thoughts of the coming race. On the Saturday, we went over on his boat to Cowes. It was my first experience of a powerboat. It was quite exhilarating. I had to concentrate every inch of the way in holding on to the front rails as we bounced from wave to wave. It wasn't at all sick-making, and an enjoyable experience.

Afterwards we went back to the Hamble Manor and into his bedroom.

I said how much I had enjoyed the trip and then he looked closely at me and said "You haven't got a line on your face." I still did look very young for my age, and he found difficulty in believing that I was 26-years-old. He was staying down after the weekend at the Hamble to do further work on his boat. There had been suggestions that I should go back with the Shand Kydds by car. After lunch he took me into his bedroom and told me that he thought it would be better for me to go back by train. He put me on the train and I was slightly annoyed, as it would have been more fun to go back with the Shand Kydds, but wished him luck with the race which he did not invite me to watch, and we parted.

It was with some shock that I read in the *Evening Standard* the following Saturday, 7th September, words to the effect that his powerboat had sunk despite leading the field for some time. I knew this would be a bitter disappointment to him, especially as it appeared to have sunk for no reason. It had a fibre-glass hull and he was leading going around the Isle of Wight. I then had a call from him asking me to come to dinner and watch the powerboat race on film, which he had arranged to show on his projector.

A letter written just after the powerboat race in August 1963 shows how seriously he took all things to do with his boat. It is particularly interesting, because it concentrates on propellers and indicates how obsessive he was:

Flat 50,
22, Park Crescent,
London, W.1.

21st September, 1963

F. Cooper, Esq.,
Beech Grove,
Brading, I. W.

Dear Mr Cooper,

I have been so involved with my boat that I have never written to thank you for your letter of August 9th giving me your recommendations for propellers. I had so many different propellers to try and at the same time difficulties with one of my engines that it was nearly all last minute work. Some of my figures appear contradictory and I can only give you a few examples.

With 14 x 17 3 bladed we obtained 40 knots at 3800 revs. on both engines. With 13 x 17 3 bladed we obtained 40 knots at 5100 revs. With 13 ½ x 17 3 bladed 42 knots at 4500 revs.. With 16.93 x 13.98 (430 x 355) 2 bladed we obtained 44 knots at 4600 revs.. We raced with the 2 bladed.

The difficulty as I see it is the absence of a firm in this country which has the technical knowledge or ability to design and produce a perfectly matched set of propellers. With one pair of English propellers we obtained 5200 revs on one engine and 4500 on the other. I foolishly spent a day going through one engine to find out what was wrong with it. We eventually put on a different set of propellers and solved the problem! The two-bladed were from Radice in Milan; they were ordered three months before the race and I got them with three days to spare.

Courtship

I had been told by Lincoln Cars (agents for Ford) that my engines developed their horse power of 400 at 4500 revs.; I later learned that this power was only obtained at 5000 revs.. With one pair of propellers a higher speed was obtained at 4600 revs than at 5000! With my new boat next year I shall spend the whole summer trying 50 different pairs and maybe I will find the right one.

Yours sincerely,

I cannot explain why, but he had quite a detailed knowledge of propellers, which leads me to believe that the propellers might well have been responsible for his body never being found following his disappearance. He obviously knew a great deal about them.

I have never read a letter more obsessive than the one I have quoted above. He was obsessive about gambling and anything he was interested in.

I arrived at his flat, 22 Park Crescent, where his younger sister Sarah (Sally), her vicar husband William Gibbs and an old army friend from National Service days in Germany and his wife were already assembled. We watched the film and he pointed out his boat and details of the race with enthusiasm. We had drinks afterwards and the army wife asked him if he was a peer. He replied very seriously that he only had a courtesy title and she said "Oh, so you're just an ordinary person like the rest of us." It was a needling attitude and I noticed it, and it seemed as though he was being attacked.

I already knew that he was not a peer and I had no feeling that we were both solitary figures, despite what I have said. A peer has a seat in the House of Lords and a courtesy title is held by the offspring of a peer. He was an offspring of the 6th Earl of Lucan.

I had the feeling that evening that he was on his own, I was on my own, and the rest were together. I was to get this feeling many times during our marriage. They looked at me curiously and we went to the Cordon Rouge in Marylebone Lane for dinner, and I sat between William Gibbs and his army friend. I turned my attention to William Gibbs, whose conversation seemed slanted at whether I should be out with his noble brother-in-law and whether I was a Christian. I made some rather unchristian replies, which appeared to stun him, and I count it as a compliment that he remembered my comments well enough to reproduce them in his affidavit for use in the custody case some ten years later.

The following weekend, on the Sunday, he asked me out to lunch and took me to the cinema in the afternoon. Then we went back to Park Crescent and he put the gramophone on and started to write letters. We must have sat there for two hours without much conversation. He made a telephone call to Stephen Raphael about the evening poker game, and then drove me home about six o'clock leaving me with a book called *All Horse Players Die Broke*, which he said I must read.

He rang me about quarter to ten the next morning and suggested dinner again. This time we talked about my off-set litho printing company and he tried to get me to talk about the company's finances, which I didn't want to do. He then told me why he had become a professional gambler and about life in the bank. It did sound rather deadly.

His Uncle Johnny Bevan had arranged for him to have an interview with William Brandts, merchant bankers, and he was taken on in the investment department of the bank where he shared an office with other men for £500 a year. He said that although the work did interest him, he could not see much future in it as he was not a Brandt, and therefore not likely to become a director as there were rather a lot of Brandts. He said he had started playing poker in a hard school at Crockfords (an old-established casino) around 1960 where he had met Stephen Raphael, who had introduced him to the Hamilton Club off Park Lane where there was a good school playing for high stakes with swings of as much as £800 a night one way or the other, although usually less.

It enabled him to live away from home in more style. He did not seem too impressed by what I had told him about the off-set litho printing company, and said he was "worried about me." He also said that he was not as conservative as he might appear. I now had a premonition that I was going to marry him - I sometimes get premonitions which I cannot explain.

I cannot say that I was especially attracted to him. He was probably more attracted to me than I was to him.

The following weekend we went down for Sunday lunch with the Shand Kydds. It was a good lunch and although we were asked for dinner, we left about 4.30pm. He drove back to London very fast and when we got closer to London and the traffic became thicker, he seemed to become more impatient and sweat appeared on his forehead. Indeed, I felt the tension that he was feeling build up in me. We got back to 22 Park Crescent and went into his flat. I sat down on the sofa in the living room, which was dominated by his grand piano, feeling unable to move. He went to the telephone and rang Stephen Raphael: "Ah... Steve?...er ...er...tell the boys I won't be coming tonight... All right? I'll speak to you in the morning."

I realised that he had done an unusual thing and cancelled his poker game. He came into the room and walked towards me, picked me up off the sofa where I was sitting and carried me into his bedroom.

We went out to dinner later and we talked about a silver trophy he intended making of his sinking powerboat. I hardly said anything and we went back to his flat to spend the night.

Early in the morning, he woke me up and said, "Will you marry me?" I didn't reply and amazingly fell asleep again. He woke me again and he asked me the same question. I replied, "Yes, I will marry you," and he went into the kitchen and made some coffee and toast for us and looked at me very lovingly. Later that morning we went to Cartier to buy my engagement ring. I said I wanted an emerald, and that is what he bought me. It was small and modern in design and I was very happy with it.

He organised the announcement to go in *The Times* by asking his father to arrange it. He then rang two of his girlfriends whilst I was with him and told them very happily that he was getting married. He rang Mrs Tucker and she asked my name, and on being told 'Veronica Duncan', she said, "It's very plain," and he said, "Yes, it is."

We faced the press and underneath the banner headline "Lord Bingham to wed business girl", he was quoted as saying that he was proud of me and that he intended to go into business himself. The announcement appeared on 14th October 1963, and it was a surprise to most people we knew. The day we got engaged he arranged to have dinner with his army friend and his wife. My husband made an excuse not to be there when they arrived, so I offered them a drink. I made an attempt to talk to them as he had suggested, but they appeared bored, disinterested and not prepared to make an effort so I suddenly told them "John and I are going to be married. Do you like my ring?" His army friend got to his feet and kissed me, and soon after my husband came into the room and without saying anything about our impending marriage, we drove to the Clermont Club to have dinner. The Clermont Club was a casino first and foremost, but you could also have dinner there.

Nothing was said throughout dinner about our marriage, and so his army friend plied him with alcohol and eventually after much prompting he told them and they congratulated him and it was clear to me that he was quite drunk... he was clearly feeling the emotional strain. We drove home and I went back to Wilton Crescent feeling anxious, a feeling I was to have throughout our marriage.

4

Introductions

A meeting was arranged with his parents at the Arts Theatre Club for dinner. His father and mother were already at the table and I was introduced. Almost immediately, my mother-in-law launched into a socialist political diatribe and it culminated as far as I can remember with my saying "So you put socialism before humanity?"

I cannot remember what they looked like, but probably like a couple of elderly old buffers. I have already stated that my mother-in-law launched into a socialist political diatribe which was one of her favourite ploys, so I cannot say that they greeted me warmly. They did not ask me any questions about myself. My husband just listened - he was probably used to this kind of behaviour from my mother-in-law. He would never have held hands under the table.

I didn't know my mother-in-law well enough to make an assessment as to whether I liked her or not.

His father had looked appalled and tried to pour oil on troubled waters... it was a bad start. There were a few other meetings - I took him to the Wheatsheaf to meet my mother and stepfather. We arrived for lunch, and the meeting was a good deal more amicable than the meeting with his parents. I don't know what they thought of my husband - but I am sure they wouldn't have said anything disparaging whatever they actually thought. I cannot remember what we ate, but I am sure they were happy for me. My husband engaged with my parents satisfactorily. We didn't stay long.

Later on I went to his parents' third floor flat in Hanover House NW8. I cannot remember why I went. It was a downright dirty flat, not just shabby but also quite large and rambling. I could see that it was not the sort of home background that you might have expected on meeting my husband. I don't know if my mother-in-law employed a cleaner, but she probably employed students to do some cleaning from time to time. They ate in the kitchen with ill-assorted chipped mugs and some cutlery with lots of dirty unwashed saucepans lying about the place.

I met the family doctor, Dr Ann Thompson, while I was there. She was a National Health GP and my husband consulted her about the large number of spots that had come out on my face and she said it was 'nerves', and when we were married they would go away. She was right, they did. She continued to be his doctor for some time after our marriage, but she never became my doctor as well. When his mother, he and I were together she dominated the conversation, mostly talking to my husband and I was on the outside, but I did not feel cut out or ostracised. His father, in 1951, had been Parliamentary Under-Secretary of State for Commonwealth Relations and was well used to putting people at their ease, and so he was not difficult to talk to. He signed the back of my passport photograph confirming it was me, although he hadn't known me for the required six years. He wasn't pompous about it and I liked him.

I then went to a dinner party arranged by one of my husband's unmarried girl friends and met his previous steady girlfriend, who seemed nice enough. We had lunch with Roxanna Vereker, wife of Sir Gordon Vereker previously mentioned, who had given him a large cheque as a wedding present of which Sir Gordon, who was very mean with his wife's money, would not have approved. I rather liked her, she was lots of fun and at the end she said "I can see why he decided to marry you, you're very pretty."

The next introduction planned was to Mrs Tucker in America and it was decided we should fly, although I am petrified of flying. My previous flight to South Africa had caused this fear. He agreed that if we flew there we could come back by boat. I didn't know much about Mrs Tucker other than he had spent the war years with her in America. He did not confide in me about the misery of being sent away during the war, and he never did. He told me very little about his life before meeting me, and I congratulate him on being reticent. I think I told him far too much about my life before meeting him.

We arrived in New York and drove to 733 Park Avenue, Mrs Tucker's New York mansion. We arrived in the afternoon and were shown to our bedrooms by an imposing butler/manservant and we rested. At about five o'clock, I started to get dressed for dinner - we were going out to her country house in Connecticut - when I heard a knock on the door. I said "Come in," and Mrs Tucker introduced herself. "You're very small," she said, and I replied "Yes." We drove in her Rolls Royce to her country house, Penwood, where I met several of her relations including her sons Carll Tucker Jr. and Luther Tucker, and their wives and various grandchildren. I wore one of the elegant dresses my husband had bought for me before we left London - it would have been a little black dress and I was pleased to have chosen it although it was very tight and I had to get my future husband to zip me up and unzip me when I wore it. I was asked if I had bought the dress in America and where I got my jewellery from.

I realised that my future husband wanted me to see a part of his background that he was proud of, and also for his substitute war mother to meet his future wife. We were taken to the theatre, a must for smart Americans and on Sunday he said I must attend the local Episcopalian church in Park Avenue to please Mrs Tucker and for her to approve of me. He did not come with us. Mrs Tucker was a civilised woman and would never have disclosed her feelings if they were not favourable. To me, Mrs Tucker was an elderly American woman.

We also attended a country wedding of one of her grandchildren at Penwood - it was charming and American, but as we passed down the line we both noticed that the bridegroom looked uneasy and shifty and the fortune hunter he was later proved to be.

The dinner table was grand at the house in Park Avenue, with many courses, all drinks served with ice and specially embroidered drink mats. There were several large portraits about the house and good heavy solid furniture.

We also visited my husband's sister Jane, who lived in a tenement block on East 66th Street. It was shabby and small, and she had two children and was very much tied to the home. I thought her quiet and shy, and she spoke with an American accent. Her husband was a very unsure of himself American, much overawed by the fact that he had married into the English nobility. I gathered the marriage had caused some distress to Mrs Tucker, who thought she could have done better. I don't think my husband and his elder sister Jane were close.

My husband told me that Mrs Tucker had indicated to him that one of her grandchildren or an American heiress would be a good idea. He explained to me that nowadays, all the American heiresses had their money tied up in foundations and it was hard to lay one's hands on the cash, and it was not worth marrying for this reason as a man would have to 'toe the line'. I think Mrs Tucker was rather disappointed that he had not married an American. He also introduced me to Lili Ohrstrom, a very attractive American girl, unhappily married whom he had taken out several times although they had not got on to intimate terms. She was a very gay, talkative and laughing girl. We went to El Morocco, which is a very well-known fashionable restaurant for dinner, and she brought a man with her. She saw us off on *The France*, a great liner and gave us a Steuben glass penguin as a parting gift. We shared a cabin and it was all very peaceful and civilised. I was not excited about being in America and the voyage took only four days, so I travelled with relatively few clothes. *The France* was like a floating hotel, everyone had their own table in the dining room. We were invited to a drinks party by the Captain.

Our engagement was short, the bare six weeks and my father-in-law arranged for my banns to be called at St Paul's Wilton Place. We were too late to book the Hyde Park Hotel for our reception and so booked the Carlton Tower instead, and arranged to be married at Holy Trinity Brompton on 28th November.

There had to be a financial arrangement made between my parents and his about the cost of the wedding. The arrangement was private so I have no idea what it was. We arranged for them to meet at the bar in the House of Lords. We arrived, then came his father and mother and last of all my stepfather and mother. It was quite terrible. After ordering drinks, there was a complete silence. I caught my father-in-law's eye and he smiled... he knew that we were feeling just the same. Somehow a desultory conversation on matters pertaining to the wedding was started, drinks completed and my parents and his went off to have lunch in the House of Lords dining room.

Afterwards, I rang my mother to ask how it went and she replied carefully, "We thought your father-in-law charming," but described my mother-in-law as going up to tables in the dining room and appearing to attack people she knew who were eating there.

It was arranged for me to spend the night before our wedding with my South Holmwood friends while my husband attended his stag party. We both felt extremely ill the next morning. He had only three days before supervised the final fitting for my wedding dress and had approved it.[1] This was typical of the interest and care he took that the wedding should be what would be expected. He had gone to some trouble about the music and hymns which would be used during the service. I was to enter to *Ode to Joy* and thought it a most appropriate choice. Neither of us had any feeling about the enjoyment of weddings, it was just something that would be expected of us by other people.[2]

I took a room in The Carlton Tower as my sister had just given birth to her first child on November 24th and she was still recovering from the birth. A hairdresser came to the hotel to dress my hair and set the tiara in place, which had been designed by Violet Lucan, on my head with the veil. We arrived at the church with much flashing of cameras[3] and my stepfather and I waited for the signal for us to

---

1   I did not like my wedding dress and thought it made me look too insubstantial. I threw it away after our wedding.

2   Human affection is very ephemeral. I was twenty-six and it was about time I got married and he was approaching twenty-nine and thought to be of an age where a man should be married, although more particularly in America than it was here.

3   There had not been much coverage of our future marriage.

process up the aisle. Something went wrong with the prompting mechanism and we did not go up to *Ode to Joy*, and half-way up the aisle I realised what had happened and almost drew back. Like many brides I did feel nervous. However, I went on and we reached the altar. My husband went forward and said something to the organist and in fact instructed him to play *Ode to Joy* on the way out.

The Reverend Prebendary Gilliatt seemed to want me to hurry through the responses, and a feeling of annoyance went through me and I spoke louder. My sister said that she heard the note of defiance in my voice. I couldn't stop a nervous cough towards the end and then we went in to sign the register. Thereupon I was faced with Princess Alice, and my memory flashed back to what I had been told that Janet, Marchioness of Milford-Haven had said to David Milford-Haven on being told that she would have to curtsey to her. She was said to have said, "I won't curtsey to your damned aunt." From this, I realised that I would be expected to do so and did so. My mother followed suit. We signed the register, my husband putting 'gentleman' as his occupation. My mother-in-law had been a lady in waiting to Princess Alice, which is why she attended, but it wasn't a big society wedding.

My mother-in-law said, almost surprised, "How nice you look." She had made an effort for her, and was even wearing a pair of diamond clips on the front of her dress. We then went out to *Ode to Joy* and posed for photographs, then drove to The Carlton Tower. The reception was held in a room with rather a low ceiling and nothing seemed to be organised. We stood there in the receiving line as the guests came past. We both had difficulty in dredging up many people to ask to the wedding, but myself particularly. It seemed as sparsely attended as did the church service. It must have been one of the shortest wedding receptions on record as we stayed for about half an hour and guests were still arriving as we left. We walked quickly down the stairs, I threw my bouquet to a former flat mate and got into the car to head for the boat train to Paris... What a blessed relief that was.[4]

We stayed two nights at the Plaza Athenee, arrived there on the morning of the 29th and slept all day as we were exhausted. I then wrote a letter thanking Aunt Margaret (Alexander of Tunis) for lending her tiara, which had been given to her by her mother who had designed it. As I did not like flying, the plan was for us to go on the *Orient Express* to Istanbul. The idea sounded romantic, but the reality was not. As we progressed out of Europe the restaurant car was taken off, and we had no relevant currency to buy food at the stops and we had no way of knowing how long the train would stay at the station. Eventually, a restaurant car was put on but the food was quite extraordinary. Goat's cheese, olives and black bread was all that was available. The train got slower and slower the closer we got to Istanbul. It was a relief to get to the Hilton Hotel in Istanbul. We visited a few mosques, wandered about the streets, noticed that the cinema hoardings were painted not printed and that the cars on the road were American and about a decade old. It didn't take us long to decide we were not enjoying ourselves and we left for home early by aeroplane as we couldn't face the return by train. The honeymoon felt strange and there seemed to be little to talk about, and my feeling was a longing for home. He seemed lost in thought, and also seemed to be rather bored.

---

4   I do not know why we left. I do not know what food was served, and cannot remember any speeches or toasts - we were not a popular couple! I remember one guest remarking in rather a loud voice, "There's nobody here!"

5
Marriage

We had some very generous wedding presents and among these were gambling chips valued at £200 from John Aspinall, Ian Maxwell-Scott and John Burke, the three directors of the Clermont Club. As soon as we returned from our honeymoon, my husband said that he had it in mind to go to the Clermont Club and play some gentle chemmy with the chips.[1]

We decided to lie low for a few days so that nobody would know that we had returned early from our honeymoon, as it might have appeared that we had not enjoyed ourselves. He left it to me to unpack the remaining wedding presents and write the 'Thank you' letters while he amused himself by playing the piano. He had become interested in music while at Eton because they had very good musical appreciation instruction, and after his National Service he taught himself to play the piano and also had lessons from a Mrs Dora Milner. He continued to have these lessons on and off until her death in 1968. My husband was not a good pianist - he mostly played Bach and occasionally Scott Joplin. His favourite opera was *Fidelio*.

The flat was not a large flat to keep clean, but he was the most untidy person one could imagine. He couldn't pick up a book and then put it back, and his clothes were always strewn about the floor. It was very disheartening and never failed to be a source of irritation for me.

---

[1] Chemin de fer is a game of pure chance where the winning card is the one closest to a value of 9. Cards are stacked in a shoe and a dealer shuffles them and the shoe moves round the table in a clockwise direction.

We did not see much of my husband's mother, although after we returned from our honeymoon she had said, "Will you lend John to me so that we can go on a trip to Russia?" I had smiled back agreeably as I could see from his face how unattractive this idea was.

One evening in early December, we went to the Clermont Club and he sat in at the 'minnows game', and I sat quietly beside him.

Before long I realised that all was not going well, as he kept calling for the changer and looking rather distraught. I did not say anything to him. Eventually he jumped from his seat and I went with him, and he approached John Burke and asked him if he could join the 'big' game. John Burke was firm. "No, John," he said. "Go home." We left and got into the car and we drove home in silence. Then he said, "I'm sorry, I'm sorry." I asked, "How much did you lose?" He replied £8,000, and then "I'm sorry." It was, to say the least, a shock. After his powerboat sunk, the Lloyds' insurers tried to salvage his boat and failed. They paid in full £9,000, which was his capital, but never insured a powerboat again.

I realised he had lost all his money and more besides. Somehow, he was being as nice to me as he had been to me since our marriage and this compensated for the shock, and I said, "Never mind, you'll win it back again," and rubbed his back as comfortingly as I could. I tried to act positively as I would consider this to be my duty as a gambler's wife. When we went to bed, he tossed and turned and I tried to reassure him. We agreed that it would be best to ring Stephen Raphael in the morning. If he couldn't pay, he was worried that Aspinall would post him on the board in the Clermont Club as a defaulter, which was very bad for a professional gambler because it meant his credit wasn't good and people wouldn't play with him.

Stephen Raphael, having suffered similar reverses, was very sympathetic and lent him the money with which to pay, or at any rate enough to keep Aspinall quiet. However, the news got out that he had lost a large sum of money. We spent a very unhappy Christmas. He decided that he must insure his father's life because his father had not made over the estate, and if he died within the seven-year period there would be heavy death duties. His father agreed to this and had the medical demanded by the insurance company, and was passed A1.

Early on the morning of 21st January 1964, he received a call from his mother saying "Daddy's dead." He had woken up at about 6 o'clock in the morning complaining of a pain in his chest, and my mother-in-law had gone to the telephone to call a doctor and when she came back he was dead. The war wound in 1918 may have taken a higher toll than the medical showed. He had a fitted steel stomach after sustaining gunshot wounds.

Pat's sister, Lady Barbara Bevan, had died the previous November of cancer and my husband went to his grandmother and told her of his father's death. It was a cruel double blow to her. She felt he had not been looked after properly by the National Health doctors her daughter-in-law had insisted on.

However, despite the heavy duties incurred because the insurance policy had not been signed and completed, he at last had some capital or land that could be sold.

My father-in-law's death initiated me into one of my more grisly experiences. I barely knew my father-in-law. This was the first cremation I had ever experienced. I felt very sorry for my mother-in-law for being widowed at a relatively early age.

He was cremated at Golders Green crematorium. When we arrived I saw what looked like a hymn number apparatus outside the funeral chapel, which read 'THE LATE THE EARL OF LUCAN'. My husband, myself, his sister Sally and his mother were the only people present. I do not know why there were so few mourners. We sat in the front right hand pew where we could see the coffin on a dais. There was some non-religious, rather esoteric music playing, and then it appeared to me that I was having an optical illusion and that the coffin appeared to be moving. Indeed, it was and it then glided a little faster out of sight. The service appeared to go very quickly. The music stopped, and we got up and walked out. As we got outside, I looked back and the hymn number apparatus now read 'THE LATE MRS BROWN'. It was all very dehumanising, I thought. I do not know what happened to his ashes. I did not see any flowers and the only condolence letter I know of was from Quintin Hogg, later Lord Hailsham, who wrote to my mother-in-law saying, "Your husband I liked and admired, but you I cannot stand."

We then had lunch in a Steak House in the Marylebone High Street, whereupon my mother-in-law burst into tears and said how some of her poorer socialist acquaintances had written offering her financial help to tide her over! My mother-in-law was not poor - she was just being toadied to by some of her socialist 'friends'. She seemed unable to release the emotion of natural sadness at her life partner's death without bringing socialism into it.[2]

I vaguely remember a meeting in the House of Lords, which seemed to serve as a memorial service for my father-in-law, but all I can remember is seeing Harold Wilson there. I wore my favourite black Fabiani suit, which I had acquired before marriage.

We had practised no form of contraception. Indeed, during our engagement we had rather a scare that I might be pregnant and he had said "I will take you to Switzerland to have the operation. No-one will be able to say of you that you had to get married." This thought for me at the time made me feel loved, wanted and protected.

My relationship with my sister was not good. It seldom was. We had had a row, although I cannot remember now what it was about. I told my husband about it and he went round to the Shand Kydds and took up the cudgels on my behalf, although I had told him not to. I don't know what my husband told my sister. My sister burst into floods of tears and Bill arranged to have lunch with my husband in order to smooth things over. She had been reduced to tears because Bill had not stood up for her when my husband had told her off. This took place many years ago and I have included it to show that our relationship was not good. Bill was still too delighted at having a noble brother-in-law. There were mixed feelings about my becoming a countess so soon after our marriage before people had got used to this possibility, and of course we were very young.

---

2   To me socialism means state ownership of everything and is connected to the Labour Party. I believe it has now gone out of fashion.

People treated me with either grovelling sycophancy or downright rudeness but mostly downright rudeness. My Aunt Elsie said "We'll have to curtsey to you next," but in a kindly tone.

    I did not conceive immediately and perhaps the memory of his mother's early inability to conceive made him rush me to a gynaecologist for tests. The doctor, on hearing we had only been married eight weeks, squeezed my ovaries and said "Go home and try again." I must have conceived very soon afterwards as our first daughter Frances was born in October of that year. One morning I woke up and, having had a cup of coffee, felt very sick, and indeed was sick. This happened three mornings running, and my husband rang his mother and excitedly told her that I had been sick and perhaps I was pregnant. They had a long discussion about my sickness and despite her doubts, I was shortly afterwards confirmed pregnant and my female private GP arranged for my confinement to be handled by an obstetrician of some repute and a bed booked for me at the London Clinic.

    I considered it my duty as a wife to have children and I did not wish we had more time together. My main duty was to produce a son and heir. It was just something that would be expected of me.

    We started looking for a house, and we found one in The Vale in Chelsea which we liked. Our preference really was for Belgravia, which is rather closer to the clubs. They were asking £25,000 freehold, but as we had been given £20,000 as a marriage settlement we needed another £5,000. The Vale did have a garden but it was rather far from central London. However, my husband had decided to go with Bill Shand Kydd to Nassau for the Miami/Nassau powerboat race in April. They had both commissioned a boat to be built by a Miami boat builder. We left for Miami and stayed at the Racquet Club, which was rather a seedy club very far from being one of the large hotels on Miami Beach. It was the sort of place where men bring their mistresses rather than their wives, and you dare not take the cover off the mattress if you were squeamish. My husband was so absorbed in the workings of the engines and the boat's performance that I might as well not have been there. I must say I found Miami and the powerboating people rather deadly.

I suffered morning sickness as most women do at the beginning of a pregnancy, but it did not last long. I rather irritated my husband by reading baby books, which I was gripped by, although I could not shop for baby clothes.

I felt extremely unhappy, and longed to go back to London and continue with our house hunting. He did not win the race or anywhere near. When we got back we drove past The Vale and we saw to our regret that during our absence it had been sold, so we took to driving about and looking at For Sale boards and then ringing up the agents. We looked at quite a few of them and a most surprising number of them were in very bad shape indeed inside. People on fixed incomes were selling and there was a slump in house prices.

Finally, one day we saw a board outside 46 Lower Belgrave Street. It was owned by a rich man called Anthony Galliers-Pratt, who had spent a lot of money on the house and it was in good enough condition for one to live in it without redecorating it. He was keen to sell. He had bought a house in the country, and number 46 had been on the market for some time. He sold it for £17,500 and we also bought the curtains and carpets. It was a bargain and we were delighted with it.

My husband was still playing in the poker school at the Hamilton Club, but it was gradually coming to a standstill - the players were running out of money - but we also visited Crockfords from time to time and we gently ticked over. We spent a lot of our time together. I was very happy about spending time with him. I did not cook as we mostly ate out. He was a creature of habit, as am I. We had lunch together most days and he was very affectionate when he came back from playing poker, especially if he had lost when he would hold me very close to him. He did not have a nickname for me, although if we left anywhere together he would say to me, "Home, James."

When my husband's parents gave up the lease of 22 Eaton Square to live in St John's Wood around 1949 in order to live somewhere more fitting to their socialist image, a large amount of furniture and pictures were stored in the Harrods depositories. After my father-in-law's death, my husband, his mother, his sister Sally and I went to the depositories to look at what was there, as it was costing quite a lot to store it. Almost at once we saw before us two pictures of a religious subject which were, in fact, by Filipino Lippi.[3] My mother-in-law and sister-in-law guffawed at these because of their religious subject, which was automatic from them. My husband did not laugh. He later sent for an expert from Sotheby's, who was delighted by this find and others from an Italian school. They were sold rather ambiguously as 'The Property of a Gentleman' for quite a lot of money. The furniture was not very good or exciting, but we all chose what we wanted and wrote with chalk on each item where we wanted it to be sent.

We were able to furnish Lower Belgrave Street with some of this furniture. Our immediate financial problems were solved, and Stephen Raphael's loan was repaid. We had had a substantial injection of money.

We moved into Lower Belgrave Street in July and I supervised the move, not that there was much to move, whilst my husband lunched with the previous owner, Anthony Galliers-Pratt. My husband was a large man and he wanted to be comfortable. His double bed in Park Crescent was rather small, which is why we invested in a large double bed from the London Bedding Centre. We hung the family portraits but there were no picture lights, and it looked a little odd and not pulled together.

I was nearly six months pregnant. One weekend my husband went off to play golf and, so I wouldn't be alone, he arranged for me to stay with his sister Sally and her husband William Gibbs in Aubrey Walk. Her husband was at that time curate at St Mary Abbott's Church, Kensington. They set me to weeding the lawn for quite some part of Saturday afternoon, and I knew the position this required was a good one for producing babies. I had not lost my baby when I went out in the powerboat in March, so hoped all was safe. The Gibbs were cool and I noticed that they talked down to me as though I was

---

3 He was an early renaissance painter of the Florentine school.

of low intelligence, telling me quite simple facts about childbirth and the upbringing of children which, of course, I knew already. It was so staggering that I had to prevent myself from gaping when they spoke. Their house was untidy and disorganised. They had a succession of sullen nannies or help of some kind, one of whom was openly rude to my brother-in-law.

It was a household that makes a major to do about the washing up. The wife has to justify her existence and show how hard she works, and therefore makes the washing up sound like a major production. This conception is both loathsome for guests and for those who live in the house, a wife who makes herself a martyr over the dishes. Properly organised it takes no time at all.

I could be in no doubt about the Gibbs' attitude towards me and I could understand it. They were, in fact, typical of many couples who get married and have children: finances are tight and realise that they are caught in anything but a tender trap, and in order to console and boost themselves must attack other people. Our way of life, although unusual, was not approved of by many people, but we wouldn't attack other people for their way of life.

Shortly after we returned from our honeymoon I was to receive a telephone call from his Aunt Meg (Meade-Fetherstonhaugh), with whom we had stayed at Uppark during our engagement for a shoot. She asked me if I would lend my husband to her as they were having the Queen Mother to lunch and were short of men. I replied that he was out but I would give him her message. When I told him he was extremely annoyed and thought that it was a slight to me so early in our marriage. He rang her back and refused her invitation but showed his irritation, which I thought a mistake. They probably were short of men. Her husband had been left Uppark by two sisters on condition he put his surname 'Meade' in conjunction with theirs, which he did and so they were able to entertain in some style. She was well known for restoring curtains with some special dyes. People from all over the country asked her to do work on their worn fabrics. My husband got the feeling that she loved Uppark a good deal more than her husband. I would not blame her if she did.

Uppark is an 17th century House with views as far south as the English Channel. One of the most interesting features of the house is the dolls' house, which gives a rare and very detailed glimpse of Georgian life both above and below stairs.

She was quite ridiculously snobbish, but it was fascinating to listen to someone who was quite so open about it and it was quite easy to take from an elderly woman. Her daughter-in-law and son were staying with her at the same time as we were, and she was addressing most of her snobbish remarks to her daughter-in-law. She was like some tiny little monument to her time.

We quite often saw the Shand Kydds for dinner and went to their house in Chester Terrace, although they very seldom came to ours. I think we were more often invited by Bill Shand Kydd as they had staff who would cook. My husband seemed happy and enthusiastic about my pregnancy, and after the initial sickness it suited me as a condition very well. He did not make many allowances for my pregnancy - long drives in the car, staying up late and whatever else he wanted. I was quite happy to do whatever he wanted.

I remember once Nanny Coles, who had been permanently reinstated with the family after the children's return from America and who now lived with my mother-in-law, listening to what he expected me to do that evening. Nanny Coles interrupted him saying "Veronica should have more rest," and he replied "She has quite enough rest," and seemed annoyed at the implied criticism.

As my sister-in-law Jane was a doctor and said to go into labour at home and then walk up the street to the nearest hospital, give birth with minimum difficulty and then walk home again, it seemed that I was going to have something to live up to.

The upstairs rooms at Lower Belgrave Street, which were to form the nursery quarters, were in a bad state of decoration and so in the three months up to the birth of our child I painted the walls, doors, windowsills and ceilings, but other than that I did not do a great deal of buying for the expected baby. I was still not sure of the state of ready cash and the shock of the £8,000 loss was still with me. However, an American boat builder and his wife gave us a crib and

Stephen Raphael and his wife a very smart coach-built pram, and so apart from buying four nightdresses and some nappies for the baby I had everything.

The due date for my expected baby was 24th October, and my husband had most unfortunately had an invitation for the beginning of November to drive a powerboat for somebody else in Miami. He was so keen to go that I felt it would be very mean to deprive him of the opportunity of driving a really fast boat with a good chance of winning. It spoilt my peace of mind, however, and I began to become anxious that I would not have my baby on time. I did an enormous amount of painting and jumping about on 21st and 22nd October, and on the evening of the 22nd started laughing uncontrollably, which I had read was a sign of impending birth, and then had my first labour pains. My husband came back from Crockfords and I told him that I thought labour had begun and started giggling again. He got rather annoyed, but the labour pains were faint and I managed to get some sleep. Early next morning, he drove me to the London Clinic and I was in labour for the whole day. My baby was born the next morning by forceps delivery. I was unconscious, and the delivery itself was painless although the part that preceded it, I thought quite appalling. I had hoped for a boy, but Frances, as we called her, was a particularly attractive baby and I soon got over the mild disappointment as my husband seemed very pleased with her.

A week later he drove me home from the London Clinic with Frances and we got into bed and I put her between us, which is what I had wanted. I had been afraid that he would go off to Miami before I could return home with our baby. He probably didn't realise how much I had been looking forward to bringing her home and sharing her with him, which you cannot do in a hospital.

After his departure - he had said "Thank you for letting me go," - there followed a very unhappy week. I had engaged a nurse to look after Frances and she was a real horror. She sent me out to buy things she considered essential for Frances when I could hardly walk because of the many stitches I had had. I also had to take her food to the top of the house, and from time to time she broke into tears and said how much she wished she had married a farmer and had several children. It really was the wrong job for her to be in, at any rate, at her time of life. She was particularly bad on Armistice Day and stayed in her room sobbing most of the time.

I had a visit from Sally and William, who asked why we had given Frances a boys' name and also asked why I wasn't looking after her myself. I didn't say anything. Surprisingly the nurse seemed to feel this to be a slight on herself and her charge, and made some fairly sharp remarks and they left.

Joy upon joy, my husband returned safe and sound early in the morning, looking bronzed and healthy, and we got into bed and were very happy.

6

Frances

We had previously interviewed a sixteen-year-old girl from the North of England to be nanny to our child. She seemed wholesome and willing, and was delighted at the sight of Frances. It was a lonely occupation for such a young girl and there was very little to do for such a young baby as it sleeps most of the time. In January, she felt she had had enough and that she could earn more money in a factory and have more free time. I could see her point. I cannot remember what we paid her, but probably £6-£7 per week. We obtained a very good temporary nanny to replace her while I set about finding a permanent nanny through the Beauchamp Nursery Bureau, a reputable bureau in Beauchamp Place. I interviewed a number of nannies, but they all turned the job down saying the bureau had told them it was a first class job. I knew why they had rejected the job. The nursery was not decorated or equipped to any standard, and it all looked rather sparse and bare. We could not afford to do much renovation at that time.

One day I had a telephone call from a Miss Jenkins, who asked to come and see me about the job at 4 o'clock. I opened the door to see a short, stout woman about 54-years-old. I took her downstairs and gave her a cup of coffee, and we started to talk as I interviewed her. She had previously worked for Mr & Mrs Robin Douglas-Home, who had divorced. They had a son called Sholto, then about two years old. Robin Douglas-Home had been granted access to his son every third weekend, and needed someone to go down to his country cottage to help him look after the child. I gathered Miss Jenkins was in sympathy with Robin Douglas-Home and not with his wife. I was to learn a good deal more about the family.

Miss Jenkins wanted a day off a week - she specified Thursday - and every third weekend before lunch on Friday to return before lunch on Monday, at a wage of eight pounds a week. She was Welsh and I thought her gossipy, and she did not give me the impression of being a first class nanny, although she had worked for a Mr & Mrs James Guinness before the Douglas-Homes for several years and her references were good. I was in no position to get a first class nanny in any case, and it was a question of who would come, rather than who I could choose.

She went upstairs and I showed Frances to her who gave her a beatific smile, and I believe this won Miss Jenkins over. She noted the lack of nursery equipment but I assured her that this would be made good in time. She accepted the job, although we would have preferred the temporary we had to stay on permanently.

I did everything I could to please Nanny Jenkins. She was given an account card for Peter Jones where she could buy any clothes she wanted for Frances, and we also opened an account at Simple Garments in Sloane Street, which she had also asked for. I felt that if she was to take a pride in her job and stay, she should be allowed some choice in her charge's clothes, as I had no strong feelings and knew myself to be a novice and to some extent I hoped to learn from Nanny Jenkins.

In early 1965 my husband received a letter from John Aspinall asking if marriage had quietened him down, and inviting him to come in to the Clermont Club one evening and have a drink. He did this, and a few days later Ian Maxwell-Scott came to the house and put forward a proposition to my husband. This meeting was tape-recorded. Aspinall wanted to have a baccarat game to start early in the evening to keep players interested and occupied until there were enough players available to go over to a chemmy game. They needed a dealer and he offered my husband a percentage of the 'bank' to do this. My husband accepted this offer, and from that time onwards there was a slow weaning away from me being the substantive person in his life to the associates he met at the Clermont Club.

He was expected to be there most nights to deal the baccarat. He wore a dinner jacket and we had dinner in the club beforehand, which was free. It was really rather a degrading thing for a peer of the realm to do and I felt a certain sorrow within me that he was prostituting himself quite so openly, but needs must and he wanted to do it and so I said nothing. He was insulted quite often but he seemed not to mind or even notice. However, the baccarat bank lost money and although the idea was fine in principle, it did not pay off sufficiently to be continued after 1965.

But the habit of going to the Clermont Club was now established, and my husband would play black jack, to which he was greatly addicted, and then go on to play later on in the chemmy game. He said the fascination of black jack was that it helped him in decision making, as one was doing this all the time whilst playing the game. I continued going to the Clermont Club every evening with my husband but I didn't learn much about a gambler's mentality except they have a tendency to chase their losses. It is considered to be 'bad luck' to cross anyone on the stairs.

The chemmy game was backed up by what were known as 'housies', who were paid five pounds a night to sit in and play with chips provided by the house to keep the game going. They were instructed not to get heavily involved and they would automatically give up their seat when a paying client arrived if there was not one available. They were paid ten pounds if the game went on later into the morning. These housies were usually young men, reasonable looking, often having had first class educations but who had somehow opted out of the 'full day's' work for a 'full day's' pay idea and liked the life. There were some older housies as well, who looked amazingly respectable and solid. They kept the fantasy that they were playing with their own money and taking quite seriously their wins and losses, which, in fact, were meaningless. They were part of a way of life. In the early days there were free cigarettes, caviar was available and they would complain that it was too salty and also decried the quality of the champagne as 'too fizzy', although it was, of course, always the best. They propagated their own fantasies in this way and if you knew how much money they owed and that they couldn't have afforded to buy themselves any caviar, it was quite amusing.

Aspinall had great style and spared no expense in making the Clermont Club as perfect as he could. John Fowler decorated the Club and he built on a pavilion as a dining room. The club fulfilled a need in a society which was changing. Few people gave grand parties any more, the civilised exclusive way of life was dying and the Clermont Club was a fantasy you could walk into and meet people who all had in common a liking for a place in the sun.

In the early days, its membership was very exclusive indeed. If you didn't have a title but you were rich, you were even more welcome. I remember that Aspinall recounted to us how he was rung up by a very rich American who asked if he should wear a dinner jacket. Aspinall laughingly said to us, "He could have come in his bathing suit if he'd wanted." Aspinall was a cruel man and controlled his club with the force of his personality.

Aspinall was married to Min (Musker) for most of the time that I knew him. She had replaced his first wife Jane, known as the Spirit of Park Lane, whom he had divorced and won custody of their two children. I never knew Jane and usually never spoke to Min, the exception being one day when I asked her why she was crying and she told me her newly born baby needed an operation. Min had had great difficulty in conceiving a child, and Aspinall would shout, "Every month there's a lot of blood and a lot of tears." Eventually she did conceive, and gave birth to a tiny infant who had a hole in her heart and died following an operation. She was buried in the grounds at Howletts. We did not go to her funeral. Our relationship with Aspinall was to do with gambling and not personal matters.

One evening a rich American was very lucky in the chemmy game and seemed unable to lose. He had been eating and drinking throughout the game when he started choking and went purple in the face. We gazed at him in shocked horror, as it appeared that he was about to have a fit. He opened his mouth and was violently sick all over the huge pile of chips in front of him. Aspinall said harshly to the chef de partie, "Get him upstairs, clean him up and bring him back again." The rest of the table sat in losing gloom. One of the players said, "I don't mind if the chips do have sick on them," but nobody laughed, for the night had been rather a bloodbath and worse was to come for he was not well enough to return and the game had to break up.

The Shand Kydds had been very pompous about our way of life but as their main interest in life apart from horses was their social life, the Clermont Club with its exclusivity had a great appeal. Shand Kydd was unsure of himself and wanted to make his mark in that exclusive milieu. The chemmy game was at its height. There was big money, and at least twice a week large sums changed hands across the chemmy table as my husband struggled to make a crust, as he called it, from the game.

Backgammon was by then being played in the afternoons, and there were a couple of tournaments where the players were auctioned for large sums twice a year. I believe they wrote cheques and IOUs. One night, Shand Kydd played in the chemmy game and won an enormous sum of money, £75,000. My husband stood beside him and told him that there were certain people that he need not 'banco'. It means to bet against another player. To my husband's embarrassment, Shand Kydd repeated the remark so the table could hear, saying, "I know, I don't have to banco." My husband went home and told me that Shand Kydd had won about £75,000. I couldn't help wishing if only it could have been us.

The next morning, I received a telephone call from my sister and she was crying. I asked, "What on earth's the matter? Haven't you won a lot of money?" Apparently Shand Kydd had left with an IOU from Aspinall for the sum he had won, but whilst driving home in the car had some thought about the IOU being no good. He returned to the surprise of the rather gloomy losing table he had left. He sat down again and began to play. His luck had changed, his bancos became wild and he lost back what he had won and much more. There was some confusion over a bet for £40,000, and Aspinall, obviously afraid that things had got out of hand, tried to make it a 'no bet'. Shand Kydd had said, "I can't pay, "I can't pay," and Lady

Osborne had said "You shouldn't play if you can't pay Billy dear." Shand Kydd was by this time distraught and agreed to the 'no bet', although my sister had said "No, no Bill, you must pay."

The disgrace was terrible, for in fact Shand Kydd did have the money with which to pay and the man who let him off the bet was a poorer man. The Shand Kydds' stock went plummeting down, and their hopes of social recognition with it. They decided to sell 33 Chester Terrace and some of their pictures to raise the ready cash with which to pay.

My husband by this time had become totally involved with the Clermont Club and the life. He had lunch every day with his professional gambler friends, and there was by then a large American professional contingent. Apparently you had to register as a professional gambler in America and were taxed accordingly. They had to think of occupations to put on their passports and there were some quite aged 'students'.

My sister told me that when my husband approached the lunch table at the Clermont, people at the table were heard to say "Ah, here comes John Lucan, he'll pay for lunch." My husband was very generous and he also felt that he had to pay to be around, because he felt he wasn't very amusing. However, as he began to establish himself as part of the 'good furniture' at the Clermont, he became more confident and he was no longer taken like this and became popular, probably for the first time in his life, with a group of people.

Although my own role in the life was rather ill defined, as a gambler's wife part of it was to aid him in getting out of a backgammon game when he was winning. He would ask one of the Clermont bar staff to telephone me and ask me to come over for dinner. I would get a taxi as fast as I could and hopefully I would be in time to rescue him from a winning backgammon game turning into a losing one.

I would go home at around twelve o'clock in the club's chauffeur-driven car, which was available for the use of clients. The backgammon game took place on the ground floor, and my husband would see me and say to the other players that he must leave to have dinner. I would sit down and ask for a glass of La Ina sherry before we went in for dinner.

The males at the Clermont Club all had their particular role, whether it was house player, professional, pigeon or dealer etc. My husband became a 'Blue', known as 'Bluecy' for short. This meant he played with half his own money and half Aspinall's, which is almost certainly illegal. He was never a house player.

There were not many women - a few good-looking girls who hung about the gamblers, but very few wives. Susan Maxwell-Scott had long ago been banished to Uckfield by Aspinall. She had a tendency to drink too much and would then talk very loudly and distractingly. Ian Maxwell-Scott had become a joke figure - his drinking and smoking made Aspinall take out an insurance policy on his life, as he felt sure that Maxwell-Scott could not survive the pace. I think Maxwell-Scott felt very much that he had been outstripped by Aspinall. His house at Uckfield was unfinished when we went to stay. There were no curtains at the windows in the bedrooms and no lampshades, bare light bulbs, and he had a brood of children to support. However, the food and drink were always good and Ian Maxwell-Scott loved golf and so did my husband, and so they got on well together.

Susan (Susie) Maxwell-Scott, daughter of Sir Andrew Clark QC, was a lover of the peerage and fancied my husband, and was consequently unfriendly to me. I think part of Ian Maxwell-Scott's appeal was that upon marriage she could then refer to the Duke of Norfolk as "Cousin Bernard." Her dinner table often included lame ducks who were quite vicious, and I didn't enjoy going there very much.

Aspinall had the only freehold house in Lyall Street and it was painted pink to indicate this - the others had to be painted the regulation Grosvenor Estate magnolia, and he owned a Georgian country house in Kent called Howletts, which included his small zoo. His mother, Lady Osborne, who was known as "Al Capone with a shopping basket" by the habituees of the Clermont Club, had a cottage in the grounds and very nice it was too if you didn't mind the nocturnal sounds of gorillas close to your back door.

Aspinall talked a good deal about his parentage, and in particular how he had been conceived as a 'love child' on the banks of the Hooglie river in India and that his father was really a General Bruce and not Dr Aspinall. I could believe this: his brother was called 'Chips' and was absolutely nothing like him, and was also a doctor like his father.

Aspinall loved the peerage but he was quite selective - he wasn't so keen on families that had Christian mottoes like 'Christ is my Hope', but preferred more ferocious ones such as 'I will Conquer', because he said that it meant they were older established noble families.

My social life outside the Clermont Club was by then non-existent. In the early days we had attempted a few dinner parties, but I was never allowed to do the cooking and a catering firm was called in to do it with a hired cook and a couple of waiters. Somehow, however hard I tried they were not successful, and the dinner parties we went to seemed to be such unhappy affairs that we were both in agreement that it was best to leave as soon as decently possible to go to the Clermont Club. It often appeared to me that we had been invited to dinner in order to be picked on. My husband would be asked what he was doing, and in order to bolster himself would boast of our holidays (at a time when there was a currency restriction), and I would sit silently in misery. None of the married couples seemed happy or content with their lot, and in a way the Clermont Club seemed a sanctuary in which we could take refuge. Stephen Raphael used to say of drink parties, "They come in, drink your drink, stamp their cigarettes out on your carpet and slang you on the way out and they aren't grateful. It's a waste of time." I fear he was a great trial to his wife, who would have liked him to socialise more, but we agreed.

I was by then feeling rather under-occupied and memories of Firefly and my relationship with her came back to me. In March 1965 I told my husband that I would like to hunt. I could keep the horse with my sister at Leighton Buzzard, and hunt with the Whaddon Chase. We bought a horse on my half-sister Hazel's recommendation. Her husband was a Master of Foxhounds, sheep farmer and horse dealer in Herefordshire. It was boxed to the Shand Kydds' Grove Stud and I used to go out and hack the horse, but it seemed to me that it was far less quiet than it had been when I had ridden it in Herefordshire. Bill's racing manager was rather annoyed that I had not bought a horse through his auspices so we started off on the wrong foot. One day I turned up unexpectedly and found the horse in a muck sweat in his box. I asked what had been going on and was told he had been exercised with the other horses. I had a feeling that he had been hotted up by galloping with Bill's point-to-pointers and I was none too pleased. I started falling off the horse whilst out hacking because it was so frisky, and my husband said he would hunt it for me and see how it went. The horse jumped like a stag, but it was uncontrollable and jumped a wire fence, catching its leg on the wire and fell, my husband falling too on to the tarmac of a disused aerodrome. He broke one arm and badly damaged the other. It was all rather distressing and I felt very sad about it.

He had to deal the baccarat with his arm in a sling. I continued to hunt on another, quieter horse, but I didn't make any friends among the hunting people and always had to drive back to London afterwards, and so the joys of discussing the day's hunting, which is so much a part of the fun, were lost. It's very much a London hunt anyway and was nothing like The Vine where I knew the country and the people, and the horse was not like Firefly and we couldn't get to know each other well. In short, it all ended very sadly indeed. It was a failure and my husband had gone to some lengths to help me make it a success but I now firmly believe there were other influences at work.

Mrs Tucker came over in February 1965 and we gave a dinner party at the house for her, and she wrote the following letter after returning to America:

> 733 Park Avenue
> 8th March 1965.

Dear Veronica,

I hated leaving England without seeing you again with never a word of appreciation for the lovely party you gave us! Horrors! I enjoyed every bit of it. The beautiful house, the delicious food & drink, good talk, the gracious hostess, so young and lovely - it was a charming picture & I shall cherish it amongst my happy memories.

I was very proud lunching with my handsome escort that last day in the elegant Ritz but missed you. How exciting to hear that you were buying a hunter! May you have fine hunting & safe riding all the seasons throughout.

My love to you three. May every blessing be showered upon you.

Devotedly, Aunt Marcia.

Nanny Jenkins seemed to be settling well, and we were establishing a relationship. We discussed the William Hickey column most days (she had her own copy of the *Express* delivered every day), and I tried to amuse her by telling her the inside story about the titled people written about. It is considered by many people, including ourselves, that to appear in a gossip column is a thing to be avoided.

She seemed to like me, and said that I took a great deal more interest in her and talked to her more than her other employers. She was having a good life. She was allowed to take taxis and go to parties with Frances whenever she wanted to.

I gave a birthday party for Frances and I attempted to arrange it as Nanny had requested. She had asked for a couple of bottles of Harvey's Bristol Celebration Cream sherry for the nannies to be given after it was all over. I did this, and saw at the end she was a little drunk and that some of the other nannies were eyeing her with some disapproval. I do not think she was very popular with the other nannies and had few close friends, and on her day off nearly always spent the day with her sister in Sevenoaks with whom she seemed to have an on-off relationship.

I gathered that Mrs Robin Douglas-Home tried to prevent, in a court action, Nanny Jenkins going to Robin Douglas-Home's cottage Meadow Brook to look after their son Sholto on access, but she showed me a good reference that Mrs Robin Douglas-Home had written for her and this had caused her application to fail. I did not forget that. She spoke to Robin Douglas-Home on the telephone about twice a month, and although she was obviously devoted to him she complained that he did not pay her for the weekends spent with him.

Life continued much the same but at some stage I noticed a new arrival at the Clermont Club. He was 26-years-old and his name was Greville Howard, a cousin of the Earl of Suffolk and Berkshire. He had a mentor who taught him backgammon, and Greville had an aptitude for it. I also heard about his rather sad background. His mother apparently abandoned Greville and his sister Amanda. Her husband had divorced her and married again, but his two children were brought up by a guardian. That sounded quite an unhappy story. He had been working for an advertising agency in Madrid and was waiting to go to South America to Brazil with a rich Spanish friend of his to make some money in a scheme they had cooked up. He sometimes brought his Spanish girlfriend to dinner. She was rather a sulky girl who apparently could speak very little English, but Greville spoke Spanish. Greville tried hard, and despite initial lack of acceptance, he oiled his way in and became known as Grovel. When he had learnt backgammon from his mentor, he became friendly with my husband, often having dinner with us in a threesome and confiding in us a great deal. At about that time, I considered that it was time to start another child as I wanted a three-year gap between my first and second child. In the December of 1966 I became pregnant.

7
George

My husband was really rather unpleasant to me during my pregnancy, but I cannot give any examples other than he ignored me. This may have been due to his anxiety that we should have a boy, or to the fact that attention is drawn to me because of my condition.

Greville, who was still dining with us regularly, became very considerate. He fetched me drinks and chairs, smiled, talked and offered to drive me home when necessary. He told me of his anxiety to get his sister Amanda married, and I can't emphasise enough the importance to girls of getting married at that time. Very few had occupations with much future, and even those with university degrees used to complain that they could only get jobs as secretaries.

She had Simon Burton in tow who was rich, but in Greville's view, vulgar. Simon Burton had suffered a motoring accident aged twenty-one and from then on was subject to epileptic fits.

Greville also talked a good deal about his aunt and uncle who were rich, lived in Kent and were to some extent substitute parents. He was four years younger than I was and I became very attached to him, and without realising it started to rely on him. I may have started to fall in love with him.

My husband got rather worse during the end of my pregnancy after taking Otto, our Doberman Pincher dog for his morning walk, would open our bedroom door and say "Jump on her." I would still be in bed, and Otto would welcome me by jumping on me - not deliberately of course.

He spent a lot of his time with Charles Benson, Philip Martyn and his girlfriend Sally Crichton Stuart (a future Begum Aga Khan). They lived together as a threesome in Bolebec House, which was Philip Martyn's flat. Philip was not an old Etonian but he was a leading backgammon professional and he needed Charles Benson, who was a socialite and Old Etonian racing figure, to be his whipping boy. His interests were motor racing, the international set and getting his photograph in *Oggi* magazine. Aspinall used to refer to Philip Martyn as 'Cardiff and Canford', as Philip's mother had, most unfortunately for Philip, met a man on a train who had persuaded her to send him to Sherborne. Philip kept Charles Benson to some degree financially, as he found it difficult to live within his income. We also subsidised him.

My husband and this threesome had lunch most days at The Mirabelle Restaurant and there was no doubt that they all basked in the glow of Sally's sophistication and beauty. Sally herself was approaching thirty, and although almost totally under Philip Martyn's thumb, they had enormous rows but somehow just missed getting married.

Sally was modelling at the time quite successfully, but when I did see her, it was clear that she felt some hostility to me, possibly because I had all that she would have liked - a husband, home and children. I felt she resented my pregnancy. In fact I got this feeling from many men at the Clermont. It was as though they were envious of me reproducing their historical monument, or 'The Old Fossil' as Charles Benson called him. I felt very alone and despairing, and had the impression from my husband if I did not have a boy, I would be out or my stock so low that I might as well be out.

We went to Yorkshire for York Races in August to stay with Robin and Juliet Hill. I remember a barbeque party and after we had eaten, we found ourselves sitting in two separate groups. Charles Benson suddenly said, "You see... the 'have's' in one group and the 'have not's' in another." He was quite right. All those with titles were sitting together and all those without were sitting together, and it had happened without any planning.

Our horse Le Merveilleux II ran at that meeting, but he did not win.

My husband's attitude towards me was unkind to say the least, and I could not understand why. He ignored me and behaved as though I was a burden and a nuisance.

He talked a little about Sally Crichton Stuart at that stage, and when I asked him if he would have liked to marry her, he replied "She would fly too high for me." I did not react and accepted what he said.

The tension was so great during this period that I lost my voice and my obstetrician agreed to induce me on 21st September. My husband drove me at lunchtime on the 21st to the London Clinic. He left me in the lift to go up alone, saying that he would ring up later to face both horrible physical pain and mental pain as well. What if it should be another girl?

My obstetrician, George Pinker, came to see me and asked where my husband was, but I did not know. He said he was going to induce my labour at 8pm. Meanwhile, I was prepared by the nurses to give birth. I lay on the table, felt a prick in my arm and woke up in my own bed. My labour started immediately with good strong contractions and it was not long before the nurse called Mr Pinker, who had me wheeled into the theatre. The head was pressing hard down into the birth canal and I called out urgently to Mr Pinker. He gave me another injection and I woke to see my husband's face looking down at me. "It's a boy." he said. I didn't believe it and said, "I don't believe it. I don't believe it," and they brought our son in for me to see and I saw that it was true, and that he was strong.

I was later told by Michael Stoop about my husband's reaction while playing bridge in Selim Zilkha's flat. The telephone rang, he answered it and Mr Pinker said, "Your wife has given birth to an 8lb 5oz boy and both are doing well." My husband replied, "The roulette wheel has been spinning for 9 months and it's come up red." Those present at the bridge evening saw a rare display of emotion from him - he is said to have danced about the room, but then sat down and finished the rubber.

I said "Thank you, Mr Pinker." And they wheeled me back into my room. I had never been so happy.

George

It wasn't long before my room was filled with flowers and telegrams of congratulation. My mother-in-law brought me a cactus in a pot, and Aspinall and the Shand Kydds sent stunning vulgarities in large baskets. Granny Lucan came to see me, and she asked who had sent which flowers and then pointed at a small arrangement of pink roses. "Sally and William," I replied. "Poor little Sally," she said.

My husband gave me a large amount of arum lilies, which I put beside my bed. I did not see very much of him, but he came briefly every day. The first time he came after the birth he informed me that our son was to be called George Charles. I did not demur. I had many letters and replied to them all in hospital. Greville Howard came to visit me and played backgammon with me, and was generally very nice. Lady Osborne came and said, "Lavinia Norfolk couldn't do it but you've done it." Aspinall wrote me a letter congratulating me on my "magnificent achievement," and said he was "looking forward to teaching Lord Bingham the games his father thinks he plays so well."

I went home a week later and was back at the Clermont Club the same evening. We saw Sally Crichton Stuart in Annabel's. She had been away, and on being told we had had a son I saw her face flicker as she looked at my husband who was beaming from ear to ear. It had been the most enormous injection of self-confidence that I had ever had and my whole being radiated with good health and vitality. But it was not to last long.

8
Otto

Dr Christian Carritt, my female GP, called at Lower Belgrave Street shortly after Frances' birth - a routine call - whilst my mother-in-law was making one of her rare visits. I introduced them. My husband was also there. My mother-in-law tried a similar tack with her as she had done with me at our first meeting, but instead of rising to the bait, Dr Carritt put an end to the conversation by saying that she was not interested in politics.

My doctor was attractive, then unmarried, intelligent and she had a private practice in Onslow Square with a great following of girls and you could say successful, for it must have been very difficult at that time to establish yourself to that degree without much money and be a woman. Her lack of success was in the fact that she was not married. My mother-in-law's conversational gambit being halted caused her to ask "Is she a good girl?" "Yes, very," replied Christian Carritt. "I wouldn't have thought so," said my mother-in-law. My mother-in-law had appeared in a high state of excitement while talking to my doctor, and I wondered if it was anything to do with her being in 'private medicine'.

Upstairs, I asked Dr Carritt what she thought of my mother-in-law. She replied carefully: "She's rather eccentric," and I congratulated her on handling the meeting so well. Downstairs my mother-in-law looked angry. I think she had a feeling that she had not shown up too well. "She was lying when she said she wasn't interested in politics," she said. "A woman like that would be interested." I didn't think it necessary to say any more. My mother-in-law had been cut short over one of her favourite ploys by a doctor in front of my husband.

My next encounter with my mother-in-law was again at home in Lower Belgrave Street. During 1965 my husband contracted yellow jaundice. I had some difficulty in getting his National Health GP to come. I produced a specimen of dark brown urine before she showed any concern. The next morning she came. My mother-in-law had arrived a few minutes before, and was already in our bedroom discussing symptoms with him. The doorbell rang and I showed his female National Health GP, Dr Ann Thompson, into our bedroom. My mother-in-law made no attempt to leave the room, so I left all three of them together. I went downstairs and in a quarter of an hour his doctor came down. She confirmed my husband had yellow jaundice, told me what he should eat and what he should not eat, and then looked at me to see if I had contracted it. She was the doctor I had met at Hanover House, my husband's parents' residence at the time, who my husband had consulted about my spots. I expect she knew the family and its eccentricities by then. I was annoyed that my mother-in-law had stayed in the room and thought it extremely uncivilised of her, but I didn't say anything either to him or her.

Shortly after Frances was born, my husband decided we should get a dog. We had been burgled earlier and he was advised that a dog was a good way of discouraging burglars. He already had a breed of dog in mind. He wanted a Doberman Pinscher. We went to see a breeder of 'Dobes', a Mrs Bastable who had kennels somewhere on the road to Newmarket. Her stud dog was called Gin and we saw him through a glass panel. His ferocious behaviour quite shocked us, and we were glad we were separated from him by a window. We told Mrs Bastable we wanted a dog for London. She said in that case we must not have a too highly bred dog, but she thought she had a litter that would have been bred for good temperament and, in short, she sold us a Doberman puppy which we called Otto.

He had a long conversation with her about the docking of their tails and the cutting of their ears to make them look sharper, which is frowned on in this country. Indeed, the Kennel Club doesn't recognise litters from dogs with cut ears. However, my husband was most anxious that his dog should look smart and ferocious, with cut ears. He arranged with a vet to have this done. Otto had looked so sweet before he went to have the operation. When he returned his ears were horribly mutilated and worse, they didn't look as though they were standing up. However, the vet had done a very professional job and in a week or so they were standing and the scars healing. It did make him look very different and I must confess that he did look smarter.

My husband went to great lengths to see that he would have a good diet. He had the best minced beef from the butcher every day, with raw eggs and biscuits. No dog could have had a better diet, and Otto grew large and strong. His teething period was most trying and he managed to demolish a set of dining room chairs and endless smaller articles before his puppyhood was over. He slept on our bed between us, and as he grew larger I began to faintly resent his presence. My husband was supposed to take him for a run in Green Park every day. Unfortunately, if there was a heavy gaming period and my husband was too exhausted to take him, Otto would be left in our paved back garden. On occasion I would look out of the window and see monstrous lumps of dog waste scattered over the yard, surrounded by flies if it was summer. If I opened the window and leaned out I would be choked by the stench and would shut it hastily and, with diptheria flashing through my mind, dash to the chemist and buy bottles of Dettol to throw all over the yard. It was unfortunate that I could not hold Otto, even with a slip chain, as he was so strong. He could easily have dragged me across the road. He began to become difficult in Green Park. We were most unpopular with the old ladies with their poodles and others.

Otto developed an irritating habit of not coming when he was called, so my husband obtained from some mushroom company in Florida a remote control device for training dogs. It consisted of a large collar with metal prongs on the inside, which stuck into Otto's neck. Antennae attached to his collar like an aerial protruded from Otto's head. He looked a curious sight as he gambolled about the park. As I jokingly remarked to acquaintances, "He's going to buy one for me next." With the remote control device in his hand, he would call Otto to heel. If there was no response, he would press mild shock, if still no response to this he would press medium shock and if this failed, he would press violent shock which was always successful as it amounted to virtual electrocution. In fact, if you had lost your temper and left your finger on the button you would have electrocuted your dog. It was all most strange, but eventually the batteries wore out or it needed to be sent for repairs and we didn't get it back for some time.

Otto, as I've previously indicated, used to sleep on our bed and he was great company as my husband did not get back from gaming until four or five or even later in the morning. He always recognised the sound of my husband's car and would leap to his feet and rush down the stairs to greet him. His black hairs were all over our blankets and he wasn't perfectly housetrained either, but he had a lovely nature and so I put up with him.

Nanny Jenkins found him a trial. He would dash up and down our narrow stairs and he could easily have sent us crashing down as he hurtled through our legs. I used to long to open the front door and say to Otto, "Go and play in the traffic," but Nanny, who took an almost religious attitude towards the cross of Otto, said, "Something will happen. We must wait."

My husband taught him to jump iron railings and took endless photographs and cine pictures of him and I really think he was more concerned about Otto than he was about me, and he went everywhere with us, which curtailed our invitations. After George was born I became more concerned if Nanny was knocked down the stairs carrying our son and heir. Fortunately, Otto was becoming interested in the other sex and one day had a fight with an Alsatian over a bitch they both fancied. He did a marvellous job on the Alsatian and the indignant owner went to the police and made a complaint. Otto, too, was not unscathed, but the police advised us that if there was another complaint there could be a magistrates order made and Otto put down.

My husband gave him back to Mrs Bastable in the hope she would find him a home in the country. There was no doubt that Otto complemented my husband as they walked down the street. Both magnificent specimens of breeding, and as Otto strained against the leash... it must have made a virile picture.

He would take Otto to the Clermont on occasions and leave him tied to a heavy marble table leg. He also liked Otto to sit in the front seat with him when we were driving anywhere, and I must confess that Otto did give me rather an inferiority complex. Perhaps as I had a child my husband felt that he would like one too and saw Otto as a substitute son, but anyway he went.

Although as previously recounted my husband used to tell Otto to jump on me in the morning as I lay in bed, I knew Otto didn't want to hurt me deliberately so I missed him. Memories of him remained... the stained and greasy carpets from his gigantic bones, and the dents in the parquet floor when he let his bone roll down the stairs, and his teeth marks in our dining table.

During 1969, I noted with some foreboding that Frances Althorp had married Peter Shand Kydd, Bill Shand Kydd's half-brother, following her divorce from Viscount Althorp. Peter Shand Kydd became stepfather to Diana, Princess of Wales, and her brother and sisters. My husband was a fifth cousin and second cousin once removed of Diana.

9
Horses

My husband lost interest, or realised that powerboating is too expensive a sport to pursue as boats are obsolete every year, and through Stephen Raphael he was introduced to Arthur Freeman, an ex-jockey who used to ride for the Queen Mother and was then trying to make his way as a trainer. He had married a well-born horsey girl and we gathered that her family disapproved of the marriage because of the wide difference in their backgrounds. Arthur Freeman had a chestnut mare in his yard called Stress Signal, and my husband bought her for me to run in my name. I was disappointed that I had not been allowed to choose a horse myself. We registered our colours Royal Blue, Gold sash and White cap.

The Freemans had a house in Newmarket and a yard. We were often invited to stay for the weekend and also for lunch or dinner. They didn't have many owners, but had had a few successes. Stress Signal was a failure and ran last in almost every race (I would never have chosen a chestnut), and she was sold as a brood mare to India. As her sire was Worden II we did not lose too much on her. We then went with the Freemans to the Deauville Yearling sales in 1968 to buy some horses with his advice. We bought three - Prince Bleu, Sebastien and Le Merveilleux II. I do not know how much my husband paid for them, and they were kept in the Freemans' yard in Newmarket. - Prince Bleu and Sebastien were later to prove useless, but Le Merveilleux II showed promise on the flat and they ran in my husband's name.

Unfortunately, his legs gave way and he broke down. There followed the most enormous number of operations on the horse.

First an operation to make a testicle descend, then an operation on his wind - he was tubed or hobdayed and then pin fired. I cannot explain more about these operations, but I have included them because they show that he needed a very long rest before racing again, when he went into training as a hurdler instead of on the flat.

My husband had been helping Arthur Freeman financially. Arthur depended to some degree on betting on his own horses, but he was unlucky and lost heavily when he punted on them. I believe my husband lent him about £4,000 and Arthur paid back the debt by keeping and training our horses for nothing. Another owner helped him as well, but it was good money after bad and Arthur went bankrupt. We were told by the liquidator to move our horses from the yard and Charles Benson introduced us to Tom Jones, a successful National Hunt trainer in Newmarket, who took Le Merveilleux II on and we sent Sebastien and Prince Bleu to the Ascot Sales.

My husband had tried to help Arthur in other ways too. He had advised him not to say appalling things on the telephone to his rich Jewish father-in-law like "My father told me England was a place for heroes to live in and not for Jews to spiv in," and not to send back their presents for the children. It is not at all surprising that his father-in-law did not come to his aid when everything closed in on him. Their marriage broke up and it was all very sad.

Stan Mellor used to ride for us, but on one occasion Lester Piggott did and when he spoke to us after the race he said, "I could have made him [Le Merveilleux II] win but he'd never have run again!"

After our first win at Market Rasen, the comment was: "Le Merveilleux was bought as a yearling at Deauville by his owner Lord Lucan who deserved this first success with the son of Wild Risk after nearly five years of waiting."

It was a great boost to our morale and we won a race in Yorkshire, and it seemed that our star was in the ascendant. We had three photo finishes and we were always successful. We followed our horse wherever he ran, and as he was not a first class horse he had to be placed rather carefully. It meant a lot of travelling, but we were usually happy together on those long drives. All in all, despite the ups and downs, the racing was a successful venture. Many people never get a winner at all.

10
Fire Auto Marine

My husband met Emil Savundra whilst powerboating.

I now quote from a letter Emil Savundra wrote to my husband shortly after his powerboat sank during the *Daily Express* Powerboat race:

> Dr. Emil Savundra, PH.D.,D.C.L.
> 80 HENDON LANE,
> FINCHLEY,
> LONDON, N.3.
>
> 14th. September 1963

Dear John,

I have been trying to get you on the telephone without success for some days.

I should be most grateful if you would give me a ring at my ex-directory private number FINchley 0946 any evening... or early in the morning before 10 a.m. (if you rise so early!)

I should be most happy to meet you again to discuss various matters, including the possibility of your joining the Board of Directors of a rather interesting new set-up.

No financial commitments are envisaged and the whole thing could be of great interest... anyway you lose nothing by discussing it with me.

The reason? Purely and simply that being an utter snob, I just like to have all the people of breeding around all the time, with the exception of what you rightly call "certain well bred/s---s"...incidentally I had the "pleasure" of meeting the most perfect specimen of that animal at Torquay, immaculately clad in reefer jacket and cap, putting on a quite nauseating display of how not to win friends and influence people! I would willingly have kicked him in the teeth... fortunately (or otherwise) we had no reason to talk to each other!

Kindest regards.
Cordially Yours,

(Signed) Emil

P.S. Having saved you from a watery grave (according to the "Times", and who am I to argue with the "Times"?) the least I can do is to feed you. Will you have dinner with us at home any evening next week? Pushpam would be delighted to meet you again, as I would too.

Emil was one of the world's most notorious fraudsters. He milked thousands of pounds of motorists' money through the Fire Auto and Marine Insurance Company, which crashed in 1966. David Frost interviewed him on television and Emil came out very badly and described the audience as 'peasants'. It was an example of trial by TV.

My husband was a director of the company, and at one stage thought he would have to commit suicide because of the disgrace.

He gave us a wedding present of a silver vase in the shape of a swan. He told us that when swans mated, if one died, the other died too of a broken heart. I thought it a very romantic idea.

Emil was a great talker and great admirer of the peerage, although he was not able to distinguish between who was respectable and who was not. He invited us to dinner at his house - he was a radio ham enthusiast and full of ideas for a revolutionary design for a fast powerboat.

As I understood it from my husband, he had conceived the idea of a computerised insurance company and indeed got IBM to supply the computers and asked my husband and various others on to the board of what was to be called Fire Auto and Marine. They used to have great lunches together. Emil was also thinking of starting a merchant bank to be called Transway and my husband was going to have a lot to do with that. It all seemed good. My husband would have an occupation: he would be a banker and it looked as though he would make some 'legitimate' money.

Emil came to dinner and it was a great success. We used our silver dinner plates and Emil admired them. I said, "I'm so glad you could come while we still have them," and after a short silence, there was a burst of laughter. Emil used to invite me to the boardroom lunches but my husband would never let me go.

In about 1966, my husband's Aunt Christine Bingham died in Rhodesia and so he went over there to oversee necessary arrangements. While he was away, I read in the press what seemed to be trouble with Fire Auto and Marine. Every day there was something about the company. Finally, Maurice Howard rang and said, "You must get hold of John and tell him to resign. All the directors are resigning." The next day their names were printed in *The Times* as having resigned from the Board of Fire Auto and Marine.

I finally traced my husband just as he was about to leave Johannesburg by aeroplane for England. I told him what I had been told, and he asked me to meet him at the airport, which I did. He said that he wished I hadn't told him before the flight as he had gone through agony wondering whether he would have to commit suicide because of the disgrace. He put on a stiff white collar and a bowler hat and went to see the Department of the Board of Trade. He had discussions with them and it appeared that it was Emil who had misappropriated funds or was responsible for making the company under-capitalised.

It was at a time when insurance companies were being looked at very closely for this. It was most unfortunate that Emil did what he did. Many people were left uninsured which was very bad. Emil's idea for computerised insurance was fine, and if he had followed the law he might have been successful. However, Emil had been involved in financial skulduggery before and leopards don't change their spots.

We lost about £4,000 overall but my husband escaped much of the publicity by not resigning with the others when, in fact, there was no useful purpose to be served in so doing. The other directors just panicked and drew attention to themselves. It was very sad. I had hoped very much that the idea was sound but it was all too good to be true.

11
Greville

I was by then beginning to see my husband as a rather strict Victorian father who often said that he was 'displeased' with me. He very rarely had a conversation with me as such, and said that that was the point of being married - you don't have to talk to the person.

I had no outlet for my emotions, which were very close to the surface following giving birth. Nanny Jenkins took over the care of the new baby, and it was clear she did not like me interfering. Sadly, Robin Douglas-Home committed suicide and this had the unfortunate effect that Nanny Jenkins no longer went away to help him at weekends, and so I was never alone for any length of time with the children. I believe Robin Douglas-Home sold a photograph of one of Aspinall's tigers to a national newspaper and was sacked. He went to live in the country and things got on top of him, which is probably why he committed suicide. Previously, he had been employed to play the piano for the entertainment of the Clermont Club's clientele.

Greville Howard continued to have dinner with us and he would arrange from time to time visits to the country, the cinema and suggested different places to have dinner. I had met his sister Amanda, who often came with us when Greville asked me to have dinner with him during my pregnancy whilst my husband played bridge at the St James's Club in Piccadilly, where he had been made a member. .

I became rather involved with the Howards' schemes to get Amanda married to Simon Burton. Amanda looked after Simon, who lived with her very well. So far, he was hedging about Amanda, who was older than he was. I cannot stress enough the importance of marriage to girls at that time. I am not an historian and cannot say why it was important - it just was.

The idea was that we shouldn't allow Simon out of our sight and to get Aspinall to accept him on the surface, which he did by saying loudly, "Hello Simon" whenever he appeared, as though he were a most welcome punter. Simon lapped this up and started to play black jack and some gentle chemmy. My husband and I would often have dinner with the three of them and attempt to give Simon the impression that he would be going up in the world socially if he married Amanda. My husband would make little cracks about Simon's family motto being "We must make more and more money," but Simon seemed to take this in good part. He was protected at all times from meeting other girls or indeed looking at them, as we watched him like hawks.

Greville continued to consider going to Brazil although he loathed the idea of the loneliness, as he had now got well in at the Clermont Club. He continued to be very friendly with me and we often spoke on the telephone during the day, and one afternoon while my husband was playing golf he came to see me at Lower Belgrave Street. We sat in chairs well apart and made strained conversation and then he asked me if he could give me a gold bracelet for Christmas. While I was replying to this, to Greville's discomfiture, my husband returned home early. Greville deflected his attention by immediately asking him for advice on some stock and my husband, who always liked to air his knowledge, gave us a twenty-minute diatribe and then Greville left.

My husband and I went downstairs afterwards and he said, "What was that fellow doing here?" I replied, "He wanted to see you, you know how he relies on you for advice." He replied "Yes, I suppose he does." In fact he relied on him for more than that, he relied on him for support in the backgammon game.

There was no doubt that I was falling in love with Greville. It put some new meaning into my life. We would see each other every evening at dinner but nothing else happened. He sent me a plant at Christmas and I wrote him a letter thanking him:

> Darling Grovel,
>
> Thank you for the lovely plant you sent us both. I put it on the centre of the dining room table on Christmas Day and although it looked strangely obscure in this position, it was warm and beautiful and reminded me of you all through lunch. I kiss you. V.

Greville lived in a flat belonging to his Aunt Rosie in Brompton Square which he shared with a chum of his from Eton who was a housie at the Clermont Club called Michael Hicks Beach. Hicks Beach was quite amusing and I enjoyed his company.

Without my realising it, my husband became aware that I was keen on Greville and he said something to Greville who cooled immediately but did not tell me why, so that I was somewhat bewildered by the change. I had by then become dependent on him and his friends for companionship. I was so distressed by all this and the collapse of my new found happiness and feeling guilty about my disloyalty of feeling to my husband that I went into a decline, took to my bed and refused to go to the Clermont any more.

In retrospect, what had happened was that Greville, as a young man, was with a young married woman whose husband was neglecting her, but was not mature enough to deal with the situation following my husband's warning. I took it to heart more than I would have done if I had had someone to discuss the situation with. I was pretty much isolated.

12

Doctors

Before this abrupt end to my burgeoning romance, I had been much fortified by the birth of our son and heir and so I instituted some 'reform bills'. I told my husband that the house must be decorated to a certain standard and so we consulted Oliver Ford of the fashionable decorating firm of Lenygon & Morant to advise, and the work was underway in a very short time.

Next, I insisted that some sort of education or insurance policy for the children should be worked out, which was done to a limited extent. Lastly, I insisted that he take his seat in the House of Lords. He seemed to spend an enormous amount of time in the company of gamblers or men who talked either about gambling or about the girls they had slept with, and I felt that this was not enough to occupy his brain.

My husband had been rather reluctant to take his seat as it meant he would have to reject his parents' socialism, and so he was hesitant about doing it. However, early one afternoon, we got dressed - he into a smart pinstripe suit with a stiff white collar, and me into something subdued with a hat - and went along to the House of Lords. I was told that I must wait outside the Chamber until prayers were said and then should come in quickly as the Oath would be said almost immediately and I could miss it. Armed with these instructions, I came in quickly and sat down in a place reserved for peeresses. My husband stood up and without doubt he looked the most beautiful man in the room. The youth had gone and there stood the man. His voice was lovely, and echoed through the Chamber with the simple oath: "I, Richard John Bingham..." and then he walked to the Conservative benches. I was proud of him, and hoped that even if he didn't speak, he would meet other people, indeed his peers, who would not be sycophantic and from whom he might broaden his outlook.

He did take the three-line whip and show up to use his words from time to time, but he didn't go there as much as I had hoped he would. He voted against going into the Common Market, but that is the only vote I can remember. He attended one Opening of Parliament in 1970 while I was confined with Camilla. He wouldn't have dreamt of collecting his House of Lords attendance money. This he considered to be for the peers who had to travel down from Scotland or the North. Several peers living in London did though. He considered making a maiden speech in favour of hare coursing and indeed wrote one, but for some reason the Bill was dropped or there were too many people speaking in favour, so he never did.

Although we had got a part of the house decorated to some standard and pulled together, not much had been done about the nurseries which meant that I was rather trapped with Nanny Jenkins, and with two children already it is rather more difficult to get another nanny. I could have looked after the children myself but somehow it seemed to be so automatic to have a nanny, and I knew that if I didn't have one I wouldn't see much of my husband, so I kept her on... but I felt the emotional deprivation.

My husband, as a result of his sedentary occupation and heredity, contracted bleeding haemorrhoids but didn't want to be examined by a woman, as we both had female doctors. Having given this impasse some thought, it seemed to me that now we were a family of two males and two females we had better find one family doctor for us all, and as women have got to get used to being looked at by men anyway, it seemed better to get one male GP. I felt very badly about Dr Carritt and dreaded meeting her in the street. My husband wrote a letter rather peremptorily dismissing her, but she replied saying that she would miss seeing me and the children, and hoped we would be happy with whoever replaced her.

One of my husband's golfing partners recommended a doctor

who practised in Basil Street, who had an older partner. The doctor recommended dealt with my husband's haemorrhoids quite satisfactorily, but seemed to want to get a medical history from me as I don't think he had my previous doctor's notes. I wasn't too pleased about this and didn't like him much. This was the doctor that my husband sent for when I went into a decline after Greville's sudden unexplained rejection. I told him about my fear that Greville might have tape-recorded our conversations. The doctor was young and thought that I had gone mad. Without my knowing, an appointment was made for me to see a psychiatrist at The Priory and on the pretext of taking me for a drive, my husband took me there. I recognised the place for what it was, a private mental hopital, as I had already heard of it when I saw the board up at the start of the drive.

However, I agreed to see him and told him the same story as I told the previous doctor. He started to say "I think you'd better come in," when I made a dash for the door, ran down the stairs and into the drive and up the street. My husband and the psychiatrist gave chase and persuaded me to come back. Anyway, it was arranged that I should have some treatment at home which they discussed, and I drove back with him. I then had my first experience of Moditen. Moditen is an anti-psychotic drug given by injection. At any rate, it probably is a successful treatment for whatever problem a patient might have as its side effects are so appalling that they would minimise a major threat to one's life.

I was unable to sleep without sleeping pills and unable to keep still either, despite the side effect pills. I was in such obvious agony that my husband drove me back to The Priory where they gave me an antidote. I was so relieved and grateful that I resumed my former life at the Clermont Club, although somewhat chastened and with some loss of spirit.

During this time, we were having a 'good run' and for the first time I was able to enjoy spending money. I bought myself clothes and things for the house. My husband bought me jewellery and a set of Louis Quinze chairs and two sofas from Mallets, and although communication between us was on rather a limited plane: "What happened?" Reply: "I lost" or "I broke even." I was happy.

The doctor who arranged the aborted Priory visit then blotted his copybook for writing something which my husband considered insolent on the bottom of the bill - he had charged for an unanswered call - my husband said that I must find another doctor as he also felt that The Priory episode had been mishandled.

We had a temporary nanny for a week while Nanny Jenkins was on holiday, and I asked her if she knew of any good GPs. She named a Dr Hay of Rawlings Street. He was well qualified and he, like our previous GP, was probably without our previous notes and also seemed to like the psychiatric or nosy approach and was always asking what I considered to be impertinent questions, so I avoided him and kept him on formal terms. I didn't see him very often, but unbeknown to me he had psychiatric conversations about me with my husband.

He obviously felt that he had not got much rapport with me and got quite het up about it and showed it by striding round my bedroom saying such non sequiturs as "I went to Gibbs, you know," letting me know he was doctor and on social terms with other patients.

During this time there were quite a lot of pigeons to be plucked at the Clermont Club, and among them an elderly man called Janni Roth who was causing a sensation by losing in the chemmy game most nights. He invited us to shoot with him at Glenlivet, Banffshire, in Scotland. For some reason, Roth knew rather a lot of foreign titles and was a title lover, and so we met some examples of European aristocracy through him, including Max of Bavaria, a Prince Quadt who had married Max's sister Lotte and Baron Gustav von Furstenberg. The shoot was run by a Major Waddington, who was about sixty and had a young wife. He would start the shoot off by saying "No loud shouting or betting." We went twice and stayed for a week both times, and it was deathly but it was an experience. My husband also had a mania for foreigners.

Our winter busman's holiday was then Gstaad, and we stayed at the leading hotel there, the Gstaad Palace. The hotel was filled with Greeks and there were practically no white Anglo-Saxon Protestants.

The quarry we had our eye on was an elderly Greek ship owner much addicted to backgammon and proud of his skill. My role in this operation was to front and appear that we were there for a pleasant ski-ing holiday together. Anyway, before lunch, we would sit in the hotel lounge with a drink making desultory conversation or possibly even reading a book, waiting for him to arrive. He would then see us and tap my husband on the shoulder and suggest a few games. I would remain sitting where I was, and when it neared one o'clock would go over and look at the score. If our pigeon was down about ten points, I knew that he would stay and try to make them back and so I would go into lunch on my own. If he was winning, he would cut short the game and we would have lost our opportunity for the day to take him for a large sum of money. The consolation was that my husband would have lunch with me. If my husband did manage to get him down, the rest of the players would come around about tea-time and take the old man on as well, and if we were lucky we would keep him down. He was a good player and fought every inch of the way. Some people would stop for dinner but my husband didn't, he was a really dedicated hustler and I would have dinner on my own and then come later on to watch and then go to bed.

I was usually so anxious that I would wake at about four o'clock and get dressed and go and see what was going on. It was usually a very seedy sight, with plates of old curled sandwiches, filled cigarette ashtrays, empty beer bottles and glasses, men with ties awry, shirts undone at the neck, with grey faces and it was usually cold, as the radiators went off in the early morning.

Just before breakfast it was usually concluded and we would go to bed happy. My husband and one of the other Greeks used to negotiate payment, and the elderly Greek was a good payer although he sometimes took a percentage of our winnings for the Greek church. His wife was very long suffering but his daughter less so, and there was quite a scene on one occasion when he lifted his stick to hit her. She had come down and said "What my mother has suffered all these years, the disgrace you are bringing on our family," and "These sharks are only taking you on for your money." All quite accurate, but he was infuriated at being spoken to like that by a woman. It had the unfortunate effect that he left early that year and we lost our opportunity to take him for a large sum of money.

On the whole, I found Gstaad the most ghastly of all our gambling holiday haunts - that is after Nassau. I don't ski and six weeks away from home with no-one to talk to, I found very depressing. The first year the children came out for a couple of weeks and that made it more bearable. The Greeks were difficult to understand, Michael Stoop was not a socialite, just a typical man's man but Bobby Sweeny (Charlie Sweeny's younger brother) was rather more of a socialite and brightened up some lunches for me.

Early on in our marriage, we twice went to Nassau to play in a poker game. That game was played in a garage and the swings were about the same as the Hamilton Club game, not much more than £800 a session. It was terribly lonely there and I spent one whole month in 1965 in a rather seedy hotel bedroom, as it rained the whole time while my husband played poker from after lunch to the early hours of the morning in the garage and then came back to our bedroom to sleep until lunchtime, and then begin the whole cycle again. I felt during that month that I was living in an unreal world and was quite frightened.

I shed tears of joy as I sat in the Boeing waiting for it to take off for London. The irony of this visit was that my husband didn't get paid for some reason, or the cheque was no good. I fear he was 'taken' by the regulars on the Island, and with hindsight he was just an injection of new money into the game, which had gone wrong. However, it had one good result - he didn't go there again, and eventually he gave up his membership of Lyford Cay, the rather exclusive and expensive country club in Nassau. It was a wonderful place with a wonderful beach, but as always there was no one to share it with and most people were rather elderly. It's the people who make the place.

Granny Lucan died just before we went to Gstaad for the last time in 1972 and I was sad. She was the most human of my husband's family. I usually represented my husband at family parties, which were held in her flat at Orchard Court while my husband was 'working'. She always welcomed me with enthusiasm, and would draw me aside to ask me how things were going in the world of gambling. She would also ask if we had managed to get any money into Switzerland for income tax was a horrific thing for her - she had once been rich and was now needing some financial support from her children. She left stickers on all her things in her flat naming the people who she wanted to have them. She left my husband two very nice pictures called 'The Card Players', which he had asked for. She left me her dressing case, which had the initials VL on the front. The 7th Earl Spencer attended her funeral. Cynthia Countess Spencer (Cynthia Spencer is the grandmother Diana believed watched over her), his wife, had died earlier, and he said to me: "I hear John thinks we've got his pictures." I thought this a very interesting opening conversational gambit. He was referring to the painting of Lady Lavinia Bingham, a distant ancestor, by Sir Joshua Reynolds, now hanging at Althorp.

Meanwhile, the good run was still continuing following the birth of George. We went to Madrid with Greville for Easter 1968 and we chartered a boat from Camper & Nicholson to go to Sardinia and cruise back along the Italian Riviera to Cannes. This trip was to set the seal on the engagement between Greville and Zoe, his first wife. Soon after our break-up he brought a sixteen-year-old model girl called Zoe Walker to dinner at the Mirabelle. She had modelled in Paris and gave the impression of being sophisticated for her age, but at the same time looking sixteen. She had long blonde hair, was quite tall with a slim figure and baby-faced. Greville decided that he must be married in order to be taken seriously and gain more respect. His courtship of Zoe involved spending a great deal of money on her, taking her for weekends with his uncle and aunt, and then his cousin the Earl of Suffolk started to invite him to stay at Charlton Park. Micky Suffolk liked girls and there was no doubt that he liked the look of Zoe, as indeed did most of the men at the Clermont. Around this time, Simon and Amanda got married with Frances as a bridesmaid.

The chartering of the *Crin Bleu* from Camper & Nicholson was to be the final swing in favour of a marriage between Zoe and Greville and to persuade her mother, who did not need much persuading that it was a good idea. On the trip we had my husband, myself, Zoe and Greville, Simon and Amanda, and Hicks Beach and his girlfriend Carolyn, whom he later married. It wasn't really a very happy holiday. It was boring, uncomfortable and altogether dreary as it rained a great deal of the time, but it achieved its objective and Greville and Zoe married in November.

I used to have golf lessons with Leslie King, the golf professional, and my husband bought me a set of clubs. When we were on holiday at Mandelieu in the South of France he played with me, giving me a large handicap and I enjoyed it. I found golf quite a fascinating game.

We decided to opt out of an English Christmas that year, and instead we went to St Moritz and stayed at Suvretta House with the two older children and Nanny Jenkins. Really, it was a waste of money as the children didn't learn to ski - they were too young and the holiday was very expensive. I had the feeling that he thought it was good for our image to be seen there. Joe Dwek and Sally Crichton Stuart came as well and stayed at the Palace. She met the Aga Khan in the King's Club, which was the discotheque in the Palace Hotel. The international set, when at a loose end, went to St Moritz at Christmas for something to do and see people they knew who would be there.

The following Easter, in 1969, we decided to do a tour of Florence, Rome and Venice, which neither of us had ever visited. We drove most of the time in silence and we ended our tour by visiting Gustav von Furstenberg, whom we had met shooting at Glenlivet. We did manage to throw three coins in the Trevi Fountain though, and I wished hard but to no avail as it turned out. I was worried during the trip because we had left Nanny Jenkins all on her own with the children, and by then I thought her to be unreliable or at any rate untrustworthy.

In November 1969 we went shooting at Banff with Janni Roth again and during the visit I felt ill. He pushed me over a five-barred gate on the pretext of helping me and I fell to the ground. That was his idea of horseplay. The others laughed. My husband seemed very happy throughout, and at one stage after dinner said to the assembled company "I'm a very happy man." It was good to hear him say that. When I returned home, I came out in spots and, being terrified it was German Measles, rang the doctor for by now I knew I was pregnant. I had been on the contraceptive pill after George's birth but the needling and incidents had begun to wear me down, and depression to be all prevailing. My husband seemed not to appreciate or understand my difficulties. Remembering the charge to my spirits after the birth of George, I tried to reproduce it. It wasn't German Measles, but I told Dr Hay that I thought I was pregnant. He went downstairs to see my husband. He returned in about quarter of an hour. "I've talked to your husband and we are both agreed that it's impossible for you to be pregnant."

He took a urine sample however, and in a day or two rang me up and said, "It's most strange, the test has proved positive." I said that I was not at all surprised, had it not occurred to him that I might have stopped taking the pill? It didn't appear to have occurred to him or my husband. I had been prescribed the pill by a doctor and, of course, I wouldn't stop taking it without consulting him first! A bed was booked for this confinement at the Lindo Wing, St Mary's Paddington.

It was rather a difficult pregnancy and I contracted a form of diabetes, which is a hazard of pregnancy, and was again induced for my safety and that of the unborn child. People often say that you feel better when you are carrying a boy. In my case they were right. I had a long labour and during it I raved a great deal and the main thought that came through was why is a birthday celebrated? It could herald the birth of someone who was going to be the cause of great misery. I was disappointed that the baby was a girl and I was not recharged in spirits.

I had come to anticipate the familiar question "What does your husband do?" followed by a smirk. I would assess my questioner according to his vulnerability. Sometimes I would say, "Gentlemen don't work." This was outstandingly successful with some people, or if he was anywhere near say in a loud voice "Why don't you ask him yourself?" or simply just "He's a professional gambler."

We had deliberately kept the birth a secret from my sister, as we by now were both agreed that this was the best course of action. I had a telegram from my husband's best man saying "You can produce the girls, we can produce the boys." I was quite unreasonably upset by this and went into a decline, and Mr Pinker was sent for and then Dr Hay came and the subject of my depression was discussed. Dr Hay arranged for a domiciliary visit by a well-known but very busy psychiatrist, a Dr Peter Dally. He talked to me for about half an hour, but Dr Hay remained in the room and I didn't really feel I could say much. When Dr Dally asked what my husband did for a living I replied "Nothing," but Dr Hay interrupted and said "He goes to the House of Lords and makes speeches you know," which completely put the psychiatrist off the scent. Anyway, he prescribed a rather large number of drugs to be taken in conjunction with one another, and then to be discontinued slowly after discussion with Dr Hay.

The pills gave me a very nasty feeling as though my eyes were staring out of my head, and a feeling of floating together with a dry mouth. My husband took me down to The Royal St George's at Guildford, Sandwich, for a weekend and I felt most peculiar. The dose was reduced but it did absolutely nothing for my depression at all. If anything, it was rather worse. I had the greatest difficulty in getting up at half past twelve to cook lunch for Nanny and the children, and every day was a struggle.

Sometimes alcohol seemed to clear away the depression for a few hours, but it always returned again very strongly the next day. But I didn't drink very much alcohol because I didn't want to spoil my complexion and often poured Vichy water into my wine at dinner.

We often went to the Ladbroke Club for dinner then - it had opened recently and they often gave us dinner on the house. My husband also went to the White Elephant, which was owned by Tony Mancini in Curzon Street, but mostly we stuck to the Ladbroke Club and the Clermont Club. They both had chauffeur-driven cars at the disposal of clients and so I could go home at any time with ease. Around this period, I pressed for the nurseries to be redecorated and I arranged it and paid for it. At this time, we also had a Frenchwoman who came in every weekday for an hour and a half to give George and Frances French lessons, and we considered the idea of employing a full time living in French Governess to replace Nanny Jenkins.

Meanwhile, I had been becoming more and more dissatisfied with Nanny Jenkins. She was even drunk on occasions, but nannies are hard to come by and I took the view 'Better the devil you know than the devil you don't.' She used to take the children to Sunday school at St Peter's Eaton Square, and one day I had a letter from someone I knew saying that they thought my nanny was too strict. I already knew Nanny Jenkins to be better with babies than with older children - she was too spinsterish and frustrated for words. She used to sigh regretfully "I'll die wondering," and tell Frances to keep her legs together even in the bath. I was long suffering and I endured Nanny Jenkins' insolence and incompetence, and considered in my mind the best moment to dismiss her - it clearly should be done when I had got my last child into playschool, and bearing this in mind, biding my time, I continued with her.

13

Camilla

On 3rd May 1971, my thirty-fourth birthday, I received a plant from my sister. I also had some red roses from my husband, which he had signed "With love from Bluecy." He was now known as 'Bluecy' as well as 'Lucky', which stood for 'Blue Lucan' and meant he played chemmy with partly his own money and partly Aspinall's. In a happy mood, I rang my sister to thank her. My mother answered and so I asked her what she was doing there and was told that my nephew Caspar had got leukaemia. It was a shock. I rang my husband, told him and said, "As you're a godfather you must do something."

He sent a basket of fruit to the hospital and said, "Oh dear, oh dearie me." I now began to feel disaster crowding in on me. I had a nasty suspicion that we were living way above our income, and I got the idea that I was holding up an edifice and if I collapsed it would come crumbling down. I asked Dr Hay to come and give me a sedative, and said that I wanted to talk to someone who knew something about human problems. He was rather annoyed that I wouldn't talk to him, but by then I had little faith in Dr Hay.

I told him my nephew had contracted leukaemia and he arranged for a psychiatrist called Dr Whitteridge to come and see me the next morning. Dr Hay arrived first. Dr Peter Dally was away on a lecture tour. My husband and I and Dr Hay sat in the drawing room. My husband and I paced about the room, and Dr Hay pointedly asked if he might sit down. He then told my husband that I had told him that my nephew had leukaemia. He clearly had not believed me. My husband replied "He does have leukaemia," and walked out on to the balcony. I asked Dr Hay what the prognosis was for this disease and he said that it was not good. I then said that I would prefer it if I could talk to Dr Whitteridge alone. When Dr Whitteridge arrived, he introduced us and then left.

Dr Whitteridge was about fifty, and I told him of my fears and asked him if there was such a thing as the Hippocratic Oath, and Dr Whitteridge said there was. I then asked him if it was possible for someone to become bankrupt because of gaming debts and Dr Whitteridge said "No." I told him that I felt very anxious and depressed and had feelings of panic, and he prescribed three Sparine, three Tryptizol and some Tuinal with which to help me sleep at night. He was one of those psychiatrists, rare in England, that a patient could ring up at any time and talk to.

I started on this course of treatment and told my husband I did not want to meet him for dinner at the Clermont any more, and would prefer it if he came home and I would cook dinner. I made some effort to introduce him to new foods, such as I found at a well-known delicatessen and during dinner attempted to make some sort of conversation with him, but I knew that he preferred the Clermont Club and the company there.

After dinner, he would take me upstairs at about eleven o'clock. We would both lie on the bed and he would give me my Tuinal sleeping pills. He would hand me a glass of water and four capsules, each valued at 200 milligrams. On the bottle it directed one to two, but I took the dose he gave me without question. As a result of this, I would fall asleep almost immediately.

I also saw Dr Whitteridge several times at his consulting rooms during this period. I began to notice certain changes in my body. I staggered or stumbled as I walked, ceased to menstruate, felt rather short of breath and rather ill. I began to think I was being poisoned. The drug dosage during the day was quite high and I began to lose my memory. I began to suspect Nanny Jenkins and wonder if she was poisoning me. I would eat a lot of fruit, as I realised that this would be impossible to poison. I even asked her if she was poisoning me, by saying at nursery tea "Did you see, I did not drink my tea? You have been poisoning it" so she would think that I had rumbled her.

The symptoms became worse and one weekend when my husband went away for a golfing weekend, I went around to Greville and Zoe and was quite hysterical. I begged them to look for me if I disappeared, which they assured me they would, and then Zoe said she would make some coffee. I noticed that she did not put any sugar in her cup but only in mine - I immediately screamed, thinking that I had discovered the real poisoner. Eventually, they calmed me down. Greville rang my husband, who told him to "get hold of Whitteridge," and was annoyed and unsympathetic. They did not do this, but drove me home instead and I became a little better.

At home again the symptoms continued. I began to hear voices and could hear what I thought was the piano in the basement playing the "Dead March" from *Saul*. If I opened the window, I would see police panda cars flashing by and men jumping out of cars and waving truncheons at me. The house seemed permanently filled with smoke. I noticed that the statues in the garden had turned pink and then I began to see everything through a pink haze, and I could smell fish. I was petrified and begged my husband not to leave me alone, and he demanded that I see Dr Whitteridge and go into hospital. I was very frightened and agreed. Dr Whitteridge had previously said to me on the telephone, "I know just the place for you. 'Greenways'."

A bed was booked for me and one hot afternoon, with much traffic on the road, my husband drove me with a packed suitcase to Greenways. It was in North London and in a very run down district indeed, with large blocks of high-rise flats with different coloured curtains at every window. Greenways itself was a house. A nurse with dyed black hair and gold teeth let us in, and I passed a room, which said on the half-opened door 'TREATMENT ROOM'. All I could see was alarming-looking electrical apparatus. We went down what seemed like a subterranean corridor full of doors and I was shown into a small room which contained a bed with a contraption like an old wireless set above it which the nurse told me I could speak into if I wanted anything. There was also an armchair, very grubby and it looked as though many a greasy head had rested on it. The room actually opened on to a garden, and I saw some women with dark glasses sitting out there. They were middle-aged and seemed strangely still, and did not turn their heads or move as I looked at them. I asked the nurse to show me where the loo was, and we left my husband in the room. I took my handbag with me, and outside I asked the nurse to show me where the front door was, "Just to know where it is." To humour me, she took me back along the narrow corridors to the Victorian front door. I opened it quietly, and then without looking back made a dash down the street.

I didn't know where I was going but I just kept on running. Suddenly I saw a bus. It was mostly filled with women but they all looked at me kindly. I bought a ticket and asked where the bus was heading. I didn't know the place. Suddenly I saw an old taxi with the FOR HIRE light showing behind the bus. I leapt out and hailed it. It stopped, I got in and asked the driver to drive to Regent's Park.

He drove through many more gloomy streets, and suddenly I saw the beautiful Nash terraces and the Park. I became calmer and then asked him to drive to Royal Hospital Gardens, Chelsea. He did and I paid him off. I started to walk about the gardens, which were in full bloom and I sang softly to comfort myself. Then I saw one of the uniformed men who patrol the gardens whom I knew and we began to talk. He seemed so normal and nice that I was much reassured. Then I walked home and on the way I bought some bananas as I was hungry. I was footsore by then. My feet had swollen and the dye had come off my shoes.

14
Dally Flood

Nanny was there when I got back, and unsurprisingly didn't seem pleased to see me. I told her how awful the nursing home had been and that I had run away. My husband came back later. He didn't say much to me, and the next morning I discovered it had been arranged for the three children to go to Westgate-on-Sea. I said goodbye to them very sadly, with everything taken out of my hands.

After they had gone, my husband left the house and I began my struggle back. I was now virtually on my own except for a Spanish-speaking daily. With her help during the day, I locked every window in the house so I was unable to throw myself out as the voices told me to do, and remained in the house petrified and alone at night.

From time to time during the day I went for long walks and my feet became blistered. Suddenly it dawned on me that thanks to Dr Witteridge's frequent holidays - he had left me with repeat prescriptions which enabled me to get Tuinal whenever I ran out - I had been taking too much of the drug, and that I had not been poisoned by anyone at all. Immediately, I stopped all the drugs and I suppose I went through withdrawal symptoms that drug addicts go through. I used to sit in a warm bath to help me relax and continued to walk compulsively during the day. I often walked in Hyde Park, and I had a curious feeling that time had gone wrong. I would look at a clock and it would say five past eleven, and then I would walk for what I would have considered to be half an hour and look at a clock and see that it was only ten past eleven. During this time I would have the feeling that I was appallingly wicked and must die.

I was picked up by a man on one of my walks and he wanted me to get in the car with him, and as we were walking towards it I started to tell him how wicked I was and he asked "Are you on drugs?" I mumbled something and he looked a bit alarmed and left me. This jolted me a little, and I went and sat in some gardens in Holland Park. Some children were playing round about and it seemed to me that they were shouting obscenities. I felt that I was in the most appalling nightmare possible. I started to walk back to Lower Belgrave Street and attempted several times to cross the road directly in front of the oncoming cars, but because of the strange time lag I was experiencing I always reached the other side of the pavement before the cars hit me.

I became a little better in that the hallucinations ceased, but I still couldn't stop walking and so finally I went to see Dr Hay on about 23rd July. I was worried because my pupils seemed enormous and I couldn't stop walking. He persuaded me to have an injection of Modecate, which is a milder version of Moditen, a drug I have previously mentioned, and gave me some DISIPAL which was said to counteract the side effects.

If only I had held out a little longer before going to see him. I was almost out of the worst part by then and as it was I was now started on another course of treatment. Modecate caused slight blurring of vision and I couldn't keep my feet still for any length of time while sitting down, and indeed during dinner at the Clermont Club several people who had been sitting next to me at dinner noticed it. I had by now agreed to return to the Clermont, as I knew he preferred it. I was supposed to have this injection monthly. After about seven months, however, I began to find the side effects more than irritating. I couldn't read and even went to an optician to be fitted for glasses. So I just didn't turn up for my next injection. In March 1972 Dr Hay wrote me a letter saying that he would refuse to continue to be my doctor if I wouldn't accept his treatment. It was a nasty letter and I threw it away because I didn't want my husband to find it. I didn't know that he had also spoken to my husband about this.

He then transferred me to his junior and less qualified partner, who was very much under his thumb. I now saw Dr Ann Dally for conversation therapy fortnightly on my depression. I used to try and amuse her and she was surprised that I did not have crying fits like most of the other women she talked to. Dr Ann Dally was Dr Peter Dally's wife and partner in the practice. She seemed puzzled by my gloom, and said that at my age I should be enjoying myself. She was a large unattractive woman in her late forties and nearly always wore ill-fitting trousers when I saw her.

Shortly after the news of my nephew Caspar's illness and my reaction to it, I was in our bedroom and my husband was lying on the bed. I opened my cupboard door and among my clothes, hanging up, was a stick with the end cut off and wrapped in plaster. I turned to look at my husband who seemed to be grinning peculiarly. At that moment, I thought "Oh my God, he is mad." I had previously had a feeling that my husband was not quite all there, and those thoughts crystallized as I looked at him. He said "I'm going to beat these mad ideas out of your head." He instructed me to take off my clothes, lean over the back of a chair with my hands on the seat while he gave me ten of the best. In fact, he could have hit harder and they were measured blows. We then got into bed whereupon we had intercourse. I was very weak at the time and did not protest. Afterwards he looked at the injuries he had inflicted and kissed me very tenderly. This was repeated twice more during this period.

In July 1972 we had decided to go to Monte Carlo for four weeks after the Clermont Club had broken up for the summer. Charlie Sweeny and his French mistress were also going, and so we would have a backgammon pigeon who might help pay for the holiday as well as a companion for my husband.

Some days before we left for Monte Carlo, I saw Dr Ann Dally and asked her for something to ease my anxiety about the holiday, as it would mean isolation for me, and no protection for my husband in a foreign casino. I was not looking forward to the holiday, and on the day before we left she gave me a shot of Moditen but without a test dose first which is the usual procedure.

It was to prove a most disastrous injection for me. Previously she had given me some small black and yellow pills but they had made me feel tired and exhausted, wanting only to rest. Nanny left for Westgate-on-Sea with Camilla after Dr Dally had given me the injection at an early morning appointment in Devonshire Place. Horror of horrors, I woke the next morning with all the side effects of the Moditen injection, which is similar to Parkinson's disease. I tried to get her on the telephone but the line was permanently engaged. We all bundled into the car to drive to Dover. We got on the boat, where my husband had reserved a cabin and I rested as best I could. We drove off at the other end heading for Paris.

I must try and describe the effect of this drug on me. Worst of all was the feeling of panic and fear which was inexplicable, the sweating, inability to keep still and blurred vision. I had taken the side effect controller Disipal, but it seemed to make matters worse. We got lost trying to get out of Paris and it took some time to get on the road south. We stopped at a motorway cafe and had a meal. By this time, I had communicated my desperation to my husband who was not sympathetic. It was as though every unconscious fear I had ever had was being brought to the surface, and driving with my husband would certainly have been one of them.

Frances changed places with me and sat in the front while I attempted to lie down in the back. She stayed awake all night helping her father with the motorway tolls. I took two 200 milligram capsules of Tuinal which I still had from Dr Whitteridge leaving me with repeat prescriptions and, blessed relief, managed to sleep the nightmare journey away.

We arrived at the Hotel Metropole and went to our rooms, where we slept a little. We had breakfast and went down to the beach by car to the cabanas. By now I could barely keep still, but I tried. My husband was being somewhat cold and I felt alone and frightened. I could hardly sit through meals at restaurants and my feet kept on with their relentless tapping. Each evening we would go with the children to the outside garden bar of the Hotel Metropole to drink orange presses, and it was difficult for me to remain calm. My husband's lack of conversation did not help to keep my mind off the problem, and his efforts to teach the children French were painful.

They had an early supper in the hotel dining room but he would not sit with them if I was there. It saddened me. He did not want to share them with me, it seemed.

As the drug, which is oil based, started to show its maximum effect, I began to be unable to sleep at night. That was unbearable, for sleep was my only time of peace. I confided the full extent of my agony one afternoon and he rang Ann Dally. She suggested I try an injection of Kemadrin, and a local French doctor was called. Kemadrin is only made in tablet form in France; the doctor prescribed me some but they had little effect. My husband rang Ann Dally again, who said I must return to London for the injection of Kemadrin. My husband drove me to the airport. I'm terrified of flying but the need to be relieved of the agony was paramount. They waited with me for a little while and then left.

I was under the impression that after one injection of the antidote Kemadrin, I would be able to return. The flight was bumpy and I was, of course, frightened and ill. I made the flight without incident and got into a taxi heading for Ann Dally and Devonshire Place. I arrived on time for the appointment, but she was an hour and a half late. When she finally appeared her attitude to me in my suffering made me very angry. She was more annoyed that her 'treatment' had not been successful than she was sympathetic to my predicament, for which she was entirely responsible. She gave me the injection and 200 milligrams of Tuinal. The side effects seemed to wear off.

I went home to Lower Belgrave Street to an empty house. I rang my mother and told her what had happened. She rang my sister and an hour and a half later she came to collect me and take me back to her house in Cambridge Square. I spent the night with her and I went to see Ann Dally in the morning. She gave me another injection of Kemadrin and I told her that I was going to stay in the country with my sister. She gave me a note to give to a doctor in the country, stating I needed four-hourly injections of Kemadrin as I was suffering from severe pseudo Parkinson's following an injection of Moditen. She gave me the phials of Kemadrin and I left.

My sister drove us to Grove, her country house, and that evening

I became very frightened and she called in her local doctor at my insistence and he gave me a shot of Kemadrin. I was afraid I wouldn't sleep and he gave me a sedative and I did. The next morning I went to his surgery and he asked why I was so lacking in confidence. He told me to "live day by day," and he gave me another shot. That was my last. I was still suffering from the side effects but feeling safer and more secure in England and able to rest.

The day before my husband was due back, my sister and I drove to London and went to see Ann Dally together. Her notes were not on her desk and she looked irritated. "Well, perhaps we'd better try one of the cheese ones," she said. My sister said "It's as hit and miss as that is it?"

We left with nothing decided. Nanny Jenkins was also due to return with Camilla and she was very late. The chauffeur-driven car had a shattered windscreen and they had waited for another car. The house had already been cleaned by a firm of professional cleaners, arranged by my sister. I had also been shopping and bought some new clothes, trousers and sweaters. My husband was cool on his return. I think he had enjoyed having the children to himself and perhaps had rather more attention without a wife than with one, and the children had proved a great asset and had been much admired, although his attention was somewhat lacking in the evenings as the purchase of two new mattresses for the Hotel Metropole indicated.

Meanwhile, the Shand Kydds thought I should see Dr John Flood at The Priory. My sister arranged a lunch and asked a manic-depressive friend, we talked of drug horror and she told me of her faith in this man who had helped her. I was still suffering from the side effects of Moditen and was therefore frightened and depressed.

One morning in late September, my sister drove me to The Priory to see Dr Flood. He saw us together and told us that he had broken his holiday to see me. I told him a bit about the story and that when I had seen Ann Dally and told her I was going to see him, she had lost her temper and said, "You upper class women are all the same, you go from doctor to doctor - you'll end up with no-one to go to." Dr Flood responded "Working class women go from Out Patients Clinic to Out Patients Clinic."

We made another appointment for him to see me at his Harley Street consulting rooms. He prescribed MARPLAN (MAOI), a monoamine oxidase inhibitor - in fact 'one of the cheese ones' that Ann Dally had referred to - three times a day. The improvement was nothing short of miraculous. I became so well that I reduced the dose myself in between consultations and he approved. My GP was annoyed that I should have bypassed him and found my own psychiatrist, and he showed his displeasure. My husband was annoyed that I was going to a psychiatrist that he had not been instrumental in finding.

I had discovered with my new-found bounce that he had cancelled an insurance policy for accident in which I would be the beneficiary of £50,000. That annoyed me, particularly as he had not told me, and so when due to go to California for the Vietor Cup Backgammon tournament, I insured his life for half a million against an aeroplane accident for while he was away. He listened in to the call - he often did this when I used the telephone - and he was annoyed. It might have spoilt his flight, thinking if the aeroplane crashed I would be crying all the way to the bank. I subsequently went to see the insurance brokers and discussed with them life insurance for the future. They said they would send a letter to him at 5 Eaton Row and a copy to me at 46 Lower Belgrave Street, and said that if he did not reply they would 'arrange' a meeting. They had noted that he didn't reply to his letters.

I had lunch with Zoe around this time as we were still friends. My wedding anniversary present was a crescent-shaped brooch in rubies and diamonds in a gold setting. It would have suited a more flamboyant woman than myself, and as brooches were seldom worn in those days, I was not pleased. It was a symptom of my cure from MARPLAN that I was slightly high and gave vent to my true feelings. I was still on the drug. I did not wear the brooch for our anniversary dinner. He did not say anything, although he must have noticed. The next day I went to the shop where he had bought it, and by subterfuge discovered how much he had paid for it - £450. I then went to a jewellers in Bond Street to look at emerald rings. I had long wanted a ring which looked something. One wears a ring all the time, brooches and necklaces seldom. I bought one I liked for £1,000 and was truly delighted. My husband was intrigued by the ring and not altogether pleased. Things were not good between us, but he did not ask me what had happened to the brooch he had given me as an anniversary gift.

Another example of my return to health occurred at the recently-sold Clermont Club. Aspinall had sold the Club to the Playboy Club in 1972. While we had been watching a TV university debate on the subject of women's liberation, a young girl undergraduate had said "It's amazing how we women continue to love men despite what they do to us." It had struck a chord, and I wanted to hear more. A girl in a white dress had continued to talk loudly to some backgammon players during this programme and so I said 'Shush,' but she ignored me and had continued her conversation, so I said 'Shush' a little louder. She then raised her glass of wine as though to throw it at me. Reacting quickly, I threw my glass of wine at her first and she then threw hers at my pale blue blouse leaving a stain.

It was all rather unfortunate and her boyfriend took her away, probably to sponge her dress. I remained sitting on a stool until the end of the programme and the atmosphere was rather still. I don't know why this should have been. I had heard of so many forms of unusual behaviour from the men that it seemed double standards were prevailing. My husband was very annoyed, and although I apologised, he did not comfort me. I went home with John Aspinall's mother, Lady Osborne, in a taxi.

Monday nights were what my husband described as his 'pink ticket nights'. He would go to the Portland Club to play bridge. Sometimes, on my husband's bridge evening, I had dinner with my sister and occasionally with my mother as well. One Monday evening my sister and my mother went with me to have dinner in the Bayswater Road. They needled me throughout the meal, and so I told them that my husband had become a multi-multi-millionaire in one of Jimmy Goldsmith's companies and that he was buying a huge estate in the country. They looked extremely distressed by this news and refused to drive me home so I hailed a taxi. When I arrived home, my husband was unexpectedly at home as well. I told him that I had "Killed them, I crucified them, they didn't know what had hit them." He asked what had happened and I told him what I had told them. I had told them this because I wanted them to have a good opinion of him, which I knew they didn't actually have. I told my husband that my mother and sister had been very nasty. I learnt later from my husband's custody affidavit that my mother had rung Dr Flood to say that she was very worried about me and what was he doing about it. She made him promise faithfully that he would on no account tell me that she had rung. Needlessly to say, this information shocked me and I did not forget it.

In November my husband went to California for the Vietor Cup, which is a backgammon tournament and during that time I spoke to the Vicar at Laleham, who told me that Granny Lucan's body was to be exhumed and moved closer to her husband's grave. Apparently it was thought by some members of the family that she had been buried too far from him, and that it might appear to future generations that they were estranged. Aunt Margaret and Uncle John had not told my husband about this, which they should have done, and the Vicar confided to me that he was a little concerned about it. My husband was a Patron of the Living All Saints church at Laleham in Middlesex, which formed part of the English Estate. The church burial grounds contained the remains of the 3rd, 4th and 5th Earls of Lucan. My husband inherited the right to appoint the vicar of All Saints.

The matter was later sorted out and I indicated to Aunt Margaret that I thought that this was not the way to go about things - behind my husband's back without consulting him. Realising that I was right, she subsequently asked us to the unveiling of a memorial tablet in the Guards Chapel to his Uncle Alex (Earl Alexander of Tunis).

The night before the unveiling, my husband and I had a row while we were both in the mews house. He said that he wished he could go away for six months to America. I said "If that is what you want, then you must go." This was the first time my husband had been physically violent and I cannot remember what the argument was about, but it developed further and he attempted to strangle me. The marks were still on my neck the next day for the unveiling of the memorial tablet.

There was a lunch afterwards and I sat next to Brian Alexander and Johnny Bevan. It was quite an enjoyable lunch but my husband looked grim and unapproachable throughout. Shane Alexander had been most helpful during the ceremony, indicating what we should do and when, and Hilary his wife had been friendly. Earl Mountbatten of Burma was there but we were not introduced, and various others whom I did not recognise. The drinks afterwards were easy, and I felt that it was good that we had been invited and had attended.

In October my sister asked me to allow George to attend her son Caspar's fifth birthday party as a reward for having looked after me while I was ill in the summer. My husband and I had made it a policy to allow our children to make their own friends, and we did not inflict their cousins on them as a matter of course. The Shand Kydds were too rich and we didn't want our children to become discontented. The same applied in reverse to the Gibbs children - we were rather richer than they were, or at any rate our lifestyle suggested that we were. However, I said that if that was what she wanted I would allow him to go. I made it a fait accompli by asking George if he would like to go to Caspar's birthday party on the day. He said he would, and when his father appeared at lunchtime and George said "I'm going to a party" or words to that effect, my husband asked "Whose?" Upon being told, he was faced with disallowing George a party or letting him go.

Barry Swaebe, a well-known photographer, was at the party and took photographs of Caspar, the Shand Kydds and George, and several of the other guests. At the end I heard him say "I'll try and get these in *The Queen* for you." "Thank you Barry," she replied. However, she was, *The Queen* magazine said, a day too late with her photographs and they didn't go in.

15

Mews House

In 1971 my husband had noticed a mews house with a For Sale board in the mews behind Lower Belgrave Street - 5, Eaton Row. We both looked at it and it was in a very bad state of repair. It would take a long time to make it fit for habitation, which is probably why it had remained on the market. We bought it. It had two bedrooms, a garage, living room, small galley kitchen and dining recess.

We decided that it would be our guest cottage and we would repay hospitality we had had from people in the country by having them to stay in London. They would be away from us part of the time, but could make bacon and eggs and do more or less what they wanted while they were there, without being on top of us. I do not remember what it cost.

It was a great idea. We had central heating put in, it was re-wired, plumbed, repaired and we redecorated the whole house, which gave me an interest. The house was habitable by August 1972, and in view of the Leasehold Reform Act as the house had a rateable value of under £400, if we had owned and occupied for five years we could buy the freehold.

In order to prove occupancy, my husband spent as many as five nights a week there but he did the occupying because he didn't get back from the Clermont until five o'clock or later and it would mean being there on my own until he came back, so I preferred to stay with the children at Lower Belgrave Street.

My husband had taken to collecting George from Eaton House School in the afternoon, but he was going to be away for a week and so he asked the linkman at the Clermont Club, Billy Edgson, to collect him instead. I was going to have lunch nearby on the Thursday, so I rang him and said I would be collecting George that day. I turned up at the school to be told that he had already been collected by a chauffeur. I went home to discover George was there and so I rang Edgson to ask why he had collected George when I had told him that I would be collecting him that day. He replied, "Lord Lucan told me to collect his son." He said this in a tone so insolent and rude that I could only believe that he had some very good reason for thinking that my husband would not be very angry when I told him what had been said and done.

From the time my husband started regularly occupying 5 Eaton Row, I lost any hope that I might have had in keeping some control over him. He slept at the back of the house so I could not make him hear me if I shouted from the mews. He would switch the telephone bell off and bolt the front door. His friends would ring up Lower Belgrave Street in the morning, as they too could not get through, and give me messages about gambling or meeting for lunch to give to him when I could. At about 11.30am he would have unbolted the front door and I would bring him his mail and his messages. He developed the habit of ringing me up if he wanted me to come over, and I realised that I was losing all dignity as a human being although I was quite amused about this development at first.

16
Jenkins Sacked

On Friday, 1st December I dismissed Lilian Maud Jenkins. She had become, in recent weeks, more and more insolent - shouting at me, she hit me on one occasion and indeed I had given up paying her myself, because I could never get her wages from my husband and I couldn't bear the unpleasantness. I told her she would have to ask him for it herself.

She was annoyed that all the children were at school, and particularly resented the daily French tuition given by Mlle Marie Christine Monteilleur, an educated woman who was waiting to get married to an Englishman. In order to augment her income, she gave the children French lessons for an hour and a half in the afternoon. Just before tea, I discovered that Marie Christine had not been. I asked Nanny Jenkins if she had rung and I was told "No." I went downstairs and asked Marie Christine on the telephone if she had rung. She replied that she had called asking to be excused as she wanted to go to Paris for the weekend. I accepted this and I went upstairs and asked Nanny Jenkins again. The answer was the same "No," in a defiant and rude tone. To reassure myself finally that I was getting the truth, I rang Marie Christine again. This time a friend answered and she confirmed that Marie Christine had rung as she had been with her. I asked Nanny again and got the same reply, and so I told her she was a liar and to pack at once.

We went upstairs and I started to put her things into her suitcases. It was an exhausting business - she appeared stunned and angry, and I carried her suitcases downstairs. I put them out on the pavement although it was raining, and found her insurance cards. I tried to get a taxi through the Clermont Club desk but failed, so I stood in the middle of the road outside Lower Belgrave Street in the rain and eventually I managed to stop one. Her suitcases were loaded in and she got in. I asked the driver to help her out at the other end. I had no money to pay her but told her to send her account in.

Nanny was a member of a residential women's club called the Helena Club in Lower Sloane Street, and so I knew she had somewhere to go. I knew of this club but not the name or address. I thought that this was the best thing to do. It's very dangerous to have a disaffected nanny under notice in your house for a month.

On the following Sunday, George told my husband at lunch that Nanny had gone to stay with her sister. He jumped to his feet and rushed upstairs to the top of the house and discovered that all her things had gone. On Monday, I tried to find out the whereabouts of the Helena Club because at that time I did not know where it was except that it was in Sloane Street. My husband had tried to elicit this information from me but I couldn't help. I sought the address all along Sloane Street and finally asked a newsvendor if he knew the whereabouts of a women's club. He did. It was in Lower Sloane Street. I went there and delivered a blue suitcase which had been given to us as a wedding present by the Dunsmures. I said I was a friend and the receptionist told me that Nanny had arrived with an injured hand and could hardly sign the register, and had been taken on Sunday to St George's Hospital.

I was a little puzzled by this, for I had noticed nothing wrong with her hand when I left her. I took a taxi to St George's Hospital and I found her in the Casualty Out Patients Department, her gross figure ensconced in a chair in the middle of the ward with her arm in a sling, which was suspended from the ceiling. I spoke to her for a few minutes and I gathered from her that some black hair dye had got into a cut on her finger and that it had gone sceptic. I was not entirely satisfied with her explanation and looked at her with some disgust. Subsequently, I discovered she had been drinking not only alcohol, but the children's milk as well in large quantities. I thought she might have deliberately sabotaged her finger to gain sympathy.

My husband was anxious to trace her, and as I had re-addressed some letters to her in front of Frances she was able to give him an approximate address. We all drove around in the car looking for ___ Sloane Street but it turned out to be a demolition area. That was the end of his search for the day. He finally discovered it, and I was later told that Bill Shand Kydd had visited her in hospital, told her I was ill and given her some money.

Meanwhile, I got babysitters every evening and looked after the children myself, which was both interesting and rewarding. However, I became more and more certain that my husband was trying to pin mental illness on me. He was quite unreasonably upset by the loss of Nanny Jenkins, whom he had never liked and had wanted to replace with a French governess. Memories fade, and I cannot quite remember the instincts and impressions which told me to protect myself. Things kept disappearing, and his attitude towards me was unpleasant and the feeling was very strong. I became desperate and rang a barrister friend from before marriage and asked him for some advice. He explained that I would need a solicitor, and gave me the name of John Elliott Brooks. I rang him, and he seemed much surprised when I asked him about the law on Committal to Lunatic Asylums. He said "He can't be going to do that as he took you out to dinner last night." However, he put on a 'one-day stay' against having me committed. It was a far seeing decision. My husband subsequently tried to have me committed by playing a tape recording of me to Dr Flood. My husband apparently made tape recordings of any altercations we had, although I did not know he was doing this. Dr Flood knew Elliott Brooks and told my husband that there was a one-day stay on having me committed.

I had had lunch with my sister-in-law Sally Gibbs that November, and I had agreed to spend Christmas with them. Not that I wanted to, but in order to be friendly and let the cousins meet. That was another disastrous decision.

Elliott Brooks came to see me at home one morning when my husband was sleeping in the mews house. He came to see me, as I could not leave the house because I was looking after the children.

I described my husband's behaviour and, with my agreement, he wrote the following letter to my husband addressed to 5 Eaton Row:

13th December 1972

Dear Lord Lucan,

I have been instructed by your wife that after a lot of ups and downs you have finally brought your marital state to an end by "bolting her out".

I live in Chelsea myself and am therefore only too well aware of the necessity for security as against burglars, but as between husband and wife as you live in adjacent premises for financial reasons, in relation to the property that you occupy, security can be covered by a Banham or Chubb lock, of which you could each have one key.

My instructions are that on the other hand, Lady Lucan has never bolted you out of the house she occupies.

In these circumstances you appear to be in desertion and I must therefore formally ask you what financial proposals you have to make in support of your wife and the children, who have always been in her care or in the care of staff which have been under her supervision.

Yours sincerely,

My husband received this letter on 14th December and rang me through on our ex-directory line, which was attached to the burglar alarm system. He was very annoyed about the letter, and from that night on he slept every night at Lower Belgrave Street. I rang Sally and told her that I had authorised a solicitors' letter. I had told her during our lunch at La Popote in November something of my husband's behaviour. I asked her if she still wanted me to come for Christmas in view of this. She said "Yes," but I could not tell her when we would be arriving as I would not know until my husband had made the decision as he would be driving us.

17

Christmas Gubbs

Family Christmases are often rather miserable affairs anyway, but the Christmas of 1972 was an outstanding example. From the moment I arrived the needling began. At the time, I felt they were trying to incite me to lose my temper and now I know that they were. In the end I took to my bedroom to get away from them.

My mother-in-law's affidavit sworn for the custody case gave some information:

> She spent most of Christmas day in bed much to the relief of the rest of the family and John took food up to her. In the evening I was sufficiently worried to telephone Dr Flood and ask if anything could be done as the situation seemed to be deteriorating fast.
>
> He was very cagey and said "You realise that if I do something wrong she'll ditch me like my five predecessors" and after asking if there had been any actual violence, he said nothing could be done unless some change happened."

My husband's affidavit for the custody case was also revealing:

> On Christmas day everyone was desperate, Veronica would not let me out of her sight and eventually I passed a note to my mother asking her to get to a telephone and ring Flood.

The culmination was when I heard George crying in the night. I went into his room and discovered that he was alone. It had been arranged that their nine-year-old son Oliver should share the room with him, but to my astonishment, the camp bed and Oliver had gone. George was coughing. He had been taken out in the cold without his anorak while I had been in bed. I took him into my bed. I also had a cough from standing out in the rain trying to get Nanny Jenkins a taxi, and we coughed in unison throughout the night. He was worse in the morning and I told my husband we must leave and take him to a doctor in London, which we did. We left on Boxing Day and my husband arranged for Dr Henderson to come at 4.30pm.

While my husband was in California in November 1972, on Greville Howard's recommendation I moved to his doctor in Basil Street and instructed Dr Hay and his partner to send our notes over. They took a week to do so - I felt I must have a doctor who was not influencing my husband.

Dr Henderson arrived at 5pm with a Miss Watson, whom he introduced as his nurse. We all went up to the nursery and Dr Henderson examined the children. My husband offered Miss Watson a cigarette and seemed to be grinning in a sinister manner. He went downstairs and then Miss Watson said she had left her cough pastilles in the car and wanted to get them. I thought it strange. First, she had accepted a cigarette when she said she had a cough and then left us with such a lame excuse.

However, she went downstairs and Dr Henderson made out the prescriptions and explained them to me. He then admired some trousers I was wearing, and I felt a warning. Flattery and not about me but about my clothes - the insolence of the man - and I turned without any more ado and ran down the stairs and into the drawing room where I found my husband and Miss Watson deep in conversation. He did not get up when I came into the room but I sat down and asked what they were talking about. My husband said "We were talking about the children's health." But it seemed they were unable to continue while I was present. We then started to go upstairs again and met Dr Henderson coming down from the nursery. Both he and the nurse seemed rather embarrassed and they rushed out of the house.

I found the whole thing rather puzzling and I attempted to find out who Miss Watson was. I suggested to my husband that Miss Watson was one of Dr Henderson's girlfriends, as his wife had recently died. I couldn't draw him out at all and so I left it.

He went to Underwood's the chemist to get the prescriptions for

Camilla and George. When they came back I saw that the dosage explained to me by Dr Henderson for George was on the bottle for Camilla and became a little worried. My husband rang Henderson who confirmed it was a mistake, and to substitute the bottles. I also took George to see a chest specialist on his advice and the specialist's attitude was most strange - George was already on the mend, but he suggested an X-ray. I said that I would prefer not if it wasn't absolutely necessary, as I had read that X-rays were bad for people. I felt that I had been discussed with this specialist from the way he talked to me and was even more suspicious.

I discovered later that in a reference my husband wrote for Nanny Jenkins, he had stated that Miss Jenkins had been dismissed "at ten minutes' notice without my knowledge and against my wishes," and said that she had been "at all times totally trustworthy, loyal, discreet, industrious and dependable," and gave her "the highest possible recommendation." This reference was probably written in January 1973 as Nanny Jenkins was dismissed on 1st December 1972, but I would have been very angry if I had known about it.

18
Flood Acapulco

On 1st January 1973 my husband and I had an appointment at The Priory to see Dr Flood. He saw us together, and recommended a six-week separation and suggested that I should employ an au pair girl to help me.

My husband did not take his advice and started persecuting me by hiding my handbag; he 'inadvertently' ran me a bath which was much too hot and scalded my foot, and incited me in other ways and said that he was 'displeased' with me. I was tired as it was the school holidays, and I was occupied with the children all day, cleaning the house and going out to dinner with him in the evening. I had sacked the daily on his instructions. "Men!" she had exclaimed as she stomped down the steps when I told her who was responsible for the termination of her services.

I would lose my temper at these incidents, and insult him and tell him what I thought of him. We were having a very normal sex life, however - he did not seem to be at all disinterested in that part of our married life. I refused to go with him to the Ladbroke Club on New Year's Eve. Before this, unknown to me, he had bought a small Sony pocket tape recorder and would engage me in conversation, trying to get me to lose my temper, and from his affidavit I learnt that the tapes, for the most part, were mild.

We had a violent argument during which he tape-recorded us both and which he later produced and played in court as evidence against me. He would edit his part in the altercation in order to make it appear that I was mentally unbalanced.

As he was tape recording me, he usually replied "Yes" or "OK," which frustrated me as I wanted to find out what he really thought about me. I responded and I was verbalising my negative feelings about him.

Recorded comments include my telling my husband: "You're a liar, with stinking breath and smelly feet," following this up by saying that he had a miserable, weak, drooping little penis. Also that "My loathing, hatred and detestation of you knows no bounds." "You're a ventriloquist's dummy with a moustache stuck on your face. You couldn't even have taken your seat without me."

Other complaints included that I wish I'd never married him and that he'd made my life a misery. I say "You're completely idealess."

I say that I thought when I met him, "How is it that someone with all these advantages in life can make so little of them." I then tell him "If you want something in life you don't sit around whining about it, you go on out there and get it."

I tell him he's "Thick, thick, thick, thick, that I never liked him and thought he was the most crashing bore when I met him," also that "I've never for one second loved you or even liked you." He asked, "What right from the start?" I said, "I was dying for a poke and I thought it was a bloody weak one." He said "You've put that very delicately I must say."

I abuse him and repeat he's thick, thick, thick... "I'm sick of conning people," say I. "You were conned!" he said, "I was the unlucky guy." I reply "Yes, you were." I complain of him sucking up to an old woman for her money (Aunt Marcia) and I say "if you succeed in this disgusting enterprise which I am not going to help you with, I want some of it."

I complain that he didn't even treat me properly: "If you'd treated me decently you'd never have known this." I describe his mother as "That bloody awful farting mother of yours, it's unbelievable that you pay attention to someone so ugly, horrible and beastly."

I tell him that he can't make me think something I don't think. I tell him he's stupid and that I'm intelligent, that's why he's got to do what I say. I abuse him over his choice of a Doberman Pinscher to enhance his masculinity, which I imply is sadly lacking. I yell at him to "Stop! Stop! Stop!" "What will become of us if you go on like this?"

I say "John Burke saved you once - there will be no-one to save you next time," and "I tell you what to do but you don't do it." I complain that he never thinks about anything. "It's completely un-understandable to me."

I say that he's killing me, and that he has no sense of rhythm, and that I'm going to break him for what he's done to me. I call him 'Poor old Bluecy'.

He usually replies "Yes" or "OK," and then I say "You've got to become a human being."

The whole tape is interspersed with expletives and abuse regarding his sexual prowess and inability to hold himself up on his arms, and complaints that he squashes me. I say "I've wasted my wonderful genes on you. I've no doubt some other girl will come along and will con you again." He replies "Yes, like you conned me." I exclaim "NO! You were the one who wanted to marry me. You rushed me into it. I never said I loved you, not once. Not once and you never asked me. I was rushed into the marriage - how did I know I was going to be Countess of Lucan for so long? I mean, your father could have lived another twenty years."

He replies "That's all right." I say "Anyway, you were penniless when I married you. I was sorry for you." He replies "All right, well that's fair." I say "And your constant golf and I mean all your friends have said nasty things behind your back; I tried to put you right, you never listened, I tried to tell you and even about the insurance brokers; you wouldn't listen, you wouldn't listen, you wouldn't listen because you were too fucking thick." He replies "Yes."

"I ask you to do one thing and you can't even do that." He said "I'm very glad then that it's come to a head over such a simple thing as running a bath..."

I say "I'm tired out, worn out and sick of life." He replies with all sweet reason: "Well naturally, you didn't get to bed, you see you played the gramophone until about six..." Then he says, "Are you going to have something to eat before we go to bed?" I reply "It's not your business what I'm going to do." He says "OK, well that's all right, up you go." I reply "I'll do what I feel like, and the sooner you get out of this house and leave me on my own the better and move into your little mews house which I've decorated nicely for you and you've turned into a kennel like you turn everything else."

We had sexual intercourse following this - he was aroused and, in retrospect, clearly very pleased that he had managed to get me on tape.

Dr Flood told him, on hearing some of the tape recording, that women often attacked their husband's sexual prowess when they were annoyed with them. It was a thing they often did.

On 2nd January 1973 I asked my husband for some money. He had given me some shares to the value of £10,000 in 1965, but later on he had had a bad run and I had signed them back to him. I felt he had not made good the loan, and I was in a very weak situation without any capital at all and I also felt that any money in my name was a good deal safer than in his. He replied that if I behaved myself for a few months, he would review the situation. I, leaning over backwards, increased the few months to one year and asked if by 2nd January 1974, if I had behaved myself, would he consider giving me some capital. He said "Yes." We agreed that I should employ an au pair girl, and Marie Christine would continue the children's French instruction. We made love for the last time, which was recorded in his custody affidavit and is why I remember it.

He was then very annoyed, for a day or so later I went to his cousin Rose Basset's memorial service. I had decided to go without him for a change, and he would in any case be in bed. It was noticed that I was alone and there was quite a stir from the pew where Stephen Raphael was sitting. Subsequently, he was told and was very annoyed with me. "I won't forget this," he said. It is quite usual for wives to represent their husbands at memorial services, and I did not see why he should have been so angry. At least, I thought, I could go somewhere without being made to look foolish by my husband.

On 7th January he came into the house at about 6.30pm and I

wanted to talk to him. He refused to listen, so I followed him about the house. On the half-landing of the ground floor I goosed him as I had often done before, which was sometimes a prelude to intercourse and usually put him in a better humour. This time however, he knocked me down with one movement of his hand. I wasn't hurt as the stairs were heavily carpeted. I jumped to my feet and said I was going to call the police, which I pretended to do. He then rang the Henderson partnership on the ex-directory line and called for a doctor. This time the youngest doctor in the partnership came, whom neither of us had met. While we were waiting, I extracted some gramophone records of Hitler's speeches at Nuremburg rallies in 1939 and replies to the charges at the Nuremburg Trials by Goering and company. When the doctor arrived, I walked into the room - brandished the gramophone record cover and pointed to the silver vase that Emil Savundra had given us as a wedding present, and said "This is the sort of thing and the sort of people I have had to endure for the past nine years."

My husband was quite taken aback by this approach and he asked the doctor if I was 'fit' to look after the children. I looked pleadingly at him and he said, "Yes." My husband rushed up the stairs, packed two canvas bags and dashed out of the house. We were never to live together again. The doctor stayed with me. He told me that he thought I ought to know that Dr Henderson had been called on Boxing Day after a conversation with my husband, and came with a psychiatric worker with the intention of having me committed under the Mental Health Act. I was stunned that he would do such a thing, but very grateful to the doctor for telling me. He said he would come and see me next week and see how I was coping. For the first time since leaving my female GP, I felt I had a real doctor.

My husband had previously been to the employment agencies to see about a daily, and shortly afterwards I had a call from an agency saying they had a Mrs Dawson who would like to come for an interview. I saw her and she seemed a perfectly nice woman, and had been working in a bank up to then. I didn't think she seemed like a typical daily. She didn't accept the job there and then, but said she would ring me the following morning at 8am. She did not do this, but instead arrived just after lunch and said she would like to start. Mrs Dawson took a very long time to make the bed and was still cleaning my bedroom where she had started an hour and a half before, and had managed to break a glass light fitting. I had a funny feeling about Mrs Dawson as she didn't seem to want to know what I wanted her to do and I didn't like her attitude, and said so and she said that she was leaving. I offered to pay her for the one and a half hours but she refused. Subsequently, I learnt that my husband had spoken to Mrs Dawson's husband who had said if he had been there he would have advised his wife to walk out. I thought it was quite incredible that a husband would interfere with his wife's domestic arrangements and discuss her with total strangers.

On 19th January 1973 he was telephoned by the headmistress of George's school, Mrs Ingham, saying that she was worried about George and had not been able to get much sense out of me and various other complaints. She had apparently been teaching for thirty-five years, and said that she had seen the occasional mother like me. My husband was well in at this school. When he collected George the schoolmistresses would fawn over him, although he was not so popular with the mothers who waited in the queue to collect their children in the afternoons. Apparently, one day he barged to the head of the queue, saying "Bloody women, like a flock of sheep." This was repeated to me by an indignant mother. That same afternoon, he went to see Dr Flood at The Priory and gave him Mrs Ingham's telephone number, and he said he would ring her and hear what she had to say. He then played a tape recording of me insulting him and asked about committal. Dr Flood told him that my solicitor had standing instructions in the event of my committal to drag all concerned in front of a tribunal to attempt my release. Apparently Dr Flood said that this could be done on day one of the twenty-eight days.

My husband was now living permanently at 5 Eaton Row, and twice a day I had to leave the house in Lower Belgrave Street unoccupied as I had to take George and Camilla to school. During this time he would follow me in the car and time it to cross the road just as we were about to do so. When I returned home I would have the feeling that he had been in the house. Things would be moved or be lost, and in particular Frances' piano music. He had a mania about Frances learning the piano. The refrigerator would defrost of its own accord and I would find water all over the floor. The breakfast things, which had been stacked on the draining board, would be back on the table. I became rather alarmed.

Meanwhile, I was still trying to get a nanny, but permanent nannies were hard to come by and the best likelihood was a daily nanny. I interviewed a couple, and finally Stefania Sawicka. She wanted a temporary daily nanny job as she was an SRN and a State Registered Nursery Nurse (SRNN) and was waiting for a suitable hospital appointment. She started her duties on 6th March. She arrived at nine in the morning and took the children to school. About three days later, she arrived saying she felt ill and so I said I would take the children to school. A few minutes after I had gone, my husband opened the door with his Yale key and saw her. It must have been a surprise to him as he did not know that I had employed anyone. He said "Are you the babysitter?" and she replied, "I look after the children." Stenya (as I called her) usually wore trousers and was about twenty-five years of age and you couldn't see her qualifications written all over her.

She told me about this when I returned, and it confirmed my suspicions that he had been doing the peculiar things in the house. I had long conversations with her about my life and she appeared gripped by what I told her, and she would go home each evening to her mother and father and tell them what I had told her. She thought it all sounded fantastic. I felt much better when she was with me as she was most companionable and when I got copies of letters from my husband's solicitors, Payne Hicks Beach, with insidious allegations against me, she would comfort me. She didn't work on Saturday or Sunday.

I saw him on 13th February and he told me that he was going to stay with Jimmy Goldsmith. He did not tell me for how long he was going or give me the address. I found out later that he thought if he left the country I would have a breakdown and so he wrote a letter to my GP and sent a copy to Dr Flood:

5, Eaton Row
London, S.W.1.
10th February, 1973

Dear Doctor,

I enclose a copy of my letter to Dr Flood. I have also written to Mrs Ingham (Eaton House), Miss Malloy (Glendower) and Miss Richardson asking them in the event of absence from school or change in the behaviour of the children to report the facts to you immediately. If any of them do not show up at school one morning it might only be a case of a bad cold. I think therefore it becomes more important to keep some disease going so that you can always drop by the house or ring up without alerting Veronica.

If you do manage to persuade Veronica to go into hospital you would have to tell her that you were sending along a fully trained nurse to look after the children in her absence. Whatever happens you cannot say that my mother is going to move in until my return. My mother's telephone number is 286 5906.

Any legal problems should be referred to Mr Leverton of Payne, Hicks Beach & Co. (tel. 242 6041).

If at any stage you and another are prepared to certify to protect the children, the following witnesses could and should be called for the appeal (assuming Flood is right in thinking that Brooks has standing instructions on this):

Miss L.M. Jenkins, Helena Residential Club, 52 Lower Sloane Street, SW1 (730 9131)

Rev. W.G. Gibbs, The Vicarage, Guilsborough, Northants. (060 122 297)

Doctors Hay and Harding.

Mrs Ingham, Eaton House School, SW1 (730 9343).

Thus apart from your own, Dr Henderson's and Dr Flood's opinions, you have evidence from a clergyman, two past G.P's, the ex-nanny (whose account of the last six years is a nightmare), a school mistress (who, with 35 years of dealing with parents, says that Veronica is on the verge of a complete breakdown) and a past psychiatrist (who prescribed modicate and moditen).

The nanny's evidence would be devalued on:

a. The fact that she had been dismissed after nearly 8 years service and turned out of the house at 15 minutes notice. The evidence might therefore be biased.

b. Drink: Miss Jenkins says that in the last weeks she so dreaded going down to lunch that she used to fortify herself with whisky (which she does not like anyway).

I myself have never seen Miss Jenkins drunk or tipsy.

My address in Mexico will be: c/o Mr J. Goldsmith, Moana, Las Brisas, Acapulco, Mexico. (telephone Acapulco 41529)

Yours sincerely, (Copy to Mr Leverton, Payne, Hicks Beach & Co.)

John's letter to Dr Flood:

5, Eaton Row
London SW1
10th February, 1973

Dear Dr Flood,

It is now five weeks since Veronica and I separated. When we both saw you at The Priory you recommended a trial separation of four to six weeks. During that period she has not employed a nanny or a daily - she did have a daily for 1 ½ hours one day who "left of her own accord". I very much doubt that if she were to employ a nanny or au pair that it would last more than a week or two.

I am naturally more than worried about the effect this is having on my children. You are already aware of the concern at George's school over the change that has occurred in him. I have talked to Frances' form mistress at the Glendower who told me that Frances is working well. Frances is happy when at school but I get the impression on the few occasions I have seen her that she is nervous and frightened at home. Camilla appears to be all right but Veronica is making an effort to please them - for example, not taking them to church, letting them watch television instead of going out in the afternoons and letting Frances stay up late.

During the last five weeks the only people whom I know she has seen are her GP, George's form mistress, Mrs Zoe Howard, her sister Mrs Shand Kydd and myself. You already know the views of her doctor and the Eaton House School. Mrs Howard saw her for an hour ten days ago and told me she appeared to be quite calm. Her sister had lunch with her on January 6th and she told me she "had never known her worse". All the old accusations against, her, her mother, my family, the medical profession, etc., but now couched, if one could think it possible, in even more vicious terms. For some reason the sister was not allowed beyond the ground floor. She stood guard at the bottom of the stairs saying "you've only come to spy on me". She had in fact been asked to come to lunch. Veronica told her that I had come round and had "had a shit on the front doorstep" which she had cleaned up. The next day "he came round and poured blood on the step. I went in today before lunch and she greeted me with "you're going to be the laughing stock of all London". I went downstairs where they were about to have lunch and she told me that she was now instructing Frances at the piano and had "taken over the French lesson". Veronica is a one finger performer on the piano and barely speaks a word of French. What worried me while she was talking was a change in her face and eyes and voice. Her sister was appalled at how thin she has become.

I saw the nanny a week ago. What she told me would fill a book but as a sample Veronica "would roll around on the nursery floor with her dress pulled up and make George kiss her bottom". I refuse to believe a 60 year old could have made that up.

I am going abroad on Wednesday 14th February. I will tell her of this on the Tuesday. Judging by her past performances when I have been out of the country something will happen. All three schools have been instructed that any sign of different behaviour in the children or their absence from school is to be reported immediately to her GP. If Veronica had to be admitted to hospital in my absence, my mother (to whom you have talked on the telephone) would move into the house and look after the children for the 36 hours it would take to return. If Veronica were to discover that you and her doctor were, for instance about to turn up at the house together, the children would, in my opinion, be endangered.

I am sending copies of this letter to my mother, the Dowager Lady Lucan, 73 Lord's View, NW8 (286 5906), to my solicitor Mr David Leverton, Payne, Hicks Beach & Co., 10 New Square, WC2 (242 6041) and to our doctor.

My address in Mexico will be c/o Mr James Goldsmith, Loaho, Las Erisas, Acapulco, Mexico, (telephone Acapulco 41520).

    Yours sincerely,

He had the doctor to ring him in Acapulco if I had to be admitted to hospital, and apparently they were all waiting around for the call, which never came. I was much relieved that he had left the country and would not be able to persecute me. He had also given his mother a key to 46 Lower Belgrave Street, in case she had to move in.

A Moment in Time

In December 1972, I had approached the Vicar of St Peter's Eaton Square, our nearest Anglican church, with a view to having confirmation instruction and being confirmed. I felt that I must have reliable professional people seeing me from time to time. As a result of this, he came every week to instruct me.

I saw my husband on 18th March. He came into the house and talked to the children, but I felt suspicious. He was grinning - I thought "He's got something up his sleeve," but didn't know what it was.[1]

We continued fairly happily through the week, I had lunch with Zoe on Friday, 23rd March, and spoke to Bill Shand Kydd on the telephone about 3pm. He sounded very jolly and was laughing away. Later my sister told me, "The whole of London knew what was going to happen."

I decided I would go and meet Stenya, who had taken the children on their usual walk to Green Park - I had a strange feeling of anxiety. Then I turned back and told myself not to be so silly, and went back into the house and closed the door, putting the safety chain in place.

The bell rang and I went to open it and I saw Stenya standing alone on the step looking distraught. "What's happened?" I asked, "Where are the children?" "Keep calm," she said, and then told me that she had been walking with George and Camilla in Green Park when she became vaguely aware that she was being followed by a man she did not recognise. After a time, it became quite obvious to her that this man was in fact following her and she became rather concerned as she could not think what his purpose might be.

Eventually, she left the park and was about to approach a policeman to complain about this man, when my husband drew up in his car. At first, she felt relief, and began to tell him of the strange man, who by then had been joined by another man, but she quickly realised that both men were in fact something to do with my husband. One of the men folded Camilla's pushchair and put it in the boot of the car. George had already got into the car, and my husband ushered

---

1 The date of the Originating Summons was 16th March.

her and Camilla into the car before she could properly understand what was going on.

She was quite frightened by the rapid and unexplained turn of events. My husband referred to a Court Order and told her that everything was all right, but she was still confused and did not understand what had happened. Within minutes she found herself back at 46 Lower Belgrave Street. She was asked to get out of the car, where she was confronted by another man who handed her a piece of paper which she took to be a copy of the Court Order. She told my husband that her key to the front door was in the carrier of the pushchair. He immediately bounded up the steps, opened the front door with his own key and said "Lady Lucan must be in the house as the door is on the safety chain," and drove away.

After hearing this story I telephoned the headmistress of Frances' school, but when I got her on the line and asked her if she had let Frances go, she couldn't reply. I put the telephone down and screamed. I then rang Gerald Road Police Station and 999. Both sets of police came, but said that they couldn't do anything in view of the Court Order, but they were very sympathetic.

I telephoned my doctor, who said that he already knew about the Order and had been going to prepare me for the news over the weekend, but the children had been taken sooner than he expected. He said he would come as soon as he could. I wrote out Stenya's cheque and said "I won't be needing you any more Stenya," and "Goodbye."

My GP came and rang a barrister friend of his for advice, who told him that it was quite rare for a husband to be granted custody, and then took me back to his house. However, it seemed that it was not convenient for me to stay there so he got his receptionist to spend the night with me at 46 Lower Belgrave Street.

My husband had returned from Acapulco on 28th February 1973, and on 23rd March 1973 he obtained the *ex parte* order which enabled him to take the children. Three days later he wrote a letter to Jimmy Goldsmith and Annabel Birley, part of which follows, dated 26th March 1973:

A Moment in Time

Dear Jimmy and Annabel,

I have been so involved since Mexico that I have had all the time in the world to write and thank you for the holiday in the land of the greasers - never do today what can be put off until tomorrow. I loved Mexico not the countryside or the climate or the alleged indigenous population or Eric's filthy messed up foreign food; but the world of BJ's and AP's that was opened to me, not orifically, to use a piece of Aspinalia, but orally via what bankers might call 'your good-selves!

I love you both and wish life could always be like that.

    J.

*Lady Lucan as a child with her mother and sister Christina
Inset: Major Charles Moorhouse Duncan MC,
1897–1939, Lady Lucan's father*

Below: Lord Lucan's mother, Kaitilin
Right: His father, the 6th Earl of Lucan
Bottom: The 6th Earl with John, 1940

*Wedding of Lord and Lady Lucan,
28th November 1963, Holy Trinity Brompton*

Mrs Marcia Tucker at Hobe Sound

Lord Lucan

Bob Run

Migrant, successor to White Migrant

Inside the Clermont Club, 1971. Kyrie Markos, Benson and Raphael

Lady Lucan in St Moritz, Christmas 1968 *Lady Lucan with Le Merveilleux II at Newmarket*

*Lord Lucan receiving the Inquestrie Challenge Cup,
won by Le Merveilleux II in 1972, presented by Viscount Inquestrie*

Lord and Lady Lucan in Venice, Easter 1969

Lady Lucan, Glenlivet 1968

Lord Lucan at Banff 1969

Lord and Lady Lucan in Venice, Easter 1969

Lady Lucan with Frances, one week old

George, Frances and Camilla

Lady Lucan with Frances

Lord Lucan with George and Camilla

Greville Howard with Frances, 1968

Christmas 1974, staying at Tredrossil, Cornwall

Lower Belgrave Street garden, 1968

Caspar's birthday, 1972:
Bill Shand Kydd, Christina, Lucinda and George

Sandra Rivett
© Mirrorpix

46 Lower Belgrave Street - Ante room leading to cloakroom

46 Lower Belgrave Street - Stairs leading to breakfast room

19
After Kidnap

Meanwhile, my husband had been back to the house and taken several of the children's toys and clothes. I spoke to my solicitor next morning, and he was very sympathetic and said "He will rue the day he ever did this."

My GP arranged through an agency that I would have constant companionship, and a nurse arrived. She was very jolly, and later Stenya appeared and said she would come every day. Another nurse came in the evening, but she was very stroppy and so I told her to leave and rang my doctor and told him, and he arranged for the jolly nurse to come back. We had lunch and talked and they all tried to comfort me. I had no idea where the children had been taken, and I realised that I must not do anything bizarre and stand outside the schools or anything.

On Monday, 26th March, my solicitor, John Elliott Brooks, brought me the affidavits which had contributed to the decision made by the judge, Mr Justice Arnold, previously a chancery judge. They made very heavy reading - my husband's, I was told, was one of the longest in the history of British Law and those of his family quite detailed. I was quite horrified by their interpretations of my behaviour, and considering I rarely saw them, I was very angry. That Christmas had been a great mistake. A great deal of what they wrote had been taken from that visit.

I learnt from one of the affidavits that my husband had passed a note to my mother-in-law during Christmas lunch asking her to get to a telephone and ring Dr Flood who was supposed to have said "Is she violent?" and on being told "No" had said there was nothing he could do at that moment.

The basis of the case was that I was seriously mentally disturbed; my husband feared in the short term for the safety of the children and thought that in the long term their interest required that he should be able to supervise their care and upbringing, as he felt it was totally wrong that our three children should remain in the custody of someone who the doctors regarded as psychotic. After reading my husband's affidavit, sworn 21st March 1973, I said to my solicitor Mr Brooks "He's mad!" Mr Brooks replied smiling "Yes, he is."

There was one particular paragraph in my husband's affidavit which is the one that seriously damaged his chances of gaining custody of our three children, and I quote it below:

> 44. I had to go away to Mexico on 14th February. As past experience has shown, my absence from the country has generally brought on a crisis. I saw no point in waiting around for the children to slowly deteriorate before anything could be done. Before going I took the most stringent precautions as can be seen from the copy letters, now produced in a bundle and shown to me marked "R.J.B.5". All three schools had a letter to say that if the children were absent or late for school our doctor was to be telephoned immediately. If the schools noticed anything they were equally to inform him. I asked the local vicar to keep his eyes open and report if necessary to the doctor. The attached to Flood speaks for itself as does the one to our GP. My mother was given the keys to Lower Belgrave Street in case she had to move in. I also saw Mlle Monteulier who had just seen the children for the first time in 6 or 7 weeks and was appalled at their demeanour and Veronica's weight loss. She agreed to go into the house and see as much of them as possible.
>
> 45. Nothing untoward happened while I was in Mexico (I returned on the 28th February 1973), but with much regret I am now forced to ask the Court to give me custody of the children. I feel it is totally wrong that my three children should remain in the custody of someone whom the doctors regard as psychotic. If the Court decides to grant me the daily care of the children I have already suitable accommodation and I have employed an experienced nanny.
>
> SWORN 21st March 1973

The Official Solicitor's Report was dated 4th May 1973, and I quote from paragraphs sixteen and seventeen below:

> Lord Lucan confirmed that his trip to Mexico on February last had been in the nature of a holiday. He admitted that he did not have to go away, as stated in paragraph 44 of his Affidavit sworn 21st March 1973, and he regretted that reference to the trip had been expressed in that way. However, after full consideration of the situation obtaining in February, he thought that he should go away on this holiday, leaving the three children with his wife, in the hope that his absence might precipitate some development in his wife's condition which would force her medical advisers to commit her to Hospital for treatment. He fully expected to return to England to find that something of this nature had occurred, but in the event it had not, and it appeared that the period of his absence had passed without incident.
>
> 17. On the subject of the matrimonial problems between himself and his wife, Lord Lucan said he had no plans at the present time to institute proceedings for divorce. There is no other woman in his life, and he is certainly not thinking in terms of re-marriage. However, if his wife should wish to divorce him, he would not oppose this. Although divorce was not in his mind, Lord Lucan felt that he could not return to live at 46 Lower Belgrave Street again, but he did not entirely rule out the possibility of a reconciliation if his wife would agree to take proper treatment for sufficiently long to effect a cure.

On 27th March, the Official Solicitor came to visit me at home with his right-hand man Mr Ditch, and they took a statement from me and looked over the house. They saw the rooms were comfortably furnished and ready for the children's immediate return. I explained that I felt very strongly about the dismissal of Miss Jenkins, and pointed out that from that date, 1st December 1972, up until 6th March 1973, I had had no assistance in the house in looking after the children. I also told him that my husband had instigated a long-standing campaign to try and show that I was mentally unbalanced.

I said that my husband appeared unconcerned with making proper arrangements for the children's education, and it had been left to me to conduct correspondence with the schools, and I produced letters addressed to myself concerning arrangements for the children's education throughout their school life.

I pointed out that my husband had gone away to Mexico from 14th to 28th February 1973, during which time I had had sole care of the children and that they had come to no harm. My husband did not "have to go away" as stated in paragraph 44 of his Affidavit; he went purely to satisfy his own pleasure.

I said that I did not agree that I told my husband to leave the matrimonial home on 7th January 1973, but asserted that he left of his own accord. I said that his occupation was as a 'professional gambler'. Backgammon was his best game. He also played poker, at which he excelled, and blackjack. I said that up until 26 years of age my husband worked for the investment branch of a merchant bank, but discovered that he could make more money in a week gambling than he could by working for a year, so he retired from the bank and had earned his living by gambling ever since.

I was not entirely clear whether the marriage had broken down irretrievably, but the subject of divorce had been tentatively discussed with my solicitor, and I said if my husband wanted a divorce I would consent. In any case, I thought that I had grounds for presenting my own petition on the basis of unreasonable behaviour, but I would in due course take the advice of my solicitor.

The Official Solicitor's representative, Mr Ditch, then spoke with Stenya, who was still attending the house even though the children were no longer there. She said she was a State Registered Children's Nurse and took up her duties with me on 6th March 1973. She confirmed that her hours were from 9am to 5pm from Monday to Friday. Frances had already left for school when she arrived, so she did not see her. George and Camilla had finished their breakfast and were dressed ready to leave for their respective schools. Stenya said she invariably walked with George to his school, and Camilla went by bus to her kindergarten. Camilla returned by bus at about 12.30pm, and on Monday and Friday of each week Stenya collected George from his school at 12.30pm, and on Tuesday, Wednesday and Thursday she collected him at 3.30pm. By the time the children had returned home I had prepared their lunch. After lunch, they became Stenya's responsibility, and weather permitting, they usually went out for a walk to Green Park.

With regard to the relationship between the children and myself, Stenya said that if for any reason I was not immediately in evidence to the children they would always ask for me, and appeared very concerned to know where I was and what I was doing.

Stenya had formed the opinion that I was perfectly capable of carrying out the duties of a mother, and in her view I ran a well-ordered household and she thought that George and Camilla were very well advanced with their schooling for their ages.

Stenya said that she had always found that I paid particular attention to the children's personal hygiene and clothing, and that she always found George and Camilla to be well turned out in clean clothing ready for school. She felt my standards of cleanliness were exceptionally high.

From her own observations since the 6th March 1973, she could find no justification for the children being taken away from their mother and said she would be happy to give evidence in Court on my behalf.

On 30th March 1973, Mr Ditch called at 72A Elizabeth Street, this being the address to which the three children were taken on 23rd March 1973, and where they still resided. He was greeted by Miss Jordanka Kotlarova, who was the nanny employed by my husband to look after the children. She said she was a Yugoslav by birth. She had attended University in Yugoslavia and obtained a degree as a teacher of small children. She had been in England approximately one-and-a-half years, and hoped to stay another two years before returning to Yugoslavia.

She said that the children had settled down straightaway and she had experienced no problems at all. She had found my three children to be particularly endearing. Miss Kotlarova said that when the children arrived at 72A Elizabeth Street they were in a neglected condition. She said they were untidy in appearance, their hair was greasy and their fingernails were long and their clothes were dirty. In particular, Frances' dress was stained and torn, and George and Camilla were not wearing under vests.

Miss Kotlarova then showed the Official Solicitor's representative around the accommodation. Every room was furnished to a very high standard and the general effect could be described as luxurious. He said he thought Miss Kotlarova was clearly enchanted, not only by the children but by the surroundings in which she then found herself.

The Official Solicitor's representative then spoke with the three children on their own in the nursery, where they were playing. All three seemed perfectly happy. He engaged Frances in conversation, and in reply to a series of questions during the course of the conversation the following information was elicited. Frances liked living at 72A Elizabeth Street, and if given the choice preferred to live with her father rather than her mother. After being pressed on the subject by Frances, George concurred. When asked why she preferred living with her father, she said words to the effect that he was more lenient with them. He allowed her to stay up watching television until 10pm and also took her out to a restaurant for dinner one evening. Frances said she "usually prepared breakfast," and by this she meant that although her mother laid the table for breakfast each morning, she poured out the cereals for each of them and made the toast. She did not now have to do this.

Mr Ditch then spoke to my husband in the ground floor sitting room. My husband said that he thought my illness started early in 1964, and referred to the various doctors and specialists I had seen over the years. He also referred to other letters which mentioned the conditions of schizophrenia and manic depression.

He said that I was a very lonely person and had great difficulty in making friends, and he pointed out that when the children were removed from my care, I did not have a single friend I could turn to for help. Arrangements for me to be attended by a nurse had been made by my doctor. He expressed regret at the very great shock and distress which his actions had caused, but felt there was no alternative.

On the subject of the matrimonial problems between himself and myself, he said he had no plans at the present time to institute proceedings for divorce. He did not entirely rule out the possibility of a reconciliation if I would agree to take proper treatment for sufficiently long to effect a cure.

Referring to my changing moods, he said that up to November 1972 I showed a total dependence on him, which after the dismissal of Miss Jenkins turned to a total aggression against him, coupled with a strongly expressed desire for financial independence from him.

He did not agree with my allegation that he saw very little of the children when living at home at Lower Belgrave Street. He said that during George's first term at school, he always walked him to school in the morning and collected him at lunchtime, and for most of the second term continued to take him to school in the mornings. He also said he collected Frances from school most days up to November 1972 when she began to use the school bus.

Prior to leaving the matrimonial home in January 1973, he admitted that he had begun to sleep at 5 Eaton Row, usually from Monday to Friday. So far as he could recall, this practice started in about June or July 1972. It was not his intention to live apart from me in the legal sense, but only to prove occupancy under the Leasehold Reform Act in order to obtain the freehold of the property.

The Official Solicitor's representative pointed out to him that no mention had been made in any of the evidence so far, particularly his own affidavit, as to the proposed arrangements for the children's education in the long term. My husband then outlined the existing and proposed future arrangements for each child. He said he considered my allegations about his laxness over making arrangements for the children's education very unfair, and he was satisfied that he had made all proper arrangements for their education. He supplied a (totally inadequate) statement in respect of each child to provide for the cost of their education.

As regards the question of where the children should live, even if I was not ill, despite his belief that I was, on the assumption that we would continue to live apart, he would wish to have care and control of the children.

With regard to the question of access, my husband said he would not oppose access by me provided that both nannies were present at all times. He would prefer access to take place either at 72A Elizabeth Street or in some public place, as he felt it would only confuse and possibly upset the children if they were taken back to Lower Belgrave Street to see me in the home surroundings, now that they had settled down and got used to the idea of living at 72A Elizabeth Street.

On 5th April 1973, the Official Solicitor's representative called upon my mother at her home in Bournemouth. My husband's affidavit was discussed with her, and she disputed some of the facts regarding herself which were stated in the affidavit.

She then proceeded to describe how she had seen me in London on 4th December 1972. She said she was shocked at my appearance. My behaviour was excitable and I was, she said, emotionally upset and she was concerned at the extreme unhappiness and loneliness displayed by me. I would say her comments in regard to me were not particularly favourable and she apparently seemed to accept that I was suffering from some form of mental illness, although she had no idea that it was anything like on the scale now being alleged by my husband and his relations.

On 12th April the Official Solicitor's representative called on my younger sister at her house in Cambridge Square. She had had more contact with me and she pulled out all stops for me. She said that she was of the opinion that my husband's gambling habits were, and always had been, the root cause of the difficulties in my marriage.

She commented that she had always observed my house to be "spotlessly clean," and would be astonished to find the children in the condition that Miss Kotlarova suggested they were in. She said the language I used was no worse than that used by my husband, in answer to the allegations that I sometimes used obscene language even in front of the children. She said that I was completely devoted to my three children and that "They are her whole life." She said she had never known of or observed any violence by me, and was prepared to give evidence in Court on my behalf.

On 5th April I applied for the Order to be set aside, but the Judge

After Kidnap

wished to hear from Dr Flood, who was in Ireland and not able to appear. I was granted access (now called contact) twice a week for four hours.

Access was one of the most appalling experiences I have ever been through. I was instructed to go to 72A Elizabeth Street, about a hundred yards from Lower Belgrave Street, at 2pm. The door was opened by Jordanka Kotlarova, the children's Yugoslav nanny he had engaged for the children.

It was a luxurious ground floor maisonette - the sort that are rented out to rich Americans or Greeks for six months. It was already furnished, but in the living room I saw he had had his grand piano installed. He had put it in store after leaving Park Crescent, and his portrait by the late Dominick Elwes was above the mantelpiece. Exotic blue paper flowers were in a vase, expensive glossy magazines all over the place. His bedroom was on the ground floor next to the living room, but it was always kept locked. There was a bathroom next door to it, which was not. Downstairs there was a large dining room, which had been converted into a playroom with two enormous cardboard maps of the world and a television set. Each of the children had their own bedroom and there were two more bathrooms. It seemed that Jordanka had the master bedroom with bathroom attached.

The children were at this time 2, 5, and 8. They seemed quite at home and quite calm on seeing me. I was not allowed to see them alone, but had to be accompanied by my own nurse and to have Jordanka present. From time to time he would ring up and ask Jordanka if "everything was all right." I had this access from two to six o'clock and then I had to leave. There was nothing to do in the cold weather except sit in the flat, and it was quite dreadful. The children came to accept my visits without much enthusiasm, and I could see that Camilla was forgetting me and George seemed to watch television all the time I was there. Frances told me that Granny Kait had been and had asked how I was and I asked "What did you say?" She replied "Very well." I was glad for that, and astonished at the evilness of my mother-in-law. Sometimes I would do imitations of people and make them laugh - so did Jordanka, but then I started on her and she looked angry.

Jordanka did not know what to cook for the children, and so I gave her some suggestions and she became a little warmer towards me. She confided that she had not had a day off since she had started, and that my husband would not lend her his car and she said that he wasn't a gentleman. I gathered that Frances soaked her bed every night and that Jordanka didn't like Frances, who could be a bit of a 'madam', and Frances didn't like her, but there was nothing I could do about it.

Meanwhile Stenya, the vicar, Rev John Graham and my doctor came to see me at regular intervals. They had all written affidavits on my behalf, and John Graham had asked the previous vicar, Rev Giles Hunt, to write a letter on my behalf as well which he had done.

One weekend, I was invited by the Shand Kydds to stay. I could not believe (although my instinct should have told me otherwise) that they were not horrified by what had happened. I arrived in a Godfrey Davis hire car, which seemed to annoy my sister and she took over the control of the driver in a proprietorial way. They said we were going to have supper in the TV room and did not want to talk about the case or anything. Their unkindness shocks me when I think of it. On the Sunday evening, Bill Shand Kydd said things like "Well you are a bit peculiar - and I'd have beaten you if you'd been my wife" and I became upset, and he said that he was going to ring Dr Flood, which he did. By this time, Dr Flood must have been getting thoroughly irritated with having calls from my relations at odd times and hours, and it was arranged that I should go to The Priory and see him that Monday. I spent most of the day at Cambridge Square, when one of my sister's 'ladies in waiting' arrived. This woman did not say anything at all to me, she must have realised that she had to follow my sister's lead.

Anyway, we drove to The Priory and I waited to see Dr Flood. He said to me "You'd better come in." I asked him how long for, and he said "About a week." I was taken to a room on the Treatment Corridor, which I was later told was for the very disturbed but I was actually put there so I could have constant observation. Each room had a glass panel through which the patient could be observed. My things were unpacked, I got undressed and got into bed and a nurse brought me a tablet and some water. "What is it?" I asked. "Largactil," she replied. "It will help to calm you." I started to go into a daze and then I opened my eyes and had the strange eyes staring out of my head feeling. I got out of bed to go to the loo and started staggering and felt terribly sick. I called the nurse and told her the effect the drug was having on me and that my mouth was dry, and to tell Dr Flood. She was kind and did not make me have any more, which she could have done.

The next morning I saw Dr Flood again and he said they had decided to start me on Lithium Carbonate, which is a salt, three times a day, and that I could get up and mix with the other patients. There was nothing wrong with my room as far as rooms go, but I didn't have one of the better ones. It had a tiny monk-like window, as it was an old priory, and the carpet had cigarette burns on it where I could imagine that previous occupants had dropped their cigarettes after night sedation.

I went down to the dining room on the ground floor. It was a large room with several long tables. You could choose where you wanted to sit, and also there was quite a choice of food. We were supervised by two nurses, who also sat at a table and had breakfast. Afterwards, they would walk round distributing the medication. I was quite shocked by the number of tablets put in front of some people. The patients were mostly middle-aged and elderly women suffering breakdowns after experiencing divorce or death, but there were some men, although no young ones when I was there. Afterwards, one sat in a communal sitting room and read the morning newspapers. The place was voluntary, and so one could walk out at any time, but of course, if one did before being officially discharged, they might refuse to have you back again.

The rooms were all heated to a high temperature, and I could feel my skin drying up. Most days I tried to sit next to somebody new. One evening I sat next to a nice-looking American about forty years of age. I asked him what he was in The Priory for. He replied "I know too much..." and proceeded to tell me an involved story about working for some company as their legal adviser. He then later on in the living room pointed to a hole in the wall, and said "They observe us through there." He then told me that he had been thrown out of every single private mental hospital he had been into, and this was his last chance at The Priory.

The patients talked about their treatment and the doctors a great deal of the time. They looked forward to seeing their psychiatrist as a major highlight of their day, and would quote him at length after their session.

On the Good Friday, Dr Flood had arranged for a leading hospital consultant to see me to back him up, for he had no hospital appointment as such. This doctor asked me various questions like "Who were the last six prime ministers?" "The names of the Queen's four children?" "Today's date?" "What I thought of my mother?" and "What did I think of my chances of remarriage?" My replies must have satisfied him that I was not psychotic.

I then met a very nice middle-aged man who seemed very normal, and when I asked him what he was in there for he said that his wife had left him and he was on BUPA and admitted himself on festivals like Easter and Christmas to get some company and be fed, as he was lonely. Apparently, he was an alcoholic and had lost his job as well, but he now knew The Priory very well and the nurses, and it was quite like a second home. He showed me the ropes, i.e. where to make tea on each floor, and told me all about the nurses; which ones were nice and which ones were not, and I told him about my case.

During lunch I would become somewhat involved with my story, and the nurse would shout "LADY LUCAN stop talking about your case," and I would have to stop until another time. He knew all about Lithium Carbonate as he had been on it (Priadel) himself, and was able to explain it to some degree. My main concern was, however, as I had not seen Dr Flood for some time, that he would not discharge me in a week. I pestered the nurses on my corridor and told them to remember that I would be seeing Dr Flood on Tuesday, and that

I would be leaving. One of the nasty nurses said that if she had her way, I would be in there for two months. My heart nearly stopped beating. The nice man had told me that the nurses gave a report to the psychiatrists on the behaviour of each patient, and I was afraid that she would give me a bad one.

On the Monday before my hopeful release date, I sat with the nice man and he comforted me, held my hand and said he was sure it would be all right and I would be discharged. I woke on the Tuesday and had breakfast, and waited in the waiting recess for my appointment with Dr Flood. He asked me what I would do at home, and I said that I would work on my case. He then took a blood sample to see how much Lithium Carbonate I had absorbed and I was discharged, and I rang for a taxi to go home.

The case had been set down for hearing on 18th May. On 3rd May I had a visit from Miss Derrick, one of the articled clerks who said that she was very sorry to have to tell me that the case had been put off due to a heavy backlog of cases, until June 11th. It was a shattering blow, which they had tried to soften by giving me a beautiful bouquet of flowers and by assuring me that this in no way represented a victory for my husband. I was confirmed that evening. I saw my lawyers rarely, but I met my counsel Mr Roger Gray and I set about answering the allegations in detail in writing for him to defend me.

At this time, my husband was still hoping for a successful outcome to the custody case and on 6th May 1973 he wrote a letter to Aunt Marcia, which follows:

> Dear Aunt Marcia,
>
> I meant to write to you after your telephone call at Easter but there has been very little to add to what I told you then.
>
> As you know, I was awarded interim 'care and control' of the children on March 23rd pending a full hearing of the case. That full hearing will start on June 11th. The best result for me would be to be given permanent 'care and control' with 4 weeks access for her - that is to say she would have them for 2 weeks in the summer and a week at Christmas and Easter. The worst result would be the return of the children to her with virtually unlimited access to me.

Both these extremes are unlikely for the following reasons: during the last month she had been under the care of a psychiatrist who has persuaded her to take a drug called Lithium. This drug... has had a beneficial effect on Veronica. The argument will therefore be that although the judge's decision to take the children away on March 23rd was correct, she is now a cured person and should have them back. Even if the judge did not go that far, he would have difficulty in refusing her a good deal of access.

On my side I have the very strong evidence of my own family, George and Camilla's headmistresses, the ex-nanny and of course Veronica's psychiatric record going back to 1962 (before I met her). We will argue that the Lithium which she is taking is only an alleviation...; what happens when she comes off the drug?

We do have against us the natural inclination of most judges to award children to the mother, but I have the best Q.C. in the country working for me and what is more important, he is not a lawyer with a reputation for being too brilliant on behalf of his client right or wrong; the judges all respect him. The fact also, that by the time the case comes up, the children will have been with me for the best part of three months, and that they are happy and contented, will weigh very much with me...

So much for my domestic problems but I think of nothing else.

    Love,

      J.

Now the better weather had come I was able to go for walks with Camilla, pushing her in her pushchair accompanied my two wardresses. It was so ghastly to walk about followed by two women that I thought that this can't be true - it's unbelievable.

I would get back to Elizabeth Street about four o'clock in time for the two older children to have returned from school. It was torture, and I rang my GP and asked for access to be discontinued. As I approached Elizabeth Street for access my husband would be waiting in the car and he would shout "Don't defend - there will be a lot of mud slinging." I would go up to the car and plead with him to drop the case and say I would have any treatment he wanted. He would then drive away. One day I met him in the chemist at Lower Belgrave Street. He tried to walk past me but I stopped him and said "It was meant that we should meet like this - please stop - please!"

He said "It's too late now," and brushed me aside. I was going grey, getting very thin and was covered in spots.

I now had to take a heavy dosage of sleeping pills in order to sleep at night as the trial was getting closer, and the loneliness, isolation and feeling of horror was always with me. The nurse and I would walk about on the summer evenings - the streets were always deserted, and I could not believe that I was so alone. I had asked my mother to come up and be with me but she had refused, giving a lame excuse that she needed a little time to sort out her domestic arrangements. She was a widow, living at home and her daughter, my half-sister Tessa, was at boarding school.

Around this time, the nurse would intercept many calls from people asking to speak to Lord Lucan, and we realised that this was a form of persecution. My finances were in a bad state and I was afraid to spend any money for fear that I would need it later. My GP also seemed more worried, and I also saw Dr Flood once more.

My sister's manic-depressive friend lived near The Priory and she asked me to lunch after my last appointment with Dr Flood. She seemed gloating and pleased to hear that the trial had been put off. Her main purpose in asking me to lunch appeared to be to show off her house and attempt to patronise me. I asked her to call for a taxi to go home and said I felt that I would be happier there.

The days wore on, and at last the Monday of June 11th dawned and I got dressed, put on a hat and took a taxi to Elliott Brooks' offices in Little Essex Street. Miss Derrick, one of the articled clerks, accompanied me to the Court. Its number was 44, and outside it said BINGHAM MINORS.

Previously, we had waited anxiously for the name of the judge allocated to hear the case, and Mr Brooks was well satisfied when he heard that Mr Justice Rees was to hear the case. He said that there were several mad judges in the Family Division, but he wasn't one of them.

The first day was taken up with the reading of the affidavits. The Judge entered and we all stood up and some of us bowed. He sat down and asked laconically "Has anybody read all this?"

Mr Brooks arranged for me to have lunch each day at the Wig and Pen across the road from the Law Courts, and either he or one of his articled clerks accompanied me. I walked home each evening from the Courts through St James's Park and thought about the events of the day.

The next day, the nitty-gritty began. My husband was called first and during his evidence a tape-recorded conversation between us was played. He tried to place the tape recorder on the judge's desk, but the Judge waved it away and he had to place it in front of himself on the stand in the witness box. He apparently pressed play and it didn't immediately respond and we could all see his horrified expression as he appeared to be afraid that it had been accidentally deleted. However, it hadn't and eventually began to play. I endured this by thinking to myself that it was a play on the wireless and not us at all. Voices sound different on tape recordings, and it was quite easy to do this but nevertheless it was very terrible to walk home after it.

Whilst being cross-examined by my counsel, at one point my husband clenched his fist and shook it threateningly at my counsel saying "You're doing a very serious thing coming between me and my children!" My counsel, Mr Gray, theatrically jumped backwards at this and the Judge could be seen to be making a note.

After three days the Judge issued a directive which showed how he was thinking - and it indicated that it was along the lines of custody with the mother together with a nanny. Mr Brooks said if my husband had been his client, he would have advised him to accept this. He kindly told me "You're a racing certainty."

The Judge had also said that he was getting annoyed at the number of human relationships the case was destroying. My husband did not accept the directive. His solicitor, Mr David Leverton, probably explained to him how the Judge was minded, but his only response was to call out, to no-one in particular, "Just you wait till you hear from my mother!"

I was not called to give evidence until the Friday. I had to endure the continuing embarrassment of being cross-examined about my medical history. I thought to myself, he's not going to get away with this unscathed and so I called out loudly, "What about his bleeding haemorrhoids then?" and I had the satisfaction of seeing him jerk involuntarily in his seat at this personal revelation. I did not finish my evidence that day and had to wait until Monday, which meant that I was not allowed to discuss the case with anyone until my evidence was finished. It was very hard and the weekend was a nightmare. I was, however, cheered to hear that the female court usher had been overheard to say outside the courtroom "There's a terrible man in there who calls himself the Earl of Lucan." I was reminded of how Mr Brooks' secretary had said to me, "Some of our clients really do need treatment!"

The days dragged on - the doctors gave their evidence on subpoena, but the other witnesses didn't. During my time at the Court I saw Nanny Jenkins, Jordanka Kotlarova, Sally and William Gibbs, my sister, my mother, Stenya, Rev John Graham, my mother-in-law and Zoe. I did speak to some of them and they were clearly all very worried.

Nanny Jenkins' evidence was on the whole favourable to me. She described the children as being "very popular" and that sometimes they asked the whole class to their parties. Jordanka Kotlarova appeared in the witness box with an interpreter and it was so ludicrous that the Judge waved them away. Sally and William were very poor. Sally said that her own view was that it would be an absolute disaster for my children to be brought up by me, and that the children should be removed from my care in their own best interests. Sally was challenged by my counsel over her version of the theft of a bottle of scent which she had taken from under the Christmas tree, a gift intended for me from my husband and answered "So that's what's bugging her is it?" William said that he had had dealings with many mentally ill people over the years and had no doubt at all that I was mentally ill. William was told that vicars of rather more prestigious parishes than his own did not share his opinion of me and he could not reply satisfactorily.

My sister did well and made the Court laugh. My mother-in-law started well. On being asked "Don't you think that a little knowledge of psychiatry is a dangerous thing?" she replied, "No knowledge of psychiatry is a dangerous thing, Mr Gray." My mother-in-law then opined that in her view, as a lay-person, I was not normal and needed treatment. Thereafter she was clearly too partial to be taken seriously. My mother appeared in the witness box as though it was a confessional. She admitted coming up to London from Bournemouth where she lived to have lunch with my husband at his invitation. She had told him that I had been kicked in the head by a horse and concussed when I was a child. She explained that she felt she could not stay with me and sympathise - it appeared that she had read my husband's affidavit and was annoyed at what had been stated in it.

Zoe Howard did very well indeed. She was not intimidated by the proceedings and described what she had seen as a result of my husband having beaten me without any hesitation, in spite of him glowering at her from his seat facing her as she stood in the witness box.

The doctors clambered into the witness box clutching their medical bags, as though to protect them from the unusual position of having to be on the other side of questioning. Last to be called was Dr Flood on the Thursday afternoon. He was asked to come back the next morning. Friday morning dawned and I was advised not to go into the Court but wait, and I sat on a seat outside. After about an hour, the doors burst open and the articled clerks came rushing out shouting "They've conceded, they've conceded." I was told to come back into the Court to hear what the Judge had to say, and I looked back before I went in through the doors and I saw my husband sitting on a bench with his head in his hands. At that moment, I wanted to turn back and say "Save your face - a reconciliation - Save your face," but by then I was too afraid. I had won so much even though it was a pyrrhic victory.

20

Jobbins

My great difficulty was that I had to employ a living in nanny, chosen by me and approved by the Official Solicitor and paid for by my husband. This formed part of the Court Order handed down by the Judge.

My GP gave me the name of an agency called the People Bureau, and I was told the person to contact there was called Mrs Greenslade. She was most sympathetic on the telephone and said that she was sure she could find a nanny for me. I was not allowed to have the children back until I had employed a nanny. Within a day or two, she sent a Miss Hazel Jobbins, who had been doing work with disturbed children. She was about thirty-two years of age, tall, heavily built, with dark hair. She had brown eyes with enormous pupils and she looked rather foreign. She had a loud discordant voice, but she seemed as though she wanted to come at a wage of £25 a week clear.

Then what was known as 'the hand-over' took place on or about 1st July. The children were about 3, 5 and 8 years of age, and were driven over in my DAF which my husband had confiscated in January and had only returned it when Dr Flood wrote a letter saying I was fit to drive. Then he had handed it back.

The children were introduced to their new nanny. Hazel had a boyfriend of colour who was a prince and he visited us quite often. Hazel had never been a nanny before and hadn't the slightest idea how to cope. She couldn't iron and was in a perpetual muddle, but we struggled along. I discovered that she and her boyfriend had slept in my bed while I spent a weekend with the Shand Kydds. I was not pleased.

It was arranged that I should have the first half of the summer holidays and the Shand Kydds invited us all to stay. The Shand Kydds had supported me over the custody case albeit rather reluctantly.

We all drove down there and arrived just before lunch. The Shand Kydds' nanny told Hazel where the vacuum cleaner was in a rather patronising way, and the result of this was that after we had had lunch and my sister and I were sitting in the drawing room having coffee, Hazel walked in and said she would like to ring for a taxi and go back to London as things were not as she had expected. This was a bombshell, but we drove with her to the railway station and we said "Goodbye." I shook her hand and she looked at me as though to say, "You're all right, you won't lose the children as you are staying with Mrs Shand Kydd." I said "Thank you Hazel."

My sister was much put out by this and it was arranged that I should go back to London the next day and find another nanny. I got back and went into Hazel's room and started packing her things, which were in a hideous mess. At the bottom of her drawer, I saw some pills which I recognised. They were DISIPAL and the memory of her large pupils flashed into my mind. I later discovered that she had recently been discharged from a mental hospital following a nervous breakdown.

Earlier, she had told me that she had been intercepted in the street by Jordanka Kotlarova, still staying with my husband, who had taken her to the flat in Elizabeth Street and shown her over it in order to encourage her to want to move with the children there. I had been given a choice of 72A Elizabeth Street or 46 Lower Belgrave Street. Lower Belgrave Street was our home, and the lease had been bought with the Marriage Settlement money so I saw no reason to move despite the fact that Elizabeth Street was probably easier to keep clean and far more luxurious.

Fortunately, I did not give way to this suggestion although Jordanka Kotlarova had told her that my husband was determined to get the children back. I got on to Mrs Greenslade again, who sent me a temporary nanny called Mrs Elizabeth Murphy. She was Irish, jolly, about fifty years of age, looked very smart and said that she was staying at the Irish Club in Eaton Square.

She agreed to come back at 2.30pm in a taxi where we would drive on to Paddington and go by train to the Shand Kydds. I had some doubt that she would appear, but promptly at 2.30pm a taxi drove up with Mrs Murphy in it and we drove to Paddington. She chain smoked Capstan and asked if there would be anywhere she could buy some whisky as she didn't like drinking other people's. When she arrived she put on a smart overall with 'The Order of St John' embroidered on it and started work. She was another one who really preferred babies to older ones. She got on well with the staff, but especially with the Shand Kydd cook whom she persuaded to leave. She didn't take any nonsense from my sister, who was prancing about ordering the children to the pink loo, blue loo or yellow loo. She would point her finger at me, saying to the children "That's your mother - over there."

Later on she asked my sister if she could go into Leighton Buzzard to buy a bottle of whisky. "I like a sundowner," she said. My sister wasn't in a good position to argue about this and was still a little chastened by Miss Jobbins' departure.

The Shand Kydds stayed in London during the week to continue with their active social life and I would be left on my own. But Mrs Murphy was kind, there was no doubt about it. I was to drive her to London on her day off and she filled the car with roses for Lower Belgrave Street as I would have to be there for a couple days to look for a permanent nanny and to pack the children's clothes in readiness for their holiday with their father in Portugal.

I received a letter from my husband, the only one he had ever written to me, dated 16th August 1973, before their holiday in Portugal. It read:

> Dear Veronica,
>
> If you want an airline ticket to go somewhere on holiday I have made arrangements with Twickenham Travel Ltd., 22, Church Street, Twickenham, Middlesex, so that you can get tickets and charge them to my account. The telephone number is 892 7606 and you should ask for Mrs Willis Smith.
>
> Yours John

The Shand Kydds were also going to the same place in Portugal. Their chauffeur had to drive down and deliver their suitcases in advance, and when he came back he told Mrs Murphy that it was quite awful and primitive and far too hot and was glad he wasn't going to have a holiday there. She repeated this to me much delighted.

Mrs Greenslade now sent two Spanish sisters for an interview called Tina and Theresa. The idea was that one would clean the house and the other would look after the children. They were thin and miserable looking, but seemed to want to come. All I had to do was buy another bed to put in the nanny's bedroom, which I did. It was arranged for them to start their duties when we were due to come back from the Shand Kydds' in mid-August.

Mrs Murphy had worked in Spain and knew the Spanish, and was able to tell them what to do although I don't know what she told them. She spent her last evening drinking with me before she returned to the Irish Club to look for more temporary work and she was very jolly and encouraging. I was quite sad to see her go.

The Spaniards were a gloomy couple but they were efficient, and I told them about the Harrods account and we started ordering food and things they considered they needed through this outlet.[1] They were paid £15.00 a week each.

Two days before the children were due to go off on holiday with their father, I went to my old luncheon haunt La Popote to see if there was anyone there that I knew. I was dreading the four-week break from the children and the terrible loneliness - shut up in a house with the two Spaniards. I saw Dickie Muir sitting at a table. He owned the place and was a Clermont member. He asked me to have a drink at his table with some friends of his, and then invited me to have dinner with him and some friends that evening which I accepted with alacrity.

We met for drinks at his flat above La Popote and then went out for a Chinese meal at a place off the Fulham Road. Then we went back to La Popote and sat at a table out in the garden and ordered some

---

[1] We had always paid in cash before for food and had not used the Harrods account.

drinks. I was getting a little bored by now and began to pay attention to the loud-voiced conversation of a couple at the table next to me. The young man seemed to be as affected as his companion, a fat girl with a slight Irish accent. I interrupted them saying they were talking nonsense. Mary Geraldine said "What degrees do you have?" and I replied "None. I married the Earl of Lucan."

I could not have chosen a better person to say this to. Mary Geraldine O'Donnell, or Mary G as she was known, worshipped the peerage and lived with the fantasy that she was the Princess of Donegal. She introduced me to her companion, Peter Geiger, who was selling second-hand Bentleys in partnership with the Marquess of Bristol's son John Jermyn (Earl Jermyn). After some conversation she discovered that I had never been to Ireland and she said she was making one of her rare visits there that weekend to stay with a great friend of hers, and would I like to join her. Her friend was called Judy Yeatman-Biggs.

21

Dublin

Well, the upshot of my meeting with Mary Geraldine O'Donnell was that after the children had gone on the Friday, I drove to the West London Air Terminal where I met Mary G and Peter Geiger and flew to Dublin where we were met by a tall, rather wild-looking girl with a strong Irish accent who drove us to her house just outside Dublin called Brackinstown. It was dark when we arrived, but I was put to sleep in a large room that had a bed with a horsehair mattress. I woke early in the morning as the curtains were torn and had been hanging for years, and I saw out of the window the most beautiful Irish landscape marred only by an enormous round blue swimming pool. I gathered that her father was a famous Dublin gynaecologist who had left the house to his four children. It appeared that they each lived in a separate part of the house and met in the large stone Irish kitchen for meals.

However, most of the catering was done separately as it appeared that they were short of ready cash. The interior of the house was quite bizarre, but in a strange way beautiful and Irish in character. Their father was a collector of obscure antiques and these were all over the house. Her brother, Tom Cross, was about thirty-two, tall, good-looking and peculiar. He wore dirty torn jeans and a tee shirt most of the time and he and his wife, two children and a nanny lived in the most civilised part of the house. If Judy wasn't there, I was ignored by the rest of the family and would sit at my place for lunch without any food. Tom always sat at the head of the kitchen table and without moving his head from his plate would say "Has she had anything to eat?" and one of the women would get up from her seat and bring me some food.

Tom spent most of his time bulling and bearing on the stock exchange and studying racing form. Mary G went back after the weekend because she had a job to go to, but I stayed on. Judy seemed to spend most of her time at the Airport, which had been newly built - it seemed a sort of social centre in Dublin - you could have your hair done and meet people you knew at the bar there. Otherwise, we would go to the Hibernian Hotel, another social centre and have tea or lunch. Judy knew rather a lot of men and would get very involved in her conversations with them, which were mostly about carnal knowledge, or rather her lack of it, but everyone drank a great deal and seemed very jolly. She took me to see Lucan House, which was just outside Dublin and is now the Italian Embassy. The butler showed us round the ground floor and I was very impressed. I remember in particular a Bossi table and the two marble pillars in the entrance hall.

Lucan House is the official residence of the Italian Ambassador to Ireland. It is one of the principal Georgian houses in the country, and it is one of the most beautiful Italian residences abroad.

At night I could hear Tom calling "Judy, Judy" from the grounds, and he would go and look for her and then he would come into my room. I had been moved to a smaller room which was filled with junk, another horsehair mattress and bats hanging from the ceiling. He would 'flash' but would go away when I spoke to him severely. If guests or visitors came he would hide and when he heard them leaving, would watch from the top of the banisters until they had gone. I had to ask the gardener to light the boiler if I wanted a bath and I managed to have one. I stayed on at Judy's invitation because my children would still be on holiday with their father.

Judy arranged to drive me back in her car to London as she was planning to go to Menorca, where she owned a house. When we got back to Lower Belgrave Street, she stayed for a week and her two children and her estranged husband came to see her there. The Spaniards were very disapproving of Judy, and her two children called Poly and Ramon annoyed them very much. Her children were about six to eight years of age. The Spaniards had been most industrious while I had been away and made new net curtains for the dining room.

My husband brought the children back at about 10pm at night. Their aeroplane had been delayed and they had been diverted to Hamburg. The Spaniards opened the door to him and so I did not see him but welcomed the children later on when they were getting ready for bed.

Since the custody case, I had seen him on just a few occasions. On the night of the end of the case on 22nd June, as I was talking to the nurse and my GP outside Lower Belgrave Street, I saw him drive by in the car so I waved to him. After staying with the Shand Kydds I visited him at his flat in Elizabeth Street and I took notes of what he said:

> "You've ruined the family."
>
> "Brooks calls himself a family solicitor."
>
> "It will take 25 years for the Family to recover from this."
>
> "It is a worse disaster than Sebastopol."
>
> "It's a mixture of Flood's fault Brooks and you."
>
> "The children are wards of court until they are 18."
>
> "I don't love you."
>
> "I will only talk to you about the children."
>
> "I am very busy with all this paper work."
>
> "You are a paraphrenic."
>
> "You drove wedges between me and other people."
>
> "Don't drive back if you are upset."
>
> "I could never live with you again."
>
> "I am getting a transcript of Flood saying that I was the cause of you being ill."
>
> "You destroyed my masculinity."

He went out half an hour later after these comments. I then saw him at 46 Lower Belgrave Street when he came to collect Frances for her music lesson with Caroline Hill, which had been initiated while he had the children. I had been given a list of their forthcoming parties and future engagements. I then rang Caroline Hill and suggested that he take Frances to her music lesson. She told him this and he did so which gave me an opportunity to talk to him when he brought her back.

In October, he invited me to have lunch with him and he collected me and we went to The Mirabelle restaurant. I told him enthusiastically about my trip to Ireland and visit to Lucan House and he smiled. I also revealed that I had been told by my South Holmwood friends that he had drunkenly accosted them in Annabel's, and they had had difficulty in getting away. He looked embarrassed when I told him this.

I then put it to him that he should leave it a decent interval and come back. I also suggested that as it was my turn to have Christmas that year, we go to St Moritz, stay in separate hotels and share the children during the day. He said "Do you think that I am made of money?" We then discussed the performance of the lawyers and the court case. All in all, it was a good lunch but it ended and I got into the car to drive back to Lower Belgrave Street. He said "I did love you once," and I replied "If you loved me once then you still do," but he made no reply. I got out of the car and he came into the house to collect his mail and kissed me for the last time gently on the cheek. A few minutes after he had gone, I went down the street to buy some cigarettes. He must have had the same idea as I saw him walking towards me on the other side of the street. He did not see me and his face was sad and I knew that he regretted the whole thing as much as I did.

Early that November, I was invited by my sister to have supper at her house in Cambridge Square. The purpose of her invitation was to ask if the children could attend Lucinda's birthday party at the end of November, and I said "Yes." The conversation developed - she was in a 'very-pleased-with herself-I'm-on-top' mood. I told her about the difficulties with the Spaniards, and I said "What do you think about giving the children to John - I cannot get a proper nanny and it all seems hopeless." I was just testing her reaction, playing devil's advocate.

She offered to drive me home, but I said that I had the DAF with me. She also said "You're not pretty any more - have you looked in the mirror lately?"

I didn't see her again before the murder of Sandra Rivett. Eleven months passed with no contact with any members of my family and particularly my sister, but I had realised there was a very cold wind blowing from that direction.

22
Arthur Jones

Later on in November, I went to see Mr Brooks and told him that it was impossible to go on with the Spaniards. They had no rapport with the children. They were very irritated by the number of birthday parties the children were invited to, and we were plagued with mice because of their eating habits. They were resentful of me and said "You have everything and we have nothing," but I couldn't explain how tenuous this 'everything' was for me.

It was part of the court order that I should employ a live in nanny. It is extremely difficult to find nannies when the children are of the age mine were. I couldn't possibly sack the Spaniards without another nanny to replace them. The children's parties involved taking the child to the party and then waiting around to take the child home again.

I explained that life was intolerable, and could he tell the Official Solicitor this. He lost his temper - he was probably drunk - and shouted at me, "If you're not satisfied, go elsewhere." I left Little Essex Street stunned and despairing, and started to cry. As I walked along the Strand, a middle-aged man in a British warm coat and wearing a bowler hat stopped me and asked what was wrong, and suggested that I have a cup of tea with him, which I did. He was very anonymous looking - he could have come from almost any walk of life. I started to tell him what had happened, became more involved and he took me for a drink at the Strand Palace Hotel, where he had arranged to meet some business acquaintances. This took my mind off things for a bit and I left him at Charing Cross Station where he was going to get a train for his sister's house in Brockley. This was the beginning of a friendship which was to last until his death twenty years later. Arthur Jones lived most of the time in Switzerland and dealt in commodities, was a shipbroker and also knowledgeable about banking. He was about 54 years of age, had been married and divorced and had two sons, one by his wife and the other by his mistress who lived in Switzerland.

He had said he would ring me in the morning. He came to the house and saw the situation for himself. The Spaniards were stroppy and unpleasant, and we discussed what I should do. Employing a living in nanny approved by the Official Solicitor and paid for by my husband formed part of the Court Order handed down by the Judge, and for this reason I could not dismiss any staff without having a replacement.

At this time, my husband flew to America to outline his proposition to 'buy me off' to Aunt Marcia in New York. I know this happened, because of books relating this. His suggestion was that I should be offered a maximum of a small flat in London, the jewellery (which was in theory mine anyway, although quite improperly insured in his name) and £100,000 capital to give up care and control of the children to him. I had no knowledge of this 'buy-off' plan.

He wrote on 24th November 1973 to Mrs Tucker's son, who was living in Germany at the time. Part of the letter read as follows:

> Dear Luther,
>
> Although I have made my proposals in the bluntest possible way as being a straight purchase of the children by your mother on my behalf, the offer would have to be dressed up in order to give Veronica the maximum amount of face saving.
>
> It may seem incredible to you that Veronica might entertain such a monstrous proposal or that it should be necessary to go to such extreme lengths when a solution should be obtainable in the courts.
>
> I regret to have to involve you and your family in my domestic problems, but I did everything I possibly could in court and although we did not have judgement given against us (we conceded after 2 weeks ruinous court action) we ran into a brick wall in the shape of the current psychiatrist, if I could have afforded to battle on, win or lose, there would have been an appeal and if we were still successful in keeping the children there would have been nothing to prevent

her going to court once a year to ask for the children back.
But I am reasonably confident that the offer would be considered by her.

Mrs Tucker thought the idea 'crazy' and refused him the cash, and the idea was never put to me. How little he understood me, if he thought that I would even consider such an offer. I wanted my family to be together again and I never lost hope of a reconciliation. I had experienced the results of divorce in my childhood. We could not afford to divorce either.

I had met, through Mary G, a man who had given me the name of a chum of his who was a solicitor, and Arthur Jones and I went together to Walter House in the Strand where the firm was located and we went up in the lift. There were about four men in the lift and I asked if one of them was Mr Swallow. A tall young man replied "Yes, I am," and we said we wanted to see him. He saw us immediately, heard my story, had his secretary type out a note authorising Mr Brooks to send my documents over which I signed and I had a new solicitor - Simon Swallow.

Arthur Jones came every day and he was very companionable. He also went with me to see Mr Ditch, the Official Solicitor's right hand man, and told him about the nuisance calls we were having and how dreadful the situation was. We had received many telephone calls asking to speak to Lord Lucan.

One Friday, the Spaniards asked for their money at about 5pm, saying they needed it to get some medicine. I gave it to them and to my horror at a quarter past five, just before the children were due to go off on access, the children told me the Spaniards had gone down the stairs with their suitcases. I was in a terrible predicament. The children would tell their father and I had only 48 hours to get another nanny and it was the weekend, to make things even more difficult. I called Mrs Greenslade in despair and she rang a very reliable young woman she knew who lived in Essex. I rang her and she understood the urgency and would get on a train and be with me on Sunday at four o'clock. She arrived on the dot and it was my first meeting with Christabel Martin.

What a joy it was to have someone nice and companionable. She was first and foremost intelligent, and she was English and understood the dreadfulness of my situation and was able to discuss it in a knowledgeable way. Christabel was tall and heavily built, and was later to meet a violent death at the hands of her husband Nicholas Boyce. She used to do temporary work in mental hospitals and would start her duties by saying "I don't take part in any ill-treatment of patients."

She met the children and we all had supper and Arthur brought some wine. Christabel was a very capable woman, she was able to drive and do many things for me like renewing my parking permit and buying necessities for the children as well as being a great builder of my morale.

At this time, my husband wrote a letter to his solicitor and here follows part of the letter:

> A note to mark your card in case you receive any complaints about 'access'. Today was Camilla's Nativity Play at the nursery school and Frances's Carol Service. Veronica informed me of neither but other parents told me. I arrived at 11.10 (for 11.15) for the Play and not seeing Veronica there I sat through it and after the performance Camilla came down from the stage to see me.
>
> If I had not gone, Camilla would have been, out of 50 children, one of two or three who did not have a parent present. Camilla's new nanny (Miss Christabel Martin) who I did not know by sight eventually came up to me and after a short time took Camilla home. In the afternoon, I went to Frances's Carol Service at 2 PM. Veronica arrived at about 2.15, stood next to me and started to tell me I was in breach of the Court Order; I told her to be quiet and at the end of the Service left without saying hullo to Frances.

On the morning of Camilla's Nativity Play, I woke up feeling rather ill and asked Christabel to go to the play instead. Christabel was very reliable and she managed the situation well. She told me that my husband had been at the kindergarten and was present at the Nativity Play but nothing untoward had occurred.

However, Christabel had to leave on 18th December and Mrs Greenslade, who by now had become a firm friend and came to see me every Friday after work before she went home, asked Mrs Elizabeth Murphy if she would come back over Christmas. Mrs Murphy agreed and she took over on 18th December and we spent as happy a Christmas as we could. Arthur and his son Nigel came for lunch, so it wasn't just a monstrous regiment of women, and we had the Harrods account so we could eat and drink well within reason.

Apparently, my sister thought it had been agreed some months before that the children and myself would spend Christmas 1973 at Grove with the Shand Kydds. I cannot explain why I saw so much of the Shand Kydds, but probably because they often invited me. Bill Shand Kydd had refused to have me on his property, but for the sake of Frances, George and Camilla had waived his ban. Trouble ensued following a telephone call between myself and my sister about the Christmas arrangements - I cannot remember the whole conversation, but I probably said that I wanted to spend Christmas at home in Lower Belgrave Street and didn't want to spend it with the Shand Kydds. However, it ended with my sister saying "I never want to lay eyes on you again," before slamming down the receiver. I never contacted her again before the murder of Sandra Rivett and she never contacted me in the ensuing eleven months. I was in a dreadful situation, but there was no support forthcoming from my sister.

Meanwhile, the nuisance telephone calls continued - Arthur intercepted one from Bill Shand Kydd asking for Lord Lucan and he listened in to all the calls, which were quite strange. We had other telephones in the house, which meant that one could listen in to other telephone calls if one lifted the receiver. After Christmas, Mrs Murphy decided she would stay on permanently at a wage of £35 a week. The Irish Club was close by and she liked the set-up at Lower Belgrave Street, although usually she refused permanent work. I never criticised her drinking habits and she was allowed to drink as much as she liked and order any food she wanted. My primary concern was to keep the current nanny happy because of the difficult Court Order with which I had to comply.

My husband took the children to Hobe Sound. Hobe Sound is in

Florida, and Mrs Tucker's beach house was also called Hobe Sound. It was ideal for a holiday with the children for his half of the holidays following Christmas 1973, and on his return from Florida in January 1974 he asked Bill if he could bring them to Grove, their country house occasionally for weekends. Bill quite rightly believed that I would not take kindly to this new arrangement, and it certainly set in stone the Christmas row. However, despite this, Bill and Christina agreed. Grove became a regular access spot and so did Horton Hall nearby, where the children swam in Bill's mother Freda's pool in the summer. Obviously, I thought that it was disloyal to me to accept such an arrangement considering the way my husband had behaved towards me. Although I didn't know it at the time, my husband was spreading malign rumours about me to anyone who would listen and I had no way of combating this. I do not know what all the rumours were, but all were untrue.

Apparently, one of the malign rumours was that my husband bought a kitten for the children from Harrods and shortly after he had delivered it to Lower Belgrave Street, it had been killed and its remains pushed through his letter box. It has been alleged that this cruel end for the kitten sent him over the edge.

Meanwhile my husband had contacted a firm of private investigators called Devlin & Co., and on 28th February 1974 they reported their progress:

Dear Lord Lucan,

Re: Lady Lucan

In accordance with your instructions, we confirm that observation was maintained upon the address of Lady Lucan during the period Saturday 23rd February 1974 - Tuesday 26th February 1974.

At 8 am on Saturday the 23rd February 1974, our Mr Cranstoun commenced observation upon 46 Lower Belgrave Street, London SW1, when he located the brown DAF motor car, Reg. No. LPK 389K, parked outside the address.

At 11.45 am a woman referred to as fitting the description of Mrs Murphy left the address with the three children, Frances, George and Camilla. Mrs Murphy was wearing a dark blue coat with a fur collar, Frances was wearing a black jacket and blue tartan trousers, George was wearing a grey jumper and grey trousers, and Camilla was wearing a fawn jumper and blue trousers.

Mrs Murphy and the children were followed to a newsagent's shop, Quinlan's at 31 Ebury Street, London SW1, and a few moments later they left those premises and were followed to The Irish Club, 82 Lyall Street, London SW1, where they arrived at 12.10 pm.

Thereafter Mr Cranstoun observed Mrs Murphy and the three children sitting at the bar drinking from glasses.

Mr Cranstoun telephoned our Mr Devlin from the club when we reported the foregoing to you as the premises are situated close to your property.

Yours faithfully,
(Signed)

My husband replied on 4th March 1974 and appeared delighted by the report and his reply follows:

Dear Mr Devlin,

Thank you for your most useful report. I would like if possible the same arrangement for next Saturday and Sunday. In fact on Saturday their most likely destination would be the health food bar at Harrods. However if the family were divided I am more interested in the hours spent inside and outside the house by the children.

Remember that my wife is extremely suspicious (the psychiatrists agree on a form of paranoia) so that if she was to go out with the three children and your man followed them he would have to be very careful.

If the whole party got in the car (assuming Mrs Murphy was with them or had gone away) it might be an opportunity to install the telephone device.

Yours faithfully
(Signed)

The Irish Club is a respectable residential club and I had no objection to Mrs Murphy taking the children for a drink there.

My husband's obsession with the children can be seen here and his quest to regain custody of them remained unabated. I did not know that I was being followed and Devlin & Co., appear to have been very discreet. Their surveillance continued from February to March until April when they were withdrawn either because of the hundreds of pounds my husband was billed for or because Mrs Murphy left.

Arthur Jones was a platonic friend who understood the terrible position I was in. He was sweet with the children - he helped Camilla with her homework and projects, and generally provided on-going male attention which would certainly have been lacking if the children's custody had been given to their father.

Arthur and I used to walk past 72A Elizabeth Street in the evenings, but did not see anything of interest. Mrs Murphy began to get very gloomy in the evening, however, and began to take a dislike to Arthur and one evening she said "either he goes or I go," and as I needed her more than Arthur he had to go and he went back to Switzerland, although we corresponded. I have explained that because of the court order I was placed in an intolerable situation and open to blackmail. I could not sack Mrs Murphy without a nanny to replace her. But I am very competent and would never place the children in danger. It was a court order which was extremely difficult to comply with.

Before Arthur went, I had noticed lights on in the mews house and although I rang the telephone number, it was out of order. One evening I went over to the house and to my surprise saw Zoe sitting in the downstairs living room. I hadn't seen much of her since the custody case but I had spoken to her on the telephone from time to time, but I gathered she was much taken up with her new boyfriend. She had split with Greville quite amicably some two years previously. I went back and told Arthur what I had seen.

I decided to go back to the mews house and asked Arthur to wait by the telephone. I rang the doorbell, Zoe was still there sitting in the living room and she answered the doorbell and let me in. I had quite a pleasant conversation with her then Greville Howard appeared from upstairs. I gathered that Greville now lived in the mews house with a girlfriend. We had an altercation and I went to the telephone and called Arthur who came rushing round. I let him in (I had said 'private detective' on the telephone), and Greville started to threaten him and asked who he was. Arthur refused to reply, and Greville said he would ring the police and Arthur stood his ground and said "Yes, you do that." Seeing that we were in earnest and that he dare not lay a finger on me because of an accusation of assault, he got into his car with Zoe and tried to persuade me to get in with them. As soon as they had gone we slammed the door and bolted it and went upstairs where we saw a girl sitting on the bed in the bedroom looking alarmed. We looked about the house a bit more and then decided to leave. We got back to Lower Belgrave Street and started to laugh about the whole thing.

Greville looked concerned and said, "I won't have anywhere to stay the night." This sort of wetness no longer worked with me. I realised that he was, by living in the mews house, preventing my husband from returning to it, from where it would have been easier to negotiate a reconciliation.

In the evening, I sometimes walked past 72A Elizabeth Street and on one occasion was doing so just as my husband's Mercedes drew up. He got out of the car with his passenger who turned out to be Caroline Hill, the piano teacher. They went into the flat and from looking through the window, I observed them watching cine films, probably of the children which he had taken on holiday. I decided to wait and got into the Mercedes and sat in the back for a while and then I tried the door and to my horror found that I could not open it. My husband had fitted safety locks to the back doors. I jumped quickly into the driver's seat and fortunately the door opened, and I was able to get out. I hid behind the car and when my husband and Caroline Hill emerged, I rose from behind the car and said to my husband "What are you doing living in that expensive flat which you cannot afford?" They both looked shocked to see me, and my husband said "Get into the car Caroline," and they drove away.

The days dragged by, but Mrs Murphy arranged for a friend of hers who was an ex-Broadmoor warder to drive the children to school in his employer's car for £3 a week. Sometimes he would come and entertain us with Broadmoor stories. In particular, I remember one about a man who had been chased by dogs before he had been caught and when the warders passed his bed they would make sounds of dogs baying and the man would go madder than he already was. These stories were rather enjoyable in a horrific kind of way, and broke the monotony of life at Lower Belgrave Street.

Mrs Murphy would ask me to get her a bottle of whisky every second day. I have explained that in order to keep staff I had to put up with some very strange requests. On occasion she would get the date wrong on the cheque and I would have to go back and ask her to change it. At about Easter she started to say things like "I feel the door of this house closing on me." Alarmed, I would ask her if she wanted to leave and she said "No," but she had a strong feeling that she wouldn't be with me for much longer.

On 2nd April, I received a letter from the Official Solicitor informing me that information had recently come to him to the effect that Miss Murphy had been dismissed from previous employment due to excessive drinking habits, and he was given to understand that she still drinks more than a lady in her position, having the care of young children, should.

In Spain 1966/67 the Marquesa de la Puenta sacked Miss Murphy for excessive drinking, heavy smoking and encouraging the child to drink, and apparently a tendency to walk nude in the house.

In Cyprus 1972 Miss Murphy worked for Mr George Tornaritis, a solicitor, and the son of the Attorney-General. She "drank to excess." "had hallucinations," and was sacked.

> If this information is correct, I should be most concerned for the welfare and indeed safety of the children, and you will appreciate that I would have to withdraw my approval of Miss Murphy as a suitable person to have the care of the children.

The Official Solicitor must have given my husband copies of Mrs Murphy's references, which he should not have done as she was solely my employee.

This was a bombshell. I later discovered that my husband had invited Mrs Murphy and the ex-Broadmoor warder to have a drink with him at Elizabeth Street and he had discovered her weakness, possibly prompted by my sister who knew of her habit of drinking sundowners, and he had checked on her references.

I told Mrs Murphy as kindly as I could, but I was informed that she had in any case to go into hospital as she had cancer. She left on 24th April.

On 28th April 1974 my husband wrote to Mr Ditch, the Official Solicitor's aide, and part of his letter follows:

> I told my wife on Friday that I was not prepared to pay a net salary of £35 a week for the next nanny. She told me it was impossible to get anyone for less and complained that I was 'sabotaging' her.
>
> In ordinary circumstances £16-£20 per week clear is the going rate. I recognise that the circumstances are not normal and that I must pay more, but there are limits. I do not have to remind you that £35 per week grossed up comes to about £2500 per annum and to this must be added the cost of housing and feeding the person. I don't know for instance how much your own department pay qualified female staff but I would guess that most would be more than happy with £3200 per annum with 8 weeks holiday on full pay.
>
> The point I wish to make is this: am I obliged to bribe someone to live in 46 Lower Belgrave Street so that my wife may comply with the Court Order?
>
> I know that the choice of nanny rests between you and my wife but I would like to comment that a very high wage is just as likely to attract the wrong woman. I would like to put a limit of £25 clear per week for the next one. If you think that this proposal is unreasonable or unfair or that it is an attempt to 'sabotage' my wife's position, I will of course withdraw it....

Apparently it is quite common for judges to make an order stating care and control to the mother together with a nanny, in my case approved by the Official Solicitor and paid for by my husband. It is an order almost impossible to comply with as they had to be interviewed and approved by the Official Solicitor and most nannies would find this difficult and would prefer an easier way to gain employment.

The children were on holiday with their father at that time and Mrs Greenslade arranged for Christabel Martin to come back. Christabel once again reinforced my morale and did more than that by being so companionable.

Mrs Greenslade now sent a plump busty French girl about twenty-five years of age called Pierrette for an interview. The Official

Solicitor approved her as she appeared demure and well-behaved. Christabel took her in the car, sitting in the passenger seat, to show her where the children's schools were and said she had noticed that when pulled up at the traffic lights, she would smile and wave to the man pulled up next to her. We put this down to her being French.

She came in May and I endured her through June and July. She spent most of the day sitting in the drawing room listening to her French-English gramophone records which were hopelessly out of date. In the evening, the demure well-behaved French girl disappeared. She would wear long evening dresses, and her face would be caked with make-up so that she looked more like a clown and would go to a pick-up joint that she had discovered.

Apparently, in his search for further information to enable him to bring the custody case back to Court, my husband made contact with her and made notes about mail which arrived.

23
Pierrette

One day, I had a telephone call from Mrs Greenslade, who started her conversation by asking "Is she out?", referring to Pierrette.

On being told that she was, Mrs Greenslade told me that she had had a letter from Pierrette. It said, in effect, that now THE LORD had approved her would Mrs Greenslade get her a job at £30.00 a week or she would go to the People Bureau where Mrs Greenslade had previously worked, and get one from them. The People Bureau would then discover that Mrs Greenslade had put Pierrette into Lower Belgrave Street for no fee.

My husband was supposed to pay the agencies for any nanny that I employed an agency fee. The People Bureau had had to issue a summons before he would even pay for the first one. There are so many people wanting nannies that the bureaus will not bother with people who are bad payers, so that I was in an even more hopeless situation because the bureau would not supply me or even send any for interviews.

Apparently, she also complained that I had not helped her with her English. We were both somewhat horrified by this development, as it was the summer and even more difficult to get a replacement.

During Pierrette's tenure as nanny, the two older children had sports days, which had to be attended. Both were in July, and the first was Frances' swimming sports. These sports were due to start at two, but I waited to allow Camilla to have a rest after lunch and so arrived at 3 o'clock. My husband was already there armed with his large cine camera. I sat next to him and then put Camilla in between us and she put her arms around both of us. The sports seemed to take ages and I made some uncomplimentary remark about the organisation, and he drew my attention to the fact that the headmistress was sitting within earshot.

I felt this to be a friendly move on his part, but at about 4 o'clock he left me saying he had had to park the car some way away from the swimming baths and would return with it. He did not come back, and at the end of the sports I went outside and found him leaning against his Mercedes deep in conversation with two of the mothers. I was rather annoyed about this and thought it bad manners. He did not acknowledge my arrival. I noticed that he looked very unkempt, his suit was not pressed, his shoes not cleaned and he was very baggy under the eyes. Frances took ages to come, and so I sat in the car with Camilla while he continued with his conversation. At last she came and we drove off, but it was clear that both of us were in an ill humour and there was no chance of any pleasant conversation.

Frances' sports day was also in July, and the day was grey and dull. Christabel was up on one of her infrequent visits to London and came to see me around lunchtime. I had had it in mind to enter the Mothers' Race that year and hoped to win. I bought a tin of baked beans to eat for lunch to give me enough energy to run, and was boosted by Christabel who drove me to the sports ground, which was behind Holy Trinity, Brompton. We arrived at about two and then Christabel left to drive home. My husband was not there, and I talked to one or two mothers and hung about watching the races.

At about 4 o'clock I saw him. He was looking quite flushed and was wearing, unusually for him, a rather jazzy tie. I went up and said cheerily "You lucky thing, you've missed most of it," and stood beside him chatting about nothing and he made no reply. Camilla was with me and we were later joined by Frances. After the children's races, the Father's race was announced and run. It was rather undignified. They had a sort of obstacle race, which was concluded by the fathers having to run with balloons in between their legs.

Then came the Mother's race. My heart was pounding as I stood in line with the other mothers, and after some argument about how the race was to be run, the women objecting to an undignified obstacle race, it was announced that we should run a straight running race. I was thankful for that and breathed in deeply and tried to relax my muscles. I was off to a bad start but began to make up ground halfway to the finish. There was just one woman in front of me and, using every ounce of my speed passed her a few yards before the finishing line. I had won and was very pleased.

My husband congratulated me and he had by then been joined by some creepy-crawly parents who usually cottoned on to him. He gave me a cigarette and I could see his hands were trembling but he looked pleased. Later I went up to get my prize. Everyone could see I had won the race and it would be difficult for a mentally disturbed person to have done so. It was not an important moment for me to establish my sanity before an audience. It was just a by-product. He drove us back in the car to Lower Belgrave Street and then left us.

George's sports day was 18th July, and I rang my husband and asked if he would drive me out to the sports ground at Richmond. I said how peculiar it would look if we arrived separately, and what would George think if we drove home afterwards without him. He agreed and arrived at about a quarter past two. I chatted to him in the car and he made very few replies but seemed friendly. We arrived at about 3 o'clock and the sports were well underway. We decided to sit on some chairs which were placed on a raised piece of concrete. As we got on to the concrete he knocked one of the chairs to the ground. Force of habit made me jump down and pick it up again, and then to my astonishment he did it again but I let him pick it up this time. I had the feeling he was slightly drunk.

From time to time he smiled at me in a most friendly way and introduced me to some hearty women who rushed up to him saying "Hullo, John" in loud and braying voices and who looked in a hostile bullying way at me. "This is my wife, Veronica," he said. I didn't know them but he quite obviously knew them and one of them said she would ring him up during the week. I was used to this sort of behaviour and didn't mind too much, and he was just as anxious as I was to get away quickly at the end.

A Moment in Time

We drove home talking parent talk to the children - Camilla had come third in the 'Little Visitors' race for the under fives. We got back to Lower Belgrave Street at about ten to five and I asked him if he would like to take the children there and then on access which was due at 5.30pm but he said "No, thank you, I've got something to do, very kind," and drove away. This was the last time we were to be anywhere together, which I confirmed at the inquest during my evidence.

Mrs Greenslade and I bided our time after receiving Pierrette's letter, and Mrs Greenslade found a very nice girl called Nadia Broome who was a student teacher and who wanted a holiday job. I interviewed her without Pierrette knowing and she accepted the job.

The next day Mrs Greenslade and I faced Pierrette with her letter. I said to her that it was not working out and she must leave the next day. She appeared absolutely shattered. She blustered "I know my rights," and "I 'ave to 'ave a week's notice," and "I 'ad my period when I wrote the letter." She knew that it was no good, as Mrs Greenslade had the letter. She had thought that Mrs Greenslade was making money out of me by supplying the nannies and did not realise that she was an ally. Pierrette tried to get me to give her her money that evening, but I refused.

Nadia Broome came the next morning and started her duties, and Pierrette took the whole day to pack her things. One of her boyfriends came in his car to collect her luggage. Two days later, my husband rang the doorbell to collect his letters - there were several for Pierrette and when I went downstairs I discovered they had gone as well and that he must have taken them. She would have gone round to him at Elizabeth Street but as nothing more came of it, I guessed that he had the same opinion of her as I did.

We spent a relaxed and peaceful summer. As it was my half of the school holidays there was no access and Nadia was good company.

24

Sandra

Shortly before Pierrette left, Mrs Greenslade had told me about a very nice girl she knew of who was looking for a job as a permanent nanny and said that she had given her my telephone number. I then had a telephone call from Mrs Sandra Rivett, who asked if she could come and see me one evening. I explained about Pierrette, and that she must pretend to be a friend. She understood this and she arrived one evening at about 7pm.

We went down into the basement and we each had a cup of coffee. I explained to Sandra about the job, and then Pierrette herself came down the stairs. She looked at her most picturesque, as she was dressed to go to her pickup joint. Sandra, who looked most respectable and well turned-out, could see without my having to say any more as it was obvious what was wrong with Pierrette.

We then went upstairs to my bedroom and talked until 11 o'clock. I told her a good deal about my situation and she told me about her husband, Roger Rivett, who was a merchant seaman and who had left her.

She was still living in their marital flat in Kenley and hoped to keep it on, but she needed to make some money to pay off hire purchase debts and so on. I liked her at once. She seemed kind and decent, and said she liked to take a pride in her work and other nice old-fashioned things, and understood the difficulties attached to my situation. We left it that she would ring me when she had come to a decision. She was working for an elderly couple near Baker Street but it was such hard work - she had to lift an old woman on to a commode - that she couldn't keep it up, although they were anxious to keep her.

She also talked about her budgerigars and cats, which she seemed very fond of. I spoke to her again while Nadia was with me, and it was arranged that she would come at the end of the summer holidays, on 9th September.

My husband was apparently now trying a more constructive way to deal with his financial problems, as can be seen from a letter dated 10th September, sent by Coutts & Co. to his solicitors Messrs Payne Hicks Beach:

> Sirs,
>
> Lord Lucan's Re-Settlement
>
> We have been asked by Lord Lucan to write to you concerning the provision of an income for Lady Lucan. We have referred to the Settlement Deed and under Clause 5 (i) there is a provision which states "that no interest in the capital of the settled property shall be appointed to any spouse widow or widower of any such issue as aforesaid", issue having been defined as the issue of the 5th Earl of Lucan. It would, however, appear to be possible for Lord Lucan to appoint income to Lady Lucan from the Settlement.
>
> We would like further time to consider the total capital and income position before being able to give you any detailed figures and we will write to you again in the matter in due course.
>
> We are,
> Sirs,
> Your most obedient Servants,
> Coutts & Co.

On 13th September 1974, by which time his Coutts overdraft had risen to more than £5,000, he approached Coutts Trustee Department asking the managers of the Lucan family trusts to release investment funds. He said that the money would be used to help pay the children's school fees. They were all at day schools - Frances was at the Glendower School, George at Eaton House School and Camilla at Young England Kindergarten. The bank informed him they would need the approval of the Official Solicitor as the children were wards of court. He immediately withdrew his request as he did not want to risk exposing his desperate financial plight to the

Official Solicitor, and the continuing gambling addiction which had contributed to this.

During this time, Nadia and I went to the RSPCA to get a kitten for George's 7th birthday. The kitten was very tiny and we were all enchanted with him, and called him Sooty. Then I got a call from Sandra and she was weeping. She had had to have one of her cats put down and while the vet was there, the other one, Tara, scenting trouble had run off. I told her about Sooty and suggested that she brought Tara with her which she duly did.

Sandra fitted into the scheme of things very well, did her work most satisfactorily and got on extremely well with Frances, who liked the nannies least. She had Thursday as her day off and every other weekend when the children were away on access from 5.30pm on Friday to 5.30pm on Sunday. She had a boyfriend that she had met while with the elderly couple near Baker Street called Ray, who took her to the Plumber's Arms, which was the pub at the bottom of Lower Belgrave Street where she also met John Hankins, who was relief manager there. He started to take her out as well. Ray was very unreliable, he would ring up and arrange to meet her on her day off but didn't show up. He would then ring a day or so later with some excuse. This intrigued for a while, but then when she did go out with him she found that he was very dull. They had gone to a pub where he met a man friend and they left her out of the conversation.

She met Lord and Lady Boothby at the pub and some of the regulars, but John Hankins, the relief manager, seemed to be taking over, though I got the impression that she was less attracted to him than to Ray.

On her free weekends, she went back to her flat at Kenley and saw her friend Rosemary Jordan, who was an assistant matron at a boys' school, and they went to a pub or a dance together. Latterly, they went to John Hankin's new pub in Chelsea. She had very few telephone calls and none from her family until the last week, when she had one from her mother.

I seldom left the house to do more than go down the street to do some shopping now the children were back at school. I sometimes saw Mary G on the access weekends, but she and Sandra didn't get on well. Mary G tried to patronise her or order her about, but Sandra was very dignified and ignored her. She was particularly disgusted when I rang Mary G on Friday after the children had left asking her to come, and she then made an excuse about a party when she had said she would come previously.

She also told me that she had overheard Mary G and a friend she had brought to the house saying that they will go into the drawing room and drink some of my sherry. She also showed her friend about the house while I was out at the chemist.

I gave a dinner party for some friends of Mary G's whom she suggested that I might like to meet, as two had sons at George's future school, Summer Fields in Oxford. She helped me polish the silver and the next day I found that she had done all the washing up after the dinner party, which wasn't really her job. She told me that Mary G was using me, and I said I knew but I could not cut myself off from the world outside entirely, and that I could see through her.

We talked a great deal about our cats - Tara slept in her bedroom with her and was fed on the best cat food, and her likes and dislikes catered to. Sooty was growing fast and the two cats were becoming friends.

On 29th September 1974 my husband wrote a letter to George's headmistress, part of which read:

> I enclose George's report. I am a little disappointed with his place in the class (ignoring the high position in French as he had a French nanny for the whole term). He has gone from 1st to 2nd to 8th in reading in three terms and his arithmetic from 84% to 72% and 45%.
>
> To keep you up to date on the domestic front, the French girl (Pierrette) left in August; they then had a temporary (Nadia) and now there is a girl (about 25 years old at a guess) called Sandra looking after them.

My husband did not seem to realise that his actions in disturbing our family almost certainly contributed to George's rather dramatic slide in reading and arithmetic.

I learnt a little about Sandra's background. She had spent part of her childhood in Australia. I gathered there were three daughters in the family but no boys, until her mother had produced one late in life. I was later to discover that this was Sandra's own child. Her son, named Stephen Hensby, was born on 13th March 1964 and was adopted by her parents on 26th May 1965. Three years later she gave birth to a second son named Gary Roger who was given up for adoption.

I understood that for some reason her father, who had previously been very fond of her, had taken against her when she was about sixteen and tried to have her committed to an asylum and that, in fact, she was put in some sort of home or other. She was very bitter about this indeed, and produced a photograph of her father asking me whether I could see any likeness to herself. She had the fantasy that he was not her real father, and that her mother had had a lover and she was the result of their union.

From the photograph she showed me I could not see much likeness, but when I saw him in the flesh at her inquest, I could see that he was her father. She said she didn't look like her sisters and that she was very much the odd one out. Sandra had the most beautiful thick red hair, which was long and she said that they used to tell her to cut her hair as she looked, according to them, like a witch. Finally she did, and they all grew theirs long. I could believe that this happened very well. There were stories about arguments on who should do the washing up and she used to end them by doing it herself.

Her life with her husband Roger Rivett sounded rather sad. He would be away at sea for some eleven months and she would stay at home waiting for him, and when he came back he would want to put his feet up and watch television and didn't want to take her out. As she was attractive, I could see that this would be most frustrating and lonely for her. He had left her in December 1972. Of course, I don't know how much of this was true, but she was so good with me that I must believe there was truth in what she said.

She never to my knowledge brought her boyfriends to Lower Belgrave Street or was late back from her time off, but she used to look very ill sometimes and not as well as a girl of her age should have looked. She had some menstrual disorder, so I would discount any allegations about promiscuity as she would have been hors de combat most of the time.

On the access weekends when she was at her flat in Kenley, she would ring me up about ten o'clock and ask if I was all right. She was really concerned about me. I used to take her to the Hurlingham Club with me to have lunch with Mrs Doris West, whom I had met that summer at Hurlingham. She was the mother of one of Frances' school friends who was called Julia, and we used to have drinks at the bar there.

She was quite an attraction and men would stop and seem to want to be introduced. My husband appeared to approve of her and it seems he liked her best of all the nannies. She told me that one afternoon when she had collected George from his school and she, Camilla and George were walking up the middle of Eaton Square, one of the children had seen him in the car and that he was apparently following them. He did not stop or say anything after they had seen him, but just blew the horn as he drove away. This disconcerted her somewhat. Also, I was rather disconcerted when I was driving home with Camilla after a children's party to see his Mercedes in the mirror. I stopped and waved but he drove off round a corner.

Sandra used to manage the access and would come downstairs after he had gone and describe his appearance to me. On Friday, he usually looked bright-eyed and bushy tailed when he came to collect the children, but sometimes he looked as though he had had a hard day's night, looking rumpled with bleary eyes and unpolished shoes. He always looked bad when he brought them back and it must have been dreadful having to be polite so that he would be asked again.

On our weekends, it was our habit to go to the Hurlingham Club on Saturday afternoon. One afternoon, we arrived back to discover that there was no milk left in the fridge, which there had been before we left, and all the bottles had been put outside. This was most puzzling but we didn't know what to think. Subsequently, I learnt that the hard-pressed Express Dairies milkman was then owed £43.80 and that my husband settled the long overdue milk account on 5th

Sandra

November, just two days before the murder.

I gathered later that Sandra had told Mrs West that my husband frightened her and she thought that he was mad. Early one evening in October, it was dark by then, I saw that the front door was open. I was very concerned because I feared that the cats would get out, but thought no more about it. It must have been another day when I had forgotten to put the safety chain on the door. On 24th October, which was Frances' birthday, I looked out of the window and I saw my husband sitting in his dark blue Mercedes outside 46 Lower Belgrave Street. He was wearing glasses or dark glasses, and then he drove away. I often glanced out of the window and saw him driving past, and the children had also seen him walking past on several occasions.

Mr and Mrs Myers came to organise Frances' birthday party that day, and Sandra and I sat together for tea and Mrs Myers asked if we were sisters. We were the same height and similar build.

On 5th November we went to a firework display at Hurlingham with the children and had supper with Mrs West. It had been Frances' half term as well. On 7th November, the school bus did not arrive to collect Frances. As it was the day after half term I thought that they would do little work, and as it would cost a pound to send her to school by taxi, I asked her if she would like to stay at home and she said "Yes." Apparently my husband rang the school and spoke to the headmistress and asked why Frances was not at school. She had apparently replied rather curtly that she had no idea why.

We spent a normal enough day at home, and then at about five o'clock Sandra said she wanted to go to the Post Office to buy some stamps, and Frances said she would like to go too. I asked them not to be long as I was already preparing supper. In fact, they did take rather a long time as they went somewhere else as well and I was getting annoyed as I thought the food would get cold. At about 5.40pm they returned and I hurried them downstairs to have supper. I usually put the safety chain on the door after Frances, the last one back from school, arrived. But she didn't go to school that day, and in the rush for supper I forgot to put the chain on.

Sandra had asked for Wednesday off instead of Thursday, because her boyfriend John Hankins had that Wednesday off and she wanted to spend time with him. I gathered she also went to see her mother who lived near Basingstoke, and her mother subsequently told me that Sandra had said she was very happy with me. I was glad of that.

After supper we went back upstairs, the children had their baths and the evening's television viewing began. That was the last time I was in the basement that evening.

25

Attack

Sandra would have put the two younger children to bed after watching television for a little while, but as Frances had not gone to school that day she was continuing to play with her game interspersed with watching television. *Top of the Pops* and *The Six Million Dollar Man* were mentioned.

I was lying on my bed in my bedroom on the second floor watching *Mastermind*, when Frances joined me on my bed just before Sandra put her head round the door at 8.55pm and asked me "Would you like a cup of tea?" This was not a usual thing for her to do, but she may have been trying to thank me for allowing her to change her day off from Thursday to Wednesday so she could go out with her boyfriend.

I watched the news at 9pm, and at about a quarter past nine, when she had not reappeared bringing the tea with her, I said to Frances that I wondered why Sandra was so long. I left the bedroom leaving the door open as the light on the landing had burnt out, and made my way downstairs to the ground floor. I looked down the basement stairs and saw that it was dark and so thought that she couldn't be there. I called her name. I then heard a sound of something or someone coming from the downstairs cloakroom, which had a washbasin with a strip light above it, a lavatory and some books and photographs.

I moved towards the sound and someone rushed out and hit me on the head about four times. I screamed and my husband said "Shut up" and thrust three gloved fingers down my throat. There were about four blows. This happened in the area at the top of the basement stairs. We started to fight. He attempted to strangle me from in front and gouge out my eye. I gasped "Please don't kill me John." We fell into the basement doorway and he tried to push me down the basement stairs. I hooked my leg around the balustrade and I remember kicking out a balustrade at the top of the basement stairs during the struggle. I clawed at his genitals and he went back, he moved back and I ended up sitting sideways between his legs. I put my hand down and felt something curved and metal wrapped in bandaging, and also felt what seemed like a great deal of my hair as well. I looked at the front door and saw the number 46 in reverse and I realised that it would not be safe to run for the door. I remember thinking, I'm thirty-seven - it's too young to die.

I asked him if I could have a drink of water as my throat hurt so much because he had thrust three gloved fingers down it. We went into the downstairs cloakroom and I had a drink. The water was hot and it was dark, although the strip lighting above the wash basin was switched on. We then had a conversation. I did not scream or shout for help. At one point, he grabbed at my sapphire and pearl necklace and I said very sharply "What are you doing with my necklace?" and he desisted. I asked him where Sandra was. He replied that she had gone out. I said that she wouldn't have gone out without telling me. He then said, "She is dead - don't look." This revelation told me that Sandra was not in cahoots with him as I had feared, and that I still had a chance of surviving. I said "Oh dear, what shall we do with the body?" I proceeded to tell him that Sandra had few friends who would make any enquiries about her, and that I could stay in the house until my wounds had healed.

I asked him "Why didn't you come back?" And he replied "No Veronica, that can never be now." He said that he had received a letter from my solicitor asking for his financial proposals as we would have been separated for two years the following 7th January, 1975. This had apparently been a motivating factor. "I'll go to Broadmoor for this," he said.

Following this, he asked me if I had any sleeping tablets and I said that I had in my bedroom. He said that he had to make a decision and asked if I would take the tablets. I said that I would. "We must go away together," he said. Then we both went upstairs. He hustled me up rather than 'helped' me up the stairs.

Frances was still up watching television in my bedroom. He sent her to bed. I said that I felt ill. At first I lay on the bed. We then went together into the bathroom and we looked at my injuries. My face was streaked with blood and it was not possible to see how much damage had been done.

After that we went back into the bedroom and he laid a towel on the pillow and I lay on it. I understood that he was going to get a cloth to clean up my face. He went into the bathroom and I heard the taps running. I realised that he would not be able to hear properly. I jumped to my feet and ran out of my bedroom and down the stairs, out of the front door and ran as fast as I could, without wasting any breath by calling anything, to the Plumber's Arms about thirty yards from the house. I burst into the Plumber's Arms at 9.50pm saying "Help me, help me, help me, I've just escaped being murdered. He's in the house!" The customers in the bar were in varying stages of inebriation and gazed at me stupefied so I said "He's murdered my nanny."

Assistance was sought, and I was taken to St George's Hospital on Hyde Park Corner. The head barman, Arthur William Whitehouse, called the police and also for an ambulance, which took me to the hospital for my head wounds to be sutured. I remained in the hospital for about a week.

I often wondered how my husband managed to keep as calm as he did when he realised after he returned from the bathroom with wet towels that I had fled. We know from Frances' statement that he went upstairs and called "Veronica, where are you?" When there was no response he went downstairs and got into the Ford Corsair and turned right into Chester Square and tried to rouse Mrs Florman, mother of one of Frances' school friends, as she knew Frances well and could have gone to the house and tried to obtain entry and take the children to her house. He must have returned to his flat in Elizabeth Street and made his first telephone call to his mother, telling her that there had been a "terrible catastrophe at number 46 and to get the children out and ring Bill Shand Kydd who would help."

He must have sponged his bloodstained flannels and then got into the Ford Corsair again without taking his passport with him. He drove to Uckfield to see Ian and Susan Maxwell-Scott. Fortunately for him, I believe, only Susan, who was enamoured of him, was at home. She let him in and listened to his version of events. She gave him writing materials and four Valium tablets and he made another telephone call to his mother, asking if she had the children and she was able to reassure him that she had. He refused Susan Maxwell Scott's offer to stay the night, but said he had to get back to sort things out. She said she would post the letters and he left her house at about 1.15am, never to be seen again.

The timelag from leaving Susan Maxwell-Scott's house in Uckfield at approximately 1.15am and arriving before 8am at Newhaven could be explained as he had taken the four Valium tablets which Susan Maxwell-Scott had given him. He would have parked the car, knowing the area well, and had a sleep. He was extremely unlikely to be found there or arrested as there was no warrant for his arrest, and no-one apart from Mrs Maxwell-Scott knew he had been in Uckfield. When he woke up, his resolve must have hardened and he wrote his last letter to Michael Stoop. He described himself in the past tense as 'destroyed'. "The fact that a crooked solicitor and a rotten psychiatrist destroyed me between them will be of no importance to the children." He also wrote "When you come across my children which I hope you will, please tell them that you knew me and that all I cared about was them." This is rather final - he did not anticipate seeing our children or Michael Stoop again.

Upon arrival at Newhaven, he would have left the car carrying his last unstamped letter addressed to Michael Stoop, looked for and found a pillar box and posted it. I believe he boarded the ferry and jumped off mid-channel in the way of the propellers - which is why his remains never surfaced.

He understood the necessity for the financial future of the family that his death should remain a mystery. His second letter to Bill Shand Kydd was headed 'Financial Matters', and proves that such matters were to the forefront of his mind. He also had an affinity with the sea, which is said by some to be a sacred place. The luck that so eluded him in life came in death.

Upon reading in a national newspaper, whilst I was still in St George's Hospital, that members of my family were about to make a bid for the custody of my three children, I was devastated. I was taken from the hospital by police to the court when the hearing was adjourned. I attended another hearing a few days later, and was again granted the already previously-won custody of my three children.

I had been visited in hospital in November 1974 by one of the then Official Solicitor's aides, who gave me the dire news that my husband had not complied with the Judge's order to produce his proposals for financing the education of the three Lucan wards within six months. No proposals had been forthcoming from the 7th Earl, and no money set aside to secure the financial position of the wards.

This was clearly a financial imbroglio, which was left in the hands of the Official Solicitor to sort out. I had told Mr Justice Rees that my husband would have committed suicide, and by January 1975 all those who knew him well were sure that he was dead. I was advised by lawyers not to say this to the press, but to say that I believed him to be 'missing'.

As a result of my husband's last letters to my brother-in-law Bill Shand Kydd, he was joined together with my sister to the wardship proceedings and he recommended Denis Gilson, a certified accountant, to be joined as well after he and other creditors had decided to declare my husband to be bankrupt.[1]

Mr Justice Rees decided that the children and I should leave London to escape press intrusion, and as a result of a letter written to me by a former flatmate it was decided that we should go to Torpoint near Liskeard in Cornwall, where she and her husband, a naval officer,

---

1 In 1993 Denis Gilson was found guilty of obtaining a valuable security by deception.

lived. Camilla could not join us in Cornwall immediately as she had been left in the bath with the hot tap running, and upon leaning forward to reach her bubble bath had scalded her arm and needed medical treatment in the interim. So much for the care provided by my sister-in-law Sally Gibbs, who was in charge at the time.

The naval couple had some children about their ages, so mine did not mind missing school at all and we spent Christmas with this family. I was very relieved when the Judge allowed us to return in January to London. The nanny order was still in force so I spent some time trying to get it removed. My husband had been declared bankrupt and so I had to discuss this matter with Mr Gilson.

Mr Gilson was very pleasant to deal with and allowed me, as the wife's share, to keep the items I wanted. The day came when some items had to be removed from Lower Belgrave Street and it was rather distressing. The men who came to collect the items wished me luck as they departed.

Mrs Greenslade had arranged for a very nice American woman to be nanny/housekeeper.

John Aspinall was quoted as saying "God knows into what red hell a man's sightly soul may sink under the bleeding attrition of a wife who's always out to reduce you and from whom you are tied merely because she has borne you three children."

I think Aspinall was a very amusing man and quite likely to say such a thing. He seemed to be enjoying the publicity the tragic events had caused. It was at his house in Lyall Street that a lunch was held the day after my husband's disappearance to discuss what action to take if he turned up at one of their residences. They comprised their host John Aspinall, Stephen Raphael, Bill Shand Kydd, Charles Benson, Dominick Elwes and Dan Meinertzhagen.

One person who most definitely was not at the lunch was Jimmy Goldsmith. *The Sunday Times* published an article just before the inquest on Mrs Rivett was held in June 1975 and erroneously said that he had. *Private Eye*, who had been publishing unflattering material about Jimmy Goldsmith for some time, innocently repeated this mistake and Jimmy Goldsmith overreacted, issued writs galore and even one for criminal libel, which became a hot topic of conversation. *Private Eye* was represented by Sir James Comyn QC, who had acted for my husband at the custody case. I was not very impressed by him, despite the fact that all the judges apparently respected him. My husband described him as the best QC in the country. Anyway, the case was settled but really all Goldsmith had achieved was to make himself unpopular, which was not what he had intended.

26

Inquest

Dr Gavin Thurston, the Coroner, said he had agonised about the difficulties of a wife giving evidence adverse to her husband. He did not share these difficulties with me and I was not told about the exception, which is that when a man had assaulted his wife she could give evidence against him. If told about this prior to the inquest, I would have said that I did not want to bring charges against my husband for the injuries he had inflicted upon myself, so presumably I would not have been called as a witness about the death of Mrs Rivett and the scientific evidence would have had to suffice in bringing the jury to a conclusion.

It seems a long time ago now, but on the morning of the opening day of the inquest, 16th June 1975, I was collected by Detective Sergeant Graham Forsyth, who had been assigned to me as a bodyguard. I was shocked to see so many photographers waiting outside my house. I was driven to the Coroner's Court and took my seat beside my bodyguard on the right hand side facing the Coroner, Dr Gavin Thurston.

I was called to the witness stand at about 11am, was invited to sit and was cross-examined for about two hours.

I confirmed my name was Veronica Mary, Countess of Lucan, of 46 Lower Belgrave Street, SW1. In response to his opening questions, I told the Coroner that I had married Richard John Bingham on 28th November 1963 and he had succeeded his father to the earldom on 21st January 1964. I said that we had had three children, but our marriage had deteriorated in recent years. He had left me on 7th January 1973 and we had not lived together since that date. The children went to live with my husband as a result of a Court Order on 23rd March 1973 but were returned to me as a result of High Court action on 1st July 1973.

I said that my husband had been very affectionate towards the children and they were very important to him. He had been allowed access to them every other weekend. He usually collected them at 5.30pm on Friday and returned them to me at 5.30pm on Sunday evening.

The Coroner then asked me a series of questions relating to when I last saw my husband, where and what he was doing, and my answers appear below, given as I sat in the witness box:

> When did you last see your husband?
>
> To speak to or with my eyes? To speak to, it must have been about 18th July, on my son's sports day.
>
> When did you last see him without speaking to him?
> On 24th October.
>
> Was this casually, in the street?
> No, I looked out of the window and saw him.
>
> What was he doing then?
> Sitting in his car. I noticed he was wearing dark glasses.
>
> Was this outside 46 Lower Belgrave Street?
> Yes.
>
> Was he looking in any particular direction?
> He was about to drive away.
>
> What sort of a car was this?
> A dark blue Mercedes-Benz.
>
> A car that you knew well?
> Yes.

The Coroner continued with his questions, and elicited the information that my husband did possess a key to number 46, and that apart from one telephone call about collecting the children, my husband had not spoken to me for several months before

7th November 1974. He then questioned me about our financial arrangements:

> Were you receiving a regular allowance from your husband?
> Yes, I was.
>
> Did he pay the rates and the telephone bill and water rates?
> That was the arrangement, that he would do that.
>
> Was that fulfilled, do you know?
> I imagine so because the water gets cuts off otherwise, doesn't it? (Actually, it doesn't get cut off)
>
> Could I ask how much you were allowed by your husband?
> £40 per month. (I should have said per week)
>
> And that payment was always perfectly prompt?
> It was erratic.
>
> Did you get the total in the end?
> In the end.
>
> Do you know anything about your husband's financial situation?
> I have read about it.
>
> Did you know from personal knowledge whether he was in financial difficulties?
> I did read an article which suggested it, in the *Daily Express*. (Groan from Press)
>
> But you didn't know from your personal knowledge?
> No.

I told Dr Thurston that my husband had owned powerboats in the past, but as far as I knew, he had never had any connection with Newhaven. I said that one of my husband's boats had sunk, and another had been smashed when it was dropped onto a quayside. I believed that he had always raced his boats out of the Hamble, near Southampton.

I wore a hat because of my rank, and told the Coroner that my husband enjoyed good health with no serious illnesses.

Inquest

Did your husband know Sandra Rivett?
He met her when he collected the children and brought them back.

And that was all as far as you were aware?
Yes, as far as I am aware.

You have had various nannies. How many nannies have you had in the last six months, until 7th November?
I had seven including temporaries.

When did Sandra Rivett come to you?
I think she came early in September.

From an advertisement, or recommendation?
One particular woman provided all the nannies I had. (Mrs Greenslade)

An agent?
An agent who was a friend.

Did you get on well with her?
With Sandra? Yes, I did.

What sort of temperament?
She had an even temperament.

Do you know if she had any men friends?
I know of two. She talked of two.

You knew she was separated from her husband?
Yes, I did.

Had any men friends come to your house?
No.

Had she asked if any could come?
No.

What was her usual night off?
Thursday night - Thursday was her day off.

Could you say anything about her stature, would she be of similar height to yourself?
We have heard her husband describe her as 5 feet 2 inches. I am 5 feet 2 inches.

A Moment in Time

> Had she tried on any of your clothes?
>
> She tried on a dress given to me by another woman. The dress was size 10. I am a size 8. It was too large for me. It fitted Sandra.
>
> Although the same height she was rather fuller built than you?
>
> Yes.
>
> On the evening of 7th November 1974, was this a Thursday?
>
> Yes, it was.
>
> This was Mrs Rivett's usual day off. Was she at home that evening?
>
> Yes, she was.
>
> Why was that?
>
> Because her current boyfriend had his day off on Wednesday and she asked if she could change hers to Wednesday as well, so she could go out with him.
>
> And there would have been at the house, yourself, the three children and Mrs Rivett?
>
> Yes. It was the first week she had taken Wednesday off instead.

I then went on to describe how the house was secured each evening. At about 6pm we usually put the safety chain on the front door, but on this evening we had forgotten to do so. There was a second door leading from the basement kitchen to outside the front of the house. This was used every day to take out the rubbish, but was then always kept bolted. In the breakfast room there were French windows, which were kept locked, and there was another door at the side which opened on to the garden.

I confirmed that escaping via the rear door into the garden would have been unlikely. I explained that there was a trellis on the wall with roses and it would have been a prickly business.

> How did you spend the evening of 7th November from about eight o'clock?
>
> Watching television.
>
> Where?
>
> In my bedroom.

Inquest

Who was watching television at eight o'clock?
My daughter Frances.

And Mrs Rivett?
She was not watching it with us.

Just you and your daughter?
Yes.

And what time did Mrs Rivett look into the room?
At about five to nine.

What did she say?
"Would you like a cup of tea?"

This was quite a usual thing, was it?
I had the habit of getting myself a cup of tea at that time. But it wasn't a very usual thing for her to do.

When she offered to get some tea, did you accept?
Yes, I did.

Your bedroom is on the second floor in the front?
Yes, it is.

Where were you when she said she would get you some tea?
I was lying on the bed.

And your daughter also?
Also.

You can place the time from the television programme at about five to nine? (*Mastermind*).
Yes.

Did Mrs Rivett take some crockery with her?
I don't know that she did.

We have the crockery (I was shown the exhibits) Do you recognise these cups?
Yes, I do.

These were taken by Mrs Rivett?
I am told that.

A Moment in Time

But had they been in your room?
She may have had them in her own room.

And then you watched the news at nine o'clock?
Yes.

And when did you begin to wonder about the tea?
At about quarter past nine.

Did you hear anything unusual during this time?
Nothing unusual.

So what did you do then?
I decided to go downstairs and find out what had happened to the tea.

And how far did you descend the house?
To the ground floor.

What did you do when you got there?
I looked down the stairs leading to the basement.

Was there anything unusual?
There was no light on at all.

Nowhere in the basement?
Nowhere.

There is a two-way switch that enables you to switch the light on from the top of the stairs and the other way round?
I believe you can. It may be possible.

Was the light usually left on?
No. You switch on the light by leaning forward through the doorway at the top of the stairs.

Did you try this switch?
No, I didn't. I just saw it was dark, and so she couldn't be there.

Did you call out?
I called her name.

What happened then?
I heard a noise.

Inquest

What sort of noise?
Just a noise of somebody, or something in the downstairs cloakroom.

This is where there is a wash-basin and lavatory?
Yes.

What happened next?
I walked towards the sound or at any rate moved towards it.

What happened then?
Somebody rushed out and hit me on the head.

Did this happen in the area at the top of the stairs, approximately?
Approximately, yes.

Was there more than one blow?
About four.

Did you hear anyone speak at that time?
Not at the time I was being hit on the head, later.

Then what?
I screamed and the person said 'Shut up'.

Did you recognise the voice?
It was my husband.

What did he do then, what happened to you?
He thrust three gloved fingers down my throat, and we started to fight.

What happened during the fight?
It's difficult to remember, it was seven months ago but during the course of the fight he attempted to strangle me.

From behind or in front?
From in front, gouge out my eye.

And all this was at the top of the stairs, was it?
Yes.

And you were on the ground by this time?
Yes.

> Do you remember sitting up between his legs with your back to him or sideways?
>
> I would say sideways.
>
> Then he desisted?
>
> He desisted, yes.
>
> There is a photograph of a top metal support on the balustrade of the stairs that has been disturbed. Can you explain that?
>
> I would have dislodged it with my leg in the struggle.

I was then asked about the aftermath of the fight. I wouldn't describe it that I asked my husband to 'help' me. I was cross-examined by Mr Watling for the police. He asked: "When you were struggling with your husband, is it right that you grabbed hold of him?" I replied "Yes." "By his private parts?" "Yes."

I was then asked what effect, if any, that had on him, and replied: "He went back. He moved back." I was then asked if he had said anything to me at that stage, but the Coroner would not allow me to reply. I was then asked about what I was hit with, and I described it as an object. It appeared to be slightly curved and hard. I was shown a photograph of the bludgeon and said that it fitted the description of what I was hit with. I agreed that I had told a police officer "I know it sounds silly, but it felt bandaged."

The Coroner continued questioning me about the aftermath of the fight.

> Did you manage to persuade your husband to help you - first in the downstairs cloakroom? (I would describe it differently not as helping me, but allowing me.)
>
> I asked him if I could have a drink of water.
>
> And what did you do? Where did you go?
>
> We went into the downstairs cloakroom and I had a drink.
>
> I believe there was only hot water available. Is that right?
>
> Yes.
>
> Was it dark in the downstairs cloakroom, or had the light been switched on?

Inquest

It was dark. (The strip lighting was very dim but it was switched on.)

Following this you both went upstairs. Is that right?
Yes.

Where did you go?
We went upstairs to my bedroom.

Who was in there?
My daughter was there.

That's Frances isn't it?
Yes.

And the television was still on?
It was still on.

What did you do when you got there?
I said I felt ill.

Did you lie on the bed?
Yes.

What did your husband say when you lay on the bed?
He didn't say anything. We went together into the bathroom before I lay on the bed and together we looked at my injuries.

And after you had done that?
After we had done that, I think I said I don't feel very well, and he laid a towel on the bed and I got on it.

Would this towel have been laid on the pillow?
Yes.

And your daughter by this time?
She was sent upstairs as soon as we came into the bedroom. The television was switched off and she was sent upstairs by my husband.

And you were now lying on the bed - did your husband say anything about helping you further?
Very vaguely I understood that he was going to get a cloth to clean up my face.

For this he would have gone into the bathroom?
Yes.

A Moment in Time

What did you do while he was in the bathroom?
I heard the taps running and I jumped to my feet and ran out of the room and down the stairs.

Where did you go then?
I ran to the Plumber's Arms.

That's only a matter of 30 yards from your house?
Yes.

From there assistance was sought - and then did you go to St George's Hospital ?
Yes.

How long were you there?
Just under a week.

Have you seen your husband since he went into the bathroom?
No, I haven't seen him.

You have no doubt that it was he?
No doubt at all.

Could Lady Lucan be shown the letters? It is not the content but the handwriting. Can you recognise it?
Yes, I would say it was my husband's handwriting.

(On being shown the sack) Have you seen this before?
I do not recognise it from before.

What was he wearing?
He was wearing a sweater of sorts, no tie and grey flannel trousers. That's the best I can do.

And you have mentioned gloves. Did he take them off?
No, he took those off before.

When you were lying on your bed?
He took them off before.

There is just one small thing. In the kitchen there is an electric kettle. Is there some defect by which, when it is switched on, the red light shows?
It does the opposite to what it should.

> The red light is showing all the time?
>
> Yes.

The Coroner then asked final questions clarifying my evidence:

> Did you see anybody else at the time apart from your husband. Did anybody brush past you?
>
> I saw nobody else.
>
> Nor at any time during that evening?
>
> No, not at any time during the evening.
>
> I am going to ask my officer to reiterate your evidence. Is there anything you want to alter?
>
> No, there is nothing.

Michael Eastham QC, retained by my mother-in-law, started to cross-examine me and appeared to be trying to work himself up into an uncontrolled fury in order to obtain a similar response from me, but I just thought it was rather an idiotic and obvious ploy. I had been told that he was a 'red-herring' man. He asked firstly:

> Lady Lucan, the separation was 7th January?
>
> 7th January 1973.
>
> And the position was that, even before the separation, you entertained feelings of hatred for your husband? (He would be referring to the tape-recorded material used in the custody case proceedings.)

My Counsel, Mr Bruce Coles, jumped to his feet to object. Mr Eastham explained that understanding my attitude to my husband was vital to the case. He said:

> I don't enjoy my task, but you know in the two written accounts, especially the one written to Mr Shand Kydd, is that Lord Lucan was really saying was that he was not the attacker but Lady Lucan was making it look as though he were the attacker, and so their relationship was relevant as to whether Lady Lucan's recollection was an honest one or a pure fabrication.

He said that his instructions were that by the beginning of 1973, I quite definitely hated my husband. [He said he could prove this.

(again referring to the tape-recorded evidence).] He said my husband only wanted to look after the children and that a large number of doctors expressed conflict. (Most were not in conflict).

I quote from my husband's main letter to my brother-in-law Bill Shand Kydd:

7th November 1974

Dear Bill,

The most ghastly circumstances arose tonight which I briefly described to my mother. When I interrupted the fight at Lower Belgrave St and the man left Veronica accused me of having hired him. I took her upstairs and sent Frances up to bed and tried to clean her up. She lay doggo for a bit and when I was in the bathroom left the house. The circumstantial evidence against me is strong in that V will say it was all my doing. I also will lie doggo for a bit but I am only concerned for the children. If you can manage it I want them to live with you - Coutts (trustees) St Martins Lane (Mr Wall) will handle school fees. V. has demonstrated her hatred for me in the past and would do anything to see me accused. For George & Frances to go through life knowing their father had stood in the dock for attempted murder would be too much. When they are old enough to understand, explain to them the dream of paranoia, and look after them.

Yours ever,
John.

Mr Eastham explained his situation and said that he knew that questions aimed at discrediting witnesses were not allowed at inquests, but he needed to pose certain questions so that my husband's name could be fully defended.

He said that he did not enjoy his task but it involved the inescapable and unpleasant duty of suggesting that what I was saying I knew to be untrue.

What he would like to have in evidence, he said, was that there was a suggestion that I suffered from paranoia, and that the situation further deteriorated in view of the long proceedings, which had gone on for eleven days. It could be made to sound a great deal worse than that.

My response to this is that it could not truthfully be made to sound a great deal worse than that. I do not suffer from paranoia. My late husband was advised by his lawyers in view of mounting costs to concede, and so custody of the three Lucan wards was awarded to me with conditions, difficult with which to comply, attached.

It became clear to me along the way that although it is not allowed at inquests, attempts were being made to discredit me. Evidence about our marital relationship and what various references in my late husband's letters meant were disallowed by the Coroner. Subsequently, Bill Shand Kydd and Michael Stoop were only allowed to give 'Yes' or 'No' answers.

Frances' statement was read to the Court by Woman Detective Constable Sally Bower, who had taken the statement some thirteen days after the murder. Her police statement disagreed with my evidence on the matter of time and elsewhere. The policewoman said that I was in the house at the time the statement was taken, and Frances was quite clear and composed, and added that she thought that she was telling the truth as she saw it.

The statement read:

> I live at 46 Lower Belgrave Street with Mummy, my brother George, my sister Camilla, and whoever is looking after us. Mummy and Daddy don't live together, but I usually see Daddy every other weekend. We stay the weekend with him at the Gibbs's house in Northampton or with the Shand Kydds or with a friend of Daddy's, Lord Suffolk, who lives in Wiltshire at a place called Charlton Park. George, Camilla and I spent the weekend of 2nd/3rd November 1974 with Daddy at the Gibbs's house in Northampton. Daddy took us home to Lower Belgrave Street at 5.30pm on Sunday 3rd November 1974. The last time I saw Daddy was on Thursday 7th November 1974. On that day I didn't go to school because the bus didn't come for me, so Mummy said I need not go. Camilla and George went to school as usual. I spent the day at home with Mummy and Sandra, our nanny. As far as I know nothing unusual happened that day and nobody came to visit us at home.
>
> On Thursday evening we, that's Mummy, George, Camilla and Sandra and I, all had our tea together. I think that was sometime around 5pm or 5.30pm. After tea I played with one of my games in the nursery. Then at about 7.20pm I watched *Top of the Pops* on the television in the nursery. Mummy, Camilla, George and Sandra were downstairs

in Mummy's room. They were watching *The Six Million Dollar Man*. I went downstairs and joined them at about 8.05pm, and we all watched the television in Mummy's room. When the programme finished at 8.30pm, I went back upstairs to the nursery and played a little more with my game. Sandra brought George and Camilla upstairs and put them to bed. I had had a bath before I started watching television and I was wearing my pyjamas after my bath. I stayed in the nursery for about five minutes only, then I went downstairs again to Mummy's room. That would have been about 8.40pm.

I asked Mummy where Sandra was and she said she was downstairs making some tea. I didn't see her go downstairs so I don't know if she took any empty cups with her. I didn't notice whether or not there were any empty cups in the room. After a while Mummy said she wondered why Sandra was so long. I don't know what time this was, but it was before the news came on the television at 9.00pm. I said I would go downstairs to see what was keeping Sandra but Mummy said no, she would go. I said I would go with her but she said no, it was OK, she would go. Mummy left the room to go downstairs and I stayed watching the television. She left the bedroom door open, but there was no light in the hall because the light bulb is worn out and it doesn't work.

Just after Mummy left the room I heard a scream. It sounded as though it came from a long way away. I thought maybe the cat had scratched Mummy and she had screamed. I wasn't frightened by the scream and I just stayed in the room watching television. I went to the door of the room and called out 'Mummy?' but there was no answer so I just left it.

At about 9.05pm, when the news was on the television, Daddy and Mummy both walked into the room. Mummy had blood over her face and she was crying. Daddy didn't say anything to me and I didn't say anything to either of them. I don't know how much blood was on Mummy's face, I only caught a glimpse of her. As far as I can remember, Daddy was wearing a pair of dark trousers and an overcoat which was full length and was fawn-coloured with brown checks. I was sitting on the bed as they came in the door and I couldn't see them very well. There were two lights on above Mummy's bed and one other sidelight on. I didn't hear any conversation between Mummy and Daddy. I couldn't see if Daddy's clothes had any blood on them. I wondered what had happened but I didn't ask.

After Mummy told me to go upstairs I got straight up and went upstairs to my bedroom, which is on the top floor of the house. I got into bed and read my book. I didn't hear anything from downstairs. After a little while, I don't know how long because I don't have a clock

Inquest

in my room, I heard Daddy calling for Mummy. He was calling out: "Veronica, where are you?" I got up and went to the banisters and looked down and I saw Daddy coming out of the nursery on the floor below me. He then went into the bathroom on the same floor as the nursery. He came straight out and then he went downstairs. That was the last I saw of him. He never came up to the top floor of the house that night, either to look for Mummy or to say goodnight to me. I didn't notice at any time whether or not Daddy was wearing gloves. The last time I saw Sandra was when she took George and Camilla upstairs to bed. I was very surprised to see Daddy at home that Thursday night, but I never asked why he was there.

During the last weekend we spent with Daddy on the 2nd and 3rd November 1974, Camilla told Daddy that Sandra had boyfriends and went out with them. Daddy asked when Sandra went out with her boyfriends and Camilla said Sandra went out with her boyfriends' on her days off. Then Daddy asked me when Sandra had her days off. I said her day off was Thursday.

Frances' statement disagreed with Mrs Maxwell-Scott's description of what my husband was wearing on the night of 7th November 1974 and also my own. Her timing was also rather muddled, despite giving references to television programmes.

Mr Whitehouse from the Plumber's Arms was the next witness, and told the court that at 9.50pm, the door of the pub burst open and I ran in. He said:

I gave her assistance. I laid her on the bench. She was head to toe in blood from head wounds but it was crusted. She was quite all right for a few minutes. I covered her with an overcoat. She then cried out "Help me, help me, help me! I've just escaped from being murdered, he's in the house. He's murdered my nanny!" No names were mentioned. I telephoned for the police and ambulance immediately. The police were ten minutes, the ambulance about twenty minutes. I called my wife down to give medical attention until the ambulance arrived.

Three more witnesses were called that day. First was Dr Michael Smith, a police surgeon, who confirmed that the body of Sandra Rivett was dead and thought that death was very recent. He said:

I received a call at 10.45pm on November 7th 1974 to go to Lower Belgrave Street at Number 46. In the basement, on the floor I saw a large canvas bag which appeared to contain a human body. I also noted bloodstains on the floor. I didn't disturb the bag in any way. I was satisfied that the body was dead and that death was not due to natural causes. I thought death was very recent, within an hour or so.

Dr Hugh Scott was called and said that he saw me about 11pm, and described my injuries. He said:

> I have looked at the photographs in C6 of Mrs Rivett. There is a laceration over the right eyebrow. There are probably two at the back of the head. There is apparently a third above the right ear. It is difficult to say from photographs but there are similarities with the wounds of Lady Lucan. From photographs they would have been produced in a similar manner.

Sergeant Baker was the first investigator on the scene, shortly after 10pm. He said he met PC Beddick on the ground floor hall. They searched the house for suspects and for the children. The first light they came to was in a double bedroom, a bedside lamp on the left hand side, the door side as they looked at the bed. There was a bloodstained towel on the pillow on the same side as the lamp.

They went to the floor above, in the nursery there was a colour television and the volume was very loud. On the floor above that were three children. In the first room Lady Frances was standing beside the bed and another little girl was in bed asleep. A police constable stayed with them.

He returned to the ground floor, near to the door leading to the basement, and he saw an object on the floor and at the time he thought it was a doll's leg, it was white. When he saw it the second time, it looked like a lead pipe with tape round it. It had changed colour, it was red. (I wonder if the reason for the change in colour was due to the fact that my husband, although wearing gloves, might have been washing the bludgeon in the downstairs cloakroom which is why it was still white when Sergeant Baker saw it the first time and that blood had seeped through when he saw it the second time?)

After this, he re-entered the basement with PC Beddick and started a more thorough search. There was a light switch slightly above the piano and he turned on the light.[1]

Eventually, he noticed what he thought was a tent bag on the floor near the piano. The top was folded over and there were bloodstains on the bag. The top was open. He said he saw the top of a human thigh in black tights. He took out an arm - it was very white. He said he could feel no pulse. There was a door leading into a back yard. He went through this. The door was closed but not locked.

---

[1] This is the switch I believe my husband used when he discovered he had killed the wrong woman.

27

Inquest Continued

On day two, Detective Sergeant Forsyth said that he was about to bring in evidence certain points about which the Coroner had made a ruling. My Counsel rose to his feet saying, quite unnecessarily, I thought, that the evidence would be an embarrassment to me, implying, I thought, that the evidence was true. I must make it clear at this stage that I do not suffer from paranoia.

The evidence was allowed and Detective Sergeant Forsyth said that my mother-in-law, when asked "Does your son live here?", replied "He's separated. The children were made wards of court and Veronica was told to continue with medical treatment for her mental complaint." "What was that?" "Manic-depressive. Not violent, except verbally. In the original court case it was thought she was a danger to the children." By so saying, she had viciously managed to slander me and misrepresent the reality of the custody case.

Detective Sergeant Forsyth read from my husband's second letter to my brother-in-law, which was headed:

FINANCIAL MATTERS

Dear Bill,

There is a sale coming up at Christie's Nov 27th which will satisfy bank overdrafts. Please agree reserves with Tom Craig.

Proceeds to go to:

Lloyds, 6 Pall Mall;

Coutts, 59 Strand;

Nat West, Bloomsbury branch,

who also hold an Equity and Law Life policy.

The other creditors can get lost for the time being.

Lucky.

The Bankers Book Evidence Act allowed Sergeant Forsyth to discover that my husband's overdraft at Lloyds was £2,841, at Coutts £4,378; at Nat West £1,290, and interestingly not included in his letter was £5,667 guaranteed by Sir James Goldsmith at the Midland Bank, Newgate Street, making a total of £14,177.

After lunch on the second day, Professor Keith Simpson, the pathologist, outlined the injuries to Mrs Rivett, which he had found during his post mortem some twelve hours after her death. Her body was clothed in a smock, short dress, brassiere, panties and black tights, and was doubled up inside the bag, death having taken place before she was placed in the bag. Her clothing had not been disturbed and there was no sign of a sexual attack. She was a healthy woman of short stature and medium build. There were three major injuries to her face - over the right eye, the right corner of the mouth and over the left eyebrow. To the head above the right ear there were two crushed splits in the scalp, two further splits in the scalp nearer the right brow but still in the hair. To the back of the head there were two splits in the scalp above the nape of the neck. There was heavy bruising from some 'near misses' on her shoulders when she had moved as she lay on the ground trying to evade the repeated frenzied strikes of the bludgeon. After she had been killed, she was gripped by the arms and bent double and placed in the bag with her head lolling between her feet. Professor Simpson thought that some minor injuries to her face had been caused by a fist or a hand slap.

The injuries were sufficient to cause deep bruising to her brain, which had caused her to inhale a large quantity of blood through her nose. The skull was not fractured, but widespread surface (and some deeper) bruising of the brain had accompanied the head injuries, and death was due to blunt head injuries. He said an unconscious person cannot clear the airwaves by coughing. He agreed that the bludgeon was 'highly likely' to have caused the injuries to both myself and Sandra Rivett.

He said that he was shown by Detective Chief Superintendent Ranson a length of lead piping, around which surgical plaster strip had been wrapped. It weighed a little over 1,000 grams and could have caused the scalp, shoulder and hand injuries described. It was bloodstained.

My mother-in-law was later called to the stand and she affirmed, getting it wrong amid laughter. She refused an invitation to sit. She continued to prevaricate throughout her evidence, and had to be reminded she would be liable to prosecution if she made any false statements. She said that she remembered that my husband had said in his first telephone call that he had interrupted a fight in the basement, which was not mentioned in her first statement:

> "John speaking. There has been a terrible catastrophe at number 46. Veronica is hurt and I want you to collect the children. Ring Bill Shand Kydd he will help." He also said "The nanny is hurt." I asked "Badly?" and he said, "Yes, I think so." That was I think the whole conversation. It was hardly a conversation I would forget.

She continued:

> I first attempted to ring Mr Shand-Kydd. I was told he was not available. This was a mistake, although I didn't speak to him. I went to 46 Lower Belgrave Street. I returned to the flat and then there was a second telephone call. This was well after midnight. I had got the children to bed first so it was not immediately after my return.

She paused, remembering something (which it would be surprising if she had forgotten), and said "I must add that in the first telephone call he said: 'I interrupted a fight in the basement'."

The coroner Dr Thurston asked:

> He used those words?

> Yes. During the second telephone call he asked "Have you got the children?" and I replied "Yes."

Cross-examination by Mr Watling for the police was interesting and revealing. He asked if "it was right that, as Detective Sergeant Forsyth has told us, you made a statement to him?"

He then read the start of my mother-in-law's first written statement. He asked her if she had said in the statement that she received the first phone call from my husband at about 10.45pm. She replied "I am sure this must be correct because this is the statement

Inquest Continued

I made at the time. But I am still under the impression that the hour mentioned is unduly late."

She was asked if it was correct that she had said in the statement that my husband had said "There has been the most terrible catastrophe at number 46." She replied "I have no recollection of that, but I have no reason to doubt it."

She was then asked if her statement had continued "This is very difficult for me to remember now but I have the impression there was a third person present but I can't be exact about this." She replied "Yes. It was my subjective impression at the time, and it remains my subjective impression now."

Mr Watling continued: "You have told the jury that in the first phone call you had from your son, he used the words: 'I interrupted a fight in the basement.'" She replied "Yes - and when asked to repeat the conversation, in some curious way I failed to explain this quite unaccountably."

Mr Watling said: "You see, you didn't use in that statement anything about your son telling you 'I interrupted a fight in the basement' did you? What you said was 'I have the impression that there was a third person present but I can't be exact about this.'"

My mother-in-law replied that the words 'I interrupted a fight' were undoubtedly his words, and she imagined that when she made this statement that the impression that there had been a third person present was an obvious deduction from the statement that he interrupted a fight in the basement. (She may have been told that my husband in his letter to Bill Shand Kydd had referred to a fight in the basement.)

"Yes," said Mr Watling, "but why did you not tell the police officer that so it could go down in the statement? No deductions, just plain statement?"

My mother-in-law replied "It is a plain statement and this is a plain statement." She said that she thought that the upshot of the two was the same.

Mr Watling replied that that may be a matter for the jury:

> The point is you did not in that statement use the words which you now tell the jury your son used.
>
> Yes, but these are the words which to the best of my recollection he used.

Mr Watling referred her to a second written statement she made several weeks after the murder: "In that statement you mention 'I remember he said he had interrupted a fight.'"

"Yes," replied my mother-in-law. She said my husband had said it close to the point in the first telephone call when he had asked her to ring Bill Shand Kydd.

Had she rung Mr Shand Kydd?

> I did subsequently get in touch with the Shand Kydds. I spoke to Mrs Shand Kydd and told her Veronica was in hospital. Her immediate reaction was: "Has she attempted to kill herself again?"[1]

An objection was raised, but although the coroner said "I shall not record that, it is prejudicial" he had no power to direct the press not to report the comment.

The lengths my own relations were prepared to go in order to discredit me were extraordinary. This prompted Mr David Webster, Counsel for the Rivett family, to say:

> This inquiry is to discover how, and when and where Mrs Rivett met her death but there seems to be a certain amount of imbalance. How and where is becoming clear. But the person who may be charged may not be clear to the jury.

Mr Watling asked if my husband had said on the phone who was fighting whom.

"No," replied my mother-in-law.

"Did he say how Veronica and Sandra came to be hurt?"

"No."

"Did you think of ringing the police at this time?"

"It crossed my mind as I drove over as I was aware there had been a violent accident."

---

[1] This was the only day my sister was in court, which gave credence to this statement.

Eventually Mr Watling sat down after saying "I need go no further. The jury will have seen this lady for themselves."[2]

Michael Eastham posed some questions to my mother-in-law, and elicited the information that she had lent my husband £4,000 towards the cost of the custody proceedings, and she agreed that my husband was 'obsessed' with his children. Returning to the dispute with Detective Sergeant Forsyth, he then asked "Do you agree that you mentioned the fight?" She replied "Yes."

She was then asked whether she had said my husband had told her that he was 'driving past' or 'passing' the house. My mother-in-law said that my husband had told her he was 'passing' the house. She assumed he was passing on foot. She said it was seven months ago and she couldn't be certain that she said 'driving'. She thought she said 'passing'.

My mother-in-law said that during the first telephone call my husband muttered "blood and mess", and some parts of it she could not follow, but she got the impression that he could not stand the blood and mess.[3] She left the witness box after answering questions for just over an hour and looked at my sister-in-law as if to elicit her approval as she took her seat beside her.

Mrs Susan Maxwell-Scott took the stand to give her version of my husband's bogus defence, which he had outlined to her during his visit to her house at Uckfield on 7th November 1974.

The Coroner asked her about his appearance and she said that he looked a little dishevelled. His hair was ruffled, he was casually dressed and wearing a light blue polo-neck, silk or nylon shirt, grey flannel trousers, a sleeveless brown pullover, but no overcoat.

He asked her if there was any marking on his clothes, and she said that while he was sitting talking she did notice, but not immediately, a damp patch on his trousers on the right side of the hip/thigh. He said he had been walking past 46 Lower Belgrave Street house on

---

2   He was made to apologise, as Michael Eastham said "That is a most improper remark for any member of the Bar to make."
3   The words 'blood' and 'mess' confirm that my husband saw the state of the breakfast room, in the basement.

his way to change for dinner. She was interrupted by the Coroner, who said that the word 'walking' was rather important. She said that she was almost certain he said 'walking', but it could have been that he said he was 'passing'. She said, "I don't know what my police statement said because that's more likely to be correct." The coroner told her that the statement said 'walking'.

Mrs Maxwell-Scott continued with the narrative provided by my husband, and started by saying, "Through the venetian blinds in the basement he said he saw what looked like a man attacking his wife. He said it was 'an unbelievable coincidence'. Mrs Maxwell-Scott said she didn't think it so extraordinary, as he had previously told her that he was in the habit of walking past the house quite regularly and sometimes going in. Mrs Maxwell-Scott said to him "It isn't such a coincidence to pass your house," and he said "Well, yes, I quite often go in to see if the children are all right."

He said he let himself in through the front door - he had a key - and went down into the basement. As he entered he slipped in a pool of blood - as he got to the bottom of the stairs, that is. She stressed that he was not telling it like a story, but that it came out in bits and pieces:

> The man he had seen attacking his wife ran off. Whether this was on hearing Lucan coming down the stairs or on seeing Lucan, I am not clear. But the man ran off. And Lucan, perhaps unfortunately, rather than chasing the man, went straight to his wife.

The Coroner asked "Did he say which way the man ran?" She replied "No. He just said the man made off. Perhaps through the back door, I don't know." (Mrs Maxwell-Scott had never visited 46 Lower Belgrave Street and so was unable to visualise the interior of the basement. If she had, she might have known it was very unlikely that he made off through the back door.)

"He then went to his wife?" asked the Coroner.

"Who was covered in blood and very hysterical" said Mrs Maxwell-Scott.

> Did he say anything further about what his wife had said?

Inquest Continued

What she had said at the time, yes. At first, she was very hysterical and cried out to him that someone had killed "the nanny". Then almost in the same breath, she accused Lucan of having hired the man to kill her. This Lucan told me was something she frequently accused him of - having "a contract to kill". He reckoned she got it from an American TV movie. He said the scene in the basement was horrific and he certainly saw the sack with Mrs Rivett's body in it. I think Lady Lucan indicated it to him. He assumed the body was in the sack but he did not go over and examine it. I think he felt squeamish with all the blood and didn't want to look too closely. He said he tried to calm her down, as I said, she was hysterical. I don't know how long all this took because he didn't tell me. He took her upstairs to a room - I assumed her bedroom - where her daughter, Lady Frances, was watching television. Lady Frances went to bed. I thought Lucan said he sent her or took her to bed. Lady Lucan was lying down. Lucan persuaded her to lie down.[4] His intention - this is what he told me - was first to get some wet towels to mop up the blood on her and see how severe her injuries were. He was then going to telephone for a doctor and subsequently telephone the police. But while he was in the bathroom he heard the front door slam and Lady Lucan out in the street shouting: "Murder! Murder!"[5]

Mrs Maxwell-Scott described his state of mind in her own words, saying he obviously panicked:

He put it another way. He felt there he was with all that blood, with the body, a murderer who had got away, and with a wife who would almost certainly try to implicate him. She had already accused him of hiring the man. He told me he reckoned no one would believe his story. I did my best to convince him that people would believe him. It was quite incredible that he should have had anything to do with it.

Cross-examined by Michael Eastham, Mrs Maxwell-Scott agreed that she had raised the question of the killer's motives:

We were discussing this probable killing and it seemed to me that it would be someone wanting to kill the nanny. But Lord Lucan said it wouldn't be someone wanting to kill her. He said she was a "good kid" or "good girl". He told me he had spoken to the official solicitor

---

4   I had gone upstairs with my husband because I wanted to lie down.
5   He told this to Mrs Maxwell-Scott in order to explain his hasty exit from the house and departure from London. I didn't waste any breath calling anything but saved it all for my run to the Plumber's Arms.

and said the children had got a nice girl for a nanny, at last. He was very pleased with her.

She was asked by the Coroner about the telephone calls my husband had made from Uckfield, and she said that he looked at his watch and said something about the time. She said she thought it was then about 12.15am. He then asked if he could telephone his mother, and used the telephone in the drawing room and spoke to her.

Apparently he asked something about the children and said "Oh, good." He then asked "Has Veronica turned up?" Mrs Maxwell-Scott said she gathered the reply must have been that she had been found and taken to hospital. Next he dialled Bill Shand Kydd's number but there was no reply.[6]

He then asked if he could borrow some writing paper.

Cross-examined by Mr Watling for the police, she was asked "Is it right that Lord Lucan at no time described to you the man he had seen attacking his wife?" "Not entirely right," she replied, "Lord Lucan did not see him clearly enough to describe him. He said he was large."

Mr Watling asked whether or not Lord Lucan knew that the nanny was dead.[7] This was underlined by Mrs Maxwell-Scott's careful assertion that they had discussed a 'probable killing'. She was asked "Did he see the sack?" She replied "Yes," and then when asked if he had examined it replied "No." She was reminded that when Lord Lucan left the house, he knew that the nanny had been killed and she said this was because Lady Lucan had told him that the nanny had been killed. She had told him that the man had killed the nanny and had attacked her. He had said that he saw the man attacking his wife, anyway.[8]

---

6   I think that was good fortune - I am not sure that Shand Kydd would have been as helpful as Mrs Maxwell-Scott.

7   If his story were true, he would not know unless he had examined the sack.

8   The use of the term 'attempted murder' presumably referred to the attack upon myself which had ceased when he had let himself into the house with his key which he still had as I had not changed the locks, hoping that he would return.

Inquest Continued

Mrs Maxwell-Scott then asked if he would like some coffee and she went and made them both some. He wrote his letters to Bill Shand Kydd and then handed them to her, asking if she would post them for him. She replied "Yes," and put them on the drinks trolley.[9]

After this, she was asked if there was general conversation on different matters, the children and so on. "Yes," she replied. She was then asked if she had offered to let him stay the night. She replied that she had tried to persuade him to stay the night and telephone the police in the morning. But after slightly agreeing, he said that he must - stressing the word "must" - get back and clear things up. When he said "get back" he did not mention London.

The Coroner asked "Did he ask you if you had any sleeping pills?"

According to Mrs Maxwell-Scott, he said he was sure that he would have difficulty sleeping and asked if she had got any. She said that she hadn't. The best she could find was some Valium, which is a tranquiliser. There were about four 2mg tablets still left. It was not a very strong dose but he took them with the water she had brought for the whisky earlier. He then said he must be getting back.

The Coroner asked "What time did he leave?" She replied "To the best of my knowledge about 1.15am." She was asked what happened then, and she said she went to bed. She was asked if she had seen him since, and replied "No." "What about your husband?" "I know he hasn't."

In the morning, she had taken the letters off the drinks trolley and stamped them. She gave them to her small daughter and asked her to post them on her way to school.

Susan Maxwell-Scott was not hostile to me nor was her husband Ian. She merely gave her evidence, and gave it very well I thought.[10]

Bill Shand Kydd was called to the witness stand next, and he told the coroner that he was a company director and that he was married

---

9   She did not query why he was writing letters to Bill Shand Kydd to his London address.
10 I sometimes wonder if Ian Maxwell-Scott had been at home when my husband called late on 7th November, if he would have taken the same view as his wife and taken different actions.

to my sister. He was asked if he saw my husband quite frequently, and he replied about every three weeks. He said he could say nothing about my husband's debts and knew nothing about his financial situation before. He was asked when he last saw him, and he replied that his memory was very unreliable but that it was probably about two weekends before 7th November.

He seemed very relaxed and spent a lot of time with the children, his and mine. He expressed pleasurable anticipation because it was his turn to have the children that Christmas. The Coroner asked if my husband was 'unusually fond' of children, and my brother-in-law replied: "I don't think so. He was very fond of his children. I think he was worried about his children and possibly considered they were not being looked after properly." My counsel Mr Bruce Coles instantly objected and the Coroner upheld the objection.

My brother-in-law told the Coroner that he had received the letters written to him by my husband at his house in Cambridge Square on Saturday morning, 9th November. He had been telephoned by Ian Maxwell-Scott, who informed him that my husband had visited his house in Uckfield and written two letters which had been posted to his London address. He immediately rang his London address and his butler told him that two letters had arrived that morning with Uckfield postmarks. He drove straight to London as he was at his country house in Leighton Buzzard, and had been since Friday evening. He read the letters, and took them to the police at Gerald Road and pointed out the bloodstains on them.

The Coroner asked if my husband ever said anything about the children's nannies. My brother-in-law replied that he always asked when my husband visited him. My husband said that Mrs Rivett was the most satisfactory one so far, and he hoped it would last. He said she was a very nice girl and the children liked her. He was then asked about my husband and he replied "I wouldn't describe him as one of my three greatest friends but I know him well and liked him." He was then asked if my husband would have approached him for financial help. My brother-in-law replied "Only if he had been in really dire circumstances, from pride I would be the last person to approach if at all possible - in extremis only."

Mr Eastham then tried to develop a line of inquiry about which the Coroner had made a ruling, but said that in view of the Coroner's ruling concerning what was admissible evidence, would he just answer "Yes" or "No."

> "Veronica has demonstrated her hatred for me in the past." Do you understand what he meant by this?
>
> Yes.
>
> "And would do anything to see me accused." Could you give evidence about it?
>
> Yes.
>
> "When the children are old enough to understand, explain to them the dream of paranoia." Did you understand that when you read it?
>
> Yes.
>
> Could you if asked give evidence about the paranoia?
>
> Yes.

He asked to be excused from the proceedings on the ground of business, and was photographed the next day in the Royal Enclosure at Ascot wearing a brown morning suit.

Mrs Eileen Sims, the next witness, a housewife, told the court about the abandoned Ford Corsair, as she was a resident of Norman Road, Newhaven, where the car was found. She had never seen it before and didn't see anyone go near it from Friday morning to Sunday. She said:

> I first saw the car at 8am on Friday 8th November, a navy blue Ford Corsair parked opposite. We do not often have strange cars parked in the road and this was particularly noticeable. The car was old and dirty. I saw nobody park the car. I saw nobody go near the car until the police came on the Sunday. I am quite sure the car was not there on the Thursday.

Detective Sergeant David De Lima, stationed at Lewes, produced a photograph of the contents of the boot exactly as he saw it, which included a bar with white tape. Inside the police had found a second piece of bandaged lead piping - like the one found at Number 46, but not bloodstained.

First in the witness box on day three was Michael Stoop, owner of the abandoned Ford Corsair, which he had lent to my husband. He said that my husband and himself were both members of the Clermont Club, and he had known my husband for about fifteen years.

He said he couldn't recall the exact date my husband had asked to borrow his car, but it was probably the 21st or 23rd of October, the night of a dinner at the Portland Club. He said:

> I had a Mercedes and I suggested that he might like to borrow that as my own Ford Corsair is a pretty dirty old banger. But I imagine through natural manners he didn't want to deprive me of my better car. He wanted the Ford specifically for that evening. I didn't ask for any reason and he didn't offer any.

On the Monday after the murder he received letters at his club, the St James's. There was no stamp on one letter. The hall porter had to pay the postage. He identified the letter and the handwriting as my husband's. He thought he must have thrown the envelope away.[11] The letter was written on both sides of a sheet of blotting paper and read out:

> My dear Michael,
>
> I have had a traumatic night of unbelievable coincidence. However I won't bore you with anything or involve you except to say that when you come across my children, which I hope you will, please tell them that you knew me and that all I cared about was them.
>
> The fact that a crooked solicitor and a rotten psychiatrist destroyed me between them will be of no importance to the children.
>
> I gave Bill Shand Kydd an account of what actually happened but judging by my last effort in court no-one, let alone a 67 year old judge, would believe - and I no longer care except that my children should be protected.
>
> Yours ever,
> John[12]

---

11 I have often wondered which pillar box probably close to Norman Road was used by my husband to have posted the letter.

12 This is my husband's suicide note, which left me in no doubt that he had committed suicide.

Inquest Continued

Mr Eastham cross-examined Michael Stoop. He explained that it was difficult to reply just "Yes" or "No" to Mr Eastham's questions. He was shown a photograph of the interior of the Ford Corsair and one of the lead piping, and he said "I have never seen that object before."[13] He said he had not lent the car to anyone else, principally because it was insured in his name only. The car would do about 24 miles per gallon on a long journey.

Next came the senior fingerprint officer at New Scotland Yard, Mr Ian Lucas. He was interesting, because he said that all the fingerprints found in the basement of number 46 were of police officers, one of the children or Mrs Rivett, so whoever attacked her left no fingerprints.[14] However, a print found in the flat at Elizabeth Street and a print found on the interior driving mirror of the Ford Corsair had probably been made by the same person. He said he would need a control sample to be definite.

Dr Margaret Pereira, a senior principal scientific officer, was next. She had an international reputation as a blood analyst. She and her colleagues had perfected a method of analysing even the smallest samples of dried blood. Mrs Rivett and myself had different blood groups, which helped matters considerably. Mrs Rivett had Group B blood, which was found in 8½% of the country's population. Mine was of the more common Group A, shared by about 42% of the population.

Following the attack upon myself by the basement door on the ground floor there was extensive blood to be found. She was able to confirm this. It was established that Group B blood was concentrated in the basement, and Mr Eastham cross-examined her about this. There was blood smearing on the arch of my shoes, and so he said "It is very probable that Lady Lucan walked through the basement?" She replied that it is certainly a likely explanation. She also said "I cannot eliminate the possibility of the shoes coming into contact with sodden garments." He then asked which was more probable:

---

13 Interestingly, no-one mentioned the biro which my husband presumably used to write his last letter to Michael Stoop.
14 This is not surprising, as my husband was wearing gloves at the time of the attack.

that that had happened, or that Lady Lucan had walked through Sandra's blood in the basement. She replied "I think that is a difficult question for me to answer. I really can't express an opinion. Perhaps if I could have the shoes... I can't tell. The bloodstaining could have come from either source." As to the blood of Sandra's group on my dress, she said "It was not heavy - it was smearing. It's consistent with contact with clothing of anyone with that blood on it."

As to the Group A blood in the basement kitchen which was described as no larger than a pinhead, it was most probably deposited by one of the cats. It had taken three days for the police to catch them. In the kitchen there were a few scattered bloodstains on the floor. A blood smear near the doorway from the breakfast room was Group B, Sandra's group. Approximately in the middle of the kitchen floor there were two spots of blood close together. Tests on samples showed one spot was Group B, Sandra's group, and the other was Group A, my group.

The lead piping found by the basement doorway was about 9 inches long, weighed 2lbs 3oz and was grossly distorted. Interestingly, tests showed that the hairs stuck to the lead piping were similar to mine but none were similar to Sandra's hair. Mine was of the fine, split-ended easily broken type of hair, and Sandra's was thick, strong coarse hair, which must have been the reason her hairs were absent from the lead piping - it had withstood the battering.

Dr Roger John Davis said:

> I am a Master of Science and Doctor of Philosophy and Senior Scientific Officer at the Metropolitan Police Forensic Science Laboratory at Lambeth. I received two pieces of piping from my colleague, Miss Margaret Pereira. I examined these. I produce my report.
>
> The piece of pipe found in the car had the light blue and royal blue paint. The short piece (46 Lower Belgrave Street) has light blue and royal blue paint, different in shade from that on the piece from the car.
>
> The corrosion in the short pipe could have been caused by its being used as a water pipe. The corrosion in the long pipe is much less than that in the short. The minor extrusion marks in the short pipe may have been removed by corrosion except the more deep ones. The

Inquest Continued

pipes may have come from the same batch or from the same length of pipe but I don't know how long that length was.

Mr Charles Genese, a money-lender, was next and told the court that on 11th September my husband asked to borrow £5,000 and was perfectly open about his commitments. He said his gross income payable through trust fund solicitors was £12,000. He said he had put some family silver up for auction and from the proceeds would be able to pay off anything he had borrowed. His only mention of further income was if he was fortunate enough at gambling. Mr Genese said he refused to lend him any money in view of his financial position. But several days later, after my husband had provided a surety, he agreed to lend him £3,000. He had to pay £120 per month, 48% per annum for a period of six months. He said he saw my husband a second time on 18th October, two days prior to the first instalment falling due. It was a Friday and he came in and paid. The next instalment was due in November by which time the events had occurred.

Andrea Demetriou, the assistant restaurant manager, said that he knew Lord Lucan as a client. He said:

> I started work at 7.30pm. I received a telephone call from Lord Lucan around 8.30pm. He said he was going to the theatre and would be rather late. I entered the booking. Lord Lucan never turned up, a party of four came and wanted an extra chair for Lord Lucan. The order was for four, and four people, not including Lord Lucan, turned up. The party of four, or one of the party, said Lord Lucan was coming.[15]

William 'Billy' Edgson was the next witness. He parked and collected Clermont members' cars for them. He often did private jobs for my husband such as taking him to the airport and collecting the children. On 7th November 1974 he was on duty at 8pm - his partner started at 9pm. At about 8.45pm my husband drove up, and Edgson said he was fairly certain he was driving his Mercedes and asked who was in the club and told him "none of the usual

---

15 This forgetfulness may indicate something of the stress my husband was under at the time.

crowd." He said that my husband was his usual self and not excited. He could not remember his dress. He said "I have driven from the Clermont in the daytime and that he could do the journey in less than ten minutes. He had never driven from the Clermont to Lower Belgrave Street in the evening. At 8.45pm it would be very quiet." The difference between 46 Lower Belgrave Street and 72A Elizabeth Street is only a few minutes, say three minutes.

Mr Watling, for the police, referred Coroner Dr Thurston to a statement which had been made to the police by Greville Howard. He was to have appeared as a witness but Mr Watling said he was "ill in hospital," so he asked for the statement to be read out in his absence. He made the submission because there had been great play made of a third person (referring to the alleged intruder). Mr Watling said there was evidence in his statement about my husband's depressed state of mind. He said that evidence was highly relevant and should be before the jury when they made their deliberation.

Michael Eastham told the coroner that he would most 'strongly object' to the proposal. There would be no opportunity for cross-examination and its prejudicial effect would outweigh its probative value. The statement was withheld.

Detective Sergeant Forsyth and I went for lunch as always to the Barley Mow which was opposite the Coroner's Court in Horseferry Road.

The final two witnesses were Detective Chief Inspector Gerring and Detective Inspector Charles Hulls, who told of experiments they had carried out a couple of days after the murder of Mrs Rivett had taken place. It was particularly important to carry out, because of ascertaining correctly what could or could not be seen through the basement window. Mr Gerring first drove a car past 46 Lower Belgrave Street and, looking towards the house, he said he could only see the top of the basement area.[16] Mr Hulls then went into the basement, stood at the bottom of the stairs and weaved backwards and forwards a few paces towards the door of the kitchen several

---

16 This proved that it was impossible to see a fight taking place in the basement.

Inquest Continued

times. From outside, Mr Gerring tried to see if he would see his colleague Mr Hulls through the venetian blinds on the kitchen window.

Detective Chief Inspector Gerring said that when the basement was in complete darkness, all he could see from outside was the red glow of a kettle. When the light over the breakfast room table was switched on, Mr Gerring continued, he could make out the figure of Mr Hulls in the area at the foot of the stairs, but then only by stooping. He said "My head was between 2 and 3 feet from the ground." "When the kitchen lights were switched on," he continued, "I could see Mr Hulls at the foot of the basement stairs and also about three or four of the steps."

He then walked past the address and on looking through the slats of the venetian blind, he could only see the kitchen and not the foot of the stairs. There was no evidence of a fight having taken place in the kitchen and there would have had to be a light on for my husband to have seen anything clearly, and so left his stated motive for entering the house without explanation and apparently untrue.

Mr Gerring told the court that he had first been to Lower Belgrave Street at midnight on the night of 7th November 1974. As far as he knew, nothing had been moved and on coming down the stairs to the basement he saw the pool of blood and the body in the sack. There was one saucer lying broken on the floor at the bottom of the stairs. Half of the saucer was on the last step, the other half on the ground. There was no sign of a fight in the basement. He said he then interviewed me at about 1.30am. I made a verbal statement to him and to Mr Ranson on the evening of Friday, 8th November at about six o'clock. He said that my understanding was extremely good. Sergeant Forsyth then took my written statement, which was remarkably close to the verbal statement.

28

Coroner

My mother-in-law, on the third day of the proceedings, remarked to reporters "I do not think this is serving any useful purpose at all."

The purpose of the inquest was to discover when, where and how Mrs Rivett met her death. It was not to use the proceedings as an opportunity to attempt to discredit me. She had clearly hoped for this, as she had instructed Michael Eastham to ask questions which arose out of my husband's last letters to Bill Shand Kydd and Michael Stoop.

The hearing resumed on the fourth and final day - Thursday, 19th June, and Dr Thurston the coroner made several observations. He said that although my husband and myself were separated, I was still his wife and that in law a wife can only give evidence in a matter concerning her husband where there had been an assault on her. I could not answer the jury's question as it was not connected to a matter concerning an attack upon myself. He continued that I was therefore not allowed to answer the jury's question "How did Lady Lucan know the nanny had been murdered?" I was disbarred as my husband's wife from clearing the matter up for them. I was allowed to answer any question relating to the assault on me, but in law a wife cannot give evidence on a matter concerning her husband.

He said:

> I have thought fit to exclude affairs which might tend to go toward family tensions. You know that Lord and Lady Lucan are separated and they have been on either side of custody proceedings since 1973. To raise family tensions would not benefit this inquiry. Simply to turn this into a forum for airing family tensions would be a wrong thing

and I do not think justice would be served by doing so.

Dr Thurston then reviewed the evidence, beginning with the fact that both Sandra Rivett and myself were five feet two inches in height. He then referred to the birdcage light fitting without a bulb and the light bulb found lying on a chair in the basement. When the light bulb was inserted into the birdcage light fitting it worked perfectly.[1] Next, he referred to the letter written to my brother-in-law beginning "Dear Bill". He said that it is evidence of what was in my husband's mind when he wrote it, but the jury should not treat the letters as proof of the statements in them. He went on, "You have heard Lady Lucan's evidence and you have had the advantage of seeing her and hearing the way she answered questions. She answered very carefully and gave questions a great deal of thought."

He recalled that I had told the jury that I came downstairs from my bedroom on the second floor looking for Sandra at about 9.15pm. I had said that there was no light on anywhere in the basement. I had said that I was attacked in the area of the hall at the top of the basement stairs, and recognised my husband's voice saying "Shut up" after I had screamed when he attacked me. I was taken into the downstairs cloakroom and this had been confirmed as my blood was found there. It was unusual for Mrs Rivett to be in the house on a Thursday, but she had changed her day off.

He reminded the jury that when my husband had asked Frances when the nanny had her day off, she had replied "Thursday." My husband's only description of the intruder was that he was 'large'. Then there was the evidence of my head injuries, which could be explained either by an attack by an intruder or my husband at this stage.

Dr Thurston asked,

> If, as Lord Lucan says, he was trying to help - and he was obviously giving her succour - would she have run crying 'Murder! Murder!' to

---

1   This indicated that the person who removed the light bulb knew about the two way switch and that you had to lean forward to switch the light on at the top of the basement stairs.

the Plumber's Arms.[2]

His next point was why hadn't my husband rung the police? Apparently he had asked his mother to telephone the police, according to Susan Maxwell-Scott.

Dr Thurston then said my evidence fitted in with what had been found scientifically, and I was 'remarkably clear' when first interviewed and never varied my statement at any time.

He then recalled experiments performed at number 46 by Detective Chief Inspector Gerring and Detective Inspector Charles Hulls. First of all, Mr Gerring drove past the house but could not see into the basement.[3] From the pavement, however, Mr Gerring had said he had been able to see into the basement when he stooped down and when the interior lights were on. But, said the Coroner, the evidence was that there was no light on in the basement. Referring to my husband's story that he had interrupted the fight he had seen between myself and my attacker, the Coroner said there was no sign of a struggle, with no furniture upset, although blood was spread over the wall.

Dr Thurston said:

> We know Lord Lucan had a key. We know he entered the house. There was no sign of a door being forced. We have not been told which way the intruder went out. It is possible to go out through a side door into the garden but also that it would be extremely difficult to scale the wall and get out of this garden without leaving traces of having done so.[4]

The Coroner said very broadly there were two main areas of blood, Group B - Sandra's blood - in the basement, and the Group A blood on the hall steps. Blood could be transferred - Sergeant Baker went down the basement stairs and it was necessary for him to pass through the blood on the stairs.

---

2   Well, I didn't and didn't waste any breath calling anything but saved it all for the run to the Plumber's Arms.
3   This proved that my husband could not have seen anyone attacking me in the basement whilst driving past the address.
4   The door was mostly kept unlocked so that we could call the cats in for meals.

Dr Pereira had suggested it would be 'a likely explanation' that I had walked through the basement, but it would not be compatible with what I had said. The Coroner reiterated that the bloodstaining on my shoes could have appeared there from walking through Sandra's blood, or it could have come from contact with soggy clothing.[5]

Dr Pereira's examination of the bloodstained length of lead piping from the hallway showed the blood to be Group AB, which could well be a mixture of blood from both women and suggested it was used to attack both Sandra and myself. Dr Pereira had found hairs on the piping which were similar to mine.

My husband had left Uckfield at about 1.15am on Friday, 8th November. A car he had borrowed a couple of weeks earlier was spotted parked at Newhaven at 8am on Friday morning. The police found it on the following Sunday and in the boot discovered a second piece of bandaged lead piping. Dr Thurston recalled in earlier evidence that the two pieces of lead pipe might have come from the same source, but not cut so as to be adjacent to each other. The adhesive tape which had been wrapped around each weapon was different. There were similarities between blood samples, hair and fibres found in the car and those found in my house.

The Coroner continued:

> You may feel it is possible that Mrs Rivett was not the objective of the assailant's attack. You have very seriously to consider the matter: "Was there an intruder which was mentioned by Lord Lucan?" The injuries on Lady Lucan and Mrs Rivett are similar. Both could have been caused by the same weapon. Lady Lucan describes herself as having been attacked without any doubt whatsoever by her husband.

Motive was a matter for conjecture, said Dr Thurston:

> There is the question of Lord Lucan's financial situation. There is no doubt that, as a result of the separation, he was having to keep two establishments going with all their outgoings. It could have eased his situation if he had only one establishment instead of two.

The Coroner told the jury:

---

5 I kicked him on his sodden flannels whilst we were fighting.

> I am going to ask you to retire. I do not think in this case, I can ask you to consider the question of accidental death.
>
> If you are satisfied on the evidence that there was an attack by another person, then your verdict would have to be murder.
>
> The second point is that you have to ascertain the person or persons, if any, to be charged with murder or manslaughter. And on the evidence you have got to decide whether you feel you can name the person responsible. You have got the facts before you, you have the possibility of an intruder, and you have got to consider what a very serious matter this is.

He referred to the possible 'stigma' that could accompany their verdict. Dr Thurston told them he would accept a majority verdict provided there were not more than two dissentients.

The six men and three women of the jury filed from the courtroom. They were out for thirty-one minutes. When they returned Dr Thurston asked for the verdict and the foreman stood up and said: "Murder by Lord Lucan."

The Coroner said "I will record that Sandra Eleanor Rivett died from head injuries, that at 10.30pm on 7th November 1974 she was found dead at 46 Lower Belgrave Street and that the following offence was committed by Richard John Bingham, Earl of Lucan - namely the offence of murder."

Then the jury was formally discharged.

I spoke briefly to Mr Roger Rivett and said how sorry I was, and then I was driven home in a police car with Detective Sergeant Forsyth. As I ran up the steps of 46 Lower Belgrave Street, an ITV reporter thrust his microphone in my face and said he was from the BBC. It didn't make any difference to me as my solicitor had given out a statement on my behalf, which I quote below:

> I am obviously very relieved that the Coroner's inquiry is over. I intend to put the past behind me so far as I can and continue to lead a family life. As to the inquiry, you have heard my evidence. My husband's interests were represented before the Coroner, and the jury have returned their verdict. I cannot say that I am pleased or displeased with the verdict. I was concerned only with establishing the facts.

That evening I was sickened to see, on the television news, my mother-in-law and sister-in-law careering down the street, following their exit from the Coroner's Court, screaming with laughter and being pursued by reporters and photographers having just heard the verdict "Murder by Lord Lucan."

Susan Maxwell-Scott gave an interview to the *News of the World* the following Sunday asking if I could have mistaken my husband for the killer. She wrote: "A person who's been hit over the head, possibly slightly concussed,[6] within an ace of being strangled and believes she might die, must be confused."[7]

Greville Howard, who had not appeared at the inquest as he was ill, made a statement to the police that he had had a conversation with my husband some months before, in which my husband had talked about getting rid of me and dumping my body in the Solent. He was apparently worried that our children might one day see him in court as a bankrupt. Greville Howard said it would be far worse for the children to see their father in court accused of murder. My husband had replied "But I wouldn't get caught."

Howard thought at the time such comments were drunken ramblings.

---

6   I was not concussed at all.
7   I was not confused at all and very clear in all my replies.

29

Imbroglio

The two older children were due to go to their respective boarding schools in the Autumn of 1975, and I could not help thinking what bad legal advice had been given to my husband, as we were to lose our children for most of the time very soon anyway.

I had a couple of meetings with my counsel but nothing seemed to ensue from the time spent. Although I had told Mr Justice Rees that my husband would have committed suicide, the difficulty remained that there was no proof that he was dead.

The Lucan family trusts were discretionary, and the Official Solicitor and Coutts, the trustees, decided to make my son the beneficiary. I received no advice about this, although I believe I should have been informed. Obviously, I thought that the trusts should have been treated as my husband's income and distributed to me, as his wife, for our maintenance. The Trustees were Messrs Coutts & Co.

I know that there was some hostility to me because of the unusual situation, and in those days people were a great deal more sexist than they are today.

I managed to get the 'Nanny Order' removed, despite opposition from the Official Solicitor. However, I still had to see the same doctor so I was still in a vulnerable position and left open to abuse.

Simon Swallow, my then solicitor, decided that I should obtain a decree of judicial separation from my husband. On 8th December 1975, as we were sitting in the Court, I read in a law book in front of me that a decree of judicial separation made the Will a nullity. I was horrified to read this, and drew my solicitor's attention to it.

Imbroglio

He advised that it was the right thing to do. However, Mr Justice Rees came to my aid and said that he could not see how somebody could be judicially separated from someone who might be dead. If this decree had been granted, every potential financial life-line I had would have been stripped away. My husband had made a Will in my favour two days before our marriage in November 1963.

Mr Gilson, my husband's trustee in bankruptcy, was easy to deal with and he allowed me to keep most of the items I chose before sending the rest for sale.

It was decided to sell 46 Lower Belgrave Street and I prepared to move into our mews house at 5 Eaton Row, which was behind but three houses down to the side of number 46. The house was sold and we moved into the mews house in January 1977 before this had been authorised, but I got a locksmith to open the front door. I had been paying the rates on the property and had also paid the electricity, gas and telephone bills left by the previous occupant.

The children were delighted by the way I had decorated the house, and when the Official Solicitor and his right hand man visited us in March 1977, he congratulated me on how comfortable I had made it.

However, I was in no doubt about the attitude of the Official Solicitor towards me, as his right hand man had yelled at me on one occasion: "The Official Solicitor doesn't give a damn about you!"

I had many letters from well-wishers which I very much appreciated, but one especially stayed in my mind. The writer was a woman and she warned me "You are not out of the wood yet." She was very right and what followed showed me the depth of feeling there was at the unusual situation that had transpired.

I had to see my GP whenever he wanted, and on 28th January 1977 he decided to change my prescription for Mogadon, a benzodiazepine sleeping pill, to Dalmane another benzodiazepine. The prescription was for 15mgs.

In July 1977 a complaint was made to the NSPCC about my ability to look after Camilla in a manner the complainant thought satisfactory. I co-operated with the NSPCC and discussed the matter with them. I was obviously horrified by this. I do not know who complained, but it was decided it was a malicious complaint and I was cleared of the allegation. When I told some of the other mothers who came to the Hurlingham Club with their children frequently, they were all very shocked and supportive.

The Official Solicitor's department always sent my maintenance cheques late and I realised that it was a ruse to destabilise me so I didn't worry, although I made a note of when I received them in my diary.

Mrs Greenslade still kept in touch, although I didn't need any more 'nannies' as my children were all at boarding school. The nanny order was removed. Mrs Greenslade would come after work on a Thursday or Friday, sometimes bringing flowers as well as alcohol. She usually brought a bottle of sherry. On 9th December, on a Friday, she arrived with a bottle of Marks and Spencer sherry and some cake from Justin de Blank, a well-known delicatessen.

I drank quite a lot of the sherry and she left. At nine o'clock that evening she rang me up and asked if I had eaten the cake. I said that I had eaten it, although I had thrown it away. I felt very ill for the next few days but managed to keep going, and I believe this was the first attempt to render me ill so that the children would have to spend Christmas with the Shand Kydds.

On 20th December 1977 I got my prescription for Dalmane from the doctor's surgery. This was the first time that I had obtained a prescription from his surgery. It was now for 30mgs instead of 15mgs as previously, but no discussion about this uprate took place between me and the doctor. I should have asked why he had increased the dose, but I didn't.

On Monday, 23rd January 1978, I received a prescription for 100 Dalmane - this was the second from his surgery. On Friday, 31st March I received my third prescription for Dalmane from the surgery.

Arthur Jones had obtained a job at The Fine Art Trade Guild, very close to where I lived and I used to go and help him, which involved typing. It provided some intellectual stimulation for me. I was subjected to long convoluted letters from the Official Solicitor - sometimes three a week - but the green file in which they were kept has been removed from my house. I went to the Fine Art Trade Guild, to help Arthur Jones and for something to do.

The year 1978 was the year that I was horrifically medically abused with steroids in conjunction with benzodiazepines. My health was damaged for the next ten years, and I became involuntarily addicted to prescribed drugs until 1984. A bruise remained on my leg for weeks and eventually appeared to run. A change had taken place in my blood. On 26th June, I visited the doctor's surgery, accompanied by George. I remarked that Dalmane was addictive but he ignored me and drew George's attention to some soldiers, which he had already seen before, and then handed me a plastic container with the capsules loosely placed inside and labelled DALNAE.

I became very tired and found it difficult to lift anything heavy like my IBM typewriter and my eyes seemed to be giving me trouble when I did any work for the Fine Art Trade Guild. I noticed my parotid gland on my right side moving up and down. Sweat, which had previously appeared under my arms, was transferred to my feet and my tights became stained because of this. If I ran downstairs, my muscles in my calves seemed to almost give way. I started to wake up very early despite taking the sleeping pill, Dalmane (Flurazepam).

In July 1978, my mother-in-law tried to get the Criminal Law Act 1977 retrospectively applied to my husband's case but was not successful. The purpose of this was to remove the stigma of my husband being legally described as a murderer. The right of an inquest jury to name anyone a murderer was abolished in 1977.

I then received a letter from Bill Shand Kydd, informing me that there were no funds to meet George's school fees for Summer Fields in the Autumn term and enclosing the bill for £673.10.

I was beginning to lose my memory, and suddenly I realised that it was possibly the 'Dalnae' that was causing my symptoms, and stopped taking it immediately. I had the most appalling headache for several days, and my eyes receded deep into my head. The orbital fat behind my eyes had gone.

I drove to Moreton-in-Marsh in the Cotswolds and stayed in a bed and breakfast there. I took the children with me. I could not find my womb and the muscles in my breasts caused them to stand up in a most surprising manner. However, I had not had a holiday for a very long time and so I think that the fresh air caused me to survive the first impact of the withdrawal.

On 28th September 1978, I attended at the Official Solicitor's Chambers with Camilla. Camilla did not go to school in the afternoon which is why I took her with me, and she used to make very interesting observations about situations. I wrote a letter to the trustees requested by the Official Solicitor, which asked Coutts & Co. to exercise their discretionary powers under the terms of the Marriage Settlement for the education, maintenance and benefit of my two daughters during their respective minorities. After I had written the letter, the Official Solicitor asked about the Summer Fields bill of £673.10 and I told him that I had dealt with it. He said "Oh, you paid it," and seemed disappointed.

On Monday, 2nd October, I saw my GP at his request and he decided to give me what he described as a 'vitamin injection'. He also gave me a prescription for 30mgs Mogadon as I had told him that 'Dalmane' did not 'suit' me and would like to change. He also took a sample of my blood.

He said he would like to see me again on Monday, 9th October at 2.30pm. He said he wanted to give me another 'vitamin injection'. Following this my eyes came out again and I started sweating normally.[1]

On Friday, 3rd November I was given 100 Mogadon from the practice nurse, Janet and 20 Redoxon. I felt rather sick as I was withdrawing from the benefits of the 'vitamin injection' or cortisone. I had an appointment with my dental hygienist and it appeared that she knew of the abuse and remarked on my skin, which had changed.[2]

---

[1] Dr Creightmore later told me that it was probably an injection of cortisone - the effects lasted a month.

[2] Efcortelan cream was later prescribed as shown in the doctor's letter of 17th March 1981.

On 22nd November I had a letter from my former solicitor J. Elliott Brooks informing me that I had to pay my own costs for the custody case, as the bankruptcy would not accept that my husband should be liable. On the 28th I gave him a cheque for £2,000 and asked for time to pay the remainder, which he allowed. He said the outstanding balance on their ledger was £2,029.

On 14th December I received a letter from my then solicitor, whom the Official Solicitor had told me he 'approved' of, saying that money was to be paid to Denis Gilson (Bankruptcy) from out of the Marriage Settlement - rather a large sum, £4,000. My written consent was not required and I began to think that I was being represented by someone the Official Solicitor knew in order to legitimise whatever he decided to do, and, on the face of it, all seeming to be above board. My best interests were not being considered although I had a solicitor, but I was not receiving independent legal advice.

On Saturday, 16th December, I discovered that most of my photographs and negatives stored in a cardboard box in the garage were missing. I was devastated and went to the police at Gerald Road where I saw a Detective Sergeant Bradley and reported this serious loss. The only time I left the house was in the afternoon when it was dusk to collect Camilla from the Francis Holland School in Graham Terrace. There was only a Yale lock. The police wondered why they had been taken, as the photographs were so easily recognisable and therefore traceable. I now believe that, as the police were in constant touch with the Shand Kydds, one of the detectives assigned to the case removed them and stored them with the Shand Kydds for George's eventual benefit.

I remember writing a letter to the Official Solicitor saying that I was concerned that he collectively referred to the trustees and himself as "we" in view of the trustees' rather hasty sale of 46 Lower Belgrave Street, and that perhaps he should be standing back and looking at them with a rather jaundiced eye. I said that I had noted that the officer concerned with the sale had been moved to a different department in the bank.

People used to stop me in the street and say things like "You were done over your house." The price paid had been widely publicised and I had been very disappointed.

On 11th January 1979 I applied for a form called Notice of Change of Solicitor, which I completed but did not name any solicitor to represent me in future.

On 16th January I ran for a bus and was completely exhausted. It was as though my adrenal glands were not working properly. Running had been a speciality of mine. I was now often sweating and feeling ill. I discussed this with my two younger children, and I decided to ring my GP, who made a home visit on 10th February, which was a Saturday, and we faced him and told him what we believed. Guilt was written all over his face. Camilla said "She couldn't have had a vitamin C deficiency, she has satsumas every day." George said "That last lot of Dalmane seemed to put the lid on it."

On the Sunday, the doctor came in the evening about 11pm. On the following Wednesday he gave me an injection which caused pain, and on Friday, 16th February 1979 the nurse Janet gave me an injection intravenously of an anti-psychotic drug which gave me the extrapyramidals, a horrible side effect. He then recommended Micronor, which is specifically contra-indicated for endocrine disorders and is a contraceptive pill.

On the 22nd, Pam Francis from the *Daily Star* recommended a Dr Robert Lefever, and I consulted him and he took me on as a patient. I did not inform the Official Solicitor.

I told a friend called Dawn Robb that I believed that I had been medically abused and she obtained an appointment for me with her doctor, Dr James Bevan. I told him about my symptoms and he said that he did not know if I could withstand the chemical disorder within my body and would like my permission to discuss this with my doctor, which I did not want to do as he would inform the Official Solicitor.

On 10th March, my doctor prescribed two Parstelin to be taken each day, together with some more Valium. Parstelin has now been removed from the list of drugs allowed to be prescribed in this country by the Committee for Safety of Medicines. It caused hypertensive crises, but I was now taking the drug regularly before this diktat.

On 21st March I saw my doctor again for a home visit. He was bullying as usual but suggested that I see Richard Bayliss, a well-known endocrinologist. We had rather a shouting match, which was overheard by Camilla.

On 23rd March I received a letter from the Official Solicitor saying that he had heard from my GP and that he was anxious on the children's behalf, and would I contact him, which I did. I went immediately to his office, arriving there at 9.15am having dropped Camilla off at school, but he was on the way out. He asked me to wait, and his secretary went to get me a cup of coffee. While he was away the telephone on her desk rang rather insistently so I picked it up, to hear my brother-in-law saying, without preamble, "Has Lady Lucan been certified yet?"

I was horrified, but I let him think that I was the Official Solicitor's secretary and said: "The Official Solicitor is out of the office at the moment" and put the receiver down. When his secretary returned with a cup of coffee, I told her what had happened and when the Official Solicitor returned she told him about this "mishap". He seemed very annoyed that this had taken place and said "Oh, Mr Shand Kydd's language!"[3]

Fortunately, thanks to Pam Francis I had already got another doctor, Dr Robert Lefever, who immediately sent a letter saying that in his opinion I was medically fit.

On 9th March I saw Dr Flood at home for the last time as he died shortly afterwards. He had said that he would one day tell me what he thought of the doctors I had seen during my marriage, but sadly he was never able to do this.

---

[3] My brother-in-law should have said, "Has Lady Lucan been "sectioned" yet?"

30

Imbroglio Continued

On 2nd May 1979, I saw Frankie McGowan from the *Evening News* and I gave her an interview, which was published on 8th May 1979, headed:

> THE VOICE SAID: HAS SHE BEEN CERTIFIED?
> Why I'm living in fear, by Lady Lucan

Frankie McGowan's exclusive ran as follows:

> In the five years since her husband's disappearance, Lady Lucan has been attempting to rebuild her life and the lives of her three children into something resembling normality.
>
> It is an effort that is, according to Lady Lucan, being constantly thwarted by repeated attempts to either prove she is incapable of caring for her children or that she is insane. This week, once again, she is in fear that such a move may succeed. She is bewildered by it all, the inevitable strain of living under such uncertainty is beginning to tell.
>
> Mentally she is totally alert, physically her appearance has changed in the past two years. Her hair is streaked with grey, her face is pale and drawn.
>
> The house in Belgravia has gone and she and her three children have moved around the corner to a small mews house where the blinds are tightly closed and Lady Lucan who is now 47, keeps everything going where once nannies and daily helps were readily available to her.
>
> "I am coping and the children have settled down well into their new life, we don't harm anyone or seek anyone out, so I can't understand why these constant attempts are made to separate us," she said.

RECOVERING

"I am not imagining it when I say that I know beyond doubt that there is a plan in operation to have me certified mentally incapable of caring for them."

"It was a chance in a million that I heard about it and I'm still recovering from the shock of it."

"I have had a very difficult relationship with my doctor for the past two years ever since I gave a newspaper interview about the circumstances surrounding my marriage and in which I made some adverse comments about some of the medical profession."

"My doctor was clearly annoyed and our relationship declined to such an extent that on March 21st I removed myself from his care."

"I didn't see him that often, just for things like sleeping pills, the odd cold. The children hardly ever."

"But on the day following our final rather difficult interview I had a letter from the Official Solicitor saying he had heard from the doctor and that he was anxious on the children's behalf and would I contact him."

Her instincts, she said, made her extremely concerned when the letter arrived.

"I went immediately to the Official Solicitor's Office arriving there at 9.15am, having dropped Camilla at school, but he was on his way out."

"However, he told me to wait and his secretary went to get me a cup of coffee. While she was away the phone on her desk rang rather incessantly so I picked it up, to hear a voice say: "This is Mr Shand Kydd. Is the certification order on Lady Lucan ready yet?"

ANNOYED

"I nearly collapsed. I didn't say anything."

"I let him think I was the secretary. As far as I know he has no idea he spoke to me. The Official Solicitor was obviously very annoyed that this had taken place and said 'Oh Mr Shand Kydd's language.'"

"No one had bothered to tell me of this latest development. Fortunately I already had another doctor who immediately sent a letter to the Official Solicitor saying in his opinion I was mentally fit."

The Lucans had three children before Lord Lucan disappeared in 1974 after their family's nanny was killed. He is wanted for her murder.

Lady Lucan said the children are aware of all the facts surrounding her husband's disappearance but they don't think he is dead.

"They think he's living in, oh, South America or somewhere."

FABRICATION

"What do I think? Well, how can you be sure of anything? His body has never been washed up, it is possible that he is alive somewhere."

Mr Bill Shand Kydd, whose wife Christina is Lady Lucan's sister, said: "On the day she mentions when I phoned the Official Solicitor's Office, I said nothing about certification. I wouldn't discuss that sort of thing with the secretary anyway. I just said: "Is the Official Solicitor there" and the voice which answered said he was busy.

"The family certainly hasn't cut her off. That is a complete fabrication. She has cut herself off from us.

"She doesn't reply to letters, she doesn't even open the door when we go round to deliver presents for the children and we have to leave them at the house opposite.

"She has always been very welcome and we would like to see more of the children but she appears to want to keep the children apart from the rest of the family."

Following the publication of this story in the *Evening News*, on 11th May 1979 I received a letter from the Official Solicitor, who was obviously annoyed by this. He wrote, "And I thought I had made it clear that I did not contemplate any application to the Court about care and control of the children. The passing of time since we met without any application being made should afford further reassurance were any needed."

On 6th July, the Official Solicitor wrote that the income received was now considerably enhanced because of the Re-Settlement of the English Estate. This was good news as it would improve our stringent living standards.

My hair kept falling out and was very greasy, so I had to wash it every day. At night my heart kept pounding and I kept dreaming and did not have a decent night's sleep even after taking two Dalmane and, of course, I was still taking two Parstelin each day.

My friend Arthur Jones formed an alliance with a Dr John Baksh, MB BS FRCS (Edin), of 79 William Barefoot Drive, Eltham, SE9, who prescribed Parstelin and Dalmane willingly for a fee. He was later convicted of murdering his wife Ruby and went to prison. He had told his second wife "I murdered Ruby for you. It was the animal in me." I thought this story was interesting.

On 22nd October 1979, the *Daily Mirror* published an article by John Penrose entitled 'New Riddles Of The Missing Earl', which referred to the theft of my photographs. Part of this article read:

> Police assured Lady Lucan that it was unlikely that anyone would take the pictures - so easily identifiable and traceable - for publication. Why then should the pictures be stolen? Did someone take them to destroy? Or were they taken and passed on to someone? Lady Lucan said, "I have no idea who took the photographs. There were four keys to the door and I had them all. The police found no sign of a break-in."

Sir John Arnold became President of the Family Division. He was the judge who gave the first order *ex parte* for my children to be removed from my care.

I saw Dr Lefever on Monday, 5th November 1979, and he told me that my eyes would "never come back." Obviously I had hoped that the maiming could be corrected and my eyes returned to normal.

Stuart Kuttner recommended a Dr Joy Edelman, who arranged for me to have tests at the Wellington Hospital and the Pathology Department, and discovered my corticosteroids were not quite normal. I still had tetany, and sweat kept pouring off my head and neck.

On Friday, 19th September 1980, I had an appointment with the police together with Arthur Jones and made a complaint about my former doctor, and they took samples of my hair and noted that I was putting on weight. I saw the police again on 22nd September and again on Thursday, 2nd October 1980.

I wrote less and less in my diary as I became more and more dependent on Parstelin. Arthur Jones made friends with some nurses at St Thomas's and I was introduced to Professor Sonkson, who headed a relevant department and who offered to take me into St Thomas's as a patient and take me off Parstelin, but as I feared losing custody of my three children I could not take up his offer.

I now quote from a letter written by my former doctor to my brother-in-law Bill Shand Kydd, dated 17th March 1981:

A Moment in Time

PRIVATE & CONFIDENTIAL

Bill Shand-Kydd Esq
235 Vauxhall Bridge Road
London S W 1

17th March 1981

Dear Bill

This letter is entirely off the record.

From March 1977 until October 1978 Veronica had a number of repeat prescriptions of Dalmane but I did not see her. The following is a list of the dates that I saw her and what I prescribed:-

2.10.78	Parentrovite & Vitamin B 12 injection. Mogadon Tabs and Redoxon Tabs
	1% Efcortelan cream
9.10.78	Parentrovite & Vitamin B 12 injection
10.2.79	Home visit
11.2.79	Parentrovite & Vitamin B 12 injection
	Tabs Mogadon x 30
19.2.79	Office visit
24.2.79	Depixol injection (refused Stelazine)
26.2.79	Parentrovite & Vitamin B 12 injection
	Haliperidol 0.5 mg ii bd x 50
1.03.79	Haliperidol 0.5 mg x 100 Inderal 40 mg at night
	Mogadon i-ii at night x 100
	Parentrovite & Vitamin B 12 injection
6.03.79	Seen by me at a friend's house in Napier Avenue
9.03.79	Home visit
10.3.79	Valium 10 mgs injection
	Parstellin 2 in morning
11.3.79	Valium 10 mgs injection
12.3.79	Valium 10 mgs injection
14.3.79	Valium 10 mgs injection
16.3.79	Valium 10 mgs injection
19.3.79	Valium 10 mgs injection
21.3.79	Home visit

That is absolutely everything that she had over this period which started with her intense anxiety as to her state of health and finished with her answering the telephone to you in the Official Solicitor's office.

> Veronica is quite right about the bill, which fits in with our rate of charges at that time.
> Yours sincerely,

The injection given intravenously to me by Janet the practice nurse on 16th February 1979 is not listed.

This letter confirms the *Evening News* interview and stated that I had indeed picked up a telephone in the Official Solicitor's office to hear my brother-in-law Bill Shand Kydd say "Has Lady Lucan been certified yet?" I removed this letter from the Shand Kydd's house.

I wrote to the law firm Pannone Napier in September 1989 enclosing a copy of the doctor's letter, and they replied that my letter was of interest because my former General Practitioner provided with repeat prescriptions without clinical reassessment.

They confirmed that they were one of six firms who comprised the Steering Committee of the Benzodiazepine Solicitors Group, who co-ordinated the actions for damages, investigated the legal issues and pursued the claims against the defendants.

As I do not qualify for legal aid, I was unable to pursue my claim for damages.

31
Conspiracy

Despite hearing my brother-in-law asking if I had been 'certified' yet, I allowed my children to see the Shand Kydds and also to visit. We lived in a tiny mews house which had only two bedrooms, and so during the school holidays we were very cramped. Camilla stayed with them and was able to learn to ride and attend their local Pony Club, which she enjoyed.

I feared that they would still try to obtain custody of my children but hoped that they wouldn't, although they had done so whilst I was lying in hospital with head injuries following the attack in November 1974. Unfortunately, I was still very addicted to Parstelin, which is not an easy drug to withdraw from. The pills were small, and being round and shiny were difficult to cut into pieces, which if I had been able to do so could have helped my withdrawal from the drug.

There was something within the drug which caused me to put on weight, and I had to wear smocks in order to hide my swollen stomach.

I remember Camilla telling me that George did not love me as much as he could, and indeed I did notice that he was not a very affectionate son. My relationship with Frances had never recovered from the influence of Nanny Jenkins, who disapproved of my role in teaching my children to read, but I do believe that the amount of publicity I had been subjected to was a factor in alienating me from the older two children.

Things started to come to a head in 1982. George used to go off on my bicycle during the school holidays to see his "friends," as he described them. I was later to discover he was visiting the Shand Kydds, who still lived when in London in Broomhouse Road, SW6. Then Frances, who was by then 17-years-old, told me one day that she was "getting out of here" and she left to stay with a friend, although I didn't know where. Later I discovered that at this time she had also been liaising with the Shand Kydds, and the result of this liaison came later.

It was in October 1982 that I received an affidavit from the Official Solicitor with allegations about my inability to cope with the children, and quoting George as saying he would "Find it much more congenial to live as part of the family of his aunt and uncle."

The Shand Kydds had succeeded in their long term objective and sustained campaign to obtain custody of the two younger children, although not Frances as she was eighteen years of age on 24th October 1982. Camilla was due to come home for half-term that October weekend, and so I told her on the telephone and she was succinct in her response. "Disgusting," she said. I didn't attend the court hearing and I didn't apply for access either. My brother-in-law Bill Shand Kydd has been quoted as saying, "It was hard work, but we got there eventually." The children were then of an age to choose where they wanted to live and they did.

Parental alienation syndrome was strongly at work because of the Shand Kydds' attitude towards me. I was, however, now free to attempt to be taken off Parstelin, and it had to be done by narcosis. I was put to sleep for about a week, and when I came to I had withdrawn from Parstelin, but the sudden chemical change caused me to lose weight suddenly. I left the hospital but they didn't send on my chequebook or money, and so I stopped eating and became very ill and was admitted to Banstead Hospital in Surrey. I stayed at the hospital for seven months and very slowly started to recover. The only drug I was given was Ativan, a benzodiazepine which is not a drug with nasty side effects.

It was planned by social workers to place me in a hostel for mentally ill persons locally. Although there was a conflict of interest as he was guardian ad litem of the wards, the Official Solicitor appointed himself my receiver while I was at the hospital and no doubt had a hand in this decision. I managed to escape from the hospital and returned to 5 Eaton Row. I discovered both property and documents had been removed in my absence, probably by my son. As he had not reached seventeen, he was unable to drive and so must have been accompanied by someone, probably my sister, to be able to remove my property and take it away. He must have stored it with them at Grange Villa, the house where they lived in South West London.

I wrote to my son's solicitors and there followed much correspondence, but finally I hired a chauffeur-driven limousine with a large boot and collected some of the stolen items from the solicitor. Sadly my documents, custody case papers, transcripts of my custody case, photographs and personal correspondence have never been returned despite repeated requests.

I reported these thefts to the police - Crime Book Entry E492 - on Saturday, 19th September 1987, and visited Gerald Road Police Station on 7th December 1987 when I saw a detective inspector and another police officer. The whole interview was most unsatisfactory. No-one could have any claim to my documents (or indeed my property), but no action was taken by the police to retrieve it.

The police knew that my son had my property but were reluctant to do anything about it. It was particularly distressing as I learnt that he was taking the view that my husband was not guilty of the murder of Mrs Sandra Rivett. I had never had a conversation with him or with any of my children about the circumstances surrounding the murder. I have no idea what their thought processes were. I think that they liked the thought of living with the Shand Kydds. They were, in effect, encouraged to go.

I was surprised to learn that my son was taking a sabbatical from the Bank where he worked, and apparently he spent six months going to libraries in order to read the books written about his father. The one person he should have been discussing his father with was me, not those who had written books for commercial reasons and had never met him. Apparently he became obsessed with the murder, and annoyed those who knew him at the time for harping on and on about it.

On 10th September 1998, my son was arrested for causing actual bodily harm to his girlfriend, Imogen Brewer. The charges were later dropped. I learnt about this from reports in the press.

I was surprised at the content of his interview with William Sitwell in 1998 and Andrew Dagnell in 2012. I quote below, firstly from William Sitwell's interview:

> He also reached the emphatic conclusion that his father was not guilty of the murder of Sandra Rivett, the young woman who had the fatal misfortune to be in the wrong house working for the wrong people at absolutely the wrong time.
>
> George has no memory of her. He says, "We had a lot of nannies as children and Sandra had only been there for a few weeks. I feel guilty because I have never contacted her parents, but by the time I was an adult, I would only have raised old wounds."

The following is an extract from his interview with Andrew Dagnell in 2012:

> While the loss of his father was difficult, somehow George says the sudden loss of his beloved nanny seemed more heartbreaking at the time. With genuine fondness, George says, "My relationship with Sandra was very good. She was lovely. From time to time, I used to bundle into her bed and crawl under the sheets with her. She was very maternal which I appreciated. She hadn't been with us for very long, only six to nine months. But she was a lovely woman."

Following my escape from Banstead Hospital, I had quite a struggle to re-establish myself after spending seven months away. I also had to wean myself off Ativan at once, which was extremely difficult. An Express Dairies milk float came early every morning so I was able to buy milk, bread, orange juice and eggs, and I managed to survive on this. Eventually, the hospital returned my chequebook and I was able to obtain money and arrange for food to be delivered to the house as I was suffering from plantyfashyitis (inflammation of the heels), which the hospital had mistaken for arthritis.

My friend Arthur Jones contacted me and came to see me. He had apparently visited Banstead Hospital in the hope of seeing me but had been told that I had returned home.

He told me about an item that had appeared in Nigel Dempster's Diary column in the *Daily Mail* dated Friday, 9th November 1984 headed 'Family Fear over Lady Lucan'. The content began: "All attempts by the family of the Countess of Lucan to maintain contact are being shunned..."

My brother-in-law Bill Shand Kydd is quoted as saying:

> Christina goes round there [to 5 Eaton Row] on a regular basis to see that Veronica is all right and is in constant touch with the local police station at Gerald Road. Veronica does not answer telephone calls or the doorbell and we are worried.

The picture editor has shown a photograph of my brother-in-law and sister laughing and drinking, and humorously captioned the photograph: "Bill and Christina: "We are worried."

It is quite true that I did not answer the door or answer the telephone. Arthur Jones rang Gerald Road Police Station and enquired of the chief police officer in charge about this, and was told "She's been no trouble on my patch."

It was astonishing that my sister should be in contact with the police about me (putting the rozzers on her sister!), but it confirmed to me that they were infuriated by my return to 5 Eaton Row and had wanted me to remain under 'supervision'. It was also clear to me that my children were being influenced to an alarming degree by the Shand Kydds. The Shand Kydds used Nigel Dempster as a conduit for providing information about my family.

In October 1985, Nicholas Boyce was accused and tried at the Old Bailey for murdering his wife Christabel, our one-time temporary nanny. The couple had two children but Nicholas, a science graduate, was unable to find gainful employment, much to Christabel's anger. They had enormous rows and during one of these, he head-butted her and she fell back, very dead. Boyce, distraught at the thought of leaving the children orphans, cooked Christabel's body in the oven and then distributed her remaining parts in skips around London. He could not deal with her head in the same way, so he covered it in concrete and dropped it into the Thames whilst walking with the children over Hungerford Bridge.

The police, however, suspected him and told him in words to the effect "We know you did it. Tell us what you've done with her and we'll see you get a lesser sentence." Boyce complied and police divers retrieved her entombed skull from the Thames. Boyce was sentenced to four years for manslaughter. I think this is interesting as Christabel took such a large part in my story.

Two books on the Lucan affair were published in 1987. *Lucan, Not Guilty* by Sally Moore was the most comprehensive, but as she had an impossible brief, as indicated by the title of her book, it is full of distortions and inaccuracies. She did not ask me for an interview, although she untruthfully states that she did. The other book, *Trail of Havoc* by Patrick Marnham, was padded out with other material not relating to the Lucan affair, presumably to make it a more substantial read.

I was very much kept out of the loop, but on 11th December 1992, Mr Justice Morritt of the High Court Chancery Division gave the Trustees of the then Lord Bingham (the 7th Earl's heir as regards the titles) liberty to administer the 7th Earl's (settled) estate under the presumption that he was dead; in addition, leave was granted to have the 7th Earl's death sworn in the High Court Family Division. My son could have styled himself 8th Earl of Lucan thereafter.

On 8th December 1998 Lord Bingham/the 8th Earl applied to the Lord Chancellor for a writ of summons to the House of Lords as Baron Bingham, of Melcombe Bingham, Co. Dorset, but was refused at the end of July 1999. He had not made out his case.

Probate was granted on 11th August 1999 and is not an official confirmation of death for all purposes; nor does it operate as if it were a death certificate. The grant is valid for probate purposes only, and is a technical requirement for the administration of the subject's estate.

I gave a copy of the grant to a reporter from *The Times* on 26th October 1999 as it was a matter of public record. By coincidence, the Hereditary Peers lost their Voting and Sitting rights at about the same time by a 140 majority.

Channel 4 produced a documentary entitled *The Hunt for Lord Lucan* in 2004. My son took part in the film and implied that my husband had been part of an insurance scam which had gone fatally wrong. The film was defamatory, as it impugned the evidence I gave at the inquest on Mrs Sandra Rivett in June 1973.

I produce my comments on the film below.

Part I

I was not hit on the head from behind but from in front, and my late husband thrust three gloved fingers down my throat, not two as stated on the programme. I was not covered in blood from head to foot. Mr Arthur Whitehouse's statement confirms this.

Only my late husband's rather more disreputable gambling associates called him 'Lucky'. This started around 1967.

Colin Ingleby-Mackenzie, who takes a rather large part in this film, was not a gambler. He was a cricketer and worked in insurance or something similar. He pretends in the film that he participated in the exploits of my husband's gambling associates, but he didn't. He occasionally played golf with my husband at weekends, and I cannot recall that we ever had dinner with him.

A police officer, Lewis Benjamin, suggests there may have been "some confusion" on my part, but the police officers at the time who interviewed me noted how clear and precise I was about the events of the night of 7th November 1974. It was indeed an "open and shut case".

Part II

My son George appears and suggests that my late husband's friends were toying with the media. Those disreputable people had never had so much publicity in their lives and appeared to revel in it, and so I would agree with his assessment on this point.

I have never heard of the rather rotund man called Richard Wall, who pretends he knows a great deal more than he actually does and bangs rather boringly on about being working class and about aristocrats. There were very few aristocrats involved in the case at all.

Colin Ingleby-Mackenzie described my husband as being popular at Eton, which he wasn't. He made very few friends at Eton. It is a huge school and it is possible to be at the school at the same time as someone else but not know them at all unless they were in your House at Eton.

Caroline Hill was a girlfriend in the 1950s but not one in the "lovey-dovey" sense. She did not marry herself until the late 1970s, after my late husband's disappearance. My husband was so in need of having people to listen to his complaints about injustice and me that anyone he could dredge up from the past who would fulfil this need came back into his life. Caroline Hill was a piano teacher and for a couple of months she gave Frances piano lessons.

Billy Edgson, the doorman at the Clermont Club at the time of the murder, appeared saying he did odd jobs for my husband which indeed he did, and was probably well paid for them.

Ingleby-Mackenzie said that my husband was "mad about his children." Well, I think one should consider this in the light of what transpired later. It is an earl's main function to raise the next generation, and I think his position was very well put by John Aspinall, who said "He loved his children not as you or I would love our children, but as his descendants."

My sister-in-law's intemperate comments followed and I think she discredited herself by saying such spiteful and untrue things. I have forgotten what spiteful and untrue things she said but her rant began "We thought she was a pathetic little person…"

I have endured films abusing me and newspaper articles vilifying me for many years, and so I don't think anyone could accuse me of mental instability. I have had to endure these injustices without the support of my family, which I think is disgraceful. I do not know why they did not support me more.

Part III

Colin Ingleby-Mackenzie appears again. I think we must all have gathered by now that my husband was chasing his losses at the gaming tables after the custody case. I was interested to learn that Caroline Hill thought that I became a focus for him in his agony, which is a possibility. At least, Ingleby-Mackenzie does agree that my husband made "a complete bog of it," referring to the murder of Mrs Rivett.

My son George appears again, looking rather shifty I thought, with some further absurd statements. The only reason Frances was up watching television as late as 9pm was that she had not gone to school that day as the school bus had not come for her, and so she had spent the day at home with her nanny Sandra Rivett, whom she liked. Usually she disliked the nannies. My husband could not have known about this internal arrangement.

I would agree with my son's statement that my husband had wanton disregard for our children's welfare. He took such a risk, which if it went wrong (and it did) would impact on his children, and for the rest of their lives as it turned out, as well as ruining mine to an even greater extent.

Billy Edgson appeared again saying that my late husband had arrived outside the Clermont Club at a quarter to nine (unlikely) and had asked if Charles Benson or Greville Howard were in the Club.

My son then addresses himself to the inadequacy of the weapon my late husband used to carry out the murder, suggesting a glass ashtray, or cricket bat would have been a better choice. The fact is, my husband chose the weapon he did and bandaged it because he did not know that heads bleed more than any other part of the body. I don't know if my husband actually rained 15 odd blows or more on Mrs Rivett, but he certainly rained many.

My husband told me that my solicitor had written to him asking for his financial proposals as we would have been separated for two years in January. This was the motivating factor. I have shown that he discovered that he had murdered the wrong woman when he was still in the basement.

There was more comment that DNA wasn't around in 1974/75 but, although this is true, it really wasn't necessary in the Lucan case as it was an 'open and shut' case. Nothing has been discovered from the alleged fingerprint found on the bludgeon. The police explained to Sally Moore that they had tried to get the bludgeon examined down at Harwell to see if there were latent fingerprints on it. And although there were finger marks, the examination was thwarted by the stretching of the adhesive tape. The binding of the adhesive material had stretched any fingerprints out of recognition.

Anthony Scrivener QC then appears, and insults all former and present psychiatric patients by implying because they have experienced such treatment, it makes their testimony in a court of law unreliable. Indeed, my testimony was never tested at a trial because my husband absconded and so no trial was ever held. I think my evidence was clear and unequivocal, and I answered all the questions put to me. I would not have been allowed to give evidence at any trial of my husband because as his wife, I would not be a competent witness.

My son George then appears and gives some rather unconvincing reasons as to why he thinks his father was not guilty of the attack and murder of Mrs Rivett. It was all rather confused. He talked vaguely of an insurance fraud, the piping was planted to suggest a broken entry, and he suggested that the bludgeon covered in bandage was to reduce the noise. He then described his father as tapping his hands on the dashboard and going into the house to investigate.

He then further describes me as being in tremendous shock (I wasn't, I fought back immediately), claiming 'by her own admission' - where have I admitted this? He said I was on heavy-duty prescription medicines, which I most certainly wasn't. That statement is particularly wicked in the light of the subsequent medical abuse I received, and the suffering I endured as a result of this abuse, which he and his sisters had first hand knowledge of. Their silence in the face of this points to the undue influence of their aunt and uncle, who have told them that the "waters can be muddied" and doubts can prevail.

He then attempts to cast doubts on what he describes as a conversation lasting 40 minutes. As I have often explained, I left the second floor bedroom at approximately 9.15pm, went downstairs and encountered my husband, and we fought probably until 9.25pm and then had a conversation before going up to the second floor bedroom when I seized my opportunity to escape whilst he was in the bathroom getting a cloth to clean up my face. I then ran down the stairs and out of the front door, turning left to run the 30 yards to the Plumber's Arms, where Mr Arthur Whitehouse described in his statement for the police that the door burst open at 9.50pm and in I came.

Chester Stern then talks further nonsense saying my husband was probably alive and living in Africa. My husband was NOT fluent in German as Chester Stern states. In fact, his command of foreign languages was extremely poor. I also learnt German at school but if you don't keep it up by speaking it every day you lose it although you may still be able to read some of it.

A reporter with a vested interest stated that he thought my husband was "revelling in the mystery he had created." Here, again, you see someone who is so far removed from the class of person he is writing about that he does not realise that my husband was a proud man who would not want to live as anything other than the 7th Earl of Lucan.

My son George appeared again to say that he believed his father to have died some 12 hours after the murder, and his intuition told him that he believed his father died in London. He used the phrase "to be honest", rather unfortunate in the circumstances.

There was talk about a full scale review, how important this was for police, and that they conduct a relentless pursuit etc, saying that the investigation fell well short of what a reasonable public could expect. They are really implying that before DNA techniques were developed, most murders were not properly investigated, which of course they were. It is all grist to their mill to justify them for taking part in the film.

There followed a few vague glimpses of my husband with a child, all to imply what a hands-on father he had been. However, until he conducted a 'legal kidnap' in March 1973, he very rarely saw our three children as he was always occupied with his gambling activities. After the custody case, he had 'compulsory' access, or contact as it is now known, and then saw more of them.

I think the whole film lacked balance and I could hear the sound of grinding axes throughout.

32

In Conclusion

Recently, Wikipedia started a new category called 'Featured Article Candidate' and chose my husband. I was not allowed to edit and will not be allowed to do so, as I have been 'blocked'. Those who are allowed to edit rely on books that have been published about my husband over the years and which are very inaccurate.

As I am now eighty years of age, I have taken this opportunity to try to 'set the record straight' by writing a book and giving my side of the story before it is too late.

I think it is wrong that my children have withheld my property. I was upset that I was not told about Camilla's impending marriage to be held at St Peter's Eaton Square, because it set the press on me without warning. I gave an interview to the *Sunday Times* about this. I was in my sixties and so shocked that it is fortunate that I didn't have a heart attack.

My daughter announced her engagement in *The Times* as "Younger daughter of the 7th Earl of Lucan wheresoever and the Countess of Lucan," although she knew that her father had been presumed deceased in December 1992. This piece of bad manners was followed a few months later by yet more, as she failed to invite me to her wedding held at a church a stone's throw from my house in Eaton Row. The press were told and when I walked past the church, which I had to do, they rushed out saying "Lady Lucan, Lady Lucan, it's your daughter." My daughter used my residential address to have a service of blessing and then did not invite me. Such lack of respect for anyone is disgraceful. She untruthfully told the vicar, the Rev

In Conclusion

Desmond Tillyer, that she had invited me.

As for my chances of remarriage in the years following my separation from my husband, I cannot think that any sensible man would want to take on three young children, a bankrupt husband who had absconded and me, even if I wanted such a thing. It was difficult enough to find a husband the first time. How on earth could I start a new life with all this baggage, not to mention the tape recording!

Arthur Jones was not a marriageable prospect. We were not lovers. We had remained friends until his death some twenty years after our first meeting in the Strand in 1973. Camilla benefitted from my friendship with Arthur Jones, who provided her with male attention as well. He used to help her with her homework and projects, and even wrote some of her lines for her. He lived in Dolphin Square, and arranged a birthday party using the swimming pool there as the focal point of the party.

I think I have shown that my son decided he wanted to live as part of another family. I received an affidavit sent through the post, dated 20th October 1982, while my three children were all at boarding school, in which my fifteen-year-old son declared that he would find it "Much more congenial to live as part of the family of his aunt and uncle."

I did not attend the Hearing on Friday, 22nd October 1982, and I did not apply for access either. I did not approve of either the late Bill Shand Kydd or my sister, and would have been very distressed at the change in my children's behaviour because of the Shand Kydds' attitude towards me.

My children, after being influenced by the Shand Kydds, would have divided loyalties if they had continued to see me and would play one person against another, which they had already started to do when my husband and I lived separately.

The Shand Kydds were using the media, with such demeaning statements as "The two girls are skint" appearing frequently, referring to Frances and Camilla. The extraordinary behaviour of my blood relations in supporting a belief in my late husband's innocence and attempting to cast doubt on my sworn evidence, and somehow portraying me as the offending party has been confirmed to me by members of the media who have interviewed them.

I was dismayed by the contents of my son's press interviews, which appeared to suggest that he did not think his father was guilty of the murder of Mrs Sandra Rivett, although he was seven-years-old when the murder took place and had never discussed the matter with me.

I believe my son bartered the accidental privilege of his birth to live as part of another family. Following his arrest in 1998 for causing actual bodily harm to his girlfriend Imogen Brewer, he explained that it was due to "this absurd name," meaning 'Lucan'!

I still cannot understand why my husband did not return to live at Lower Belgrave Street if he was so concerned about the welfare of our children.

I will eternally regret that an innocent woman died because of my relationship with my husband.

Index

Alexander, Brian, 126
Alexander, Howard, first Earl Alexander of Tunis, 125–6
Alexander, Shane, 126
Alice, Princess, Countess of Athlone, 6, 60
All Saints church, Laleham, 125
Annabel's (nightclub), 49, 87, 175
Arnold, Mr Justice, 149
Arnold, Sir John, 261
Aspinall, Jane (John Aspinall's first wife), 76
Aspinall, John: background, 80; and Clermont Club, 62, 74, 76, 99; marriages, 76; residences, 79; on Philip Martyn, 85; and birth of George Bingham, 87; sacks Robin Douglas-Home, 99; sells Clermont to Playboy Club (1972), 124; hosts lunch for Lucan's friends, 206; on Lucan's love for his children, 271
Aspinall, Min (née Musker; John Aspinall's second wife), 76
Atkinson, John, 45

baccarat, 74–5
backgammon, 29, 77
Baker, Sergeant, 224–5, 246
Baksh, Dr John, 260–1
Banstead Hospital, Surrey, 265, 268
Basset, Rose, 139
Bastable, Mrs (dog breeder), 89, 91
Bayliss, Richard, 257
Beach, Michael Hicks, 101, 109
Beauchamp Nursery Bureau, 73
Beddick, PC, 224
Benjamin, Lewis, 270
Benson, Charles, 84–5, 94, 206

Benzodiazepine tranquilliser drugs, 251, 252, 253, 254, 262–3, 265
Bevan, Dr James, 256
Bevan, Johnny (Lucan's uncle), 5, 19, 28, 52, 125, 126
Bingham, Barbara (later Bevan; Lucan's aunt Barbara), 5, 11–12, 14, 19; death, 64
Bingham, Camilla (Lucan's daughter): birth, 110; father gains custody of, 146–7; Nativity Play, 180; with father in Florida and at Shand Kydds, 181–2; at school sports day, 189–90, 192; scalds arm, 206; at Official Solicitor's Chambers, 254; on mother's illness, 256; visits to Shand Kydds, 264; marriage, 276
Bingham, Charles (1830–1914) see Lucan, 4th Earl of
Bingham, Christine (Lucan's aunt), 98
Bingham, Frances (Lucan's daughter): birth, 71–2; holidays, 109, 120; French lessons, 112; at school, 144; interviewed by Official Solicitor's aide, 153–4; access visits from mother, 157; dislike of Jordanka, 158; music lessons, 174–5; Carol Service, 180; with father in Florida and at Shand Kydds, 181–2; at school sports day, 189–90; and Sandra Rivett, 195; birthday party, 199; actions on day of murder, 199–201, 203, 213, 217, 224; statement at inquest, 221–3; relationship with mother, 264
Bingham, George Charles (1800–1888) see Lucan, 3rd Earl of
Bingham, George Charles (1860–1949) see Lucan, 5th Earl of

Index

Bingham, George Charles Patrick (1898–1964) *see* Lucan, 6th Earl of
Bingham, George (Lucan's son): birth, 86–7; holidays, 109; French lessons, 112; attends Caspar Shand Kydd's fifth birthday party, 126; chest infection, 133–4, 135; father gains custody of, 146–7; interviewed by Official Solicitor's aide, 153–4; access visits from mother, 157; with father in Florida and at Shand Kydds, 181–2; at school sports day, 191; school report, 196; made beneficiary of Lucan family trusts, 250; school fees, 253; prefers to live with Shand Kydds, 265, 277; removes documents and photographs from Eaton Row, 266, 278; view on Lucan murder case, 266, 267, 278; obsessed with case, 266–7; assault charges, 267, 278; bid to take father's seat in House of Lords, 267, 269; conflicting press statements about Sandra Rivett, 267; in *The Hunt for Lord Lucan*, 271, 272, 273–4
Bingham, Hugh (Lucan's brother), 6, 11, 14
Bingham, Jane (Lucan's sister) *see* Griffin, Jane
Bingham, John (Lucan's uncle), 5
Bingham, Kaitilin (Lucan's mother) *see* Lucan, Kaitilin, Dowager Countess of
Bingham, Margaret (*later* Countess Alexander of Tunis; Lucan's aunt Margaret), 5, 61, 125
Bingham, Richard John *see* Lucan, 7th Earl of
Bingham, Sarah (Sally; Lucan's sister) *see* Gibbs, Sarah
Bingham, Violet *see* Lucan, Violet, Countess of
Birley, Annabel, 147–8
black jack, 75
blood analysis evidence, 239–40
Bournemouth, 31–2, 33, 34, 41–2, 156
Bower, Detective Constable Sally, 221
Boyce, Nicholas, 180, 268–9
Bradley, Detective Sergeant, 255

Broadmoor stories, 185–6
Brooks, John Elliott, 131–2, 149–50, 163–4, 177, 179, 255
Broome, Nadia (nanny), 192, 195
Brudenell, Anne, 3
Burke, John, 62, 63, 138
Burton, Amanda *see* Howard, Amanda
Burton, Simon, 84, 99–100, 108–9

Cardigan, 7th Earl of, 3, 4
Carlton Tower, The, 58, 59, 60
Carne, Judy, 43
Carritt, Dr Christian, 66, 88, 103
Caterham Guards Depot, 21
Charge of the Light Brigade (1854), 3–5
Chatfield, Dorothea (*later* Bingham; Lucan's aunt Dodo), 5
chemin de fer, 62*n*
Chester Terrace (No. 33), 70, 78
Clermont Club: description and atmosphere, 75–6, 111; Bill Shand Kydd at, 77–8; Greville Howard at, 83, 100; Lucan at, 54, 63, 74–5, 77, 78–9; Robin Douglas-Home at, 99; Veronica at, 54, 63, 75, 85, 118, 124; women at, 79; sold to Playboy Club (1972), 124
Coleridge, Fred, 20
Coles, Bruce (QC), 219, 236
Coles, Flora: appointed nanny, 10; with Bingham children in USA, 11, 12–13; sent back to England, 15; reinstated with family, 70
Collegiate School, The, Port Elizabeth, 37–8
Comyn, Sir James (QC), 207
'contract killer' theory, 233
Corsair, Ford, 203–4, 237–8, 239
Coutts and Co, 194, 227, 250, 254
Crichton Stuart, Sally, 85, 86, 87, 109
Crimean War, 3–5
Criminal Law Act 1977, 253
Crockfords casino, 28, 52, 67
Cross, Tom, 172–3

Dagnell, Andrew, 267
Daily Express Powerboat Race (1963), 49, 50
Daily Mail, 268

Index

Daily Mirror, 261
Dally, Dr Ann, 118–20, 121, 122
Dally, Dr Peter, 111
Dartrey, 1st Earl of, 2
Dartrey earldom, 5
Davis, Dr Roger, 240–1
Dawson, Edward, 2, 5
Dawson, Kaitilin *see* Lucan, Kaitilin, Dowager Countess of
Dawson, Mrs (daily help), 140–1
de Lima, Sergeant David, 237
deck quoits, 38
Demetriou, Andrea, 241
Dempster, Nigel, 268
Derrick, Miss (articled clerk), 161, 163
Devlin & Co (private investigators), 182–3
Diana, Princess of Wales, 92
Diocesan School for Girls, Grahamstown, 38
Ditch, Mr (Official Solicitor's aide), 151–6, 179, 187, 251
Douglas-Home, Robin, 73, 82; suicide, 99
Douglas-Home, Sandra, 73, 82
Douglas-Home, Sholto, 73, 82
Downshire, 8th Marquess of (Robin Hill), 29
drug treatments: Ativan, 267–8; Dalmane, 251, 252, 253, 260; Disipal, 118; Kemadrin, 121–2; Marplan, 123; Moditen, 104, 118, 119–21, 122; Mogadon, 251, 254; Parstelin, 256–7, 260, 264, 265; Sparine, 114; Tryptizol, 114; Tuinal, 114; Valium, 256
Dublin, 171–3
Duncan, Christina (Veronica's sister) *see* Shand Kydd, Christina
Duncan, Colonel T.A. (Veronica's grandfather), 30
Duncan, Hazel Patricia (Veronica's half-sister), 31, 80
Duncan, Major Charles Moorhouse (Veronica's father), 30–1, 32–3
Duncan, Mary Clementina (*née* Shaw; Veronica's grandmother), 30
Duncan, Pamela Jean (Veronica's half-sister), 31

Duncan, Thelma (*née* Watts; Veronica's mother): early life, 31–2; marriage to Charles Duncan, 32; birth of daughter Veronica, 30; death of husband, 32; birth of daughter Christina, 33; raises children, 33, 35; buys house in Bournemouth, 34; relationship with Jim Margrie, 36; takes family to South Africa, 36–7, 38; takes over running of Wheatsheaf Hotel, North Waltham, 39; meets John Bingham, 55; and daughter's wedding arrangements, 58–9; relationship with daughter, 124–5; interviewed by Official Solicitor's aide, 156; refuses to meet with Veronica, 163; evidence at custody hearing, 166
Duncan, Violet Louisa (*née* Handcock; Charles Duncan's first wife), 31
Dunsmure, James, 20
Dwek, Joe, 109

Eastham, Michael (QC), 219–20, 231, 233, 237, 239–40, 242
Eaton Row (No. 5) mews house: Lucans buy and renovate, 127; Lucan occupies, 127, 128, 141, 155; Veronica 'bolted out', 131–2; altercation between Veronica and Greville Howard, 184–5; Veronica moves into (January 1977), 251; property and documents removed from, 266, 278; Veronica shuns family, 268
Eaton Square (No. 22), 16–17, 67
Edelman, Dr Joy, 261
Edgson, Billy, 127–8; evidence at inquest, 241–2; in *The Hunt for Lord Lucan*, 271, 272
Elizabeth Street (No. 72a), 154, 156, 157, 168, 185, 186, 203–4
Elwes, Dominick, 157, 206
Eton, 8, 17, 19–20, 62, 271
Evening News, 258–60

Fine Art Trade Guild, 252–3
fingerprint evidence, 239
Fire Auto and Marine Insurance

Index

Company, 96–8
Firefly (pony), 40–1
Flood, Dr John: treats Veronica, 122–3, 158–9, 160–1, 163; and Veronica's family, 125, 133, 149, 158; Lucan plays tape recordings to, 131, 139, 141; recommends trial separation, 136; Lucan writes to, 144–5; evidence at custody hearing, 166; confirms Veronica fit to drive, 167; death, 257
Florman, Madelaine, 203
Forsyth, Detective Sergeant Graham, 208, 226–7, 242, 243, 248
France, The (liner), 58
Francis, Pam, 256, 257
Freeman, Arthur, 93, 94
Frost, David, 97
Furstenberg, Gustav von, 105, 109

Galliers-Pratt, Anthony, 67, 68
Gascoigne-Smith, Barry, 37
Gascoigne-Smith, Joan (*née* Margrie), 33, 37
Gascoigne-Smith, Sidney, 33, 37
Geiger, Peter, 171–2
Genese, Charles, 241
Gerald Road Police Station, 147, 236, 255, 266, 268
Gerring, Detective Chief Inspector David, 242–3, 246
Gibbs, Oliver, 133
Gibbs, Sarah (Sally; *née* Bingham; Lucan's sister): evacuated to USA, 11; upbringing with Tucker family, 11–15; returns to England after the War, 16; provided with marriage settlement, 28; meets Veronica, 51; at father's funeral, 64; relationship with Veronica, 68–9, 72, 131; sends flowers on birth of George, 87; evidence at custody hearing, 165; takes charge of children after murder, 206; reaction to inquest verdict, 249; in *The Hunt for Lord Lucan*, 271–2
Gibbs, William, 51–2, 68–9, 72, 87, 165
Gilliatt, Reverend Prebendary, 60
Gilson, Denis, 205, 206, 251, 255

Gloucester Place, 43
Goad, Tim, 20
Golders Green crematorium, 64–5
Goldsmith, Jimmy, 124, 142, 147–8, 206–7, 227
Gordon-Lennox, Cecilia, 2–3
Graham, Rev John, 158
Gray, Roger, 161, 164, 166
Green Park, 90, 146
Greenslade, Mrs, 167, 168, 179, 180–1, 187, 189, 192, 193, 206, 252
Greenways (nursing home), 115–16
Griffin, Jane (*née* Bingham; Lucan's sister): birth and early life, 10; evacuated to USA, 11, 12; upbringing with Tucker family, 11–15; returns to England after the War, 16; in New York tenement, 57–8; and birth of children, 70
Grove (country house), 121–2, 182
Gstaad, 105–7

Hamble Manor Hotel, 49
Hamilton Club, 28, 52, 67
Hankins, John, 195, 200
Hanover House, 55–6, 89
Harrison, Miss (nursery governess), 11, 12
Harvey School, Connecticut, 15
Hay (friend of Kaitilin Lucan), 10
Hay, Dr, 105, 110, 111, 113–14, 118
Helena Club, Lower Sloane Street, 130
Henderson, Dr, 134–5, 140
Hensby, Albert (Sandra Rivett's father), 197
Hensby, Gary Roger (Sandra Rivett's son), 197
Hensby, Sandra *see* Rivett, Sandra
Hensby, Stephen (Sandra Rivett's son), 197
Hill, Caroline, 29, 174–5, 185, 271, 272
Hill, Juliet, 85
Hill, Robin (*later* 8th Marquess of Downshire), 29, 85
Hogg, Quintin, Lord Hailsham, 65
Holy Trinity, Brompton, 47, 59–60
horse racing, 85, 93–5
Horton Hall, near Leighton Buzzard, 47, 48, 182

Index

Hotel Metropole, Bournemouth, 31–2, 34
Hotel Metropole, Monte Carlo, 120–1
House of Lords, 4, 59, 65, 102–3, 267, 269, 270
'housies' (in-house gamblers), 75
Howard, Amanda (*later* Burton), 84, 99–100, 108–9
Howard, Greville: background, 83; friendship with Lucans, 83–4, 87, 99, 100–1; at Clermont Club, 83, 100; warned off by Lucan, 101; courtship and marriage to Zoe Walker, 108–9; Veronica calls on, 115; split with Zoe, 184; altercation with Veronica at mews house, 184–5; statement withheld at inquest, 242; and Lucan's 'wanting to kill his wife' remark, 249
Howard, Maurice, 98
Howard, Michael, 21st Earl of Suffolk, 108
Howard, Zoe (*née* Walker), 108–9, 115, 123, 146, 166, 184–5
Howletts (country house), 76, 79
Hulls, Detective Inspector Charles, 242–3, 246
Hunt, Rev Giles, 158
Hunt for Lord Lucan, The (documentary), 270–5
Hurlingham Club, 198, 252
Hyde Park, 45, 117–18

Ingham, Mrs (headmistress), 141, 196
Ingleby-Mackenzie, Colin, 270, 271, 272
inquest into death of Sandra Rivett (1975): inquest opens, 208; Lady Lucan gives evidence, 208–19; questions aimed at discrediting witnesses disallowed, 219–21, 244; Frances' statement, 221–3; evidence of Arthur Whitehouse, 223; evidence of Dr Michael Smith, 223–4; evidence of Dr Hugh Scott, 224; evidence of Sergeant Baker, 224–5; evidence of PC Beddick, 225; evidence of Kaitilin Lucan, 226, 228–31; financial evidence, 226–7, 241; post mortem findings, 227–8; evidence of Susan Maxwell-Scott, 231–5; evidence of Bill Shand Kydd, 235–7; evidence of Eileen Sims, 237; evidence of Sergeant David de Lima, 237; evidence of Michael Stoop, 238–9; fingerprint evidence, 239; blood analysis evidence, 239–40; evidence of Dr Roger Davis, 240–1; evidence of Andrea Demetriou, 241; evidence of Billy Edgson, 241–2; Greville Howard's statement withheld, 242; police experiments refute Lucan's defence, 242–3; Lady Lucan disbarred from answering questions unrelated to her assault, 244–5; coroner's summary, 245–8; jury verdict, 248; Lucan named as murderer of Sandra Rivett, 248; jury discharged, 248
insurance scam theory, 270
Irish Club, Lyall Street, 169, 170, 181, 183
Istanbul, 61

Janet (practice nurse), 254, 256, 263
Jenkins, Lilian (nanny): and Robin Douglas-Home family, 73, 82; appointed nanny to Lucan children, 74; relationship with Veronica, 82, 264; and Otto, 91; as nanny, 99, 103, 109, 122; Veronica increasingly regards as unreliable, 109, 112; Veronica suspects of poisoning, 114; sacked, 129–30; injury to finger, 130; given money by Bill Shand Kydd, 131; Lucan writes reference for, 135; devalued testimony at custody hearing, 143–4; evidence at custody hearing, 165
Jews: and Parliamentary Oath reform, 5
Jobbins, Hazel (nanny), 167–8
Jones, Arthur: meets Veronica, 177–8; background, 178; supports Veronica, 179, 181, 261, 268; friendship with Veronica, 184, 277; Mrs Murphy takes a dislike to, 184; altercation at mews house, 184–5; employed at Fine Art Trade Guild, 252–3; alliance with Dr Baksh, 260; death, 277
Jones, Tom, 94

Jordan, Rosemary, 195
Judd, Veronica, 31

King, Leslie, 20, 109
Knecht, Nanny (Swiss nanny), 34
Kotlarova, Jordanka, 153–4, 157, 158, 168; evidence at custody hearing, 165
Krefeld, West Germany, 22–7
Kuttner, Stuart, 261

La Popote (restaurant), 132, 170–1
Ladbroke Club, 111
Laleham, 125
Le Merveilleux II (racehorse), 85, 93–4
Lefever, Dr Robert, 256, 257, 261
Leverton, David, 164
Lippi, Filipino, 68
Llandovery Castle, SS, 38
London Clinic, 66, 71, 86–7
Lower Belgrave Street (No. 46): Lucans buy and furnish, 67–8; nursery quarters, 70–1; Otto at large, 90, 91, 92; decorated, 102, 103; surveillance of, 182; night of murder, 199–203, 212–19; police search, 224–5; body found, 225; blood spatter evidence, 239–40; police experiments, 242–3; contamination of crime scene, 246–7; sale of, 206, 251, 255–6
Lucan, Kaitilin, Dowager Countess of (*née* Dawson; Lucan's mother): birth and family background, 2; socialist beliefs, 5, 15; ambitions of becoming a doctor, 5–6, 12, 16; relationship and marriage to Pat Bingham, 6–8, 9; letters to husband, 9, 10; views on Pat's mother, 9; first pregnancy, 9–10; birth of daughter Jane, 10; birth of son John, 1; and separation from children during the War, 12; and son's disturbed behaviour, 17; meets Veronica Duncan, 55–6; at Hanover House, 55–6; attacks diners in House of Lords, 59; at John and Veronica's wedding, 60; and death of husband, 64–5; sends cactus on birth of George, 87; cut short by Dr Carritt, 88; at Lower Belgrave Street, 89; affidavit for custody case, 133; evilness, 157; evidence at custody hearing, 165–6; Lucan telephones after murder, 203–4; evidence at inquest, 226, 228–31; remark to reporters, 244; reaction to inquest verdict, 249; attempt to have inquest verdict retrospectively removed, 253
Lucan, 3rd Earl of (George Charles Bingham), 3–4, 5
Lucan, 4th Earl of (Charles Bingham), 2–3
Lucan, 5th Earl of (George Charles Bingham), 2
Lucan, 6th Earl of (George Charles Patrick Bingham; Pat): birth, 2; military career, 6; relationship and marriage to Kaitilin Dawson, 6–8, 9; diary, 8–9; letters from wife, 9, 10; birth of daughter Jane, 10; birth of son John, 1; seeks psychiatric help for son, 16–17; on son's development, 17–18; succeeds to earldom, 19; gives access to family papers, 23*n*; releases capital for Sarah and John, 28; meets Veronica Duncan, 55–6; life insured, 63–4; death and crematorium service, 64–5
LUCAN, 7th EARL OF (Richard John Bingham):
early life (1934–55):
family background, 2–9; birth, 1; infancy, 10–11; evacuated to USA, 11; upbringing with Tucker family, 11–15; at Harvey School, Connecticut, 15; returns to England after the War, 16; childhood years in London, 16–18; sees child psychiatrist, 16–17; injures hand playing with chemicals, 17; at Eton, 19–20; decides against University, 20; National Service (1953–5), 20–7; lifestyle, 24, 26, 27, 28; love of card playing, 28; passes out as 2nd lieutenant, 28
young adulthood (1955–63):
bank career, 28, 52; at Crockfords casino, 28, 52, 67; meets Stephen

Raphael, 28; receives money from father, 28; becomes professional gambler, 28; takes flat in Park Crescent, 29; appearance and dress sense, 29, 47; introduced to Veronica Duncan, 47; courts Veronica, 48–9, 51–3; powerboat racing, 15, 29, 49, 50–1, 63, 66–7; engagement, 53–4; meeting the parents, 55–6; takes Veronica to New York, 56–8; reticence about life before Veronica, 56–7; wedding day, 59–60; honeymoon in Paris and Istanbul, 60–1

married life (1963–73):
lies low after honeymoon, 62–3; as piano player, 62; untidiness, 62; at the Clermont Club, 63, 74–5, 77, 78–9; and death of father, 64–5; sells family paintings, 68; house hunting, 66, 67; buys and furnishes 46 Lower Belgrave Street, 67–8; and birth of daughter Frances, 71–2; baccarat dealer, 74–5; insecurity and lack of confidence, 78; nicknames, 79, 113; riding accident, 81; treatment of Veronica during second pregnancy, 84, 86; lunches at Mirabelle, 85; and birth of son George, 86; contracts yellow jaundice, 89; and Otto, 89–92; as racehorse owner, 85, 93–5; and Fire Auto and Marine affair, 96–8; married relations, 99, 104–5; warns off Greville Howard, 101; takes seat in House of Lords, 102–3; career as Peer, 103; haemorrhoids, 9, 103, 104, 165; takes Veronica to The Priory, 104; shooting parties on Janni Roth's estate, 105, 109–10; gambling holidays, 105–7; European trips, 108–9; beats wife with stick before sex, 119; holiday in Monte Carlo, 119–21; enjoys having children to himself, 122; life and accident insurance policies, 123; physically assaults Veronica, 125–6, 140; moves into Eaton Row, 127–8; instigates campaign to portray Veronica as mentally unbalanced, 131, 134–5, 140, 141; tapes wife's conversations, 131, 136–7; in desertion, 132; moves back into Lower Belgrave Street, 132; deteriorating marital relations, 136–40; sex life, 139; interferes in wife's domestic arrangements, 140–1; separation from wife, 140, 152; surveillance of wife, 142; sends 'precautionary' letters, 143–5; holiday in Mexico, 145

custody battles (1973–74):
gains temporary custody of children, 146–7; collects toys and clothes from house, 149; affidavit for custody case, 133, 149–51; interviewed by Official Solicitor's aide, 154–6; writes to Marcia Tucker about impending custody hearing, 161–2; gives evidence, 164; concedes case, 166; 'hand-over' of children, 167; letter to Veronica, 169; holiday with children in Portugal, 169–70, 174; contact with Veronica after custody case, 174, 175; 'buy-off' plan, 178–9; complains about access arrangements, 180; takes children to Florida and to Shand Kydds, 181–2; spreads malign rumours, 182; engages private investigators, 182–3; accosted by Veronica in Elizabeth Street, 185; digs up dirt on Elizabeth Murphy, 186; proposes reduced childcare rate, 187; continued surveillance, 188, 198, 199; delays payments to childcare agency, 189; at children's sports days, 189–92; financial problems, 194–5; writes to headmistress about George's school report, 196; access visits, 198

murder case and disappearance (1974–):
actions on day of murder, 199; attacks Veronica, 201–2; aftermath of fight, 202–3; flees scene, 203–4; writes letters to Bill Shand Kydd, 204, 205, 220, 226; writes 'suicide note' to Michael Stoop, 204, 238; at Newhaven, 204; commits suicide, 204; no financial provision for

Index

education of children, 155, 205; bankruptcy, 205, 206; overdrafts, 226–7; bogus defence, 231–3; debts, 241; named as murderer of Sandra Rivett, 248; 'wanting to kill his wife' remark, 249; legal status, 250; family trusts, 250; Will, 251; son considers not guilty of murder, 266, 267; presumed dead, 269; family granted probate over estate, 270; books on case, 269, 276; 'contract killer' theory, 233; insurance scam theory, 270; in Africa theory, 274; relationship with his children, 275

LUCAN, VERONICA, DOWAGER COUNTESS OF (*née* Duncan):

early life (1934–54):

birth and family background, 30–2; orphaned, 32; early childhood, 33–6; at Queensmount School, Bournemouth, 34; poor health, 35; air travel/fear of flying, 36–7, 56, 121; in South Africa, 36–8; returns to England by steam ship, 38; parents take over running of Wheatsheaf Hotel, North Waltham, 39; at St Swithun's School, Winchester, 39–40; Pony Club activities, 40–1; leaves school, 41

young adulthood (1955–63):

art student in Bournemouth, 41–2, 43; helps out behind bar at Wheatsheaf Hotel, 42; first love (Tony), 42–3; modelling career, 43, 44; flat sharing in London, 43, 44–5; works as receptionist/secretary, 44; relationship with parents, 45; director of printing company in Brompton Arcade, 45; meets Bill Shand Kydd, 46; introduced to John Bingham, 47; courted by Bingham, 48–9, 51–3; first powerboat ride, 49; engagement, 53–4; meeting the parents, 55–6; trip to New York to meet Tucker family, 56–8; wedding arrangements, 58–9; wedding day, 59–60; honeymoon in Paris and Istanbul, 60–1

married life (1963–67):

lies low after honeymoon, 62–3; and husband's gambling, 63, 78; and death of father-in-law, 64–5; relationship with sister, 65; becomes Countess of Lucan, 65–6; pregnant with Frances, 66, 67, 70; house hunting, 66, 67; trip to Miami, 66–7; buys and furnishes 46 Lower Belgrave Street, 67–8; stays with Gibbs family, 68–9; birth of daughter Frances, 71–2; nannies employed by, 71–4, 142; at Clermont Club, 75, 78, 118; social life outside Clermont Club, 80, 81–2; hunting, 80–1; relationship with Nanny Jenkins, 81; pregnant with George, 84; falls in love with Greville Howard, 84, 100–1; attends York Races, 85; birth of son George, 86–7; and Otto, 89–92; as racehorse owner, 93–5; married relations, 99, 104–5; plans children's education, 102; accompanies Lucan to House of Lords, 102–3

married life (1967–73):

isolated and goes into decline, 101, 104; taken to The Priory and prescribed anti-psychotic drugs, 104; relationship with Dr Hay, 105, 118; shooting parties on Janni Roth's estate, 105, 109–10; gambling holidays, 105–7; European trips, 108–9; pregnancy and birth of Camilla, 110; post-natal depression, 110, 111, 114; sees psychiatrist Dr Peter Dally, 111; increasingly dissatisfied with Nanny Jenkins, 109, 112; thirty-fourth birthday, 113; feels 'disaster crowding in', 113; sessions with psychiatrist Dr Whitteridge, 113–14; fears of being poisoned, 114–15; hallucinations, 115, 118; flees from Greenways nursing home, 115–17; alone at Lower Belgrave Street, 117; drug withdrawal, 117–18; begins another course of drug treatment, 118; conversion therapy for depression, 119; husband beats with stick before sex, 119; holiday in Monte Carlo, 119–21; 'disastrous' injection of Moditen, 119–21, 122; recuperates at sister's house in country, 121–2; sees Dr John Flood, 122–3; life and accident insurance policies, 123; spurns husband's wedding anniversary gift, 123–4; throws wine over girl at Clermont Club, 124; physically assaulted by husband, 125–6, 140; attends unveiling ceremony at Guards Chapel, 126; husband moves into Eaton Row, 127–8; sacks Nanny Jenkins, 129–30; husband seeks to portray as mentally unbalanced, 131, 134–5, 140, 141; husband tapes her conversations, 131, 136–7; claims Lucan in desertion, 132; family Christmas (1972), 133–5; deteriorating marital relations, 136–40; sex life, 139

custody battles (1973–74):
Christian confirmation, 146, 161; husband gains temporary custody of children, 146–7; affidavits for custody case, 133, 149–51, 158; interviewed by Official Solicitor, 151–2; applies to Court to have children returned, 156–7; access visits, 157–8, 162; books stay at The Priory, 158–61; full hearing delayed, 161; days leading up to hearing, 162–3; custody hearing, 163–6; gives evidence at hearing, 164–5; awarded custody, 166; negotiates series of temporary nannies, 167–70, 177, 179–81, 187–8, 192–3; 'hand-over' of children, 167; summer holiday at Shand Kydds, 168, 169; trip to Dublin, 171–3; contact with Lucan after custody case, 174, 175; estrangement from Christina, 176, 181; friendship with Arthur Jones, 177–8, 179, 181, 184–5, 277; and Lucan's 'buy-off' plan, 178–9; hires Simon Swallow, 179; nuisance phone calls, 179, 181; altercation with Greville Howard in mews house, 184–5; accosts Lucan in Elizabeth Street, 185; at children's sports days, 189–92; hires Sandra Rivett, 193–4; relationship with Sandra Rivett, 198

murder case (1974–76):
actions on day and evening of murder, 199–200, 212–14; attacked by Lucan, 201–2, 215–16; aftermath of fight, 202–3, 216–17; flees to Plumber's Arms, 203, 218, 223; taken to St George's Hospital, 203; injuries sustained, 224; statements to police, 243; High Court grants custody of children, 205; moves with family to Liskeard to avoid press, 205–6; returns to London, 206; gives evidence at inquest, 208–19; debarred from answering questions unrelated to her assault, 244–5; reaction to inquest verdict, 248; refutes being confused or concussed after attack, 249; and Lucan family trusts, 250; gets 'Nanny Order' removed, 250; seeks decree of judicial separation from husband, 250; and husband's Will, 250–1

at Eaton Row (1977–2017):
moves into 5 Eaton Row, 251; changes in prescription medication, 251, 252; fears plot to render her ill, 252; malicious complaint against, 251–2; medically abused with steroids and benzodiazepines, 252, 253, 254, 256–7, 260, 261; helps out at Fine Art Trade Guild, 252–3; bills and fees, 253, 254, 255; holiday with children in the Cotswolds, 254; and theft of her photographs and negatives, 255, 261; and plan to have her certified, 257–60, 263; puts in complaint about former doctor, 261; declines treatment at St Thomas's, 261; letter from former doctor detailing drug regime, 262–3; does not pursue claim for damages against former doctor, 263; addicted to Parstelin, 264, 265; relationship with children, 264; loss of children to Shand Kydds, 265; admitted to Banstead Hospital, 265; returns to Eaton Row, 266; property and

Index

documents removed from house, 266; addiction to Ativan, 267–8; shuns children after loss of custody, 268; comments on *The Hunt for Lord Lucan* (documentary), 270–5; and Lucan's Wikipedia entry, 276; not invited to Camilla's wedding, 276; interview in *Sunday Times*, 276; reflections in later life, 277–8
Lucan, Violet, Countess of (Lucan's grandmother): marriage to 5th Earl of Lucan, 2, 3; children, 5; perpetual complaints, 9; and grandson's accident with chemicals, 17; and 6th Earl's socialist leanings, 19; tiara, 59; visits Veronica after birth of George, 87; death and bequests, 107–8; body moved, 125
Lucan House, Dublin, 173, 175
Lucas, Ian, 239
Lyall Street, 79, 206
Lyford Cay, Nassau, 107

Mancini, Tony, 111
Mangan, Miss (nanny), 34
Margrie, Gwen (Jim's first wife), 36
Margrie, Jim (Veronica's stepfather), 33, 36–7, 38, 55
Margrie, Joan (Jim's sister) *see* Gascoigne-Smith, Joan
Margrie, Tessa, 45
Marnham, Patrick: *Trail of Havoc*, 269
Martin, Christabel (nanny), 179–80, 187–8, 190, 269
Martyn, Philip, 84–5
Maud, Humphrey, 25, 26
Maxwell-Scott, Ian, 62, 74, 79, 235, 236
Maxwell-Scott, Susan, 79, 204, 223; evidence at inquest, 231–5; interviewed by *News of the World*, 249
McGowan, Frankie, 258–60
Meade, Elizabeth, 2, 5
Meade-Fetherstonhaugh, Margaret, 69–70
Meinertzhagen, Dan, 206
Melbury Road flat, 44–5, 47
Mellor, Stan, 94
Miami/Nassau Powerboat race (1964), 66
Migrant (powerboat), 15
Milford-Haven, Janet, Marchioness of, 60
Milner, Dora, 62
Mirabelle Restaurant, 85, 175
Moditen (anti-psychotic drug), 104, 118, 119–21, 122
Monteilleur, Marie Christine, 112, 129, 139
Moore, Sally: *Lucan, Not Guilty*, 269
Morritt, Mr Justice, 269
Muir, Dickie, 170–1
murder weapon (lead piping), 216, 224, 227–8, 237, 240–1, 247, 272–3
Murphy, Elizabeth (nanny), 168–9, 170, 181, 182–3, 184; Lucan digs up dirt on, 186; hospitalised with cancer, 187
Myers, Mr and Mrs (party organisers), 199

Nassau, 66, 107
Newhaven, 204, 210, 237, 247
News of the World, 249
Nolan, Captain Louis, 4–5
NSPCC, 251–2

Oakley, Hampshire, 40–1
Odlum, Dr Doris, 35
O'Donnell, Mary Geraldine ('Mary G'), 171–2, 173, 196
Official Solicitor (Norman Turner), 251, 253, 254, 255, 265–6; interviews Veronica, 151–2; report (4 May 1973), 150–1; concerns over Elizabeth Murphy, 186; Lucan conceals financial plight from, 194–5; and Lucan family trusts, 250; and plan to have Lady Lucan certified, 257, 259–60 *see also* Ditch, Mr (Official Solicitor's aide)
Ohrstrom, Lili, 58
Orient Express, 61
Osborne, Lady, 78, 79, 87, 124
Otto (dog), 84, 89–92

Pannone Napier (law firm), 263
Park Avenue (No. 733), New York

(Tucker mansion), 11, 57
Park Crescent flat (No. 22), 29, 51, 52, 53, 68
Parliamentary Oath reform, 5
Parstelin (antidepressant), 256–7, 260, 261, 264, 265
Penrose, John, 261
People Bureau, The (childcare agency), 167, 189
Pereira, Dr Margaret, 239–40, 247
Pierrette (nanny), 187–9, 192–3
Piggott, Lester, 94
Pinker, George, 86, 111
Playboy Club, 124
Plumber's Arms (public house), 195, 203, 223, 274
poker (card game), 28, 52, 107
Portland Club, 124
powerboat racing, 15, 29, 49, 50–1, 63, 66–7
Prince Bleu (racehorse), 93, 94
Priory, The (clinic), 104, 122, 136, 141, 158–61
Private Eye, 206–7
propellers, 50–1

Queen, The (magazine), 126
Queensmount School, Bournemouth, 34

Racquet Club, Miami Beach, 66
Raglan, Lord, 3–4, 5
Ranson, Detective Chief Superintendent Roy, 243
Raphael, Stephen, 11, 28, 52, 53, 63, 68, 71, 80, 93, 139, 206
Ray (Sandra Rivett's boyfriend), 195
Reason Why, The (Woodham-Smith), 23, 25
Rees, Mr Justice, 163–4, 205, 250, 251
Rivett, Roger, 193, 197, 248
Rivett, Sandra (*née* Hensby; Lucans' nanny): hired by Veronica, 193–4; background, 193–4, 196–7; social life, 195; menstrual disorder, 197–8; relationship with Veronica, 198; frightened of Lucan, 198, 199; changes day off, 200, 212; actions on day of murder, 199, 201, 213; murdered, 202; body found, 225; body examined at scene, 223–4; injuries sustained, 224; post mortem findings, 227–8; inquest (*see* inquest into death of Sandra Rivett (1975)); George Bingham's conflicting statements over, 267
Robb, Dawn, 256
Rosalind, Duchess of Abercorn, 19
Roth, Janni, 105, 109–10
Royal Free Hospital, London, 12, 16
Royal Hospital Gardens, Chelsea, 116
Rusty (pony), 40

Sail, Miss (Veronica's governess), 34
Savundra, Emil, 96–8, 140
Sawicka, Stefania ('Stenya'; nanny), 142, 146–7, 149; interviewed by Official Solicitor's aide, 152–3
Scott, Dr Hugh, 224
Scripts Limited (printing company), 45
Scrivener, Anthony, 273
Sebastien (racehorse), 93, 94
Shand Kydd, Bill: meets and marries Christina Duncan, 46–7; hosts house and dinner parties, 48, 70; and powerboat racing, 66; at Clermont Club, 77–8; knowledge of impending custody grab, 146; unkindness towards Veronica, 158; Lucan writes to after murder, 204, 205, 220, 226; wardship proceedings, 205; lunch with Aspinall (8 November 1974), 206; evidence at inquest, 235–7; sends Veronica bill for George's school fees, 253; and plan to have Lady Lucan certified, 257–60, 263
Shand Kydd, Caspar, 113–14, 126
Shand Kydd, Christina (*née* Duncan; Veronica's sister; Bill's wife): birth, 33; early childhood, 34; in South Africa, 37–8; shares flat in London with Veronica, 44; meets and marries Bill Shand Kydd, 46–7; warns Veronica about Lucan, 48; birth of children, 59; relationship with sister, 65, 124–5; takes Veronica to Grove House to recuperate, 121–2; interviewed by Official Solicitor's aide, 156; evidence at custody

Index

hearing, 165; Veronica and children stay with, 168–9; estrangement from Veronica, 175–6, 181; wardship proceedings, 205
Shand Kydd, Frances, 92
Shand Kydd, Peter, 92
Shand Kydds: awarded custody of children, 265, 277; use of media, 277–8
Shepherd, Nanny, 36
Simpson, Professor Keith, 227–8
Sims, Eileen, 237
Sitwell, William, 267
Smith, Dr Michael, 223–4
Sonkson, Professor, 261
Sooty (cat), 195, 196
South Africa, 37–8
Spaniards, the (Tina and Theresa; nannies), 170, 173–4, 177, 178, 179
St George's Hospital, 130, 203, 205
St James's Club, Piccadilly, 99, 238
St Mary's Hospital, Paddington, 110
St Moritz, 27, 29, 109
St Peter's church, Eaton Square, 146
St Swithun's School, Winchester, 39–40
St Thomas's Hospital, 261
Stern, Chester, 274
Stoop, Michael, 86, 107, 204, 221; evidence at inquest, 238–9
Stress Signal (racehorse), 93
Summer Fields School, Oxford, 196, 253
Sunday Times, 206, 276
Swaebe, Barry, 126
Swallow, Simon, 179, 250–1
Sweny, Bobby, 107
Sweny, Charlie, 11, 119

Tara (cat), 195, 196
Thompson, Dr Ann, 56, 89
Thurston, Dr Gavin (Coroner), 208, 209–19, 228, 230, 231–2, 235, 236, 244; summary at inquest hearing, 245–8
Tillyer, Rev Desmond, 276–7
Times, The, 4, 53–4, 98, 270, 276
Tina and Theresa (nannies) *see* Spaniards, the
Tony (Veronica's boyfriend), 42–3
Tucker, Carll, 11

Tucker, Carll, Jr, 11, 57
Tucker, Luther, 11, 57, 178–9
Tucker, Marcia ('Aunt Marcia'): brings up Lucan children, 2, 11–15; Lucan visits in 1960, 28; and Lucan's marriage intentions, 53; Lucan and Veronica visit, 56–8; visits Lucans in England, 81–2; Lucan writes to on custody case, 161–2; and Lucan's 'buy off' plan, 178, 179
Turner, Norman *see* Official Solicitor

Uckfield, Sussex, 30, 32, 79, 204, 236
Uppark, 69–70

Vale, The (Chelsea house), 66, 67
Vereker, Roxana, 29, 56
Vereker, Sir Gordon, 29, 56
Vine Hunt, 41

Walker, Zoe *see* Howard, Zoe
Wall, Richard, 271
Walter House, Strand, 179
War Office Selection Boards (WOSBs), 27
Watling, Mr, 216, 228–31, 234, 242
Watson, Miss (psychiatric worker), 134, 140
Watts, Elna (Veronica's aunt), 32
Watts, George James (Veronica's grandfather), 31–2
Watts, Muriel (Veronica's grandmother), 31–2, 35–6
Watts, Ronald (Veronica's uncle), 32
Watts, Thelma (Veronica's mother) *see* Duncan, Thelma
Webster, David (QC), 230
West, Doris, 198, 199
Westgate-on-Sea, 117
Whaddon Chase, 80–1
Wheatsheaf Hotel, North Waltham, 39, 42, 55
White Elephant (London club), 111
White Migrant (powerboat), 15, 49, 50, 63
Whitehouse, Arthur William, 203, 223, 270, 274
Whitteridge, Dr, 113–14, 115
Wilbraham, John, 29

290

Index

William Brandt's bank, 28, 52
'William Hickey' (gossip column), 82
Wilson, Harold, 65
Wilton Crescent bedsit (No. 34), 47
Winnicott, Dr D.W., 16, 17
Woodham-Smith, Cecil: *The Reason Why*, 23

World War I, 6, 30–1
World War II, 11, 34, 36
Worsted Farm, Uckfield, 30, 32

Yeatman-Biggs, Judy, 171, 173

CW01371486

FIGHTING FOR THE FUTURE

Liverpool Science Fiction Texts and Studies, 67

Liverpool Science Fiction Texts and Studies

Editor David Seed, *University of Liverpool*

Editorial Board
Mark Bould, *University of the West of England*
Veronica Hollinger, *Trent University*
Rob Latham, *University of California*
Roger Luckhurst, *Birkbeck College, University of London*
Patrick Parrinder, *University of Reading*
Andy Sawyer, *University of Liverpool*

Recent titles in the series

47. Sonja Fritzsche, *The Liverpool Companion to World Science Fiction Film*
48. Jack Fennel: *Irish Science Fiction*
49. Peter Swirski and Waclaw M. Osadnik: *Lemography: Stanislaw Lem in the Eyes of the World*
50. Gavin Parkinson (ed.), *Surrealism, Science Fiction and Comics*
51. Peter Swirski, *Stanislaw Lem: Philosopher of the Future*
52. J. P. Telotte and Gerald Duchovnay, *Science Fiction Double Feature: The Science Fiction Film as Cult Text*
53. Tom Shippey, *Hard Reading: Learning from Science Fiction*
54. Mike Ashley, *Science Fiction Rebels: The Story of the Science-Fiction Magazines from 1981 to 1990*
55. Chris Pak, *Terraforming: Ecopolitical Transformations and Environmentalism in Science Fiction*
56. Lars Schmeink, *Biopunk Dystopias: Genetic Engineering, Society, and Science Fiction*
57. Shawn Malley, *Excavating the Future: Archaeology and Geopolitics in Contemporary North American Science Fiction Film and Television*
58. Derek J. Thiess, *Sport and Monstrosity in Science Fiction*
59. Glyn Morgan and Charul Palmer-Patel, *Sideways in Time: Critical Essays on Alternate History Fiction*
60. Curtis D. Carbonell, *Dread Trident: Tabletop Role-Playing Games and the Modern Fantastic*
61. Upamanyu Pablo Mukherjee, *Final Frontiers: Science Fiction and Techno-Science in Non-Aligned India*
62. Gavin Miller, *Science Fiction and Psychology*
63. Andrew Milner and J.R. Burgmann, *Science Fiction and Climate Change: A Sociological Approach*
64. Regina Yung Lee and Una McCormack (eds), *Biology and Manners: Essays on the Worlds and Works of Lois McMaster Bujold*
65. Joseph S. Norman, *The Culture of 'The Culture': Utopian Processes in Iain M. Banks's Space Opera Series*
66. Jeremy Withers, *Futuristic Cars and Space Bicycles: Contesting the Road in American Science Fiction*

FIGHTING FOR THE FUTURE

Essays on *Star Trek: Discovery*

SABRINA MITTERMEIER
AND MAREIKE SPYCHALA

LIVERPOOL UNIVERSITY PRESS

First published 2020 by
Liverpool University Press
4 Cambridge Street
Liverpool
L69 7ZU

Copyright © 2020 Sabrina Mittermeier and Mareike Spychala

The right of Sabrina Mittermeier and Mareike Spychala to be identified as the editors of this book has been asserted by them in accordance with the Copyright, Designs and Patents Act 1988.

All rights reserved. No part of this book may be reproduced, stored in a retrieval system, or transmitted, in any form or by any means, electronic, mechanical, photocopying, recording, or otherwise, without the prior written permission of the publisher.

British Library Cataloguing-in-Publication data
A British Library CIP record is available

ISBN 978-1-78962-176-1 cased

Typeset by Carnegie Book Production, Lancaster
Printed and bound by CPI Group (UK) Ltd, Croydon CR0 4YY

To our Star Trek family (in all its iterations),
and especially Ken Mitchell who reminds us that
all we have is time.

Contents

Preface: Unheimlich *Star Trek*   1
   Sherryl Vint

Introduction: 'We Get to Reach for the Stars': Analyzing *Star Trek: Discovery*   5
   Sabrina Mittermeier and Mareike Spychala

'Boldly Going Where No Series Has Gone Before?' – *Discovery*'s Role Within the Franchise and Its Discontents

Looking in the Mirror: The Negotiation of Franchise Identity in *Star Trek: Discovery*   21
   Andrea Whitacre

A *Star Trek* About Being *Star Trek*: History, Liberalism, and *Discovery*'s Cold War Roots   41
   Torsten Kathke

The Conscience of the King – Or: Is There in Truth No Sex and Violence?   61
   John Andreas Fuchs

These are the Voyages? The Post-Jubilee *Trek* Legacy on the *Discovery*, the *Orville*, and the *Callister*   81
   Michael G. Robinson

> 'Just as Repetition Reinforces Repetition, Change Begets Change' – Modes of Storytelling in Canon and Fanon

From Series to Seriality: *Star Trek*'s Mirror Universe in the Post-Network Era ... 105
Ina Batzke

'Lorca, I'm Really Gonna Miss Killing You': The Fictional Space Created by Time Loop Narratives ... 127
Sarah Böhlau

Discovery and the Form of Victorian Periodicals ... 145
Will Tattersdill

To Boldly Discuss: Socio-Political Discourses in *Star Trek: Discovery* Fanfiction ... 165
Kerstin-Anja Münderlein

> 'Infinite Diversity in Infinite Combinations?' – Negotiating Otherness in *Star Trek: Discovery*

Afrofuturism, Imperialism, and Intersectionality

Interview with Dr. Diana A. Mafe on 'Normalizing Black Women as Heroes' ... 191

The Cotton-Gin Effect: An Afrofuturist Reading of *Star Trek: Discovery* ... 201
Whit Frazier Peterson

The American Hello: Representations of U.S. Diplomacy in *Star Trek: Discovery* ... 221
Henrik Schillinger and Arne Sönnichsen

'Into A Mirror Darkly': Border Crossing and Imperial(ist) Feminism in *Star Trek: Discovery* ... 243
Judith Rauscher

Interrogating Gender

Star Trek Discovers Women: Gender, Race, Science, and
    Michael Burnham   267
    Amy C. Chambers

Not Your Daddy's *Star Trek*: Exploring Female Characters in
    Star Trek: Discovery   287
    Mareike Spychala

'We Choose Our Own Pain. Mine Helps Me Remember': Gabriel
    Lorca, Ash Tyler, and the Question of Masculinity   307
    Sabrina Mittermeier and Jennifer Volkmer

Queering *Star Trek*

'Never Hide Who You Are': Queer Representation and
    Actorvism in *Star Trek: Discovery*   331
    Sabrina Mittermeier and Mareike Spychala

'I Never Met a Female Michael Before': *Star Trek: Discovery*
    between Trans Potentiality and Cis Anxiety   351
    Si Sophie Pages Whybrew

Veins and Muscles of the Universe: Posthumanism and
    Connectivity in *Star Trek: Discovery*   373
    Lisa Meinecke

Coda: *Star Trek* and the Fight for the Future   391
    Sabrina Mittermeier and Mareike Spychala

Notes on Contributors   393

Acknowledgments   399

Index   401

Preface
Unheimlich *Star Trek*

Sherryl Vint

From its first moments, it is clear that *Star Trek: Discovery* (2017–ongoing) strives to be something new, to reinvent and reinvigorate the *Star Trek* mythos for the twenty-first century. It opens not with the Federation, but with pre-unification Klingons and its first scene is spoken in Klingon with English subtitles ('The Vulcan Hello,' 1x01). The first scene with Federation personnel seems designed to put the audience at ease in a familiar *Star Trek* environment: Captain Philippa Georgiou (Michelle Yeoh) and her Number One, Michael Burnham (Sonequa Martin-Green), are on an away mission to aid a pre-warp civilization. They casually banter as they find their way to a well that has become sealed, which they will prime to flow again and thus save from extinction the planet's native species, all accomplished without making contact so as not to violate the prime directive (general order #1) of non-intervention in other cultures.

Both of these first two scenes prepare the audience for a new perspective on the Federation, in ways that are only fully apparent upon subsequent viewing. In the first, the Klingons rally together against the threat they see in contact with those who bring the threatening greeting, 'we come in peace.' In the second, a peculiar precision that fans have come to associate with *Star Trek*, especially characters such as the logical Spock (Leonard Nimoy) or the android Data (Brent Spiner), dominates: the coming storm will arrive in one hour, 17 minutes and 22 seconds, the coming drought will last for 89 years, and a phaser burst of 0.17 seconds at level 14.5 is required to release the water from the well. Although this last proves exactly right, the storm approaches much more quickly than predicted, disrupting communications and requiring Georgiou to outline the *Star Trek* insignia via footprints in the sand so they can be evacuated. This image, just before the opening credits, encapsulates the project of *Star Trek: Discovery* – the outlines of the familiar Federation are there, but written in an unstable medium and subject to change. Visible only from the air, this symbol tells us that everything is about perspective.

And changing our perspective on the *Star Trek* universe is precisely what this series is about. Roughly contemporary with *The Original Series* (*TOS*) in canon timeline, *Discovery* sets out ambitiously to perpetuate all that is most beloved and culturally valuable about the franchise – its interest in social justice and equality, its utopian vision of a future of prosperity and inclusion, its commitment to pushing the boundaries of media diversity – while at the same time acknowledging the ways that the franchise's embrace of mainstream liberalism has allowed it to be complicit in white supremacist and imperialist ideologies. The Klingons are not wrong when they recognize the lie in the Federation's claim to come entirely in peace, given the Federation's blithe presumption of the superiority of their own cultural value, which are foundationally those of middle-class American whiteness. *Discovery* takes us back to the early days of the Federation, in diegetic and franchise timelines, to offer us a new vantage point on the Federation as a vision of the future.

By episode 2, we leave the familiar *Star Trek* milieu and enter an unfamiliar and disconcerting *Star Trek* at war: while Burnham discussed getting her own command in the first episode, by the second she is a disgraced traitor, seemingly imprisoned for life. The science exploration vehicle *Discovery* is repurposed as a military flagship. Georgiou is dead and, instead, we have Captain Lorca (Jason Isaacs), an authoritarian who commands with a subtle malice that seems uncomfortably non-*Star Trek*.

When I first watched 'The Vulcan Hello' I wanted to immerse myself into the comfortable *Star Trek* universe, to see how Michelle Yeoh's Captain Georgiou would build upon the model of integrity and principle embodied by Captain Picard (Patrick Stewart), my favorite of the franchise's captains. It was the *Star Trek* I wanted, but it was not the *Star Trek* I needed.

Rather, as the insightful and original essays collected here demonstrate, by wrenching viewers away from the familiar, *Discovery* has been able both to critique limitations of the franchise narrative as it unfolded and find new and better ways to embody the ideal of a better future that has always been at the franchise's core. Putting a woman of color at the center of a *Star Trek* series requires more than just the optics of leadership, the strategy adopted by *Deep Space Nine* (1993–1999) and *Voyager* (1995–2001), of widening the parameters of who is viewed as the fundamental moral agent without questioning the qualities deemed to mark one as thus central. With Burnham and with the prominent role the Mirror Universe plays in the first season, *Discovery* actively questions how and why the Federation should be valued, revealing the darker side of liberal humanism and its connection to Cold War politics, as *Fighting for the Future* ably demonstrates.

With essays on questions of race and racialization, sexuality and the politics of gender identification, and the new storytelling possibilities of television in the post-network era, this volume shows how *Discovery* engages the history of the *Star Trek* canon and reinvents the series through the new critical perspectives of twenty-first century cultural politics. These are smart discussions not only of *Discovery* and its themes, but of the central place the *Star Trek* franchise has occupied in utopian visions of the future, both for better and for worse.

In 'Lights and Shadows' (2x07), Tyler (Shazad Latif) suggests, 'We're in the middle of a fight for the future' as a way to describe the interventions made by the Red Angel. This is also an apt tag line for the place of *Discovery* in the *Star Trek* canon. The series does not always get it right, as the careful critiques collected here reveal, but it does more than simply update the franchise for the new television landscape that calls for more ambiguity, for antiheroes, and for 'gritty' reboots such as Ron Moore's *Battlestar Galactica* (2003–2012). Certainly, *Discovery* does these things, but it also continues to fight for the better future that *Star Trek* has long emblematized in the public imaginary. It strives to be a little less naïve and a little more realpolitik than its predecessor, but the overwhelming desire for the Federation insignia to continue to symbolize a future of justice, inclusivity, and peace remains. Both familiar and strange, *Star Trek: Discovery* encourages us to ask questions about means and ends along the path to this future, to recognize the costs attendant to the project of modernity that were cloaked for Roddenberry and other showrunners who could not see the damage inherit in race-blind, supposedly neutral visions of future humanity.

Fighting for the Future illuminates both the familiar and the uncanny in how *Discovery* revisits and reinvents the franchise. As these essays show, we may not always feel at home when watching the series, but such discomfort may well be its most important affect.

Episodes Cited

'The Vulcan Hello.' *Star Trek: Discovery*, written by Bryan Fuller and Akiva Goldsman, directed by Davis Semel, CBS Television Studios, 24 September, 2017.

'Light and Shadows.' *Star Trek: Discovery*, written by Ted Sullivan and Vaun Willmott, directed by Marta Cunningham, CBS Television Studios, 28 February, 2019.

Star Trek: The Original Series. 1966–1969. Gene Roddenberry. Desilu Productions, Paramount Television.
Star Trek: Deep Space Nine. 1993–1999. Rick Berman and Michael Piller. Paramount Television.
Star Trek: Voyager. 1995–2001. Rick Berman, Michael Piller, and Jeri Taylor. Paramount Television.
Battlestar Galactica. 2004–2009. Ronald D. Moore and David Eick. David Eick Productions.

Introduction
'We Get to Reach for the Stars'
Analyzing *Star Trek: Discovery*

Sabrina Mittermeier and Mareike Spychala

Fighting for the Future: Essays on Star Trek: Discovery brings together 18 essays engaging with *Star Trek: Discovery* (2017–ongoing), the newest series in the long-running and influential *Star Trek* franchise (at the time of writing). It collects contributions from a variety of disciplines, such as cultural studies, literary studies, media studies, fandom studies, history, and political science that engage with aspects such as representations of gender, shifts in storytelling, race, and depictions of diplomacy, often in contrast to older entries into the *Star Trek* canon.

Unlike the three feature films (*Star Trek,* 2009; *Star Trek: Into Darkness,* 2013; and *Star Trek: Beyond,* 2016) produced between the final episode of *Star Trek: Enterprise* (2001–2005) and the arrival of *Star Trek: Discovery,* which focus on and reimagine iconic characters like Captain Kirk (Chris Pine), Spock (Zachary Quinto), and Dr. McCoy (Karl Urban) in an alternate timeline, the first two seasons of *Star Trek: Discovery* present a prequel set ten years before the events covered by *Star Trek: The Original Series* (1966–1969). Through two self-contained narrative arcs, the first centered on the war between the Klingon Empire and the United Federation of Planets and the second on the investigation of seven mysterious signals, a being referred to as 'the Red Angel,' and the struggle against a rogue A.I., explore the road leading up to the utopian future fans and critics have come to expect from the franchise. As producer and writer Ted Sullivan stated in an interview with *Wired* (Kamen, 2017):

> We're trying to do a *Star Trek* that represents modern day society, which is we have to find a way to interact and learn and be and coexist ... Our hope is that this story represents where we are, and where we can go, in a hopeful way because Star Trek at it's [sic] core is a very hopeful series.

Another marked difference between *Discovery* and the above movies is that the latter fall squarely into the trends David M. Higgins has outlined, especially 'the trope of the alien encounter' which, he argues, 'is reformulated and redeployed … to address an environment of spectacular and indeterminate omnicrisis' (2015, 45). What is more, the first two of these movies do not expand the existing canon so much as they present an alternate timeline in which some of the events known to fans from the original *Star Trek* and older movies, such as *Star Trek II: The Wrath of Khan* (1982), are revisited.

Star Trek: Discovery (*DSC*) repeatedly gestures to and evokes these older iterations of the franchise, but nonetheless presents its own take on it, updating, for example, the look of the Klingons and the interior of the ships for the visual tastes of the twenty-first century. The show's evocation of *Star Trek* canon is maybe most obvious in the second part of the first season when the characters are stranded in the so-called Mirror Universe, a parallel universe first visited in the 1967 episode 'Mirror, Mirror' (2x04) that presents the dystopian alternative to the idealized future presented from the original *Star Trek* onwards. Through this contrast, *Discovery* further complicates the questions of good and evil, friend or foe, already raised by the war storyline dominating the first half of the season. In season two, the show goes one step further and adds a young Spock (Ethan Peck) as well as other characters featured in *TOS* and even the *Enterprise-A* to the mix.

As every new *Star Trek* show since the end of *TOS*, *DSC* has been met with intense scrutiny from fans and critics alike. This scrutiny began even before the first episode aired in September 2017, after promotional material revealed that the show's lead character, Michael Burnham (Sonequa Martin-Green), would not only not be the captain of the eponymous starship *U.S.S. Discovery*, but also a black woman. This was heralded as a continuation of the franchise's longstanding commitment to diversity, with Emma-Ann Cranston noting that the human and alien diversity seen on *DSC* 'breaks the stigma surrounding *Star Trek*' (2018). Some segments of the fan base, however, reacted with hostility to precisely this move away from mostly white and mostly male leads.[1] While one could see this development with Justin Everett as another instance of 'the reclamation of Star Trek by its fanbase' and the fact that 'Star Trek as a television

---

[1] *Star Trek: Voyager*'s (1995–2001) Captain Kathryn Janeway (Kate Mulgrew) is so far the only female Captain featured as a series regular. Benjamin Sisko (Avery Brooks), an African American man, also fell out of the roster of the usual idea of a Starfleet captain since he commanded a star base rather than the usual spaceship on *Star Trek: Deep Space Nine* (1993–1999).

and movie megatext diverged from the fan megatext' (2007, 195), the enthusiastic response to the show from the overwhelming number of *Star Trek* fans that could be observed in online communities and at conventions in the United States and Europe rather seems to indicate the franchise's continuing resonance with and relevance to its fans and the fan megatext. Additionally, the backlash against *DSC* is part of a contemporary dynamic across a variety of pop culture fandoms in which the increasing inclusion of women, people of color, and LGBTQ people has repeatedly led to outpourings of misogynist, racist, and queerphobic hate that were not always necessarily driven exclusively or even primarily by disgruntled fans, but more likely by reactionary forces from outside the fandoms. It is for all of these developments in the ways in which *DSC* engages with the *Star Trek* franchise, changes its storytelling conventions, and reverberates through the fandom that it warrants academic attention.

Criticism, both from fans and scholars, continued after the first season of *DSC* had aired. Lyta Gold (2018), while raising some valid criticisms – for example the fact that the bridge crew remains underexplored in the first season – also seems to disregard the larger implications of the first season's arc. She laments that

> the problem with contemporary SFF [i]s a failure of imagination, but in the case of *Discovery*, the problem isn't a failure as much as a pointed refusal. The *Star Trek* template already exists; utopias, ..., are difficult to write, but *Star Trek* is a plug-and-play. Why refuse to engage with Roddenberry's beloved vision, the socialist universe that inspired contemporary fandom? (2018, n.p.)

What Gold misses is the fact that *DSC*, in its first season, uses its status as a prequel to engage with questions of how the *Star Trek* universe we know from older series comes to be and how easily that utopian future might be lost due to complicity and a willingness to sacrifice one's values in the name of security. This is especially the case because it turns out that the ship's captain, Gabriel Lorca (Jason Isaacs), originally hails from the Mirror Universe; his influence on Starfleet as well as his ultimately successful plan to return to his home dimension not only puts his entire crew at risk, they also invite questions about the moral compass at the heart of the *Star Trek* franchise. Lorca's actions, motivated by his larger plan to succeed as the ruler of the fascist Terran Empire, recast and condemn some of his earlier, ambiguous behavior, complicating the other characters' and the viewers' implicit trust in Starfleet and Starfleet personnel and their willingness to go along with this morally questionable captain.

Burnham standing up to Admiral Cornwell in the finale of season one (1x15, 'Will You Take my Hand?') is the culmination of this rising doubt about the direction Starfleet has taken. She insists on the principles of the Federation and thus echoes earlier such instances in the franchise. Burnham tells her superior, who at that moment is ready to betray everything Starfleet and the Federation stand for by committing genocide against the Klingons: '[a] year ago... I stood alone. I believed our survival was more important than our principles. I was wrong. Do we need a mutiny today to prove who we are?' This is reminiscent of Captain Jean-Luc Picard's (Patrick Stewart) resistance to orders he receives from Admiral Dougherty (Anthony Zerbe) in *Star Trek: Insurrection* (1998):

> We are betraying the principles upon which the Federation was founded. It's an attack upon its very soul. And it will destroy the Ba'ku. Just as cultures have been destroyed in every other forced relocation throughout history ... How many people does it take, Admiral, before it becomes wrong? A thousand? Fifty thousand? A million? How many people does it take, Admiral? (1998)

Thus, while the tone in *DSC*'s first season is indeed darker and more dystopian than what fans and scholars have been used to from most earlier entries into the franchise's canon, the show also grapples with some of the same questions that *Star Trek* has always asked.

One could even argue that simply focusing on another instance of the well-known *Star Trek* utopia in *DSC* – as Gold and many fans would have preferred – would have been the easy way out. In keeping with the preceding *Star Trek* shows, which, as M. Keith Booker reminds us, 'ha[ve] always been about the here and now, maintaining an especially close contact with contemporary reality' (2018, xix), *DSC* asks questions that are born out of the current climate, both the lingering after-effects of 9/11 and the 'War on Terror' – Admiral Cornwell's speech about the need to defend the Federation against a possible Klingon attack (1x14, 'The War Without, the War Within') seems to echo the Bush doctrine – and the current right-wing resurgence in the United States and several European nations. While David Banks notes that '[g]ood Trek, pre-9/11 Trek was, at base, all about not even needing optimism because *of course* everything would work out: humanity was part of a galactic federation of peace and exploration' (2019, n.p.; original emphasis), it can be argued that the complacent assumption that everything will work out would be misplaced for a science fiction show written in and addressing the (political) realities of the twenty-first century. Rather, *DSC*'s first season asks and attempts to answer the question 'What can a climate of war and insecurity do to even the most utopian civilizations and how do we counter those developments?' Ultimately, *Star Trek: Discovery* serves as a reminder that the idealistic future so central to *Star Trek* as a whole is not a foregone conclusion and that it takes individual and collective action to arrive at, and preserve, a more hopeful future.

In addition, while it is understandable that some audience members and scholars miss the more overtly positive notes of earlier *Star Trek* shows, it also needs to be asked in how far their assessment of earlier shows and the topics they dealt with is tinged with nostalgia. Many of those having grown up watching *Star Trek* – whether that still meant *TOS*, or *The Next Generation* (*TNG*), *Deep Space Nine* (*DS9*) or *Voyager* (*VOY*) – claimed *DSC* was simply #NotMyTrek and voiced concern about the directions the show was taking online, but as is argued by several authors throughout this volume, this claim is not necessarily true. *The Orville* (2017–ongoing), meanwhile fills the void for those longing for the past, particularly for the *TNG* era's *Enterprise* and its crew, inciting a rivalry between the two shows; at least for those claiming it, rather than *DSC*, is the 'real' *Star Trek*. Without wanting to delve into a deeper discussion of the underlying ideas of authenticity and the larger repercussions this might have for the *Trek* fandom, it seems like this nostalgia is more overtly catered to in *DSC*'s second season. The appearance of a young Spock, as well as Captain Christopher Pike (Anson Mount), Number One (Rebecca Romijn), and an updated version of the *Enterprise* – which painstakingly recreates details of the old set down to the buttons (*Trek Movie*, 2019) and leads Mirror Georgiou (Michelle Yeoh) to quip 'Orange, really?' (2x13, 'Such Sweet Sorrow, Part One') – at least seems to suggest that some of these critical voices were heard by the powers that be. Yet the show nevertheless manages to avoid some of the retrofuturistic pitfalls that *Enterprise* (2001–2005) stumbled into. As Sharon Sharp points out,

> *Enterprise*'s retrofuturism entails an intertextual revisiting of many of the visions of the future represented in previous installments of the *Star Trek* universe. *Enterprise* nostalgically appeals to Roddenberry's utopian vision of the future. While the last two series, *DS9* and *Voyager*, explored more dystopian visions of the future, *Enterprise* returns to the original series' humanist visions of technological progress, where the white captain teaches other alien races thinly veiled moral lessons about the 'American Way.' (2011, 31)

While Pike captains the *Discovery* for most of season two – together with First Officer Saru (Doug Jones) in what he calls 'a joint custody situation'

(2x01, 'Brother') – it is still Michael Burnham who is central to the season's plot and its resolution and through whom viewers absorb most of the points the show tries to make. What is more, the crew's decision to accompany Burnham and the *Discovery* 930 years into the future in the second season's finale (2x14, 'Such Sweet Sorrow, Part Two') for now seems to leave Pike, the *Enterprise*, and most of the nostalgia attendant to them, in the past – at least within the scope of *Discovery*. Plans to expand the franchise are ever-growing, and the upcoming *Star Trek: Picard* (slated to be released in early 2020) seems designed to tap into this need to relive old times.

Given these constant negotiations with, and interrogations of *Star Trek* canon within both its text and paratexts, we have devoted the first section of this collection to *Star Trek: Discovery*'s role within the franchise. The chapters in this section entitled '"Boldly Going Where No Series Has Gone Before?" – *Discovery*'s Role Within the Franchise and Its Discontents' thus engage with the show's role within canon from a variety of perspectives and disciplines. Andrea Whitacre's chapter deals with how *Discovery* grapples with the franchise's identity as a whole; Torsten Kathke explores *Discovery*'s Cold War roots and connections to the original *Star Trek* series; John Andreas Fuchs engages with the use of profanity and depiction of violence in the franchise; and Michael G. Robinson explores the show's legacy and its ties to two contemporary homages to *Star Trek*, *The Orville* and the *Black Mirror* (2011–present) episode 'U.S.S. Callister.'

A second section entitled '"Just as Repetition Reinforces Repetition, Change Begets Change" – Modes of Storytelling in Canon and Fanon,' explores the series' ways of storytelling compared to earlier instalments, but also the way in which narrativization has generally changed in television over the past decades (with the advent of recording devices, cable television, and now, streaming platforms) and how this shift influences not only character development, but also the audience's reception of the series' characters and its narrative. Ina Batzke uses the Mirror Universe to interrogate how serialized television in the post-network era of television affects *Discovery*. Sarah Böhlau's chapter focuses on science fiction's time-honored tradition of time loop narratives, analyzing its use in the show's much lauded seventh episode 'Magic That Makes the Sanest Man Go Mad' (2017). Meanwhile, Will Tattersdill engages with *Discovery*'s serialized storytelling, by looking at the same episode and providing a comparison to earlier forms of periodical science fiction narratives, such as H.G. Wells's *War of the Worlds* (1898). Finally, Kerstin-Anja Münderlein's chapter analyzes fan fiction inspired by *Discovery* and looks at how the wider social and political issues addressed in the show are taken up and elaborated on in these fan texts.

As established above, the *Star Trek* franchise has long been known for its portrayal of a utopian vision of the future and its commitment to progressive ideals. Creator and executive producer Gene Rodenberry, quoted in *The Making of Star Trek* (1968), described 'the "message" basic to the series' in the following way: '"We must learn to live together or most certainly we will soon all die together"' (Whitfield, 112) The original *Star Trek* is recognized for featuring the first interracial kiss on American television in the episode 'Plato's Step-Children' (1968, 3x10), and for featuring an African woman on the bridge with Lieutenant Uhura (Nichelle Nichols), as well as Japanese and Russian officers with Lieutenant Sulu (George Takei) and Ensign Chekov (Walter Koenig), respectively. A few decades after the Second World War and in the midst of the escalating Cold War, this inclusive group of characters was chosen deliberately to represent a future in which humans had overcome the differences shaping the twentieth century. However, much of this diversity seemed to be 'cosmetic' – sexism was often rampant in *TOS*, and Nichelle Nichols almost dropped out of the show for lack of character development, or often even any significant speaking lines. Sexism continued to be an undercurrent in *TNG*, where female characters, particularly in the early seasons seemed to play second fiddle, and racist or orientalist portrayals of alien species in particular continued in *TOS*'s tradition, also outside of the now infamous 'Code of Honor' (1x04). This episode, among others, illustrates Katja Kanzler's claim that *Star Trek*,

> being a product of the entertainment industry, with its principal interest in economic success, ... will never adopt a radical position on multicultural issues. It rather articulates what I call a 'popular multiculturalism,' whose structure results, on the one hand, from *Star Trek*'s generic and media-related characteristics, and, on the other hand, from the socio-cultural context of changing public discourses on 'race,' ethnicity, and gender. (2004, 6)

Trek's continued expansion of its underlying idea of an idealized, equal future and its use of storylines set in the future to interrogate contemporary issues or darker chapters of human history, then, is due to these 'changing public discourses,' as Kanzler also notes (6). Notable examples from subsequent *Star Trek* series are *TNG*'s 'Measure of a Man' (1989, 2x09), *DS9*'s two-parter 'Past Tense' (1995, 3x11 and 3x12), and *VOY*'s 'Nemesis' (1997, 4x04). Still, as Daniel Bernardi has pointed out, '*Star Trek*'s liberal-humanist project is exceedingly inconsistent and at times disturbingly contradictory' (211). In light of all these arguments, it is not surprising that the earlier series and films belonging to the *Star Trek* franchise continuously fell short of their stated goal of being inclusive and representing a wide variety of ethnic groups and other minorities when it came to, for example, the representation of LGBTQ persons – despite the efforts by long-time writers such as David Gerrold. While Hikaru Sulu, one of the characters with the longest history in the franchise, was revealed as being in a same-sex relationship at the end of *Star Trek: Beyond*, the moment was brief. *DSC*, by contrast, features the franchise's first fully-fledged queer characters in the form of (later Lieutenant Commander) Paul Stamets (Anthony Rapp) and Dr. Hugh Culber (Wilson Cruz), and, from the second season onwards, Commander Jett Reno (Tig Notaro), yet, as several of the chapters in this book also argue, it still leaves a lot of room for more diverse queer representation.

In other ways, too, *DSC* is different from former *Trek* shows and other contemporary science fiction television. Its first season seemingly starts out relying on the 'trope of the alien encounter' (2015, 45) that Higgins has detected in most post-9/11 science fiction, and especially on the persistent representation of alien races as 'incomprehensibly difficult to understand' (2015, 46). Unlike the villains in the movies and television shows Higgins talks about, however, *DSC* presents the war from both the human and the Klingon perspective from the beginning, humanizing the Klingon characters, and thus complicating the war storyline and avoiding a representation of them as simply racialized others or villains. By deliberately blurring the line between humans and Klingons through the character Ash Tyler (Shazad Latif) in a way that is reminiscent of the blurred boundaries between humans and robots in *Battlestar Galactica* (2004–2009), another recent reboot of a classic science fiction series, *DSC* engages with, and dismantles discourses surrounding the Other that are often present in science fiction in the twenty-first century. Like *Battlestar*, *DSC* 'explor[es] the possibility that the self/other binary that structures the show's central conflict may be artificially constructed, and therefore able to be transcended' (Higgins, 2015, 50). While it does so more prominently in the first season, *DSC*'s second season also contains several subplots during which the crew encounters alien species that at first seem like a threat, until it is revealed that there is a miscommunication or misinterpretation of motives. Only in the representation of Control, a rogue A.I., in the second half of season two does *DSC* fall back on older tropes that frame the Other as incomprehensible threat.[2] In this and some other

---

[2] The fact that there was a showrunner change from Gretchen J. Berg and Aaron Harberts to Alex Kurtzman during the first half of season two after

cases, then, the show still finds itself stuck in *Star Trek*'s liberal humanist framework, from which it has so far been unable to disentangle itself completely. Overall, however, the show's interrogation of differences and divisions between the self and the Other on the narrative level is yet another way in which the series resonates with contemporary political and cultural debates, continuing the franchise's commitment to diversity and progressive storytelling.

Consequently, a significant number of the chapters in this book engage with issues of diversity and representation in *DSC*. These are collected in the third section, '"Infinite Diversity in Infinite Combinations?" – Negotiating Otherness in *Star Trek Discovery*.' For the sake of clarity, this section is divided into three further sub-sections encompassing chapters on Afrofuturism, the show's engagement with gender roles, and its representation of queer characters, respectively. The first sub-section, 'Afrofuturism, Imperialism, and Intersectionality,' includes an interview with Diana A. Mafe that will expand upon her deeply researched and incisively argued monograph *Where No Black Woman Has Gone Before: Screening Black Femininity in Twenty-First-Century Speculative Cinema* (2018) to include *DSC*'s lead character Michael Burnham. Whit Frazier Peterson then presents an Afrofuturist reading of the series that examines the ways in which it deals with the treatment of the black body and what he terms the 'cotton-gin effect.' Henrik Schillinger and Arne Sönnichsen focus on the ways in which American models of diplomacy are reflected in *DSC*, raising the question whether the show lives up to the franchise's progressive reputation. Finally, Judith Rauscher's chapter interrogates imperial feminisms, border crossings, and the politics of race and gender underlying the newest addition to the *Star Trek* franchise.

The second subsection, 'Interrogating Gender,' collects essays focusing on representations of gender and gender identities. Amy Chambers traces the roles of women scientists in *Star Trek* and science fiction in general, with a particular focus on Michael Burnham as not only a female, but a black female scientist. In addition, Mareike Spychala's analysis of *Discovery*'s varied female characters and their departure from existing archetypes and tropes is complemented by Sabrina Mittermeier and Jennifer Volkmer's chapter engaging with two of the show's male leads, Gabriel Lorca and Ash Tyler, dealing with its representation of pervasive

---

the writing staff had complained about abusive behavior might account for some of the discontinuous and uneven storytelling in season two. It remains to be seen how this change, and the addition of Michelle Paradise as second showrunner, will shape the show's third season.

ideas of masculinity, and how it subverts and problematizes existing tropes of the male action hero in film and on television.

In the third of these sub-sections, 'Queering *Star Trek*,' Sabrina Mittermeier and Mareike Spychala analyze the representation of openly gay characters in *DSC* and what could be seen as an explicit and implicit unearthing of a queer subtext present in the original *Star Trek* and subsequent iterations. At the same time, this essay also looks at the 'actorvism' of some of the cast members. Highlighting further opportunities for representation in the franchise, Si Sophie Pages Whybrew explores the ways in which *Star Trek* has been haunted by the absence of transgender characters and how *DSC* might ultimately transcend the franchise's and reviewers' aversion to trans identification. Finally, Lisa Meinecke analyses the tardigrade, an alien animal featured in the show, Lieutenant Stamets, and the mycelial network through a transhumanist lens that relies on the framework of the rhizome.

As these 18 essays and the interview with Diana A. Mafe attest, the first two seasons of *Star Trek: Discovery* represent an expansion of the *Star Trek* franchise, updating it narratively, via the seasons' serialized, self-contained storylines, to appeal to audiences' changed viewing habits in the streaming age. In addition, the storylines' topical nature, and the broad range of socio-political issues they engage with, allow for wide-ranging scholarly engagement with and examination of this relatively new series. As discussed above, *Discovery*, over the span of only two seasons and (at the time of writing) roughly two years of existence, has garnered a lot of praise but also incited controversy, and the essays we have brought together here in many ways reflect this. The authors in this collection work in a variety of disciplines, including American and British cultural and literary studies, political science, and cultural history. They also come from a variety of European and North American backgrounds and are at different stages in their careers. What is more, while they all have a vested interest in *Star Trek*, not all of them would describe themselves as fans. This diversity is reflected in their writing and we, as editors, felt this was important to preserve in the tone of the essays. As a consequence, not only do the writing styles across these essays diverge from each other, but so do the analyses of and opinions about *Star Trek: Discovery* expressed in them. What emerges, therefore, is a lively scholarly debate about a series that has itself already gone through a significant number of changes and, at times, seems to be engaged in a discussion not only with the franchise it belongs to, but also with itself. The variety of approaches and opinions gathered together in this book are a testimony to this and, at the current moment, when the (narrative) future of the series is yet again wide open, presenting a multiplicity of voices seems the only way to fruitfully start discussing it.

So, while the essays collected here represent some of the most salient angles for investigation that presented itself, several of the authors gathered here also had to factor out potentially fascinating lines of analysis for the sake of length. Much like *Discovery* itself, which seemingly has revitalized the *Star Trek* franchise, we see this collection only as a new starting point for scholarship into this phenomenon and its fans, both of which are going more boldly than ever before.

Works Cited

David Banks, 'Some Disconnected Thoughts About Star Trek: Discovery', *Cyborgology*, 18 February (2019), https://thesocietypages.org/cyborgology/2019/02/18/some-disconnected-thoughts-about-star-trek-discovery/.

Daniel Bernardi, '*Star Trek* in the 1960s: Liberal-Humanism and the Production of Race', *Science Fiction Studies*, 24.2 (1997): 209–25.

M. Keith Booker, *Star Trek: A Cultural History* (New York: Rowman & Littlefield, 2018).

Emma-Ann Cranston, 'Star Trek Discovery: Boldly Going Where No Series Has Gone Before', *Literary Cultures*, 1.2 (2018): n.p., https://journals.ntu.ac.uk/index.php/litc/article/view/129.

Justin Everett, 'Fan Culture and the Recentering of *Star Trek*', in Lincoln Geraghty (ed.) *The Influence of Star Trek on Television, Film, and Culture* (Jefferson, NC: McFarland, 2007): 186–98.

Lyta Gold, 'The Dismal Frontier', *Current Affairs*, 13 May (2018), https://www.currentaffairs.org/2018/05/the-dismal-frontier.

David M. Higgins, 'American Science Fiction after 9/11', in Eric Carl Link and Gerry Canavan (eds.) *The Cambridge Companion to American Science Fiction* (Cambridge: Cambridge University Press, 2015): 44–57.

Matt Kamen, 'Inside *Star Trek: Discovery*'s mission to bring hope back to TV', *Wired*, 23 September (2017), http://www.wired.co.uk/article/inside-star-trek-discovery-netflix-uk.

Diana A. Mafe, *Where No Black Woman Has Gone Before: Screening Black Femininity in Twenty-First-Century Speculative Cinema* (Austin: University of Texas Press, 2018).

Sharon Sharp, 'Nostalgia for the future: Retrofuturism in *Enterprise*', *Science Fiction Film and Television*, 4.1 (2011): 25–40.

'How the U.S.S. Enterprise Bridge Was Brought to Life for Star Trek Discovery', *TrekMovie.com*, 12 April (2019), https://trekmovie.com/2019/04/12/how-the-uss-enterprise-bridge-was-brought-to-life-for-star-trek-discovery/.

Stephen E. Whitfield, *The Making of Star Trek* (New York: Ballantine, 1968).

Episodes and Films Cited

'Mirror, Mirror.' *Star Trek*, written by Jerome Bixby, directed by Marc Daniels, NBC, 6 October, 1967.

'Plato's Step-Children.' *Star Trek*, written by Meyer Dolinsky, directed by David Alexander, Paramount Television, 22 November, 1968.

'Code of Honor.' *Star Trek: The Next Generation*, written by Katharyn Powers and Michael Baron, directed by Russ Mayberry and Les Landau, Paramount Television, 12 October, 1987.

'Measure of a Man.' *Star Trek: The Next Generation*, written by Melinda M. Snodgrass, directed by Robert Scheerer, Paramount Television, 13 February, 1989.

'Past Tense, Pt. 1.' *Star Trek: Deep Space Nine*, written by Robert Hewitt Wolfe, directed by Reza Badiyi, Paramount Television, 8 January, 1995.

'Past Tense, Pt. 2.' *Star Trek: Deep Space Nine*, written by Robert Hewitt Wolfe and Ira Steven Behr, directed by Jonathan Frakes, Paramount Television, 15 January, 1995.

'Nemesis.' *Star Trek: Voyager*, written by Kenneth Biller, directed by Alexander Singer, Paramount Television, 24 September, 1997.

'The War Without, the War Within.' *Star Trek Discovery*, written by Lisa Randolph, Sean Cochran, and Kirsten Beyer, directed by David Solomon, CBS Television Studios, 4 February, 2018.

'Will You Take My Hand?' *Star Trek: Discovery*, written by Gretchen J. Berg and Aaron Harberts, directed by Akiva Goldsman, CBS Television Studios, 12 February, 2018.

'Brother.' *Star Trek: Discovery*, written by Gretchen J. Berg, Aaron Harberts, and Ted Sullivan, directed by Alex Kurtzman, CBS Television Studios, 17 January, 2019.

'Such Sweet Sorrow, Part One and Two.' *Star Trek: Discovery*, written by Michelle Paradise, Jenny Lumet, and Alex Kurtzman, directed by Olatunde Osunsanmi, CBS Television Studios, 11 April, 2019.

Star Trek II: The Wrath of Khan. 1982. Directed by Nicholas Meyer. Paramount Pictures.

Star Trek: Insurrection. 1998. Directed by Jonathan Frakes. Paramount Pictures.

Battlestar Galactica. 2004–2009. Directed by Ronald D. Moore and David Eick. David Eick Productions.

Star Trek: Beyond. 2016. Directed by Justin Lin. Skydance Media.

'Boldly Going Where No Series Has Gone Before?' – *Discovery*'s Role Within the Franchise and Its Discontents

Looking in the Mirror
The Negotiation of Franchise Identity in *Star Trek: Discovery*

Andrea Whitacre

Introduction

The opening episodes of *Star Trek: Discovery* (*DSC*) establish it as a story about identity and power, on both fictional and metafictional levels. The very first scene of the new show invites viewers to examine Starfleet's identity from the outside, through the perspective of the Klingon Empire. Conducted entirely in Klingon with English subtitles, this opening is a comment on the nature of Starfleet as potential conqueror or colonizer despite (or rather because of) their ubiquitous friendly greeting: 'We come in peace.' This invitation to question Starfleet's identity is quickly linked to Michael Burnham's (Sonequa Martin-Green) own quest to find herself, as the episode segues from the Klingon council of war to first officer Burnham and her captain, Philippa Georgiou (Michelle Yeoh), on an away mission. Burnham unknowingly echoes the Klingons' words: 'We come in peace, that's why we're here. Isn't that the whole idea of Starfleet?' It is spoken earnestly, but it is also framed as a question – *is* that the whole idea of Starfleet? Burnham's own identity is also a work in progress. Georgiou thinks she is ready to command, but their situation on the planet offers a metaphorical commentary that suggests Burnham does not quite know yet where or who she is: 'I trust you with my life, Commander Burnham,' says Georgiou, 'but it doesn't change the fact that you are lost. Very lost.' They are saved when Georgiou marks their position with a giant Starfleet insignia in the sand for their ship to locate. The twin openings, pairing xenophobic Klingon skepticism with utopian Starfleet earnestness, suggest that through this story and the lens of our main character Starfleet identity is both an object of critique and the means of salvation.

The metanarrative of the show, especially in its casting and marketing, aspires to a reinvention of *Star Trek*'s larger identity as a franchise. The initial series advertising and interviews showcased the new ground the show was breaking in casting its first woman of color as a lead character with Burnham, its first woman of color captain with Georgiou, and its first gay lead characters with Dr. Hugh Culber and Lieutenant Commander Paul Stamets, the *U.S.S. Discovery*'s spore drive specialist. In another departure from *Star Trek* precedent and American television history more generally, both characters are also played by openly gay actors, Wilson Cruz and Anthony Rapp, respectively.

But the power Burnham has on this metanarrative level contrasts with her lack of power in the show's story. Unlike past *Star Trek* leads, she is not in a central position of authority within the ship's hierarchy, or even an official part of that hierarchy at all. She is a prisoner, serving a life sentence of labor for Starfleet. The show's design, in its casting as well as in its self-critical narrative, is bound up in contradictory representations of power and its role in Starfleet and *Star Trek*. Each of those flagship characters – Burnham and Georgiou, Culber and Stamets – experience shocking negations of their initial power over the course of the first season. Burnham loses her position and her freedom. Culber and Stamets are separated by Culber's tragic onscreen death. Captain Georgiou does not even survive the pilot episodes. The Mirror Universe is both the source and the solution for many of those contradictions, serving not just as an extended callback to past *Trek*s, but as a tool for mediating what *Star Trek* has been and what it wants to become. For each of these characters, the loss they experience is followed by a renewal and restoration of power. They die, literally or figuratively, so they can be resurrected.

Much of *Star Trek*'s recent renewal in film and now on television has concerned itself with how to portray *Trek*'s human utopia for a modern audience. Both the reboot films and season one of *DSC* share plotlines in which characters grapple with Starfleet's military nature. *Star Trek: Into Darkness* (2013) explores the way Kirk and his crew deal with an attempted military exploitation of Starfleet's mission. In an interview with the cast on science fiction news site *io9*, Simon Pegg, who plays Chief Engineer Montgomery 'Scotty' Scott, made his own tongue-in-cheek critique of the film's darker tone: 'I had this idea. I think we might all be in the Mirror [Universe] crew' (Anders, 2013). In the film, Scotty openly questions whether militarism should be part of Starfleet's identity: 'Is that what we are now? Cause I thought we were explorers.' Compare the numerous similar expressions of dismay at the military repurposing of Starfleet in *DSC*, as in 1x02 when an injured crewman (Sam Vartholomeos) laments to Burnham, 'Why are we fighting? We're explorers, not soldiers' (1x02, 'Battle at the Binary Stars'). The question could well be posed to the writers of *DSC* and the reboot films: why are we fighting? Why is modern *Star Trek* drawn to dystopian military narratives that question the utopian underpinnings of Starfleet and *Star Trek*? More and more, *Star Trek* finds itself turning to its evil twin universe in order to articulate its own contradictions and to attempt to earn its utopia.

DSC is a *Star Trek* reflective of its own origins, seeking both to reiterate and question the franchise's guiding principles and the nature of its utopian subjectivity – a balancing act that is as ambitious as it is fraught. This reflectiveness finds its literal expression in the Mirror Universe, through which the characters previously marginalized by the franchise regain the power they lost in their series introduction. In this story of mirrors, there exists an inherent duality in the way *DSC* wants to explore identity. The show is chewing on a problem of power inherent to *Star Trek*: How do you reinvent the franchise's identity while remaining recognizably that franchise? How do you rebuild the house while still living in it? It is the difficulty and complexity of this challenge that creates duality within this mirrored narrative, in which marginalized characters earn their redemption – and that of Starfleet and *Star Trek* – through suffering, hardship, and even death.

The Mirror Revisited: The History of an Alternate Universe

The Mirror Universe, named for its first appearance in the *Star Trek: The Original Series* (hereafter *TOS*) episode 'Mirror, Mirror' (2x04) is recognizable to longtime viewers by its continuity across *Star Trek* series as well as its consistent use of visual imagery: military-style uniforms, sidearms, and, more dramatic, often darkened, set lighting.[1] The Mirror Universe's Terran Empire is consistently portrayed as a fascist empire that sustains itself through military conquest. Junior officers gain promotion through assassination; their commanders maintain power through surveillance and torture. Women in the Mirror Universe exert significant power, but do so primarily through sexual manipulation, and they are in turn offered to the viewer as a sexualized spectacle (Cutler-Broyles, 2017, 49). *DSC* maintains most of these tropes, though it leans away from the sexualization of women. It also emphasizes more

---

[1] For the purposes of this essay, 'Mirror Universe' will refer specifically to the parallel universe established in the *TOS* episode 'Mirror, Mirror,' while 'Prime Universe' will refer to the timeline of the regular series episodes in all series and in the *TOS* and *TNG* films. For all other divergences from the Prime timeline within *Star Trek* canon, I will use the term 'alternate universe.'

than any other series the xenophobia of the Empire, articulated in racial terms as human supremacy over all alien species.

From its origins in *TOS*, the Mirror Universe has always been a place for intertextual play between and about the different *Star Trek* series, a kind of connective tissue for continuity and meta-commentary. The extensive use of alternate universes in television shows like *Star Trek* and *Doctor Who* suggests that the trope is particularly suited to long-running and well-established stories, allowing the internal 'mirror' to reflect not only the social and political situation of contemporary audiences but the nature of the 'normal' world of the television series (Byrne and Jones, 2018, 259). As such, *Star Trek*'s Mirror Universe and other alternate story worlds always play more to fans than to general audiences. As Steffen Hantke argues, the alternate universe in *Star Trek* becomes a tool for establishing franchise identity:

> The intertextual play – which, within the confines of the franchise, is really more an intratextual play – raises the profile of each individual series, under the umbrella of the entire franchise, to a level of self-consciousness that exceeds straightforward dramatic and narrative pleasures. In such episodes the franchise comments upon itself *as a franchise*. (2014, 563; original emphasis)

In fact, the *Star Trek* series which produce the most Mirror Universe episodes tend to be those whose relationship to the core franchise is most central or most fraught. *Star Trek: Deep Space Nine* (1993–1999) (*DS9*), whose unconventional setting and moral complexity continually raise questions of its *Trek* credentials among viewers, was the first series to revisit the Mirror Universe, and *Star Trek: Enterprise*'s (2001–2005) (*ENT*) Mirror Universe episodes can be seen as an extension of its nature as a prequel series heavily invested in returning to the origins of *Star Trek* (Kotsko, 2016, 357). With its even more extensive integration of the Mirror Universe into its first-season plot, *DSC* appears to have an even greater desire to examine its intertextual relationship to its predecessors.

DSC takes the Mirror Universe far more seriously than its sibling series, both in terms of the tone and in terms of the threat it poses. Formerly, the Federation was portrayed as threatening to the established order of the Terran Empire, and Prime characters inevitably improve the conditions of the Mirror Universe with their superior ideals. While the Empire was evil in *TOS*, it was not a very competent evil. Kirk's (William Shatner) Mirror Universe double is easily apprehended in 'Mirror, Mirror' (2x04), while Prime Kirk passes himself off relatively smoothly: 'it was far easier for you as civilized men to behave like barbarians than it was for them as barbarians to behave like civilized men,' Spock (Leonard Nimoy) informs him on his return. Before he leaves, Kirk quickly convinces Mirror Spock of the superiority of Federation ideals. In subsequent Mirror Universe episodes in *DS9* and *ENT*, the Prime Universe is always more technologically and socially advanced than the Mirror Universe. The fledgling rebellion of *DS9* gains most of its key victories through the aid of the Prime crew, and in *ENT* the Mirror Universe is shaken to its core by access to more advanced Federation technology and its principles of equality. The intended purpose of the Mirror Universe in these shows is to highlight the natural longevity, efficiency, and efficacy of the Federation.

In *DSC*, however, the purpose of the Mirror Universe is to reveal the Federation's instabilities. In contrast to the Mirror Kirk of *TOS*, Lorca (Jason Isaacs) successfully impersonates a Starfleet captain for months. What is more, when the truth comes out, Admiral Cornwell (Jayne Brook) concludes that Prime Lorca must be dead, because no Starfleet officer could survive long alone in such a universe ('The War Without, The War Within,' 1x14).[2] *Discovery* eventually learns that the Empire's experimentation with the mycelial network threatens all the parallel universes in existence. Likewise, the Mirror Universe's amoral values of strength and domination threaten to infect Starfleet's higher principles through Captain Lorca's authoritarian and military style of command, as well as Emperor Georgiou's insidious influence and Burnham's personal crisis of identity later on in the season. Through Lorca's influence, in particular, characters like Commander Saru (Doug Jones), Burnham, and Stamets must negotiate between the principled ideals for which they joined Starfleet and the pragmatic expediency which war demands.

As a proxy for the Federation's larger ethical battle against its darker impulses, Burnham fights to hold onto her sense of self and her identity as a Starfleet officer while immersed in the necessary violence of the Mirror Universe. As she performs her role as the ruthless Captain Burnham of the *I.S.S. Shenzhou*, she reflects in voice-over on the crisis of identity her duties inspire:

> It's been two days, but they're already inside my head. Every moment is a test. Can you bury your heart? Can you hide your decency? Can you continue to pretend to be one of them, even as little by little it kills the person you really are? ... I've continued

---

[2] The second *Discovery* novel's (Dayton Ward's *Drastic Measures*, 2018) coda at least suggests Prime Lorca is still alive.

to study their ways, read all I can. It's getting easier to pass, which is exactly what I feared the most. ('The Wolf Inside,' 1x11)

In the same episode, Burnham loses confidence in the essential difference between herself and her evil Mirror Universe counterpart: 'We're all human here. We all start out with the same drives, the same needs. Maybe none of us, no matter what world we're from really know what darkness is waiting inside.' Whereas previous series, from *TOS* to *DS9* to *ENT*, uniformly emphasized the potential for knowledge of the Federation to inspire rebellion within the Mirror Universe, *DSC* asserts the opposite, that participation in the Empire could corrupt even the most devoted Starfleet officer and reveal an inner potential for destruction within the Federation itself. Whereas in previous series we were dangerous to the Mirror Universe, in *DSC* the Mirror Universe becomes dangerous to us.

The Empty Throne: *Star Trek* Subjectivity and *Discovery*'s Captaincy

The Mirror Universe creates a void at the heart of *Star Trek*: the captain's chair. The captain has long served as the figure for *Star Trek*'s liberal humanistic view of the future, the philosophy famously instilled by creator Gene Roddenberry and expressed in the show's narrative project of gradually extending human values and rights to a widening circle of human and alien Others. In *TOS*, Captain Kirk's position at the center of the bridge surrounded by his officers becomes an expression of ego, rationality, and individuality, his unique ability to observe and act. He is, in other words, the humanist subject. For Kirk and later for Captain Picard in *Star Trek: The Next Generation* (*TNG*), the captain's chair signifies one's position as the emblem and arbiter of the best kind of humanity. To occupy this position, as Daniel Bernardi has shown in his study of race in *Star Trek*, one must be socially normative: white, male, straight, able, and human.[3] Around the captain's chair are his crew, who for the liberal humanist project should represent 'diversity' of various kinds – deviations from the captain's central identity position. They represent an extension of human subjectivity and its privileges, but generally possess

---

[3] The trope of the Starfleet captain is also further discussed in another chapter of this book, Sabrina Mittermeier and Jennifer Volkmer's '"We Choose Our Own Pain. Mine Helps Me Remember": Gabriel Lorca, Ash Tyler, and the Question of Masculinity.'

less power in the hierarchy of the ship and in the narrative of the show (Bernardi, 1998, 68).

As Lynne Joyrich notes in 'Feminist Enterprise? *Star Trek: The Next Generation* and the Occupation of Femininity,' the franchise as a whole tends to express its commitment to diversity and humanist ideals by gradually bringing these 'Others,' from women to people of color to aliens, into the circle of human subjectivity represented by the *Enterprise* (1996, 67). This pattern also informs the metastructure of the *Star Trek* franchise, which tends to use white male captains to establish its flagship shows before spinning off into new series like *DS9* and *Voyager* (*VOY*). Even with these shows' Black male and white female captains, one can see their relationship to the humanist subject – each are permitted only one deviation from the norm at a time.

DSC's choice of protagonist, then, is a radical break from the humanist subjectivity of *Star Trek*'s past. As a Black woman, Burnham decenters the white male subjectivity of previous series. Perhaps even more radically (from the standpoint of *Star Trek*'s typical narrative structure), she is not a captain. Moreover, her relationship to captaincy and the Starfleet power hierarchy is fraught, marked by her initial mutiny on the *U.S.S. Shenzhou*, her amorphous unranked position on the *U.S.S. Discovery*, and her uneasy impersonation of the captain of the Mirror *I.S.S. Shenzhou*. Among the crew of the *Discovery*, it is difficult to find Kirk's brand of normative, default human subjectivity anywhere. *DSC*'s casting and characterization signal its departure from the humanist reference points of past franchise installations, moving toward a modified vision of humanity that science fiction critic Annalee Newitz calls 'posthuman' (Newitz and Anders, 2018). It speaks of a conscious effort to move beyond the benevolent and conditional inclusiveness of Roddenberry's liberal humanist version of the future, where diversity orbits a normative center symbolized by the captain's seat.

The show itself seems ambivalent toward the idea of captaincy, hesitant to fill the chair. Season one features a veritable revolving door of captains: first Georgiou aboard the *Shenzhou* before her untimely death, then Lorca on the *Discovery*, then Saru while Lorca is kidnapped, then Tilly (Mary Wiseman) on the *I.S.S. Discovery* and Burnham on the *I.S.S. Shenzhou*, then Saru again, then Cornwell after their return to the Prime Universe, then Emperor Georgiou posing as Captain Georgiou. At the close of the season, the crew is en route to pick up their new captain on Vulcan, when Captain Pike (Anson Mount) of the *Enterprise* commandeers their vessel and serves as interim captain for the bulk of season two. Pike, however, carefully and frequently acknowledges the limits of his claim to *Discovery* and declines to name a replacement when he returns to the *Enterprise* at the end of the season. Almost every major character gets a chance to sit in the big chair, but no one stays there.

In refusing to name a permanent captain from among the crew, *DSC* is also revising the typical *Trek* ideal of the solitary, predestined leader. When Saru is first placed in command early in season one, for instance, he asks the ship's computer for a list of the most highly decorated captains and their shared outstanding traits. He initiates a computer program that will evaluate his actions as captain based on this metric. However, after using his own unique prey instincts to recognize a fleeing enemy ship as Lorca's, he cancels the computer's evaluation, stating, 'I know what I did' ('Choose Your Pain,' 1x05). Saru, and the other captains in this series, will chart their own path rather than emulating the typical characteristics of previous *Star Trek* luminaries. While Kirk and Picard's captaincies and the hierarchy of their officers seem preordained and immutable, *DSC* is in a constant state of flux. Its captains command based on expediency and situational need, not destiny or innate qualifications alone.

The show's second season extends this de-centering of the captaincy. Although Pike commands the *Discovery* for almost the entirety of the season and embodies a return to the (white, male, canonical) captain as a figure of human exemplarity and wise authority, he also holds the reins lightly. When he comes aboard, he asks Saru's permission before taking the captain's seat. He startles the bridge crew by asking them to sound off with their names, then explains that with danger ahead he wants to know who he is facing it with. The scene fosters a sense of solidarity and teamwork among the bridge crew, with Pike even instructing that they 'skip your ranks, they don't matter' ('Brother,' 2x01). The episode contrasts him with the arrogant Lieutenant Evan Connolly (Sean Connolly Affleck), whose shuttle is destroyed by an asteroid after he ignores Burnham's warning. Pike listens, and lives. His introduction also contrasts him, pointedly, with Lorca, as Pike acknowledges the crew's trauma from their previous experiences and promises to be a different kind of leader – one with an explicitly temporary role as their captain.

When Pike returns to the *Enterprise* at the end of the season, he leaves his replacement open-ended. Before exiting the bridge, he raises the 'housekeeping' question of the captaincy. The camera pans around the faces of the officers, lingering on Burnham, Spock, and finally, resting on Saru – but no further word is spoken before the cut to commercial.[4] When the scene returns to the bridge, Pike begins, seemingly, to formally

---

[4] Unlike Netflix, which distributes *DSC* outside of the United States, CBS's *All Access* platform offers a subscription that includes commercial breaks.

instate Saru as captain, but Saru interrupts: 'I would prefer we focus on our respective tasks for now and discuss the captaincy later. There are many things to consider' (2x13, 'Such Sweet Sorrow, Part One'). Pike accedes, and the captaincy remains formally vacant. The captainless ship then launches itself toward the far future, signaling *DSC*'s desire to effect further change to the franchise's power structures beyond the canonical limits of its prequel-era setting.

But the setting of the show – the adventures of a largely autonomous starship governed by a naval hierarchy – still requires a captain in order to function. Within this new posthuman and de-centralized perspective on *Trek* subjectivity, the captain's chair represents an unresolved question of franchise identity: when you attempt to move beyond the exclusions of humanist frameworks, what do you do with their symbol? *DSC*'s answer, at least in season one, is to replace it with a warped funhouse mirror version – Gabriel Lorca.

On the surface, Lorca looks like a Kirkish kind of captain, albeit with some rougher edges. He is notably the only straight, white, human man on the crew, ostensibly serving as the humanist center of the ship and the show. Further, like Kirk he has a way with women, shown in an onscreen tryst with his longtime friend Vice Admiral Katrina Cornwell, in his closeness to Commander Ellen Landry (Rekha Sharma), and in his keen personal interest in Burnham. But from Lorca's first introduction, these traits are undercut by mistrust and suspicion, aligned with the secretive military nature of his newly repurposed science vessel. Burnham observes the disconnect between Starfleet ideals and the ship's operations: 'Starfleet doesn't keep its engineering labs classified,' she notes. 'This is *Discovery*,' a crew member responds ('Context is for Kings,' 1x03). As a scientist, Stamets openly objects to Lorca's style of leadership, setting the captain's militarism in opposition to *Star Trek*'s mission of peaceful exploration. Lorca shuts him down with a reminder of his power as captain: 'This is not a democracy. You understand?' When Burnham questions the reasoning behind Lorca's decisions, Saru tells her, 'The captain keeps his own council.' Previous captains, too, had the final word aboard their ships, but Lorca's authority is not framed as exemplary but as tyrannical. Burnham, not Lorca, is the viewpoint character, and through her eyes the captain is a figure of mystery – sometimes admirable in his effectiveness, but never fully trusted. Even before the reveal that Lorca is actually from the Mirror Universe, *DSC* works to subtly compromise what Lorca and his chair represent. It subverts viewer expectations of captaincy and its subject position, creating a void where there used to be a center. Within the Mirror Universe, Lorca's Kirk-like traits are unmasked, and their sinister side laid bare, retroactively implicating the nature of the captain's seat he filled in the Prime Universe.

But it is hard to stage a mutiny. In depicting the captaincy and Lorca's style of masculine authority as dangerous and opposed to Federation ideals, the show is working against decades of franchise history, against the way audiences have been trained to read not only *Star Trek* but fictional leadership more broadly. Even Pike's democratic captaincy, in its loving portrayal of the captain's unshakeable sense of loyalty and duty, is as much a fulfillment of traditional masculine subjectivity as it is an inversion of it. The ways in which Lorca echoes past *Trek* captains, especially Kirk, often plays more as an homage than a critique, and many fans respond to it in this light. His ready-room and weapons lab, for example, are a Trekkie Easter egg hunt of references to *TOS*, including a Gorn skeleton and a tribble, items that are meant to suggest his mysterious connections, but that also connect him in a positive way to Kirk's brash style of leadership. The CBS-run recap and discussion show *After Trek* (2017–2018) had a marked interest in Lorca throughout the season, often reveling in exactly these kinds of Easter eggs and in Lorca's military and sexual conquests.

This interest is most disturbing when it overwrites violence toward the show's marginalized characters. After the death of Commander Landry, host Matt Mira's first gleeful question for actor Rekha Sharma asked her to confirm the character's implied sexual relationship with Lorca. He frames Landry's death as a kind of throw-back reference to another ill-fated female security officer, *TNG*'s Tasha Yar: 'But, I mean, listen, it's *Star Trek* and, you know, security chief sometimes is a deadly position to have in season one. We've seen this. We also know that sometimes those actors come back again and again and again' (1x03, 'Episode 3'). Both as the captain's conquest and as a female security officer, Mira jokingly suggests, Landry should accept and expect an unceremonious death (and, in a prophetic moment for Mira, a return) as just the way things are in *Star Trek*. Lorca actor Jason Isaacs plays along with this positioning of his character: 'Thanks for all your, uh, loyal service. I think you know what I'm talking about,' he quips to audience laughs.

This is not to say that no fun can be had at Landry's exit, especially on what is essentially a comedy-oriented recap show, but that the show's ambivalent portrayal of Lorca – and the powerful appeal of the captain's chair – allow viewers to sweep past the show's intended critique of him to revel in precisely the qualities being criticized. As a tool of critique, Lorca has the same weakness as the Mirror Universe itself: they are both too much fun. Lorca is as much an opportunity to enjoy the dark side of the captain's chair as to critique it, and his similarity to laudable *Trek* captains like Kirk makes it easy to glide over his deeper problems – like the dead and damaged women he leaves in his wake.

The *After Trek* discussion also highlights a crucial faultline in *DSC*'s approach to critiquing and revising the franchise: it criticizes the past by recreating its casualties. To invoke Audre Lorde (1984, 110), *DSC* wants to critique *Star Trek*'s relationship to power and to who gets to have it, but it wants to use the same toolset in order to do so. In the following sections, I will show how this approach creates some difficult contradictions: just as Lorca remains sympathetic and charismatic despite the show's critique and eventual condemnation of him, characters like Burnham and Culber must relive the deprivations and violence of previous *Trek*s in order to regain the power the franchise previously denied them. In order to depict these characters, the show ends up drawing on narratives of their own erasure.

The Symbolic Queer Gets Literally Buried: Culber and the Mirror

Star Trek's approach to LGBTQ characters evolved over the decades from *TOS* to *ENT* from explicit exclusion to ever-postponed promises for inclusion. Every producer since Roddenberry on *TNG*, up to and including J.J. Abrams on *Star Trek* (2009) and *Star Trek: Into Darkness* (2013), has made promises of onscreen inclusion that never materialized (Jenson, 2011; Maloney, 2013). Ultimately, there would be no queer characters in *Trek* until Abrams' third film, *Star Trek: Beyond* (2016), and then only in a much-touted but brief onscreen moment that relies more on implication than on explicit representation.

In between the refusal and the delayed promises, *Trek* relied mainly on the symbolic – and, with it, the tragic. Symbolism is *Star Trek*'s preferred method for addressing social issues of all kinds, and the alien space adventure is in many ways a medium designed for mainly metaphorical discussion of humanity. In episodes like *TNG*'s 'The Host' (4x23) and 'The Outcast' (5x17) or *ENT*'s 'Stigma' (2x14) and 'Cogenitor' (2x22), alien culture and biology become a stand-in for exploration of human homosexuality and gender identity. *DS9*'s 'Rejoined' (4x06) perhaps comes closest to breaking through the metaphorical to the representational when Jadzia Dax (Terry Farrell) kisses another woman from her symbiont's past life – but this encounter is still cloaked in the guise of the 'alien taboo.' For much of *Trek*'s history, queerness was the thing that could not be represented literally – the thing that could only be figured, never embodied. Further, all of these symbolic episodes end in tragedy, ranging from romantic rejection to forced 'reeducation' to death. *DSC* makes an important stride in breaking through the symbolism and unreality of these previous depictions.[5] But there is also a troubling aspect to the way *DSC* makes queerness visible: it makes this implicit violence part of the explicit level of the text.

Aside from Sulu's (John Cho) very brief moment in *Star Trek: Beyond*, Stamets and Culber are *Star Trek*'s first canonically gay characters, and they are the first to appear in any *Trek* television show. There is much to celebrate in their depiction: it is utterly unsensationalized, almost quotidian. The first onscreen confirmation of their relationship is a scene in which they brush their teeth together. Both characters are portrayed with enough depth that one can perhaps forgive that this is more a Straight-plus world, still using heterosexuality as its default, rather than a truly queer future. (In 1x07, 'Magic to Make the Sanest Man Go Mad,' for instance, Burnham is asked at a party about her old boyfriends. Her discomfort, we are meant to understand, is with her lack of romantic history, not with the heteronormativity of the question.) One of the show's most delicate and touching moments is an improvised ballroom dance between Stamets and Burnham in 1x07, in which he tells the story of how he met Culber: 'Never hide who you are. That's the only way relationships work.' It is a moment that subtly speaks to the new way forward for the franchise: this is the only way *Star Trek* works.

But *DSC* is still intent on using tragedy to explore that new visibility. In a shocking onscreen moment, Culber is killed by a crewmate in episode 1x09. His neck snaps. He falls to the floor. I found it very difficult to watch, all the more so because the show seems intent on showing the image of his death over and over in flashbacks and recaps. In all, it is shown onscreen five times in season one and twice more in season two. His loss becomes a centerpiece of the plot resolution in season one, with Culber's multiverse echo guiding Stamets back to *Discovery* and then guiding *Discovery* back to the Prime Universe. The storyline seemed to be a textbook instance of the trope of 'burying your gays,' constructing tragic deaths for any queer characters in a story,[6] especially those in a

---

[5] For a further analysis of LGBTQ representation on *DSC*, see Sabrina Mittermeier and Mareike Spychala's essay '"Never Hide Who You Are": Queer Representation and Actorvism on *Star Trek: Discovery*' published in this volume.

[6] The phrase 'bury your gays' as a name for this media trope originates in fandom and was popularized by the online site *TV Tropes*, largely replacing the previous fandom moniker of 'Dead Lesbian Syndrome.' Both describe a common cliché in fictional narratives in which queer characters, especially women, frequently die in sudden or tragic circumstances within the story.

romantic relationship, so much so that Culber actor Wilson Cruz and showrunners were quick to assure fans that Culber would return, and that the narrative payoff would be worth the heartbreak (1x09, 'Episode 9'). It is the brutality of Culber's death, more than anything else, that lingers at the close of the season, an echo of the tragic symbolic ends of other queer-adjacent characters in *Star Trek*. In season two, the show introduces the character of Commander Jett Reno, played by Tig Notaro, who talks about her wife. But her wife, too, is dead, another victim of season one's Federation–Klingon War.

Culber receives his promised resurrection in 'Saints of Imperfection' (2x05), in which Burnham and Stamets enter the mycelial network and discover that the spore-world has preserved his consciousness in a new body. For all the reassurances about his return from death, the mechanism of his return feels oddly perfunctory: it follows an arc in which Tilly is haunted and eventually kidnapped by a spore alien inhabiting her body, but the arc forms a narrative cul-de-sac that has no long-term connections to the ongoing plot of the season, in which the spore drive and mycelial network hardly factor. It is, fairly transparently, a plot device for returning Culber, making his return feel more like a side plot than a major part of the ongoing narrative.

Although the show explores his struggle to cope with his trauma and resume his old life, it continues to do so mainly in the background of other events. Culber and Stamets go through a painful separation, and Culber moves out of their shared quarters and makes plans to transfer to another ship. Many of these scenes, such as the one in which Reno tells Culber about her wife and pushes him to reconcile with Stamets ('Through the Valley of Shadows,' 2x12), are tender and emotional, giving real weight to the characters' sense of loss and love for each other. However, they are also consistently set against a backdrop of pain and tragedy, which forms the core of the show's interest in these characters and relationships. Culber's pivotal decision to stay with Stamets happens offscreen, recounted to a wounded, half-conscious Stamets in a brief scene of reconciliation (2x14, 'Such Sweet Sorrow, Part Two'). To be fair, the two-part episode is already packed with action and the resolution of other major characters' storylines. But the brevity and secondary treatment of Culber's true moment of return speaks to the show's priorities regarding the character – they are far more interested in Culber's death and trauma

---

The trope has a long history in science fiction and fantasy television: one of its first uses in fandom referred to the death of the character Tara on the show *Buffy the Vampire Slayer*, and other notable examples include *Babylon 5*, *Battlestar Galactica*, and, more recently, *The 100*.

than in its amelioration. His story arc over the first two seasons, the promised epic love story, relies alarmingly on the same tragic narratives that fuel *Star Trek*'s earlier symbolic queer episodes.

Michael Burnham: Pain, Power, and Black Womanhood in *Star Trek*

Burnham is an inherently dual character, existing at the center of the narrative but at the margins of Starfleet's power structures. She is at once a reflection of *Star Trek*'s historical humanist hierarchy and a rebuttal to it – a reflection in that her position on the crew is marginal to its power structures, a rebuttal in that this marginal position is now the main perspective of the entire show. As such, there is a duality as well in what the show is claiming for the franchise's identity through her character and casting. On the one hand, through *Trek*'s humanist philosophy of diversity, the show can credibly claim that their casting and character choices are a continuation of Roddenberry's legacy, something that has always been part of *Trek*. In response to racist criticism of Martin-Green's casting as Burnham, for instance, fans pointed to *TOS*'s Uhura as evidence that *Trek* has always been inclusive (Andrews, 2017, para. 5). This is entirely true, but it also cheats the real newness of Martin-Green's position in *Trek*, and the extent to which Uhura's role remained largely marginal in terms of narrative space onscreen. There is a famous anecdote about Nichelle Nichols meeting Martin Luther King, Jr., who convinced her to stay on the show when she was planning to leave after its first season (Ohlheiser, 2015, para. 7). Though this anecdote underlines the groundbreaking nature of Uhura's role in *TOS*, and is often told in order to demonstrate *Star Trek*'s anti-racist credentials, it also tends to overshadow the reasons Nichols intended to leave in the first place, as she watched her lines trimmed and cut from every script: 'It finally got to the point where I had really had it. I mean I just decided that I don't even need to read the FUCKING SCRIPT! I mean I know how to say, "hailing frequencies open"' (qtd. in Bernardi, 1998, 40). Martin-Green and Michael Burnham are contending with both sides of Black womanhood in *Trek*: their central role in the show's legacy and their marginal role in the show's content.

Not coincidentally, 'Mirror, Mirror' is one of Uhura's most significant episodes, in which she receives her own subplot complete with action and espionage, a reprieve from 'hailing frequencies open.' Within the Mirror Universe Burnham, too, experiences a reprieve from her powerless status, commanding the *I.S.S. Shenzhou* with absolute authority. The Mirror

Universe rewards her with the captaincy she forfeited with her mutiny against Starfleet, extravagantly returning her lost power. For both Uhura and Burnham, it is a space of possibility as well as hardship, where the usual strictures of the universe can be lightened and bent.

But like Burnham's own rhetorical purpose within the show, the Mirror Universe is a two-sided tool in her narrative. It grants her the power Starfleet denied her, but it also punishes her, allowing her to make amends to Starfleet. She works off Starfleet's debts in a chillingly literal way – her work on the *Discovery* is, after all, a kind of prison labor – by serving them at their darkest hour and by undergoing a personal journey that (also very literally) reflects her choices back at her (Capener, 2018). Troublingly, the show makes her exile from centers of power her own fault, something she must atone for, when in fact it largely reflects the implicit treatment of all women of color in *Star Trek*. Her storyline in season one is partly a tacit acknowledgement of that checkered franchise history, reiterating the violences of the past in order to show Burnham triumphing over them and remaking Starfleet in the process. At the same time, the show makes Burnham into a stand-in for Starfleet itself, with her ethical struggles and lessons mirroring those of the Federation. She is the embodiment of Starfleet's struggle between pragmatic, fearful aggression and moral principles, but she is also the embodiment of the people *Star Trek* has historically marginalized in its onscreen depictions of the future. Her struggle to regain the power and status she lost in the series opener suggests the lingering shadow of *Star Trek*'s past, a need for Burnham to earn what is given freely to others. For Burnham, this future does not look utopian yet.

Through the Mirror Universe plotline, Burnham plumbs the potential for darkness within herself and within Starfleet. When she ultimately rejects it to embrace the value of true Federation ideals, it is portrayed as a reinforcement of not just her own identity, but that of *Star Trek* as a whole. In the final scene of season one, an inverse mirror to the dark staging of her military tribunal in the series opening, Burnham is now honored and praised by the institution that formerly condemned her (Capener, 2018). She and Starfleet are each redeemed by the other, with service saving Burnham from ethical compromise and Burnham saving Starfleet from the same. The connection is clear to the point of heavy-handedness in Burnham's final speech:

> The only way to defeat fear is to tell it no. No, we will not take shortcuts on the path to righteousness. No, we will not break the rules that protect us from our basest instincts. No, we will not allow desperation to destroy moral authority. I am guilty of all these

things. ... We will continue exploring, discovering new worlds and new civilizations. Yes, that is the United Federation of Planets. Yes, that is Starfleet. Yes, that is who we are, and who we will always be. ('Will You Take My Hand,' 1x15)

The original values of *Star Trek*, Burnham's speech asserts, are rediscovered and reaffirmed through her own struggles. But this ending fails to reckon with Starfleet's own role in that suffering. The way the series chooses to work through the problems of *Star Trek*'s humanist framing is by repeating and then reclaiming the violences visited upon marginalized characters. The result is a fragmented doubling, a character who highlights the value of *Star Trek* ideals and its failure in these ideals.

Death and Resurrection, or Can We Really Return from the Mirror?

The purpose of modern *Trek*'s many journeys downward into dystopia – the wars, the deaths, the moral ambiguity, the Mirror Universe – is so it can return. *Star Trek* travels through the Mirror Universe so that it can come back changed and renewed, its values affirmed or demons exorcized. For individual characters, the return may take the form of resurrection (or at least a doppelganger), restoration of rank and status, or resumption of scientific exploration. So, what are the characters given in return for their shattering voyage through the mirror? By the end of the season the answer is power, both in terms of in-world authority for the characters and in terms of narrative centrality within the franchise. This is especially true for Burnham, who receives a restored rank and a more confident understanding of herself and her place in Starfleet. There is an important payoff for the narrative hardships that she, Georgiou, and Culber endure. And yet it still troubles me that the way the show chooses to tell these characters' stories is by hurting them, by taking away their power and making them earn it back.

Burnham, Georgiou, and Culber are embodiments of a crisis of identity within *Star Trek*. These characters serve as staging-grounds for correcting the inequalities and exclusions of the past, and for bringing *Star Trek* more in line with its own ideals – paradoxically, changing it by making it ever more what it already was. But they are also collateral damage in *DSC*'s reiterative impulse, its desire to repeat the past in the process of revising it. *DSC* does not just want to be a show that fixes the franchise, it wants to be a show *about* fixing the franchise – which means they have to break these characters before they can empower them, and they end up reiterating some of *Trek*'s worst impulses even as they attempt to rewrite them. *DSC* desires to fix the problems of the past but is not able – yet – to fully imagine the future.

Works Cited

Charlie Jane Anders, 'Simon Pegg's Star Trek Reboot Theory: Is this the 'Mirror' Crew?', *io9*, 9 May (2013), https://io9.gizmodo.com/simon-peggs-star-trek-reboot-theory-is-this-the-mirro-499064330.

Travis M. Andrews, 'Some white "Star Trek" fans are unhappy about remake's diversity', *Washington Post*, 23 June (2017), https://www.washingtonpost.com/news/morning-mix/wp/2017/06/23/star-trek-fans-anger-at-remakes-diversity-proves-they-dont-understand-star-trek/?noredirect=on&utm_term=.cba484118ae5.

Daniel Bernardi, *Race-ing Toward a White Future* (New Brunswick, NJ: Rutgers University Press, 1998).

Aiden Byrne and Mark Jones, 'Worlds Turned Back to Front: The Politics of the Mirror Universe in *Doctor Who* and *Star Trek*', *Journal of Popular Television*, 6.2 (2018): 257–70.

Sean Christopher Capener, 'Star Trek: Discovery is Optimism, But Not for Us', *Itself*, 5 March (2018), https://itself.blog/2018/03/05/star-trek-discovery-is-optimism-but-not-for-us/.

Teresa Cutler-Broyles, 'What We See When We Look in the Mirror: Star Trek's Alternative Sexuality', in Nadine Farghaly and Simon Bacon (eds.) *To Boldly Go: Essays on Gender and Identity in the Star Trek Universe* (Jefferson, NC: McFarland, 2017).

Steffen Hantke, '*Star Trek*'s Mirror Universe Episodes and US Military Culture through the Eyes of the Other', *Science Fiction Studies*, 41.1 (2014): 562–78.

Michael Jenson, 'Gay Star Trek Character? J.J. Abrams Promises AfterElton He'll Explore the Possibility for Next Film', *NewNowNext*, 4 August (2011), http://www.newnownext.com/gay-star-trek-character-jj-abrams-promises-afterelton-hell-explore-the-possibility-for-next-film/8/2011/.

Lynne Joyrich, 'Feminist Enterprise? *Star Trek: The Next Generation* and the Occupation of Femininity', *Cinema Journal*, 35.2 (1996): 61–84.

Adam Kotsko, 'The Inertia of Tradition in *Star Trek*: Case Studies in Neglected Corners of the "Canon"', *Science Fiction Film and Television*, 9.3 (2016): 347–70.

Audre Lorde, "The Master's Tools Will Never Dismantle the Master's House', in Audre Lorde (ed.) *Sister Outsider: Essays and Speeches by Audre Lorde* (Berkeley, CA: Crossing Press, 1984): 110–13.

Jamie Lovett, '*Star Trek: Discovery* Cast Promises Return to Familiar Trek Tone, Ideals in Season 2', *Comic Book*, 22 October (2018), https://comicbook.com/startrek/2018/10/22/star-trek-discovery-season-2-optimism/.

Devon Maloney, '*Star Trek*'s History of Progressive Values – And Why It Faltered on LGBT Crew Members', *Wired*, 13 May (2013), https://www.wired.com/2013/05/star-trek-lgbt-gay-characters/.

Annalee Newitz and Charlie Jane Anders, 'Hope, Dread, and *Star Trek: Discovery*', *Our Opinions Are Correct Podcast*, 15 March (2018), https://www.ouropinionsarecorrect.com/shownotes/2018/8/4/episode-1-hope-dread-and-star-trek-discovery.

Abby Ohlheiser, 'How Martin Luther King Jr. convinced "Star Trek's" Lt. Uhura to stay on the show', *The Washington Post*, 31 July (2015), https://www.washingtonpost.com/news/arts-and-entertainment/wp/2015/07/31/how-martin-luther-king-jr-convinced-star-treks-uhura-to-stay-on-the-show/?noredirect=on&utm_term=.ba1518d1c795.

StarTrek.com staff, '*Discovery* Heads to Blu-ray: Sonequa Martin-Green', *StarTrek.com*, 12 September (2018), http://www.startrek.com/article/discovery-heads-to-blu-ray-sonequa-martin-green.

Episodes and Films Cited

'Mirror, Mirror.' *Star Trek: The Original Series*, written by Gene Roddenberry and Jerome Bixby, directed by Marc Daniels, Paramount Television, 6 October, 1967.

'Skin of Evil.' *Star Trek: The Next Generation*, written by Joseph Stephano and Hannah Louise Shearer, directed by Joseph L. Scanlan, Paramount Television, 25 April, 1988.

'The Host.' *Star Trek: The Next Generation*, written by Michel Horvat, directed by Marvin V. Rush, Paramount Television, 13 May, 1991.

'The Outcast.' *Star Trek: The Next Generation*, written by Jeri Taylor, directed by Robert Scheerer, Paramount Television, 16 March, 1992.

'Crossover.' *Star Trek: Deep Space Nine*, written by Peter Allen Fields and Michael Piller, directed by David Livingston, CBS Televison Studios, 15 May, 1994.

'Rejoined.' *Star Trek: Deep Space Nine*, written by Ronald D. Moore and René Echevarria, directed by Avery Brooks, Paramount Television, 30 October, 1995.

'The Emperor's New Cloak.' *Star Trek: Deep Space Nine*, written by Ira Steven Behr and Hans Beimler, directed by LeVar Burton, CBS Television Studios, 3 February, 1999.

'Stigma.' *Star Trek: Enterprise*, written by Rick Berman and Brannon Braga, directed by David Livingston, Paramount Television, 5 February, 2003.

'Cogenitor.' *Star Trek: Enterprise*, written by Rick Berman and Brannon Braga, directed by LeVar Burton, Paramount Television, 30 April, 2003.

'In A Mirror Darkly, Parts 1 and 2.' *Star Trek: Enterprise*, written by Mike Sussman, directed by James L. Conway (part 1) and Marvin V. Rush (part 2), Paramount Television, 22 April, 2005 (part 1), 29 April, 2005 (part 2).

'The Battle of the Binary Stars.' *Star Trek: Discovery*, written by Gretchen J. Berg and Aaron Harberts, directed by Adam Kane, CBS Television Studios, 24 September, 2017.

'Context is for Kings.' *Star Trek: Discovery*, written by Gretchen J. Berg, Aaron Harberts, and Craig Sweeny, directed by Akiva Goldsman, CBS Television Studios, 1 October, 2017.
'The Butcher's Knife Cares Not for the Lamb's Cry.' *Star Trek: Discovery*, written by Jesse Alexander and Aron Eli Coleite, directed by Olatunde Osunsanmi, CBS Televison Studios, 8 October, 2017.
'Episode 3.' *After Trek*, hosted by Matt Mira, CBS Television Studios, 8 October, 2017.
'Choose Your Pain.' *Star Trek: Discovery*, written by Kemp Powers, directed by Lee Rose, CBS Television Studios, 15 October, 2017.
'Magic to Make the Sanest Man Go Mad.' *Star Trek: Discovery*, written by Aron Eli Coleite and Jesse Alexander, directed by David Barrett, CBS Television Studios, 29 October, 2017.
'Into the Forest I Go.' *Star Trek: Discovery*, written by Bo Yeon Kim and Erika Lippoldt, directed by Chris Byrne, CBS Television Studios, 12 November, 2017.
'Episode 9.' *After Trek*, hosted by Matt Mira, CBS Television Studios, 7 January, 2018.
'The Wolf Inside.' *Star Trek: Discovery*, written by Lisa Randolph, directed by T.J. Scott, CBS Television Studios, 14 January, 2018.
'The War Without, The War Within.' *Star Trek: Discovery*, written by Lisa Randolph, Sean Cochran, and Kirsten Beyer, directed by David Solomon, CBS Television Studios, 4 February, 2018.
'Will You Take My Hand?' *Star Trek: Discovery*, written by Gretchen J. Berg and Aaron Harberts, directed by Akiva Goldsman, CBS Television Studios, 12 February, 2018.
'Brother.' *Star Trek: Discovery*, written by Gretchen J. Berg, Aaron Harberts, and Ted Sullivan, directed by Alex Kurtzman, CBS Television Studios, 17 January, 2019.
'Saints of Imperfection.' *Star Trek: Discovery*, written by Kirsten Beyer, directed by David Barrett, CBS Television Studies, 14 February, 2019.
'Through the Valley of Shadows.' *Star Trek: Discovery*, written by Bo Yeon Kim and Erika Lippoldt, directed by Doug Aarniokoski, CBS Television Studios, 4 April, 2019.
'Such Sweet Sorrow, Part One and Two.' *Star Trek: Discovery*, written by Michelle Paradise, Jenny Lumet, and Alex Kurtzman, directed by Olatunde Osunsanmi, CBS Television Studios, 11/18 April, 2019.

Star Trek. 2009. Directed by J.J. Abrams. Paramount Pictures.
Star Trek Into Darkness. 2013. Directed by J.J. Abrams. Bad Robot Productions, Skydance Productions, K/O Paper Products.
Star Trek: Beyond. 2016. Directed by Justin Lin. Skydance Media, Bad Robot Productions, Sneaky Shark Productions, Perfect Storm Entertainment.

A *Star Trek* About Being *Star Trek*
History, Liberalism, and *Discovery*'s Cold War Roots

Torsten Kathke

At the height of the Cold War, the original *Star Trek* series (1966–1969) provided viewers with a utopian, racially inclusive and altogether progressive alternative to the contemporary standoff among superpowers. Yet, at the same time it was caught within the bipolar world system.[1] *Star Trek* may have interrogated U.S. policy in the Cold War, frequently posing the question of what its heroic protagonists were supposed to do given morally tenuous options, but it never questioned that the crew the show portrayed in fact was heroic, and good.

In the Western movie analogy that creator Gene Roddenberry used to sell his brainchild to NBC, *Star Trek* was a 'wagon train to the stars' (Gibberman, 1991, 109). From set design to story tropes to music and stuntmen's fighting techniques, the genre was dutifully reproduced in *Star Trek*. As were its precepts: exploration of space was equated with historian Frederick Jackson Turner's American western frontier (in its guise, here, as 'the final frontier') and as a necessary drive for humanity (Bonazzi, 1993, 153; Turner, 1998, 31–60). The need for the trek in the name of progress itself was never doubted. The original *Star Trek*'s emphasis on diversity, too, remained rooted in its age. The show sought to include additional groups into the purview of male, liberal, American whiteness while never truly portraying them as co-creators of its quasi-utopian future.

After the original run, *Star Trek* remained a narrative corollary to popular imaginaries of history. Trends, fads, and new focus points in historiography frequently cropped up in its iterations. *The Next Generation*'s (1987–1994) emphasis on cultured diplomacy, for example, coincided with a slew of academic and popular histories focusing on

---

[1] Bipolarity always had limits (Westad, 2018, 7). As John Lewis Gaddis contends, however, the Cold War world *appeared* to be a bipolar one (Gaddis, 2005, 120). This mattered for how it was portrayed in popular culture.

America's role in the world, while *Deep Space Nine*'s (1993–1999) location as an outpost on the frontier depicted a meeting ground of cultures, as if ripped from the pages of any number of works of the then-ascendant *New Western History*.

2017's *Star Trek: Discovery* takes a deliberate departure from the colorful and successful, but philosophically lackluster alternative universe incarnation depicted in the series of movies helmed by J.J. Abrams from 2009 onward. *Discovery* (*DSC*), I argue, operates on an added meta level that is not found in any of the other editions of the franchise. It is not just political in the sense that it takes stances in its narratives and challenges viewers' preconceptions regarding current political issues. It also pointedly reasserts *Star Trek*'s role *as* a societal force that can, and wants to be, part of such a discourse.

In this chapter I explore how, in doing this, *DSC* harkens back to the idea of a unitary mainstream American society, continued into the future as a utopian ideal. In turn, the series builds not only on a tradition of exceptionalism present in America's constitutive canon of writings, but more specifically on a tradition of political thought regarding the idea of liberalism; a tradition dominant in public discourse during the 1960s, the decade of *Star Trek*'s original conception.

To trace this intellectual history, I will first put *DSC* into its social and political context. I then elaborate on *Star Trek*'s roots in Cold War America, highlighting the notion of liberalism described by Louis Hartz and its attendant claim that the United States was a nation solely founded on the thought of Enlightenment philosopher John Locke. A description of the cultural creation of the original series follows, as well as a brief section on how the legacy of this genesis was preserved throughout later series. Finally, I return to *DSC* itself, developing my argument that the series continues this tradition while also adding a further level of reflection and self-awareness of its status in the canon. The conclusion links both series through a common set of ideological positions and shows that, while *DSC* strays from some principles that former versions held fast to, it both actively reproduces the core framework of *Star Trek* and cannot escape the franchise's philosophical underpinnings even where it attempts to depart from them.

The Limits of *Star Trek*

DSC's first season pointedly creates a universe in which the predictable normalcy of the benign protectorate offered by the United Federation of Planets, the various series' stand-in for, depending on the context, the United Nations or the United States (Scharf and Robert, 2003, 76; Crothers, 2015, 66–67; Wills, 2015, 3), is out of kilter. The storyline begins with the start of a dire war against the original series' favorite baddies, the Klingons. This provides dramatic fodder for season one. Picking up the baton of a cadre of shows never overly inventive in terms of structure, this iteration of *Star Trek*, too, happily follows Campbellian formulas of the hero's journey (Campbell, 2008, 210).

Sonequa Martin-Green's character Michael Burnham is the audience proxy, a second-favorite child who has proven herself. A human adopted by Sarek (James Frain), biological father of quintessential *The Original Series* (*TOS*) character Spock, Burnham has advanced through the rungs of the exclusive Vulcan Science Academy and through Starfleet, becoming a trusted first officer to Michelle Yeoh's Captain Philippa Georgiou. Buoyed by a bout of exploratory enthusiasm and imbued with a penchant for reckless adventure, she accidentally sets off a war between the Federation and the newly resurgent Klingon Empire, getting her captain killed in the process. The events of *DSC*'s first season then follow Burnham as she redeems herself. Rescued from spending a good portion of her remaining life in a penal colony by starship *Discovery*'s Captain Gabriel Lorca (Jason Isaacs), she becomes a member of the ship's crew, attempting to prove her worthiness to both her complement of comrades and herself.

On the surface, *DSC* ticks all the boxes of progressive fantasy – it is literally and figuratively inclusive: it features a black female main character, a gay couple, and various alien species, as well as cybernetically enhanced humans who are accepted without prejudice, as members of the crew. Its underlying politics, however, are those of the 1960s original and, with infrequent exceptions, those of the hundreds of episodes that followed: they create an ever-more inclusive liberal ideal world. They do not, however, fundamentally critique that vision. Said vision is one of Cold War internationalism that preserves the primacy of the nation-state at its core while only adding layers of inclusion on top, not making them central to an altogether more open conception of political involvement. *Star Trek*'s vision of the future in 2017 tells forward the tale of Turner from 1893, by way of Kennedy's 1960 *New Frontier*.

This frontier has through the decades consistently opened for settlement to a growing number of groups and individuals once excluded from the Western movie masculinity that overtly dominated the original run. Inclusion in *DSC* has its limits, though, and they are strikingly similar to the limits *TOS* established in the 1960s. Mike O'Connor has argued that a liberal color-blindness affected the series, while Daniel Bernardi has analyzed the racism inherent in *Star Trek*'s supposedly post-racial society (Bernardi, 1997; O'Connor, 2012). If one accepts these assessments, one is then prompted to conclude that the series fared well where it could grandstand on principle, and where it could incorporate otherness into its liberal conventions. If Captain Kirk in *TOS*'s 'Plato's Stepchildren' (3x10) asserts that 'where I come from size, shape, or color makes no difference,' it is an expression of that color-blindness. Where questions of personhood beyond a performative assertion in the style of the American founding belief that 'all men are created equal' were concerned, however, the stumbles into racism and sexism were frequent. This is sometimes painfully visible, as when in 'The Menagerie, Part Two' (1x12) a character remarks of green-skinned Orion women held as slaves that 'they're like animals, vicious, seductive. They say no human male can resist them.' He casually embraces an orientalist and misogynist worldview also tacitly accepted by the scene's interlocutor James Kirk. *Star Trek* presents a society outwardly accepting of forms of co-existence and cohabitation not traditionally presented in the American twentieth or twenty-first century mainstream. Yet, it also always painstakingly circumscribes the way in which these can be experienced. Thus, in *DSC* the *Trek* television universe's first gay couple among series regulars, Dr. Culber (Wilson Cruz) and Lieutenant Stamets (Anthony Rapp), is shown to us in images invoking the tame, idealized domesticity of 1950s family sitcoms; matching pajamas and all.

The original *Star Trek*'s janus-faced overt moralizing on topics of inclusion and diversity – the latter even literally in its championing of the Vulcan concept of 'Infinite Diversity in Infinite Combinations' – while at the same time often failing to create room for minority characters to be allowed the same possibilities for development as those representing white America, has been tempered in later series. What *Star Trek* can never fully escape, however, is its philosophical grounding in American liberalism, as defined by political scientist Louis Hartz at mid-century. That liberalism lay at the heart of its ideology and that *Star Trek* reproduced in space major constellations of the Cold War has been argued convincingly (Worland, 1988, 112; O'Connor, 2012). With definitions of liberalism notoriously slippery, however, its use to describe *Star Trek*'s undergirding rationality demands elaboration.

Cold War Liberalism

Harvard scholar Louis Hartz's 1955 *The Liberal Tradition in America* became a citation classic almost immediately. It is a sweeping waltz through the weeds of U.S. elite learnedness in the middle of the twentieth century.

In the service of his main argument, Hartz nonchalantly name-checks over 60 thinkers and writers like Locke, Beard, Marx, Peggy Hutchinson, John Adams, Margaret Kennedy, Aristotle, and Sir Walter Scott. (Hartz, 1955, 3–13). That argument: what set America apart from other countries was a single factor that showed itself as two: the absence of feudalism and the presence of classical liberalism (Hartz, 1955, 20–21).

Where Arthur Schlesinger's contention in his 1949 *The Vital Center* was that liberalism was necessary to provide a bulwark against fascism and communism, Hartz's contention was that the United States's core political system functioned as a push-and-pull of two different variants of liberalism, the progressive liberalism of the left in the mold of FDR's *New Deal* (today almost synonymous with 'liberalism'), and liberal free-trade conservatism (Gunnell, 2005, 196; Horowitz and Schlesinger, 2017). Both were ingrained in U.S. political culture from the founding of the republic and both could unite large enough swathes of the U.S. population at any one time. This was why they could forever form the foundation of the country's political discursive sphere, including and co-opting even the fringes and providing extreme points that were still within the purview of liberalism. Alexander Hamilton's elitist finance capitalism and its disciples may have battled Jeffersonian yeoman agrarianism, but 'in a liberal society the individualism of Hamilton [was] also a secret part of the Jeffersonian psyche' (Hartz, 1955, 12).

Any detractors of liberalism needed to still look to liberalism as their one avenue to gain a share of power. America may have fought over the soul of the country, Hartz would admit, but all the fighting had been done on one controlled battlefield, with pre-defined rules that made sure the outcome would be a dialectical outgrowth of liberalism, nothing outside it. Accordingly, American ideology, warts and all, was liberalism, and liberalism was Americanism (Hartz, 1955, 12–14).

James T. Kloppenberg observed in 2001 that Hartz's book 'provides an inadequate account because its analysis is too flat and too static. Hartz focused exclusively on issues of economics and psychology and missed the constitutive roles played by democracy, religion, race, ethnicity, and gender in American history' (Kloppenberg, 2001, 460). But despite such disparagement by academic interpreters of American society, Hartz held on. More than that: he was duly rescued for the 50th jubilee of his book. Philip Abbott, in 2005, found that he could use 'his basic concepts' as 'powerful analytical tools, which continue to provide the most compelling analysis of recent American political development' despite Hartz's own flawed takes on American history (Abbott, 2005, 93). Assessing Hartz 50 years after the book's publication, Corey Robin had to admit that 'The evidence weighs heavily against Hartz, but the picture he paints seems inescapably right.' He pointedly wondered: 'How can a book that gets so much wrong nevertheless seem so right?' (Robin, 2005, 2). Part, if not all, of the answer here is certainly the popularity of Hartz's thesis. Whether a correct and useful assessment of American society or not, Hartz's Lockean United States has been an influential view. Cited frequently, if grudgingly, even by its critics on both the left and the right, it also inserted itself into popular culture.

If for Hartz America was mainly beholden to a liberal consensus, how then could it develop 'that sense of relativity, that spark of philosophy which European liberalism acquired through an internal experience of social diversity and social conflict'? If the dialectic of growth could not be internal in America, where liberalism was 'absolutist' as much as it was 'irrational' (Robin, 2005, 3), then where could relativity and spark come from? For Hartz, it had to come from outside America's borders. The only question was whether this external tempering of liberalism would be enough, 'whether a nation can compensate for the uniformity of its domestic life by contact with alien cultures outside it' (Robin, 2005, 14).

Star Trek's alien cultures are literal aliens. They allow for progress, externalized from a politically (if not culturally) uniform United Federation of Planets. It is this uniformity, this supposed mainstream consensus that most profoundly defines *Star Trek*. Under the auspices of a benevolent Federation all peoples can prosper. Yet they prosper according to human values and human rules, ethical continuations of America's assumed liberal tradition.

The long shadow of Hartz is felt most acutely in the rules the imaginary future society's organs have set themselves. Starfleet heeds a 'prime directive' of non-intervention. The Federation is a political platform that combines a number of species, some of them former enemies. The philosophical basis on which they meet is never made completely clear, while *Star Trek*'s economic system has been called everything from libertarian to socialist, even communist (Tracinski, 2014; Worstall, 2015; Somin, 2016; Gittlitz, 2018). Yet it is always obvious that philosophically, the Federation is a joint venture of individualists – not outright libertarians, but certainly no communists. *TOS*'s Klingons were originally meant to represent the Soviet Union, while *TNG*'s Borg are by design a collective. Spock (Leonard Nimoy), in a storyline connecting the original crew's second motion picture outing, *The Wrath of Khan* (1982), and its third, *The Search for Spock* (1984), is contradicted in his assertion that 'the needs of the many outweigh the needs of the few' by his captain. Kirk (William Shatner) defies orders and the natural order of things to resurrect his friend from the dead.

'The needs of the one' here clearly 'outweigh the needs of the many' (Meyer, 1982; Nimoy, 1984).

Individualism alone, though, does not Lockeanism make. Property, the other necessary constituent part of Locke's political project, is harder to square with *Star Trek*'s supposedly post-mammon society. In the *Declaration of Independence*, Locke's emphasis on property was transmogrified into the Thomas Jefferson-penned *pursuit of happiness*. In this guise of self-improvement, Lockeanism is present in each iteration of *Star Trek*. Moreover, the moneyless economy of *Trek* seems to explicitly allow for property.

When Captain Jean-Luc Picard (Patrick Stewart) returns home in *TNG*'s 'Family' (4x02) after the ordeal of being absorbed into the Borg collective, that home is an idyllic French family-owned vineyard. Healing from the multitude's grip, it appears for him involves rejuvenation through exposure to the family home, a hallmark of ownership society. Similarly, when Avery Brooks's Commander Sisko transfers to the *Deep Space Nine* station in the pilot episode, he has crates of African art shipped to decorate his quarters ('Emissary'). *Discovery*'s Captain Lorca even stems from a family of producers of fortune cookies ('Context is for Kings,' 1x03).

An early draft of the original show's iconic opening narration has the 'United Space Ship Enterprise' on a 'five year patrol of our galaxy' during which it 'visits Earth colonies, regulates commerce, and explores strange new worlds and civilizations' (Cubé, 2016). Here the impulse to explore is mediated by the ship's assignments to visit colonies and, pertinently to Lockean liberalism, 'regulate commerce.' Though the latter phrase did not remain in subsequent drafts, it does show that Roddenberry thought of his starship as something in the mold of an early modern era Royal Navy cruiser or a late nineteenth century American gunboat that could be deployed to bolster the nation's economic interests.

As Stefan Rabitsch notes, C.S. Forester's maritime *Hornblower* novels, set in the late eighteenth and in the first half of the nineteenth century, were a cultural touchstone for Roddenberry and a source of inspiration for *Star Trek* and its 'nostalgic, gentlemanly form of military hierarchy.' In those novels, the Royal Navy – the very force through which the British Empire for centuries enforced its trading interests – was portrayed as a 'benign and seemingly disinterested "meddler"' and guarantor of 'peace for all' (Rabitsch, 2018, 64). While thus outwardly given fully to the development of knowledge and mind, under the surface *Star Trek* has always also been about the protection of interests, monetary or otherwise.

Do Mention the War

TOS is set several years after a devastating war – the same one portrayed in depth in *DSC*, making the newer series a prequel of sorts. *Star Trek*'s inaugural series shows a time in which the peace-seeking but battle-prepared Starfleet coasts from colony to colony, keeping a peace thinly established and always in need of defense and nurture. There is no small overlap of the political undercurrent of that time with that of the era of its making, which, per Henry Luce's *American Century* saw a United States, sometimes reluctant, sometimes fueled by missionary zeal, fielding its role of world policeman (Schulman, 2014, 13).

In both the original series and the newest one, moreover, *Star Trek* is openly defined by the vocabulary and reality of the *frontier*. The Federation's mission, though purportedly peaceful, carries with it always a measure of colonialism: its representatives are, to various degrees, colonizers of a virgin land, 'where no man has gone before.' The drive of the show is subsumed under this lodestar. Though often problematized and complicated, the *frontier* is always present in the series (Wills, 2015, 2, 5, 9). The crew of the *Enterprise* is cast variously as a cavalry force keeping the peace or as a scrappy, multicultural expedition. We can see them in the vein of an idealized view of Lewis and Clark: explorers first who only meddle with existing political structures when absolutely necessary. The goal of the Federation that backs the five-year mission, however, is not only little different from that of colonial land grabs or American national expansionism in the nineteenth century, it is specifically modeled on them (Scharf and Robert, 2003, 76). Humanity and its ally species must stake out their territory in the Milky Way galaxy and defend against rival powers – not French, Spanish, or Russian, but Klingon, Romulan, or Tholian.

Star Trek's Western movie analogy in this context has to be read in two ways: first, as just that, a reference to America's supposed pioneering spirit, evoked through the centuries in multiple ways, from John Winthrop down to Barack Obama; second, as a reference to the Cold War world system and the nation's defense against the Eastern Bloc. Western television series in the 1950s and 1960s provided a canvas for both the home front of the Cold War to be portrayed, as well as a mental space in which a larger conversation about America's place and role in the world could be acted out (Georgi-Findlay, 2018, 214, 221–22). The original *Star Trek* series, with its overt political commentary and its clear lineage originating from the Hollywood television factories that gave the nation *Have Gun, Will Travel* (1957–1963) (for which series creator Gene Roddenberry previously had written) or *Bonanza* (1959–1973), therefore is doubly infused with American ideology.

The Long 1960s

The 1960s have rightly been seen as a time of an explosion of developments in American society. A spectrum of white America, having been given a boost up the horse of personal progress by the GI Bill and massive government subsidies towards homeownership, was just comfortable enough to see enemies at the gates, invading 'traditional' values and the supremacy of educated white male elites and their witting or unwitting allies.

Another large section of that populace of people in power saw a future of perhaps an immediate abyss of humanity, but certainly of long-term progress. Post-war economic science boosterism, a strategy by corporations whose size and manufacturing capacities had ballooned in the Second World War, was the order of the day (Seefried, 2015, 50–51). Captains of industry lobbied local and state governments and especially the federal government in Washington for stabilizing handouts (Bickell, 2002, 138).

This boosterism and the Cold War coincided with and fed off of each other. The era during which Dwight D. Eisenhower was president has too often been seen as a kind of national holding pattern, a long moment in waiting until the Kennedy and Johnson years and their concomitant social movements and unrest brought in the plane for landing. But in its own way, Eisenhower's supposedly staid governance was radical in its expansion of both the military capacity of the United States as well as its economic base.

Weapons research and space flight had gone hand in hand in America as they had in Nazi Germany, where Wernher von Braun, a moral weathervane of a scientific mind, had early sought his luck with the military in order to make his dreams of conquering space feasible. Through a combination of smart maneuvering, luck, and an American government not so much set on punishing Nazi scientists, but rather on winning them for its own projects, he emerged out of the war unscathed and immediately set to work on proving his worth to America, and to again further his schoolboy interest in spaceflight (Laney, 2015, 75, 230).

Working through the 1950s and 1960s, American and German rocket engineers, test pilots, and scientists built up U.S. spacefaring capabilities. In tandem, American marketing experts, sometimes working for the government outright, and sometimes for companies seeking government contracts or merely peddling their wares to consumers, created a decidedly optimistic view of humanity's future in space. The story was an easy one to write. America's frontier myth had never fallen out of favor since the dime novels of the late 1900s, and had only gained salience with the spread of movies, radio serials, and especially television. To extend it to space, the Kennedyian *New Frontier* (and *Star Trek*'s *Final Frontier*, inspired by a government publication emerging out of exactly this kind of mindset) was as much a natural progression as it was a genius stroke of marketing. The progress narrative, an enlightenment staple since the eighteenth century, active in force during the nineteenth century, had been favored until the dual catastrophes of the two world wars. It did not remain underground for long. As the United States sought to position itself against the Soviet Union, it used negative propaganda against the Soviet system as much as it used positive examples of American greatness to set itself apart from it (Gaddis, 2005, 161–63).

These positive examples, however, were always fraught, laden with the ballast of their point of origin in stories of American Exceptionalism and imperial notions of the 'white man's burden.' *Star Trek*'s original run, conceived in the early and mid 1960s and airing from 1966 to 1969, presented a self-consciously 'enlightened' version of the future, in which race, gender, social status, or, quite literally, alien behavior and looks, were no longer disqualifying factors. In truth, and on purpose, that twenty-third century world had more in common with the America of the early 1960s than any imaginable far-off future. Series creator Gene Roddenberry's worldview aligned closely with the establishment liberalism of the Kennedy and early Johnson years. *Star Trek*'s original pilot episode, 'The Cage,' was finished in early 1965. Its copyright date is given as 1964. This means that the pilot was conceived and produced within a few months of July 1964's Civil Rights Act, and finished while the August 1965 Voting Rights Act was debated. *Star Trek* was a contemporary of the most triumphal few months of a long, often opposed movement toward an expansion of civil rights in the United States, a winning streak for progressives not to be repeated throughout the rest of the century.

Celebrating such seemingly measurable successes in humanity's progress, the program took on an often triumphant air of inevitably positive outcomes of human history. It dealt constantly with issues of the day, be they nuclear war and atomic military buildup, the clear and present racism of the American South, sexism, or other problems humanity had supposedly transcended before heading to space. The casual racism of the original series, easily visible in its transposed identity of purportedly gentle ribbing of Leonard Nimoy's Spock, the only member of the main cast portraying an alien, however, attest to the fact that this was only ever skin-deep.

Breaking New Ground But Few Rules

When *Star Trek* premiered on television in 1966, it did not set itself apart through revolutionary storytelling. Rather, what the series did masterfully was to package a liberal consensus zeitgeist prevalent in American society – at least in the echelons of popular culture producers and policy-making elites – into a cross between a Western drama and a sci-fi anthology show. Presenting a mixture between spacey adventure and philosophical morality plays became the series' hallmark. In this it owed much to the 'Golden Age of Science Fiction' in the United States. One-time writer and prolific editor John W. Campbell had begun his run as the might at the helm of *Astounding* science fiction magazine in 1937, publishing a gamut of writers from Isaac Asimov to Robert A. Heinlein to a then still firmly bread-and-butter sci-fi L. Ron Hubbard. This would lay the groundwork for the ascent of the science fiction genre at mid-century (Nevala-Lee, 2018, 6–14). At the beginning of the 1960s, science fiction was beginning to be taken somewhat more seriously by television. In the United Kingdom, the BBC in 1962 commissioned an internal survey as to how science fiction, despite being 'overwhelmingly American in bulk,' could be made usable for the company (Frick and Bull, 1962). Still, the genre was typically considered exclusively scientific, rational, aseptic almost. Character development was low on writers' priority lists, leading to hackneyed and heavy-handed moralizing as well as stilted dialogue. Science fiction, for all its dreams of worlds and worlds of dreams was devoid of blood and emotion. It was coded as male, but not fit for most adults, skewing towards boys instead.

Star Trek wanted to address adults. Although *TOS* finished before the first moon landing, it epitomized the hopes of the space age at the same time that it told morality tales about the dangers of the atomic bomb and racism. Fully infused by Enlightenment thinking and Cold War liberalism, it had, only half on purpose, hit a nerve in a country that still mourned John F. Kennedy and was ready to follow his successor's opinions that civil rights and a full-on attack against poverty were in order. *Star Trek* was born of the Kennedy optimism, and it carried on through the progressive social policies as well as the escalating Vietnam War of Lyndon B. Johnson, incorporating always a criticism of vague but definite threats – allegories on racism but also a hardly disguised jeremiad on Nazi Germany, through the mirror of its fiction. The zeitgeist had been what formed *Star Trek*'s vision, cribbed from NASA press releases as much as from the pages of page-turners set in outer space. Now, the show itself would become part of the zeitgeist, and become enmeshed with America's self-described mission of a peaceful conquest of space.

Out of Time

As the liberal project waned and the United States became mired more and more in the seemingly unending Vietnam War, *Star Trek* disappeared from the airwaves. It was a future out of time. What kept it alive was its dedicated fan base of viewers who sought moral clarity as much as they sought escapist adventure to take them out of a troubled and troubling time. When the historical developments that congealed into the moment and appellation of 'the sixties' reached its clamorous peak in 1968, *Star Trek* had begun its third and last season. NBC had been persuaded to renew the series once, but it would not be persuaded again.

When *Star Trek* reemerged on the other end of the era-cleaving 1970s, first as a series of movies, then a series of television shows, it was variously updated in terms of changing economies of attention and of distribution. Yet it had changed very little otherwise. There were captains, ships, space adventure stories, tales of the indomitability of the human spirit, and parallels to current politics and historical events. Movies based on *TOS* produced from 1978 through 1991 meandered across genres, from effects-laden self-importantly serious science fiction (*The Motion Picture*, 1979) to adventure stories (*The Wrath of Khan*, 1982; *The Search for Spock*, 1984) to topical comedy (*The Voyage Home*, 1986), to ambitiously weird but ultimately corny allegory (*The Final Frontier*, 1989) to era-relevant political drama (*The Undiscovered Country*, 1991, an analogy to the fall of the Berlin Wall, filmed at the time the Soviet Union was crumbling during the summer of 1991).

On television, *The Next Generation* (1987–1994) accompanied the last years of the Cold War and its end, the show's run clearly marked by a transition from a known Manichean power universe to a Habermasian new complexity of politics (Habermas, 1985). New enemies emerged, both foreign – most prominently the assimilating cyborg race of the Borg – and domestic; unrest at the Federation frontier led by outlaw citizens unhappy with a border settlement, styled the 'Maquis.' These storylines were picked up in both the franchise's other 1990s entries, *Deep Space Nine* (1993–1999) and *Voyager* (1995–2001) – one an exploration of war and war crimes, of secularism and religion, the other an exploration of a region of space heretofore unknown to the *Trek* universe.

Star Trek post 9/11 then veered in the same flag-waving direction as much of popular culture. Not to be outdone by the likes of Kiefer-Sutherland-starring torture-porn *24* (2001–2010), *Enterprise* created a multiseason story arc surrounding an attack on Earth by the multispecies Xindi, playing out a version of 9/11 in space. This incongruous marriage of *Trek* with the neoconservative now did not sufficiently excite viewers, who were more and more turning away from network television, and *Enterprise* was canceled after a shortened run of four seasons. More than 12 years would elapse until a new *Star Trek* television show appeared again.

When it did, that show, *DSC*, had to navigate a thoroughly changed media landscape. *DSC* debuted in September 2017 on the CBS *All Access* streaming service in the United States and on Netflix internationally. Formerly an online DVD lender, Netflix had launched its video-streaming product in 2007. CBS's service had been in operation since 2014, but had languished for lack of content. *DSC* was a product of the streaming age. Unlike its predecessors, it would not consist of seasons in excess of 20-odd episodes each year, producing 15 instalments during season one instead, with the number further reduced to 14 for the second season. The show's creators, chiefly former *Voyager* staff writer Bryan Fuller, consciously experimented with the storytelling mode of the series. Initially planned as the first glimpse into an anthology universe, *DSC* during development became a more saleable straightforward story (Hibberd, 2017). Its change of perspective from emphasizing the captain or commander of a crew as the central character (most pronounced on *Deep Space Nine*, in which Benjamin Sisko even becomes a pivotal figure of religious veneration for the nearby Bajoran civilization) to spotlighting Burnham, an outcast and convicted criminal, remained its most immediately obvious narrative innovation within the *Star Trek* canon.

The new show was thoroughly self-aware in terms of its role as a guiding light of inclusion and progressive ideals. Despite leaving the show before its premiere, Fuller got his way in the casting of Sonequa Martin-Green to play the first black female lead in a *Star Trek* series (Hibberd, 2017). In the run-up to the release, the importance of inclusion and diversity being a mainstay of *Star Trek*'s overall DNA was repeatedly stressed. Martin-Green even called the series 'a form of activism' (Zalben, 2017). *Discovery*'s 2017 premiere was consequently accompanied by laudatory fanfare as well as by the shrieks of self-described fans from the right-wing fringes of internet culture who complained about 'social justice warriors' ruining what some now disparagingly referred to as *Star Trek: Diversity* ('Morgoth's Review,' 2017). Beyond the unavoidable backlash from the fringe, a function mostly of the changed discursive sphere offering easily accessible platforms for such views since the early 2000s, could the tried-but-tired premise of humanity's trek to the stars still literally fly in the age of cord-cutting and on-demand video? And, if so, how different would it be from *Star Trek*'s past?

Outwardly, *DSC* is organized much differently from other *Trek* shows. It begins with the start of a war and features a crew whose captain dies within the series' first 90 minutes. Its main protagonist is not the accomplished commanding officer of a ship, but an up-and-coming second in command who makes a fatal mistake. The titular ship and its hands-on captain only show up in the third episode. The focus on Burnham and her story of redemption as the audience's window to the world of the series is new for *Star Trek*, if it is in keeping with the narrative tendencies and complicated moralities of television in the second decade of the twenty-first century. As is its whole-season story arc. *DSC*'s Captain Gabriel Lorca in Jason Isaacs's swaggeringly broken portrayal is a war-torn presence who throughout the series appears manipulative and has no compunction about leaving his friend and lover, Vice Admiral Cornwell (Jayne Brook), to be tortured and possibly killed by the Klingons. Seemingly, as the whole of television became grittier, more morally ambiguous, and darker, so the new *Star Trek* followed suit.

At a closer look, however, *DSC* merely takes the long way around to living up to *Star Trek*'s founding credo. More than that, it restates emphatically the *Star Trek* mission. The manipulative captain turns out to have come from a dystopian Mirror Universe, a parallel dimension that was visited multiple times before during several of the predecessor series. By episode 12 ('Vaulting Ambition'), he has been revealed as an interloper, and by episode 13 ('What's Past is Prologue'), his second in command, Saru (Doug Jones), virtually embodies the ideal of a Starfleet captain: composed, determined, morally unimpeachable, and with an uncanny ability to give rousing speeches about what defines Starfleet and the Federation. Lorca, it turns out, was a new kind of Starfleet captain simply because he was not a Starfleet captain at all. Through this disclosure, the arc of the moral universe is bent back to where it belonged in all other entries into the *Star Trek* canon.

The introduction of Anson Mount as Captain Christopher Pike in season two further emphasizes the useful aberration. Portrayed as the epitome of an officer and gentleman beyond reproach, Pike is the first captain created for *Star Trek*, and *DSC* purposely uses his character to reconnect with *Trek*'s past. The connection is made plain at the beginning of season two's 'If Memory Serves' (2x08), which features footage from *Star Trek*'s 1965 original pilot episode 'The Cage' in which Jeffrey Hunter, portraying Pike, is featured prominently. After this, the action cuts directly to Mount's Pike. By placing much of season two's focus on Pike, a white male American leader figure not just in the mold of, but in fact the same character as, a 1960s *Trek* commanding officer, *DSC* in its second season seems to course-correct perhaps a bit too eagerly in order to dispel any notion that its deconstruction of the figure of the *Star Trek* captain in season one was permanent.[2] In doing so, *DSC* continues to negotiate the meaning of *Star Trek* in a changed cultural landscape through the lens of its own Cold War origins.

The season one plot twist preceding Pike's entrance into the series is *DSC*'s initial solution to the dilemma of reconciling *Star Trek*'s Hartzian streak with the demands of modern audiences: to be *Star Trek* it needs to fulfil the franchise's promise of a positive future, of heroines and heroes that can be emulated and celebrated, of a middle-class mainstream idealized American citizenry. Yet, to provide present-day viewers with a taste of the less than perfect protagonists that abound in current filmed entertainment, and that they therefore expect, it needs to be able to portray such persons as significant characters. Much like Hartz, in order for his concept of American liberalism to hold fast, needed to turn to other nations to find relativity with which the politics of the United States could contrast itself, the move here is to bring in alien elements that through negative example illuminate the positive.

By largely externalizing the evil within its ranks, *DSC* can have its cake and eat it, too. It can exploit the more complicated characters a newly complex television landscape makes possible while staying true to *Star Trek*'s idealism. In the end it cannot but circle back to the inherent heroism of Starfleet officers who may stray from the righteous path here and there but always return to it. An ambiguous non-Mirror Universe Captain Lorca making problematic choices due to and during the war would have been a noticeable deviation from *Trek*'s established playbook – though not a total innovation, as the actions of *Deep Space Nine*'s Captain Sisko in the sixth season episode 'In the Pale Moonlight,' in which he compromises his constancy in order to convince an ally to join another multi-episode arc war effort, make clear (Lobl). Revealing the Lorca we have seen for nine episodes to have emerged from outside the normal *Trek* universe instead, however, merely reaffirms the goodness of the 'real' Starfleet officers portrayed.

DSC cleverly avails itself of two kinds of audience expectations. The expectation of a general streaming television audience is for multifaceted, complex characters, while that of *Star Trek* fans is for a *Star Trek* show that is infused with the franchise's spirit. Playing these off against each other, *DSC* threads the needle the only way it can. By having the mirror version of Captain Georgiou, the Mirror Universe's ruthless emperor, survive and take the identity of the deceased Prime Universe's Georgiou,

---

[2] See also, in a similar vein, Sabrina Mittermeier and Jennifer Volkmer, '"We Choose Our Own Pain. Mine Helps Me Remember": Gabriel Lorca, Ash Tyler, and the Question of Masculinity' in this volume.

it further frees itself to explore more stories of moral ambiguity in future instalments while again externalizing villainy.

These moves set *DSC* up to not only discuss the issues of the day – as it has done, for example, in refashioning the backward-looking Trumpian 'Make America Great Again' slogan, both initially as 'Remain Klingon' and then again as Lorca's less than subtle 'Make the Empire Glorious Again' – but to open up a dialectic of meaning-making from within the text. Through deconstructing multiple elements of what *Star Trek* has represented in the past, *Discovery* tests the limits of its narrative niche's affordances. By probing what *Star Trek* can get away with in the twenty-first century, *DSC* orbits back around to defining what *Star Trek* is, jettisoning negative constraints on the original vision and shoring up its positive qualities. *Discovery* argues that *Star Trek* has been flawed all along. By aiming to fix these deficiencies, it presents an even stronger definition of what *Star Trek*'s liberal foundations ultimately are. In doing this, the show emerges as not simply another entry into the long-running franchise, but as a *Star Trek* that is deliberately about being *Star Trek*.

Conclusion

A *Star Trek* series that overtly embraces the ideas of its twentieth century creation will necessarily always contain within it that inherently twentieth century original text, born of the liberal idealized politics of the 1960s United States. The inaccuracy of Louis Hartz's analysis of the American national past notwithstanding, as a creation of that time, it was then and still is now an astute description of an important thread in the quilt of American self-mythologization. *Star Trek* may change its attitudes to a certain degree, pulling into the fold of inclusion more and more marginalized groups. But in this it promotes rather than rejects in the name of true diversity the American post-Second World War conception of a unitary mainstream society which all should aspire to be a part of, modeled on an enlargement of American, white, male, elite ideals of progress.

As a product of 1960s popular culture, if it is to retain some semblance of continuity in its internal canon, *Star Trek* can never fully escape this origin. Hardly any voices have been more vocal about criticizing *Star Trek*'s many deficiencies than its fans. As Constance Penley puts it: 'No one knows the object better than a fan and no one is more critical' (1997, 3). What they have glommed onto in criticizing *DSC* has presented as an impossible dichotomy: it is too much unlike other *Star Trek*s in order to belong among them, while being too much like the *Star Trek* of old for some contemporary viewers (Handlen, 2017; Rasmus, 2017). In truth, however, this dichotomy is a dialectic. It is a productive exchange about what makes *Star Trek* as a whole, which results in an expanded but altogether affirmed definition of what *Star Trek* is. For good and ill, in jumping forcefully on the ice of convention, *DSC* finds it to crack but not break, and to freeze solid even more strongly in support of its weight.

Works Cited

Philip Abbott, 'Still Louis Hartz after All These Years: A Defense of the Liberal Society Thesis', *Perspectives on Politics*, 3.1 (2005): 93–109.

Daniel Bernardi, '"Star Trek" in the 1960s: Liberal-Humanism and the Production of Race', *Science Fiction Studies*, 24.2 (1997): 209–25.

Lara Bickell, 'Eugene Pulliam, Municipal Booster', in Benson Tong and Regan A. Lutz (eds.) *The Human Tradition in the American West* (Lanham, MD: Rowman & Littlefield, 2002): 137–53.

Tiziano Bonazzi, 'Frederick Jackson Turner's Frontier Thesis and the Self-Consciousness of America', *Journal of American Studies*, 27.2 (1993): 149–71.

Joseph Campbell, *The Hero with a Thousand Faces* (Novato, CA: New World Library, 2008).

Lane Crothers, 'From the United States to the Federation of Planets: Star Trek and the Globalization of American Culture', in Douglas Brode and Shea T. Brode (eds.) *Gene Roddenberry's Star Trek: The Original Cast Adventures* (Lanham, MD: Rowman & Littlefield, 2015): 63–72.

Caroline Cubé, 'To Boldly Go: The Hurried Evolution of Star Trek's Opening Narration', *UCLA Library*, 11 October (2016), www.library.ucla.edu/blog/special/2016/10/11/to-boldly-go-the-hurried-evolution-of-star-treks-opening-narration.

Alice Frick and Donald Bull, '*Science Fiction*', BBC, March (1962), http://www.bbc.co.uk/archive/doctorwho/6400.shtml. BBC Archive.

John Lewis Gaddis, *The Cold War: A New History* (London: Penguin UK, 2005).

Brigitte Georgi-Findlay, 'Politische Bildung durch Bonanza & Co.?', in Anja Besand (ed.) *Von Game of Thrones bis House of Cards: Politische Perspektiven in Fernsehserien* (Wiesbaden: Springer Fachmedien, 2018): 207–23.

Susan R. Gibberman, *Star Trek: An Annotated Guide to Resources on the Development, the Phenomenon, the People, the Television Series, the Films, the Novels, and the Recordings* (Jefferson, NC: McFarland, 1991).

A.M. Gittlitz, '"Make It So": "Star Trek" and Its Debt to Revolutionary Socialism', *The New York Times*, 20 January (2018), www.nytimes.com/2017/07/24/opinion/make-it-so-star-trek-and-its-debt-to-revolutionary-socialism.html.

John G. Gunnell, 'Louis Hartz and the Liberal Metaphor: A Half-Century Later', *Studies in American Political Development*, 19.2 (2005): 196–205.

Jürgen Habermas, *Die neue Unübersichtlichkeit* (Berlin: Suhrkamp, 1985).
Zack Handlen, 'Another Episode with Too Much Star Trek, Not Enough Discovery', *The A.V. Club*, 22 October (2017), www.avclub.com/another-episode-with-too-much-star-trek-not-enough-dis-1819758431.
Louis Hartz, *The Liberal Tradition in America* (New York: Harcourt, Brace and Company, 1955).
James Hibberd, 'Bryan Fuller on "Star Trek: Discovery" Exit: "I Got to Dream Big"', *EW.Com*, 28 July (2017), ew.com/tv/2017/07/28/bryan-fuller-star-trek-discovery/.
Irving Horowitz and Arthur Schlesinger, *The Vital Center: Politics of Freedom* (Milton Park: Taylor & Francis, 2017).
James T. Kloppenberg, 'In Retrospect: Louis Hartz's "The Liberal Tradition in America"', *Reviews in American History*, 29.3 (2001): 460–78.
Monique Laney, *German Rocketeers in the Heart of Dixie: Making Sense of the Nazi Past during the Civil Rights Era* (New Haven, CT: Yale University Press, 2015).
Morgoth, 'Star Trek Diversity: We Are the Klingons Now!', *Morgoth's Review*, 30 September (2017), nwioqeqkdf.blogspot.com/2017/09/star-trek-diversity-we-are-klingons-now.html.
Alec Nevala-Lee, *Astounding: John W. Campbell, Isaac Asimov, Robert A. Heinlein, L. Ron Hubbard, and the Golden Age of Science Fiction* (New York: HarperCollins, 2018).
Mike O'Connor, 'Liberals in Space: The 1960s Politics of Star Trek', *The Sixties*, 5.2 (2012): 185–203.
Constance Penley, *NASA/Trek: Popular Science and Sex in America* (London: Verso, 1997).
Stefan Rabitsch, *Star Trek and the British Age of Sail: The Maritime Influence Throughout the Series and Films* (Jefferson, NC: McFarland, 2018).
Daniel Rasmus, '"Star Trek: Discovery" Dazzles But Fails to Engage', *PopMatters*, 4 November (2017), www.popmatters.com/star-trek-discovery-dazzles-but-fails-to-engage-2497172172.html.
Corey Robin, 'Louis Hartz at 50: On the Varieties of Counterrevolutionary Experience in America', *Schmooze 'Tickets'*, March (2006), digitalcommons.law.umaryland.edu/schmooze_papers/19.
Michael P. Scharf and Lawrence D. Robert, 'The Interstellar Relations of the Federation: International Law and "Star Trek: The Next Generation"', in Robert H. Chaires and Bradley Stewart Chilton (eds.) *Star Trek Visions of Law and Justice* (Denton, TX: University of North Texas Press, 2003): 73–100.
Bruce J. Schulman, 'Introduction', in Bruce J. Schulman (ed.) *Making the American Century: Essays on the Political Culture of Twentieth Century America* (New York: Oxford University Press, 2014): 1–15.
Elke Seefried, *Zukünfte: Aufstieg Und Krise Der Zukunftsforschung 1945–1980* (Berlin: De Gruyter Oldenbourg, 2015).
Ilya Somin, 'Star Trek Is Far from Libertarian – Here's Why', *Learn Liberty*, 22 July (2016), www.learnliberty.org/blog/star-trek-is-far-from-libertarian-heres-why.

Robert Tracinski, 'Is Star Trek Really Anti-Libertarian?', *The Federalist*, 22 October (2014), thefederalist.com/2014/10/22/trekonomics-is-star-trek-really-anti-libertarian.

Frederick Jackson Turner, *Rereading Frederick Jackson Turner: 'The Significance of the Frontier in American History', and Other Essays* (New Haven, CT: Yale University Press, 1998).

Odd Arne Westad, *The Cold War: A World History* (London: Penguin, 2018).

John Wills, '"Wagon Train to the Stars": Star Trek, the Western Frontier, and American Values', in Douglas Brode and Shea T. Brode (eds.) *Gene Roddenberry's Star Trek: The Original Cast Adventures* (Lanham, MD: Rowman & Littlefield, 2015): 1–11.

Rick Worland, 'Captain Kirk: Cold Warrior', *Journal of Popular Film and Television*, 16.3 (1988): 109–17.

Tim Worstall, 'Star Trek Economics Is Just True Communism Arriving', *Forbes*, 5 October (2015), www.forbes.com/sites/timworstall/2015/10/05/star-trek-economics-is-just-true-communism-arriving.

Alexander Zalben, 'From Dr. Martin Luther King, Jr. to Discovery, Star Trek's Diversity Is "A Form of Activism"', *TVGuide.Com*, 10 September (2017), www.tvguide.com/news/star-trek-discovery-diversity-sonequa-martin-green-activism.

Episodes and Films Cited

'The Menagerie, Part Two.' *Star Trek*, written by Gene Roddenberry, directed by Robert Butler, Desilu Studios, 24 November, 1966.

'The Cage.' *Star Trek*, written by Gene Roddenberry, directed by Robert Butler, Desilu Studios, 4 October, 1988.

'Family.' *Star Trek: The Next Generation*, written by Ronald D. Moore, directed by Les Landau, Paramount Television Studios, 29 September, 1990.

'Emissary.' *Star Trek: Deep Space Nine*, written by Michael Piller, directed by David Carson, Paramount Television, 3 January, 1993.

'In the Pale Moonlight.' *Star Trek: Deep Space Nine*, written by Michael Taylor, directed by Victor Lobl, Paramount Television Studios, 15 April, 1998.

'Context is for Kings.' *Star Trek: Discovery*, written by Gretchen J. Berg, Aaron Harberts, and Craig Sweeny, directed by Akiva Goldsman, CBS Television Studios, 1 October, 2017.

'Choose Your Pain.' *Star Trek: Discovery*, written by Kemp Powers, directed by Lee Rose, CBS Television Studios, 15 October, 2017.

'Vaulting Ambition.' *Star Trek: Discovery*, written by Jordon Nardino, directed by Hanelle M. Culpepper, CBS Television Studios, 21 January, 2018.

'What's Past is Prologue.' *Star Trek: Discovery*, written by Ted Sullivan, directed by Olatunde Osunsanmi, CBS Television Studios, 29 January, 2018.

'If Memory Serves.' *Star Trek: Discovery*, written by Dan Dworkin and Jay Beattie, directed by T.J. Scott, CBS Television Studios, 7 March, 2019.

Star Trek II: The Wrath of Khan. 1982. Directed by Nicholas Meyer. Paramount Pictures.
Star Trek III: The Search for Spock. 1984. Directed by Leonard Nimoy. Paramount Pictures.

The Conscience of the King
Or: Is There in Truth No Sex and Violence?

John Andreas Fuchs

After two rather different seasons *Star Trek: Discovery* (2017–ongoing) has firmly established its rightful place within the *Star Trek*[1] universe. The writers and producers have made nods to the original series and the rest of the franchise right from the start. Between mentioning the captains April (*TAS*), Archer (*ENT*), Decker (*TOS*), and Pike (*TOS*) in episode 1x05 ('Choose Your Pain'), or the *Enterprise* in episode 1x06 ('Lethe') to bringing back Pike (Anson Mount), Spock (Ethan Peck), and the *Enterprise* in season two there have been Easter eggs for fans in almost every episode. Lorca (Jason Isaacs) telling Stamets (Anthony Rapp) to leave the ship when Stamets complains about the *Discovery* and his research being conscripted for war (1x04) is similar to Scotty (Simon Pegg) threatening to leave the *Enterprise* because Starfleet had confiscated his research and the *Enterprise* has been given a military mission while he thought, 'we are explorers' (*Star Trek: Into Darkness* (2013)). This nod even to J.J. Abrams' reboot is remarkable[2] since 'JJ-Trek,' as hardcore fans call it, is rather unpopular with the fandom.

---

[1] In the text *Star Trek* is used for the whole franchise. The different *Star Trek* series are mentioned by their official abbreviations: *TOS* for the original *Star Trek* TV show, *TAS* for *Star Trek: The Animated Series* (1973–1974), *TNG* for *Star Trek: The Next Generation* (1987–1994), *DS9* for *Star Trek: Deep Space Nine* (1993–1999), *VGR* for *Star Trek: Voyager* (1995–2001), *ENT* for *Star Trek: Enterprise* (2001–2005), and *DSC* for *Star Trek: Discovery*. Although the fan made *Star Trek* encyclopedia *Memory Alpha* uses the more common *VOY* for *Voyager* and *DIS* for *Discovery*, John van Citters (VP *Star Trek* Brand Development at CBS Studios) lists the official abbreviations on his twitter account as given above (Van Citters, 2016). When feature films are mentioned the whole title is given. To avoid confusion the first reboot will be mentioned as *Star Trek* (2009).

[2] Yet hardly surprising since the movie was co-written by *DSC* showrunner Alex Kurtzman.

But unlike the reboot, *DSC* avoids many of its mistakes: as sticklers to canon will notice, the *Enterprise* has the right size, its phasers are rendered in the correct color, and when planets are mentioned they are where they should be, unlike Delta Vega in *Star Trek* (2009). When it is at its best *DSC* gives its references to *TOS* tongue-in-cheek. While on *Star Trek* (2009) it is still the famous red shirt, engineer Olson (Greg Ellis), that has to die during the away mission over Vulcan, *DSC* acknowledges the fact that security officers and engineers only seem to die more often than blue and gold shirts. When Pike tells Nhan (Rachael Ancheril), 'Get your red shirt into an EV suit, Nhan. You are with us' (2x01, 'Brother'), everybody expects her to die, especially since the descent to the asteroid is rather reminiscent of the space jump towards the drill that results in Olson's death in *Star Trek* (2009). But instead the blue shirt, science officer Connolly (Sean Connolly Affleck), bites the asteroid dust.

Not all references are welcomed by the fandom; since *Star Trek: The Animated* series is not seen as canon, mentioning Captain Robert April twice (*DSC* 1x05, 2x01) on the show was not very popular. The only other mention of April as captain of the *Enterprise* before Pike took over takes place in the *TAS* episode 'The Counter-Clock Incident' (2x06) when April (James Doohan, voice) and his wife Sarah (Nichelle Nichols, voice) are passengers onboard the *Enterprise*. The strongest link to *TAS*, however, is Michael Burnham (Sonequa Martin-Green)'s love for *Alice in Wonderland*. Her foster-mother, Amanda (Mia Kirshner), used to read it to her and Spock. In 'Once Upon a Planet' (*TAS* 1x09) Kirk (William Shatner, voice) is surprised that Spock (Leonard Nimoy, voice) knows the difference between the books *Alice in Wonderland* and *Through the Looking-Glass*. Spock tells him, 'My mother was particularly fond of Lewis Carroll's work.'[3]

Canon aside the fans' biggest problem with *DSC*, especially with season one, is the darker tone and the more military appearance: 'Don't be fooled into thinking you can watch this with your family. It's [sic] tone is dark, there's blood and gore (Ep 3) – and now they've dropped the F-bomb!' (Maven, 2017). They tend to forget, that – Damn it, Jim! – cussing, sex, and violence have been a part of *Star Trek* since the 1960s. The only thing that has changed is their depiction. And even the militarism is not new:

---

[3] Although there have been minor references to *TAS* on *TNG*, *DS9*, and *ENT* the 'canonization' on *DSC* might be due to the fact that CBS is planning a new animated *Trek*-series.

Is Star Fleet [sic] supposed to be military all of a sudden? Everyone wears the same color uniforms with metal badges, the phasers fire in pulses now and the story is brooding and self-important. One of the leads is super depressed and can't get over the past. There is so much hate and revenge. Crew members are getting killed violently in space battles and throats are being slit! Everything is saddled with some kind of deeper meaning instead of just being space adventure. They try to connect it to real *Trek*, but they get the details wrong. It's almost like they are only doing it lip service! Then they went and killed a character we liked ...

...*The Wrath of Khan* was just way too dark for *Star Trek*. (Gaska, 2018; emphasis added)

During its over 50 years on screen *Star Trek* has become a good indicator for the role of sex and violence in U.S.-American science fiction. It also clearly shows what viewers will tolerate while highlighting the cultural differences of its audience at the same time. Depictions acceptable in the United States are not necessarily accepted in Europe and vice versa. While *TOS* often showed its audience things far more sexual than fans of the time were accustomed to seeing on television – Dr. 'Bones' McCoy (DeForest Kelley)'s cabaret chorus girls dressed in nothing but pink and yellow fur outfits with matching panties come to mind ('Shore Leave' 1x15[4]) – its depiction of violence 'was not controversial in the United States,' although 'it was seen as such in other countries' (Finley, 2018, 161). The depiction of sex, violence and swearing evolved with the viewers' tastes and their times. From Bones' 'damns' and 'hells' and the forced kiss between Uhura (Nichelle Nichols) and Kirk (William Shatner) in 'Plato's Stepchildren' to other censored episodes like 'Conspiracy' (*The Next Generation* (*TNG*) 1x25, censored for violence in the UK), 'Rejoined' (*DS9* 4x06, first same-sex kiss on *Star Trek*, censored in the US South), or 'To the Death' (*DS9* 4x23, censored for violence), the use of sex and violence as a narrative element on *Star Trek* has been progressing with the times and is evocative of the decades each show was produced in.

[4] Even though *Memory Alpha* lists *TOS* episodes according to their production number thus making 'Where No Man Has Gone Before' (prodno. 6149–02) season one, episode 1, I follow the order in which the episodes where aired. Thus 'The Man Trap' (prodno. 6149–06) is given as 1x01 making 'Where No Man Has Gone Before' episode 1x03 and 'Shore Leave' episode 1x15. The production number 6149–01 belongs to the rejected first pilot 'The Cage', which first aired on October 4, 1988 and will be given as 0x01.

Seen in the context of the zeitgeist the newest addition to the franchise is not any more violent, gory, or even vulgar than any of the other series or feature films were in their time. Sex and violence have always been an integral part of *Star Trek*'s storytelling and are a vital part of showing its positive message of humanity's future. And that is what *DSC* keeps boldly doing. While season one explores war in all its gruesomeness – just like *DS9* did in 'Nor the Battle to the Strong' (5x04) and 'The Siege of AR-558' (7x08) – season two focuses on two other typical *Trek*-topics: exploration and religion. Everything seen on *DSC* has been seen on *Star Trek* before. Georgiou (Michelle Yeoh) and Nhan's illogical fisticuffs with Leland/Control (Alan van Sprang) (2x14) – phasers can hardly harm him so fists can? – as well as Leland/Control's sexist remark 'Women, stop talking!'? Been there, done that.

'There's a stain of cruelty on your shining armor, captain' (Lenore Karidian (Barbara Anderson), 'The Conscience of the King,' *TOS* 1x13)

While a lot of *TOS* seems to be rather harmless and could even be seen as wholesome family fun from today's point of view, in its day it sometimes seemed rather inappropriate. When the BBC first aired 'Miri' (1x08) in 1970 they received so many complaints from viewers that they checked the rest of the episodes and decided to remove 'The Empath' (3x12), 'Whom Gods Destroy' (3x14), 'Plato's Stepchildren' (3x10), and 'Miri' from the broadcast schedule because 'they all dealt most unpleasantly with the already unpleasant subjects of madness, torture, sadism and disease' (BBC quoted in Cockburn, 2014, 33). 'The Empath,' 'Whom Gods Destroy,' 'Plato's Stepchildren' first aired in 1992 and 'Miri' was not rerun until 1993 (cf. Cockburn, 2014, 33; Berkman, 2016, 42).[5]

---

[5] In 'Miri' the *Enterprise* discovers an Earth-like planet that was devastated by a horrific degenerative disease and is now populated entirely by children. Everybody reaching puberty succumbs to the disease becomes insane and dies. In 'The Empath' Kirk, Spock, and McCoy become the subjects of an alien experiment whose mysterious intention involves a beautiful, empathic woman. She is able to heal wounds empathically by transferring the wound and the pain to her own body. In order the see if she is willing to do so Kirk, Spock, and McCoy are tortured by aliens. In 'Whom Gods Destroy' Kirk and Spock are held captive in an insane asylum by a former Starfleet hero who tortures Kirk. 'Plato's Stepchildren' features the famous kiss between Kirk and Uhura.

TOS had a rather violent start, which was no coincidence. During the first episode 'The Man Trap' (aired September 8, 1966) four crewmen – none of them a redshirt by the way – and one civilian are killed by a salt-sucking alien. The salt-vampire also brutally attacks Spock (Leonard Nimoy) and Captain Kirk before being shot and killed by Dr. McCoy. Gene Roddenberry described *Star Trek* as '"*Wagon Train* to the stars"' (Altman and Gross, 2016a, 31), a Western in a science fiction setting. Space has become 'the final frontier' setting the tone for the series. The frontier 'makes us Americans,' claims Thomas Doherty. 'We have to have initiative and inventiveness and youth and strength and canniness to survive on the frontier – and also we also [sic] have to kill the Indians' (Altman and Gross, 2016a, 33). Violence is part of the American DNA.[6] Thus, the death toll for the first episode could have been even higher. In 'Where No Man Has Gone Before' (aired September 22, 1966), intended to be the pilot, 12 members of the *Enterprise*-crew are killed. However only three deaths are witnessed by the audience; nine are reported by Spock. NBC executives felt that 'Where No Man Has Gone Before' was 'too expository in terms of the series concept and characters' (Solow and Justman, 1997, 162) and decided that the show should start with either 'The Man Trap' or 'The Naked Time' (1x04, aired September 29, 1966; only one crewman killed). Assistant director and later producer Bob Justman agreed with NBC's decision to choose the first after favoring the latter and suggests in *Inside Star Trek: The Real Story* that it was 'scarier and more exploitable than the others' (1997, 163). The third episode 'Charlie X' (1x02, aired September 15, 1966; two deaths, possibly more since a ship is destroyed) had also been a candidate for first episode, but was seen as 'too gentle a tale' (1997, 163) since it only dealt with the problems of an adolescent. There even had been one candidate without any casualties, 'Mudd's Women' (1x06), but this episode was not considered to lead off the franchise because it dealt with a rather salacious story about drugs and selling women, or as Herb Solow eloquently puts it: 'an intergalactic trader-pimp... [and]... three beautiful women-hookers selling their bodies throughout the galaxy' (65–66). Its overall 'eroticism' (59) had also meant the end for the first *Star Trek* pilot 'The Cage,' especially the 'scantily clad green dancing girls with the humps and grinds' (61). Not only had 'The Cage'

---

[6] As the frontier myth has always been a part of *Star Trek*'s DNA ('Space, the final frontier...'). Richard Slotkin explores the origins of the frontier myth and highlights the parallels between Westerns and science fiction, especially *Star Trek*, in *Gunfighter Nation* (1998, 635–36).

been too sexy it also did not provide enough hands-on violence as Gene Roddenberry recalls:

> I should actually have ended it with a fistfight between the hero and the villain if I wanted it on television ... because that's the way shows were being made at the time. The great mass audience would say, 'Well, if you don't have a fistfight when it's ended, how do we know that's the finish?' and things like that. (Asherman, 1988, 10)

Sex, or any allusions to it, could not be tolerated, but violent fistfights would have been fine; as long as the depicted violence was not 'gratuitous' as NBC's Programming department demanded. 'However,' Bob Justman recalls, 'the word *gratuitous* was open to interpretation ... After all, if we removed all "gratuitous" violence, the average hour episode would run approximately seventeen minutes' (Solow and Justman, 1997, 199). Yet another NBC department, Broadcast Standards, always knew what gratuitous meant, especially when it came to sexual connotations: 'no open mouth kissing, no nudity – not even exposure of an inner thigh now and then, and definitely no nipples. Genitalia did not, do not, and would not ever exist' (Solow and Justman, 1997, 200). That is something that has not changed as viewers' reactions to *DSC*'s fifth episode 'Choose Your Pain' show:

> I was deeply disappointed when *'Trek'* reverted to using a specific f-word on the most recent... *Star Trek* has always been a family show – ... it ... didn't have to rely on extreme profane language (comparing Bones saying 'damn' doesn't compare) just for shock value such as obscene cursing or showing T&A [tits and ass] to get its point across. If I'm blessed to one day have a child / children I can't show them *'Discovery'* like my dad could *TOS* and growing up with *TNG* because of the vulgarity – nor would I want to. ... I'm assuming now it's just a matter of time before we see full body nudity. I'd love to introduce my potential future children to *Trek* and a belief in a better future – unfortunately, it can't be this series. (Perry, 2017; emphasis added)

Perry's complaint is one among many of its kind to be found on Facebook's *Star Trek* group. *Star Trek* is falsely seen as a family show and *DSC* criticized for not qualifying as such. The focus of Perry's criticism is the use of 'fuck' – and the possibility that there even might be 'full body nudity' in future episodes. Many of the negative comments on 'Choose Your Pain' and 'Into the Forest I Go' (1x09) criticize Stamets and Culber

(Wilson Cruz) kissing as well as their homosexual relationship. The majority of the complaints are about sex or allusions to it.[7] This narrow perspective does not go unnoticed. On Facebook, Ben Taylor responds to Perry's post: 'In the same episode we had someone get beaten to death [and his head smashed by a Klingon boot], we had Lorca being tortured and we had the rape of a prisoner of war, but yes let's freak out because a grown woman said "fuck."' What Taylor does not mention is L'Rell (Mary Chieffo)'s phaser-burned face and the abuse of a sentient being as a means of propulsion. By using the tardigrade as a living computer and gravely harming it in the process, the *Discovery* crew is doing something very similar to the crew of the *U.S.S. Equinox* on *Voyager* (*VOY*) who were killing sentient beings to boost the output of their warp drive in order to get home from the Delta Quadrant ('Equinox' 5x26 and 'Equinox, Part Two' 6x01). Those who do not care about the profane language do not care about the different forms of violence either: Morgan Jurmalietis comments on Perry's post, 'I watch this show with my 4 year old [sic]. If she ever works on a spore drive[,] I have NO PROBLEM [sic] with her referring to it as "fucking awesome"' and Ian DelBianco adds, 'I watched it with my 10 year old daughter. Tilly cursed, stamets [sic] cursed, she giggled, I shrugged and we moved on.'

What was true for 'The Cage' is still true for *DSC*. You can have fistfights, but you cannot have sex, nudity, or any allusion to it. Nevertheless, there has been even worse on *TOS*: sexism, sexist violence, sexual assault and rape. As common as fistfights with barely connecting fists were in the 1960s, so was sexism. Although *TOS* presented its audience with an African-American woman serving as communications officer it remained a child of its time and especially a child of its creator Gene Roddenberry:

---

[7] Here are two examples from *Parent Reviews for Star Trek*: 'Previous series have all shown great character and have wonderful lessons in them. Imagine my surprise watching this, and in the fifth episode they drop not one but two f bombs. Then to top it off the very first romantic relationship is introduced and it is two men. Had to have a talk with my son after watching that episode about language and choices. Definitely not appropriate for children' (Wes V., 2017). 'If you have traditional Christian morals, you should know that there is, as in most modern series, a central gay couple. The hero of the first series is gay, the doctor and he kiss on the final episode. They say that they love each other a couple times. The thing that irritated me most is that there are Klingon boobs. I'm not talking about the low cut [sic] leather, or the side, or cleavage, but the top view of a fully bare breast. It is in the middle of a traumatic flashback, but it certainly wasn't necessary. It's the straw that broke this camel's back' (Brian F., 2017).

Gene Roddenberry claimed to be progressive when it came to sexual politics, but his actual practices belied it. He wanted the actresses in the show to be visual sexual objects. Even uniformed female crew members were not exempt. They were chosen on the basis of their looks, and their costumes were designed to emphasize feminine physical qualities: short skirts and high-heeled boots to show off their legs, nipped-in waists and well filled tunics to emphasize [sic] their female figures. (Solow and Justman, 1997, 216)

For female aliens it was even worse. Their costumes were designed to 'expose their bodies and accentuate their breasts' (Solow and Justman, 1997, 216); one of the best examples being Sherry Jackson's outfit in 'What Are Little Girls Made Of?' (1x07) Jackson's android Andrea is also one of the many examples of female adversaries being overpowered by Captain Kirk's charm. Women – no matter the species – are clearly marked as inferior to men. The few strong female characters 'are almost invariably represented as evil and/or emotionally unstable,' Anne Cranny-Francis tells us (1985, 280). In 'The Changeling' (2x03) the *Enterprise* crew encounters Nomad an intelligent probe seeking perfection. Nomad tries to absorb Lieutenant Uhura's knowledge leading to the following conversation:

> Nomad: That unit is defective. Its thinking is chaotic. Absorbing it unsettled me.
> Spock: That unit is a woman.
> Nomad: A mass of conflicting impulses.

If the Vulcan Spock had said, 'That unit is human,' it might have been an understandable though speciesist twenty-third century remark. As it stands it is nothing but 1960s' sexism. And yet again it is Spock who utters the following when the crew tries to catch a serial killer in 'Wolf in the Fold' (2x14): '... I suspect [it] preys on women because women are more easily and more deeply terrified, generating more sheer horror than the male of the species.'

It is a small step from sexism to sexual assault. In the 'too gentle' episode 'Charlie X' Charles 'Charlie' Evans (Robert Walker), a teenager raised by Thasians and given special mental powers, sexually assaults Janice Rand (Grace Lee Whitney), the captain's yeoman.[8] His assaults – like slapping

---

[8] Editors' note: There are persistent rumors that Gene Roddenberry sexually assaulted Grace Lee Whitney on set of *TOS*, and consequently wrote her out of the show. These rumors are fueled, in part, by allegations she made

Rand's bottom – are explained away by Captain Kirk as mere adolescent problems and overreactions. Charlie keeps pursuing Rand who finally slaps him. He then uses his powers and makes her disappear, claiming: 'Why did she do that? I loved her, but she wasn't nice at all.' In Charlie's eyes it is Rand's own fault. She had to be punished. That is a classic depiction of the victim–offender relationship. The victim has given offense. She has provoked the offender. Nevertheless, this scene is not discussed or even seen in the context of sexual assault. In the episode 'The Enemy Within' (1x05) a transporter-generated evil duplicate of Kirk tries to rape Janice Rand (who previously had been returned by the Thasians). After the situation is resolved and Kirk is one person again Spock remarks: 'The, er, impostor had some interesting qualities, wouldn't you say, Yeoman?' Spock's completely out-of-the-place remark did not cause a stir at the time the episode aired. Seen today it might be considered worse than the rape flashbacks on *DSC*. With them it is clear that they are not desirable moments, while Spock's remark suggests otherwise. *TOS* is the real wolf in sheep's clothing. Everything that is criticized about *DSC* is already there; less bloody, less graphic, less explicit, but therefore left to the audience's imagination.

The stage for nudity was not set by L'Rell on *DSC* either, but by the hint of Nancy Kovack's breast in *TOS* episode 2x19 'A Private Little War.'[9] *TOS* kept pushing the borders of what was possible on television, advancing the 'final frontier' of Broadcast Standards. While being progressive in many ways it still had to pander to the zeitgeist,[10] and appeal to the audience's sensationalism. Maybe next time it would not just be ten seconds of nude bathing.

>   in her autobiography *The Longest Trek: My Tour of the Galaxy*, in which she describes being sexually assaulted by a man she calls 'The Executive' (1998, 5–6).
> [9] 'In "A Private Little War," Marc Daniels had directed a scene in which a shapely primitive maiden ... [Nancy Kovack] ... bathed beneath a small waterfall. ... if the viewer strained very hard, an occasional small portion of Nancy's breast could be seen.' The producers went out of their way to get the scene past Broadcast Standards as Solow and Justman recall. Before submitting the episode, they added another ten seconds to the scene. 'When the restored episode was screened by Broadcast Standards, their reaction was predictable. "You can't show this sort of thing on television. Why you can actually see part of her... her..." "Tit?" "Breast, Bob, breast. You have to lose the shot"' (1997, 355–56). Broadcast Standards could be convinced that the scene was necessary for the story and agreed to keep it if it was shortened by ten seconds.
> [10] Though there were many female lieutenants besides Nichelle Nichols' Lieutenant Uhura, they often were relegated to the sidelines and women were generally still seen as weaker than men.

'Do you know the Klingon proverb that tells us revenge is a dish that is best served cold? It is very cold in space' (Khan (Ricardo Montalban), *Star Trek II: The Wrath of Khan*)

As soon as the *Enterprise* boldly went to the silver screen it adapted to its customs and the need to pander to a broader audience. In 1977 *Star Wars* had set high standards concerning special effects. It even used CGI for the simulated swoop through the Death Star trench. *Star Trek* had to follow suit and set even higher standards. *Star Trek: The Motion Picture* (1979) was almost only set as a stage for showing off special effects. The story, the action, and the characters suffered – the movie flopped. With *Star Trek II: The Wrath of Khan* (1982) the producers remembered the idea of Kirk as a Captain Hornblower in space.[11] The *Enterprise* is styled more like a battleship than a ship of exploration.[12] While *Star Wars* fashioned space battles like air fights, *Star Trek II* kept with the naval tradition. The *Enterprise*'s battle with the *Reliant* in the Mutara Nebula is not only reminiscent of submarine battles, but also of the battle against a Romulan warbird in one of the most popular *TOS* episodes 'Balance of Terror' (1x14). While *DSC* is true to this concept during the Battle at the Binary Stars (1x02) – Starfleet and the Klingons engage in battle like ships of the line – it goes *Star Wars* in 'Such Sweet Sorrow, Part Two' (2x14). Here the focus is on aircraft-like shuttles and fighters deployed by the starships. In *Star Trek II*, violence finally has become hurtful and bloody. During Khan's early surprise attack on the *Enterprise* a lot of cadets get killed in the engine room. One of them, Peter Preston (Ike Eisenmann), is critically wounded and while dying leaves a blood stain on Kirk's uniform. Preston's bloodied face is a first for *Star Trek*. Khan torturing Captain Terrell (Paul Winfield) and Chekov (Walter Koenig) underlines the difference between Kirk's crew – enlightened, peaceful human beings – and Khan, the genetically enhanced despot from the past. Just as Gul Madred (David Warner) torturing Picard (Patrick Stewart) in 'Chain of Command Part One and Two' (*TNG* 6x10, 6x11)

---

[11] Gene Roddenberry had read *Hornblower* when the novels were first published in the United States in 1939 and the English captain soon became his favorite literary character. In 1945 he even published a poem titled 'Sailor's Prayer' (for more cf. Rabitsch, 2019, 63).

[12] While science fiction often dealt with the military, military science fiction gained a lot of popularity during the 1970s and 1980s. Works like David Drake's *Hammer's Slammers* series (starting 1979), Orson Scott Card's *Ender's Game* (1985), and Lois McMaster Bujold's *Vorkosigan* saga (starting 1986) helped to established military science fiction as a subgenre.

does for Starfleet officers and 'evil' Cardassians. At the same time the graphic depiction of violence fulfills the producers' need to present the audience with something new. In order not to get boring *Star Trek* has to become either more violent – i.e. show more deaths – or more realistic and detailed – i.e. show more blood, more gore (cf. Eisermann, 2001, 34–35). These two elements culminate naturally on *DSC*. The violence is not Starfleet's violence but forced upon them. As early as *Star Trek VI: The Undiscovered Country* (1991) the next level had been reached. Handheld phasers no longer disintegrate the targets, but pierce them, leaving dead Klingons spinning and bleeding in zero gravity. The critics liked it: 'the Klingons' spilled blood floats in the air in eerily beautiful purplish globules; it's space-age Sam Peckinpah' (Howe, 1991, N53). The *Star Trek* movies followed Paramount's need to attract a wider audience and quite naturally adapted to the action and special effects-oriented style of the cinema logically leading to the action oriented theatrical reboot in 2009.

'If you can't take a little bloody nose, maybe you ought to go back home and crawl under your bed' (Q (John de Lancie), 'Q Who,' *TNG* 2x16)

When *Star Trek* returned to television in 1987 a lot of things had changed. Klingons were now friends and allies, the captain was French (notwithstanding Patrick Stewart being British), men wore skirts known as 'skants' (but only in season one) and the crew was even more diverse than before. But the more things change, the more they stay the same – *TNG* is no exception. The *Enterprise*-crew kept pushing the final frontier and meeting strange new aliens; some of whom still wore skimpy dresses ('Justice'), and even female crew members were still experiencing prejudice (e.g. using flower pots as weapons in 'Qpid' 4x20) and had to live up to the male audience's salacious phantasies (Deanna Troi (Marina Sirtis) does not wear a proper uniform till season six). Nevertheless, there were attempts to have stronger female roles on *TNG*. Just like the *Star Trek* movies were influenced by the new standards for special effects, *TNG* was influenced by other science fiction genres and tried to meet the viewers' new demands. After watching *Aliens* Gene Roddenberry told David Gerrold (author and story editor) about actress Jeanette Goldstein, 'That woman created a whole new style of feminine beauty. We should have something like that in *Star Trek*.' Supervising producer Robert Justman agreed:

> If we could get her, she could be a member of the Enterprise's onboard Marine contingent or MP contingent.[13] This would enable her to serve in a military capacity within our landing parties. Her feistiness, coupled with her earthy physicality, could create interesting opportunities for drama. (Altman and Gross, 2016b, 55)

Thus, the character of Tasha Yar, chief of security played by Denise Crosby, was born. The problem was that Gene Roddenberry wanted 'armaments and militarism to be deemphasized over previous *Star Trek* series and very much deemphasized over the *Star Trek* movies.' He wanted to 'go back to the flavor of the previous series' first year when emphasis was on 'strange new worlds' rather than on space villains and space battles' (Altman and Gross, 2016b, 62). This led to Denise Crosby being '"bored to tears"' on set. 'Fifteen-hour shoots on the bridge where she had a few technical lines to repeat left her feeling "brain dead" as a performer' (Green). Adding to the problem was the fact that *TNG*, like *TOS*, should revolve around three male characters – Picard, Riker (Jonathan Frakes), and Data (Brent Spiner) – as Roddenberry told Crosby during their final conversation leading to Crosby's departure. Tasha Yar became the first regular *Star Trek* cast member to be permanently killed off ('Skin of Evil' 1x23).[14] Boredom was not the only problem. Crosby pointed out, '"I think they would have been very happy for me to wear really tight outfits and heels and stick my tits out – believe me, they suggested it, those very words were actually used."' According to Michelle Green she 'noted that the franchise has not escaped this mentality yet [in 1997], given the catsuits worn by Nana Visitor on *Deep Space Nine* and Jeri Ryan on *Voyager*' (Green; emphasis added). As far as strong female lead characters are concerned *Star Trek* has come a long way to reach Michael Burnham, Philippa Georgiou, Sylvia Tilly (Mary Wiseman), and Katrina Cornwell (Jayne Brook).[15]

---

[13] This foreshadowed the placement of MACOs (Military Assault Command Operations) on the *Enterprise* on *ENT* as well as Starfleet's more military attitude on *DS9*.

[14] Although she later returned briefly in a time travel/parallel universe plot twist. Something which becomes a major plot element on *DSC* (cf. Georgiou's death and return).

[15] For a more in-depth analysis of the variety of female characters in *DIS* see Mareike Spychala's essay '"Not Your Daddy's *Star Trek*:" Exploring Female Characters in *Star Trek: Discovery*' also published in this volume.

On *TNG*, rape is also a topic. In 'Violations' (5x12)[16] Deanna Troi is telepathically violated by an Ullian (Ben Lemon). The scenes were clearly recognized as rape and provoked matching viewer reactions.

> 'Violations' led to a temporary ban on *TNG* in my household when I was about eight years old. The repeated 'mind rape' scenes weren't well-received by my father at the dinner table and led him to exclaim, 'this isn't for you! This isn't for any of us!' Which was funny in retrospect, since the only people home were him, me, and the family dog. (RapidNadion, 2010)

On *Star Trek: Nemesis* it is again Deanna who is telepathically assaulted. The scene in *Nemesis* marks a change in the treatment of characters since Captain Picard in essence asks Troi to endure further rape attacks by Shinzon (Tom Hardy) in order to gain an advantage over him. This 'the end justifies the means' attitude is something Picard would not yet have done on *TNG*. It is, however, something Emperor Georgiou would do without hesitation.

Although the *Enterprise-D* is a far less dangerous ship to serve on – 57 crew killed in seven seasons compared to Kirk's 53 crew killed in only three seasons[17] – the depiction of violence is more graphic than on *TOS*. During the first season there are a number of scenes with violence gorier than anything on *TOS*. In 'Conspiracy,' which was cut and censored in the United Kingdom as well as in Germany and preceded with a viewer discretion warning in Canada, Picard and Riker confront an officer, Lieutenant Dexter Remmick (Robert Schenkkan), hosting a parasite. Rather unlike Starfleet officers they immediately

---

[16] Telepathic rape has first been explored in *The Undiscovered Country* during Spock's forced mind meld with Lieutenant Valeris. The *ENT* episode 'Stigma' (2x14) confirms the interpretation of Spock's actions as rape. T'Pol is accused by the Vulcan High Command of having contracted Pa'nar Syndrome, a mind-affecting disease. Pa'nar Syndrome is transmitted during mind melds just like a STD. Not only did T'Pol become infected during a forced mind meld, but Vulcans in the twenty-second century consider melding a 'unnatural practice' ('Fusion' 1x17, 'Stigma'). For more on the topic of telepathic rape and rape on *TNG* cf. Sarah Projansky, 'When the Body Speaks. Deanna Troi's Tenuous Authority and the Rationalization of Federation Superiority in *Star Trek: The Next Generation* Rape Narratives', in Taylor Harrison et al. (eds.) *Star Trek: The Next Generation Rape Narratives. Enterprising Zones: Critical Positions on Star Trek* (Boulder, CO: Westview Press, 1996): 33–50.

[17] Only counting crew members who stayed dead. In both series there have been a lot of revivals.

open fire with their phasers. Remmick's head is vaporized and partly explodes. When his body begins to dissolve the parasite breaks through his chest *Alien*-style. Picard and Riker fire again vaporizing the alien leaving Remmick's exploded smoldering corpse showing his intestines, ribs, and spine.

Gene Roddenberry wanted *TNG* to be believable and more realistic than *TOS*. Part of this realism is the addition of conflict and graphic violence; the audience expected as much since, as Rick Berman puts it, '[t]elevision has grown up a lot. The cynical part of television' (Altman and Gross, 2016b, 115). Although *TNG* still followed Gene Roddenberry's cardinal rule that there should not be any conflict between the main characters – something *DS9* and *VOY* circumvented by introducing non-Starfleet crew members like the Bajoran militia on *DS9* and the Marquis on *VOY* – Starfleet officers were now allowed to explore their dark sides. Cruel and violent acts were still reserved for (non-human) adversaries, however, leading to the creation of one of *Star Trek*'s most infamous alien races: the Borg, a cybernetic pseudo-species. When Captain Picard is assimilated by the Borg and turned into a drone he is physically and mentally violated and forced to commit unthinkable cruelties ('Best of Both Worlds' *TNG* 3x26, 4x01). As a drone Picard helps the Borg to destroy 39 starships causing more than 11,000 deaths. Given *Star Trek*'s emphasis on each individual's value, to take away one's identity, one's individualism, is the greatest possible violation in *Star Trek*, even more terrible than death.[18] This experience changes Picard and leaves a permanent mark as can be seen in his violent outburst in *Star Trek: First Contact* (1996) when he kills two assimilated crew members with a tommy gun. He does not only want to stop the Borg from taking over his ship, but he is on a personal quest for vengeance. On *TNG* the producers still followed Roddenberry's no-conflict rule and until *First Contact* it had been the Klingon Worf (Michael Dorn) who provided the necessary friction. Not being human but hailing from a warrior race enabled him to not be as perfect as the other Starfleet officers onboard. In *First Contact* it is Worf who wants to do the reasonable thing, abandon the *Enterprise*, activate

---

[18] For more on the loss of individualism and the Borg cf. Fuchs, 2016, 167–70. Also, rescued Borg drones, like Picard and Seven of Nine (Jeri Ryan), are left with a severe case of PTSD and never fully regain their humanity as seen in the following dialogue between Seven and Picard on *Star Trek Picard*: 'After they brought you back from your time in the collective… do you honestly feel that you regained your humanity?' 'Yes.' 'All of it?' 'No. But we're both working on it… aren't we?' 'Every damn day of my life.'

the self-destruct sequence and destroy the Borg. Picard disagrees: 'You want to destroy the ship, and run away. You coward.' Lily Sloane (Alfre Woodard), a twenty-first century survivor of the Third World War, confronts Picard in his ready room due to the crew following his orders and calls him 'Ahab.' Picard smashes a display case in anger promising: 'I will make them [the Borg] *pay* for what they've done!' He comes to realize he is indeed acting like Ahab and is able to suppress his dark instincts and the enlightened twenty-fourth century human can take over again. These violent outbursts, these insights into the darker corners of Picard's soul make him more human and are necessary to make *Star Trek*'s idealistic future more believable.

Starting with *TOS*'s 'Mirror, Mirror' the crossover episodes fulfilled the same function and were highly popular with the cast, authors, and audience alike. *TNG*'s co-producer Hans Beimler argued for more conflict from the very beginning: 'I always said to Gene Roddenberry that Shakespeare works three hundred years later because the things that motivated human beings then still motivate us today' (Altman and Gross, 2016b, 114). The Mirror Universe episodes gave the authors the opportunity to explore the darker sides of the main cast. The Mirror Universe is always a place of more violence, eroticism and sex. Even Intendant Kira (Nana Visitor) and Ezri Teagan (Nicole de Beor) kissing in the Mirror Universe ('The Emperor's New Cloak,' *DS9*, 7x12) did not raise a storm of protests like Lenara Kahn (Susanna Thompson)'s and Jadzia Dax (Terry Farrell)'s passionate kiss in the Prime Universe ('Rejoined,' *DS9*, 4x06) did. Deviant behavior is acceptable for 'evil' Mirror-characters; however, none of the 'good' Prime Universe characters should act in such unacceptable ways. Teresa Cutler-Boyles points out that in Roddenberry's vision for the future 'sexuality will be a non-controversial subject, perhaps open, always vanilla' (2017, 43). The characters of the Mirror Universe, however, practice a more '*deviant* sexuality' (2017, 42). But neither the Prime Universe characters, nor the viewers have to be threatened by the Mirror characters since at the end of each episode the Prime characters find their way back through the Mirror and 'the status quo is reinstated, and everyone breathes a sigh of relief' (2017, 50). This leads one to wonder if there would have been similar outcry by *Star Trek*'s more hypocritical fans if it had been 'evil' Lorca and 'evil' Stamets kissing on *DSC* instead of Prime Stamets and Culber.

'I'm going, I'm going, get off my ass! Sir. Get off my ass, Sir' (Jett Reno (Tig Notaro), 'Such Sweet Sorrow, Part Two,' DSC 2x14)

With *Star Trek: Discovery*, *Star Trek* has arrived in the twenty-first century. It not only uses narration techniques and effects suitable for its new audience, it also keeps boldly doing what *Star Trek* has done: holding up the mirror to society with all its strengths and weaknesses. It also allows for a much more human depiction of humanity. By taking Emperor Georgiou through the mirror and essentially making her a Prime character, *DSC* allows for the fact that even the darkest personality might have some good in them. Georgiou reminds the viewer of not getting too comfortable. With her there is no 'sigh of relief' just as today there does not seem to be one for humanity yet. *DSC* refreshes the franchise and comments – tongue-in-cheek – on some of the wrongs in *TOS*. Those criticizing it for not being canon might try to watch 'Badda-Bing, Badda-Bang' (*DS9*, 7x15) where Kasidy Yates (Penny Johnson) tells Ben Sisko (Avery Brooks):

> I know [it] isn't a totally accurate representation of the way things were, but it isn't meant to be. It shows us the way things could have been. The way they should've been. ... it reminds us that we're no longer bound by any limitations, except the ones we impose on ourselves.

If that does not help, quote Jett Reno.

Works Cited

Mark A. Altman and Edward Gross, *The Fifty-Year Mission, The First 25 Years. The Complete, Uncensored, Unauthorized Oral History of Star Trek* (New York: Thomas Dunne Books/St. Martin's Press, 2016a).
—— *The Fifty-Year Mission, The Next 25 Years. The Complete, Uncensored, Unauthorized Oral History of Star Trek* (New York: Thomas Dunne Books/ St. Martin's Press, 2016b).
Allan Asherman, *The Star Trek Interview Book* (New York et al.: Pocket Books, 1988).
Marcus Berkman, *Set Phasers to Stun. 50 Years of Star Trek* (Boston, MA: Little, Brown and Company, 2016).
Paul F. Cockburn, 'Trek Britain: 45 Years on British TV', *Star Trek Magazine*, 177 (2014): 28–33.

John van Citters, 'TOS, TAS, TNG, DS9, VGR, ENT, DSC', *Twitter*, 23 July (2016), https://www.twitter.com/jvancitters/status/756983274208198656.

Anne Cranny-Francis, 'Sexuality and Sex-Role Stereotyping in Star Trek', *Science Fiction Studies*, 12 (1985): 274–84.

Teresa Cutler-Broyles, 'What We See When We Look in the Mirror: Star Trek's *Alternative Sexuality*', in Nadine Farghaly and Simon Bacon (eds.) *To Boldly Go: Essays on Gender and Identity in the Star Trek Universe* (Jefferson, NC: McFarland & Company, 2017): 41–53.

Jessica Eisermann, *Mediengewalt, Die gesellschaftliche Kontrolle von Gewaltdarstellungen im Fernsehen* (Opladen: Westdeutscher Verlag, 2001).

Brian F., 'Why Do They Have to Add the Garbage?', *Parent Reviews for Star Trek: Discovery*, 20 October (2017), https://www.commonsensemedia.org/tv-reviews/star-trek-discovery/user-reviews/adult#.

Laura L. Finley, 'Star Trek', in Laura L. Finley (ed.) *Violence in Popular Culture: American and Global Perspectives* (Westport, CT: Greenwood, 2018): 160–61.

John Andreas Fuchs, '"Suddenly Human:" The Importance of Individualism and Humanitas in the *Star Trek* Universe (1966–today)', in Marko Trajkovic and Joost van Loon (eds.) *Faith and Reason: An Interdisciplinary Construction Of Human Rights* (Sankt Augustin: Academia Verlag, 2016): 163–73.

Andrew E. Gaska, 'Star Trek', *Facebook*, 21 May (2018), https://www.facebook.com/groups/Trek1701/permalink/10155412877266053/.

Michelle Erica Green, 'Denise Crosby's Trekkies: The Deep Impact of Tasha Yar', *The Little Review*, n.d., littlereview.com/getcritical/trektalk/crosby.htm.

Desson Howe, 'Trek Still Boldly Going', *The Washington Post*, 6 December (1991).

M. Maven, 'Not Family Viewing!', *Parent Reviews for Star Trek: Discovery*, 20 October (2017), https://www.commonsensemedia.org/tv-reviews/star-trek-discovery/user-reviews/adult#.

Memory Alpha, November 2003, memory-alpha.wikia.com/wiki/Portal:Main.

Jason F. Perry, 'Star Trek', *Facebook*, 18 October (2017), https://www.facebook.com/groups/Trek1701/permalink/10154908186621053/.

Sarah Projansky, 'When the Body Speaks. Deanna Troi's Tenous Authority and the Rationalization of Federation Superiority in *Star Trek: The Next Generation* Rape Narratives', in Taylor Harrison et al. (eds.) *Enterprising Zones: Critical Positions on Star Trek* (Boulder, CO: Westview Press, 1996): 33–50.

Stefan Rabitsch, Star Trek *and the British Age of Sail: The Maritime Influence Throughout the Series and Films* (Jefferson, NC: McFarland & Company, 2019).

RapidNadion, 'TNG's Most Violent Episodes & TV-14 Ratings', *The Trek BBS*, 12 October (2010), https://www.trekbbs.com/threads/tngs-most-violent-episodes-tv-14-ratings.130332/.

Richard Slotkin, *Gunfighter Nation: The Myth of the Frontier in Twentieth Century America* (Norman: University of Oklahoma Press, 1998).

Herbert F. Solow and Robert H. Justman, *Inside Star Trek: The Real Story* (New York et al.: Pocket Books, 1997).

Wes V., 'No Longer Family Appropriate', *Parent Reviews for Star Trek: Discovery*, 20 October (2017), https://www.commonsensemedia.org/tv-reviews/star-trek-discovery/user-reviews/adult#.

Grace Lee Whitney, *The Longest Trek: My Tour of the Galaxy* (Clovis, CA: Quill Driver Books, 1998).

Episodes and Films Cited

'The Man Trap.' *Star Trek*, written by George Clayton Johnson, directed by Marc Daniels, Desilu Productions, 8 September, 1966.

'Charlie X.' *Star Trek*, written by Gene Roddenberry, directed by Lawrence Dobkin, Desilu Productions, 15 September, 1966.

'Where No Man Has Gone Before.' *Star Trek*, written by Samuel A. Peeples, directed by James Goldstone, Desilu Productions, 22 September, 1966.

'The Naked Time.' *Star Trek*, written by John D.F. Black, directed by Marc Daniels, Desilu Productions, 29 September, 1966.

'The Enemy Within.' *Star Trek*, written by Richard Matheson, directed by Leo Penn, Desilu Productions, 6 October, 1966.

'Mudd's Women.' *Star Trek*, written by Gene Roddenberry, directed by Harvey Hart, Desilu Productions, 13 October, 1966.

'What Are Little Girls Made Of?' *Star Trek*, written by Robert Bosch, directed by James Goldstone, Desilu Productions, 20 October, 1966.

'Miri.' *Star Trek*, written by Adrian Spies, directed by Vincent McEveety, Desilu Productions, 27 October, 1966.

'Plato's Stepchildren.' *Star Trek*, written by Meyer Dolinski, directed by David Alexander, Desilu Productions, 22 November, 1966.

'The Conscience of the King.' *Star Trek*, written by Barry Trivers, directed by Gerd Oswald, Desilu Productions, 8 December, 1966.

'Balance of Terror.' *Star Trek*, written by Paul Schneider, directed by Vincent McEveety, Desilu Productions, 15 December, 1966.

'Shore Leave.' *Star Trek*, written by Theodore Sturgeon, directed by Robert Sparr, Desilu Productions, 29 December, 1966.

'The Changeling.' *Star Trek*, written by John Meredyth Lucas, directed by Marc Daniels, Desilu Productions, 29 September, 1967.

'Mirror, Mirror.' *Star Trek*, written by Jerome Bixby, directed by Marc Daniels, Desilu Productions, 6 October, 1967.

'Wolf in the Fold.' *Star Trek*, written by Robert Bosch, directed by Joseph Pevney, Desilu Productions, 22 December, 1967.

'A Private Little War.' *Star Trek*, written by Jud Crucis, directed by Marc Daniels, Desilu Productions, 2 February, 1968.

'The Empath.' *Star Trek*, written by Joyce Muskat, directed by John Erman, Desilu Productions, 6 December, 1968.

'Whom Gods Destroy.' *Star Trek*, written by Lee Erwin and Jerry Sohl, directed by Herb Wallerstein, Desilu Productions, 3 January, 1969.

'Once Upon a Planet.' *Star Trek: The Animated Series*, written by Chuck Menville and Len Janson, directed by Hal Sutherland, Filmation, 3 November, 1973.

'The Counter-Clock Incident.' *Star Trek: The Animated Series*, written by John Culver, directed by Bill Reed, Filmation, 12 October, 1974.

'Justice.' *Star Trek: The Next Generation*, written by Ralph Willis and Worley Thorne, directed by James L. Conway, Paramount Pictures, 9 November, 1987.

'Skin of Evil.' *Star Trek: The Next Generation*, written by Joseph Stefano, directed by Joseph L. Scanlan, Paramount Pictures, 25 April, 1988.

'Conspiracy.' *Star Trek: The Next Generation*, written by Robert Sabaroff, directed by Cliff Bole, Paramount Pictures, 9 May, 1988.

'The Cage.' *Star Trek*, written by Gene Roddenberry, directed by Robert Butler, Desilu Productions, 4 October, 1988.

'Q Who.' *Star Trek: The Next Generation*, written by Maurice Hurley, directed by Rob Bowman, Paramount Pictures, 8 May, 1989.

'Best of Both Worlds, Part One and Two.' *Star Trek: The Next Generation*, written by Michael Piller, directed by Cliff Bole, Paramount Pictures, 18 June/24 September, 1990.

'Qpid.' *Star Trek: The Next Generation*, written by Randee Russell and Ira Steven Behr, directed by Cliff Bole, Paramount Pictures, 22 April, 1991.

'Violations.' *Star Trek: The Next Generation*, written by Shari Goodhartz, T. Michael, and Pamela Gray, directed by Robert Wiemer, Paramount Pictures, 3 February, 1992.

'Chain of Command, Part One and Two.' *Star Trek: The Next Generation*, written by Frank Abatemarco, directed by Robert Scheerer, Paramount Pictures, 14/21 December, 1992.

'Rejoined.' *Star Trek: Deep Space Nine*, written by René Echevarria, directed by Avery Brooks, Paramount Pictures, 30 October, 1995.

'To the Death.' *Star Trek: Deep Space Nine*, written by Ira Steven Behr and Robert Hewitt Wolfe, directed by LeVar Burton, Paramount Pictures, 13 May, 1996.

'Nor the Battle to the Strong.' *Star Trek: Deep Space Nine*, written by Brice R. Parker, directed by Kim Friedman, Paramount Pictures, 21 October, 1996.

'The Siege of AR-558.' *Star Trek: Deep Space Nine*, written by Ira Steven Behr and Hans Beimler, directed by Winrich Kolbe, Paramount Pictures, 18 November, 1998.

'The Emperor's New Cloak.' *Star Trek: Deep Space Nine*, Ira Steven Behr and Hans Beimler, directed by LeVar Burton, Paramount Pictures, 3 February, 1999.

'Badda-Bing, Badda-Bang.' *Star Trek: Deep Space Nine*, written by Ira Steven Behr and Hans Beimler, directed by Mike Vejar, Paramount Pictures, 24 February, 1999.

'Equinox, Part One and Two.' *Star Trek: Voyager*, written by Rick Berman, Brannon Braga, and Joe Menosky, directed by David Livingston, Paramount Pictures, 26 May/22 September, 1999.

'Fusion.' *Star Trek: Enterprise*, written by Rick Berman and Brannon Braga, directed by Rob Hedden, Paramount Pictures, 27 February, 2002.

'Stigma.' *Star Trek: Enterprise*, written by Rick Berman and Brannon Braga, directed by David Livingston, Paramount Pictures, 5 February, 2003.

'Battle at the Binary Stars.' *Star Trek: Discovery*, written by Bryan Fuller, directed by Adam Kane, CBS Television Studios, 24 September, 2017.

'The Butcher's Knife Cares Not for the Lamb's Cry.' *Star Trek: Discovery*, written by Jesse Alexander and Aron Eli Coleite, directed by Olatunde Osunsanmi, CBS Television Studios, 8 October, 2017.

'Choose your pain.' *Star Trek: Discovery*, written by Gretchen J. Berg, Aaron Harberts, and Kemp Powers, directed by Lee Rose, CBS Television Studios, 15 October, 2017.

'Lethe.' *Star Trek: Discovery*, written by Joe Menosky and Ted Sullivan, directed by Douglas Aarniokoski, CBS Television Studios, 22 October, 2017.

'Into the Forest I Go.' *Star Trek: Discovery*, written by Bo Yeon Kim and Erika Lippoldt, directed by Chris Byrne, CBS Television Studios, 12 November, 2017.

'Brother.' *Star Trek: Discovery*, written by Ted Sullivan, Gretchen J. Berg, and Aaron Harberts, directed by Alex Kurtzman, CBS Television Studios, 17 January, 2019.

'Such Sweet Sorrow, Part Two.' *Star Trek: Discovery*, written by Michelle Paradise, Jenny Lumet, and Alex Kurtzman, directed by Olatunde Osunsanmi, CBS Television Studios, 18 April, 2019.

'Stardust City Rag.' *Star Trek: Picard*, written by Kirsten Beyer, directed by Jonathan Frakes, CBS Television Studios, 20 February, 2020.

Star Wars. 1977. Directed by George Lucas. Lucasfilm.
Star Trek: The Motion Picture. 1979. Directed by Robert Wise. Paramount Pictures.
Star Trek II: The Wrath of Khan. 1982. Directed by Nicholas Meyer. Paramount Pictures.
Aliens. 1986. Directed by James Cameron. 20th Century Fox, Brandywine Productions.
Star Trek IV: The Voyage Home. 1986. Directed by Leonard Nimoy. Paramount Pictures.
Star Trek VI: The Undiscovered Country. 1991. Directed by Nicholas Meyer. Paramount Pictures.
Star Trek: *First Contact*. 1996. Directed by Jonathan Frakes. Paramount Pictures.
Star Trek: *Nemesis*. 2002. Directed by Stuart Baird. Paramount Pictures.
Star Trek. 2009. Directed by J.J. Abrams. Paramount Pictures.
Star Trek: Into Darkness. 2013. Directed by J.J. Abrams. Paramount Pictures.

These are the Voyages?
The Post-Jubilee *Trek* Legacy on the *Discovery*, the *Orville*, and the *Callister*

Michael G. Robinson

A network television series was noticeably absent from *Star Trek*'s half-century anniversary. By 2016, the primary output of the *Trek* franchise was a set of commercially successful feature films that had retconned a substantial portion of the early series' history and consequently left later spin-off television series adrift in continuity limbo. One year later, or perhaps one year too late, three programs emerged to take up the mantle of *Trek*. This essay explores how these series make a claim to a familiar science fiction formula legendary for diverse themes and progressive ideologies even while deviating from some elements of that formula. Plagued by production delays, *Star Trek: Discovery* (2017–ongoing) arrived as the official heir apparent. Set shortly before the original adventures of the *U.S.S. Enterprise*, *Discovery* banks upon viewer nostalgia for *Trek* while also challenging long established storytelling patterns through a serial narrative and by having that narrative focus upon a female executive officer in a complex crisis with personal ramifications. This program also carried the weight of hustling for an online access system. *The Orville* (2017–ongoing) was promoted as a *Galaxy Quest*-style parody in the mode of its creator, Seth McFarlane, but the show baffled those expectations by producing one of the most ardent tributes to late era *Trek*. While humorous in tone and laced with asides, this series often seems like a *Trek* program in disguise on another network. Finally, the 'U.S.S. Callister' (2017) episode of *Black Mirror* (2011–ongoing) challenged toxic themes at the heart of the classic space exploration story while honoring the formula in a modern era.

Wrestling with a broad popular culture topic like *Trek* requires a large academic perspective. As the legacy of *Trek* is central to this analysis, mythology is a good starting point. In *To Boldly Go* (2018), Djoymi Baker sees the franchise as a powerful circulator of past mythology and, simultaneously, a creator of its own mythology. This process is neither latent nor implicit. The various commercial forces that seek to profit from *Star Trek* increasingly promote these ideas. *Star Trek* sells the epic and the epic sells *Star Trek*. In one analysis, Baker examines the various opening credit sequences of the *Trek* television programs in great textual detail. Baker finds a trend towards increasingly Earth-centric imagery: 'the "real" cosmos is subsumed into the *Star Trek* cosmos, a mythic realm in which the strange promises to be rendered familiar and safe, and where, ultimately, there's no place like home' (140). In another analysis, Baker explores the interactive *Star Trek: The Experience* installation at the Las Vegas Hilton. This attraction allowed visitors to immerse themselves in *Trek*-style environments and to enjoy ride experiences that put participants into an adventure as the guardians of future *Trek* continuity in their role as a possible ancestor of future *Enterprise* Captain Jean-Luc Picard (Patrick Stewart). Baker argued,

> [t]he timeline, the succession of series and films, the physical artefacts that are both fictional and real, and the real physical experience of a fictional *Star Trek* within the rides, all serve to uphold the reality of *Star Trek* as historical future: a mythological Neverland that is both situated in time and yet is also timeless and eternal. (167)

While optimistic about the potential for fans to create meaning in this case, Baker is careful to acknowledge that these *Trek* elements are largely in the control of commercial industries. In essence, Baker argues that there are qualities that are definable as *Trek*. While Baker's goal is to situate the modern mythologizing of the *Trek* franchise into the broader study of mythology, the understanding that these elements are also commercialized and promoted leads to an interesting corollary. Towards the end of the book, while commenting on the franchise's recent films and the hints of *Star Trek: Discovery* to come, Baker states '*Star Trek* is constantly coming up with these reimaginings, new beginnings and further adventures that nonetheless draw upon its past, such that any 'end' feels entirely provisional' (190). As a franchise, *Trek* continues to reinvent itself, but in ways that also comfortably situate the new in what has come before.

In fact, in this way, the initial trailers for *Discovery* invite the connection to the past. Baker observes: 'By calling *Discovery* a "new chapter in the *Star Trek* saga" the trailer continues the promotional strategy of the series that followed after *TOS*, which similarly sought to link the franchise with myth, legend, and saga' (191). Another way to see this observation is to argue that *Trek* itself has a certain kind of rhetorical force. Curiously, any new *Trek* can prove itself by linking to the old *Trek* that passed before.

That paradox is reminiscent of John Cawelti's ideas of formula. Cawelti sees the propagation of a formula across popular culture as a balancing act between convention and innovation. Certain set elements exist in any story formula. For *Trek*, these might be iconic items like Federation starships or themes about humanism, diversity, and exploration. Cawelti maintains that in order to prevent staleness, formulas must innovate. Again, for *Trek*, this might be moving the narrative even further into a future setting like *Star Trek: The Next Generation* (1987–1994) did when it jumped a century ahead or it might be adding more diverse actors in leadership roles as in *Star Trek: Deep Space Nine* (1993–1999) and *Star Trek: Voyager* (1995–2001).

While Cawelti tends to look backwards across formula changes, allowing them to emerge in his study, this analysis seeks a more imminent perspective. As *Discovery* arrived in 2017, creators made a tautological case for this show's inclusion in the franchise's myth by invoking the myth. Or changes to the formula were rationalized as being in the spirit of the formula. Roughly simultaneously, two other properties arrived, Fox's new show *The Orville* and *Black Mirror*'s episode 'U.S.S. Callister.' These texts also invoked the spirit of *Trek* while challenging *Trek*, thereby demonstrating ways that *Trek* exceeds the grasp of its owners.[1]

Discussing the legacy of *Trek* also requires a consideration of its legator. Throughout much of the *Trek* franchise's history, that role was assigned to its originator, Gene Roddenberry.[2] Roddenberry is undeniably central to the myth of *Trek*. Consider, for example, the way that Roddenberry

---

[1] Another way that the franchise exceeds its creators' grasp it through fan creations. See, for example, Kerstin-Anja Münderlein's '"To Boldly Discuss...": Socio-Political Discourses in *Star Trek: Discovery* Fanfiction' in this volume.

[2] A full recounting of Roddenberry's history with *Trek* is beyond the scope of this paper, but interested parties may find many authorized and unauthorized histories available to understand the complex ways in which Roddenberry was involved in the show from its earliest moments. This analysis does not wish to fall for the traps inherent in auteur studies and assign the role of the sole author of *Trek* to the so-called 'Great Bird of the Galaxy.' Many creative people were involved in the shaping of *Trek*. This analysis will also not explore the politics of that creativity nor will it examine Roddenberry's own attempts to secure that role for himself. Readers are again encouraged to explore *Trek* histories for the many battles Roddenberry waged with studios and the many battles other creators within *Trek* waged with him.

appears in *The Making of Star Trek*. Co-authored by Stephen E. Whitfield and Gene Roddenberry and published in 1968, the book purports to be 'the first such attempt to tell the history of a television series' (13). It is very simple to tell when one of the co-authors communicates. Words by Whitfield, which dominate the book, are printed in normal fashion. Roddenberry is revealed to us through internal communications from the series. When he communicates directly, Roddenberry's words appear in all caps. Here, for example, is Roddenberry talking about the first series' commitment to diversity,

> INTOLERANCE IN THE 23RD CENTURY? IMPROBABLE! IF MAN SURVIVES THAT LONG HE WILL HAVE LEARNED TO TAKE A DELIGHT IN THE ESSENTIAL DIFFERENCES BETWEEN MEN AND BETWEEN CULTURES. HE WILL LEARN THAT DIFFERENCES IN IDEAS AND ATTITUDES ARE A DELIGHT, PART OF LIFE'S EXCITING VARIETY, NOT SOMETHING TO FEAR. IT'S A MANIFESTATION THAT THE GREATNESS OF GOD, OR WHATEVER IT IS, GAVE US. THIS INFINITE VARIATION AND DELIGHT, THIS IS PART OF THE OPTIMISM WE BUILT INTO STAR TREK. (23)

To our modern eyes, all caps is the format of shouting and angry debate, but our communication conventions did not exist then. Instead, this quote and all the other all caps utterances in *The Making of Star Trek* suggest importance. This is like receiving the direct pronunciations of the god of *Star Trek*. Such is the position of Roddenberry in the *Trek* mythology.

Roddenberry died in 1991, roughly the mid-point of *Trek* as a franchise. *Deep Space Nine, Voyager,* and *Enterprise* aired after this time. However, they were created by a finely tuned *Trek*-producing culture industry at Paramount. What makes *Discovery* particularly compelling is the gap that occurred before it arrived.

The *Discovery*

In its jubilee year, *Trek* was curiously both everywhere at once and nowhere to be seen, a bizarre quantum state that was perhaps fitting for a science fiction show. The story of *Trek* as a television engine that could was well known. That the original NBC series somehow survived three years and generated a massively successful franchise was a testament to the imagination of its creators and the tenacity of its fans. Yet, all those decades later, there was no new *Star Trek* for the jubilee.

Metaphorically speaking, there were plenty of old favorites to ride in the jubilee parade. Yet there was something hollow about that. There had been renewed motion picture success since J.J. Abrams' *Star Trek* blasted onto the screens in all its lens flare glory in 2009, but these films present retcons of the original series characters.[3] That new *Trek* started as old *Trek*. While there had been a consistent wave of new *Trek* programs after *Star Trek: The Next Generation* arrived in 1987, television production in the *Trek* franchise had stopped with the cancellation of *Enterprise* in 2005. An entire decade of the 50-year history had passed without any new programming until *Discovery* debuted on September 24, 2017.

Unsurprisingly, there were legal reasons for this. As James Hibberd reported in 'The Story of How Star Trek Returned to TV After 12 Years,' the Viacom conglomerate broke up in 2005, shedding Paramount Pictures and CBS into separate entities. Paramount got the film rights to *Trek* while CBS held onto the television rights. An agreement explicitly prevented CBS from bringing any new series forward until January 2017.

While it seems unlikely that fans would have minded an abundance of *Trek* on their big and small screens, corporations like protection. As Paramount preserved its creative space, CBS slowly drew up plans to bring a new *Trek* series to the public. Their mission was to seek out new viewers and new subscribers, to lucratively go where other streaming services had gone before. CBS launched its *All Access* streaming service in 2014 but there had been no compelling reason to use it beyond its archive of classic television episodes. As Daniel Holloway reported, *Discovery* was intended to be the first show with original content on the platform. New *Trek* would be the lure that drew subscribers in to the archival site. Delays in development meant that *Discovery* lost that opportunity to the legal spin-off *The Good Fight* (2017–ongoing), but expectations for the newest Trek were high. Les Moonves, chairman and CEO of CBS at the time 'had set a goal of 4 million subscribers for All Access by 2020' (Holloway, 2017, 8).

Trek television had been in this position before. *Star Trek: The Next Generation* was a pioneering program in the direct syndication market when it was released in 1987. *Star Trek: Voyager* was the draw for the fledgling UPN network when it arrived in 1995. Still, the risks were considerable. As Holloway (2017) summarized:

---

[3] This is commonly called the 'Kelvin Timeline' after the name of the *U.S.S Kelvin*, a ship captained by Kirk's father. Its destruction marks the change in continuity.

> For CBS, however, the question looming over 'Discovery' is whether the decision to place one of the most expensive shows in TV history on a platform where it will be initially exposed to fewer than 2 million potential U.S. viewers is a good business move. Part one of the premiere will debut on CBS, with part two available to watch immediately after on All Access, where all subsequent episodes will debut weekly. (8)

Holloway reported that Moonves further contextualized the risk by noting that other networks such as the CBS television network, Showtime, Amazon, and Netflix all wanted the show. Moonves was essentially stating that there was no reason to worry about something so desirable.

However, as Jordan Zakarin reported in a September 2017 story for *SYFY Wire*, there was fan resistance to the entire idea. *All Access* requires just that, access. Stereotypically tech savvy Trekkers presumably have reliable internet. However, these fans were being asked to shell out more gold-pressed latinum to see the newest instalment in their beloved franchise. *All Access* costs, as Zakarin notes, $5.99 a month or $9.99 a month for commercial-free viewing. *Discovery*'s diabolically commercial weekly release schedule meant that it would not be possible to buy a free trial and binge out new episodes immediately as one might with desirable series on other streaming platforms. Zakarin reported that fans on Twitter announced they would watch the pilot on CBS, take the trial service for the second episode, and then quit *All Access*.[4]

Other viewers must have been similarly affected. Anthony D'Alessandro reported that while no specific numbers were given, the CBS network stated that *Discovery* 'drove a record number of single day signups at CBS' digital streaming subscription service' (1). D'Alessandro also stated that the show was also part of a very good month for that network: 'In addition to its single-day record, CBS All Access saw its best week and month ever for signups thanks to *Star Trek: Discovery*, the fall kickoff of the NFL on CBS, and the season finale of *Big Brother* and *Big Brother Live Feeds*' (1). *Discovery* also drove increased mobile phone sign ups, levels that Janko Roettgers described that 'CBS was able to almost double the mobile subscription revenue' (1). Matthew Jackson speculated that these numbers may be higher because they do not include people who subscribed through the CBS website. Jackson also wondered if some

---

[4] Anecdotally, that was this author's plan too. Unfortunately, this author failed to reckon with the awesome power of the almighty serial format. Subscription occurred immediately, driven by his and his wife's fear that someone would eventually spoil the show for them in the future.

of the increase was from people who forgot to cancel the service after the free trial.

Discontent with *All Access* continued though. Not everyone chose to experience the show in legal ways. As Hibberd reported for a September 2017 *Entertainment Weekly* article entitled 'Star Trek: Discovery Already Getting Pirated A Lot,' right after the pilot's premiere, people worked around the system: '*Star Trek: Discovery* is on the verge of cracking Pirate Bay's Top 10 most illegally downloaded shows in less than 24 hours' (1). Resistance continued. A few months after the premiere, in 'Star Trek Fans, It's Time to Get Over Your CBS All Access Hangups,' Jamie Lovett argued that the economic reasons for resisting the *All Access* service were unfounded by comparing the cost of watching *Discovery* favorably against the price of other activities such as movie viewing, gaming, and comic book reading. Lovett also noted one particularly interesting argument:

> For some fans, the answer seems to be that its [sic] a matter of principle. Star Trek: Discovery being on a streaming service somehow goes against the egalitarian spirit of Star Trek as creator Gene Roddenberry envisioned it. Some even claim that Star Trek: Discovery only exists to convince people to sign up for CBS All Access. Those people are probably right. But so what? (4–5)

While there were some controversial qualities to the way *Discovery* arrived on screen, this was just the tip of the iceberg for the differences in this show.

From its very conception, *Discovery* was designed to break expectations. The original showrunner Bryan Fuller had envisioned a very different kind of project. As Hibberd explained in his 'The Story of How Star Trek Returned to TV After 12 Years' article, Fuller's initial pitch was for 'multiple serialized anthology shows' (2017, 4). Modelled after the format taken by the *American Horror Story* (2011–ongoing) franchise, these different programs were to be set in many different eras of *Trek*, from a period before the original series into a future never shown by *Trek* before.

CBS did not approve that idea but the network did greenlight a new *Trek* series under Fuller's guidance. As Holloway describes Fuller: 'He is not known as someone who prioritizes deadlines and budgets above all else. In short: He is not a typical CBS showrunner' (2017, 5). What followed, therefore, was a fairly complicated creative relationship with the network, leading to a series of delays in which *Discovery*'s premiere kept being pushed back because Fuller saw it as not ready. When Bryan

Fuller left the show in October 2016, Lesley Goldberg reported it as an amicable decision based on Fuller being unable to dedicate time to the *Trek* series and to *American Gods* (2017–ongoing) on STARZ. But Holloway also noted that 'sources close to Fuller and within CBS say that he was pushed out' (2017, 5). New showrunners Gretchen J. Berg and Aaron Harberts had worked with Fuller and, as reported by Holloway, sought his approval before taking over the show.

There was an awareness of the new nature of the program and its potential to rupture expectations among other creative people on the show. Sonequa Martin-Green, for example, expressed a certain kind of reverence for the show in her pre-release press conversations. As the star of the show, the future Commander Michael Burnham, stated:

> Anyone doing a new iteration of 'Star Trek', you have to understand how deep it is; you have to understand how important it is. You have to understand how much of a pillar it is to our culture. I think you need that in order to really give it the weight it deserves and I think that—I hope that more than anything—people get the sense of how serious we take this. (quoted in Holloway, 2017, 5)

Given the changes ahead in *Discovery*, it is almost as if Martin-Green is making proactive reassurances.

While it was unusual for a *Trek* series to focus on a character that was not the highest ranking officer on the ship, the fact that an African-American actress was the lead on the program felt like a natural continuation of *Trek*'s commitment to diversity, a line of change that at least stretched back through *Voyager*'s Captain Janeway (Kate Mulgrew) and *Deep Space Nine*'s Captain Sisko (Avery Brooks). As Zakarin discussed in a January 2018 article, *Discovery* did get caught up in an anti-diversity backlash that had heightened over the past few years in popular culture.[5] Zakarin called this activity, a 'dull, hateful background drone' (5) and noted how the new *Trek* series had joined a group of other genre texts that had come under fire from alt-right groups. Zakarin also rightly suggested that these racist opinions were antithetical to *Trek*'s long-standing commitment to diversity, calling it 'the franchise that has most embodied those ideas' (2018, 5).

How that main character ended up narratively speaking at the end of the first two episodes was, however, more shocking. At the beginning of 'The Vulcan Hello' (1x01), already vested deep in continuity as the

---

[5] For example, readers prepared to be disappointed in some of their fellow humans may wish to explore the Gamergate and Comicsgate phenomena.

foster-daughter of Spock's (Ethan Peck) parents Sarek (James Frain) and Amanda (Mia Kirshner), Commander Michael Burnham seemed about to follow a standard *Trek* plot about career advancement as Captain Philippa Georgiou (Michelle Yeoh) spoke to her about her readiness to take on command of her own vessel. By the end of 'Battle at the Binary Stars' (1x02), Burnham was Starfleet's first official mutineer. Struggles within the chain of command were not new thematic territory for *Trek* either. Much of the excitement of the original series' episode 'The Doomsday Machine,' for example, comes from Spock's (Leonard Nimoy) efforts to find a way within Starfleet's hierarchical command structure to oust the unhinged and vengeful Commodore Decker from command of the *U.S.S. Enterprise* before Decker can recklessly obliterate the ship as he did his own before it. As that classic episode exemplified, such *Trek* stories always led to the vindication of the character. *Discovery* ended its first two episodes with the main character tried, convicted, and headed for incarceration.

In an interview with James Hibberd entitled 'Star Trek: Discovery Producer Explains Those First Two Episodes,' series producer Alex Kurtzman explained what he saw as the central dilemma in adding to the *Trek* franchise:

> It's been 12 years since a new iteration of *Trek* has been on television and understandably there have been a lot of crossed arms about it. *What are you guys doing? How are you going to make it different? How are you going to make it the same? How are you going to honor Star Trek?* And those are the right questions. I had the same questions. Even before [executive producer Bryan Fuller] was hired, I raised with CBS that we cannot do a new version of *Trek* until we have a reason to do it, a really solid idea and a movement that feels new. (2017, 1; original emphasis)

Kurtzman explained that he and Fuller believed 'there's something very powerful about setting the audience up to believe they were going to be able to predict what was going to happen' and then surprise them (2017, 1).

Kurtzman was careful to avoid characterizing this as a stunt though, locating the decision in the needs of drama. Kurtzman continued:

> The chain of command exists for a reason, and once you break the chain of command you are jeopardizing the lives of your crew. It's a tricky debate, and that's part of what Star Trek is about – controversial debate and moral quandary. *The Original Series* and

best versions of Trek were always complicated morality plays. It felt like the right idea to launch a series. (2017, 2–3)

Thus, the innovation was a little more conventional than viewers realized or wanted to acknowledge. The most shocking thing to happen in *Trek* was therefore the most *Trek* that *Trek* could be.

A similar explanation could be found in regards to a longstanding rule about interpersonal conflict on *Trek* series. As Hibberd summarized it in 'Star Trek: Discovery to Ditch a Long Frustrating Trek Rule':

> As part of Trek creator Gene Roddenberry's utopian vision of the future (and one that Trek franchise executive producer Rick Berman carried on after Roddenberry's death in 1991), writers on Trek shows were urged to avoid having Starfleet crew members in significant conflict with one another (unless a crew member is, say, possessed by an alien force), or from being shown in any seriously negative way. (2017, 1)

The injunction was considered stifling to the creative process. As Hans Beimler, co-producer of *Next Generation* explained: 'On Next Generation, my argument with Gene Roddenberry was that he felt we were going to solve too many of our problems. Human characteristics like greed and that kind of thing were going to be gone' (quoted in Altman and Gross, 2016, 114). Jonathan Frakes, an actor on and director of various *Trek* projects echoed these sentiments more succinctly when he described the creative atmosphere on *Next Generation*: 'They were deathly afraid of conflict and that's the heart of good drama' (quoted in Altman and Gross, 2016, 115).

Harberts explained to Hibberd that these restrictions were cast off in order to make complex drama: 'People have to make mistakes – mistakes are still going to be made in the future. We're still going to argue in the future' (2017, 2). And yet, Berg maintained in the same article that this was not a violation of a sacred Roddenberry edict. Rather, it was in the very spirit of Roddenberry and thus *Trek*,

> The handling of these inner-Starfleet conflicts will still draw inspiration from Roddenberry's ideals, however. The thing we're taking from Roddenberry is how we *solve* those conflicts. So we do have our characters in conflict, we do have them struggling with each other, but it's about how they find a solution and work through their problems. (2017, 2; original emphasis)

Hibberd concludes the article by reminding the reader that *Discovery*'s serialized format is not so unusual for *Trek* either, harkening back to those seasons of *Deep Space Nine* in which the show took on a serialized approach to the Dominion War story arcs.

The *Orville*

Where *Discovery* arrived as the heir apparent to the *Trek* legacy with some potentially problematic elements, *The Orville* slipped in under the guise of a *Trek* parody. It might be tempting to see *The Orville*'s premiere two weeks earlier than *Discovery* on September 10, 2017 as a pre-emptive bid on the part of Seth MacFarlane to take over the *Trek* legacy. The two-week head start is more likely due to the vagaries of network scheduling. Also, prior to the debut, there was very little to suggest that *The Orville* was serious about anything.

Consider, for example, the trailer for the show. It begins with what should be a moment of honor as MacFarlane's Ed Mercer is assigned by Admiral Halsey to lead *The Orville* but quickly shifts to embarrassment comedy as Mercer is told he is not the first choice for the job and then in his nervousness mistakes a marble for a mint. The remainder of the trailer intersperses sci-fi imagery from future episodes with moments of comedic smart alec remarks or situations. If those moments are not enough to drive home the comedic intent of the series, at one point the network-inserted cards in the trailer force a pun, telling us that 'The universe has a crew loose' (*Rotten Tomatoes TV*, 2018). Everything signaled a *Galaxy Quest*-style spin on *Trek* through MacFarlane's unique lens.

What eventually became clear after the premiere though was that *The Orville* was really MacFarlane's ardent tribute to *Next Generation*-era *Trek*. Critics initially pounced on the tone of this new program, often implying a lack of identity for the series. Kelly Lawler said:

> The biggest problem with *The Orville* is that it can't strike a consistent or engaging tone, at least in the first three episodes made available for review. There are too few jokes for it to truly feel like a comedy (despite appearing that way in the early promos), but attempts at humor muddy the series' ambitions as a pure sci-fi adventure. (2017, 2)

Eric Deggans noted 'a bro-centered style to this comedy that feels odd, and stands at odds with *Trek* tradition' (2017, 3). Caroline Framke notes:

> Every time The Orville starts to settle into something resembling a rhythm in its *Trek* replications, MacFarlane will spit out some reference to 20th-century pop culture – despite this show taking place [vague mumbling] years into the future – or some variation on #what a bitch my ex-wife is, amirite? (2017, 3)

Both Framke and Deggans also implied that *The Orville* may have just been a gift to MacFarlane from Fox, a vanity project greenlit in gratitude for MacFarlane's track record of success for the network.

For his part, MacFarlane seemed resigned to the negative criticism. As he told Erik Kain: 'It happens almost every time I release a movie or a TV show. I've grown to expect it from critics and so it's not something that really fazes me anymore' (2017, 1). Lightening that blow for MacFarlane was no doubt the surprising early success of the series. Kain reported that although critics had slammed the show, it had an impressive 8.6 million viewers for its debut and it had earned a 91 percent fresh rating from audiences (2).

Comparatively speaking, *The Orville* felt like the safer, easier to access alternative to *Discovery*. As Mike Hale described it:

> Mr. MacFarlane's hourlong comedy emulates the original 'Trek' series to a degree somewhere between sincere homage and creepy necrophilia. Its sets, costumes, and characters are so Trekker-esque that it makes this fall's officially sanctioned 'Star Trek: Discovery' (on CBS All Access) look like a radical departure. (2017, 1)

In the *Geek's Guide to the Galaxy,* John Joseph Adams joked about *The Orville*, 'I would have bet you money that a good number of these scripts were unused *Star Trek: The Next Generation* scripts' (2017, 3). In the same source, Melinda Snodgrass, a veteran writer from that era of *Trek*, also saw similarities between old stories and the new Fox show.

Perhaps none of this should be surprising. Brannon Braga, a creator associated with every modern television incarnation of *Trek* in some way or another is executive producer on *The Orville*. If there were files of unused *Trek* stories, Braga would have them. More importantly, MacFarlane is a diehard *Trek* fan. As MacFarlane told Kain, shortly after completing his movie *Ted 2*, MacFarlane approached CBS about letting him take on the series. Ideas for *The Orville* started when CBS declined the offer. In his foreword to an oral history of *Trek*, MacFarlane relishes the opportunity he had to play a character called Ensign Rivers on *Enterprise*. More importantly, he effusively praised the franchise. In drawing parallels between Gene Roddenberry's philosophy and that of

Martin Luther King, Jr., MacFarlane called *Trek* 'that rare Hollywood product that means something to mankind' (xv).

Framke dismissed *The Orville* as 'a show that might as well be about a band of enthusiastic cosplayers' (2017, 1). Who has more love for a series than its fans though? *The Orville* is ultimately a show that gets as close to being a *Trek* program as it legally can. Dana Walden, a chief executive at Fox admitted as much at the Television Critics Association press tour, saying 'We obviously have a big legal team' (quoted in Hale, 2017, 1). Watching the program just requires a slight decoding. The 'Planetary Union' is obviously *Trek*'s United Federation of Planets. The multicolored uniforms of the Orville crew suggest their general function on the ship, but the colors are just different, an experience not unlike going from *Star Trek* to *Next Generation*. While the Orville itself is supposed be some kind of run-of-the-mill ship, its sleek design and fantastic maneuverability puts it in the same league as *Trek* vessels. Only the three rounded drive units break from Federation starship design traditions. Characters evoke classic *Trek* archetypes. In fact, Isaac, the Orville's mechanical crewman, so sounded like *Next Gen*'s Data that this author swore Brent Spiner was somehow back until he saw the program's cast list.

While the critics are right in that *The Orville* has some trouble balancing its comedic elements, the weird obsession with twentieth century popular culture is only strange within the context of the show. Of course, it has to be that way. Seth MacFarlane wrote it. More importantly though, modern viewers are watching it. Meanwhile, the series has produced some remarkably *Next Gen*-style storytelling. 'About a Girl' (1x03) may feature silly visuals about male aliens nesting, but it also hits right at contemporary issues about gender identity and sex reassignment surgery when a rare female child is born to the ship's Moclan member Bortus and his husband. 'Majority Rule' (1x07) metaphorically examines contemporary social media ranking practices through the lens of an alien society with a legal system based on such rankings.

The *Callister*

The other heirs to the *Trek* legacy had been around for a few months when the 'U.S.S. Callister' episode of *Black Mirror* streamed its way onto television screens on December 29, 2017. *The Orville* had completed its 12-episode run on Fox. *Star Trek: Discovery* was in the midst of the intermission it took between the first and second halves or its first season.

The episode was the debut of the highly anticipated fourth season for the popular science fiction anthology series with a notably bleak take on the possible impact of technology in our lives. Right away, the episode signaled something very different from the typical episode of the series. The official trailer for the episode highlighted a brightly colored space opera epic in the mode of the original *Star Trek* as new characters interacted on a ship's bridge, braved a rocky alien world, and cheered their Captain Daly. There was also a tinge of sarcasm in Nannette's (Cristin Milioti) reaction. More worrisome though, was the hint of menace to some camera angles in the very beginning. Something was going to go wrong. After all, on *Black Mirror*, something always does.

This episode broke its own formula though by breaking the patterns already established in the show. As Anne Thompson noted, the episode was long, involved science fiction, and, most importantly, switched protagonists in the story (2018, 4–5). What appears to start as a contrast between the dreary real-world life of programmer Robert Daly (Jesse Plemons) and his more effective, virile avatar Captain Daly, who is living out his *Space Fleet* fantasies online, suddenly changes gears part way through the story when the viewer discovers that Daly is a horrible human being in both worlds. The supporting characters on the virtual *U.S.S. Callister* are digitally cloned from DNA samples that Daly surreptitiously collected in real life so that he might gain control of these beings in his fantasy world in disturbing ways reminiscent of the omniscient little boy in the *Twilight Zone* episode 'It's a Good Life' (3x08). Given the generally dark endings of the series, Daly's latest virtual victim Nannette leads a surprisingly successful rebellion that ends with the avatar crew free to explore cyberspace and the real Daly presumably dead.

Like most *Trek*, the message of the episode is delivered directly and clearly. The defeat of Daly, who Zack Handlen succinctly calls an 'arrested development manchild' (2017, 4), by a diverse crew of rebels led by a woman is the thematic takedown of particular types of toxic masculinity that have become all too familiar. These are, for example, the droning fans noted previously by Zarkarian, unable to process the progressive expectations of their program. Nick Statt also likens this to what he sees as an imminent cultural issue:

> This Black Mirror episode suggests that while some big tech names, like Bill Gates and Elon Musk worry about a superintelligent [sic] AI enslaving or destroying humanity, the more immediate threat is human beings, who misuse modern tools every day to manipulate and harm people in ways an AI would never dream of. (2018, 7)

As is often the case, *Black Mirror* shows us people are awful.

The episode's take on *Trek* is trickier to spot. Dany Roth (2017), for example, creates a long list of references to *Trek* in the episode. Roth notes clear references like the William Shatner-esque mode of speaking actor Jesse Plemons exhibits when he appears as Captain Daly in the cyberworld to more oblique connections between the wormhole important in the conclusion of 'U.S.S. Callister' to the famous wormhole on *Deep Space Nine*. Where some see a love of *Trek*, others see a necessary deconstruction of the franchise. Darren Franich argues that there is an interesting moment happening to the space opera. Franich is tired of re-examinations of characters that really do not produce anything other than the reaffirmation of that character, like Luke Skywalker in *Star Wars: The Last Jedi* (2017). Considering *Trek*, Franich says:

> Look, I love a lot of *Star Trek*, and it's pointless to make any broad statements about any story cycle that has lasted through so many years and permutations. Then again: if we've learned one thing this year, it's that we can would maybe [sic] be better off if we started to throw out some of pop culture's most sanctified legacies. Or at least question them? (2017, 9)

Franich sees the end of Robert Daly as symbolic of the end of our devotion to old types and tropes.

These types of readings led to concerns by the creators of the episode though. In an interview with Louisa Mellor, *Black Mirror* creator/showrunner Charlie Brooker and producer Annabel Jones were careful to point out that this episode was not targeting *Trek*. Brooker clearly states: 'We wanted it to feel more like an homage than an attack' (2017, 1). Any negative comments about the *Trek* surrogate *Space Fleet* in the episode are not about the show and thus not about *Trek*. Instead, as Brooker explains, they are condemnations of Daly:

> It's *his* interpretation of the show, rather than what that show would have actually been, it's his simplistic fable version of it and it's quite reductive and out of date. We're not saying that shows of that nature are reductive and out of date, because they were actually very progressive at the time. (2017, 3)

It is a now familiar refrain. Really, the only thing Brooker fails to do here is mention Roddenberry.

Their Continuing Missions

Like space itself, our popular culture universe is full of bright, long-lived objects. Cinematic universes and franchises are commercially desirable to culture industries and beloved by fans. *Trek*'s longevity is impressive, particularly given its beginnings as a science fiction television underdog. *Trek* certainly seems like a contender to live longer and prosper more.

As *Star Trek: Discovery* demonstrates, the evolution necessary to keep the franchise fresh is fraught with risks. These changes are not so much smoothed over as they are paradoxically revealed as part of the intent all along to create the same old *Trek*. Invoking nostalgic elements and the spirit of Roddenberry are key parts of continuing this mythology. Along the way, programs like *The Orville* or *Black Mirror* may also take up that mythology as their own.

Like most things about *Black Mirror*, the future of the *Callister* remains unclear. It is, after all, an anthology program. Meredith Jacobs reported that Brooker and Jones would neither confirm nor deny that a possible sequel to the story might happen. The highlight of *Black Mirror*'s next season was 'Bandersnatch,' a disturbing exploration of the fracturing of a young game designer's psyche that plays out interactively for the viewers. The remainder of that season came nowhere near *Trek*.

The Orville continued its mission as well. The second season trailer opened with Captain Mercer making a grand speech to a table of dignitaries: 'In the vast emptiness of the universe, we have found a fullness of cultural diversity. And when a first contact unfolds, the cosmos becomes a living, breathing organism. And we become a way for the universe to know itself.' When complimented on the speech by his first officer, Mercer replies, 'Yeah thanks. I plagiarized it from like nine different things.' The only thing MacFarlane did not do there was wink at the audience.

Interestingly, repercussions of the decisions in 'About a Girl' (1x03) carried into subplots, but *Orville*'s second season still felt like more *Trek*. The speech above is from 'All the World is Birthday Cake' (2x05), a very *Trek*-like story in which the new civilization bizarrely obsessed with its own kind of astrology oppresses citizens via their birth signs. Season enders 'Tomorrow and Tomorrow and Tomorrow' (2x13) and 'The Road Not Taken' (2x14) entertainingly explore the consequences when a time travel accident disrupts Mercer and Grayson's (Adrianne Palicki) relationship by bringing a past version of Grayson into the future, but it is easy to see its pedigree as *Next Generation*'s 'Yesterday's Enterprise' (3x15) by way of 'Second Chances' (6x24).

The Orville will move exclusively into streaming space for its third season when the program moves to *Hulu*. It is tempting to see this as a move to imitate *Discovery*, but *Variety*'s Joe Otterson (2019) and *Deadline*'s Denise Petski (2019) reported that the move has more to do with accommodating Seth MacFarlane's busy schedule.

Discovery's second season took up the surprises revealed at the end of 'Will You Take My Hand?' (1x15) when the newest series' ship rendezvoused with the *U.S.S. Enterprise*. The second season narrative arcs revolved around the Red Angel, an enigmatic time traveler from the future that was eventually revealed to be Michael Burnham herself, and a battle against an artificial intelligence created by the Federation's shadowy Section 31 with nihilistic ambitions to destroy all intelligent organic life. Along the way, the series revisited and expanded upon Captain Christopher Pike (Anson Mount), the *U.S.S Enterprise*'s captain before Kirk. It also took up the ambitious task of integrating Spock (Ethan Peck) into the *Discovery* storyline, allowing the program to flesh out Burnham's childhood relationship with *Trek*'s arguably most popular character ever.

Playing with such iconic elements risked narrative confusion and fan disappointment. However, all was still *Trek*. As Beth Elderkin reports, before the second season began, new showrunner Alex Kurtzman was already assuring viewers that while this Spock may not seem like the Spock we know, there is no reason for concern. Kurtzman says, 'And that's really exciting to us because it in no way violates cannon, it just builds on what's been set before' (2018, 2). This quote, would perhaps, make a good mantra for *Discovery* overall.

The constraints of continuity have become creatively tiresome though. *Discovery* is taking its voyages elsewhere. Or, said more accurately, 'else-when.' The climactic events of 'Such Sweet Sorrow,' the two-part second season finale, necessitated the *U.S.S Discovery* and its main crew to leap 930 years forward into the future. As Kurtzman told Mike Bloom:

> We love playing within canon. It's a delight and a privilege. It's fun to explore nooks and crannies of the universe that people haven't fully explored yet. That being said, we felt strongly that we wanted to give ourselves an entirely new energy for season three within a whole new set of problems. We're farther than any *Trek* show has ever gone. (2019, 3)

Kurtzman returns to familiar assurances, 'Star Trek is about optimism, hope, and a brighter future. Even if the future turns out to be not as bright as we hope, we are always striving to protect and preserve the best version of it' (2019, 8). Jonathan Frakes reinforced these positive sentiments at a panel at Fan Expo Canada. As quoted by Jamie Lovett in 'Star Trek: Discovery Season 3 Will Be More Optimistic, according to Jonathan Frakes,' the series director and *Trek* icon invoked the ultimate *Trek* icon saying 'The optimism that Gene infused in all of his shows and in all of us may not be as obvious as it once was, but it's certainly the driving force of his vision and the franchise' (2019, 2).

The great tautology remains. Even when they are not obviously *Trek*, these voyages continue because *Trek* is always *Trek*. And like the greatest of myths, that is how *Trek* will always survive.

Works Cited

Mark A. Altman and Edward Gross, *The Fifty Year Mission: The Next 25 Years* (New York: Thomas Dunne Books/St. Martin's Press).

Djoymi Baker, *To Boldly Go: Marketing the Myth of Star Trek* (New York: I.B. Taurus, 2018).

Black Mirror – USS Callister: Official Trailer [HD]. *Netflix*, 5 December (2017), https://www.youtube.com/watch?v=qgTtyfgzGc0.

Mike Bloom, 'How the "Star Trek: Discovery" Finale Pulled Off the Franchise's Boldest Leap Yet', *Hollywood Reporter*, 18 April (2019), www.hollywoodreporter.com/live-feed/star-trek-discovery-season-2-finale-time-jump-explained-1203166.

John G. Cawelti, *Adventure, Mystery, Romance* (Chicago, IL: University of Chicago Press, 1976).

Comic-Con 2018 Official Trailer: THE ORVILLE Season 2. 21 July (2018), www.youtube.com/watch?v=lavy7qZ1ao0.

Anthony D'Alessandro, '"Star Trek: Discovery" Fuels Record Signups for CBS All Access', *Deadline Hollywood*, 24 September (2017), deadline.com/2017/09/star-trek-discovery-cbs-all-access-record-sign-ups-1202176110/.

Eric Deggans, 'Make It So-So: Fox's The Orville', *NPR*, 10 September (2017), www.npr.org/2017/09/10/549407699/make-it-so-so-foxs-the-orville.

Beth Elderkin, '*Star Trek: Discovery*'s Showrunner Promises This Spock "In No Way Violates Canon"', *Io9*, 16 October (2018), io9.gizmodo.com/star-trek-discoverys-showrunner-promises-this-spock-in-1829782919.

Caroline Framke, 'Seth MacFarlanes's The Orville Isn't the Spoof Fox Advertised. It's Much Weirder—and Worse', *Vox*, 10 September (2017), www.vox.com/culture/2017/9–8/16267782/the-orville-seth-macfarlane-review-lol-what.

Darren Franich, 'In Praise of "USS Callister," the *Black Mirror* Space Opera to End All Space Operas', *Entertainment Weekly*, 29 December (2017), ew.com/tv/2017/12/29/black-mirror-uss-callister-star-trek/.

Geeks Guide to the Galaxy, 'Don't Give Up on The Orville Too Quickly', *Wired*, 30 December (2017), www.wired.com/2017/12/geeks-guide-orville/.

Lesley Goldberg, 'Bryan Fuller Out as "Star Trek: Discovery" Showrunner', *The Hollywood Reporter*, 26 October (2016), www.hollywoodreporter.com/live-feed/bryan-fuller-as-star-trek-discovery-showrunner-941587.

Mike Hale, 'Review: Fox's "The Orville" is Star Trek, the Next Regurgitation', *New York Times*, 8 September (2017), www.nytimes.com/2017/09/08/arts/television/the-orville-tv-review.html.

Zack Handlen, 'Black Mirror Beams into a Familiar Nightmare as Season 4 Begins', *AV Club*, 29 December (2017), www.avclub.com/black-mirror-beams-into-a-familiar-nightmare-as-season-1821633354.

James Hibberd, 'Star Trek: Discovery Already Getting Pirated A Lot', *Entertainment Weekly*, 25 September (2017), ew.com/tv/2017/09/25/star-trek-discovery-pirated.

—— 'Star Trek: Discovery Producer Explains Those First Two Episodes', *Entertainment Weekly*, 24 September (2017), ew.com/tv/2017/09/24/star-trek-discovery-premiere-interview/.

—— 'Star Trek: Discovery to Ditch a Long Frustrating Trek Rule', *Entertainment Weekly*, 23 June (2017), ew.com/tv/2017/06/23/star-trek-discovery-rules/.

—— 'The Story of How Star Trek Returned to TV After 12 Years', *Entertainment Weekly*, 22 August (2017), ew.com/tv/2017/08/22/star-trek-discovery-cover-story/.

Daniel Holloway, 'Can "Star Trek: Discovery" Help CBS Boldly Go Into a Streaming Future?', *Variety*, 29 August (2017), variety.com/2017/tv/features/star-trek-discovery-preview-cbs-all-access-sonequa-martin-green-1202540540/.

Matthew Jackson, 'Star Trek: Discovery Nearly Doubled CBS All Access Subscription Rates', *SYFY Wire*, 4 October (2017), www.syfy.com/syfywire/star-trek-discovery-nearly-doubled-cbs-all-access-subscription-rates.

Meredith Jacobs, 'Will "Black Mirror's USS Callister" Become a Series? Creator Teases There Could Be a Future', *Newsweek*, 10 September (2018), www.newsweek.com/uss-callister-spinoff-possible-1114207.

Erik Kain, 'Interview: Seth MacFarlane on The Orville's Unique Tone, "Star Trek" Roots', *Forbes*, 16 September (2017), www.forbes.com/sites/erikkain/2017/09/16/seth-macfarlane-on-the-orville-going-boldly-where-no-tv-show-has-gone-before/#14e08d7e5357.

Kelly Lawler, 'Review: Seth MacFarlane's "Star Trek"-inspired "The Orville" Flies Off Course', *USA Today*, 6 September (2017), www.usatoday.com/story/life/tv/2017/09/06/review-seth-machfarlane-the-orville-star-trek-fox/633304001/.

Jamie Lovett, '"Star Trek" Fans, It's Time to Get Over Your CBS All Access Hangups', *Comicbook.com*, 12 November (2017), comicbook.com/startrek/2017/11/12/star-trek-discovery-cbs-all-access/.

Seth MacFarlane, 'Foreword', in Edward Gross and Mark A. Altman, *The Fifty Year Mission: The First 25 Years* (New York: St. Martin's Press, 2016): xiii–xv.

Louisa Mellor, 'Black Mirror season 4: USS Callister "More Homage Than Attack"', *Den of Geek*, 29 December (2017), www.denofgeek.com/uk/tv/black-mirror/53682/black-mirror-season-4-uss-callister-more-homage-than-attack.

Orville Season 1 Trailer, *Rotten Tomatoes TV*, 6 March (2018), sdwww.youtube.com/watch?v=cYRL93Ayp_g.

Janko Roettgers, '"Star Trek: Discovery" Almost Doubled CBS All Access Mobile Subscription Revenue', *Variety*, 3 October (2017), variety.com/2017/digital/news/star-trek-discovery-cbs-subscription-revenue-1202579644/.

Dany Roth, 'Black Mirror's USS Callister is a Bigger Homage to Star Trek Than You Thought', *SYFY Wire*, 30 December (2017), www.syfy.com/syfywire/black-mirrors-uss-callister-is-a-bigger-homage-to-star-trek-than-you-thought.

Nick Statt, 'In Black Mirror's USS Callister, the True Villains are Real-World Tech Moguls', *The Verge*, 2 January (2018), www.theverge.com/2018/1/2/16841938/black-mirror-uss-callister-review-netflix-season-4-jesse-plemons-crtistin-milioti.

Anne Thompson, '3 Ways Netflix's "Black Mirror" Broke the Rules with "USS Callister"', *Indie Wire*, 23 July (2018), www.indiewire.com/2018/07/netflix-black-mirror-uss-callister-star-trek-emmys-jesse-plemons-1201987029/.

Trekmovie.com Staff. '"Star Trek: Discovery" USS Enterprise Design Change Clarified as Creative Decision, Not Legal One', *Trekmovie.com*, 17 April (2018), trekmovie.com/2018/04/17/star-trek-discovery-uss-enterprise-design-change-clarified-as-creative-decision-not-a-legal-one/.

Stephen E. Whitfield and Gene Roddenberry, *The Making of Star Trek* (New York: Del Rey, 1968).

Jordan Zakarin, 'A Lot of Star Trek Fans are Mad about Having to Pay for CBS All Access', *SYFY Wire*, 25 September (2017), www.syfy.com/syfywire/a-lot-of-star-trek-fans-are-mad-about-having-to-pay-for-cbs-all-access.

—— 'How the Alt-Right and Nostalgic Trolls Hijacked Geek Popular Culture', *SYFY Wire*, 17 January (2018), www.syfy.com/syfywire/how-the-alt-right-and-nostalgic-trolls-hijacked-geek-pop-culture.

Episodes and Films Cited

'It's a Good Life.' *The Twilight Zone*, written by Rod Serling, directed by James Sheldon, CBS Television Network, 3 November, 1961.

'The Doomsday Machine.' *Star Trek*, written by Norman Spinrad, directed by Marc Daniels, Desilu Productions, 20 October, 1967.

'Yesterday's Enterprise.' *Star Trek: The Next Generation*, written by Ira Steven Behr, Richard Manning, Hans Beimler, and Ronald D. Moore, directed by David Carson, Paramount Television, 19 February, 1990.

'Second Chances.' *Star Trek: The Next Generation*, written by René Echevarria, directed by LeVar Burton, Paramount Television, 24 May, 1993.

'About a Girl.' *The Orville*, written by Seth MacFarlane, directed by Brannon Braga, Fuzzy Door Productions, 20th Century Fox Television, 21 September, 2017.

'Battle at the Binary Stars.' *Star Trek: Discovery*, written by Gretchen J. Berg and Aaron Harberts, directed by Adam Kane, CBS Television Studios, 24 September, 2017.

'The Vulcan Hello.' *Star Trek: Discovery*, written by Bryan Fuller and Akiva Goldsman, directed by Davis Semel, CBS Television Studios, 24 September, 2017.

'Majority Rule.' *The Orville*, written by Seth MacFarlane, directed by Tucker Gates, Fuzzy Door Productions, 20th Century Fox Television, 26 October, 2017.

'U.S.S. Callister.' *Black Mirror*, written by William Bridges and Charlie Brooker, directed by Todd Haynes, Netflix, 29 December, 2017.

'Will You Take My Hand?' *Star Trek: Discovery*, written by Gretchen J. Berg and Aaron Harberts, directed by Akiva Goldsman, CBS Television Studios, 11 February, 2018.

'Bandersnatch.' *Black Mirror*, written by Charlie Brooker, directed by David Slade, Netflix, 28 December, 2018.

'Such Sweet Sorrow, Part One and Two.' *Star Trek: Discovery*, written by Michelle Paradise, Jenny Lumet, and Alex Kurtzman, directed by Olatunde Osunsanmi, CBS Television Studios, 11/18 April, 2019.

'Tomorrow and Tomorrow and Tomorrow.' *The Orville*, written by Janet Lin, directed by Gary S. Rake, Fuzzy Door Productions, 20th Century Fox Television, 18 April, 2019.

'The Road Not Taken.' *The Orville*, written by David S. Goodman, directed by Gary S. Rake, Fuzzy Door Productions, 20th Century Fox Television, 25 April, 2019.

Galaxy Quest. 1999. Directed by Dean Parisot. DreamWorks.
Star Trek. 2009. Directed by J.J. Abrams. Paramount Pictures.
Star Wars: The Last Jedi. 2017. Directed by Rian Johnson. Lucasfilm.

'Just as Repetition Reinforces Repetition, Change Begets Change' – Modes of Storytelling in Canon and Fanon

From Series to Seriality
Star Trek's Mirror Universe in the Post-Network Era

Ina Batzke

To Boldly Go Where No Television Series Has Gone Before

Until the first season of *Star Trek: Discovery* aired in September 2017 on CBS, all previous *Star Trek* television series typically conformed to the prevalent narrative formats of their historical periods, i.e., most episodes comprised single, self-contained narrative units. When this format was ever abandoned, for example, in two-part episodes such as 'The Menagerie' (*The Original Series*, 1x11 and 1x12), this most often resulted not from a desire for narrative innovation, but rather from budgetary constraints (cf. Pearson and Davies, 2014), or to generate cliffhangers at the end of a season (for example, *The Next Generation*, 'Time's Arrow, Part 1 & 2,' 5x26 and 6x01). With *Star Trek* moving to CBS, and particularly its *All Access* platform,[1] however, this traditional format – in parallel to other television series adaptations for streaming services – changed significantly: for the first time, *Discovery* intentionally was created as a post-network serial, instead of a traditional television series with 'extended seriality' (Pearson and Davies, 2014, 128).[2] Akiva Goldsman,

---

[1] Only the first episode aired on the CBS network in a preview broadcast on September 24, 2017. Following this cable network premiere, subsequent first-run episodes of the first season were streamed weekly on *All Access*, CBS's subscription streaming service, through February 2018.

[2] While the latter concept, 'extended seriality,' refers to *Star Trek*'s longstanding capacity to form narrative links among the television series and, occasionally, the feature films, the 'post-network' or 'serial' format differs in that it is 'distinct for its use of narrative complexity as an alternative to the conventional episodic and serial forms that have typified most American television since its inception' (Mittell, 2006, 29). For the reassessment of seriality in this project, however, I found it most useful to not categorize television series as 'serials' or 'series,' but understand them – and single episodes – as operating within a 'series–serial' continuum. The

(former) executive producer of *Discovery*, confirmed this observation in a *New York Times* interview accompanying the release:

> On a vintage 'Star Trek' episode like 'The City on the Edge of Forever,' in which Kirk must allow a character played by Joan Collins to die, [Kirk] is shattered. But he's not allowed to carry those feelings to the next episode.' [On] 'Discovery,' [we] don't reset every week. Because serialization replicates life. (quoted in Itzkoff, 2017)

In this chapter, I investigate how this intentional move from a traditional series format to a post-network production with a pronounced focus on seriality influenced not only the narrative structure, but particularly the worldbuilding strategies and possibilities inherent in *Star Trek*. While worldbuilding has always been a significant element of the canon-heavy series, which thus far built worlds across seven television series, thirteen feature films and various other media,[3] I argue that the post-network character of *Discovery* allows it to transcend, complicate, and even contradict already established *Star Trek* story worlds and rules over the course of the entire series. By doing so, particularly the first season of *Discovery* blends into the oeuvre of second wave post-network series that avoid promoting rather clear-cut Manichean binaries. In contrast to a first wave of post-network series, that oftentimes have been direct reactions to the 9/11 events (cf. Espinoza Garrido, 2018) and that were informed by discourses surrounding the 'war on terror' narrative and its justifications, productions belonging to this second wave are not direct reactions to 9/11, but offer more nuanced interrogations not only of the attacks themselves but also of their socio-political aftermath.

Looking at the first season,[4] this becomes particularly prominent

---

post-network format hence put *Discovery* further toward the serial terminus of the series–serial continuum, which in turn enabled it to enhance its world-building strategies significantly.

[3] Since this chapter zooms in on *Star Trek* as a television series, it does not consider the various other instantiations of the story world in other texts, such as comic books or feature films, as such consideration would be outside of the scope of this investigation.

[4] Since this article explores the Mirror Universe, it sets its central focus on the first season of *Discovery*, as only there the Mirror Universe is presented as a main setting for the entire season. In the second season, only one character (Georgiou) links the story from the first season to the Mirror Universe; apart from that, it does not play a central role. Thus, this article will only link observations to the second season when appropriate.

when comparing the story world of the Mirror Universe, a fictional universe that has haunted the *Star Trek* characters since *Star Trek: The Original Series* (1966–1969). Traditionally, the Mirror Universe served as an evil, dystopian counterpart to the Prime *Star Trek* universe: While it was so named because most characters and places that existed in the Prime Universe also existed in its counterpart, they often were their antithesis, i.e., everything that was considered 'good' in the Prime Universe was 'evil' in the Mirror Universe, and vice versa. In *Discovery*'s post-network version of the Mirror Universe, however, this strict dichotomy is blurred, arguably enabling a more apt questioning of the right- and wrongness of moral and ethics, which notably is prototypical for second wave post-network adaptations in general.[5] To illustrate this argument, this chapter will firstly introduce what is referred to as the 'pre-*Discovery*' Mirror Universe, by focusing briefly on all episodes that have featured it: *The Original Series*' 'Mirror, Mirror' (2x04), five episodes from *Deep Space Nine* (1993–1999; 'Crossover,' 2x23, 'Through the Looking Glass,' 3x19, 'Shattered Mirror,' 4x20, 'Resurrection,' 6x08, and 'The Emperor's New Cloak,' 7x12), and *Enterprise*'s (2001–2005) two-part episode 'In a Mirror, Darkly' (*Enterprise*, 4x18 and 4x19). I then turn to the post-network instantiation of the Mirror Universe in the first season of *Discovery*, explain its different function in the series, and shed light on how the serial character of the show enabled the Mirror Universe to be expanded and complicated.

The Pre-*Discovery* Universe

The Mirror Universe[6] comprises a parallel universe in which the plots of several *Star Trek* television episodes have taken place. When it was

---

[5] The Mirror Universe and how the show uses it to represent and interrogate (imperial) feminisms is also explored in Judith Rauscher's essay '"Into A Mirror Darkly": Border Crossing and Imperial(ist) Feminism in *Star Trek: Discovery*' published in this volume.

[6] As pointed out, *Star Trek*'s Mirror Universe is named after 'Mirror, Mirror,' a *The Original Series* episode in which it first appeared. It should be noted, however, that the term 'Mirror Universe' has never been used on screen. On screen, in the earlier series, 'parallel universe' and 'the other universe' have been used (*The Original Series:* 'Mirror, Mirror,' *Deep Space Nine*: 'Through the Looking Glass'). Later, also terminology such as 'alternate reality/universe,' 'the other side,' and 'The Terran universe' appeared (*Enterprise*: 'In a Mirror, Darkly,' *Deep Space Nine*: 'Crossover,' 'Shattered Mirror,' 'Resurrection,' 'The Emperor's New Cloak,' *Discovery*: 'The War Without, The War Within').

first introduced in the *The Original Series* episode 'Mirror, Mirror' (2x04) in 1967, it marked a narrative milestone, as the episode offered a 'spectacular narrative that brought together not only different textual-actual-world timelines but for the first time alternate-possible-world timelines as well' (Pearson and Davies, 2014, 145). In the episode, a transporter malfunction sends Captain Kirk (William Shatner) and three of his crew members into a parallel universe that exists almost simultaneously with the Prime Universe, but on another dimensional plane. Already at first glance, this parallel universe is strikingly different from its Prime counterpart: Kirk is welcomed back by a Mirror First Officer Spock (Leonard Nimoy) with a mustache and goatee, who is in the midst of ordering his crew to attack a humanoid civilization for their refusal to collaborate – and thus clearly does not act according to the guiding principles of Starfleet. To prove this assumption, he then punishes one of his own crew members for an error by putting him in an agonizer booth – an instrument of torture that, since then, has become one of the most significant characteristics of the Mirror Universe.

While most characters, ships, and places that exist in *The Original Series*'s Prime Universe hence also exist in its parallel counterpart, at the same time, it is instantaneously obvious to both Captain Kirk and the viewer that the parallel universe poses as an antonym to the Prime Universe. Whereas the Prime Universe represents an utopian future in which the United Federation of Planets values 'toleration,' 'peace,' and 'social progress,' (cf. The Charter of the United Federation of Planets), 'Mirror, Mirror' introduces its authoritarian counterpart, the Terran Empire, which values conquest, war, and despotism instead. In line with this, mirror characters showcase characteristics that reverse those of their Prime Universe equals, as they are mistrustful, aggressive, and opportunistic in personality. Officers, for example, can achieve promotion only when assassinating their superiors. Finally, the oppositeness is also marked visually: the mirror crew presents different crew uniforms and looks, which arguably underline their evil behavior, and the Terran Empire identifies itself by a logo that features an aggressive sword instead of the laurel of peace of the United Federation of Planets' logo.

All in all, the episode thus not only familiarizes *Star Trek* viewers with the concept of a parallel universe in general, but already

---

Although the term itself is also not used throughout *Discovery*, the crew at least refer to their vessel's counterpart as the 'mirror *Discovery*' ('Despite Yourself'). Editors' note: DSC became the first show to use the term on screen in 2x13.

establishes the Mirror Universe as an 'evil twin'[7] to the Prime Universe, and as such as a particular story world with rules other than those valid in the Prime Universe.[8] At the same time, Kirk's encounter with the Mirror Universe has no impact on other *The Original Series* episodes or storylines. At the end of the episode, Kirk and his crew manage to beam themselves back to the Federation universe, where he learns that aboard the Prime Universe's *U.S.S. Enterprise,* Spock had placed their Mirror Universe counterparts in confinement. When asked by Kirk how he was able to identify the intruders from the Mirror Universe, he explains they were easy to expose because of their distinct alterity: 'It was far easier for you as civilized men to behave like barbarians, than it was for them as barbarians to behave like civilized men. ... They were brutal, savage, unprincipled, uncivilized, treacherous...' ('Mirror, Mirror'). This marked difference between Mirror and Prime characters, that is emphasized here by the characters themselves, is upheld in the five *Deep Space Nine* episodes that feature the Mirror Universe in its twenty-fourth century version: 'Crossover' (2x23), 'Through the Looking Glass' (3x19), 'Shattered Mirror' (4x20), 'Resurrection' (6x08), and 'The Emperor's New Cloak' (7x12). While it is beyond the scope of this chapter to summarize all five Mirror Universe episodes of *Deep Space Nine,* it should suffice for the following argument to state that their instantiations of the Mirror Universe resembled that shown in *The Original Series* (1966–1969). Most importantly, the viewer always follows a Prime character into the Mirror Universe, or vice versa ('Resurrection'), but there is never an interaction between the two universes, except on the level of single character contact. What is new is the fact that in contrast to Kirk's visit in *The Original Series,* visiting

---

[7] Traditionally, in literary studies, the 'evil twin' concept refers to an antagonist that is a physical copy of a protagonist, but with fundamentally inverted ethics and moralities. By using it here to refer to the Mirror Universe as a whole, the concept is borrowed but applied to a whole story world that is antagonistic to its prime counterpart.

[8] This makes sense, as from its very beginning, the Mirror Universe was read as a possibility to deviate from Gene Roddenberry's *Star Trek* rulebook (1987). Gene Coon, a co-producer and writer of *The Original Series,* summarized Roddenberry's worldbuilding in the following words: 'He created an entire galaxy and an entire rule book for operating within that galaxy, with very specific laws governing behaviors, manners, customs, as well as science and technology.' Rules, collected in what Roddenberry himself titled the *Star Trek* 'bible,' included that writers must 'stay true to the prime directive,' and that characters must be 'very committed to their ship, their crewmates, and their mission' (Roddenberry, 1987, 11) – all aspects that are mistreated in the Mirror Universe.

the Mirror Universe in *Deep Space Nine* is, except for the first visit, no longer accidental, but intentional. Moreover, *Deep Space Nine*'s visits to the Mirror Universe introduced the idea that people who died in the Prime Universe might be alive and well in the Mirror Universe (cf. 'Through the Looking Glass' and 'Shattered Mirror'). Despite these two narrative novelties, however, the thematic foundation of all *Deep Space Nine*'s Mirror Universe episodes rests on the idea that, by going to the respective Mirror Universe, one can achieve positive effects for the other universe. Examples include when Prime Sisko is decoyed into the Mirror Universe to help build the *U.S.S. Defiant* ('Shattered Mirror'), or when a thief is sent to the Prime Universe to steal a Bajoran orb, believing it would permit Mirror Intendant Kira (Nana Visitor) to unite Bajor under her rule ('Resurrection'). Such effects, if they are achieved at all, are, however, always short-term, and, as in 'Mirror, Mirror,' do not influence grander strands of narrative continuity in the Prime Universe. This also explains why the Mirror Universe episodes are spread over several seasons of *Deep Space Nine*; each episode repeats the same Mirror Universe, sometimes even with the same Mirror Universe characters, but remains self-contained: 'No serial effect is produced because no [Mirror Universe] episode story branches beyond or reveals an awareness of events occurring in prior episodes' (Ndalianis, 2005, 88).[9]

This changes slightly in the two-part Mirror Universe episode of *Star Trek: Enterprise*, entitled 'In a Mirror, Darkly' (Part 1: 4x18 and Part 2: 4x19), which introduces the early developments of the Mirror Universe (twenty-second century). In a notable difference to its first occurrences, this time viewers do not follow a Prime Universe character into the Mirror Universe, but are exposed to it right from the beginning of the episode, as a prologue revisits *Star Trek: First Contact*: by reusing the very same footage from the 1996 feature film, we see the Vulcan ship landing on Earth in 2063. Instead of returning the peaceful greeting of the Vulcans, however, one and a half minutes into the episode the original footage is abandoned, and we instead watch Zefram Cochrane (James Cromwell) shoot the leader of the Vulcans. This scene thus opposes everything a viewer knows about the first contact as it had happened in the Prime Universe, and by doing so triggers the conclusion that the scene must have happened in the Mirror

---

[9] Note that, nevertheless, some degree of seriality is implied through 'the repetition of characters and narrative patterns beyond single episodes' (Ndalianis, 2005, 88, also cf. Pearson and Davies' 'extended seriality' [2014]).

Universe. This is confirmed by the fact that the prologue is followed by a special mirror opening credits sequence, which chronicles the history of warfare and interstellar domination of the Terran Empire, the repressive interstellar government dominating the Mirror Universe in the twenty-second century.

In fact, both 'In a Mirror, Darkly' episodes feature these special opening credits and accordingly are set solely in the Mirror Universe. In the first part of 'In a Mirror, Darkly,' the *I.S.S. Enterprise*[10] crew learns that a Starfleet ship from the future of the Prime Universe has arrived in the Mirror Universe – the *U.S.S. Defiant*, which had disappeared from the Prime Universe in 2268 (cf. 'The Tholian Web,' *The Original Series*, 3x09) – and seeks to obtain the ship from Tholian space. While part of the crew beam onto the *U.S.S. Defiant*, at the conclusion of the first episode, the Tholians fight back by creating an energy web and eventually manage to destroy the *I.S.S. Enterprise*. The second part then sees the surviving crew on board of the *U.S.S. Defiant*, seeking to get the advanced weaponry of the ship to work to eventually fight back against the Terran Empire. Thematically, the two episodes thus seem to serve a clear purpose. As the fourth season of *Enterprise* is 'engaged with the idea that the utopian ideals of the Federation are no longer a "given" in the way that they had been during the broadcast of *Star Trek* or *The Next Generation*' (Darren, 2016), 'In a Mirror, Darkly' confronts the viewer with a universe in which those ideals have never taken hold. In that sense, this two-part Mirror Universe episode is markedly similar to its predecessors, as it approaches the Mirror Universe not primarily in terms of continuity, but in terms of philosophy and outlook, intervening into the respective series at a point where Starfleet ideals are questioned by presenting the opposing alternative. While the two episodes do establish an unprecedented continuity for the Mirror Universe as they tie together two episodes from the original series ('Mirror, Mirror' and 'The Tholian Web'), and even a key scene from *Star Trek: First Contact*, there is still no crucial interaction between Prime and Mirror Universe, as the two episodes do not even see *Enterprise* Prime Universe characters moving between the two parallel universes this time. The only Prime Universe object that crosses into the Mirror Universe, the *U.S.S. Defiant*, has no relevance for the *Enterprise* timeline whatsoever, and the Prime characters of *Enterprise* do not even learn about the instance narrated in 'In a Mirror, Darkly.'

---

[10] Instead of U.S.S., the Mirror spaceships are marked by the abbreviation I.S.S., which stands for 'Imperial Star Ship.'

All in all, with the exception of *The Next Generation* (1987–1994)[11] and *Voyager* (1995–2001), all *Star Trek* television series have visited the Mirror Universe and, by doing so, have created a coherent parallel world with its own history and rules. While arguably 'this is worldbuilding of such a scale that no other television series could hope to equal it' (Pearson and Davies, 2014, 145), at least not while maintaining the format of self-contained episodes, at the same time, all those pre-network Mirror Universe episodes were largely irrelevant for continuity development or character building, as its storylines and characters never overlapped with the Prime Universe. Quite to the contrary, the writers of *The Original Series*, *Deep Space Nine*, and *Enterprise* were careful to clearly mark the strict differentiation between the Prime and the Mirror Universe, be it through differing dress codes, hair styles, logos, and opening credits, or by carefully pointing out to the viewer who belongs to which universe. Only by keeping up this strict demarcation the series arguably was able to reach the antithesis effect it was trying to create with the Mirror Universe: If one understands the 'outcome goal of the show to arrive at the utopian principles that ... are endemic to "Star Trek"' (Goldsman quoted in Velocci, 2017), the Mirror Universe's prime purpose in pre-network times was to pose as a dystopian counterpart to the Prime Universe, thereby emphasizing *Star Trek*'s utopian features even more clearly.

The Post-Network Mirror Universe

Traditionally, the Mirror Universe thus has been clearly demarcated from the Prime Universe, visually, narratively, and sometimes even cinematographically. The pre-network Mirror Universe episodes comprised separate stories, that were concluded at the end of each episode – as is typical for traditional television series' episodes in general. When moving to the Mirror Universe in *Discovery*'s first season, it is therefore at first glance most striking that here the Mirror Universe does not span just a single episode, but that instead the whole series is influenced by it and almost all episodes are either set in the Mirror Universe or at least

---

[11] Indeed, it seems that the writing staff of *Next Generation* deliberately did not explore the option of a Mirror Universe episode: 'We were a little frightened at doing it, and doing it badly, and maybe never really figured out what the Next Generation take would have been on it,' writer/producer Brannon Braga explained in a 2017 interview (in Wright, 2017). Only novelizations and comics have so far dealt with a Mirror version of *The Next Generation* characters.

feature characters from it. At the same time, it should be noted that even an experienced viewer is unaware of this until episode 12. Only the first two episodes, which are set roughly six months before the rest of the serial and provide a kind of back-story to Michael Burnham (Sonequa Martin-Green), the mutineer, do not feature any Mirror Universe aspects.[12] In the third episode, set about a decade before the events of *The Original Series*, viewers meet *U.S.S. Discovery* Captain Gabriel Lorca (Jason Isaacs) for the first time, who rescues Michael Burnham from her prison transfer and takes her on aboard his ship. It is nine minutes into this episode that a first hint at the Mirror Universe is dropped, which, however, is undetectable even for the most erudite *Star Trek* fan: Lorca mentions his photosensitivity, which is later explained to be the 'singular biological difference' ('Vaulting Ambition,' 1x12) between humans from the Prime Universe and humans from the Mirror Universe. Since this feature has never before been part of the other Mirror Universe mythology, however, and is not explained until the 12th episode of the first season of *Discovery*, at this point, it might at most make a viewer suspicious.

The viewer gets another instance of this kind of suspicion when at the end of the episode Lorca states that '[u]niversal law is for lackeys, context is for kings,' a dictum that also gave the episode its title ('Context is for Kings,' 1x03). Being so contradictory to Starfleet values, this indeed led to first speculations in *Star Trek* forums about whether Lorca could be from the Mirror Universe.[13] These speculations aside, throughout the following six episodes, and thus until the mid-season break,[14] the

[12] In the first two episodes, which can be considered as a set-up for the rest of the series, we get to know protagonist Michael Burnham, at the time first officer of the *U.S.S. Shenzhou*, and how she investigates an ancient vessel drifting in space, which reveals itself to be a Klingon artefact. This eventually leads to Burnham attempting to fire on an approaching Klingon vessel, against the wishes of her captain, Philippa Georgiou – she is arrested for mutiny, the *U.S.S. Shenzhou* is destroyed.

[13] First reactions and theories were that the whole episode was set in the Mirror Universe (cf., e.g., the discussion 'What are the odds that *Discovery* is actually set in the Mirror Universe?' on Reddit that was started just hours after 'Context is for Kings' was made available on CBS *All Access*. Not much later, first speculations occurred that named Lorca as a Mirror Universe character. One user, for example, posted the following theory: 'I think that Lorca ... is originally from the Mirror Universe and something happened where he got sent to the main universe when his last ship blew up. It also explains why he took an interest in the main universes Michael' (r/startrek, 2018).

[14] CBS *All Access* promoted the first nine episodes as chapter one, and the six

viewer is confronted with a variety of controversial actions by Lorca that both confirm and deny that he might indeed have something to hide. On the one hand, Lorca, for example, convinces as a *Star Trek* captain by being able to cite Starfleet regulations by heart ('Choose your Pain,' 1x05), and by supposedly showing compassion for an endangered species when he tries to find a solution to help the Pahvans ('Into the Forest I Go,' 1x09).[15] On the other hand, he is constantly disobeying Starfleet superiors, which makes especially old acquaintance Admiral Katrina Cornwell (Jayne Brook) suspicious of him. She even questions him in his private quarters about his behavior ('I don't think you've been the same'; 'Lethe,' 1x06), but he manages to respond somewhat convincingly that he has passed his psychological appraisal. He eventually manages to seduce her, thus arguably patching up their relationship, but the mood changes once again when Lorca threatens Cornwell with his phaser after waking up: 'Cornwall [screaming]: "You sleep with a phaser in your bed, and say nothing's wrong? ... I have ignored the signs, but I cannot any more. The truth is, you are not the man I used to know"' (1x06). While the scene thus ends with a Cornwell who is once again convinced that something about Lorca is not right, it surely does not help that for all these contradictions in his character, skeptics are offered a somewhat reasonable explanation from episode 1x06 onwards, when it is suggested that Lorca suffers from PTSD[16] as a result of his loss of the *U.S.S. Buran* under his command.

Up until episode 9 and thus the midseason finale of season one, the divided opinions about Lorca by different *Discovery* crew members hence mirror the mixed feelings viewers might have about Lorca

episodes following the midseason break as chapter two. While all previous network *Star Trek* seasons also featured similar breaks over the holidays, *Discovery*'s first season broadcast break is the first that serves as a cliffhanger in a *Star Trek* series.

[15] Two other essays in this collection that deal with the figure of the captain in the *Star Trek* universe and Lorca specifically are '"We Choose Our Own Pain. Mine Helps Me Remember": Gabriel Lorca, Ash Tyler, and the Question of Masculinity' by Sabrina Mittermeier and Jenny Volkmer and 'Looking in the Mirror: The Negotiation of Franchise Identity in *Star Trek: Discovery*' by Andrea Whitacre.

[16] I want to note here that this representation of PTSD as being synonymous with malignance and perfidy is certainly problematic, as is the fact that symptoms of PTSD and other mental health issues are portrayed in *Discovery* as not being distinctive from villainy. This is not necessarily surprising, as contemporary American science fiction, but also other media, has commonly misrepresented morally ambiguous actions or violence by persons suffering from PTSD as common place.

when watching: while Cornwell, Dr. Hugh Culber (Wilson Cruz), and Lieutenant Paul Stamets (Anthony Rapp) clash with Lorca in several scenes, Burnham seems to be supportive of him,[17] and Stamets eventually also falls back in line and supports his plan to jump. At the same time, Starfleet clearly has been destabilized, and it is hard for viewers to gauge what is happening based on prior knowledge of *Star Trek*. This becomes especially obvious in different readings of a key scene of 'Into the Forest I Go,' namely when Starfleet presumably validates Lorca's actions:

> Admiral Terral: 'The war is not won yet, but you have increased the likelihood of a victory for Starfleet, despite your unorthodox methods.' Lorca: 'I'm gonna take that as a compliment.' Admiral Terral: 'You will find that your accomplishments have not gone unnoticed. Starfleet Command would like to award you with the Legion of Honor.'

On the one hand, the award of the medal can be read as Lorca's absolute approval by a Starfleet official. On the other, it can be read as a ploy. As some argued after the episode was screened, Admiral Terral (Conrad Coates) arguably only promised Lorca the medal to lure him back to the Starbase to take his command away. As one viewer put it: 'when Terral spoke the words "Legion of Honor," it felt like there was no sincerity in it' (OhMally, 2018). The scene also ends with a stretching close-up of Lorca, whose facial expression is anything but a jubilant one, despite just having been awarded one of the highest honors in Starfleet.[18] Then again, others have argued against such an interpretation as it would, for example, defy the traditional *Star Trek* maxim that 'Vulcans cannot lie.' Whatever side of this interpretation one feels more comfortable with, in all, the first nine episodes left many *Star Trek* viewers with a lack of explanation for the discrepancies in the world of *Discovery* from the world of previous *Star Trek* series, materialized first and foremost in the character of Lorca and his corresponding actions, which are anything but adhering to the *Star Trek* rulebook (cf. Roddenberry's 'bible,' 1987).

---

[17] After all, Lorca appeals to the mutineer Burnham's strongest desires, redemption, or at least a chance to right wrongs, when he enlists her.

[18] This rather subjective reading can also be supported by the fact that Terral concurrently informs Lorca that Cornwell, who has been most skeptical of Lorca, has arrived at the Starbase and will make a full recovery. That piece of information in turn makes Lorca – and *Discovery* viewers – wonder if Cornwell already told Terral about Lorca, thus spurring on the speculation about a ploy.

As one review put it: 'This doesn't feel like the Federation or Starfleet we know and love because it isn't' (Burt, 2017).

These speculations are not resolved until the very last scene of episode 9, which climaxes in one final spore drive jump to get the crew back to safety and a shot that clearly shows Lorca overriding the co-ordinates.[19] After all, it can hardly be a coincidence that Lorca's 'Let's go home' are the last words spoken before the jump is ordered. And indeed, when after the jump violent Vulcans attack the *U.S.S. Discovery* without warning, it becomes clear that Lorca's previously mentioned 'home' is 'not our universe' ('Despite Yourself,' 1x10). Moreover, visual hints finally also confirm this observation to viewers: We encounter the usual logo of the Terran empire, and see Tilly (Mary Wiseman) switching into a Terran uniform in order to pose as her Mirror counterpart. As in all other *Star Trek* series, viewers are thus now confronted with a clearly marked oppressive, racist, and xenophobic Mirror Universe, that makes use of the world-building strategies viewers know from the previous series, such as the agonizer booths and the killing of officers as the only way of career advancement. To confirm this traditional function of the Mirror Universe as an evil counterpart of the Prime one, in the following episodes, we follow Burnham overseeing the deaths of prisoners and must realize that Kelpiens are slaves in the Mirror Universe. Even though episode 11, 'The Wolf Inside,' also focusses heavily on the subplot of Tyler (Shazad Latif) actually being the Klingon Voq, episode 1x10, 1x11, and 1x12's main aim is to once again portray the Mirror Universe as an evil counterpart to the Prime Universe. This background arguably makes the revelation about Lorca's true identity, which comprises the climax of episode 1x12, even more appalling: Once again situated as the climax of the episode, it is Emperor Georgiou's (Michelle Yeoh) reaction to light that makes Lorca's betrayal become clear to Burnham by pointing out that extreme sensitivity to light is one way to tell Mirror Universe characters apart from Prime Universe ones:

> [cross-cut to flashback scene where Saru and Lorca discuss the 'fortunate coincidence' that the spore drive jumps identified the coordinates for the Mirror Universe, then cross-cut back to Emperor Georgiou, who is blinded by light]. Burnham: 'You're sensitive to light.' Georgiou: 'Only compared to a human from your universe. It's the singular biological difference between our two races.' [cross-cut to another flashback: Lorca blinking, injecting himself

---

[19] The shot shows the control panel, where the line before jump 133, the final jump, reads 'OVERRIDE – LORCA, G.'

with a serum that helps fight his photosensitivity]. ('Vaulting Ambition')

This key scene thus simultaneously reveals Lorca to be from the Mirror Universe, explains his erratic nature and actions over the first part of the series, and repeats the hints that were spread about his mirror identity throughout the first nine episodes using flashbacks. This moment of anagnorisis hence enables both Burnham but also the viewer to read scenes from the first half of the series differently, and manages to release the potential tension that viewers felt about 'the discrepancies in the world of *Discovery*' (see above). In the end, Lorca and his actions felt different because he *was* different, having only posed as his mirror counterpart from the Prime Universe.

This is a narrative novelty that deserves further attention. In contrast to sudden plot twists, which are common to *Star Trek* series, *Discovery*'s writers here instead have focused on a slow burn.[20] The revelation of Lorca being from the Mirror Universe, though, which was hinted at for more than half of the series, but only revealed in the last third, has lasting impact and moreover changes what viewers thought about the first half. The *Macbeth*-inspired title of the revelation episode, 'Vaulting Ambition,' therefore is appropriate on at least two levels: it applies to Lorca's actions, which now all can be read in a different light (to 'save' the Pahvans, to make the 'final' jump, to 'help' Burnham), but it also describes what can be considered the riskiest plot twist a *Star Trek* series has ever delivered: Instead of presenting a concluded storyline for each episode, with this Mirror Universe storyline, *Discovery* connects, extends, and *changes* the story world continuously over the entire serial. Structurally, the first season of *Discovery* thus is not leaning on the old conventions of the franchise, is not a reiteration of previous series of *Star Trek* with the self-contained episode format, but presents a series that has adapted to twenty-first century post-network rules with a focus on seriality and gradual plot progression.

This, in turn, has important consequences for the story world itself: the Mirror Universe can no longer just be read as the evil twin of the

---

[20] While sudden plot twists, such as the deaths of Captain Georgiou and Culber, certainly exist as well, even those have significant impact on the following storyline. Captain Georgiou's death, for example, might be read as a motivation for bringing Mirror Georgiou into the Prime Universe, and Culber's death even has repercussions throughout both seasons of *Discovery*: towards the end of season one, his 'ghost' helps Stamets navigate within the mycelial network, and in season two he reappears when Tilly is dragged into the network as well and the crew manages to resurrect him.

Prime Universe that fulfills its aim when confirming the progress and utopian qualities of the latter by presenting its contrary alternative. Rather, a clear-cut dichotomy between 'good' and 'evil,' between Mirror Universe and Prime Universe, must be rejected for the first season of *Discovery*. As explored above, for the first eight episodes, this is done through deceiving the Prime characters – and the viewers – by adding Mirror Lorca into the Prime Universe. Since clear visual or narrative clarifications are lacking, and arguably plausible explanations are given for Lorca's sometimes unusual behavior, a viewer can identify with Lorca and can see him as part of the Prime Universe. While he might not be seen as an entirely 'good' character, he also certainly cannot be categorized as clear-cut 'evil,' as the contradictory examples I provided above have outlined. Of course, the context of the Federation–Klingon War is important here, as it sets the background against which Lorca can justify his actions in the first place (cf. his 'context is for kings' dictum), which certainly do not meet Starfleet's traditional principles. But that is exactly what the first season of *Discovery* is arguably about. It asks whether it is always possible to draw a strict division between 'good' or 'bad,' between 'utopian' and 'dystopian,' or whether, sometimes, context might decide and might blur these clear divisions.

While it is Mirror Lorca in the first half of season one that enables this blurring of dichotomies, after the Mirror Universe is revealed, another Mirror character replaces his function: it is the reentry of Philippa Georgiou, now as Emperor in the Mirror Universe, that substitutes Lorca's role in the second half of the series. Notably, the viewer's – and the protagonists' – relation to Mirror Georgiou is different than that to Lorca, as firstly, we know her true (mirror) identity at once and, secondly, we have gotten to know her Prime Universe counterpart during the first two episodes of season one. As captain of the *U.S.S. Shenzhou*, Prime Georgiou was introduced as a compassionate but forceful woman, who was Burnham's guide and role model.[21] It is with this prior knowledge that the viewer, together with Burnham, meets Georgiou's mirror counterpart in 'The Wolf Inside.' After Burnham tried to save the lives of a group of rebels whom she was ordered to destroy by the Terran Empire while maintaining her cover as her mirror counterpart, the *I.S.S. Shenzhou* (which Burnham is commanding while serving as her Mirror self) crew receives a transmission from the emperor, who until

---

[21] Notably, *Discovery* opens the first episode with Georgiou and Burnham on an expedition, which has no other narrative relevance than to establish the closeness between Burnham and Georgiou, and moreover Georgiou's role as a role model for Burnham.

then was described as faceless. The episode concludes when a visibly upset and shocked Burnham is confronted by a holographic Georgiou about her cowardness, anticipating the emotional tension that will develop between Prime Burnham and the mirror counterpart of her former captain in the following episodes.

In the subsequent episode, 'Vaulting Ambition,' the viewer is informed that Burnham afterwards was summoned to the *I.S.S. Charon* to explain her cowardly behavior, with Lorca, who had staged a coup in the Mirror Universe before being transported to the Prime Universe, as her bounty.[22] In the beginning of the episode, Georgiou is clearly presented as the cruel, evil emperor she was said to be, as she hits Lorca and punishes him with the agonizer booth, and thus meets expectations of a Mirror Universe character. Only seconds later, however, the mood in the scene changes significantly, as Georgiou approaches Burnham: 'You could have died hunting that traitor across the universe. I am so happy you didn't. ... Everything will be the way it was, dear daughter' ('Vaulting Ambition').

Both Georgiou's emotional speech, and her physical contact to Burnham when she caresses her cheek, confirm that this is not the evil, faceless Emperor Georgiou, but that she is impersonating a caring mother, an emotional protector of Burnham – and she is doing so quite deliberately since she later attempts to sentence Burnham to death when Burnham fails to call her 'mother' before she can prove that she is from the Prime Universe. In this earlier scene, however, Georgiou reminds both Burnham and the viewer of her Prime Universe counterpart. Especially for Burnham, this representation is highly ambiguous, as she is clearly struggling with the contrast between the Georgiou she knows and Mirror Georgiou, and with Mirror Georgiou being so personal and referring to her as her 'daughter.' Once again, one is thus confronted with ambiguous feelings for a Mirror Universe character, as the viewer is not only exposed to clear cruelty, but humanity, compassion, and a wounded pride. When the viewer looks at Georgiou in this scene, it is through Burnham' eyes, who sees both a trusted mentor and friend – and the leader of the xenophobic Terran empire.

This emotional connection is enhanced throughout the following episode, when Burnham manages to destroy the *I.S.S. Charon*'s power core in order to use its energy to get back to the Prime Universe. She ultimately refuses to let Mirror Georgiou die, but instead takes her with

---

[22] Burnham impersonating her Mirror counterpart (who is presumed dead) is reminiscent of Benjamin Sisko impersonating his presumed dead counterpart in *Deep Space Nine*'s mirror episode 'Through the Looking Glass.'

her aboard *U.S.S. Discovery*. Once again, a Mirror character has thus traversed into the Prime Universe, even though this time unwillingly but owing to Burnham's emotional attachment: 'The truth is, I couldn't watch her die again, Saru [Doug Jones]. I wanted to offer her more' ('The War Without, The War Within,' 1x14). As we follow the story to its finale, however, we understand that Mirror Georgiou's transfer to the Prime Universe also serves another purpose. When the *U.S.S. Discovery* finally manages to return to the Prime Universe at the conclusion of the episode, the crew immediately realizes that they overshot by nine months and that, in the meantime, the Klingons have all but won the war against the Federation. Starfleet is withdrawing and is advising the *U.S.S. Discovery* crew to do the same, but when they arrive at Starbase One, they find it has been destroyed by Klingons from House D'Ghor.[23] This leads Burnham to her realization that 'the time for peace has passed,' and she asks Georgiou to tell her how she defeated the Klingon Empire in her universe.

Once again, we have thus reached a point in the first season of *Discovery* where the unconditional conformity to Starfleet directives is rendered futile under current conditions, and in order to bypass them, it can arguably only be a character from the Mirror Universe that can offer a viable solution. Indeed, the following finale sees Starfleet agreeing to Georgiou's proposition to strike against Qo'noS to end the war. The official plan is to release a drone on Qo'noS to map the planet for military targets that then can be attacked by Starfleet. To do so, the Federation Council even allows Georgiou to assume the identity of her Prime counterpart to lead the attack, and she is reinstated as captain of the *U.S.S. Discovery* by Admiral Cornwell. Notably, in quite striking contrast to Lorca, Georgiou never tries to fit into the Prime Universe: she keeps up her antagonistic behavior when she, for example, enters the bridge of the *U.S.S. Discovery* for the first time at the beginning of 'Will You Take My Hand' (1x15). Within seconds of her taking command, she repels Saru and the rest of the crew by calling out the helm, who previously served under Prime Georgiou on the *U.S.S. Shenzhou*, for calling Qo'noS the Klingon 'home world.' She emphasizes in her harsh emperor voice that in her view, 'Klingons are animals, and they don't

---

[23] By the time the *U.S.S. Discovery* returns from the Mirror Universe, the Klingons do no longer fight as an alliance, but their houses are divided once again. As Sarek (James Frain) explains: 'They quarrel among themselves, hence the indiscriminate nature of their aggression. But their collective aim seems clear. To compete for dominance by seeing which house can destroy the most Federation assets' ('The War Without, The War Within').

have homes,' and that, under her rule, Qo'noS is to be called the 'enemy planet.' Mirror Georgiou thus is clearly not embodying or adjusting to Federation ideals, as Saru poignantly points out only seconds later, after he is also verbally attacked by Georgiou. When later she continues to act against Starfleet principles when she restrains and tortures L'Rell (Mary Chieffo) in the presence of Burnham, the latter also begins to question Georgiou's motives and her decision to bring Georgiou to the Prime Universe. And indeed, soon after Burnham, Georgiou, Tilly and Tyler have arrived on Qo'noS to release the drone, they discover that Georgiou's true objective is it to detonate a hydro bomb instead of a drone to destroy the Klingon home planet once and for all. Burnham immediately contacts Admiral Cornwell and argues that genocide is not the Starfleet way, even when trying to end the war. Cornwell and, through her, Starfleet, responds by saying that the Federation is close to defeat and that they, under these circumstances, do not have the 'luxury of principles' ('Will You Take My Hand'). Burnham refutes by arguing that principles are all that they have, and that Cornwell sent Mirror Georgiou on the mission because she knew that only a Terran from the Mirror Universe could execute what Starfleet officers could not:

> Cornwell: 'Terms of atrocity are convenient after the fact. The Klingons are on the verge of wiping out the Federation.' Burnham: 'Yes, but ask yourself: Why did you put this mission in the hands of a Terran...? It's because you know it is not who we are.'

This scene shows remarkable parallels to Lorca's controversial place in the first half of *Discovery*. Even though he clearly disregarded Starfleet principles and mentioned similar questionable motifs for his behavior, nevertheless, he also had the partial support of his crew and (arguably) Starfleet. At the time, however, Starfleet and the Discovery crew believed Lorca to be from the Prime Universe. With Georgiou now, the situation differs slightly, but significantly: Burnham knows (and most of the crew probably suspects) that she is from the Mirror Universe, while Starfleet still tries to pass her off as her Prime counterpart. Burnham's experience with Mirror Lorca hence enables her to see through Georgiou's *and* Starfleet's wrong morals. As a consequence, she threatens a mutiny to prove what Starfleet stands for, and, in strong contrast to what happened in the first half of the series, the crew of the *Discovery* stands to support her, instead of their interim captain Georgiou. It is in the conclusion of the last episode in Burnham's speech in front of the Starfleet council that she sums up her lessons learnt from the exposure to the Mirror Universe:

We are no longer on the eve of battle. Even so, I come to ask myself the same question that a young soldier asked the general all those years ago: 'How do I defeat fear?' The general's answer: the only way to defeat fear is to tell it 'no.' No. We will not take shortcuts on the path to righteousness. ... No. We will not allow desperation to destroy moral authority. ... We have to be torchbearers, casting the light so we may see our path to lasting peace. ('Will You Take My Hand?')

We can thus understand the function of the Mirror Universe in the first season of *Discovery* as going far beyond simply presenting an antagonistic twin to the Prime Universe that was key to previous instantiations of the Mirror Universe in *The Original Series, Enterprise,* and *Deep Space Nine*. Instead, particularly the first season of *Discovery* uses two instantiations of a mirror character operating in the Prime Universe – and the *Discovery*'s journey into the Mirror Universe itself – to probe the assumption that it is possible to easily delineate the Prime Universe as 'good' and the Mirror Universe as 'evil,' especially under special circumstances such as 'the eve of battle,' i.e., war. Both Mirror Lorca and Mirror Georgiou function to not unquestioningly reinforce the validity of Prime values and morals by presenting their 'evil' opposite, as characters from the pre-network Mirror Universe would have done. Instead, they offer foils on which to question them – and also, on a broader level, to question previous rather clear-cut instantiations of the Mirror Universe as the evil twin of the indisputably 'good' Prime Universe.

Conclusion

The Mirror Universe and its mirror characters in season one of *Discovery* are hence a prime example of how an already established world in *Star Trek* can be recycled and adapted to blur boundaries and challenge clear-cut Manichean binaries in the post-network era. Going beyond the Mirror Universe, one could ask whether the combination of the Klingon Voq and Ash Tyler, as hosting both 'good' and 'evil' characteristics in one body, could be read as another of such instantiations. Expanding the argument to season two, one could also investigate the prolonged role that Mirror Georgiou plays in the story, especially in relation to Starfleet's Section 31, a black ops organization that first appeared in *Deep Space Nine* and that is also known for being a counterweight to the utopian ideals of the federation. Notably, both Tyler and Mirror Georgiou are reintroduced to the viewer in season two as part of Section 31, and they continue to act as controversial, non-Manichean characters that push the boundaries of what is accepted within Starfleet's directives.

While both investigations unfortunately lie beyond the scope of this chapter, it shall suffice to conclude that such complicated story worlds and character constellations enable *Discovery* in both season one and two to impeach the simple, affective dichotomies that have provided the discursive basis for earlier *Star Trek* television series, and instead offer complicated interrogations into the right and wrongness of ethics and morals – or, to be more specific, the otherwise unquestioned validity of Starfleet principles – that seem more appropriate in an post-9/11 era (Espinoza Garrido, 2018).

I would like to close by exploring the overarching question of how it was particularly a post-network series that was able to present such a changed function of the Mirror Universe for *Star Trek*. When we go back to comparing the pre- and post-network instantiations of the Mirror Universe, we firstly must realize that the long-term orientation of post-network serials have of course enabled such slow-burn experiments that we encountered especially with the trickster figure of Lorca during the first half of *Discovery*. In the traditional format, the Mirror Universe always had to be strictly demarcated from the Prime Universe, using various cinematographic and narrative devices such as dress code, behavior, objects, logos, or even different opening sequences; otherwise, single episodes could not have captured the concept. Only because this logic of self-sustained episodes was abandoned for the first time in *Discovery*, a world-building approach towards the Mirror Universe could be developed that went beyond simply presenting an antagonistic twin to the Prime Universe. Instead, both the protagonists of the Prime Universe and the viewers should not know that an important character is actually from the Mirror Universe. The first season of *Discovery* thus was able to trick us into identifying with a character from the Mirror Universe, and in turn, managed to question our previous assumptions about the Mirror Universe as an all-bad twin to the Prime Universe. Similarly, with Georgiou, the series was able to frame us by firstly introducing Prime Georgiou in the first two episodes, and then attaching our sympathies for her to her Mirror counterpart in the second half of the series. Both strategies include world and character building of such a scale that it can only be accomplished over multiple, successive episodes and, as such, would have been impossible in *Star Trek*'s traditional television format.

Works Cited

Katyl Burt, 'Star Trek: Discovery Episode 9 Review: Into the Forest I Go', *Den of Geek*, 14 November (2017), https://www.Denofgeek.com/us/tv/star-trek-discovery/268934/star-trek-discovery-episode-9-review-into-the-forest-i-go.

Darren. 'Star Trek: Enterprise – In a Mirror, Darkly, Part II (Review)', *The Movie Blog*, 30 May (2016), https://them0vieblog.com/2016/05/30/star-trek-enterprise-in-a-mirror-darkly-part-ii-review.

Lea Espinoza Garrido, 'Luke Cage as Postpost-9/11 TV: Spatial Negotiations of Race in Contemporary U.S. Television', *Current Objectives in American Studies* 19.1 (2018), https://copas.uni-regensburg.de/article/view/292.

Dave Itzkoff, 'On "Star Trek: Discovery," a Franchise Boldly Goes into the Serial TV Era', *New York Times*, 21 September (2017), https://www.Nytimes.com/2017/09/21/arts/television/star-trek-discovery.html.

Jason Mittell, 'Narrative Complexity in Contemporary American Television', *The Velvet Light Trap*, 58.1 (2006): 29–40.

Angela Ndalianis, 'Television and the Neo-Baroque', in Michael Hammond and Lucy Mazdon (eds.) *The Contemporary Television Series* (Edinburgh: Edinburgh University Press, 2005): 83–101.

OhMally, 'The Captain's Secret', *Fanfiction.Net*, 6 August (2018), https://www.fanfiction.net/s/12685215/72/The-Captain-s-Secret.

Roberta Pearson and Máire Messenger Davies, *Star Trek and American Television* (Berkeley, Los Angeles, London: University of California Press, 2014).

'r/startrek', '[Spoilers] I Think that Lorca…', *Reddit*, 29 January (2018), https://www.Reddit.com/r/startrek/comments/7p5bo6/spoilers_i_think_that_lorca.

Gene Roddenberry, 'Star Trek. The Next Generation. Writer/Director's Guide', *TV Writing*, 23 March (1987), leethomson.myzen.co.uk/Star_Trek/2_The_Next_Generation/Star_Trek_-_The_Next_Generation_Bible.pdf.

Carli Velocci, 'Why "Star Trek: Discovery" Will Be Franchise's "Most Serialized" Version', *The Wrap*, 1 August (2017), https://www.thewrap.com/star-trek-discovery-will-franchises-serialized-version.

Matt Wright, 'STLV17: Brannon Braga On How Kirk Should Have Died, "Star Trek: Enterprise" Regrets and More', *TrekMovie*, 11 August (2017), https://www.trekmovie.com/2017/08/11/sltv17-brannon-braga-on-how-kirk-should-have-died-star-trek-enterprise-regrets-and-more.

Episodes and Films Cited

'The Menagerie, Pt. 1.' *Star Trek: The Original Series*, written by Gene Roddenberry, directed by Marc Daniels, NBC, 17 November, 1966.

'The Menagerie, Pt. 2.' *Star Trek: The Original Series*, written by Gene Roddenberry, directed by Robert Butler, NBC, 24 November, 1966.

'Mirror, Mirror.' *Star Trek: The Original Series*, written by Jerome Bixby, directed by Marc Daniels, NBC, 6 October, 1967.

'Crossover.' *Star Trek: Deep Space Nine*, written by Peter Allan Fields, directed by David Livingston, Paramount Television, 15 May, 1994.

'Through the Looking Glass.' *Star Trek: Deep Space Nine*, written by Ira Steven Behr and Robert Hewitt Wolfe, directed by Winrich Kolbe, Paramount Television, 17 April, 1995.

'Shattered Mirror.' *Star Trek: Deep Space Nine*, written by Ira Steven Behr and Hans Beimler, directed by James L. Conway, Paramount Television, 22 April, 1996.

'Resurrection.' *Star Trek: Deep Space Nine*, written by Michael Taylor, directed by LeVar Burton, Paramount Television, 17 November, 1997.

'The Emperor's New Cloak.' *Star Trek: Deep Space Nine*, written by Ira Steven Behr and Hans Beimler, directed by LeVar Burton, Paramount Television, 3 February, 1999.

'In a Mirror, Darkly.' *Star Trek: Enterprise*, written by Michael Sussmann, directed by James L. Conway and Marvin V. Rush, UPN, 22 April, 2005.

'Despite Yourself.' *Star Trek: Discovery*, written by Sean Cochran, directed by Jonathan Frakes, CBS, 7 January, 2017.

'The Wolf Inside.' *Star Trek: Discovery*, written by Lisa Randolph, directed by T.J. Scott, CBS, 14 January, 2017.

'Vaulting Ambition.' *Star Trek: Discovery*, written by Jordon Nardino, directed by Hanelle M. Culpepper, CBS, 21 January, 2017.

'The War Without, The War Within.' *Star Trek: Discovery*, written by Lisa Randolph, directed by David Solomon, CBS, 4 February, 2017.

'Choose Your Pain.' *Star Trek: Discovery*, written by Gretchen J. Berg, Aaron Harberts, and Kemp Powers, directed by Lee Rose, CBS, 24 September, 2017.

'Context is for Kings.' *Star Trek: Discovery*, written by Bryan Fuller, Gretchen J. Berg, and Aaron Harberts, directed by Akiva Goldsman, CBS, 1 October, 2017.

'Lethe.' *Star Trek: Discovery*, written by Joe Menosky and Ted Sullivan, directed by Douglas Aarniokowski, CBS, 22 October, 2017.

'Into the Forest I Go.' *Star Trek: Discovery*, written by Bo Yeon Kim and Erika Lippoldt, directed by Chris Byrne, CBS, 12 November, 2017.

Star Trek: First Contact. 1996. Directed by Jonathan Frakes. Paramount Pictures.

'Lorca, I'm Really Gonna Miss Killing You'
The Fictional Space Created by Time Loop Narratives

Sarah Böhlau

The Time Loop Narrative

In his recent book about the history of time-travel narrative James Gleick notes: 'Time travel feels like an ancient tradition, rooted in old mythologies, old as gods and dragons' (Gleick, 2016, 4). And it does feel like the idea of travelling through time must always have been a part of the human imagination, always a well-known storytelling device. One glance at the rich intertextuality of *Star Trek: Discovery*'s (2017–ongoing) season two shows how deeply and widely the narrative device is still entrenched in contemporary popular culture.

But in fact, the trope is very much a modern fantasy, born out of the scientific and philosophical discourses and narrative innovations of the late nineteenth century. Its sub-trope, the recursive time loop, is even younger, originating in the early 1990s. As a narrative phenomenon in popular culture, the recursive time loop is most often associated with Harold Raimi's movie *Groundhog Day* (1993) – the online database *TV Tropes*, for example, refers to the trope as the '"Groundhog Day" Loop.' A *Groundhog Day* time loop occurs when the temporal fabric of a narrative world enfolds one or several characters in a recurring circular loop, while for the rest of the storyworld time flows in its natural direction. This generates a peculiar fictional space within a narrative, where – as time travel often does – known variables like cause and effect, risk and reward, even life and death follow a new set of rules. Without any external consequences for their actions, the time looper finds himself promoted to a godlike gamemaster – and simultaneously cursed to a Sisyphus-like existence.

But despite the close cultural association with *Groundhog Day*, the trope actually originates from a *Star Trek* episode airing the year before. *Star Trek*, never a franchise to shy away from bold narrative tools, introduced what is wildly acknowledged as the first time loop narrative in *The Next Generation* (*TNG*) (1987–1999) season five episode 'Cause and Effect' (1992). Series writer Brannon Braga remembers scripting the episode: 'I love time travel stories and I don't know who doesn't. We wanted to do a time travel story that had never been done before. Being trapped in a time loop is one I've never seen before' (Gross and Altmann, 1995, 241). In the episode the *Enterprise* is caught in a 'temporal distortion,' trapping her in a day-long loop which ends in a deathly collision with another spaceship. Famously, 'Cause and Effect' starts *in medias res*, several loops in. Picard barely has time to command to abandon the ship before the *Enterprise* explodes, killing everyone on board. Writer Ron Moore is especially proud of this bold episode opener: 'You will never be able to beat that teaser. That's the definite one' (Gross and Altmann, 1995, 241). Time then resets, as it already has, we will find out later, many times. There is no sole looper in 'Cause and Effect,' the whole ship is unaware of the temporal circumstances, until the feeling of *déjà vu* seeps into the awareness of several characters, allowing them to eventually break the circle.

During the repeated loops, several identical (or near identical) scenes are shot from different angles in an attempt to prevent the narrative becoming 'dangerously repetitive' (Gross and Altmann, 1995, 242). Central to the episode is a poker game between senior officers Riker, Crusher, Worf and Data. The experience of *déjà vu* sharpens from Dr. Crusher winning, smugly telling Riker she 'just had a feeling' he was bluffing, to all players being able to correctly predict each of the 'sufficiently randomized' cards Data deals.

Since 'Cause and Effect,' the trope has become a well-known storytelling device. Television formats that have utilized the time loop range from science fiction series (*Stargate SG-1*, 1997–2007), space operas (*Farscape*, 1999–2003) and mystery (*X-Files*, 1993–2018) to fantasy series like *Buffy the Vampire Slayer* (1997–2003), *Supernatural* (2005–ongoing) or even *Xena: Warrior Princess* (1995–2001). Current cinematic examples of the trope include the 2011 movie *Source Code* by director Duncan Jones and Doug Liman's *Edge of Tomorrow* (2014).[1] And, most recently, the Netflix production *Russian Doll* (2019) dedicated a whole series to the narrative device. While the time loop is certainly centered in the fantastic genres – as all of the examples listed above indicate – there are some unexpected branches into realistic narratives like comedy (*The*

---

[1] Will Tattersdill also reflects on time loop narratives and their relation to changes in the way TV shows are structured and narrated in his essay '*Discovery* and the Form of Victorian Periodicals' published in this volume.

Suite Life on Deck, 2008–2011). And one might even hesitate to classify *Groundhog Day* as a fantasy film rather than a realistic one using a singular fantastic trope.

Beside the time-travel concept itself, there is another significant narrative influence present in time loop stories, which happens to be directly addressed in the time loop episode of the TNT fantasy series *The Librarians* (2014–2018). In episode 2x08, 'And the Point of Salvation' (which, like 'Cause and Effect,' was directed by Jonathan Frakes), it takes the looper in question only a few moments to diagnose his current situation, even dutifully namedropping notable examples of the trope in other television shows: 'It's a time loop. We're trapped in a time loop. We're repeating the day over, just like in that movie "Groundhog Day" ... or "Star Trek" or "X-Files" or "Buffy"' (The Librarians, 2x08). But he is wrong. His team is, in fact, trapped in a computer game. He realizes this after, during the nervous breakdown that inevitably occurs at a certain point of the loop narrative, he kicks a nearby box and it turns – accompanied by the appropriate sound effect – into a med pack.

But the looper's initial mistake is an easy one to make, as the adventure computer game and the time loop are relatives, narratively speaking. According to Martin Hermann, the advent of computer games into the cultural awareness clearly aided in the birth of the time loop narrative (Hermann, 2011, 146), The fictional space created by time loops takes on a 'game-like quality' (Hermann, 2011, 149), as it presents the looper with conditions similar to the virtual surroundings of a computer game. Loops resemble game levels to be navigated again and again until everything unknown is detected, everything unexpected is anticipated, and the mastery over the space is absolute. Of course, these plots also usually deny the looper the kind of agency a player is accustomed to:

> The options denied to the protagonist as user in time-loop narratives in comparison to real adventure computer game users are all located outside the fictional world of the computer game and concern the missing game menu options. Game menu options are, for example, to start the game, to exit, to save, etc. (Hermann, 2011, 155)

Any kind of time travel constitutes a narrative paradox, as it goes against what are considered facts about temporality. As Marie-Laure Ryan summarizes, there are four generally accepted beliefs about time:

1. Time flows, and it does so in a fixed direction.
2. You cannot fight this flow and go back in time.
3. Causes always precede their effects.
4. The past is written once and for all. (Ryan, 2009, 142)

The time loop narrative breaks with all four of these rules, excepting the looper from them. As Ryan further points out, even paradoxical narratives show a clear 'resistance to irrationality' (2009, 159). The paradox of the time loop only works well if it emerges from an otherwise coherent narrative: 'Narrative paradoxes are like the holes in a Swiss cheese: they only exist as holes because they are surrounded by a solid texture of rational events' (Ryan, 2009, 160). The looper is the cheese in this metaphor. While everything else resets – the time, the space, its inhabitants, even the looper's body – his own personal time and memory continue in a forward direction. For him, cause and effect are still in their natural order. Therefore, he is the one element within the loop who is able to keep knowledge, to change, to develop. This marks him as 'a kind of linear and stable factor within the repeated or multiplied universes' (Eckel, 2013, 282).

Paul Stamets (Anthony Rapp), the looper in *Discovery*'s 'Magic to Make the Sanest Man Go Mad' (1x07), succeeds in outsmarting Harry Mudd (Rainn Wilson), the person who controls the loop, by spreading this stabilizing factor – the cheesiness, to borrow Ryan's metaphor – to the other crew members. They, too, have access to the information gathered by the repeating iterations of the same timeline.

'Magic to Make the Sanest Man Go Mad'

Most crucial in many of the time loop narratives listed above is the question of emotional development and human connection, both equally enabled and denied by the time loop. This is also the case in *Discovery*'s stellar episode 'Magic to Make the Sanest Man Go Mad.' Mudd having full control over the loop is an unusual example of the trope. In most instances the time loop is either caused by an unspecified cosmic entity (*Groundhog Day*), random temporal anomaly (*TNG*), or controlled by an outsider, be it a rogue angel (*Supernatural*), malfunctioning computer game (*The Librarians*), or trio of wannabe supervillains (*Buffy*). In each loop, Mudd enters the *Discovery* as a parasite, twisting the societal rules and technical structures that govern her space to his needs, harvesting the particular information he desires, before abandoning the loop by carelessly destroying the whole system.

The time loop therefore does not end randomly but is marked by the deliberate destruction of the *Discovery* and the death of everyone on board. Mudd, as the one controlling the loop, is not exempt from this; every loop essentially ends with his suicide, as he dies with the others in each explosion. As we later learn from Tyler (Shazad Latif), Mudd is an experienced looper, who has likely used the same method for a prior bank heist (1x07), which results in Mudd displaying a high level of confidence: thus, he readily pulls the trigger. Each new reset creates a new *Discovery* and a new Mudd, who, armed with the knowledge of his predecessors, can once again infest the ship in search of more advantages. In terms of narrative spaces, then, there is not one Mudd, but rather a consecutive queue of Mudds, whose knowledge carries into the loop following their death.

Stamets' piggybacking on Mudd's time loop due to his infusion of tardigrade DNA in an earlier episode (1x05, 'The Butcher's Knife Cares Not for the Lamb's Cry'), essentially enables him to do the same, but his situation is fundamentally different. Martin Herrmann distinguishes between *time loop quests* and *time loop prisons* (Hermann, 2011, 146). While the former is structured around a certain (internal or external) goal to be reached, the latter is about overcoming an antagonistic force. Hermann qualifies *Groundhog Day* as an example of the internal quest time loop. Bill Murray's thoroughly unpleasant weatherman Phil is forced to relive the titular day until the weight of repetition and boredom forces him to transform himself into a more caring, conscious human being. While he is certainly imprisoned in many ways, as Linda Thompson states, the obstacles Phil is facing are all situated in his own character traits: 'In effect, for the purposes of narrative causality, Phil is literally his own worst enemy – protagonist and antagonist rolled into one' (Thompson, 1999, 133). While Mudd is on a quest of his own design, Stamets is very much imprisoned in the loop. Furthermore, it is a captivity with a definite release date. He is very aware that there is a finite number of loops until Mudd has everything he wants. Equally, there is a definite quest-like quality to Burnham (Sonequa Martin-Green) overcoming her fear of social interaction and approaching Tyler.

Within the episode, an exact loop count is difficult, since the only hint given is Mudd bragging about killing Lorca (Jason Isaacs) 53 times ('But who's counting?'), which occurs in the third-to-last loop (1x07). Assigning the iterations Greek alphabet letters, I will henceforth call the first loop, the original iteration of the time frame, loop α. The last loop, which ends with Mudd deactivating the device he uses to control the time distortion and everyone reentering normal time, loop ω. Loop ω is the only permanent timeline, therefore allowing everyone to keep their memories.

Loop	Memorable Quote
loop α (first one)	Mudd: 'Did you miss me as much as I missed you?'
loop π	Stamets: 'It all starts with a gormagander, okay? A gormagander!'
loop φ	Stamets 'Tell me a secret. Something that will immediately prove to you we've had this conversation.'
Loop χ	Stamets: 'Dance with me. For science.'
Loop ψ	Tyler: 'This night's gotten weird. But also, very interesting.'
Loop ω (last one)	Lorca: 'Lieutenant Stamets has shown us your success is a universal certainty.'

The episode opens with Burnham recording her personal log, her voice-over establishing key elements of the starting point that every iteration will inevitably revert to. Even if certain areas are resolved in some matter, like Stamets successfully convincing Burnham he is not suffering from mushroom-fueled hallucinations, the next loop will reset these efforts. Burnham remarks: 'Lieutenant Stamets' ability to pilot the ship's spore drive has given him access not just to all of space, but to unseen parts of his personality as well' (1x07). Stamets has already deviated far from his – as Tilly (Mary Wiseman) puts it in a later episode – 'persnickety, grumpy self' (1x08, 'Si Vis Pacem, Para Bellum'), and the whole ship is aware of it. This will complicate matters considerably for him, as being established as emotionally compromised prior the time loop prevents him from being taken seriously.

Central in Burnham's initial musings are her problems with social interaction. Routinized professionalism is the space where she is most comfortable in and she is relieved to have found it on the *Discovery*: 'Despite my fears to the contrary, I seem to have found my place on this *Discovery*. An air of routine has descended on the ship and even I am a part of it' (1x07). The accompanying companionable scenes in the cafeteria with Tilly and Tyler are still within a professional context, allowing Burnham to relax. She also acknowledges her interest in Tyler. But for Starfleet's first mutineer the safety of routine has also taken on the quality of a prison, as Burnham (Sonequa Martin-Green) is fighting a very deep feeling of social isolation: 'I am among the others, but also apart' (1x07). Another shot mirrors the previous scenes with Tilly und Tyler, but here Burnham is sitting alone at the mess hall table. The log entry ends with Burnham steeling herself for 'one of my greatest challenges so far' (1x07) and entering the crew party. Here, the space deviates much from the usual aesthetics: party floodlights and sparklers illuminate the room, Wyclef Jean's 1997 single 'We Trying to Stay Alive' blasts loudly through speakers, forcing the partygoers, variously wearing uniform and civilian clothes, to bend closely together to converse. Tilly's social nature only shines brighter in the relaxed atmosphere of the party, and we see her confidently moving through the room, taking part in party games and flirting with tactical officer Lieutenant Rhys (Patrick Kwok-Choon).

The lights flickering indicate Mudd activating the time loop device and we enter the timeframe of loop α. Tilly α drunkenly prods a visibly uncomfortable Burnham α about her romantic interest in Tyler, which Burnham unconvincingly tries to transfer back into a professional setting. Tyler α's speech about camaraderie and shared experiences only further highlights her isolation: 'We're all lucky to be here tonight, surrounded by our brothers and sisters-in-arms. Laughing. Dancing' (1x07). He joins Burnham α for a few moments, until a comm announcement calls both of them to the bridge, with Tyler α accurately, but not unkindly, joking about her being 'saved from the horrors of small talk by duty' (1x07).

On the way to the bridge, while awkwardly trying to explain her social insecurity to Tyler α, she crashes into a very happy and hyper Stamets α, who is accompanied by Culber α (Wilson Cruz). He waves off her polite apology and reaches into Burnham's personal space to draw her into a tight hug: 'Why would you apologize for a random act of physical interaction? These are the moments that make life so gloriously unpredictable' (1x07). Said glorious unpredictability will, of course, soon be lost to the time loop. Stamets α proceeds to cross over more social boundaries: He mentions Tyler's experience as a victim of prolonged torture and highlights the tension he notices between him and Burnham. His personality change is a well-known fact among his co-workers, but Culber α's apologetic remark about his partner being 'different' further underlines this point (1x07). Burnham α likely tolerates the unfamiliar physical affection as a side-effect of Stamets' link to the spore drive.

On the bridge, the gormagander – gormagander α, just to be thorough with the labelling – is identified and established as an obvious projection for Burnham's personal struggles: 'They spend their lives feeding on alpha particles in solar winds. They're often so consumed by this task that they ignore all other instincts. Including reproduction' (1x07). A disinterested Lorca α allows Burnham α to take charge, and she heads down to the cargo bay as the animal is beamed in. As mentioned above, Burnham not only feels safer in professional settings, it also enables her to display emotions she would otherwise not be comfortable with. In the prior episode 'Lethe' (1x06) we see her acting as Tilly's training partner and mentor, a role that allows her to openly show care and affection, using parameters like breakfast nutrition. When later requesting Tilly to accompany her on the mission to save Sarek (James Frain), she admits to Lorca that, in addition to Tilly's competence, she also needs the younger woman's 'moral support' (1x06). Similarly, feeling safe in her position of a scientist examining a wounded animal, Burnham α now displays empathy for the gormagander ('she is all alone'), tenderly calling the space whale a 'sweet girl' (1x07).

Mudd α emerges from inside gormagander α and proceeds to shoot his way through the ship. Being confronted by Lorca α over the comm system, he readily lays out his plans to steal and sell the *Discovery* and, additionally, to kill Lorca 'as many times as possible' (1x07). Mudd α does not hesitate to detonate the ship from the inside, killing himself in the process as well. In this case he uses an explosive device he has brought with him, but in later iterations he prefers using the *Discovery*'s own systems against her: 'There are so many ways to blow up this ship. It's almost a design flaw' (1x07). The explosion marks the end of loop α.

An exterior shot of the undamaged *Discovery*, zooming in on the windows of the room housing the party, and the refrain of the now subtext-laden 'We Trying to Stay Alive' establish that time has been reset. This is the second loop we see, but the narrative has skipped an untold number of iterations in between, likely dozens. I somewhat arbitrarily assign this loop the number π. Mudd π has made significant headway in taking over the ship's systems and narrowed the *Discovery*'s secret down to Stamets' lab, where he is able to activate the spore drive, but cannot use it. Stamets π meanwhile has yet to find 'a win for the home team' (1x07) and is increasingly frustrated. He has, however, succeeded in keeping Mudd's attention away from himself as both co-looper and the crucial component missing from the spore drive. Loop π begins with the same party conversations we have seen before, but, as a visual nod to 'Cause and Effect,' they are shot from different angles. The first visible deviation from loop α occurs when, instead of colliding with Burnham π and Tyler π in front of the elevator, Stamets π catches up to them moments later, alone. His frantic warnings are collectively dismissed as part of his condition and he is quickly dragged off by an approaching Culber π, but not before mentioning the gormagander. This strange premonition causes the next point of divergence: An alarmed Tyler π accompanies Burnham π down to the cargo bay and gormagander π. Mudd π meanwhile has gained enough information on and control over the ship to simply beam into Stamets' lab, where he activates the spore drive. When Lorca π orders the nearby Tyler π to the scene, he and Burnham π confront him together. Here Stamets π, who has been hiding in the background, and proceeds to shoot Mudd π from behind, learns the crucial information about Tyler's shared past with the invader, finally gaining an angle to work with.

It is unclear how many returns pass between loop π and the next one we see. Apparently, Stamets does try to approach Tyler himself (unfortunately, there is no montage sequence of those attempts), but between Stamets' compromised credibility and the lack of prior contact between the two men, he seems to have been unsuccessful. Stamets thus has to borrow another person's personal connection with Tyler to get him to talk, and Lorca is not a good option, for multiple reasons. This only leaves Burnham, whose 'deal' with Tyler he has picked up on in loop α (1x07). The next loop shows Stamets chasing her down to acquire her help. This is the fourth-to-last iteration, loop Φ in my classification. Stamets Φ catches up to Burnham Φ on her way down to the gormagander and spends most of the remaining time convincing her of his coherence, the direness of the situation, and the need for her to retrieve the information from Tyler.

He does get Burnham Φ to believe him, but loop Φ is almost over, so the weight of acting has to be shifted to the next loop (χ). Knowing that Stamets χ cannot repeat the lengthy explanation process with Burnham χ again, he asks for a piece of information to carry over the result of their conversation – his credibility – into the next loop: 'Something that will immediately prove to you we've had this conversation. Something you've never admitted to anyone' (1x07). Meanwhile, Mudd Φ has also changed tactics. He lures Lorca Φ from the bridge to get access to his 'man cave' (1x07), hoping to find the missing information to the spore drive there. Under Mudd's growing corruption of the *Discovery*, the safe environment of the ship has turned against its inhabitants. He can determine their location on – or in Lorca's case, off – the ship, fake communications, and invalidate the crew members' commands, therefore negating their very purpose on board. The montage of him killing Lorca showcases his increasing mastery over the systems. While only using a phaser in the beginning, at the end he is able to beam the captain into open space with only a handwave.

With the shortcut provided by Stamets Φ, Stamets χ can skip the time-consuming task of getting Burnham χ to believe him, and he is able to narrow it down to a few sentences:

> We've been caught in a 30-minute time loop, and I'm the only one who realizes it. I have witnessed you and Lorca and Tyler die at the hands of a criminal named Harry Mudd, who is trying to take over our ship. I need to know you believe me, because if I have to explain this again, I'm gonna throw myself out an air lock. (1x07)

While Burnham χ is quickly convinced and goes to talk to Tyler χ, Stamets χ's added assurance of Tyler reciprocating her interest causes her to freeze: 'I had one chance to fix all this and I blew it' (1x07), she states miserably. Stamets χ doesn't disagree, and he shifts the focus to preparing the next iteration, collecting intel for Stamets ψ. Since any coaching he provides Burnham cannot exceed the 30-minute window, he can hardly teach her anything new: 'I need to see what I'm working with' (1x07). Picking up on Burnham's preference for professional settings, he asks her to dance with him 'for science' (1x07), essentially mixing the private and the professional. They settle on the strategy of honesty, since Stamets knows it to be key for a relationship and Burnham already possesses this trait: 'I'm good at honesty' (1x07). This is not something she has to learn within the very narrow time frame. Being very honest with each other as well, Burnham χ and Stamets χ grow closer emotionally during the scene. Notably, their hands stay linked as the ship explodes around them, restarting time once again.

Loop ψ starts with Burnham ψ marching determinedly up to Tyler ψ and pulling him to the dance floor. Stamets ψ seems to have engaged in a bit of audio-environmental manipulation himself, as the soundtrack of the party changes from Wyclef Jean to a song suitable for slow dancing, Al Green's 'Love and Happiness' (1972). This further positions Stamets as Mudd's moral counterpoint: While he also takes control of the environment and uses the loop-acquired knowledge to further his own plans, Stamets does so in order to save the whole ship and, additionally, to play matchmaker for a pair of lonely and traumatized colleagues. His mission is one of love and salvation. Mudd on the other hand not only uses the ship's systems to repeatedly and sadistically destroy it, he also does so while hiding from his own familial obligations. As the reunion with his wife shows, Stella (Katherine Barrell) – in her own, forceful way – offers Mudd the very thing Stamets underlines as the key for a successful relationship: unconditional love without the need to 'hide who you are' (1x07). This is something Stamets has found with Culber and which Burnham also longs for. Yet Mudd is trying to escape from it.

Following Stamets' word of advice regarding honesty, Burnham ψ forgoes small talk and summarizes the threat presented by Mudd, ending with an admission of her interest in him. Tyler ψ believes her and, while he echoes Stamets' (π) earlier statement of the situation being 'weird,' he also quickly hones in to the fact that within the space provided by the time loop, all the normal repercussions of actions are somewhat suspended, and initiates a kiss: 'If time really is repeating, this won't matter' (1x07). This proves incorrect, since Stamets ψ witnesses the scene and Stamets ω makes sure to carry this particular information out of the loop. At the end of the episode, Tyler both negates and confirms the reality of the timelines contained within the lost loops, as he tells Burnham: 'I'm just sad we missed our first kiss' (1x07). Their intimate moment in loop ψ is interrupted by the comm ordering them to the bridge. In a reversal of earlier loops, the report to duty is now an unwelcome interruption, and Burnham ψ actively pulls Tyler back when he tries to draw away: 'Please, ignore it. We have to' (1x07). They continue dancing as Tyler ψ recalls the tales Mudd has shared during their shared captivity.

Intermixed with this, Mudd ψ is shown deftly evading the crew's walking patterns with the surety of a player navigating a well-known level of a computer game. The hints provided by Tyler allow Burnham ψ to identify the likely source of Mudd's technology as a 'time crystal' (1x07). Meanwhile on the bridge, as Lorca ψ wonders aloud about his missing personnel, the arrival of Mudd ψ is heralded by loud opera music (Richard Wagner's *Lohengrin* (1850)) over the comm. 'Captain Mudd' has complete control over the environment now, and the crew finds itself locked out of the systems. Notably, Mudd ψ spares Lorca's life here, as does Mudd ω in the last loop. It seems that for Mudd, the repeated murder of Lorca is a part of the suspended space within the time loops. He even expresses first signs of fatigue: 'I never thought I would say this, but I'm actually tired of gloating' (1x07). With victory in his sights and, therefore, the high probability of the current iteration being the last and permanent one, he takes steps to ensure Lorca's survival, probably to prolong his suffering by forcing him to reenter Klingon captivity. When Stamets ψ, Burnham ψ and Tyler ψ interrupt

Mudd ψ threatening the crew for the missing information, he kills his former cellmate. This proves too much for Stamets ψ: 'I can't watch you kill any more people' (1x07). He reveals himself as part of the spore drive, ending Mudd's quest. He does this either in confidence that Burnham ψ will find a solution or, more likely, because he has reached his limit.

It is important to remember here that Stamets is not just imprisoned in a time loop, but in a traumatic experience, witnessing the safe space of the *Discovery* violated and his partner Dr. Culber, their colleagues, and himself being killed over and over. Much of the traumatic aspect that often colors time loop narratives resides in the complete lack of consequences outside of the psychological. If no cause has a permanent effect in the physical world, the most damaging, unforgivable actions can be repeated infinitely, damaging the mind while leaving the body intact. This allows a much higher concentration of traumatic experiences. For most of the loops, Stamets has no strategy but to keep himself to the background, enduring the repeated murders without the ability to intervene. After he shoots Mudd in loop π in his lab, he walks up to Burnham π and Tyler π, searching physical closeness, but turns his back on them as the ship explodes, not wanting to see them die.

As far as temporality is concerned, traumatic memory and the time loop narrative have some structural similarities. The involuntary reliving of a painful memory and the inability to move on is symptomatic of trauma. As such, the traumatic experience tends to undercut the spatial and temporal structures of human memory (Luckhurst, 1998, 44–46). In fact, 'one of the most estranging aspects of trauma is its impact on the subjective experience of time, both during the moment of wounding and afterward' (Chu, 2010, 174). Through the use of narrative devices such as time travel, science fiction (and fantasy) narratives can provide a 'literalization of trauma's atemporality' (Chu, 2010, 176), packaging the cognitive mechanics associated with PTSD, for instance, into the metaphor of a time loop prison. For Stamets, escaping the trauma can only be achieved by ending the time loop. And the only way he can get Mudd to do this is to give himself up.

Incidentally, time travel as the central theme of *Discovery*'s second season is also closely connected to trauma. As a season-framing arc, the appearances of the Red Angel turn out to be part of a (singular) loop that Burnham ultimately has to close herself. The imprisoning and, even more salient, the traumatizing quality of time is especially evident in the story of Dr. Gabrielle Burnham (Sonja Sohn). No matter how many temporal jumps Michael's mother attempts, she will always be dragged forward into the desolate future, separated from her own time and her family. As she warns her daughter: 'People think time is fragile. Precious. Beautiful. Sand in an hourglass, all that. But it's not. Time is savage. It always wins' (2x11, 'Perpetual Infinity').

Between Burnham, Tyler and Stamets, the information gathered in ψ is enough for the crew to devise a strategy to defeat Mudd, but it only becomes viable in the next loop. Also, while Tyler ψ is dead, Burnham ψ is very aware that he will only 'really be dead' if the current loop is the final one. Since Mudd has gotten everything he wants out of the current iteration, Burnham ψ must now change his priorities to something he will be unable to carry out of loop ψ. Therefore, she provides him with lucrative information and makes sure he can only act on it in yet another reset. Revealing her identity and successfully establishing herself as the (in terms of monetary reward by the Klingons) most valuable part of the *Discovery*, Burnham ψ quickly kills herself, forcing an annoyed (but not worried) Mudd ψ to reset the time loop one last time, initiating loop ω (1x07). Being the last loop, this is the timeline that everyone on the *Discovery* will remember.

While a yawning Mudd ω once again goes through the motions of infiltrating the ship, the critical knowledge about his intrusion is quickly spread among the crew. When Mudd ω arrives on the bridge, the space has lost its predictability: they are already expecting him. Through the whole episode, Mudd underlines his position of superiority by addressing the crew members as 'kiddies,' or mockingly using nicknames like 'Gabe' (Lorca) or 'Petunia' (Burnham) (1x07). Realizing he has had a stowaway, he similarly now scolds Stamets ω like a misbehaving student: 'You. Hmm. You've been cheating. Passing notes in class to save your friends' (1x07). Signaling the reversal of Mudd's fortunes, Tyler will later address him as 'Harry' and his wife Stella drags him away as a 'naughty boy' (1x07). When he enters the bridge for the last time, however, he is still feeling secure in the reset power of the time crystal: 'Well, whatever you think you've come up with, I'll find a workaround. I'll keep resetting time until I do' (1x07). But Mudd claiming dominion over the *Discovery* includes a division of the space into important and unimportant, critical and non-critical parts. In a space where one knows exactly what move to make and what to pay attention to, the looper equally knows what to ignore. Anticipating this, the crew uses the 'non-critical' systems to falsify the signal Mudd ω uses the hail the waiting Klingons. In a reversal of Mudd Φ calling Lorca Φ away from the bridge with a false message from Culber, Mudd ω now falls victim to a similar trick. With the crew seemingly surrendered and the Klingons on their way, he ends the time loop, giving up his ability to reset. The ship enters normal time and, with it, the moment for the crew of the *Discovery* to gloat.

Without the device, Mudd has to face the consequences for his actions; he can no longer prevent the effects of the causes his actions yield.[2] As Burnham smugly tells him: 'Now you don't have your time crystal, you can't learn from this mistake' (1x07).

As we have seen, the space created by the time loop presents a unique narrative. The characters within the loop have to navigate through a space where the normal rules governing not just temporality, but human interaction and experiences, have been twisted to a partly traumatizing degree. With the way Mudd uses the looping device, each loop is aimed at the securing of information for the next – the space loses its independent value, but also offers whole new possibilities to learn.

Learning is central for both those trapped in a time loop prison as well as those following a time loop quest. A way to end the loop is always connected to the knowledge the unique temporal space allows the looper to learn. Whatever the looper finds out will ultimately be responsible to break the spell, find the hidden door, trick the villain, escape the temporal distortion. Mudd's quest is centered on the knowledge he gains about the *Discovery*'s systems and the movements of her crew. The more he knows, the greater his power over the space and the possibilities to twist it to suit his own needs. As the one controlling the loop, Mudd can hit replay any time he wants, but he still needs to reach a certain goal before he is willing to end it.

Trapped in a time loop prison meanwhile, Stamets not only needs to find a way to end the loops, but also to make sure to alter Mudd's desired outcome. And this necessitates gaining critical knowledge about Mudd himself. This creates a sub-quest for Burnham, who has to overcome her social insecurity to approach Tyler as the person most intimately connected to the intruder. Human connection proves to be a critical point not only for Stamets and Burnham, and Burnham and Tyler, but also for Mudd himself. Unaware of his temporal stowaway, Mugdd carelessly exposes his plans, strategies and private information. He becomes predictable himself, allowing the crew to collect the information necessary to defeat him and carry it over to the final loop. The prison doors are opened.

---

[2] While Starfleet seems keen to keep the whole matter from being publicly known, in the *Short Trek* 'The Escape Artist' (2019) it is revealed that the charge of 'penetrating a space whale' has somehow found its way onto the official records pertaining to Mudd.

Works Cited

Seo-Young Chu, *Do Metaphors Dream of Literal Sleep? A Science-Fictional Theory of Representation* (Cambridge, MA: Harvard University Press, 2010).

Julia Eckel, 'Twisted Times. Non-Linearity and Temporal Disorientation in Contemporary Cinema', in Julia Eckel (ed.) *(Dis)Orienting Media and Narrative Mazes* (Bielefeld: Transcript, 2013): 275–91.

James Gleick, *Time Travel. A History* (New York: Pantheon, 2016).

Edward Gross and Mark A. Altman, *Captains' Logs. The Unauthorized Complete Trek Voyages* (London: Little, Brown, 1995).

Martin Hermann, 'Goes Computer Game: Narrative Remediation in the Time-Loop Quests *Groundhog Day* and *12:01*', in Jan Alber (ed.) *Unnatural Narratives – Unnatural Narratology* (Berlin and Boston, MA: De Gruyter, 2011): 145–61.

Roger Luckhurst, 'The Science-Fictionalization of Trauma: Remarks on Narratives of Alien Abduction', *Science Fiction Studies,* 25.1 (1998): 20–52.

Marie-Laure Ryan, 'Temporal Paradoxes in Narrative', *style,* 43.2 (2009): 142–64.

Kristin Thompson, *Storytelling in the New Hollywood: Understanding Classical Narrative Technique* (Cambridge, MA: Harvard University Press, 1999).

Star Trek Episodes Cited

'Cause and Effect.' *Star Trek: The Next Generation*, written by Brannon Braga, directed by Jonathan Frakes, Paramount Television, 21 March, 1992.

'The Butcher's Knife Cares Not for the Lamb's Cry.' *Star Trek: Discovery*, written by Jesse Alexander and Aron Eli Coleite, directed by Olatunde Osunsanmi, CBS Television Studios, 8 October, 2017.

'Lethe.' *Star Trek: Discovery*, written by Joe Menosky and Alex Kurtzman, directed by Douglas Aarniokoski, CBS Television Studios, 22 October, 2017.

'Magic to Make the Sanest Man Go Mad.' *Star Trek: Discovery*, written by Aron Eli Coleite and Jesse Alexander, directed by David M. Barrett, CBS Television Sutdios, 29 October, 2017.

'Si Vis Pacem, Para Bellum.' *Star Trek: Discovery*, written by Kirsten Beyer, directed by John Scott, CBS Television Studios, 6 November, 2017.

'The Escape Artist.' *Star Trek: Short Treks*, written by Michael McMahan, directed by Rainn Wilson, CBS Television Studios, 3 January, 2019.

'Perpetual Infinity.' *Star Trek: Discovery*, written by Alan McElroy and Brandon Schultz, directed by Maja Vrvilo, CBS Television Studios, 28 March, 2019.

Notable Time Loop Episodes in Television Shows Not Named *Star Trek* Cited

"Twas the Night Before Mxymas.' *Lois & Clark: The New Adventures of Superman*, written by Tim Minear, directed by Michael Vejar, December 3rd Productions, Gangbuster Films Inc., Roundelay Productions, and Warner Bros. Television, 8 May, 1998.

'Been There, Done That.' *Xena: Warrior Princess*, written by Hilary J. Bader, directed by Andrew Merrifield, Renaissance Pictures and MCA TV, 15 November, 1998.

'Déjà Vu All Over Again.' *Charmed*, written by Constance M. Burge and Brad Kern, directed by Les Sheldon, Spelling Television, 3 October, 1999.

'Monday.' X-*Files*, written by Vince Gilligan and John Shiban, directed by Kim Manners, Ten Thirteen Productions, 20th Television (1993–1995), and 20th Century Fox Television (1995–2002, 2016–2018), 27 December, 1999.

'Back and Back and Back to the Future.' *Farscape*, written by Babs Greyhosky, directed by Rowan Woods, The Jim Henson Company, Nine Films and Television, and Hallmark Entertainment, 26 September, 2000.

'Window of Opportunity.' *Stargate SG-1*, written by Joseph Mallozzi and Paul Mullie, directed by Peter DeLuise, MGM Television, Double Secret Productions, Gekko Film Corp. (1997–2005), Sony Pictures Television (2005–2006), 4 July, 2001.

'Life Serial.' *Buffy the Vampire Slayer*, written by David Fury and Jane Espenson, directed by Nick Marck, Mutant Enemy Productions, Sandollar Television, Kuzui Enterprises, 20th Century Fox Television, 9 October, 2002.

'International Date Line.' *The Suite Life on Deck*, written by Jeny Quine and Dan Signer, directed by Ellen Gittelsohn, It's a Laugh Productions, 24 October, 2008.

'Mystery Spot.' *Supernatural*, Season 3, Episode 11, written by Jeremy Carver, directed by Kim Manners, Kripke Enterprises, Wonderland Sound and Vision (2005–2013), and Warner Bros. Television, 9 March, 2009.

'I Do Over.' *Eureka*, written by Thania St. John, directed by Matt Earl Beesley, Universal Cable Productions (2008–2012), Universal Media Studios (2007–2008), and NBC Universal Television Studio (2006–2007), 27 July, 2009.

'Audrey Parker's Day Off.' *Haven*, written by Nora Zuckerman and Lilla Zuckerman, directed by Fred Gerber, Big Motion Pictures Productions, Entertainment One Television, Piller/Segan/Shepherd, Universal Networks International, Canwest Global (2010), and Shaw Media (2011–2015), 15 December, 2011.

'…And the Point of Salvation.' *The Librarians*, written by Jeremy Bernstein, directed by Jonathan Frakes, Kung Fu Monkey Productions and Electric Entertainment, 13 December, 2015.

'Lullaby.' *12 Monkeys*, written by Sean Tretta, directed by Steven A. Adelson, Division Street (season 3–4), Atlast Entertainment, and Universal Cable Productions, 6 June, 2016.

'The Lotus Eaters.' *Cloak & Dagger*, written by Joe Pokaski and Peter Calloway, directed by Paul A. Edwards, Wadnering Rocks Production, ABC Signature Studios, and Marvel Television, 13 July, 2018.

Discovery and the Form of Victorian Periodicals

Will Tattersdill

The most successful character in episode 7 of *Discovery* is the one who has seen it already, many times.

'Don't you see what's happening?,' Paul Stamets (Anthony Rapp) asks, 'we have been here before – all of us' ('Magic to Make the Sanest Man Go Mad,' 1x07). Alone among the crew, Stamets has been connected to the mycelial network and, in consequence, only he can tell that his ship is caught in a temporal loop, the same 30 minutes repeating themselves over and over again. When he puts his emphasis on 'all of us,' though, Stamets makes clear that he is not referring only to the crew of the *Discovery*. *Star Trek* aficionados will immediately recall 'Cause and Effect' (5x18) the 1992 episode of *The Next Generation* (*TNG*; 1987–1994) in which the *Enterprise*'s Dr. Crusher (Gates McFadden) negotiates an almost identical situation, and they may recall, too, *Voyager*'s (1999–2001) riff on that theme in 'Coda' (1997, 3x15). Those with broader palates will remember the *Stargate SG-1* episode 'Window of Opportunity' (2000), the *X-Files* episode 'Monday' (1999, 6x14), or the *Fringe* episode 'White Tulip' (2010, 2x18). There are so many other examples of this phenomenon that it has been given a name – the 'Groundhog Day episode' after the Bill Murray film which, as Trekkies never tire of mentioning, postdates 'Cause and Effect' by several months – and a lengthy page on *TV Tropes* ('"*Groundhog Day*" Loop,' 2018). 'All of us' have indeed been here before: watching our favorite characters negotiate time loops, over and over again, is a staple component of the experience of SFF television, one beginning to be discernible at the time of writing even in 'capital-L' literature outside the genre (see, for instance, Atkinson, 2013).

It is suggestive that *Discovery*'s groundhog 'day' is a mere '30-odd' minutes in length. The loop in 'Cause and Effect' is long enough to include a poker game, the night after it, and a meeting the next morning; in 'Window of Opportunity' it is stated that the loop lasts ten hours.

Discovery's shorter interval accelerates the familiar situation to a degree that, if we may use the phrase in such a context, strains credibility: Stamets must work on his solution with a crew who not only forget the problem every half-hour but need to be convinced of its existence from scratch.[1] From a scriptwriter's perspective, though, the acceleration is justifiable, even necessary, because the audience is used to it by now. Stamets is successful not only because of the Starfleet proclivity for trust and teamwork but also because he is, as we are, an experienced reader of the Groundhog Day episode.

Consider Mudd (Rainn Wilson), the villain of the episode and operator of the time loop device, disparagingly calling the minor character Bryce (Ronnie Rowe Jr.) 'random communications officer man' during one of his tirades. When this episode aired, Bryce had not yet been named – he is listed in the end credits as 'Comm Officer #2.' To be outside the time loop is to be in on the joke: Mudd's tone here is not that of *Star Trek* but exactly that of the fan paratexts that surround it (Mudd utters his insult while pointing a weapon at Bryce, reminding him of his own 'redshirt' status, his narrative dispensability). The more independent a character is of the flow of repeating time, the more their condition approaches that of the primary-world viewer. Stamets, too, evinces this tendency in the scene where he wearily convinces Burnham (Sonequa Martin-Green) of their plight by matching her apparently extemporized dialogue word for word, inflection for inflection. It is the action of a frustrated colleague in a desperate and unusual situation, but it is also the action of one fan demonstrating rote proficiency in a show in order to convince another of their ardor: I know the words of the episode off by heart; I, too, am part of your community. From their position above and beyond on-screen deaths, Mudd and Stamets bear not only the show's self-reflexivity but that of its audience.

It is this self-reflexivity, at least in part, that permits the episode's accelerated pace. In 'Cause and Effect,' we can identify the moment where the characters meaningfully come to terms with the problem at around 26 minutes; in 'Magic to Make the Sanest Man Go Mad' the equivalent moment is at around 17 minutes.[2] Two things in particular

---

[1] For an exploration of 'Magic to Make the Sanest Man Go Mad' as a time loop episode, see Sarah Böhlau's essay '"Lorca, I'm Really Gonna Miss Killing You" – the Fictional Space Created by Time Loop Narratives' in this volume.

[2] Exactly how you define 'meaningfully come to terms' in this context will, of course, move these times around slightly. Fastidious readers will hopefully take my general point that the *Discovery* episode proceeds at a

account for *Discovery*'s acceleration: firstly, the characters do not require the *Enterprise* crew's lengthy process of coming to terms with the idea that they might be in a loop (we see this in Stamets' ability repeatedly to convince and organize them in half-hour intervals); and, secondly, neither does the audience, trained in the genre by 25 years of Groundhog Day episodes (we see this in the writers' decision to show us only a couple of instances of Stamets convincing or organizing somebody, relying on our ability to infer their continuing and repeated presence). The first of these things is true because the second is true. 'Magic to Make the Sanest Man Go Mad' is a time loop but, unlike 'Cause and Effect,' it is not *about* time loops – it builds character relationships and plotlines from earlier in the season and gently furthers the overall arc of the season. It is able to do this because of the groundwork laid by the *TNG* episode and its successors.

Still, though, it is striking that going into the mid-point of its first season (episode 7 of 15), *Discovery* offers us its only episode with a reasonably self-contained plot, its only episode that can intelligibly be watched out of sequence ('I think the time loop episode is the only one that kind of works on its own,' wrote *io9* (Trendacosta, 2018)). This episode is about a group of people who are experiencing time in short chunks they are unable to remember or to relate to each other – more, it is about the power (for good or ill) of the people able to see beyond the immediate moments they are stuck in and order them as part of a bigger story. Even without the constant and temporally complex shadow of 'Cause and Effect' – both the episode's precedent and (in universe) its distant successor – the commentary on the changing experience of watching *Star Trek* is unmissable.

***

It is a commonplace throughout this essay collection that *Discovery* is both like and unlike previous iterations of *Star Trek*. The first television series in the franchise since *Enterprise* (2001–2005), it also faces the unusual challenge of competing with the alternative visions of *The Original Series* (1966–1969) represented by the Kelvin timeline movies (2009–present) and *The Orville* (2017–ongoing). Combining more than a

---

faster pace – especially given that the first few minutes of 'Magic to Make the Sanest Man Go Mad' are not in the loop, which seems to start at around 4 minutes, while the *TNG* episode begins at the end of a loop that is already happening.

decade of hindsight with a spread of simultaneous reinterpretations, the current moment provides the most visibly thorough working through of the franchise's history and potential since at least the release of *Galaxy Quest* (1999). Against this background, it is not surprising to find that *Discovery* conducts a discussion with its fans about where the true heart of *Star Trek* is to be found. It does this quite openly – never more so than in the liturgical repetition of the phrase 'We are Starfleet' during the season one finale (1x15, 'Will You Take My Hand') – but its perorations on the subject more often feel like icebreakers than like lectures. In other words, *Discovery* wants its viewers to think actively about what *Star Trek* is for, perhaps even about what science fiction is for. It has an answer in mind, but it is sincere engagement with the question, rather than blind agreement, that the show is seeking.

My approach in this chapter is to try and substantiate this claim solely via a discussion of form – in particular, *serial* form – examining the history behind *Discovery*'s episodic structure and suggesting that the show engages with that history very openly and very deliberately. My attention to seriality is informed by my research background in late-Victorian periodicals, and a secondary aim of this chapter is to convince you that the relationship between nineteenth century magazines and twenty-first century sci-fi TV is a little closer than might at first be presumed. Principally, though, my purpose is to articulate the conversation that *Discovery* initiates with its predecessors and with its readers via its form. It is a conversation, I argue, that materially changes the *Star Trek* universe: worldbuilding may be most obviously discernible in plots, settings, and backstories, but the way we are asked to see those details – and, particularly here, the *rhythm* in which we are asked to see them – has every bit as great a role.

From here, the chapter proceeds in four more sections. I first discuss the critical conversation around Victorian serials and television, arguing that science fiction in general and *Star Trek* in particular could profitably be added to these exchanges. I then outline the distinction between the 'serial' and the 'series,' and the possibility for reading twenty-first century television that those terms offer us. After that, I examine the awkward ways in which *Discovery* does and does not conform to those terms, suggesting a third analogue in the writings of H.G. Wells. Finally, I focus on the most important aspect of periodical publishing – the gap *between* episodes – in an effort to understand some of the dissatisfied responses to *Discovery* (and the show's own conflicted formal attitude).

In the 12-year lacuna that separated the end of *Enterprise* from the beginning of *Discovery*, the organization of the television industry underwent considerable disruption – the emergence of 'prestige TV,' the rise of Netflix, and the transformation of YouTube from 'video-sharing site' into 'network TV alternative' are only the headlines.[3] Interlaced changes in everything from casting to advertising and distribution have left their mark on the way stories are told on television, although the shift has not been total and numerous older practices continue undiminished. One of the more obscure consequences of this shift in television's topography has been a heightened awareness among academic Victorianists to what Caroline Levine calls 'the new serial television' and Michael Z. Newman calls the 'Prime Time Serial (PTS)' (Levine, 2013, para. 3; Newman, 2006, 17). The notion is that placing these shows – the most frequently cited examples are *The Wire* (2002–2008) and *Mad Men* (2007–2015) – alongside Victorian novels such as *Bleak House* (1852–1853) and *Middlemarch* (1871–1872) allows us to think about previously unnoticed similarities between the two historical periods, the ahistorical continuities of literary form, or both. In the case of *The Wire*, Levine's favorite example, the large cast of interconnected yet socially divergent characters, the embedded pleas for social and judicial reform, and the journalistic background of the creator, David Simon (to say nothing of an actual mention of Dickens in an episode title), do indeed render a comparison with *Bleak House* persuasive.[4]

Levine makes it clear that the goal is not simply to understand contemporary television as the 'descendent' of the Victorian serial but rather to view both texts 'as responding to comparable social environments' (Levine, 2013, para. 4). All the same, the discussion runs the risk of appearing to be an exercise in canon formation, an attempt, in Jason Mittell's words, to 'legitimize and validate the demeaned television medium by linking it to the highbrow cultural sphere of literature' (2011). Levine has herself acknowledged this difficulty,[5] but it

---

[3] These changes are discussed at book length in Lotz, 2014.
[4] Levine's full treatment of *The Wire* is in Levine 2015: chapter 5.
[5] '[Mittell] worries that what is motivating the comparison between television and fiction is a matter of status: we want the new work to acquire the cachet of the older, more respected one. In a shameful bid for social distinction, we push for *The Wire* to be ranked among high-class works of art. ... Thus it is my hypothesis that on political and social grounds it is more important to set two particular examples side by side than to invite broad genre and media comparisons' (Levine, 2011).

does not help that her examples are universally drawn from the realm of capital-L literature – Dickens, Eliot, Charlotte Brontë. Most of the television shows involved in her analysis, too, as the moniker 'prestige TV' implies, are 'paradigmatic of a critical darling,' pulling in rapturous reviews but not necessarily achieving high Nielsen ratings (Mittell, 2011). The scholarly conversation has legitimized its unorthodox comparison of Victorian seriality and contemporary television by applying a marked small-c conservatism in its choice of examples.

It is not my intention to criticize this tendency: an article can only fight so many battles at once, arguments work best and travel farthest when readers are familiar with the primary texts, and *The Wire* and *Bleak House* are superb terrain on which to conduct exactly this kind of discussion (as the existence of this chapter hopefully suggests, I am also enthusiastic about any efforts made towards transhistorical analysis in the currently over-periodized world of literary criticism).[6] At the same time, and with the exception of *Lost* (2004–2010), science fiction's almost total absence from Levine's conversation seems to be worth pausing over. *The Wire* is an almost exact contemporary of Ronald D. Moore's reboot of *Battlestar Galactica* (2004–2009), a show that, despite its considerable differences from Simon's *magnum opus*, is every bit as amenable to a discussion about character networks, social reform, and the frustrations of the serial format. Something similar might be said of *Fringe* (2008–2013), *Heroes* (2006–2010), *The 4400* (2004–2007), or *Orphan Black* (2013–2017), for example.[7] It is hardly fair to blame Levine for the omission of the more recent shows that, since her work was published, have moved science fiction even closer to the heart of prestige television – *Westworld* (2016–), *Stranger Things* (2016–), *The O.A.* (2016–2019), *The Man in the High Castle* (2015–2019), and the numerous shows associated with the Marvel Cinematic Universe, for instance – but a discussion about the televised renewal of the Victorian 'serial' over the 'series' format that fails to mention *The X Files* (1993–2002), *Buffy the Vampire Slayer* (1997–2003), and *Star Trek: Deep Space Nine* (*DS9*; 1993–1999) – shows that paved the way for the storytelling format in which the PTS thrives – is certainly missing an important part of the picture.

---

[6] A superb example of the kind of transhistorical analysis I mean here, which has absolutely nothing to do with the subject under discussion, is Burge, 2016.

[7] I have kept my focus on North American science fiction TV here, but it needs saying that *Doctor Who* (1963–1989; 2005–) cries out for comparison with Victorian fiction – not least during its numerous episodes set in the Victorian period (eg. 'The Snowmen,' 2012; 'The Talons of Weng-Chiang,' 1977).

In other words, this discussion is owed some science fiction. Structurally, *Discovery* seems very much part of the new generation of high-budget 'prestige' content – but it is not entirely or comfortably so. To understand why, we first need to understand the formal point that distinguishes the shows mentioned in the above paragraph from their predecessors; we need to understand the difference between a 'serial' and a 'series.'

***

Another name surprisingly absent from the academic discussions around Victorian television has been that of Sherlock Holmes. Holmes is a Victorian indelibly present in today's television culture – Netflix has just, at the time of writing, announced yet another new adaptation (Carr, 2018) – but the *form* of Arthur Conan Doyle's original stories reverberates far more widely than even their famous protagonist. The crucial innovation was the 'series' format, which Conan Doyle explained this way in his autobiography:

> [I]t had struck me that a single character running through a series, if it only engaged the attention of the reader, would bind that reader to that particular magazine. On the other hand, it had long seemed to me that the ordinary serial might be an impediment rather than a help to a magazine, since, sooner or later, one missed one number and afterwards it had lost all interest. Clearly the ideal compromise was a character which carried through, and yet instalments which were each complete in themselves, so that the purchaser was always sure that he could relish the whole contents of the magazine. I believe that I was the first to realize this and 'The Strand Magazine' the first to put it into practice. (Conan Doyle, 2012, 95–96)

In fact, Conan Doyle's idea was not wholly unprecedented ('there is nothing new under the sun,' as Holmes remarks, himself quoting Ecclesiastes 1:9 (Conan Doyle, 1974, 40)), with Edgar Allan Poe's 1830s tales of C. Auguste Dupin often cited as an influence (including by Conan Doyle himself). Poe, though, wrote only three Dupin stories, published at uneven intervals in different periodicals.[8] The key to Holmes' formal

---

[8] 'The Murders in the Rue Morgue' appeared in the April 1841 edition of *Graham's Magazine*, 'The Mystery of Marie Rogêt' in the *Ladies' Companion*

(and therefore commercial) success was the alliance with the *Strand*, which assured readers of a different yet unrelated case in every issue and promised the return of familiar characters with none of the commitment of a Dickens-style serial.[9]

Keeping old readers in a periodical rhythm while also welcoming in new ones with no knowledge of prior happenings, the 'series' is vitally distinct from the Dickens model in not requiring the reader to hunt down back issues or the writer to incorporate recaps of long-ago plot points into later instalments. It also has the important effect, as Conan Doyle himself implies in the above quotation, of elevating character and situation over plot as the principle source of attraction for viewers; the formal shift in emphasis meaningfully alters the world of the story (a point to which I shall return). Though Conan Doyle developed it for print, the series model became central to twentieth century television: *TV Tropes* calls it 'Monster of the Week' ('[it] can be seen as the complete antithesis of a Story Arc'), and by the debut of *Star Trek* in 1966 it was one of the default modes of franchise storytelling, amenable not only to casual viewing but also to syndication, the environment for which *TNG* was produced in 1987 and in which it flourished ('Monster of the Week' 2018).[10] The stand-alone, watch-in-any-order episode, in other words, is what allowed *Star Trek* to build a fanbase and profitability that far exceeded its original four-year run and eventually permitted the creation of sequels.

By 1993, the year after *TNG* aired its time loop episode, Tudor Oltean felt able to write that '[a] series requires a different story which is concluded in each episode, while the serial is provided with continuous storylines – normally more than one – that continue each episode' (Oltean, 1993, 14). By adding that '[s]eries and serial are thus two different types of series,' though, Oltean tacitly indicates that the situation was already more complicated than this implied (14). Like many other shows, *TNG* had begun introducing two-part adventures and allowing character growth to take place across episodes and seasons. Even in Conan Doyle the 'pure' notion of the genuinely independent episode was doomed: Holmes' 'death' in 'The Final Problem' (December 1893) and return in 'The Empty House' (October 1903), for

between November 1842 and February 1843, and 'The Purloined Letter' in the *Gift* annual for 1845.
[9] For more on the form of the *Strand*, see Ashley, 2006, 196–97.
[10] *TNG* was produced on the basis of the original series' success in syndication (it had not done well on its first run) and was released straight into syndication rather than being broadcast on a network first (Teitelbaum, 1991).

instance, necessarily created a metanarrative, and it is hard to get much out of the latter story if you have not already read the former.[11] As the 1990s went on, *Star Trek* and other science fiction television became less and less comfortable with the monster of the week: *Buffy*'s model of the 'Big Bad' allowed discrete adventures to be linked together by a common adversary – a kind of compromise between series and serial – but by the end of its run in 2001 even *Buffy* was telling multipart, complex stories hard to decipher at the level of the episode. The last half-season of *DS9* (aired in 1999) is effectively a nine-part serial. This tendency across science fiction television became one of the hallmarks of the streaming revolution: 'if there is one thing within the media that is metamorphosing right before our eyes,' Veronica Innocenti and Guglielmo Pescatore noted by 2014, 'it is surely televized [sic] seriality.' '[M]any TV series,' they wrote, 'have moved increasingly closer to the structure of the serial.' The changes in viewing habits wrought by Netflix and others have removed the original impetus which drove Conan Doyle's innovation, since previous episodes which may be necessary for understanding the story are all available for streaming at any moment by anyone with the appropriate subscriptions (Innocenti and Pescatore, 2014, 1). Dickens, we might say, has won the battle: like *The Wire*, the majority of science fiction television today is now told in novel-style serials.

Is it this change that drives the interest in today's television from Victorianists? Levine, certainly, mentions the importance of distribution format for her comparison, albeit somewhat incidentally.[12] The point that I hope I have made here, though, is that if it really is the case that television has switched to a nineteenth century model of serialized storytelling, the model it switched *from* also has its roots in the pages of Victorian periodicals.

---

[11] Other examples of not-quite-independent Holmes stories: 'His Last Bow' (September 1917) contains almost no action and lacks nearly all of its affective punch without some knowledge of its precursors; 'The Adventure of Wisteria Lodge' (1908) was originally published as a two-part 'Reminiscence of Mr. Sherlock Holmes' separated by a month and the words '*To be concluded*' (Conan Doyle, 1908, 250). For considerably more on the metanarrative of Holmes in relation to its series format, see Saler, 2012, 95.

[12] 'Just as *The Wire* appeared first in regular instalments [sic] on television and then became available on DVDs for purchase or rental, *Bleak House* first appeared in nineteen monthly periodical parts, later to be available in bound volumes that could be bought or borrowed from circulating libraries' (Levine, 2011).

***

Although its episodes are difficult (or impossible) to understand out of sequence, there is an important way in which the serialized *Discovery* is not formally akin to Dickens. *Bleak House* depicts the intersection of numerous spheres of life and points of view, even alternating between third and first person in its enunciations of the complex social web that is London; *Discovery*, meanwhile, is pared back even by the standards of *Star Trek*, largely restricted to the point of view of a single character rather than maintaining, like its predecessors, focus on an ensemble cast. Although the temptation to read the show's idolization of the mycelial network as a quest for Dickensian interconnectedness is real, *Discovery* is ultimately too focused (and its attention to the spore drive too superficial) for the analogy to be convincing. In terms of pure length, *Discovery* is also far less of a 'sprawl' either than Dickens or earlier *Trek*: *Bleak House* is 67 chapters in 20 instalments (Miriam Margolyes' audiobook is 43 hours 12 minutes) while the 15 episodes of *Discovery*'s first season (roughly 11.5 hours) are dwarfed by the first season of *TNG* (roughly 19.5 hours; typical for a 1980s US television series). Since it is still running, *Discovery* always has the potential to get bigger in both senses, but season two is roughly the same length as season one and, if anything, even more single-minded in its focus on Burnham. At the time of writing, it seems fair to describe *Discovery* as less formally expansive than either the Holmes or Dickens models, so a third point of comparison with Victorian periodicity is therefore warranted.

Fortunately, a perfect candidate is available in one of science fiction's foundational texts. H.G. Wells' *The War of the Worlds* appeared in *Pearson's Magazine* between April and December 1897 and has exerted a consistently powerful influence on science fiction writing ever since. As a serial, it resembles *Bleak House* in being difficult to read out of sequence, but is unlike it in following a strictly linear progression – the progression, in fact, of the Martians from Horsell Common into the center of London, which can be (and has been) drawn as a dotted line on a map (see Wells, 2017, xxxvii). Though the narration is handed between brothers at some points, the text is very far from a Dickensian 'network,' relying for its effect on the unitary force of its plot and the subjective experiences of a very small number of characters. This is reflected not only in a shorter total length (around 60,000 words; *Bleak House* is around 350,000) but, more crucially, in a difference of composition: Wells wrote the entire novel in advance, paying scrupulous attention to geographical details, while Dickens composed his instalments as he went along (Parrinder, 1972, 6).

Wells did dabble in the Holmes-style series model (his *Stories of the Stone Age*, for example, appeared in *The Idler* between May and November 1897), but the preponderance of his short stories were stand-alone and all but one of his famous scientific romances of the 1890s were serialized in a similarly predetermined fashion to *War of the Worlds*.[13] Although *Pearson's* published small summaries of the previous action at the beginning of each instalment (analogous to 'previously, on...' montages common in television, including on *Discovery*), *War of the Worlds* was a text that knew where it was going and that made few concessions to any reader who could not keep up. *Pearson's* clearly saw this fact as a potential selling point, with one editorial from the middle of the run reminding audiences that '[t]his wonderful serial is becoming more and more exciting month by month' (Pearson, 1897, 344A). This is precisely the feature, however, that is at the root of Katharine Trendacosta's difficulty with *Discovery*:

> I watched last week's episode with a friend who hadn't seen any others. And the look on her face when I tried to explain everything she needed to know was unreal. There are very few episodes which wouldn't run into that problem. (2018)

Trendacosta's observation – that *Discovery* asks to be watched completely, attentively, and in order – presents as a 'problem' because it stands against the kind of casual viewing enabled by the monster of the week. What *Pearson's* saw as a virtue – repaying sustained audience attention – has, for Trendacosta, become a liability: casual attention is impossible.

There is another difficulty, though. *Discovery*'s episodes are indecipherable if watched out of order, but they are also sometimes abrasive if watched too closely together. For example, the first words of 'New Eden' (2x02) ('As a child, I had what my mother called nightmares') are a personal log of Spock's previously heard in the climactic scene of the previous episode – a quick recap for a viewer returning after a week, but a jarringly obvious moment of repetition for anybody moving directly from episode to episode. The clumsiness of this transition, which is invisibly smooth if the episodes are not watched in immediate succession,

---

[13] *The Time Machine* first appeared in the *New Review* (January–May 1895), *The Invisible Man* in *Pearson's Weekly* (12 June–7 August 1897), and *The First Men in the Moon* in the *Strand* (December 1900–August 1901). *The Island of Doctor Moreau* (1896) was never serialized. These, of course, are only the highlights: Wells's relationship with the periodical culture of his day was profound in scale and is documented at book length in Smith 2012.

introduces us to the final element in my argument. Having discussed the series and serial in terms of their differences, it is also important to consider the thing that unites them: the gap between instalments.

***

However discrete or connected, television episodes – up until recently – have shared one defining feature: the interval. In Oltean's words, television series:

> make it irresistibly clear that the specific feature of television experience is not exactly 'flow' but 'flow and regularity', and should be regarded in terms of movement and stasis. ... The relationship between movement (direct presentation of events, or enactment) and stasis (what happens in-between the episodes, interval of narrative non-belligerance [sic]) forms the fundamental dialectics of the serial paradigm. (Oltean, 1993, 13)

This is every bit as true for print serials of the nineteenth century as it is for twentieth century television, as Sean O'Sullivan notes when comparing the two – he calls this same phenomenon 'the gap,' or 'the between, ... the animating energy, the time and space separating publications that distinguishes serial fiction from every other form' (O'Sullivan, 2013, para. 14). It is in the gaps, and not the parts, that Dickens corresponds with readers about the construction of future numbers; it is between instalments that Holmes readers start having dinner parties and *The Original Series* (*TOS*) *Star Trek* fans begin writing fanfiction.[14] The suspense generated by these gaps is, as Levine has herself helped to point out (2003), one of the cornerstones of Victorian fiction.[15] Summing up the whole phenomenon, Innocenti and Pescatore (2014) write that:

> [w]hile the idea of trekkies [sic] once seemed like a folklore phenomenon, ultimately a little naive and marginal, today we are well aware that serial products are projected as inhabitable

---

[14] Respectively (and for instance) on these topics, see Dawson, 2016, 761–78 and Saler, 2012, 116–17.
[15] For my application of Levine's ideas around suspense to periodicals, see Tattersdill, 2016, 86–88.

environments, in which spectators/users can circulate, gather information, play and develop affective bonds. (12)

Crucially, the gap is the aspect of seriality that the *Netflix* revolution truly dispenses with, and what *Discovery* strives to preserve.

Since at least the American version of *House of Cards* (2013–2018), it has become increasingly normal for new shows to emerge onto streaming services an entire season at a time, allowing viewers to choose the pace at which they consume the serial instalments. Some binge-watch, a technique inherited from the DVD box set (although still with an analogue in Victorian print culture: buying the book edition after the serial ends). Others retain a kind of routine – an episode a day, say – or choose a more irregular pattern of consumption to fit their lifestyle (as you can with a book edition). *Discovery*, released on the new CBS *All Access* service in the United States and on Netflix in most other territories, has defied this trend by airing a new episode every week, just as Roddenberry's original series had in the 1960s. This is important: though it feels the epitome of the current mood in terms of its serial structure and narrative arc, *Discovery* is actually a little old-fashioned in cleaving to the 'movement and stasis' model shared by all of its *Trek* forebears. This exaggerates the independence of the episode as a unit of storytelling even while other aspects of the new television environment (not least *Netflix*'s 'Skip Credits' button) conspire to make it less visible. For people watching the show as it aired, the episode reemerges in another important way: group conversations about what was going to happen next were rife online, since everybody was on (or, rather, *off*) the same page.

The cultural consequences of this decision are evident in the episode-by-episode reviews of *Discovery* on *Den of Geek*, or the more honestly titled weekly 'recaps' on *Vulture* – the sense in these pieces is of having to keep up with (and lead) fan speculation around where the show might be going.[16] Such writings, though, represent only the most visible form of 'water-cooler' discussions that were happening among fans for the entirety of the run – discussions that on Netflix-model shows are now limited to developments between seasons. When you think about it, it is *Discovery*'s form, simultaneously restricting both the viewpoint and velocity of its audience, that allows it to have its major plot twists, just as it is its form that encourages viewers to discuss those twists both before and after they take place. One particularly good example of this is the show's creation of 'Javid Iqbal,' the actor credited with playing

---

[16] See, for example, Hunt, 2018; Ortberg, 2018.

Voq in the episodes before it was revealed that Ash Tyler (Shazad Latif) had been Voq all along. On one level, this shows the real-life deceptions that the show was willing to perpetuate on its fans in order to keep them surprised; on another, Latif's selection of 'Javid Iqbal' – his father's name – for the alias resulted in a furor of fan theorizing and speculation and suggests, more than a little, a code meant to be cracked (see Ling, 2017; Britt, 2018). What the show wanted was the conversation.

This returns us to my earlier insistence that episodic structure meaningfully alters the world of the story. The Voq twist is impossible in *TNG*'s format: there is a hint of it in, say, 'Conundrum' (5x14), but such things have to stay contained within individual episodes and our trust in the status quo can never waver. By *DS9*, this balance began to shift, as evidenced by the frighteningly uncertain number of fifth season (1996–1997) episodes during which Julian Bashir (Alexander Siddig) was, we later learn, replaced by an alien impostor. The kind of slow-building tension that ends in Georgiou's (Michelle Yeoh) return or Lorca's (Jason Isaacs) treason, though, goes further by leading the audience into the *expectation* of such reversals: the structure creates not only a more focused space but a more paranoid one, in which viewers watch every moment for clues and develop a critical eye for discrepancies (intentional or otherwise) in the narrative, then amplify their affect by poring over them with other fans in the gaps between episodes. If *Discovery* has a 'darker, more serious tone,' then, this is one of the reasons (Liptak, 2018). Its Federation feels bleaker than *TNG*'s not only because of superficial details of tone, plot, and characterization, but because of the relationship with the viewer that its serial structure creates. Form is itself a world-building technique, and changing the form of this franchise has changed the world of *Star Trek* every bit as much as the transformations in tone, continuity, costume, writing, effects, makeup, music, and so on.

As well as pointing out the relationship with worldbuilding, my discussion of form also explains some of the dissatisfaction with which *Discovery* was received. It is not just that the new tone is off-putting: it is also the case that, as O'Sullivan points out regarding *Bleak House* and *Lost*, satisfaction itself is 'antithetical to the structure and attractions of seriality as a practice' (O'Sullivan, 2013, para. 2). In a complete and isolated novel, like *War of the Worlds*, the plot travels smoothly towards an ending: the end of the narrative, the end of the Martian invasion. In a serial of indefinite length, though, we have 'flow and regularity' – we exist as readers in the rhythm of the publication, with conclusions continuously deferred into the future and resolution experienced as a kind of threat. The deliberate positioning of *Discovery* between these two stools – pre-planned enough for time-travel plotlines but open enough to leave each season on a cliffhanger; hemmed into time and continuity by its status as a prequel but potentially able to escape them with the right retconning and plot devices – is understandably frustrating for the viewer who just wants to watch 'an episode of something.' That *Discovery* itself feels this frustration is demonstrated, I think, by the existence of the *Short Treks*, interstitial stories defined precisely by (1) their independence from the periodical rhythm of the main series, and (2) their independence from each other at the level of plot – like *TOS* and *TNG* episodes, they can be watched in any order. No previous *Star Trek* series has felt the need to reinsert this older kind of storytelling between its seasons. By the end of *Discovery*'s second year, though, half of the *Short Treks* have already been retrospectively incorporated into the main plot (as have the characters and settings of a few early season two episodes, like 'New Eden,' 2x02 and 'The Sound of Thunder,' 2x06, which appeared relatively independent at first glance). 'Runaway,' in particular, is now all but required viewing if the season two finale is to make sense. *Discovery* cannot stop looking at the series format, but is always too interested in a serial relationship with its reader to seriously commit to it.

Nothing demonstrates this better than watching *Discovery*'s first season for the *second* time: with the gaps between episodes eliminated and the big twists already known, it is in this moment that we reconcile all the various hopes and worries that accompanied the drip-feed of episodes with the complete object created by the finale. Despite some jarring moments of superfluous recap, the show's hope and optimism comes through more strongly when it is experienced in this way – the removal of suspense is also a removal of the paranoia that is naturally a product of the show's hybrid format. In other words: despite the effort that it puts into surprises and twists, *Discovery* is a show that desperately wants *re*watching. Its weekly release encourages active discussion and speculation, an explosion of possibilities; its serial format requires us to return from these discussions to a unified, organized text, and then to learn to see it as such.

Formats are not chosen at random, and every show (and the world it offers) is shaped by the way it asks to be watched. *Discovery*, I have suggested here, wants us *aware* of that process, which is why it narrativizes it in 'Magic to Make the Sanest Man Go Mad.' The tension between the arc and the episode becomes the tension between Stamets and the rest of crew: unlike *TNG*'s characters in 'Cause and Effect,' who are all caught together in the episodic time loop and must realize the severity of their continually resetting status quo entirely from the inside,

Discovery includes a character who is able to transcend the individual, half-hour episodes the rest of his crew is trapped in and commend to them a larger, more worked-through 'serial' universe. 'Don't you see what's happening?', he shouts. 'We have been here before ... I cannot be the only person who recognizes this' (1x07).

***

An incidental second in the same episode has become one of my favorite moments in *Discovery*. It happens just under 19 minutes in: Lorca gets summoned from the bridge, apparently by Culber (Wilson Cruz), and steps into the turbolift. The instant before his journey is interrupted is one of the very few in which we see the captain by himself in the Prime Universe, without the need to dissemble. He does not mustache-twirl or cackle into the camera – that would ruin the coming surprise for first-time viewers. Rather, his actions resemble those of a somewhat beleaguered actor: he draws in his breath, adjusts his stance, gets ready for the next scene. It is a wonderful glimpse into the private life of somebody who has been acting every waking minute for the longest time. If you know what is coming, you can almost hear him bucking himself up, getting himself ready to spin the next lie, to carry out the next stage in his Byzantine plan. If you do not know, though, it is completely invisible, denuded of any of the cues of lighting, camera angle or music we are habituated to: just a tired guy standing in an elevator. For some, perhaps, the pause in *Discovery*'s relentless pace was long enough to constitute a clue, another in a series of little hints that would eventually grow into certainties. For the majority of viewers, though, it is only good the second time you see it. It's only good if you have been here before.

Works Cited

Mike Ashley, *The Age of the Storytellers: British Popular Fiction Magazines 1880–1950* (London: The British Library, 2006).
Kate Atkinson, *Life After Life* (London: Doubleday, 2013).
Ryan Britt, '"Star Trek: Discovery" Secret Voq Actor Finally Reveals Everything', *Inverse*, 14 January (2018), https://www.inverse.com/article/40200-shazad-latif-star-trek-discovery-ep-11-voq-tyler-spoilers.
Amy Burge, *Representing Difference in the Medieval and Modern Orientalist Romance* (Basingstoke: Palgrave Macmillan, 2016).

Flora Carr, 'Netflix Is Planning a New Sherlock Holmes Series Called The Irregulars', *Radio Times*, 20 December (2018), https://www.radiotimes.com/news/on-demand/2018-12-20/netflix-the-irregulars-sherlock-holmes/.

Arthur Conan Doyle, 'A Reminiscence of Mr. Sherlock Holmes: I. The Singular Experience of Mr. John Scott Eccles', *Strand Magazine*, 35.213 (1908): 242–50.

—— *A Study in Scarlet* (London: John Murray and Jonathan Cape, 1974).

—— *Memories and Adventures* (Cambridge: Cambridge University Press, 2012).

Gowan Dawson, 'Dickens, Dinosaurs, and Design', *Victorian Literature and Culture*, 44 (2016): 761–78.

'"Groundhog Day" Loop', *TV Tropes*, https://tvtropes.org/pmwiki/pmwiki.php/Main/GroundhogDayLoop.

James Hunt, 'Star Trek: Discovery Episode 15 Review: Will You Take My Hand?', *Den of Geek*, 13 February (2018), https://www.denofgeek.com/uk/tv/star-trek/55277/star-trek-discovery-episode-15-review-will-you-take-my-hand.

Veronica Innocenti and Guglielmo Pescatore, 'Changing Series: Narrative Models and the Role of the Viewer in Contemporary Television Seriality', translated by Dom Holdaway, *Between*, 8.4 (2014): 1–15.

Caroline Levine, *Forms: Whole, Rhythm, Hierarchy, Network* (Princeton, NJ: Princeton University Press, 2015).

—— 'From Genre to Form: A Response to Jason Mittell on The Wire', *Electronic Book Review*, 1 May (2011), http://electronicbookreview.com/essay/from-genre-to-form-a-response-to-jason-mittell-on-the-wire/.

—— *The Serious Pleasures of Suspense: Victorian Realism and Narrative Doubt* (Charlottesville: University of Virginia Press, 2003).

—— 'Television for Victorianists', *Romanticism and Victorianism on the Net*, 63 (April 2013), https://id.erudit.org/iderudit/1025613ar.

Thomas Ling, 'Shazad Latif Addresses THAT Star Trek Voq Theory: "I Met Javid Iqbal at a Party"', *Radio Times*, 12 November (2017), https://www.radiotimes.com/news/tv/2017-11-12/star-trek-discovery-shazad-latif-voq-tyler-fan-theory-javid-iqbal/.

Andrew Liptak, 'By Going Dark, Star Trek: Discovery Freed Itself to Look at the Future in a New Way', *The Verge*, 4 March (2018), https://www.theverge.com/2018/3/4/16699294/star-trek-discovery-stargate-universe-battlestar-galactica-realism-storytelling-television-essay.

Amanda D. Lotz, *The Television Will Be Revolutionized*, 2nd ed. (New York: New York University Press, 2014).

Jason Mittell, 'All in the Game: The Wire, Serial Storytelling, and Procedural Logic', *Electronic Book Review*, 18 March (2011), http://electronicbookreview.com/essay/all-in-the-game-the-wire-serial-storytelling-and-procedural-logic/.

'Monster of the Week', *TV Tropes*, https://tvtropes.org/pmwiki/pmwiki.php/Main/MonsterOfTheWeek.

Michael Z. Newman, 'From Beats to Arcs: Toward a Poetics of Television Narrative', *The Velvet Light Trap*, 58 (2006): 16–28.

Tudor Oltean, 'Series and Seriality in Media Culture', *European Journal of Communication*, 8.1 (March 1993): 5–31.

Mallory Ortberg, 'Star Trek Discovery Season 1 Episode 15 Finale Recap', *Vulture*, 12 February (2018), https://www.vulture.com/2018/02/star-trek-discovery-season-1-episode-15-finale-recap.html.

Sean O'Sullivan, 'Serials and Satisfaction', *Romanticism and Victorianism on the Net*, 63 (2013), https://www.erudit.org/en/journals/ravon/2013-n63-ravon01450/1025614ar/.

Patrick Parrinder (ed.), *H.G. Wells: The Critical Heritage* (London: Routledge, 1972).

C.A. Pearson, 'The Editorial Mind', *Pearson's Magazine*, 4.21 (1897): 344A.

Michael Saler, *As If: Modern Enchantment and the Literary Prehistory of Virtual Reality* (Oxford: Oxford University Press, 2012).

David C. Smith. *The Journalism of H.G. Wells: An Annotated Bibliography*, edited by Patrick Parrinder (Haren: Equilibris, 2012).

Will Tattersdill, *Science, Fiction, and the Fin-de-Siècle Periodical Press* (Cambridge: Cambridge University Press, 2016).

Sheldon Teitelbaum, 'How Gene Roddenberry and His Brain Trust Have Boldly Taken "Star Trek" Where No TV Series Has Gone Before: Trekking to the Top', *Los Angeles Times*, 5 May (1991), https://www.webcitation.org/5ybc7Wqbr?url=http://articles.latimes.com/print/1991-05-05/magazine/tm-2100_1_star-trek.

Katharine Trendacosta, 'Star Trek: Discovery Wraps Up a Wildly Uneven First Season with a Wildly Uneven Finale', *io9*, 12 February (2018), https://io9.gizmodo.com/star-trek-discovery-wraps-up-a-wildly-uneven-first-sea-1822923909.

H.G. Wells, *The War of the Worlds*, edited by Darryl Jones (Oxford: Oxford University Press, 2017).

Episodes and Films Cited

'Conundrum.' *Star Trek: The Next Generation*, written by Barry Schkolnik, directed by Les Landau, Paramount Television, 17 February, 1992.

'Cause and Effect.' *Star Trek: The Next Generation*, written by Brannon Braga, directed by Jonathan Frakes, Paramount Television, 21 March, 1992.

'Coda.' *Star Trek: Voyager*, written by Jeri Taylor, directed by Nancy Malone, Paramount Television, 29 January, 1997.

'Monday.' *X-Files*, directed by Kim Manners, written by Vince Gilligan, John Shiban, 20th Century Fox Television, 28 February, 1999.

'Window of Opportunity.' *Stargate SG-1*, written by Jopseh Mallozzi and Paul Mullie, directed by Peter DeLuise, MGM Television, 4 August, 2000.

'White Tulip.' *Fringe*, written by J.H. Whyman and Jeff Vlaming, directed by Thomas Yatsko, Bad Robot Productions, 15 April, 2010.

'Magic to Make the Sanest Man Go Mad.' *Star Trek: Discovery*, written by Aron Eli Coleite and Jesse Alexander, directed by David Barrett, CBS Television Studios, 29 October, 2017.

'New Eden.' *Star Trek: Discovery*, written by Vaun Wilmott and Sean Cochran, directed by Jonathan Frakes, CBS Television Studios, 24 January, 2019.

Groundhog Day. 1993. Directed by Harold Ramis. Columbia Pictures.

To Boldly Discuss
Socio-Political Discourses in *Star Trek: Discovery* Fanfiction

Kerstin-Anja Münderlein

Introduction

When *Star Trek* first conquered American television in 1966, it boldly went where no one had gone before and took its ever-growing fanbase with it. Not only did the show introduce an exceptionally diverse cast, it actively engaged in socio-political discourses of the day, such as the age-old question of ethics in science, namely 'is science allowed to do everything it can do?,' which is a pivotal question of the plotline centering on the genetically modified Khan Noonien Singh.[1] Since then, *Star Trek* has continued to include contemporary discourses on society, science and politics in its shows and movies. This development is no product of chance, as *Star Trek* creator Gene Roddenberry pointed out in 1991. In an interview with *The Humanist,* Roddenberry stated that his 'intention was to express his philosophy [that humans are able to take control of their destiny and their future] in *Star Trek,* but [he had] to keep this intention secret lest the network pull the plug on him' (quoted in Jindra, 1994, 34). From the original series onwards, Roddenberry's philosophical convictions (and those of his collaborators and, eventually, his successors) have been embodied within the socio-political layout of the utopian future depicted in the franchise. '*Star Trek*'s social utopianism,' as Robert V. Kozinets (2001, 71) writes

> is metonymically glossed by the IDIC acronym ['Indefinite Diversity in Infinite Combinations']... a Vulcan religious philosophy that was presented in the original *Star Trek* series. The egalitarian IDIC

---

[1] This character first appears in the *The Original Series* episode 'Space Seed' (1x22) and is centralized and further explored in *Star Trek II: The Wrath of Khan* (1982).

philosophy holds that diversity should be embraced, and not simply tolerated.

Diversity, unity, and the overcoming of differences still provide some of the socio-philosophical core aspects of *Star Trek* and the new addition to the canon, *Star Trek: Discovery* (2017–; *DSC*), is no exception. In this series, cast and characters were further diversified, the ethics of war and science take center stage through the Klingon War as do the use of the controversial spore drive or Terran fascism in the Mirror Universe, to name only a few examples of the prevalent topics debated in the first season. *DSC* thus proves Christian Wenger's claim (2006, 342) that the program itself provides ways for further human development and is understood by fans as a call to action for improving their own lifestyles. By engaging with the problems negotiated in *Star Trek*, viewers cannot escape contemporary socio-political criticism and the more actively they debate these issues, for example through fan art, the more critically aware they can become. Wenger (2006, 342) thus contends that *Star Trek* is in itself a social utopia that allows for a potentially ideal future without presenting it uncritically or naïvely; neither do its fans. *Star Trek* presents tolerance and idealism but not a future devoid of potential snares the protagonists need to be aware of and counteract to hold on to this utopia (2006, 343). In 2018, *Star Trek* is as political as ever and cannot be divided from its capacity for socio-political discussion.

Yet, not only the showrunners of *Star Trek* contribute to these discourses, the fans do so as well. In engaging with (contemporary) socio-political issues, *Star Trek* offers its fans material for self-reflection as members of a post-traditional community (Wenger, 2006, 343). Their fan culture has incorporated these discourses and has demonstrated its active social awareness. *DSC*'s fans are no exception in providing material pertaining to or exceeding the ethical and political problems negotiated in the series. In the canon, *DSC* seamlessly joins the rank of its predecessors in questioning power and monoglossia. In the fanon, contemporary fan writers have done the same and continue the tradition of political fanfictions in *Star Trek*, as this paper aims to show. Through the analysis of *DSC*-specific fanfictions according to the socio-political discourses mentioned or discussed in them, this paper will show that *DSC*'s fanbase is typical of *Star Trek* or, more specifically, *Star Trek* fans' active engagement with current debates of critical issues in ethics, science, politics, and society that mirrors the series' potential for criticism itself.

Star Trek: A Political and Contested Fandom

From its inception, 'Star Trek fandom seemed akin to some kind of movement. It certainly was not a political movement, but it had political aspects. It was something broader than that, more like a religious movement' (Jindra, 1994, 30). Jindra's appraisal of *Star Trek* fandom as more than just the passive consumption of content provided by a production company can certainly not be disputed. Henry Jenkins even goes so far as to show dissatisfaction with *Star Trek*'s 'inability to keep pace with the political growth of its audiences' (Jenkins and Tulloch, 1995, 21), thereby claiming that the fans surpassed the canon in their political activism or awareness. Whether this holds true for *DSC* remains to be seen, but my results at least imply that fans match the political actuality of the series.[2]

The influence *Star Trek* fans have had on the formation of fan culture in the twentieth century and the understanding of fan culture in general should not be (and is generally not) underestimated. While the study of fan culture and its products, fan art in all its forms, has been of note since at least the 1970s with Camille Bacon-Smith's *Enterprising Women*, the fans' importance for the phenomenon *Star Trek* has increased. 'Twenty years on, fan texts are no longer read as underground publications but as new, supplementary works in their own right' (Coker, 2012, 83). Through their own derivative works, fans dispute and add to the socio-political discourses of the franchise while at the same time including absent topics, such as the canon's failure to show same-sex couples before *Star Trek: Beyond* (2016). Generally, 'by examining fan texts closely, we will see both exceptional readings and exceptional counter-readings of source texts as fans actively engage their chosen material with their personal

---

[2] It must also be mentioned that at the start of *DSC*, self-declared fans of *Star Trek* lashed out against several aspects of the new series, such as its allegedly unnecessarily diverse cast (also described as 'white genocide,' quoted in Hibberd, 2017) or its alleged over-abundance in strong female characters (or, as one user wrote: 'Is everything going to have females in every fucking thing?' quoted in Saadia, 2017). This backlash has been commented on and strongly rejected by fans and cast members alike. Jason Isaacs (Lorca) publicly called such untoward comments 'endless white isolationist hate-spew' (quoted in Bradley, 2018) whereas Sonequa Martin-Green (Burnham) has appealed to the authors of such hate speech citing the idealism of *Star Trek*: 'I would encourage them to key into the essence and spirit of *Star Trek* that has made it the legacy it is – and that's looking across the way to the person sitting in front of you and realizing you are the same, that they are not separate from you, and we are all one' (quoted in Hibberd, 2017).

politics' (2012, 83). Despite the growing importance of fandom for the development of the series, fans were also met with public negativity:

> The more successful fans were in broadening the market for the series, the more marginal they became to its overall reception. What emerged from this tension was the stereotype of the 'Trekkie,'[3] a grotesque embodiment of everything that critics feared about mass culture – blind consumerism, obsessive commitment to the trivial, a loss of dignity and respect, a retreat from reality into the world of the 'boob tube.' (Jenkins and Tulloch, 1995, 13–14)

The lack of control over fandom and fan works must thus be read in conjunction with the general fear producers have of fans and agents beyond consumers. 'The fans' transgression of bourgeois taste and disruption of dominant cultural hierarchies insures that their preferences are seen as abnormal and threatening by those who have a vested interest in the maintenance of these standards' (Jenkins, 2013, 17).

In becoming active participants in a subculture they themselves have structured, through fan conventions or through a regular exchange in fanzines, for instance, these fans were more than passive consumers of a television show. Especially in fanfiction, *Star Trek* fans inhabit a pioneering position among fans of television programs. With its long tradition, *Star Trek* fandom provides a lot of in-group cultural memory, which is accessible through fanfiction websites, making them 'community archives that similarly safeguard the cultural memory of groups left out of the official archives of culture' (De Kosnik, 2016, 142). More than 50 years after the first *Star Trek* fanfiction appeared in print, the means of publishing fan art have changed dramatically, especially with the advent of Web 2.0. Since fan culture provides a broad spectrum of means of active participation and varying degrees of self-commitment, fans experience different degrees of communization and identity formation through their subculture (Wenger, 2006, 322); the internet, however, must be regarded as the global, inter-cultural and inter-generational 'meeting place' of fans today. 'Fan culture [thus] muddies ... boundaries, treating popular texts as if they merited the same degree of attention and appreciation as canonical texts' (Jenkins, 2013, 17). The internet provides fans with a variety of platforms on which to celebrate their fandom and publish their works, while at the same time

---

[3] As opposed to the self-denomination 'Trekker,' which presents a 'more affirmative identity' than the label attached to the fans from the outside (Jenkins and Tulloch, 1995, 15).

serving 'as critically important community archives for female and queer cultural creativity' (De Kosnik, 2016, 135). The digital infrastructure provided by internet fanfiction and fan culture has helped marginalized voices to be heard and opens up a virtual space for acceptance. *DSC* fandom already has these means of communication at its disposal, so it stands to reason that the fans make use of them.

Despite Judith Fathallah's caveat (2017, 23) that studying fanfiction always runs the risk of either over-politicizing the stories under scrutiny or, conversely, treating them as any other form of literature, thereby disregarding their special purpose as fanfictions, some scholars regard the mere existence of fan writing as a political statement:

> In a context free from editorial or branding oversight and free from commercial gain, the meaning making is open to anyone who can hold a pen, use a keyboard, or post a manuscript. The shift is not just an aesthetic one, but also political. (Falzone, 2005, 251)

Falzone's appraisal of fanfiction as free of editorial oversight seems rather naïve from the perspective of fan studies. While it is true that the influence of the producers is slight, the meaning-making process is still regulated through the fanon. Like the canon, the fanon does not exist in a social vacuum and the intertextual references and dependencies of fanfiction are not only tied to the canon, but to other fans' writings as well. Fanon does not only reproduce canonical elements, it is equally self-preservative and hence part of a larger fan network influenced by but different from the canon. In addition, the position of the fan writer among their personal network has changed in the same degree as the singularity of fanfiction writers among the people they regularly interact with (explicitly excluding other fans) has declined. Coppa (2017, 1) summarises this development:

> Fanfiction has become an increasingly mainstream art form, and fandom itself is moving fast from subculture to culture. More people than ever participate in some form of organized fan activity like reading or writing fanfiction ... – or if they don't do these things themselves, they likely know someone who does. [Thus, necessarily,] more critics are coming to recognise, then, that fanfiction should not be hastily generalized as radical. (2017, 26)

In addition, Bertha Chin points out that 'it is crucial to remember that fandom is not homogeneous, and one observation of hierarchical relationships among fans is not representative of the entire fandom'

(2018, 244). Her analysis shows how the access to different media discloses the social foundations of fan culture and establishes a hierarchy among themselves. Fans can show a high degree of ethical and political awareness, as the *Star Trek* fandom has shown, but that does not make them inherently good (as the backlash on *DSC* illustrates). When researching fan culture, scholars must therefore be careful not to either idealize or damn fans as a homogenous group.

Socio-Political Discourses in *DSC*

From the very first episode of *DSC*, the series set down its own standard regarding the depiction of socio-political issues of the twenty-third century and, especially, the Klingon War. Despite being set in the distant future, the problems protagonist Michael Burnham and the other crew members on the *U.S.S. Discovery* face show a high degree of actuality in 2017 and beyond. As such, the new series ties in neatly with its predecessors in depicting global tensions and solutions to overarching situations of threat, such as the Borg or the Dominion War represented in the 1990s. Today, issues of cultural and racial purity are as relevant as ever and in the light of the refugee movements from the Middle East due to the war in Syria, which has intensified discussions about the compatibility of different cultures and religions. Therefore, the Klingon strife for unity through cultural purity rings a bell with audiences. The rejection of the Other, which *Star Trek* idealistically presented as resolved on Earth in *The Original Series* (*TOS*), is centralized in *DSC*. With the character of Voq/Ash Tyler (Shazad Latif), *DSC* presents an interesting take on the sacrifices a fanatic (Voq) is ready to make to achieve his aim (the unity of all Klingons): he allows himself to be transformed into a human (Tyler) to infiltrate Starfleet. Racial and cultural purity thus needs to be overcome temporarily by one character to be achieved for a whole group. As such, the series questions the desire for cultural and racial integrity through Voq's infiltration plan. Besides the Klingon desire for cultural purity, humanity in the Mirrorverse is also shown as a fascistic tyranny (the Terran Empire) centered on racial purity. Thus, *DSC* does not open up the binary of self and Other through Humans (usually associated with the Federation) and Klingons with casting one race as good and the other as bad. Yet, interestingly, the battle that sparks off the Klingon War is aptly called the 'Battle at the Binary Stars' in the eponymous episode (1x02). While this binary starts the war between the Federation and the Klingons, the solution of the war is only found in the collaboration of Starfleet and the Klingon L'Rell (Mary Chieffo) in an again aptly titled episode, 'Will You Take My Hand?' (1x15). Throughout the whole series, inter-species (read: inter-cultural) collaboration, introduced with the human-born and Vulcan-raised Burnham, idealistically provides the only means of solving conflict.

During this struggle for power, the series also manages to include several crucial ethical discussions through the *Discovery*'s unique means of transportation, the spore drive. With the spore drive, the ship is able to jump anywhere in the blink of an eye and hence holds an advantage over the rest of the fleet. However, the spore drive only works properly through the abuse of a sentient being, the tardigrade, which is specifically kept imprisoned to be experimented on and turned into a biological weapon (1x04, 'The Butcher's Knife Cares Not for the Lamb's Cry' and 1x05, 'Choose Your Pain'). To spare the creature more pain, Paul Stamets (Anthony Rapp) sacrifices his health (initially unbeknownst to himself) and substitutes for the tardigrade in piloting the spore drive. The usage of both beings due to the necessity of war is highly questionable and questioned in the series and picks up on the well-established ethical question of how far science can and should go.[4]

When *DSC* started airing in 2017, it was the first *Star Trek* series to show a same-sex couple, Dr. Hugh Culber (Wilson Cruz) and Lieutenant Paul Stamets, but it was not the first instalment of *Star Trek* to do so (in the last reboot film, Sulu has a male partner, but their appearance is only brief and in passing). With this inclusion of Culber and Stamets as a couple, sharing rather normative couple dynamics while living together aboard the ship, *DSC* catered to the long-standing fan demand of including LGBTQ representation in the series.[5] Beforehand, as P.J. Falzone (2005, 256) writes,

> the corporate caretakers of these characters have proven themselves, to a broad readership, unwilling to realize the 'particular style of the 23rd century' as one in which queer love is acceptable love. And so, for close to forty years [as of 2005], an active and activist readership has been doing it for them through the creation of an aberrant folklore that they believe adheres more closely to the spirit of the narrative's utopian origins. It has fallen upon the fan

---

[4] For an analysis of the spore drive, the mycelial network it relies on, and Stamets' connection to both as a rhizome, see Lisa Meinecke's essay 'Veins and Muscles of the Universe: Posthumanism and Connectivity in *Star Trek: Discovery*' in this volume.

[5] For more on LGBTQ representation, see the chapter by Sabrina Mittermeier and Mareike Spychala on '"Never Hide Who You Are": Queer Representation and Actorvism in *Star Trek: Discovery*' in this volume.

to become creator, the reader to become the author, and the author to become active in the reuniting of this divided self.

Besides the above-mentioned discourses, *DSC*'s premise necessarily includes depictions of the effects of war on individuals. The series investigates these effects, using individual characters as focalizers. Thus, it provides discourses of war trauma through the character Tyler, grief over lost ones through Stamets, responsibility for actions in war through Burnham, otherness and the difficulties of fitting in through Sylvia Tilly (Mary Wiseman), ruthlessness and Machiavellianism through Gabriel Lorca, and eventually the integrity and idealism associated with Starfleet through the whole crew of the *U.S.S. Discovery* (especially episodes 1x14, 'The War Without, the War Within' and 1x15, 'Will You Take My Hand?'). Naturally, a brief summary of the socio-political and ethical discourses provided by *DSC* cannot do justice to the depth with which these (and more) critical issues are presented in the series. Thus, before continuing with an analysis of the fanfictions on *DSC*, I would refer to the other essays in this collection for further reference.

DSC Fanfiction: Methodology

To collate the sample of fanfiction stories published on the internet, I chose to access the two biggest databases for such writing, *fanfiction.net* as well as *archiveofourown.com*, and then use the pages' browse by fandom function. While *fanfiction.net* only yielded 115 results for the fandom 'Star Trek: Discovery' (as of October 8, 2018), *archiveofourown.com*[6] (*AO3* for short) yielded 1,181 results on the same date. Since the latter database

---

[6] Besides yielding more stories and being the 'fastest-growing multifandom archive online [as of 2016]' (De Kosnik, 2017, 131), *AO3* is also preferable as a database because it is a non-profit fans-for-fans platform that does not capitalise on the easy marketability of fandom and fanfiction (2017, 132–33). It thus provides a 'fannish' infrastructure free from censorship and content control. In comparison, 'from the mid-2000s to the mid-2010s, the for-profit archive FanFiction.net (FF.net) conducted multiple "purges," deleting thousands of stories that site moderators decided were too sexually explicit' (2017, 132). To counteract the increasing monetization of fandom, the Organization of Transformative Works was founded by fans for fans as a non-profit organisation to 'serve the interests of fans by providing access to and preserving the history of fanworks and fan culture in its myriad forms' (quoted in De Kosnik, 2017, 133). Aca-fan and fanfiction scholar Francesca Coppa is one of the founders of *AO3* (Coppa, 2017, 15).

has surpassed the former in its popularity, I used the more popular website and set the filters to 'Completion Status: Complete Works only' and 'Language: English' to analyze only finished works accessible to the majority of readers, assuming that English as the international lingua franca will reach the most readers. From the resulting 965 stories, I selected 10 percent (96 stories), that is, every tenth story to have a representative sample.[7]

Eventually, I arrived at a sample consisting of 418,180 words since most of the stories (74 stories, equalling 77.1 percent of all stories) did not exceed a word count of 5,000 words. Splitting the stories up based on their word count, 28 stories (29.2 percent) counted below 1,000 words, roughly half of the stories (46 stories making up 47.9 percent) ranged between 1,000 and 4,999 words, 12 stories (12.5 percent) covered more than 5,000 but fewer than 10,000 words and ten stories (10.4 percent) exceeded the 10,000-word mark. For a fandom this young, the existence of such long stories points to an active engagement of fans with the content.

When collating the results, one story out of 96 proved to be unsuitable for consideration. 'At the Going Down of the Sun,' by LauramourFromOz used the wrong categorization within *Star Trek* as it is a *The Next Generation* (*TNG*) story. 12 more stories did not provide any discussion or inclusion of socio-political topics, partly because they were retellings of *DSC* scenes, partly because they just did not venture into any critical discussions. The remaining 82 stories, however, picked up a plethora of socio-political discourses, ranging from the importance of home (Radiolaria's 'we sleep like wine in the conches') to vegetarianism (30MinuteLoop's 'The Struggle to Stay Human') with a strong focus on the normativity of same-sex relationships (49 percent of stories). In the following, these topics picked up in the fanfictions will be contextualized in comparison with the dominant discourses provided by the canon.

---

[7] The 96 stories were written by 79 writers, of which 68 writers only appeared once in the sample. The remaining 11 writers contributed two (KrisL, mswyrr, indiegal85, MiaCooper, stellaviatores, Pixie (magnetgirl), AndYetNotBeingDisenchanted, and White_Noise) or three stories (BlackQat, llha) to the sample with one writer, TFALokiwriter, contributing six stories in total.

Socio-Political Discourses in *DSC* Fanfiction

The overall assessment of the socio-political relevance of the stories yields rather positive results. Only 12.5 percent of stories do not contribute any such discourses, whereas more than double that number (25 stories, 26 percent) reference at least two or more ethical or socio-political issues. Mainly, these issues derive from the discourses provided by the series itself, yet they also transcend the canon and include contemporary criticism not related to *Star Trek*. The stories that can only be summarized as 'other' or 'miscellanea' account for 37.5 percent (36 stories) of the sample.[8] One such example, and the only one to touch upon this specific topic, would be criticism of entertainment electronics in 'Streaks,' a brief and playful story about Paul replicating an iPhone and sending nudes to Hugh. Here, the criticism is very subtle: 'Once everything was in working order [on the iPhone] he decided it was time to play around with some of the apps that took up so much of the time from people of those days' (holloway88).[9]

Another story, again the only one mentioning this specific problem, narrating the fictional courtship of Hugh and Paul, 'in hues of liquid caramel and oxidized soda,' provides criticism of the (American) university system through showing the financial problems Starfleet cadets (in this case Hugh) might face:

> Most cadets in the medical track don't do their mandatory internships while attempting to complete Starfleet's highly demanding curriculum, but then again most cadets don't come from small mining colonies in the Dolara system where every day with food on the table is seen as a gift. (apollothyme)

Besides highlighting the workload necessary for poor students to keep up, the story implies a classist criticism of Starfleet by noting that only few cadets come from poor regions. Both stories, centered on Paul and Hugh, exceed the limits given by *DSC* in either setting the story in the characters' free (thus off-screen) time or in the past to allow for narrative freedom. Still, the freedom these writers create is not apolitical and the characters encounter problems different from those seen in the series. Aside from these diverse stories, there are three clearly identifiable

---

[8] These categories are not mutually exclusive, that is, these 37.5 percent of stories can also present several topics.

[9] Since none of the stories provides any page numbers, all stories are quoted only referencing the author.

trends, namely stories about same-sex relationships, stories about war and trauma, and stories about ethics and idealism. The majority of these follow the socio-political discourses opened up in the canon, but employ very different narrative means of negotiating their criticism.

Same-Sex Relationships

Given *Star Trek*'s history of slash fanfiction, it is hardly surprising to find that same-sex relationships comprise the single most often used socio-political discourse in the sample. Of all stories, 49 percent (47 stories) either feature same-sex couples in crucial roles or significantly allude to them. Specifically, the normativity of a same-sex relationship deriving directly from the canon was eagerly taken up in *DSC* fanfiction. Thus, the heretofore dominant reading of slash as a 'rebellion and utopian rewriting' (Falzone, 2005, 250) must be revalued in the light of this significant alteration of the canon. If slash were only regarded as rebellion against the absence of same-sex relationships in the canon, *DSC* fanfiction should provide significantly less slash because the desire for representation has already been fulfilled by the series itself. The opposite, however, holds true.

Consequently, slash fiction needs to be reappraised. Even though slash has been associated with rebellion and writing against the grain, this can no longer apply for a series with a same-sex couple in its main personnel. Besides this inclusion of a gay couple into the canon, the constant use of slash in *Star Trek* fanfiction has also already undergone a genre formation process. Slash stories are no longer only forms of political rebellion, they are also an integral part of the fanon and must be regarded as a generic element of *Star Trek* fanfiction as a whole. As such, they do not only react to the content's failure to provide same-sex couples, but they reference the genre itself in adding to the already vast amount of slash fictions written by previous generations of fanfiction writers. At the time of writing, denoting all slash fiction as rebellious is thus too limited and disregards the mechanisms of genre formation in literature as well as the social structures within fandom that establish the fanon and thus codify certain pairings before others. In the light of this history of slash, the overwhelming presence of slash stories presenting normative relationships rather points to a desire for writing a meaningful relationship devoid of discriminations targeting sexuality or gender instead of a form of rebellion. It is highly conspicuous in my sample to see that the stories thematizing same-sex relationships (not only the canonical Paul/Hugh stories) foreground love and relationship issues beside pornographic stories centering on sex scenes, so-called 'smut' stories. In addition, the characters in such stories are generally equalized in their relationship with neither character usually occupying a subordinate role.

Since the number of stories about same-sex relationships is so high, the following story shall serve as an illustration of how normative and caring such a relationship is generally presented in the sample. As such, these stories do not veer from the canonical representation of Hugh and Paul's relationship, thereby illustrating the aforementioned decreased necessity for slash as rebellion against the canon. On the contrary, the canon is eagerly taken up to narrate stories of an idealized and equal love. In 'I've Got You,' the *Discovery* crew rescue Paul's niece Jeanie (an original character) after Klingons attack her home and kill her parents. When talking to the crew members, Jeanie's position on who her uncle/s is/are makes her a spokesperson for the normativity of same-sex relationships in implied comparisons to heterosexual couples:

> 'You're Lieutenant Stamets' niece right?' Jeanie nodded. 'Uncle Hugh's niece too.' 'Of course.' Detmer said … 'The shuttle docked and they told us all to get off. Someone said 'Welcome to Discovery' and I looked around and saw Uncle Hugh.' 'That would be Doctor Hugh Culber, who's your Uncle Paul Stamets' partner.' 'Uncle Hugh is my uncle too,' Jeanie said firmly. (tptigger)

Through repeating Jeanie's statement about Hugh in two parts of the narrative, her point is strengthened. The crew's easy acceptance of her assertion, however, clashes with the clarifications they initially attempt in stressing the blood relation between Jeanie and Paul. Yet, through this accentuation of the girl's understanding of Paul and Hugh's relationship versus the crew's enquiry about blood status, the story does not devalue the normativity of same-sex results but instead highlights how normatively Paul and Hugh's relationship should be regarded. Thereby, the story follows the canon in showing their life together as perfectly ordinary (disregarding their extraordinary jobs for the moment). Generally, the stories in the sample handle Paul and Hugh in this way and there is no story that questions their relationship other than by showing minor jealousies of former partners or the other's work taking up more room.

War and Trauma

Apart from the stories on normativity in same-sex relationships, stories about war and trauma make up a considerable part of the sample, namely 20.8 percent (20 stories). They range from passive suffering through torture to questions of personal responsibility and the difficulties of coming to terms with one's own wartime actions. The characters in these stories vary greatly and the dilemmas they are faced with usually derive directly from the series. While Burnham and Cornwell have to work through the decisions they had to take in war, Tyler is always presented as a victim of war and torture.

In 'A Prison of Her Own Design,' Burnham struggles with her guilt about starting the war and losing Georgiou. As the title indicates, the prison she creates out of her own guilt locks her in more thoroughly than the Federation prison and she apparently desires harsher treatment, which her foster-home planet would offer:

> In a Vulcan prison facility, she would be let alone to meditate on her failure, fed gruel and denied daylight. Solitary confinement is deemed inhumane by joint Federation standards, but still common on Vulcan. ... Since the system does not do it for her, she denies herself as much as she can. (strangeallure)

By using Burnham as the focalizer in this story, the reader shares in her perceived guilt but at the same time pities her for the magnitude of her guilt since she begins to have hallucinations of Captain Georgiou in her cell. Burnham is thus torn between loss and guilt.

Besides Burnham, Admiral Cornwell's wartime experiences occur in some of the stories. 'The Morning after the Night Before' and 'Whatever fate the stars are weaving' counterpoint her deliberation on the necessity of decisions made in war. While the first story shows her struggle for integrity, the second one focuses more on her regret at having had to take such actions, as the following comparison shows:

> *Our peace-oriented leadership needs to come to grips with this,* she thinks. *The Klingon people do not care about our sense of morals or outrage. They don't care about lives that are not Klingon.* Then, almost despairingly: *What do we do against such an enemy? Do we compromise our values?* (BlackQat; original emphasis)

Apart from the anti-Klingon and rather racist thoughts in the first sentence, Cornwell's dilemma here is caused by the enemy, the Klingons. By asking what to do against such an enemy, Cornwell in this story shares her own responsibility or guilt by claiming that she is forced to abandon her values because of the enemy. 'Whatever fate' tackles this responsibility very differently:

> There are things she has done, things that have been done to her that she will never forget. Her thoughts unwillingly go to Qo'noS again. She still can't believe she and the rest of the Federation Council sanctioned the destruction of a whole planet. It goes against everything she's been taught and believes in and yet she had still given the order because she'd been so desperate for peace. (Ailendolin)

Here, Cornwell is ashamed of her decisions but freely admits to the responsibility. The degree of insight into the character in both stories is similar, but the inferences the respective writers draw from the same canonical figure differ. This is ever more apparent with the fannish reimaginations of Ash Tyler.

In fanfiction, Tyler is one of the more difficult figures to analyze since he was revealed to be a Klingon (1x10, 'Despite Yourself') and more specifically the fanatic Voq (1x11, 'The Wolf Inside') only late in season one when some of the fanfiction had already been written. One story, 'Duty,' written before the revelation, claims that there has been a fan theory about Tyler/Voq and uses this for its premise. In this story, Voq is presented as an agent who has to sacrifice himself to achieve his aims. He is prepared to suffer for honor and a place in the Klingon society:

> Perhaps this is his punishment for letting his lord die. He tells himself his reward will be the unification of the Klingon empire, and he will earn forgiveness and a place of honor on the black fleet by making T'Kuvma's vision a reality. ... His sacrifice will mean nothing if it does not win for the Klingon empire the *Discovery*, and the only way to do that as a solitary spy is by ingratiating himself with the members of the crew, and winning their trust. (darthpumpkinspice)

As the focalizer of the story, Voq shares his repulsion with the reader, specifically when his sexual contact with Burnham is described as more than a sacrifice:

Tyler feels warm, wet, human tightness around him, and the reality of this situation hits him – he's inside the woman who killed T'Kuvma. He hopes she interprets his grunt of disgust as one of arousal. This is an act of duty, he reminds himself. ... He endures this for his lord and his empire, as he would endure any torture. (darthpumpkinspice)

The explicit use of 'torture' here highlights the desperate measures Voq, the cultural fanatic, is prepared to take, but it also shows that both sides of the war are prepared to do what they have to, yet also that both sides suffer from it. As such, this story provides much scope for an analysis of the Klingon antagonists, which is mostly absent in the sample. The other stories about Tyler focus on his trauma endured during his captivity on the Klingon ship, which must be read as real trauma since Voq's mind was hidden beneath Tyler's (1x12).

Two very exact representations of PTSD are given in relation to Tyler in the sample stories. In 'i have loved the stars too fondly (to be fearful of the night),' Burnham informs Tilly very matter-of-factly about what Tyler is going through: 'Ash has been experiencing vivid flashbacks with concurrent somnambulism for the past two weeks. The symptoms began after he met one of the Klingons who tortured him aboard the Ship of the Dead' (mswyrr). The description of PTSD serves to explain Tyler's behavior to Tilly but, by having Burnham explain it, it denies Tyler the chance to voice it himself. Similar to this story, 'Vulnerability,' besides its very apt title, fails to openly name PTSD, yet highlights Tyler's suffering at the hands of L'Rell in his own words when he experiences a flashback while being intimate with Burnham: '"I don't like ... being on my back," he admits finally. "I ... In ... When I was a Klingon POW..."' (lorenzobane).

While 'Vulnerability' goes slightly further in giving Tyler a voice, the representation of PTSD is still rather indirect and tied to the character's reaction without providing a direct reference by himself. Even though more stories about Tyler's PTSD fail to express his trauma in his own words, one story openly addresses it. In 'Nothing is Stopping You Except What's Inside, I can Help you but it's your Fight,' Tyler himself admits that he has flashbacks: 'I keep going back to the Klingon ship, to what they did to me, what L'Rell did and made me do' (Archaeodigit_dima). Moreover, his emotional reactions to these flashbacks are narrated, gaining immediacy by showing them from a first-person perspective:

> I had waited till L'Rell had fallen asleep and then gotten dressed. I hated what she had done and I hated myself for allowing her. Bile rose into my

throat as I thought of it and I had to force my mind away. (Archaeodigit_dima; original emphasis)

It is apparent that Tyler suffers from his experiences, but his agency in depicting his trauma is not taken away and he remains in possession of the narrative sovereignty of his own story. As with Burnham and Cornwell, the stories' presentation of the characters' inner life varies significantly and even though the same topics are negotiated, their overall presentation and thus evaluation differs.

Ethics and Idealism

Another important cluster of stories outlining the effects of ethics and idealism, especially regarding the ethics of science and the idealism of Starfleet, forms a significant percentage of the sample (14.6 percent; 14 stories). The closeness of this discourse with that of war is apparent in 'Falling Tides,' the story that also provides the most convincing statement about war, integrity, and responsibility. In this story about the budding romance between Joann Owosekun and Keyla Detmer, Joann contemplates the effects of the war from the perspective of a junior officer who has to negotiate her ideals with the orders she received:

> 'What happened... what we did... this was my second Starfleet posting, and I spent it serving under a murderer. And now... the war is over... and Lorca is gone... and it's just... us. What's left. And what's left is...' She stares down at her hands. 'People who did what we did. People who lost what we lost. What's left... it's everything Lorca and the war and the other universe just... left behind. And now they're all gone and... and what? What do we do? Who are we, now that we're not fighting or surviving or disguised or escaping or, or complicit in what they were doing? What happens now?' (m_class)

By showing Joann's insecurity about how to process her wartime experiences and contrasting them with her Federation ideals, m_class' story forms a unique contribution to the sample in that it gives a voice to the show's minor characters. In so doing, it highlights the fundamental influence of the war on everybody affected, not just the central characters. War and its necessities, hence, are discussed profoundly, especially regarding personal responsibility: 'I'm just one more junior officer who was almost complicit in an atrocity' (m_class). In addition,

Joann debates the righteousness of following orders, thereby refusing to accept some of the responsibility: 'But Lorca got away with what he did because he was in command. He was our captain, and we had sworn an oath when we joined the service to follow orders' (m_class). Joann is torn between her guilt about the atrocities she nearly participated in and her desire to share the blame by referring to Starfleet's hierarchy, which apparently demands obedience. It is not specifically her idealism that is being tested, but Starfleet's mission of idealized utopia that has been found wanting throughout the war.

This criticism of Starfleet is made even clearer in 'Rise in Perfect Light' through the character Saru, who struggles with the predicaments of his job:

> As acting captain, I gave orders that I knew would cause direct harm to a sentient being, the only known member of its species. I am a first contact specialist. I should have been the one advocating for the tardigrade, not the one denying its most basic rights. But as the captain, I had to give those orders if any of us were to live. How can any captain make these choices so often? (HopefulNebula)

Saru's deliberations combine the ethics of command and science while adhering to the dictum of prioritizing the needs of the many over the needs of the few, which in itself is a very utilitarian ideology. Apparently, Saru did what he thought was demanded of him, but feels uncomfortable with his choice. Regardless of Saru's idealism or ethics, he has to give in to utilitarianism to fight the war and prevent more damage. Ethics and idealism thus take a subordinate role to necessity, thereby questioning the standards of Starfleet in general.

In the tradition of *Star Trek*, the stories centering on ethical deliberations and the questioning of the characters' (and, by extension, the reader's) convictions, tend to negotiate between what is necessary and what is (ethically or morally) right. The stories here tie this criticism to canonical characters and show them either in situations of doubt or in the aftermath of the war. As in the other two categories examined, ethics and idealism form a core value of Starfleet, and fanfiction's critical evaluation thereof is not surprising. The overall quality of the stories under scrutiny is high and the negotiation of socio-political discourses is generally very well done regarding content and narratology.

Conclusion and Further Research

The results of this 10 percent study on *DSC* fanfiction on *AO3* show that *DSC* fans follow their fannish predecessors in the franchise in actively engaging with the series' socio-political criticism. Certainly, not all stories provide such a discussion and some only copy canonical discourses, yet the majority of stories negotiates such fundamentally important discourses as ethical behavior in science and war, trauma, racial purity, or, specifically in *Star Trek*, same-sex relationships. The overall sample shows much awareness of the problems the characters of the series face, such as identity crises after the war, or questions of personal responsibility. Besides taking up the problems presented in *DSC*, some stories also offer contemporary criticism or combine both. Despite the broad variety of results this study yielded, it can only offer a glimpse into the whole fandom, especially because the number of online platforms on which fan engagement takes place has risen considerably. The interaction of fans on *Tumblr* or *Twitter*, as opposed to *AO3*, is more direct, but must be examined with different methods than the literary approach used here. However, because of the importance of such media platforms and the direct communication thus established between producers and fans, further research in this area is necessary to arrive at a more comprehensive view on the *DSC* fandom. For the moment, the first year of *DSC* fanfictions allows the conclusion that although fans are not going where no one has gone before, they continue to venture boldly into the space opened up by fans more than 50 years ago.

Works Cited

Camille Bacon-Smith, *Enterprising Women: Television Fandom and the Creation of Popular Myth* (Philadelphia: University of Pennsylvania Press, 1992).

Bill Bradley, 'Jason Isaacs Says Racist "Star Trek" Haters "Can Go F**k" Themselves', *Huffington Post*, 8 October (2017), huffingtonpost.com/entry/jason-isaacs-says-racist-star-trek-haters-can-go-fck-themselves_us_59d9bbe0e4b0f6eed350ce3b?guccounter=1.

Bertha Chin, 'It's About Who You Know: Social Capital, Hierarchies and Fandom', in Paul Booth (ed.) *A Companion to Media Fandom* (Hoboken, NJ: Wiley & Sons, 2018): 243–55.

Catherine Coker, 'The Angry! Textual! Poacher! Is Angry! Fan Works as Political Statements', in Katherine Larsen and Lynn Zubernis (eds.) *Fan Culture: Theory/Practice* (Newcastle upon Tyne: Cambridge Scholars, 2012): 81–96.

Francesca Coppa, *The Fanfiction Reader: Folk Tales for the Digital Age* (Ann Arbor: University of Michigan Press, 2017).
Abigail De Kosnik, 'Memory, Archive, and History in Political Science Fiction', in Jonathan Gray, Cornel Sandvoss, and C. Lee Harrington (eds.) *Fandom. Identities and Communities in a Mediated World*, 2nd ed. (New York and London: New York University Press, 2017): 270–84.
—— *Rogue Archives: Digital Cultural Memory and Media Fandom* (Cambridge, MA: MIT Press, 2016).
P.J. Falzone, 'The Final Frontier is Queer. Aberrancy, Archetype and Audience Generated Folklore in K/S Slashfiction', *Western Folklore*, 64.3/4 (2005): 243–61.
Judith May Fathallah, *Fanfiction and the Author: How Fanfic Changes Popular Cultural Texts* (Amsterdam: Amsterdam University Press, 2017).
James Hibberd, '*Star Trek: Discovery* Star Replies to Show's Racist Critics', *Entertainment Weekly*, 22 June (2017), ew.com/tv/2017/06/22/star-trek-discovery-diversity/.
Henry Jenkins, *Textual Poachers: Television Fans and Participatory Culture. Updated Twentieth Anniversary Edition* (London and New York: Routledge, 2013).
Henry Jenkins and John Tulloch, 'Beyond the *Star Trek* Phenomenon: Reconceptualizing the Science Fiction Audience', in Henry Jenkins and John Tulloch (eds.) *Science Fiction Audiences: Watching Star Trek and Doctor Who* (London and New York: Routledge, 1995): 3–24.
Michael Jindra, 'Star Trek Fandom as a Religious Phenomenon', *Sociology of Religion*, 55.1 (1994): 27–51.
Robert V. Kozinets, 'Utopian Enterprise: Articulating the Meanings of *Star Trek*'s Culture of Consumption', *Journal of Consumer Research*, 28.1 (2001): 67–88.
Manu Saadia, 'For Alt-Right Trolls, "Star Trek: Discovery" Is an Unsafe Space', *The New Yorker*, 26 May (2017), newyorker.com/tech/annals-of-technology/for-alt-right-trolls-star-trek-discovery-is-an-unsafe-space.
Christian Wenger, *Jenseits der Sterne: Gemeinschaft und Identität in Fankulturen. Zur Konstitution des Star Trek-Fandoms* (Bielefeld: transcript Verlag, 2006).

Fanfictions Cited

30MinuteLoop, 'The Struggle to Stay Human', *AO3*, 2 February (2018), archiveofourown.org/works/13487700.
Ailendolin, 'Whatever fate the stars are weaving', *AO3*, 25 February (2018), archiveofourown.org/works/13797006/chapters/31718475.
Apollothyme, 'in hues of liquid caramel and oxidized soda', *AO3*, 31 October (2017), archiveofourown.org/works/12577376.
Archaeodigit_dima, 'Nothing is Stopping you Except What's Inside, I can Help you but it's your Fight', *AO3*, 21 December (2017), archiveofourown.org/works/13085625/chapters/29935446.

BlackQat, 'The Morning After the Night Before', *AO3*, 25 April (2018), archiveofourown.org/works/14436096/chapters/33343026.
Darthpumpkinspice, 'Duty', *AO3*, 19 October (2017), archiveofourown.org/works/12408957.
Holloway88, 'Streaks', *AO3*, 24 November (2017), https://archiveofourown.org/works/12809598.
HopefulNebula, 'Rise in Perfect Light', *AO3*, 3 February (2018), archiveofourown.org/works/13563705.
LauramourFromOz, 'At the Going Down of The Sun', *AO3*, 11 November (2017), archiveofourown.org/works/12690399.
Lorenzobane, 'Vulnerability', *AO3*, 7 November (2017), archiveofourown.org/works/12658062.
M_class, 'Falling Tides', *AO3*, 23 August (2018), archiveofourown.org/works/15775800.
Mswyrr, 'i have loved the stars too fondly (to be fearful of the night),' *AO3*, 27 November (2017), archiveofourown.org/works/12843207/chapters/29326380.
Radiolaria, 'we sleep like wine in the conches', *AO3*, 3 April (2018), archiveofourown.org/works/14199567.
Strangeallure, 'A Prison of Her Own Design', *AO3*, 2 March (2018), archiveofourown.org/works/13848060.
Tptigger, 'I've Got You', *AO3*, 25 May (2018), archiveofourown.org/works/14749410/chapters/34102077.

Episodes and Films Cited

'Space Seed.' *Star Trek: The Original Series*, written by Gene L. Coon and Carey Wilber, directed by Marc Daniels, NBC, 16 February, 1967.
'Battle at the Binary Stars.' *Star Trek: Discovery*, written by Gretchen J. Berg, and Aaron Harberts, directed by Adam Kane, CBS Television Studios, 24 September, 2017.
'The Butcher's Knife Cares Not for the Lamb's Cry.' *Star Trek: Discovery*, written by Jesse Alexander and Aron Eli Coleite, directed by Olatunde Osunsanmi, CBS Television Studios, 8 October, 2017.
'Choose Your Pain.' *Star Trek: Discovery*, written by Gretchen J. Berg, Aaron Harberts, and Craig Sweeny, directed by Lee Rose, CBS Television Studios, 15 October, 2017.
'Despite Yourself.' *Star Trek: Discovery*, written by Sean Cochran, directed by Jonathan Frakes, CBS Television Studios, 7 January, 2018.
'The Wolf Inside.' *Star Trek: Discovery*, written by Lisa Randolph, directed by T.J. Scott, CBS Television Studios, 14 January, 2018.
'Vaulting Ambition.' *Star Trek: Discovery*, written by Jordon Nardino, directed by Hanelle M. Culpepper, CBS Television Studios, 21 January, 2018.

'The War Without, The War Within.' *Star Trek: Discovery*, written by Lisa Randolph, directed by David Solomon, CBS Television Studios, 4 February, 2018.

'Will You Take My Hand?' *Star Trek: Discovery*, written by Akiva Goldsmith (story), Gretchen J. Berg, and Aaron Harberts (story and teleplay), directed by Akiva Goldsmith, CBS Television Studios, 11 February, 2018.

Star Trek II: *The Wrath of Khan.* 1982. Directed by Nicholas Meyer. Paramount Pictures.

Star Trek: Beyond. 2016. Directed by Justin Lin. Paramount Pictures.

'Infinite Diversity in Infinite Combinations?' – Negotiating Otherness in *Star Trek: Discovery*

Afrofuturism, Imperialism, and Intersectionality

Interview with Dr. Diana A. Mafe on 'Normalizing Black Women as Heroes'

Dr. Diana A. Mafe is Associate Professor of English, Black Studies, International Studies, and Women's and Gender Studies at Denison University and the author of Where No Black Woman Has Gone Before – Subversive Portrayals in Speculative Film and TV *(University of Texas Press, 2018) and* Mixed Race Stereotypes in South African and American Literature: Coloring Outside the (Black and White) Lines *(Palgrave Macmillan, 2013).*

This interview has been edited for clarity.

In an essay for Media Diversified you have written that *'Discovery* normalizes a black female hero in space. Evading the extremes of paragon and pariah, the show gives us a nuanced figure and places her at the very center of the story' (2018a, n.p.). Can you go into a bit more detail for us as to how Burnham (Sonequa Martin-Green) transcends both the other black women within the *Star Trek* franchise (both the new and original) Lieutenant Uhura (Nichelle Nichols) and Guinan (Whoopi Goldberg)?

I think the obvious answer to that is that she is the protagonist. That's what really sets her apart from characters that have come before. Uhura is the pioneering black female figure in *Star Trek*, and there are many ways – which I talk about in my book – that she deserves to be called a pioneer because she was breaking all kinds of barriers in the 1960s, but on the show, she still had a very limited role: she was certainly part of the main cast, but never the central figure. And there are different ways in which she was sexualized, exoticized. In interviews that she [actress Nichelle Nichols] gave later, she talked about her own frustration with not being able to really tap into potential for that role; for instance, her lines were being cut, so there were limits. In that way, she was a product of her time. And then you look at a character like Guinan and, again, she was in some ways even more of a minor character than Uhura, because she was not in every episode, she was the bartender; she was wise, she gave advice. Sometimes they would include her in more elaborate storylines, but she, too, was certainly not an essential player. So, speaking from both a post-colonial and a critical race perspective, it is important to try and put Other people at the center of the story, the center of a history, and that is what Burnham does. She *is* our protagonist; she is the character we follow from the beginning to the end. That's amazing, and it's pioneering, and it has never been done before. And it's very cool.

And to say one last thing to this: the notion of normalizing the black female hero, the point of it is not to make this perfect person, this paragon who does everything right. The fact that she's the hero doesn't mean she's always the proverbial 'good guy' – the point is just to have her at the center, regardless of what she does. Whether she's a tragic hero, whether she does or doesn't do the right thing, the point is that she gets to have her story. And that it's the main story.

To add to that, there were people online complaining that she was a 'Mary Sue' and that she is the one who solves all the problems and who can do everything, but she mutinies in the second episode. And Burnham has this network of other characters – and specifically other female characters – that allow her to do some of the things that she does. And some of that criticism was underpinned by racism or people not being able to deal with a central female character and trying to find some way of criticizing her that's not just saying 'I don't like a female character.'

That's really interesting. And I agree. The notion of a 'Mary Sue' is that she's some sort of cookie-cutter character who does everything and fixes everything. But that's not Burnham. She's much more complex than that. She rebels against her captain at the very beginning of the story; she's a mutineer and commits treason. She certainly pushes against any easy readings of her as this perfect, good, character who is always doing the right thing.

When writing about *Doctor Who* (1963–1989; 2005–ongoing) and *Firefly* (2002–2003), you point out that characters like Martha Jones (Freema Ageyman) and Zoë Washburne (Gina Torres) 'frame a[n] ... intervention in what is otherwise a grand narrative of male mastery and control' as the male protagonists on these shows '... themselves present patriarchy and leave little room for

alternatives' (2018b, 17). **Is there a similar effect with Burnham and *Discovery*, particularly in regard to Gabriel Lorca (Jason Isaacs)?**

Yes. Absolutely, and probably, in some ways even more so than characters like Martha Jones and Zoë Washburne. To get a reading of those two characters as empowered and subversive and central, I had to acknowledge and work with the fact that they were secondary, always secondary. They were sidekicks (for lack of a better word), companions, so it was always obvious that they were not at the very center. So that makes it even harder to read them as important and crucial in their own right. My reading of it is that you have to look for the subtle empowerments in those shows, and you have to shift the gaze a bit to see what they are doing that makes them important, that makes them heroes in their own right. That's a little bit more work to do. That's this intervention in a grand narrative of male mastery and control. With *Discovery*, it's easier because she [Burnham] is the hero. So, you don't have to do this shift, where you start out by saying, 'she's not the center, but I'm going to make her the center.' Here, we can say 'she is the center.' And Lorca, despite carrying the title of captain, is clearly not the main character. He's certainly interesting, and you get the sense at different points in the show that he is trying to control her, pull her strings, manipulate her. But she is very much the core. And so, even more so than shows like *Doctor Who* or *Firefly*, she talks back against a history of television in which white men tend to be the captain and the hero – and if there are black women included, they tend to be the sidekick and the marginalized figure. So, [*Discovery*] is really inverting that in a way that I think is very rare, and I can't think of a whole lot examples where you can see that in television. That's very unusual.

And people may have wondered, why not just make Burnham the captain, why not have a show with the black woman as the captain, why not start there. But the way it is made it more interesting – having her as the captain would have made it easy, more formulaic. This way, she gets to perform this range of roles, including rebel, and mutineer, and it does not have to be this obvious idea of her being the black woman, her being the hero, so she must be the captain – they wrote a much more interesting role for her in this show. The key is not so much the title she has, as the roles she gets to play.

How do you view Burnham's relationship to Spock (Ethan Peck) as his step-sister? Does it simply legitimize her within *Star Trek* canon or do you see the fact that she was raised by the white

Vulcan Sarek (James Frain) and white human Amanda Grayson (Mia Kirshner) (and the consequential absence of her black birth parents)[1] as problematic/potentially reinforcing stereotypes?

I think, on the one hand, it's true that you don't get to see her history within her own family unit. So, if you want to talk about giving credit for the kind of person she becomes, that she's brilliant, that she can fight, and that she's technically gifted, we can credit all of this to her growing up Vulcan, and to Sarek. And that he had a strong hand in raising her and turning her into the person that she was. I don't know that it necessarily undermines her character, that it reinforces stereotypes. You do get a sense that she had a birth family that she loved and that were massacred by the Klingons, so there is enough of a narrative there that you get a sense of where she really came from, as well as her adoptive experience. For me, I think, the real sense of that was to connect her to the world of Spock, to the *Star Trek* universe, the *Star Trek* lore. That was just another way for them to ground the character in the canon, by making her that close to a canonical character. So maybe it's a bit of a gimmick, 'oh, she's Spock's sister,' but it worked for me. I don't think it contributed too much to stereotyping, it was more in the service of the *Star Trek* narrative. Part of it is to lay out this struggle she has between the logic of being a Vulcan, or being raised like a Vulcan, and the fact that she's still human and has human emotion that she is grappling with. And that provides a nice counterpoint to Voq/Ash (Shazad Latif) – they both have this dual nature in themselves.

From a feminist point of view, how do you see Burnham's relationship to other female characters like Georgiou (Michelle Yeoh), Tilly (Mary Wiseman), and L'Rell (Mary Chieffo)?

To start with Georgiou, since she's her captain, that's the woman we first see – when the trailer was released, that first shot of the two women of color in the desert triggered all kinds of backlash before the show had even aired. I think the show is being careful not to isolate Burnham, as a feminist character, a feminist icon. She gets to foster interesting relationships with the other women in the show. I think it would be different if she was always on her own, doing her own thing

---

[1] This interview was conducted before season two of *Discovery* aired and Michael Burnham's mother gets a more prominent role – this does however not affect her actual upbringing as a child as discussed here.

and, on some level, she does – but she has very deep, if complicated, relationships with the other women. Georgiou is another strong woman of color, in her own right, who has another interesting story arc. Theirs is initially almost a kind of maternal relationship, on Georgiou's part, we certainly see that in the Mirror Universe. And then you have the betrayal because Burnham mutinies, she gets punished, and Georgiou dies. So, you see ways in which all the strong women in the show are complex. It's never as easy as good and bad; good guy, bad guy. All of them are complex, all of them are strong, Tilly as well. She starts out as this sort of peppy, naïve character, but she has a growth arc over the course of the story. And L'Rell, of all the characters, is probably the most interesting in terms of her relationship to Burnham, because they are archenemies, but by the end they are collaborating. You get a real range with the other female characters and Burnham's relationship to them. And the other thing is that it's not predictable, it's not cliché, it's not them arguing over a male character, if you think about the Bechdel test and questions of how female characters are interacting. I think [the show] keeps it very nuanced. And none of these characters fall into any easy, obvious, cliché roles, and that strengthens the feminist implications of the show.

You write that 'sexuality continues to be a prerequisite for modern SF heroines' (2018b, 66). Would you say that *Discovery* avoids this sexualization of Burnham (and its other female characters)?

Yes! In my book I talk about the history of how black women have been portrayed on screen, and yes, that prerequisite remains true. There is the idea that you must be scantily clad, or you can fight, but do it in short shorts. There are enough really cliché movies out there that claim a strong female character, but also a clearly sexualized one. And it's not so much that a character cannot have sexuality, I don't think that's the point – it's about whether it's stereotypical, and it's about the audience the show or film is trying to appeal to. Burnham eventually has a romantic relationship with Ash Tyler, and they do have a sexual relationship, but as a character, she is not unnecessarily sexualized; whether you look at her demeanor, her attire, her language. If anything, she initially is really channeling that Vulcan persona, which is very strait-laced, and she doesn't seem to have much of a sense of humor. It certainly pushes back against any easy readings of her as just a sexual object. She's never objectified. That's another plus for the show that it doesn't feel like it needs to put her in some outfit to make her interesting to the audience. Looking at Uhura in the 1960s, however interesting she was, she and all the other female characters were to a certain degree sexualized [through] the mini skirt that she had to wear. To go from that to a character like Burnham is really interesting for the *Star Trek* universe. And it proved that that doesn't have to be a prerequisite for a strong, female character in a science fiction show – she'll still be interesting without the mini skirt. And the point is not to make them asexual, the point is to make them interesting, but not to rely strictly on a kind of sexualization. So, the fact that she has the romance with Ash Tyler is important, because it is another way of humanizing her, and showing her desire and emotion. It's not that she's completely washed out in terms of sexuality, but she's made interesting and sexuality is not her cornerstone.

With regard to *Doctor Who*'s Martha Jones, you write that 'negative fan reactions ... simply reiterate her ability to challenge viewers when it comes to hegemonic models' (2018b, 136). Would you say the same is true for negative fan reactions to Burnham?

Yes, absolutely. Martha Jones was the first black female companion for the Doctor, and she was constantly being compared to her immediate predecessor, Rose. So, fans did not seem to like Martha Jones. It was interesting to me, I thought she was great, I loved Martha Jones as a character. But fans had an issue with her, and part of that was just always comparing her to what had come before. I took that as another sign of her subversiveness – she was riling people up, people did not like her. And the same can be said about Burnham, that this is a character who is very different from the women, certainly black women, that have come before in the *Star Trek* universe, and so the fact that people were complaining about the show before the first episode had even aired tells you something. It was just sort of a kneejerk reaction to two women of color [in the trailer] and, ultimately, to a black woman as a hero, at the center of a *Star Trek* show. And this reaction to it shows that people weren't ready for that. But I think that's to the credit of a character like Burnham, and it's true for all change – people are never ready for that, and you will always get some level of backlash to doing something different. And in terms of juxtaposing black women and white women on screen, there is a long and often insidious history of comparison there, and that's another aspect that comes into play – you are used to seeing a certain thing, and then you see something completely different.

You use the terms 'subversive spectatorship' and 'oppositional gaze' (2018b, 10) in your book. Were these strategies of watching speculative fiction necessary when you watched Star Trek: Discovery **and, if not, what does that say about the show and how it (potentially) changes the genre?**

For everything I looked at as case studies for the book, part of the reason I used an oppositional gaze is that it was kind of required because, again, the black women were not the central characters. It always means you have to do a little bit of extra work to not just see these characters but empower these characters. And again, *Discovery* makes that easier. On the one hand, Burnham's still a black woman, she still lives in a kind of universe where her race and her gender carry a certain symbolic weight, so you still need a certain subversive perspective to watch the show. On the other hand, you don't have to do all this extra work to say 'oh, she's important, despite what the show tells me.' Here, she's important and the show affirms that. And that's unusual. So, in that sense, it is a game changer, because it is so rare to have a black female hero. I would say that an oppositional gaze is still useful, but you don't have to work so hard, because the show itself is saying she's the hero.

The Klingons have traditionally been racialized on successive Star Trek **shows. Do the redesigned Klingons on Discovery change that or would you say that they still occupy a racialized position? And if so, would you say that Burnham and L'Rell coming to compromise and work together (to some extent) at the end of season one is a similar dismantling of 'white paternal law' (2018b, 48) as you argue for in** Alien vs. Predator **(2004)?**

The Klingons on *Discovery* looked very different from the Klingons that have come before. Reading reactions to the show, I noticed that there was some outrage about the 'new Klingon' being more stylized, more barbaric, more savage, even less 'civilized' than previous versions. I think the portrayal of the Klingons is an old issue within the *Star Trek* universe and I don't think that *Discovery* does a lot to resolve that. If you come from a tradition of reading the Klingons as racialized characters, then *Discovery* just extends that even further with, for instance, the kind of makeup they used to imagine the Klingons. In that sense, I don't think that they are particularly progressive. The Klingons get a lot of screen time and they are crucial to the narrative, I mean, really the whole first season, the big plot is the Klingons vs. the Federation in this war, and how to solve it. But that means they are the bad guys who are on the other side of the line, opposite to the Federation. There is a history of racialization there and I don't think that the show necessarily defuses that. On some level they are still playing into a kind of 'flat' version of the Klingons. That being said, obviously we do get close-ups of some of the characters, with L'Rell and Voq. If the show fails a bit in the broad portrait of the Klingons, it compensates by giving us some very interesting closer looks at some very nuanced Klingon characters. And the fact that Burnham and L'Rell end up working together was a very interesting twist given the arc they had over the course of the show. It was another way of evading what I have termed 'white paternal law' in the book – if we get to the end of the show, and a white male hero is not at the center, that's unusual. That certainly is similar to my argument on *Alien vs. Predator* that, at the end of it all, you have the black female character as the last one standing, and the Predator as heroes to root for, because there is nobody else left to root for. So, I do think *Discovery* does something similar.

One more question about Mirror Georgiou. There's the scene in the brothel on Qo'noS and she takes these two sex workers with her – would you say that veers too closely to established portrayals of women of color (and bisexual people) as using sex to get what they want?

I remember the scene – it certainly fit with her new character as evil. So, on that level they're clearly trying to portray her as creature of excess. This is Bad Georgiou. She does whatever she wants to do, she feeds her carnal appetites, so it fit with her new persona. But I certainly take your point of the risk of, at the same time, feeding into stereotypes; I can understand the discomfort with it as well. So, it fit with her character. I think it would have been a lot stranger if it had been Burnham. I at least appreciated that they were strategic with the sexuality of these characters – for Burnham it was this relationship with Ash Tyler, and then you have Mirror Georgiou using sex slaves. I think this was just another layer to her character, but I think you're right to be cautious. You look back to the traditions of cinema and how women of color are portrayed and notions of sexual excess – it's a fine balance.

We would like to thank Dr. Mafe for taking the time to do this interview with us and for her insightful answers to our questions and analyses of Star Trek: Discovery *and the character of Michael Burnham.*

Works Cited

Diana A. Mafe, 'Normalizing Black Women as Heroes: Star Trek Discovery as Groundbreaking', *Media Diversified*, 6 March (2018a), https://mediadiversified.org/2018/03/06/normalising-black-women-as-heroes-star-trek-discovery-as-groundbreaking/.

——, *Where No Black Woman Has Gone Before: Subversive Portrayals in Speculative Film and TV* (Austin: University of Texas Press, 2018b).

The Cotton-Gin Effect
An Afrofuturist Reading of *Star Trek: Discovery*
Whit Frazier Peterson

The recent success of the film *Black Panther* (2018) has catapulted Afrofuturism to the forefront of our current cultural conversations, even if it is not always clear what is meant by this term. It was coined by Mark Dery in his article 'Black to the Future' (1994), and the 'psychogeography of Afrofuturism' (187), as Dery puts it, covers territory ranging from music, to fashion, to film, to literature. In this chapter I will broadly define Afrofuturism as anything that explores the crossroads of identity politics, history, technology, and the African diaspora; and in the United States it can be argued that Afrofuturism has been a part of the African American aesthetic ever since John Henry took on the steel drill.[1] That is to say that the African American aesthetic has to some extent always been concerned with the way technology intersects with issues of race, because technology and race have always been connected in American society, as African slaves were brought to the United States to operate functionally as machines and not as human beings.

Recent approaches to Afrofuturism have included looking at it as a subcategory of the broader category of all Black Speculative Fiction (see the essay collection *Afrofuturism 2.0* (2016) edited by Reynaldo Anderson), a move that seems useful as the definition of Afrofuturism continues to expand. Indeed, to some extent, to mention Afrofuturism at all is to evoke the entire spectrum of Black Speculative Fiction. In this essay, I am interested in somewhat expanding the definition even further, and moving beyond looking at Afrofuturism as just a type of cultural aesthetic or philosophy, but also as a means of critical analysis. There is

---

[1] The John Henry legend is from African American folklore, and tells the story of John Henry, a railroad worker, who dies attempting to lay down track faster than a steam drill. For an interesting discussion of the John Henry myth throughout history, see Nikola-Lisa's 1998 article 'John Henry: Now and Then.'

some precedent for this. Lisa Yaszek's article, 'An Afrofuturist Reading of *Invisible Man*' (2005) and Isaiah Lavender's article, 'An Afrofuturist Reading of Zora Neale Hurston's *Their Eyes Were Watching God*' (2016) are both examples of articles where scholars take traditional works of the African American literary canon and apply Afrofuturist readings to them. In the case of Yaszek's article, we see how Ellison's book concerns itself with race and technology, despite the fact that Ellison specifically wanted to discourage any science-fictional reading of his novel (Yaszek, 2005, 298); likewise, in the case of Lavender's article, Lavender shows how many of the tropes of black science fiction appear in Hurston's novel. In this article, I will be going a step further; where these articles follow Alondra Nelson's prescription that Afrofuturism as a means of critical inquiry should attempt to 'explore futurist themes in black cultural production and the ways in which technological innovation is changing the face of black art and culture' (Anderson, 2016, 92), I am interested in how Afrofuturism as a means of critical inquiry can be used to look at pop culture products that are concerned with technology and how we can analyze these products in order to interrogate our concepts not only of blackness, but also of whiteness. To that end, I will look at the new television series *Star Trek: Discovery* (2017–ongoing) and investigate the liberal-humanist philosophy underlying both the fictional Federation of Planet's worldview, as well as the show's producers' worldview.

I will begin my examination with an analysis of the troubling relationship Captain Gabriel Lorca (Jason Isaacs), the starship captain in the first season, has with women of color, particularly Michael Burnham (Sonequa Martin-Green). Lorca's sense of propriety over the black body has a history that goes back to slavery and, in this series, this sense of propriety manifests itself not only across time, but also across alternate universes. That this sense of propriety goes unnamed, and thus unrecognized and unchallenged, especially in a time when such racial distinctions are supposedly a thing of the past, speaks to the way that technological progress, while purportedly using science to move us beyond race, often hides racist assumptions and ensconced patterns of behavior within its very design. This is what I identify as the cotton-gin effect, where technology and/or behavior, seemingly benign and interested in the advancement of progress, actually operates within the parameters and paradigms of a racist society and at the expense of an oppressed people. I will argue that the unchecked behavior of Lorca towards Michael makes his appearance akin to that of the slave-owner, who views the black body as technology and property; moreover, the fact that Lorca is actually from the highly racist Mirror Universe (a fact at first hidden from the viewer), makes his easy assimilation into the Prime Universe, and the way his behavior is tolerated in the Prime Universe, telling of the hidden ideologies in the Prime Universe itself.[2] I will also argue that the abuses of technology in the show, latent in the Prime Universe and explicit in the Mirror Universe, as well as the very balancing act that the *Star Trek* franchise has done since its inception, of promoting liberal-humanist ideals in a supposedly post-racial future, while simultaneously playing by the race-inflected rules of the era in which the shows were filmed, all create a cognitive dissonance for the viewer that is similar to that of the cotton-gin effect, in that the good intentions of the shows' producers, while exposing some of the racist assumptions and ensconced patterns of behavior in television production in general, hide others.[3] To that end, the liberal-humanist philosophy of the show itself creates something of a cotton-gin effect, where the world we live in as viewers is just the idealized view we have of ourselves; what *Star Trek* ultimately, and unintentionally, reveals to us is that the liberal-humanist world we as viewers live in is just a Mirror Universe masquerading as a Prime Universe, just like Mirror Lorca masquerades as Prime Lorca; the difference being Lorca is aware of his deceit, whereas

---

[2] It should be noted that Admiral Katrina Cornwell does actually notice and comment on Lorca's recent behavior; the relationship between these two will also be examined in the course of this paper.

[3] Dr. Diana Mafe identifies some of these issues in previous *Star Trek* series when she discusses the role black women have played in them. See the interview with Dr. Mafe in this book, in which she says: 'Uhura is the pioneering black female figure in *Star Trek*, and there are many ways – which I talk about in my book – that she deserves to be called a pioneer because she was breaking all kinds of barriers in the 1960s, but on the show, she still had a very limited role: she was certainly part of the main cast, but never the central figure. And there are different ways in which she was sexualized, exoticized. In interviews that she [actress Nichelle Nichols] gave later, she talked about her own frustration with not being able to really tap into potential for that role; for instance, her lines were being cut, so there were limits. In that way, she was a product of her time. And then you look at a character like Guinan and, again, she was in some ways even more of a minor character than Uhura, because she was not in every episode, she was the bartender; she was wise, she gave advice. Sometimes they would include her in more elaborate storylines, but she, too, was certainly not an essential player.' In this chapter I will be arguing that despite the fact that in *Star Trek: Discovery* a black woman is now the main protagonist, there are still areas of improvement that are overlooked in the justifiable celebration of increased diversity in the show, and that it is often this very self-congratulatory as opposed to self-critical attitude that causes the producers to overlook these possible areas of improvement.

we are in the grip of the cotton-gin effect, and cannot always see this clearly ourselves.

Star Trek: Discovery's first season follows a story arc involving Michael Burnham, a young Starfleet science officer aboard the *U.S.S. Shenzhou* and later a science specialist on the *U.S.S. Discovery*. Burnham is an African American woman who was raised by Sarek (James Frain), Spock's (Ethan Peck) father, after the murder of her own parents by Klingon soldiers. This traumatic event informs much of Burnham's thinking throughout the season, despite her training on Vulcan, where she learned to temper her emotions. Thus, in the two pilot episodes, when the *Shenzhou* comes across Klingon warships, Burnham, despite being a Starfleet officer, and thus committed to a moral philosophy of non-violence whenever possible, attempts to take control of the ship and attack the Klingon vessels, a maneuver known as the 'Vulcan Hello' (also the title of the first episode). The Vulcan experience with Klingons had always been adversarial, Burnham learns in a conversation with her step-father, and the Vulcans are aware that any confrontation with Klingon starships means inevitable battle; thus, in order to gain the upper hand in a conflict situation, the protocol of the Vulcan government is to attack Klingon ships as soon as they are spotted, even if they have not attacked first (1x01, 'The Vulcan Hello'), a response that clearly echoes the United States' own controversial post-9/11 policy of 'pre-emptive strikes' that characterized the 'Bush Doctrine' (Gupta, 2008, 181).

This reference is intended of course. Throughout the season, viewers are given glimpses of policy approaches that echo some of the United States' own (foreign) policies, and the corrections to U.S. policy are meant to be evident in the liberal-humanist philosophy of Starfleet, which is dedicated to peace, non-violence, philanthropy, and exploration.[4] Thus, the arc of Michael's story is from her reactionary mutiny, to once again defying Starfleet at the end of the season when Starfleet, under danger of destruction by the Klingon Empire, approves a plan to destroy the Klingons' home planet of Qo'noS, thereby rendering the Klingon Empire too weak to continue their thus far successful campaign against the Federation. Michael, in essence, learns a lesson that Starfleet command has adopted, but has not fully internalized. How Michael acquires this wisdom is the fundamental story arc underlying the season. This story involves a number of complicated relationships Michael has with

---

[4] For a discussion of U.S. foreign policy and *Star Trek* in general, and *Discovery* in particular, see also 'The American Hello: U.S. Representations of Diplomacy in *Star Trek: Discovery*' by Henrik Schillinger and Arne Sönnichsen in this volume.

members of her crew; and, as in the reboot *Star Trek* film series, which imagines the original *Star Trek* cast in an alternate universe, *Star Trek: Discovery* assumes the existence of the multiverse as well, an infinite number of parallel universes where historical differences have led to differences in the characters. The existence of this multiverse allows us to analyze the relationships between the characters in two differently imagined universes and see what tropes surface in both, and what tropes emerge slightly changed.

An Armageddon: As Now

The first thing that has to be mentioned when discussing this season from an Afrofuturist perspective is that there is no mention made of different races between humans. This needs to be analyzed because Michael's race is not immaterial to the actual product we, as viewers, are watching. Co-creator Bryan Fuller made it clear in the production of the show that not only did he want the main character to be female, he also wanted her to 'represent diversity.' In a statement before the actual airing of the show, he said:

> *Star Trek* started with a wonderful expression of diversity in its cast ... our lead of the show is going to be subject of that same level of who's the best actor and also what can we say about diversity on the show. We haven't cast her yet, so we don't know what level of diversity she will be, but that's forefront in our minds. (Hibberd, 2017)

So it is no accident that an African American woman, Sonequa Martin-Green, is playing this lead role, and yet within the context of the show itself, at least explicitly, there is no mention made of race at all. We are supposedly in a future time where questions of race between humans are no longer relevant, and even the most unenlightened humans do not see racial categories between humans as a fundamental issue anymore.[5]

What is troubling about this approach, however, is the cognitive dissonance between the cultural moment in which the show appears, where identity politics are paramount to our global conversation, and

---

[5] It should be mentioned that this is only so in the Prime Universe. In the Mirror Universe, racism appears to be a very prominent issue, although we never really learn what is meant by racism in a universe characterized by interactions between highly sentient creatures from myriad planets.

the world of *Star Trek*, where xenophobia manifests between alien species but not between human 'races.' This is perhaps most evident in the relationship Michael Burnham has with Captain Gabriel Lorca, a rogue captain who has managed to travel across universes, and uses Michael, as well as the *Discovery*'s experimental spore drive, to help him get back to his own universe, hoping in the process to continue his campaign against the Terran Empire, which is the counterpart to the Federation. The fate of Prime Gabriel Lorca remains a mystery, at least on the television show, but it becomes obvious in the second half of the season that Lorca has had a relationship with Michael Burnham in the Mirror Universe (1x12, 'Vaulting Ambition'), and this relationship is one that he assumes he can reignite in some way with the Burnham from the Prime Universe.

Michael is in fact being transferred from one prison to another for her attempted mutiny against her original captain, Captain Georgiou (Michelle Yeoh), aboard the *U.S.S. Shenzhou* when she is taken aboard the *U.S.S. Discovery*, which Captain Lorca commands. There, she encounters some of her old shipmates, who now have taken a very cold and unfriendly attitude towards her. After a fight in the mess hall, Michael is taken to see Captain Lorca, and the viewer is witness to the first meeting between Michael from the Prime Universe and Captain Lorca from the Mirror Universe (1x03, 'Context is for Kings').

His first words to her are themselves ironic: 'No matter how deep in space you are, I always feel like you can just see home' (1x03), the irony being two-fold: first, that Lorca's eyes have trouble adjusting to the light, as he is from an alternate universe and, second, that being from an alternate universe, there is, of course, no way he could imagine himself 'seeing' home across any distance. There is also the additional meaning that by seeing Michael again in this universe where she is still alive, he is once again seeing a 'home' that he had lost.[6] At the start of the ensuing three-minute exchange between the two characters, we see Lorca evading Michael's questions, and behaving in a way that can almost be considered bashful; for example when Michael asks, 'What am I doing aboard this ship?' Lorca answers, glancing furtively behind his back, 'I guess you might have to ask that storm out there.' Michael counters with, 'I received no warning that I'd be transferred to another prison facility, which is customary. My shuttle changed course halfway through the journey,' to which Lorca cryptically responds, 'Maybe the

---

[6] It should be noted that this irony is not apparent to the viewer until later on in the season, as on a first viewing it is not clear at this point that Lorca's character is from an alternate universe.

universe hates waste.' 'Sir?' asks Michael, and here Lorca coquettishly smiles and cocks his head to the side, responding, 'The question is: what am I going to do with you?' Lorca says this with something of a lascivious smile, then appears to run this question through his mind out loud – what is he going to do with her – dismissing the possibility of putting her in the brig, and deciding instead to put her to work on the ship.

Up to this point in this exchange, Lorca has played something of a flirt. His attitude has been friendly, non-threatening and, in general, that of a confidante. When Michael refuses to work, with a simple, 'no,' however, we see an immediate change in his disposition. 'Excuse me?' he says, his eyes narrow, and he gives her a sidelong, indignant glance. For the African American viewer who is aware that Michael is playing a role that is meant to celebrate diversity, we are confronted with a situation that is all too familiar: The African American woman is simply not allowed to question the use of her body in the institutional chains of power in which she finds herself. And so one cannot help but think of bell hooks' comment from 1992 in *Black Looks*, that 'there are few films or television shows that attempt to challenge assumptions that sexual relationships between black women and white men are not based solely on power relationships which mirror master/slave paradigms' (74). Historically, the *Star Trek* series have been interested in looking at tropes in popular culture and subverting them, and yet, even in 2017 (when *Star Trek: Discovery* first aired), the *Star Trek* franchise is still not able to subvert this trope. Right away, within the first few minutes of their meeting, Lorca has turned their relationship into one that echoes the master/slave paradigm, and Lorca exhibits the white male sense of propriety over the black female body by combining flirtatiousness with a quick willingness to pull rank and thus establish power dynamics within the context of this sexually charged exchange.

The scene continues with Michael immediately showing a subservient attitude by not only responding with 'No thank you, respectfully,' but responding in what amounts to no more than a whisper. She continues in this whispered voice, 'I owe a debt for my crime and it'd be best... I'd prefer to serve my time without getting involved.' Lorca, for his part simply laughs when she says this and responds, 'Think I care what your preferences are?' He then walks away from her, and says, 'Until your vessel is repaired, you'll be assigned to quarters and put to work' (1x03). This sounds eerily reminiscent of slavery, if there were still any lingering doubts, and even hearkens back to the neo-slavery of not only the Black Codes of American Reconstruction, where an African American violating the vagrancy laws could be 'put to work,' but also to the neo-slavery built into the language of the 13th Amendment, where in Section 1, it is written, 'Neither slavery nor involuntary servitude, *except as a punishment for crime whereof the party shall have been duly convicted*, shall exist within the United States, or any place subject to their jurisdiction' (*U.S. Constitution.* Art./Amend. XIII, Sec. 1; emphasis added). Thus, Michael becomes the only character in the entire first season to be subjected to involuntary servitude, and this is imposed on her by a white superior officer who has had an intimate relationship with her double in a parallel universe. 'You were once a Starfleet officer,' Lorca continues, 'I would use you or anything else I can to achieve my mission' (1x03). Once again, the language here dehumanizes Michael, in effect calling her a thing, an especially chilling attitude to take towards a sexual partner. This, too, has a long historical precedent; bell hooks observes that black women in European society were never considered human by the white male:

> They are not to look at her as a whole human being. They are to notice only certain parts. Objectified in a manner similar to that of black female slaves who stood on auction blocks while owners and overseers described their important, salable parts, the black women whose naked bodies were displayed for whites at social functions had no presence. They were reduced to mere spectacle. Little is known of their lives, their motivations. Their body parts were offered as evidence to support racist notions that black people were more akin to animals than other humans. (1992, 62)

At this point in the conversation Lorca says that his mission is to send everyone home 'safe and happy,' then he dismisses Michael with a curt nod of his head. All sense of playfulness or flirtatiousness has now dissipated, and his body language, standing above her with arms held akimbo, is one of a person in authority speaking to a subservient, which is, of course, the actual power dynamic between them. What Lorca does know, and what Michael (and we as viewers), at this point, are unaware of, is that there is already a sexual component to this relationship and this power dynamic makes the scene, upon a second viewing, even more perverse, and centers it historically within the tropes of black female slave and white male master paradigms. The look on Lorca's face when Michael leaves the room is one of disgust, lust, and curiosity.

These kinds of scenes are familiar enough to us as modern people and consumers of popular culture. Whether we focus on minor microaggressions like white people fawning over and touching black hair without permission, or cultural memes that reappear in music videos showing black women twerking, which are then subsequently satirized and turned into a kind of *booty-blackface* in countless *YouTube* videos and commercial products (consider for example the mechanical twerking Santa Claus or a mechanical twerking Christmas Bear), or the very real power dynamics in play that cause women of color to die at three times the rate of white women in childbirth (Martin, 2018), black women are devalued in American society, and this devaluation is emphasized and reemphasized through our media outlets. Even Michelle Obama, one of the most inspiring contemporary public figures in recent history, discusses how, as a successful and powerful black woman, she had to deal with the 'angry black woman' trope being applied to her (Obama, 2018, 265). What makes this interesting from an Afrofuturist perspective is the way this trope plays out in the *Star Trek* universe, not just within one universe, but across universes. In a series in which the Federation finds itself eventually facing Armageddon, we have a black female who has been living through Armageddon her entire life. Borrowing from Public Enemy's line 'Armageddon been in effect,' and referencing music writer Mark Sinker, tobias c. van Veen writes in 'The Armageddon Effect':

> For Sinker, the very genesis of Afrofuturism develops from the tension that 'Armageddon been in effect.' Armageddon commences with Africans abducted by aliens to a strange land; everything that follows is played out in a post-apocalyptic dystopia. The phrase is taken from 'Countdown to Armageddon,' the dystopic, shell-shocked opening to *It Takes A Nation of Millions to Hold Us Back* (1988). Professor Griff unleashes the flow: 'Armageddon been in effect. Go get a late pass. Step! / This time around, the revolution will not be televised. Step!' For Sinker as for Public Enemy, the alien ships had already landed. (2016, 68–69)

Thus, Michael's story begins with Armageddon, as do all African Americans' stories – specifically, in Michael's case, with the murder of her parents.[7] African Americans of course, also have to deal with their displacement from the motherland. This is to say all African Americans are in the position of the motherless child, and all African Americans have been, to some extent, like Michael, raised by an alien intelligence. When Captain Lorca decides to take Michael, and indeed the entire ship

---

[7] Michael's mother is actually alive, as will be revealed in the second season; the viewer, however, does not realize this at the moment, nor does Michael. Even in the second season, Michael remains something of a 'motherless child,' as she is forced to lose her mother a second time.

and its crew, with him to his universe, the theme of abduction takes center stage. Once again, we see the white male in position of power asserting his authority in order to wrest a black female from her home and implant her in his own. He has lost her in one universe and feels he can simply take her alternate as his lover in another. It is a position that only someone with an extreme sense of propriety over the black body could assume, and the relationship between Michael and Lorca then takes on an even darker cast once the two of them find themselves in the Mirror Universe. At this point, Michael goes from simply being an out-of-reach potential black female sex slave for Gabriel Lorca, to a very within-reach potential black female sex slave. They are no longer in the liberal-humanist universe of the Federation. They are now in the very aptly named Mirror Universe, a universe that shows us what the Federation really is when it looks itself in the face.

In the universe Lorca comes from, the Terran Empire is built on an 'oppressive, racist, xenophobic culture that dominates all known space' (1x10, 'Despite Yourself'). The Mirror Universe is a universe that, for Federation officers from the Prime Universe at least, is also an Armageddon universe. They all have counterparts in this universe, counterparts who are generally cruel and manipulative, and yet they are forced to play these roles themselves if they are to survive in this new environment. For Captain Lorca, this is just a return to normal, but for the rest of the crew it becomes an existential nightmare. In this new universe, Lorca was the right-hand advisor of Terran Emperor Phillipa Georgiou, who had been Burnham's captain on the *Shenzhou* back in the Prime Universe, and Lorca and Georgiou raised Michael together as an adopted daughter after Michael's parents were killed. At some point, however, Lorca developed a more than paternal affection for Michael, and this led to a rift between Emperor Georgiou and Lorca. This rift comes to a head when Lorca attempts a coup against Georgiou, Michael is sent by Georgiou to stop him, and Michael is killed in the process. This leads to Lorca escaping into the Prime Universe, and leaving his ship, the *I.S.S. Buran*, in the Mirror Universe to be destroyed (1x12, 'Vaulting Ambition').[8]

Lorca's relationships with various other women are also worth a bit of scrutiny at this point. The one relationship that Lorca has that the

---

[8] The reference to the Cold War Soviet Shuttle 'Buran' is certainly intentional; the original Soviet Buran was destroyed in a hangar accident in 2002 (www.space.com). The implications of this Cold War reference to questions of liberal-humanist philosophy, while beyond the scope of the present study, are certainly of interest.

viewer actually sees consummated in the first season is his relationship with Admiral Katrina Cornwell (Jayne Brook), a high-ranking Starfleet officer, who also once worked as a psychiatrist. Their intimate moment comes in episode 6, 'Lethe,' when Cornwell boards the *Discovery* in order to check on the mental and psychological health of Lorca. It seems that Lorca is interested in two kinds of relationships, and both of these involve explicit power dynamics: On the one hand, he enjoys relationships with women who are not of the same rank as he is, subordinates, whom he can use and discard at will – this characterizes his relationship with Michael, with Commander Ellen Landry (Rekha Sharma) and with a woman from the Mirror Universe, Ava, who is mentioned only once and never makes an appearance;[9] on the other hand, he seems to enjoy relationships with women in power as well, women who rank higher than he does. Both Emperor Georgiou in the Mirror Universe and Admiral Cornwell in the Prime Universe rank higher than he does, and those are the only other two women we see him involved with. In the scene where Lorca and Admiral Cornwell meet to discuss what he has been up to, Lorca at one point suggests they talk like friends, and breaks out a bottle of scotch. Admiral Cornwell then tells him, 'I worry about you, Gabriel. Some of the decisions you've been making lately have been troubling' (1x06, 'Lethe'). Lorca pushes back against this, suggesting that war requires some quick minute creative thinking, but Cornwell is able to see past his attempts at dissembling. 'I don't think you've been the same since the *Buran*,'[10] she says. At this point Lorca laughs somewhat nervously, leans forward and can only offer, 'I've passed every test. Cleared for duty every time. But you know that don't you, Doc,' thus moving the discussion away from the personal and back into the professional. Cornwell replies that she has indeed seen his evaluations, but that what really concerns her is that 'less than a week

---

[9] The question of who Ava is is itself worth asking. Her brother, Captain Maddox (Dwain Murphy), a dark-skinned man, releases Lorca from the torture chamber in order to personally exact revenge on behalf of his sister, a woman whom Lorca apparently used as a sexual object and discarded. Maddox repeatedly demands that Lorca acknowledge his sister by saying her name. Lorca, after coming out of the torture chamber and gaining the upper hand in a tussle with Captain Maddox says, 'Her name was Ava. And I liked her. But you know how it is. Somebody better came along' (1x12, 'Vaulting Ambition'). The assumption here is that this 'somebody better' was Michael; this dismissive way of talking about black women seems to support the idea that Lorca feels a sense of propriety over the black body and is easily able to dehumanize black women as objects.

[10] In the Prime Universe the *Buran* was also destroyed.

ago you were being tortured, now you're back in the chair. How do you feel about that?' Lorca's response to this is to laugh again and say, 'Are we in a session? I didn't know you were practicing again, because if I have your undivided attention for fifty minutes, I can think of a whole bunch of other things we could be doing.' At which point he commences to seduce her and thus to completely deflect the conversation away from himself.

This scene is interesting to compare with the previous scene involving Michael, because both scenes showcase Lorca's manipulative way of dealing with women – in the case of Michael, dealing with a subservient, and in the case of Admiral Cornwell, dealing with a superior officer. In both instances what we see at play is Lorca's enjoyment of the back and forth of the male/female power struggle. In the case of Michael, his obsession with her, and thus the coquettish manner in which he addresses her at first, allows her an initial advantage, to the point where she even feels like she can refuse to help him onboard the ship, an advantage which he quickly shuts down by a shift in his demeanor as soon as she denies him. In the case of Cornwell, he realizes that his point of power comes from her feelings for him. However, it does not seem likely that he has any actual feelings for Admiral Cornwell, as they do not appear to have had any relationship in the Mirror Universe,[11] and so he uses her affection for him as a means of manipulating her – not only by disarming her line of inquiry into his behavior and disposition (since he, unbeknownst to her, has assumed the place of Prime Lorca), but also by having her question her own expertise and objectivity in relation to him.

This is evident when Lorca is sleeping after they have made love, and Cornwell examines a scar on his back. His reaction is to flip around and pull a phaser on her; in essence, he wakes up experiencing a moment of trauma, a trauma that may seem like extreme PTSD to Cornwell. She responds by saying, 'The truth is you are not the man I used to know' (1x06). Once again, Lorca tries to turn this around by admitting, 'You're right. It's been harder on me than I let on, and I need help.' Cornwell responds, 'I hate that I can't tell if this is really you.' Cornwell, as Lorca's lover and as a trained psychologist, intuits something is amiss, but she cannot really see what is troubling him, because she is not able to name and identify the sense of propriety Lorca feels he has over Michael. This is to say, what seems to really trouble Lorca in this scene is the possibility of losing the *Discovery*. He knows he cannot lose the ship because, if he does, he loses the opportunity to return to the Mirror

---

[11] This is only made apparent to the viewer later in the season.

Universe, and to do so with Michael. There is a bond between Michael and Lorca, as Lorca sees it, that is fated to exist across multiverses. As he himself says, 'Different universe, and yet somehow the same people had a way to find each other. It's the strongest argument I've ever seen for the existence of destiny' (1x10, 'Despite Yourself').

That Lorca brings his Armageddon-inflected mind to the Prime Universe and exercises his sense of propriety over Michael in this new world is no surprise; what is worthy of note, however, is that Michael accepts his behavior as normal and allows it to go unchallenged. Michael, in the Prime Universe, is already in a state of Armageddon as a black woman in a white universe, as a human who has been raised as a Vulcan, as a young woman who witnessed the murder of her parents, and as a Starfleet officer who intuits that Starfleet itself is only one catastrophe away from abandoning its own principles. The fact that race is never mentioned is itself testament to the sense of complete Armageddon haunting Michael in the Prime Universe. After all, there is no way that the crew of the *Enterprise*, in the year 2257, reflects the diversity that the planet Earth will have in 250 years unless there was a literal Armageddon for people of color on the planet. In fact, Michael is the only black female on the ship that we as viewers get to know; the only other afronaut of note on the ship, Dr. Culber (Wilson Cruz), is killed off fairly early by Michael's love interest, Tyler (Shazad Latif).[12] On the one hand, one can argue that this is a television show made in 2017, where we are all fully aware that African American actors receive, in general, short shrift; but on the other hand, *Star Trek*, as a franchise has always concerned itself with the question of diversity, and to cast the crew of a starship that reflects diversity patterns in 2017 and call it 2257 suggests that, in the future, the issue of cultural diversity has been perhaps subsumed and supplanted by the enlightenment ideology of scientific progress over spiritual and moral progress.

The Intersection of Race and Technology

Much mention has been made in this chapter of the 'black body.' This phrase has come under scrutiny by several academics in recent years, and so, before moving into an examination of race and technology, it

---

[12] Dr. Culber does reappear in the second season and, while other minority characters are introduced in the second season, the point remains that the amount of diversity reflected in the show does not match what one would expect from 2257.

is first important to stop and examine this concept of the 'black body,' because the black body was technology in the United States before the industrial revolution; it was technology in every sense of the word as used today, in that the black body was used for labor, for education, for childcare, for entertainment and for enjoyment. Like Robin D.G. Kelley, I suspect the phrase has come into popular use lately largely because of Ta-Nehisi Coates' book, *Between the World and Me* (2015) (Kelley). Coates writes (to quote the exact same passage Kelley quotes in his article):

> In America, it is traditional to destroy the black body – it is heritage. Enslavement was not merely the antiseptic borrowing of labor – it is not so easy to get a human being to commit their body against its own elemental interest. And so enslavement must be casual wrath and random manglings, the gashing of heads and brains blown out over the river as the body seeks to escape. It must be rape so regular as to be industrial. ... The spirit and soul are the body and brain, which are destructible – that is precisely why they are so precious. And the soul did not escape. The spirit did not steal away on gospel wings. (Coates, 2015, 103)

Kelley writes, in response:

> I do not deny the violence Coates so eloquently describes here, and I am sympathetic to his atheistic skepticism. But what sustained enslaved African people was a *memory of freedom*, dreams of seizing it, and conspiracies to enact it – fugitive planning, if you will. If we reduce the enslaved to mere fungible bodies, we cannot possibly understand *how* they created families, communities, sociality; how they fled and loved and worshiped and defended themselves; how they created the world's first social democracy. (2016; original emphasis)

For Kelley, focusing on the concept of the black body removes agency from the actual individuals who not only created families and legacies and dynasties, but overcame slavery, overcame Black Codes, overcame Jim Crow and launched the Civil Rights, Black Arts, and Black Power movements. Similarly, in an interview with *Ploughshares*, Fred Moten argues:

> When I hear that phrase, 'the black body,' I kind of want to say, 'Well there's no such thing,' or, if there is such a thing, it's something that is imposed upon and conferred upon us at the

moment of our death. The moment of death is also the moment of individuation. To me, that's how come it was so horrific they left Michael Brown's body on the street for so long. What it did was it imposed upon on [sic] us the radical knowledge of how fundamentally alone he was at that moment. (Duplan, 2016)

For Moten, the black body only becomes a 'thing' when that 'thing' has ceased to have being as an actual individual, and then, paradoxically enough, through the presence of this black body, the individuation becomes agonizingly evident. I am sympathetic to both Kelley and Moten's takes on the weird dichotomy of the black body as object and the black body as belonging to a subject, but the thing to remember about Coates' argument is that Coates is investigating whiteness. The idea of the 'black body' is almost nonsensical from a black perspective because for the black subject the black body is simply a human body, not a trope of academic wonder; but when interrogating whiteness, the black body becomes something (like technology) worthy of academic study, because it has a significance in the white imagination beyond just the banal fact of it being another body.

Indeed, in the white American imagination, the black body is wondrous and frightening at the same time – a kind of non-human Frankenstein creation unleashed by Western overreach. Thus, when James Baldwin tells white America,

> If I'm not a nigger here and you invented him, you, the white people, invented him, then you've got to find out why. And the future of the country depends on that. Whether or not it's able to ask that question (Baldwin, 2017)

it is this black body he is referring to as the *nigger* – this bogeyman of technology and progress that the white American has created. Thus, I would argue that Coates' examination of the 'black body' as a trope is probably the most important addition to the conversation he gives us in his book *Between the World and Me*, because it helps black Americans deconstruct this myth of the black body that white America has created, so that we are better able to examine the relationship between race and technology, and how the arbiters of technology use racist structures from racist institutions to create a technology that is supposed to be post-racial, but that instead simply supports the hegemonic power structures that have always been in place in the United States.

When we look at the role of technology in *Star Trek: Discovery*, and try to analyze it through the Afrofuturist lens of what I have previously identified as the cotton-gin effect, we see that the major technological innovation introduced in the world of *Star Trek: Discovery*, the spore drive, is an insidious device that, like the cotton-gin, advances productivity at the expense of humanity, *on the backs of bodies*. The spore drive is a kind of warp engine that assumes that, at the quantum level, biology and physics are not really different fields of study, and thus travel through space involves movement along a mycelial network, instantly transporting the ship anywhere in the universe or, as it turns out, into other universes as well. In order for the drive to operate, however, a living creature has to connect to it. Initially the creature the science team on the *Discovery* uses is a tardigrade, an alien similar to the eponymous earth creature, which has a biological makeup uniquely suited to travel the mycelial network and can keep a large number of co-ordinates in its head. The travel causes the creature an enormous amount of pain, however, and damages the creature's frontal lobe, and so the astromycologist Lieutenant Paul Stamets takes over the job of navigating the spore drive. The ethical questions that arise from such technology are clear, and become even clearer as Lieutenant Stamets suffers the effects of repeated jumps with the technology. It is easy enough to see how the cotton-gin effect applies to this technology: in order to be able to pilot the spore drive, Stamets has to add some of the creature's biological makeup to his own, thus making him, in effect, something *other* than human. If the spore drive technology were to be taken up by Starfleet in all of its ships (at the time of *Discovery* only two ships had been outfitted with it, and one of them, the *U.S.S. Glenn*, crashed while using it), it would require pilots, either tardigrades or genetically altered humans; these pilots, whether human or not, would thus be sacrificed for the efficient operation of the machinery. Moreover, it is a technology that has the potential of not just destroying one universe, but several, and is used in just such a destructive manner by the Terran Empire in the Mirror Universe. Thus, this troubling technology has obvious parallels with technologies that not only have the potential for a cotton-gin effect, but also technologies in our time that accelerate global climate change. The Terran Empire in general represents the cotton-gin effect run amok. Not only are the Terrans using their technology irresponsibly, they have turned it into actively malicious technology. There is an echo of this in the episode 'What's Past is Prologue' when Lieutenant Stamets comes to the realization that the Terrans 'have created a super-mycelial reactor on the *Charon*, and it's destroying the network.' As he grimly notes, 'When it goes, it takes all life with it, in all universes' (1x13, 'What's Past is Prologue').

Conclusion

The *Star Trek* franchise offers an extraordinarily rich array of material for Afrofuturist analyses of whiteness. On the one hand, *Star Trek* has always been on the cutting edge of liberal-humanist philosophy, and Starfleet has always been meant to be the torchbearer of that philosophy. On the other hand, African American thinkers have often had to view Western liberal-humanist philosophy with a certain critical skepticism because, too often, liberal humanism loses sight of the human being in the face of liberal-humanistic ideology, and becomes blindsided to its own biases and ideological assumptions built into the very fabric of its institutions. Perhaps more insidiously, what gets taken for liberal-humanist philosophy sometimes hides neo-conservative outlooks on the world. This is an argument Daniel Leonard Bernardi makes about *The Next Generation* (1987–1994) in his book, *Star Trek and History: Race-ing toward a White Future* (1998), in which he writes:

> And for all its rhetoric of humanism, diversity, and plurality, *The Next Generation* present us with a future where everything from the multicultural past to the assimilation of dark aliens smacks of a neoconservative project. Perhaps this is most visible in the representation of human evolution as white, particularly with gods like Q, even though the beginning of life is brown, as represented in 'The Chase.' The point: wherever we come from, the course of evolution, of advancement and sophistication, is literally and metaphorically, physically and socially, white. (136)

Indeed, there is a tension and cognitive dissonance in the *Star Trek* series between what Starfleet preaches, Bryan Fuller's self-congratulatory instead of self-critical analysis of diversity in the *Star Trek* canon, and what we as viewers experience. This cognitive dissonance can be considered one example of the cotton-gin effect in *Star Trek's* production. The actual lack of diversity[13] aboard the *Discovery*, despite the extreme amount of diversity that is supposed to be represented, is another example of the cotton-gin effect in the show's production; the

---

[13] While *Discovery* has a greater diversity than many other television shows, and more diversity than previous *Star Trek* series, as mentioned, for a supposedly 'post-racial' future, the ratio of darker-complexioned characters reflects 2018/2019 trends more than the likely scientific reality of a racially color-blind 2257 and, as Bernardi points out, the course of evolution in *Star Trek The Next Generation* (and I would extend his analysis to *Star Trek: Discovery* as well) is ultimately white.

sense of propriety over the *Other* exemplified by Captain Lorca's behavior with Michael, and her acceptance of his behavior is an example of the cotton-gin effect in the plot of the show itself;[14] and finally the way technology continues to be used as a means of scientific progress instead of as a means of moral or spiritual progress is another example of the cotton-gin effect in the plot of the show itself. Thus, the cotton-gin effect's presence in the plot of the show seems almost to serve as an unintentional cautionary tale about the cotton-ginning of liberal-humanism in general, even in the production of the very show itself. What *Star Trek* ultimately shows us is a future very much a Mirror Universe of our own present Terrenean universe, where the black mind is still in a state of Armageddon, and where a post-post-racial Federation is still living in fear of a black planet.

Works Cited

Reynaldo Anderson and Charles E. Jones, *Afrofuturism 2.0: The Rise of Astro-Blackness* (Lanham, MD: Lexington Books, 2016).
Daniel Leonard Bernardi, *Star Trek and History: Race-ing toward a White Future* (New Brunswick, NJ: Rutgers University Press, 1998).
'Buran: The Soviet Space Shuttle', *Space*, Future US, Inc. (2015), https://www.space.com/29159-buran-soviet-shuttle.html.
Ta-Nehisi Coates, *Between the World and Me* (New York: Spiegel & Grau, 2015).
Mark Dery, 'Black to the Future', in Mark Dery (ed.) *Flame Wars: The Discourse of Cyber Culture* (Durham, NC: Duke University Press, 1994): 179–222.
Anaïs Duplan, 'A Body that is Ultra-Body: In Conversation with Fred Moten and Elysia Crampton', *Ploughshares*, 13 July (2016), http://blog.pshares.org/index.php/a-body-that-is-ultra-body-in-conversation-with-fred-moten-and-elysia-crampton/.
Sanjay Gupta, 'The Doctrine of Pre-Emptive Strike: Application and Implications During the Administration of President George W. Bush', *International Political Science Review*, 29.2 (2008): 181–96.
Ricardo Guthrie, 'The Real Ghosts in the Machine: Afrofuturism and the Haunting of Racial Space in *I, Robot* and *DETROPIA*', in Reynaldo Anderson and Charles E. Jones (eds.) *Afrofuturism 2.0: The Rise of Astro-Blackness* (Lanham, MD: Lexington Books, 2016): 45–60.
James Hibberd, 'Star Trek: Major Details Revealed About New TV Show', *Entertainment Weekly*, 27 July (2017) https://ew.com/article/2016/08/10/star-trek-tv-series/.

---

[14] The issue of sexism is one that could also benefit from analysis and interrogation – a kind of Astrofeminism that examines the intersection of gender and technology.

bell hooks, *Black Looks: Race and Representation* (Boston, MA: South End Press, 1992).

George Joseph and Mustafa, 'FBI Tracked an Activist Involved with Black Lives Matter as They Travelled Across the U.S., Documents Show', *The Intercept*, 19 March (2018), https://theintercept.com/2018/03/19/black-lives-matter-fbi-surveillance/.

Robin D.G. Kelley, 'Black Study, Black Struggle', *Boston Review* (2016), http://bostonreview.net/forum/robin-d-g-kelley-black-study-black-struggle.

Isaiah Lavender, 'An Afrofuturist Reading of Zora Neale Hurston's *Their Eyes Were Watching God*', *Literature Interpretation Theory*, 27.3 (2016): 213–33.

Nina Martin, 'U.S. Black Mothers Die in Childbirth at Three Times the Rate of White Mothers', *National Public Radio,* 7 December (2017), https://www.npr.org/2017/12/07/568948782/black-mothers-keep-dying-after-giving-birth-shalon-irvings-story-explains-why?t=1543239362293.

W. Nikola-Lisa, 'John Henry: Then and Now', *African American Review*, 32.1 (1998): 51–56.

Michelle Obama, *Becoming* (New York: Crown Publishing Group, 2018).

Tobias c. van Veen, 'The Armageddon Effect: Afrofuturism and the Chronopolitics of Alien Nation', in Reynaldo Anderson and Charles E. Jones (eds.) *Afrofuturism 2.0: The Rise of Astro-Blackness* (Lanham, MD: Lexington Books, 2016).

Lisa Yazek, 'Afrofuturist Reading of Ralph Ellison's *Invisible Man*', *Rethinking History*, 9.2/3 (2005): 297–313.

Episodes and Films Cited

'The Vulcan Hello.' *Star Trek: Discovery*, written by Bryan Fuller and Akiva Goldsman, directed by David Semel, CBS Television Studios, 24 September, 2017.

'Context is for Kings.' *Star Trek: Discovery*, written by Gretchen J. Berg, Aaron Harberts, and Craig Sweeny, directed by Akiva Goldsman, CBS Television Studios, 1 October, 2017.

'Lethe.' *Star Trek: Discovery*, written by Joe Menosky and Ted Sullivan, directed by Douglas Aarniokoski, CBS Television Studios, 22 October, 2017.

'Despite Yourself.' *Star Trek: Discovery*, written by Sean Cochran, directed by Jonathan Frakes, CBS Television Studios, 7 January, 2018.

'Vaulting Ambition.' *Star Trek: Discovery*, written by Jordan Nardino, directed by Hanelle M. Culpepper, CBS Television Studios, 21 January, 2018.

'What's Past is Prologue.' *Star Trek: Discovery*, written by Ted Sullivan, directed by Olatunde Osunsanmi, CBS Television Studios, 29 January, 2018.

I Am Not Your Negro. 2017. Directed by Raoul Peck. Magnolia Pictures.

The American Hello
Representations of U.S. Diplomacy in
Star Trek: Discovery

Henrik Schillinger and Arne Sönnichsen

Introduction[1]

Space: the final frontier. These are the voyages of the starship Enterprise. Its five-year mission: to explore strange new worlds. To seek out new life and new civilizations. To boldly go where no man has gone before!

ghoSlI' chaH. ngIq HeySelmaj' e' nuSev 'ej nuqat 'ej nutaHmoHbogh Hoch lunge'. (1x01, 'The Vulcan Hello')[2]

Star Trek: Discovery (*DSC*) begins with an act of estrangement. Not only are its opening words delivered in the alien Klingon language (with English subtitles), but they invert *Star Trek*'s iconic prologue. *Star Trek*'s distinguishing theme of peaceful exploration, of 'seeking out' new civilizations, is, from the Klingon perspective, marked as expansionism and a danger to cultural identity: 'They are coming ... and take all that we are' (1x01, 'The Vulcan Hello'). This opening sets up *DSC*'s first season to confront one, if not *the*, leitmotif of *Star Trek*: diplomacy.

Diplomacy is at the core of the politics of *Star Trek*. The show posits a diplomatic understanding of the world/universe. A diplomatic

---

[1] We thank the editors, Sarah Earnshaw and Lisa Scholz, for their valuable input and editorial work.

[2] T'Kuvma (Chris Obi): 'They are coming. Atom by atom they will coil around us and take all that we are. There is one way to confront this threat. By reuniting the 24 warring houses of our own empire. We have forgotten the Unforgettable the last to unify our tribes: Kahless. Together, under one creed: remain Klingon. That is why we light our beacon this day. To assemble our people. To lock arms against those whose fatal greeting is: "We come in peace"' (1x01, 'The Vulcan Hello').

understanding of the world presupposes the 'plural fact': people live under 'conditions of separation' as peoples/worlds – and even hold different interpretations of the respective ideas that constitute any people's identity (Sharp, 2009, 10). Conditions of separation require 'relations of separation' to manage the encounters with those strange new worlds and alien civilizations (Sharp, 2009, 10): enter diplomacy understood as the mediation of estrangement (Der Derian, 1987, 42–43). This understanding of diplomacy is not restricted to the deeds of ambassadors in service of the state or international conferences (though *Star Trek* offers its share of these). Rather, it includes any attempt by a political 'us' to come to terms with 'strangers,' 'Others' at the borders (or even 'the frontier').

Through its leitmotif of diplomacy, *Star Trek* speaks to political discourses of foreign policy by offering a fictional account of a non-fictional essential political issue: how to manage relations of separation. By studying diplomacy in *DSC* as the most recent iteration of a long-running and highly popular franchise, we seek insights into the politics of *Star Trek* in our time. What does *DSC* suggest to its viewers as the stakes in managing 'our' relations to alien others? Revisiting Iver B. Neumann's earlier studies on diplomacy in *Star Trek* (Neumann, 2001, 2003), we shall argue that *DSC* keeps the tradition of privileging a liberal 'new diplomacy' with universal pretensions distinctive of *Star Trek* – but at a time when this proposition has ceased to represent the consensus on the principles of U.S. foreign policy. While earlier *Star Trek* shows *reproduced*, and occasionally criticized U.S. representations of diplomacy (Neumann, 2001, 2003), *DSC* takes sides in a highly contested political debate to *reaffirm* a once consensual but now seriously challenged, if not already marginalized, political position.

A burgeoning field of research in the discipline of International Relations (IR) posits that the fictional politics of popular culture have implications for 'real' world politics – and how we can understand it. The genre of science fiction holds a special quality for investigating world politics. Science fiction 'texts' are 'grounded in the same cultural reservoir of meanings' (Weldes, 2003, 15) as political discourses but offer a sense of de-familiarization, estrangement, and extrapolation that encourages a rethinking of political issues (Livingston, 1971; Saunders, 2015). Different approaches have emerged to conceptualize the 'sci-fi/ world politics nexus' (Carpenter, 2016), which can be split broadly into positive approaches 'using' culture as data on or illustration of world politics – and constitutive approaches according to which 'popular culture provides diffuse knowledge that people bring to bear on political issues' (Neumann and Nexon, 2006, 16) by informing, naturalizing, and enabling social repertoires of meaning and action (Carpenter, 2016).[3] Popular culture, in other words, makes politics by making meaning. Constitutive approaches have mostly emphasized how popular culture reproduces and so legitimizes prevailing political understandings (cf. Erickson, 2007). The study of *DSC*, and *Star Trek* in general, suggests a more independent role especially for long-running franchises in constituting the sci-fi/world politics nexus.

The following section revisits Neumann's study of diplomacy in *Star Trek* with a critical view on his depiction of the *Star Trek*/U.S. foreign politics nexus. The first three sections discuss *DSC*'s reflection on different paradigms of diplomacy and how these combine into a reaffirmation of a universalist liberal 'new diplomacy.' We conclude by briefly discussing the implications for the study of the sci-fi/world politics nexus.

Previously on *Star Trek*: Revisiting Neumann

A broad perspective on diplomacy has been applied to *Star Trek* as 'America in space' (Buzan, 2010) before – including studies of the frontier myth in *Star Trek* (Kapell, 2016), the show's liberalist underpinnings (Weldes, 1999), and its implicit colonialism (Inayatullah, 2003), interventionism (Lagon, 2011), and militarism (Hantke, 2014). Most explicitly, however, Neumann has analyzed diplomacy in *Star Trek* – drawing on, explicitly and implicitly, Der Derian's understanding of diplomacy (Neumann, 2001, 2003).[4]

According to Neumann, *Star Trek* reproduces two major U.S. representations of diplomacy that, combined, shape U.S. foreign policy. 'Old world' diplomacy is represented as an instrument of the particularistic reason of the state. In order to advance *the* national interest, diplomacy in this sense relies on subterfuge and threats, persuasion and, occasionally, force – covered in the perfunctory rituals, codes, and symbols of a diplomatic culture originating from and conductive to the power politics of the European state system. The 'new diplomacy' of the American republic, by contrast, is dedicated to the universal interest of all mankind – grounded in a liberal discourse of universal rationality and universal rights (and obligations). This representation of diplomacy drives the United States' exceptional role in world politics: 'If there exists

---

[3] For recent categorizations see: Weber, 2014; Caso & Hamilton, 2015; Carpenter, 2016.
[4] The two publications differ only slightly in emphasis. We shall mostly refer to the more recent iteration.

a universal rationality, and if the United States make a point of living up to it by being a republic with universal significance, then the United States is a model to the world' (Neumann, 2003, 36).

U.S. foreign policy discourse and *Star Trek* both privilege 'new diplomacy' as rational and progressive. Universal rationality is represented to drive qualitative progress – the 'betterment' of individuals and nations/planets alike – that will eventually overcome (rather than mediate) estrangement. Universalist 'new diplomacy,' thus, is essentially 'anti-diplomatic' (cf. Der Derian, 134–52). In that sense, it is only a matter of time that the Federation/United States will be loved by everyone (Neumann, 2003). Meanwhile, however, it is, occasionally and reluctantly, necessary to fall back on 'old world' diplomacy, which sometimes requires even ambassadors to 'grab a phaser' (Neumann, 2001). U.S. foreign policy discourse, in other words, relies on combining both representations and weighting them against each other. The uneasy combination of anti-diplomatic rationalist universalism and accommodating the structural requirement of 'old world' diplomacy characterizes the 'neo-diplomacy' of revolutionary newcomers in the international system (Der Derian, 1987, 134–98) such as the United States.

Star Trek, according to Neumann occasionally not only identifies different U.S. representations of diplomacy but reflects on the surprising closeness between seemingly irreconcilable understandings of diplomacy. Here, *Star Trek* shows a critical and reflexive potential that sets it apart from 'run-of-the mill' approaches to U.S. foreign policy in academic and political discourses – and moves it beyond mere reproduction (Neumann, 2003, 48).

Neumann's argument rests on his analysis of U.S. foreign policy discourse. While his depiction of the distinctiveness of U.S. representations of diplomacy aligns with findings from the general theory of diplomacy (cf. Der Derian, 1987), U.S. diplomacy and foreign policy analysis (cf. Mead, 2002; Wisemann, 2011; Farrow, 2018), and studies of U.S. exceptionalism (cf. Restad, 2014; Cha, 2015; Jansson, 2018), the specifics are contingent on the time of his writing. Neumann's perspective on U.S. representations of diplomacy reflects the post-Cold War consensus on U.S. foreign policy of the Bush Sr. and Clinton administrations attempting to establish a new, liberal world order at the 'end of history' (Fukuyama, 1992) – in line with a post-Second World War American internationalism writ large.

> Bush's New World Order and Clinton's various formulations – 'assertive humanitarianism,' 'selective engagement,' 'democratic enlargement,' 'assertive multilateralism,' 'engagement and

enlargement' – were all attempts to keep expansive US internationalism alive in the post-Soviet environment. They were also efforts to articulate a foreign policy which looked beyond narrowly conceived national interest. (Dumbrell, 2018, 108)

In other words, after the end of the Cold War, U.S. foreign policy and diplomacy clearly privileged universalist diplomacy and an exceptionalist foreign policy – but integrated it into 'classical' international diplomacy through multilateral institutions. Ultimately, this consensus broke in the wake of 9/11 (Schmidt, 2018). Since then, the foreign policy doctrines and grand strategies of the Bush Jr., Obama, and Trump administrations have deviated from the former consensus to different degrees – and in various directions ranging from hyper-liberal neo-conservatism to realism, Jeffersonianism and neo-isolationism (cf. Layne 2006; Miller, 2010; Lofflmann, 2015; Brands, 2017; Clarke and Ricketts, 2017; Walt, 2017; Beinart, 2018; Peterson, 2018).

The new doctrines have been driven by a number of domestic and international challenges emerging in academic and political discourses. Firstly, critics pointed to the 'dark side of exceptionalism' (Bacevich, 2002) as unilateral and multilateral attempts to assert the new world order brought mixed success and collateral damage – literally and figuratively – that undermined its liberal principles. The promotion of universal values came to be seen as 'westoxification' by some (Katzenstein and Keohane, 2007) and created 'blowback' by facilitating resistance against the universal imposition of 'Western values' and U.S. imperialism (Johnson, 2000). Secondly, U.S. foreign policy debate has seen a return of religion and myth to foreign policy – to mytho- and proto-diplomacy (cf. Der Derian, 1987, 50, 68–72). This includes the growing political influence of the Christian right (Marsden, 2011), the religious coding of world politics in the construction of a Muslim Other (Bettiza, 2015; Zahid, 2016), or the invocation of lost greatness and unity in Trump's slogan 'Make America Great Again.' Thirdly, the return of great power politics with the rise of China and Russia (cf. Allison, 2017) and of imperial overstretch (cf. Peterson, 2018) with the dragged-out wars in Afghanistan and Iraq prompt debates on a return to 'old world' particularistic diplomacy of managing an international balance of power system and entering into reciprocal diplomatic relations with actors such as the Taliban or ISIL (cf. Norland, 2019).

Where Neumann's analysis of U.S. representations of diplomacy in *Star Trek* reflected a post-Cold War consensus in U.S. foreign policy, *DSC* is set against the background of a highly contested political playing field – and antagonistic political and academic discourses on the size and scope of the challenges confronting U.S. relations of separation.

Binary Diplomacies

Building on the sense of estrangement that the Klingon introduction creates (both, in terms of language and perspective), *DSC*'s pilot juxtaposes a Klingon particularism ('remain Klingon') with a Federation universalism ('we come in peace'). The pilot offers a clash of different paradigms of mediating estrangement – and a reflection on how to manage relations of separation as the defining plot problem for the show's first season. Equality and freedom are the foundations of Federation law, as a Federation admiral later in the show states in 'The War Without, the War Within' (1x14) – making explicit that *Star Trek* has always mirrored the (supposedly) self-evident and universal principles of the U.S. liberal creed (cf. Weber, 1999). *DSC* introduces the view from the other side. For the Klingons, equality and freedom are particular Federation principles that undermine and negate Klingon identity: 'Our purity is a threat to them. They wish to drag us into the muck, where Humans, Vulcans, Tellarites, and filthy Andorians mix' (T'Kuvma, 1x01).

The racist undertones aside, *DSC* studiously vindicates the Klingon perspective – even while inviting viewers to identify with its Starfleet protagonists and their belief in the Federation's universal mission. The second scene of the pilot introduces Captain Georgiou (Michelle Yeoh) and Commander Burnham (Sonequa Martin-Green, the show's designated protagonist) as saving an 'underdeveloped' species from the effects of a cosmic mining accident. The Federation proves itself as an 'indispensable nation' – interfering, doing the morally 'right' thing even if it is against its own law. In this case, they violate the Federation's prime directive, which prohibits contact in order to protect indigenous cultural development – all in the name of saving lives and justified by good intentions: 'we come in peace.' The righteousness of representing universal values, later, is shown to drive Burnham's insistence on investigating an unknown object at the Klingon border, which she justifies with the mission 'to discover, to explore' – or in the self-assuredness with which Captain Georgiou requires the Klingons to either enter dialogue or leave the location of an ancient Klingon artefact.

The Klingons are shown to take this insistence on 'disinterested' exploration as proof of Federation interference, expansionism and hypocrisy – as illustrated by the scene immediately preceding the titular 'Battle of the Binary Stars' (1x02):

> T'Kuvma [listening to a Federation message aboard the Klingon flagship with House leaders in attendance]: 'Here it comes, their lie.'
> Captain Georgiou: '... we come in peace.'

> T'Kuvma: 'No! They do not! They come to destroy our individuality. Shall we rise up together and give them the fight they deserve?'
> House Leaders: 'Remain Klingon!'
> T'Kuvma: 'Fire!' [Klingon ships open fire]

In this scene, the diplomatic problem of the 'plural fact' is showcased as *DSC*'s plot problem: a universalist representation of diplomacy might appear as just another particular interest – at least to 'alien' Others – and even an expansionist and hypocritical one legitimating itself in terms of a universalist ideology. Also, it indicates how a liberal universalism dedicated to maintaining difference and diversity can appear as a threat for parochial identities – and engender resistance. As *DSC* has the Klingon leader L'Rell (Mary Chieffo) put it: 'We fight to preserve Klingon identity. ... [T]he Federation cannot help itself. It seeks universal homogenization and assimilation' (1x14). On a deeper level, *DSC* points to the anti-diplomatic aspects of a universal representation of diplomacy: agents of universal truths do not so much need to mediate estrangement, but to transcend it – acting on the exceptional insight into the rights and obligations of a higher (natural) law and aiming at a utopian state beyond estrangement and separation (cf. Der Derian, 1987, 134–67).

As a tale of two diplomacies, *DSC* hits Neumann's mark for progressive *Star Trek* as it juxtaposes the two major representations of diplomacy and addresses how they ironically overlap (cf. Neumann, 2003, 48). In contrast to most former iterations of *Star Trek*, *DSC* treats this irony not as an afterthought (mostly offered by a secondary character) but accords it the center stage as the explicit plot driving conflict with either side represented by major characters. In this, it reflects the contested state of U.S. foreign policy and, in particular, the debate on the pathologies of exceptionalism and the impending 'end of diplomacy' (Farrow, 2018).

But *DSC*'s pilot goes further than forwarding a critical over a merely reproductive take on U.S./*Star Trek* representations of diplomacy. Not only does it show the ironic similarities between the two major U.S. representations of diplomacy and how this provokes interference and resistance, but it makes contestation an explicit plot point taking the form of a debate about proper diplomatic policy on the *Discovery*'s bridge (i.e. the center of decision making). This is possibly the most explicit departure from *Star Trek*'s utopian vision according to its creator Gene Roddenberry, which anticipated a post-conflict enlightened society (Hibbard, 2017) – and yet another comment on the contested state of contemporary U.S. foreign affairs.

The debate takes the form of an argument between Captain Georgiou holding on to a universalist idea of diplomacy and Commander Burnham advocating a particularistic approach in dealing with the Klingons. Georgiou insists that 'we come in peace,' that 'Starfleet never fires first' as a matter of principle, and that any conflict can be solved through dialogue– even after the Klingons have appeared in force and the first shots have been exchanged. Burnham, on the other hand, advises a 'Vulcan Hello' as a lesson from (the planet Vulcan's) history. The 'Vulcan Hello' means to shoot on sight whenever a Klingon ship is encountered. The intention is nonetheless (old-world) diplomatic as it seeks to prompt the Klingons into accepting a reciprocal relationship – even though Burnham calls it a soldier's view as opposed to Georgiou's perspective 'as a diplomat.'[5]

Burnham advises a particularistic diplomacy that corresponds to the historical paradigm of classical European diplomacy as a secular and reciprocal cultural practice to manage a system of states 'united with and against each other' by an 'equal and mutual estrangement and a complex general balance of power' (Der Derian, 1987, 113). It is also a paradigm that as 'continental realism' is distinctively not American (Mead, 2002, 35–41). Burnham proposes to replace the universal representation of diplomacy privileged by the Federation with a particularistic diplomacy based on the principle of reciprocity. As Neumann reminds us, *Star Trek* is sensitive to the 'historical fact' (sic) that diplomacy comes at a cost of at least one side having to compromise on its identity and 'erases specificity' (Neumann, 2003, 47). Against the narrative grain of *Star Trek*, Burnham's proposal requires the Federation to become estranged from itself in order to mediate estrangement from the Klingons. Consequently, in symbolic terms, the only way to implement her proposal, ultimately, is a mutiny.

Her superiors, including Captain Georgiou, by contrast, insist on the Federation's universalist diplomacy. And yet, they are not inclined to retreat (as advised by Commander Saru (Doug Jones)) but are willing to defend the Federation's (particularistic) territorial claims. They also address the problem of 'unknowns' in mediating estrangement, the irrational trust in the Other required by any first attempt at diplomacy (Der Derian, 1987, 144), as they point out how the realpolitik approach of the 'Vulcan Hello' relies on worst-case thinking. Their insistence on Federation principles, thus, is shown not as a case of blind idealism, but aware of the dangers of first contact. Diplomacy originates from encounters only when heralds and messengers are excepted from the general injunction to kill and eat all outsiders (cf. Sharp, 2009, 17) – something that the Federation in *DSC*'s pilot accidentally fails to do

---

[5] A classical dichotomy in diplomacy studies and IR (cf. Aron, 1966).

(Burnham kills the 'torchbearer') and the Klingons outright ignore – up to the point of eating Captain Georgiou (1x04).

However, the Federation is shown to hold a neo-diplomatic and exceptionalist worldview. At the frontier between civilization and wilderness (rather than a border between civilizations), the representatives of universal civilization decide unilaterally on the conditions of interaction – against all evidence of being in the territory of a foreign people and against the diplomatic principle of reciprocity (i.e. requesting the Klingons to parley or to leave a system with an ancient Klingon artefact). It is a worldview that also implies a liberal model of civilizational progress – which requires alien Others to accept *the* standard of civilization as a precondition to reciprocal diplomatic relations. *DSC* both subverts and subtly reaffirms this worldview as Burnham explicitly points to Klingon 'nature' (rather than 'culture') as an impediment for diplomatic talks and advises to literally force the Klingons into accepting the Federation's understanding rather than relying on cultural progress.

DSC's pilot, thus, offers a reflection on the contested state of U.S. foreign policy as its proponents debate the challenges of newly emerging great powers, and the limited success of exporting universal liberal values by force – and how a universalist diplomacy *cum* liberal exceptionalism may not only be inconveniently close to the rejected 'old world' diplomacy of the national interest, but also engenders resistance and a blowback.[6]

Remain Klingon: Mytho-Diplomacy in *Star Trek: Discovery*

The Klingon approach to mediating estrangement in *DSC*'s first season is loaded with religious terminology pointing to yet another paradigm of diplomacy: mytho-diplomacy. It refers to the mediation of estrangement between man and God and between man and man through sacred symbols and rituals (Der Derian, 1987, 50). The fear of death (by nature or by strangers) is transferred to the atemporal plane of religious belief and mediated through rituals, sacrifices and ceremonies – mostly worshipping a super-societal figure (Der Derian, 1987, 50). Religiously defined rights and obligations form the core of a particular cultural identity, confer political power to priests and divine monarchs, and are also projected outwards onto other peoples (Der Derian, 1987, 52).

---

[6] Cf. also the latest movie *Star Trek: Beyond* (2016) featuring 'This is where the frontier pushes back' as its antagonist's signature line.

Thus, mytho-diplomacy is also particularistic, but different from the 'narrow' realpolitik diplomacy (as offered by Burnham) as it is non-reciprocal and one-sided. For 'mytho-diplomats' God is always on their side, heathens must be converted, and estrangement fixed through ritual – which is mytho-diplomacy's ongoing legacy for modern diplomacy (Der Derian, 1987, 57). A universalist representation of (neo-)diplomacy, for example, also shows mytho-diplomatic traits as it grounds its one-sided and non-reciprocal approach to mediating estrangement in a myth of universal values. The often religiously coded and loaded mythology of liberal U.S. exceptionalism (the 'city upon a hill') illustrates this mythological side of 'new diplomacy.'

The encounter of Klingon mytho-diplomacy and Federation neo-diplomacy, thus, is a clash between two empires that are founded on exclusive belief systems. Each postulates its paramountcy and cannot recognize differing values and interests. Indeed, suzerainties commonly assert their identity by alienating internal division to another suzerainty (Der Derian, 1987, 122). The combination of non-recognition and alienation is distinctive of *DSC*'s depiction of the Klingons. In the Klingons, *DSC* reimagines the medieval and early-modern Papacy's proto-diplomacy of appealing to a lost greatness and mythical unity of Christianity against a Muslim Other as an attempt to manage an emerging system of mutually estranged and increasingly secular feudal states (Der Derian, 1987, 104).

DSC abounds with mytho-diplomatic references. The pilot introduces the Klingon leader T'Kuvma as a self-anointed 'next Klingon messiah' (1x01). T'Kuvma attempts to restore the unity of the Klingon Empire against the feudal houses by reviving a common Klingon Creed centered on worshipping the legendary unifier Kahless. He rests his claim to political leadership over all Klingons on his mytho-diplomatic proficiency as a priest of the cult of Kahless, which transcends any feudal obligations to a particular House: 'My house is open to all' (1x02).

This proficiency is demonstrated in his knowledge of how to 'light the beacon' – activating an ancient artefact that signals a danger to the Empire and rallies the houses in defense. The artefact itself, though technical in nature, is described in decidedly mythological terms, requiring a ceremonial guardian (the 'torchbearer'), and appearing as a 'new star' instantly visible across galactic distances. Also, T'Kuvma is proficient in funeral rites, which he meticulously applies in the wake of battle. From a mytho-diplomatic perspective, the priest does not only reproduce cultural identity by ritually mediating the boundary between life and death. He or she is also politically mandated to safeguard and defend it. T'Kuvma's mandate is vindicated by his mastery of the 'Ship of the Dead.' This spaceship is a powerful mytho-diplomatic symbol. Decked in the sarcophagi of Klingon warriors from all ages, it signifies the transcendental identity of the Klingon civilization itself because 'society itself comes to represent the transcendence of individual mortality; invested with the codified information of ancestors, it perpetuates a collective cultural consciousness' (Der Derian, 1987, 52).

Restaging the history of mytho- and proto-diplomacy, T'Kuvma does not recognize the Federation as equal but sets it up as a threat to Klingon identity – an identity that obviously is already jeopardized by internal division and secularism. The leaders of the different houses are visibly reluctant to subordinate themselves to T'Kuvma's leadership and openly ridicule his religious zeal. By presenting a common enemy who embodies a universalizing ideology and who itself will not and cannot recognize differing values, T'Kuvma offers an existential threat – and a paradigm to organize around. A holy war against the Federation is the mytho- and para-diplomatic means to restore Klingon unity and lost greatness.

In the story of T'Kuvma's crusade, *DSC* offers a subversion of *Star Trek's* concept of civilizational and technological progress that is closely linked to its representations of diplomacy. This resembles a three-tiered model of U.S. exceptionalism that sees the United States as the endpoint of civilizational progress (Cha, 2015). In *Star Trek*, reciprocal diplomacy is a first step that leads to eventually transcending estrangement (and loving the Federation). But entering into diplomatic relations (with the Federation) already requires a conforming standard of civilization. This standard depends on a specific level of technology – to travel faster than light – which is linked to a notion of scientific progress (Neumann, 2003, 38). Many *Star Trek* episodes explicitly address religion and myth as superstitions impeding scientific progress and, consequently, social progress towards the 'normal' standard of civilization embodied by the Federation. In this sense, *Star Trek* represents a rational anti-mythic version of the U.S. frontier myth (Kapell, 2016, 145–49). Debunking false utopias based on superstition and setting stagnant religious societies back on the track of scientific progress is the most frequent trope in the original series (Kapell, 2016, 149).

In offering a story about the politics of myth as the anachronistic return of religion to Klingon diplomacy, *DSC* undermines the liberal representation of civilizational progress as working ultimately in favor of universal diplomacy. The writers' choice of the Klingons emphasizes this subversion. The Klingons take a special place in *Star Trek's* progressive future history of diplomacy. They are, according to Neumann, 'liminars' in terms of diplomatic commensurability – a warlike species barely meeting the civilizational requirements for diplomacy. *Star Trek* tells, across many iterations, the story of 'taming' the Klingons, bringing them increasingly into the fold of Federation universalist diplomacy (Neumann, 2003, 42–43).

By offering a mytho-diplomatic (and para-diplomatic) perspective through Klingon eyes, *DSC* invites reflection on the mythological quality of the Federation's universalist 'American' diplomacy. *DSC* gives an account of the complex dynamics of the politics of religion, especially pointing to the dialectics between producing cultural identity by creating an 'alien Other' that abets radical fundamentalism and 'crusades.' This represents a turn away from *Star Trek*'s notion of history as a linear progress from mythology to rationality. In the revival of the Klingon Creed, mytho-diplomacy is represented not so much as an anachronism but as a timeless paradigm to mediate estrangement that might resurface at any time to challenge seemingly more progressive representations of diplomacy – either the realpolitik of the 'Vulcan Hello' or the neo-diplomacy of 'we come in peace.' *DSC*, thus, offers a reflection on the ongoing political relevance of quasi-religious myths. Be it in terms of 'Remain Klingon' or 'Make America Great Again,' the appeal to a lost unity and greatness is shown as an instrument to mobilize political support, offer identification, and project an exceptional status abroad. By unveiling its contingent, 'constructed' character, *DSC* also rejects any easy essentialism in understanding the dynamics of cultural clashes and identity politics.

The War Within – Universalism Redeemed

The setup of *DSC*'s first season focuses on how the 'new diplomacy' approach of the Federation is contested by particularistic diplomacies – either the realpolitik of Burnham's dissident 'Vulcan Hello' or Klingon mytho-diplomacy. But, true to *Star Trek*'s legacy, *DSC* also offers an answer to this challenge – a take-home moral of the story. This moral basically is, as we argue, that a universalist liberal diplomacy *should* be privileged.

The first lesson *DSC* teaches about diplomacy is that going down the road of a particularistic diplomacy (including war against the Klingons) in the guise of universalism ultimately undermines universalist values. It is a lesson taught by the *U.S.S. Discovery*'s detour to the Mirror Universe (MU). The MU is a basically evil version of the original *Star Trek* universe – including evil doppelganger characters. The Federation is replaced by the militarist and fascist Terran Empire. The diplomacy of the Empire is particularistic to the extreme – it recognizes neither reciprocity nor equality in its relations of separation. Estrangement is not mediated but eradicated as the xenophobic Terrans conquer, enslave, or extinguish strange new worlds. The Empire is, as Hantke suggests, both a 'reverse affirmation' of core liberal values represented in *Star Trek*, and a means to disclose the moral hypocrisy of militarized U.S. foreign policy (Hantke, 2014, 568).

DSC uses doppelganger characters from the MU to show how easily the liberal universalism of the Federation is subverted in times of crisis. Captain Lorca (Jason Isaacs) of the *U.S.S. Discovery* is a doppelganger who has replaced his original version under cover to become a decorated war hero in the original universe – one of few Starfleet officers there to succeed in the war against the Klingons. Free of the Federation's moral restrictions, he can do whatever seems necessary to win the war, i.e. he is press-ganging unwilling scientists and engineers into contributing to the war effort and enslaving a sentient life-form to navigate the spore drive. Lorca thus co-opts and distorts Starfleet's mission of scientific exploration as he makes explicit in 'The Butcher's Knife Cares Not for the Lamb's Cry:' 'The Discovery is no longer a science vessel' (1x04). Another doppelganger, Emperor Georgiou, convinces Starfleet Command that the only way to win the war against the Klingon is a genocidal plan to destroy the Klingon home world (getting a career with a Federation secret service in return). Both characters exhibit a moral ruthlessness incompatible with the Federation's liberal values and universalist diplomacy – which a Federation at the brink of defeat readily accepts according to a reasoning in terms of ends over means. The doppelganger stories in *DSC*, thus, are an allegoric tale that points to the vulnerability of universal liberal values and diplomacy. It is a *Star Trek* version of the proven trope that accepting necessary evils eventually undermines what is supposed to be protected.

When Burnham and the crew of the *U.S.S. Discovery* stand up against Starfleet Command and reject Emperor Georgiou's plan for genocide, *DSC* manifests its moral for season one. A universalist diplomacy must not be compromised by particularistic national interest – even in its defense. Or it risks to become a dark mirror version of itself: an extreme particularism like the Terran Empire's, rather than a neo-diplomacy that can accept reciprocity and compromise on the way to transcending estrangement. It takes another mutiny by Burnham and the crew to remind Starfleet Command of the Federation's universalist creed 'we come as friends.' This time, however, the mutiny is keeping up Federation values – as opposed to Burnham's first mutiny. It prompts Starfleet and the Federation to renew their pledge of universalist diplomacy. Estrangement from the Klingon will not be 'mediated' by genocide.

This leads to the second moral lesson *DSC* teaches. Again, it is deeply committed to a universalist representation of diplomacy and a 'new diplomacy.' Burnham experiences that Klingons are capable of a basically universalist diplomacy. Again, it is a lesson from the MU. There, resistance against the Empire is led by the so-called 'Firewolf,' none other than Mirror Voq (Shazad Latif), who has been the prophet T'Kuvma's stoutest follower in *DSC's* original universe. Where the original Voq is a religious zealot who seeks to continue T'Kuvma's crusade to 'Remain Klingon,' by contrast, Mirror Voq leads a coalition of different species (including founding species of the original Federation) in a common fight against the Empire. The roles of Humans and Klingons, thus, are reversed in the MU, with the Klingons leading a coalition that transcends estrangement between different species. Even though it is not based on a universalist representation of diplomacy, but the realpolitik logic of alliances against common enemies – Mirror Voq engages at the least in a kind of extended reciprocity as leader of a multispecies coalition. The Klingons, demonstrably, are not warlike by nature but by culture, and can be brought into the folds of diplomacy.

This point is further underlined by the character of (original) Voq. In the aftermath of the Battle of the Binary Stars, Voq is biologically and psychologically altered to take the identity of a killed Federation officer, Ash Tyler, and planted as sleeper agent onboard *Discovery*. Note that one of the oldest definitions of diplomat is 'honorable spy' (Der Derian, 1987, 2). Tyler/Voq's character development takes several turns, but ultimately shifts his allegiances to the Federation and, consequently, even purging the Voq-side from his consciousness (though the attempt does not fully succeed). The reformed Tyler (*sans* Voq) then provides *Discovery*'s crew topographical intelligence necessary for the destruction of the Klingon homeworld. Tyler, retaining memories of Voq and his knowledge of Klingon culture and language, becomes a hybrid, walking between both worlds. He dedicates himself to keeping the Federation safe – which leads him first to accept a position as advisor to the Klingon chancellor and later a career with the Federation's secret service. If the stoutest follower of T'Kuvma's ideology of 'Remain Klingon' can turn to Federation's values, who cannot? In order to facilitate and symbolize Voq/Tyler's turn to the Federation, *DSC* has him even fall in love with Burnham – and out of love with the Klingon spy master L'Rell, who transformed him into a hybrid in the first place.

Reflecting one of the graver concerns of any diplomatic (and secret) service, Voq/Tyler identifies too much with his target and 'goes native.' From the perspective of the Federation's (or any) universalistic diplomacy, however, this attests to the universal appeal and validity of its values.

DSC, thus, reaffirms the core of the Federation's U.S. representation of diplomacy: to know it, is, given time, to love it – and wanting to become like it (Neumann, 2003, 45).

Of course, not all Klingons can or will embrace the Federation's universalism – at least not immediately. Civilizational progress takes time and, under conditions of separation, reciprocal diplomacy will be necessary for the time being. The character development of L'Rell, in turn, is tied to the solution of the season's plot problem of diplomacy. At first, her zealotry is similar to T'Kuvma's, but in 'Into the Forest I Go,' she expresses unease with the dishonorable behavior of the Klingons (1x09). In the final episode of the first season, Burnham offers her control of the planet-busting device planted by Starfleet, which L'Rell accepts. By threatening to destroy her homeworld, L'Rell uses this gift to seize leadership of the Empire and ends the war with the Federation. The second season has her engaging in a co-operative effort by the Federation and the Klingons to destroy an artificial intelligence bent on eradicating all life across the universe – a diplomatic step even beyond peaceful co-existence to co-operation.

This plot development reimagines an important link between the rational anti-diplomatic utopianism underlying 'new diplomacy' and the 'old world' practice of classical diplomacy: 'The 'first' diplomat must commit a highly irrational act when he decides to parley with rather than kill an enemy' (Der Derian, 1987, 144). By forgoing the power to destroy the Klingon homeworld, Burnham instigates a ritual exchange of gifts, planet-buster against peace – and on a symbolic level the mutual recognition of insecurity (Der Derian, 1987, 41) – that transforms the naked exercise of power into a ritual normalizing and rationalizing her act of trust as a first step towards reciprocal diplomacy between the Klingons and the Federation: A first step on the ladder of progress towards embracing the universal values embodied by the Federation – which is vindicated by the Klingon's co-operativeness in the second season (cf. (2x03, 'Point of Light'; 2x12, 'Valley of Shadows'; 2x14, 'Such Sweet Sorrow, Part 2').[7]

On the level of character development, *DSC* tells us stories of becoming 'first' diplomats – most notably in Burnham, but also in Tyler/Voq and L'Rell. *Star Trek*, according to Neumann, typically relies on equating individual progress with social progress (Neumann, 2003). While this

---

[7] The final episode of season one also had a scene with Klingon and Federation representatives signing a peace treaty – engaging in an act of formal diplomacy, which was cut from the broadcast version (Korporaal, 2018).

can be in part explained by the narrative economics of a television show focused on its characters, there are more fundamental reasons in the notion of qualitative progress privileged by *Star Trek*. The focus on individuals 'growing' with experiences is a liberal legacy of the universalist U.S. representation of diplomacy. Individuals only change in the sense of having learned something that makes them 'better' people – which in turn leads to social and political progress, i.e. embracing the Federation's universal values (Neumann, 2003).

DSC in its first season plot thus combines typical tropes of *Star Trek* into an explicit reaffirmation of U.S. 'new diplomacy' privileging a liberal universal over a particularistic representation of diplomacy – which in former iterations has mostly been reproduced without much reflection. It does so at a time when this privilege has become highly contested in U.S. foreign policy discourses. And it appeals to personal learning as a way to overcome the supposed dangers and impossibilities imposed by encountering strangers under conditions of separation.

Conclusion and Implications

Our discussion of diplomacy in *DSC* shows that this latest iteration of the *Star Trek* franchise reproduces major U.S. representations of diplomacy only in a very general sense. As central tenets of U.S. foreign policy and diplomacy have become essentially contested in political and academic discourses, and as supposedly anachronistic paradigms of diplomacy – ranging from power politics to the return of mythology – are seeing a political revival, *DSC* offers an estranged and de-familiarized picture of a domestic political debate. Neumann's conclusion on *Star Trek* therefore still holds 20 years later – only that there is no longer a consensus to be reproduced, but a political context of sometimes antagonistic dispute and contestation on the past, present, and future of U.S. foreign relations. A longstanding consensus of U.S. diplomacy as privileging a universalist liberal understanding has become challenged if not already marginalized. What Neumann found in the early 2000s in *Star Trek* – occasional subversion and critique – can be said to be the new normal in U.S. foreign policy discourse. Consequently, we found an explicit reflection of political contest around different representations of diplomacy, including 'old world' power politics, liberal neo-diplomacy, and mytho- cum para-diplomacy, at the center of *DSC*'s first season.

DSC solves its plot problem of challenges to an idealized U.S./ *Star Trek* universalist neo-diplomacy by moving from *re*-production to re-*production*, to reaffirmation, in other words. *DSC* rejects alternative, and particularistic, modes of mediating estrangement by explicitly reaffirming a 'new diplomacy' that aims to overcome estrangement. It, ironically, subverts U.S. foreign policy discourse by reproducing and relegitimizing a once consensual, but now contested representation of diplomacy. *DSC*'s reaffirmation of new diplomacy, however, is not blind. The pilot offers a balanced debate on the relative merits of particularistic and universalist paradigms of diplomacy. But ultimately, the first season's finale is clear in combining the protagonist's personal redemption with 'normalizing' the relations of separation to the Klingons through 'classical' diplomatic relations of reciprocity. In *Star Trek*'s notion of progress, this establishes a 'normal' civilizational evolution that, ultimately, will integrate the Klingons into the Federation's cosmopolitan community of peoples. Consequently, season two of *DSC* normalizes the Klingons by reintroducing their established look (hair) and iconic design of their latter (and more co-operative) iterations – and includes them in the reciprocal diplomacy of (secret) power politics (2x03) and co-operation (2x12, 2x14).

DSC suggests that a constitutive perspective on popular culture and world politics cannot be limited *ex ante* to a study of reproduction, with popular culture mostly mirroring the state of politics. Rather, works of popular culture should be treated as political statements in their own right directed towards a citizen-audience – particularly in times of political dissent. Most constitutive studies emphasize the social construction of world politics in popular culture as outcome rather than process (Carpenter, 2016, 57–58). Such studies mostly tend to give only passing mention to the dynamic politics of popular culture in their analytical frame. However, culture is not static 'but composed of potentially contested codes and representations; it designates a field on which battles over meaning are fought' (Weldes, 2003, 6).

Works of (U.S.) popular culture, in other words, do not simply 'evoke dominant U.S. cultural norms, but they also either implicitly or explicitly represent, and at times embrace, the cultural norms held by countercultures in the United States' (Erickson, 2007, 201–02). What is lost in the attempt to fix the meaning of culture rather than mapping the battles fought over it, is popular culture's potential to be openly critical or subversive vis-à-vis dominant political representations – including the reaffirmation of once consensual but now contested representations. The study of *DSC* as the latest iteration of a franchise running for nearly six decades and still going strong indicates that items of popular culture may add persistence to political positions. In order to evaluate the politics of franchises (and reimaginations) further studies beyond *Star Trek* are required.

Works Cited

Graham T. Allison, *Destined For War: Can America and China Escape Thucydides's Trap?* (New York: Scribe Publications, 2017).

Raymond Aron, *Peace and War: A Theory of International Relations* (London: Weidenfeld and Nicolson, 1966).

Andrew J. Bacevich, *American Empire: The Realities and Consequences of U.S. Diplomacy* (Cambridge, MA: Harvard University Press, 2002).

Peter Beinart, 'Trump Takes His Party Back to the 1920s', *The Atlantic*, 14 June (2018).

Gregorio Bettiza, 'Constructing Civilisations: Embedding and Reproducing the "Muslim World" in American Foreign Policy Practices and Institutions since 9/11', *Review of International Studies*, 41.3 (2015): 575–600.

Hal Brands, 'The Unexceptional Superpower: American Grand Strategy in the Age of Trump', *Survival*, 59.6 (2017): 7–40.

Barry Buzan, 'America in Space: The International Relations of Star Trek and Battlestar Galactica', *Millennium Journal of International Studies*, 39.1 (2010): 175–80.

Charli Carpenter, 'Rethinking the Political / -Science- / Fiction Nexus: Global Policy Making and the Campaign to Stop Killer Robots', *Perspectives on Politics*, 14.1 (2016): 53–69.

Frederica Caso and Caitlin Hamilton (eds.), *Popular Culture and World Politics: Theories, Methods, Pedagogies* (Bristol: E-International Relations Publishing, 2015).

Taesuh Cha, 'The Formation of American Exceptional Identities: A Three-Tier Model of the "Standard of Civilization" in US Foreign Policy', *European Journal of International Relations*, 21.4 (2015): 743–67.

Michael Clarke and Anthony Ricketts, 'Shielding the Republic: Barack Obama and the Jeffersonian Tradition of American Foreign Policy', *Diplomacy & Statecraft*, 28.3 (2017): 494–517.

James Der Derian, *On Diplomacy: A Genealogy of Western Estrangement* (Oxford: Blackwell, 1987).

John Dumbrell, 'America in the 1990s: Searching for a Purpose', in Michael Cox (ed.) *US Foreign Policy* (Oxford: Oxford University Press, 2018): 82–96.

Christian W. Erickson, 'Counter-Terror Culture: Ambiguity, Subversion, or Legitimization?', *Security Dialogue*, 38.2 (2007): 197–214.

Ronan Farrow, *War on Peace: The End of Diplomacy and the Decline of American Influence* (New York: W.W. Norton & Company, 2018).

Francis Fukuyama, *The End of History and the Last Man* (New York: Free Press, 1992).

Steffen Hantke, 'Star Trek's Mirror Universe Episodes and US Military Culture through the Eyes of the Other', *Science Fiction Studies*, 41.3 (2014): 562–78.

James Hibbard, 'Star Trek: Discovery to Ditch a Long Frustrating Trek Rule', *Entertainment Weekly*, 23 June (2017), https://ew.com/tv/2017/06/23/star-trek-discovery-rules/.

Naeem Inayatullah, 'Bumpy Space: Imperialism and Resistance in *Star Trek: The Next Generation*', in Jutta Weldes (ed.) *To Seek out New Worlds: Exploring Links Between Science Fiction and World Politics* (New York: Palgrave Macmillian, 2003): 53–75.

David Jansson, 'Deadly Exceptionalisms, or, Would You Rather Be Crushed by a Moral Superpower or a Military Superpower?', *Political Geography*, 64 (2018): 83–91.

Chalmers Johnson, *Blowback. The Costs and Consequences of American Empire* (New York: Metropolitan Books, 2000).

Matthew Kapell, *Exploring the Next Frontier: Vietnam, NASA, Star Trek and Utopia in 1960s and 70s American Myth and History* (New York: Routledge, 2016).

Peter J. Katzenstein and Robert O. Keohane, *Anti-Americanisms in World Politics* (Ithaca, NY: Cornell University Press, 2007).

Angie Korporaal, '"Star Trek: Discovery" Designers Discuss Modern Look For USS Enterprise, Reveal Alternative Designs And More', *TrekMovie*, 5 September (2018), https://trekmovie.com/2018/09/05/star-trek-discovery-designers-discuss-modern-look-for-tos-era-reveal-alternative-designs-and-more/.

Mark P. Lagon, '"We Owe It to Them to Interfere": Star Trek and U.S. Statecraft in the 1960s and the 1990s', in Donald M. Hassler and Clyde Wilcox (eds.) *Political Science Fiction* (Columbia: University of South Carolina Press, 2011): 234–50.

Christopher Layne, *The Peace of Illusions: American Grand Strategy from 1940 to the Present* (Ithaca, NY: Cornell University Press, 2006).

Dennis Livingston, 'Science Fiction Models of Future World Order Systems', *International Organization*, 25.2 (1971): 254–70.

Georg Lofflmann, 'Leading from Behind – American Exceptionalism and President Obama's Post-American Vision of Hegemony', *Geopolitics*, 20.2 (2015): 308–32.

Lee Marsden, 'Religion, Identity and American Power in the Age of Obama', *International Politics*, 48.2–3 (2011): 326–43.

Walter Russell Mead, *Special Providence: American Foreign Policy and How It Changed the World* (New York: Routledge, 2002).

Benjamin Miller, 'Explaining Changes in US Grand Strategy: 9/11, the Rise of Offensive Liberalism, and the War in Iraq', *Security Studies*, 19.1 (2010): 26–65.

Iver B. Neumann, '"Grab a Phaser, Ambassador": Diplomacy in Star Trek', *Millennium*, 30.3 (2001): 603–24.

—— '"To Know Him Was to Love Him. Not to Know Him Was to Love Him from Afar": Diplomacy in Star Trek', in Jutta Weldes (ed.) *To Seek out New Worlds. Science Fiction and World Politics* (New York: Palgrave Macmillan, 2003): 31–52.

—— and Daniel H. Nexon, 'Introduction: Harry Potter and the Study of World Politics', in Daniel H. Nexon and Iver B. Neumann (eds.) *Harry Potter and International Relations* (Lanham, MD: Rowman & Littlefield, 2006): 1–26.

John Peterson, 'Present at the Destruction? The Liberal Order in the Trump Era', *International Spectator*, 53.1 (2018): 28–44.

Hilde Restad, *American Exceptionalism: An Idea That Made a Nation and Remade the World* (London and New York: Routledge, 2014).

Robert Saunders, 'Imperial Imaginaries: Employing Science Fiction to Talk About Geopolitics', in Frederica Caso and Caitlin Hamilton (eds.) *Popular Culture and World Politics. Theories, Methods, Pedagogies* (Bristol: E-international Relations, 2015): 149–59.

Brian Schmidt, 'Theories of US Foreign Policy', in Michael Cox (ed.) *US Foreign Policy* (Oxford: Oxford University Press, 2018): 5–20.

Paul Sharp, *Diplomatic Theory of International Relations* (Cambridge: Cambridge University Press, 2009).

Stephen M. Walt, 'The Global Consequences of Trump's Incompetence', *Foreign Policy*, 18 July (2017).

Cynthia Weber, *International Relations Theory*, 4th ed. (London and New York: Routledge, 2014).

Jutta Weldes, 'Going Cultural: Star Trek, State Action, and Popular Culture', *Millennium-Journal of International Studies*, 28.1 (1999): 117–34.

—— 'Popular Culture, Science Fiction, and World Politics: Exploring Intertextual Relations', in Jutta Weldes (ed.) *To Seek out New Worlds. Science Fiction and World Politics* (New York: Palgrave Macmillan, 2003): 1–27.

Geoffrey Wiseman, 'Distinctive Characteristics of American Diplomacy', *The Hague Journal of Diplomacy*, 6.3–4 (2011): 235–59.

Zahid Mehmood Zahid, 'U.S.A. Versus "Them": Fomenting an Enemy for the Hegemonic Discourse', *Ipri Journal*, 16.2 (2016): 105–18.

Episodes and Films Cited

'The Vulcan Hello.' *Star Trek: Discovery*, written by Bryan Fuller and Akiva Goldsman, directed by David Semel, CBS Television Studios, 24 September, 2017.

'Battle at the Binary Stars.' *Star Trek: Discovery*, written by Gretchen J. Berg and Aaron Harberts, directed by Adam Kane, CBS Television Studios, 24 September, 2017.

'The Butcher's Knife Cares Not for the Lamb's Cry.' *Star Trek: Discovery*, written by Jesse Alexander and Aron Eli Coleite, directed by Olatunde Osunsanmi, CBS Television Studios, 8 October, 2017.

'Into the Forest I Go.' *Star Trek: Discovery*, written by Bo Yeon Kim and Erika Lippoldt, directed by Chris Byrne, CBS Television Studios, 12 November, 2017.

'Point of Light.' *Star Trek: Discovery*, written by Andrew Colville, directed by Olatunde Osunsanmi, CBS Television Studios, 31 January, 2019.

'Through the Valley of Shadows.' *Star Trek: Discovery*, written by Bo Yeon Kim and Erika Lippoldt, directed by Doug Aarniokoski, CBS Television Studios, 4 April, 2019.

'Such Sweet Sorrow, Part 2.' *Star Trek: Discovery*, written by Michelle Paradise, Jenny Lumet, and Alex Kurtzman, directed by Olatunde Osunsanmi, CBS Television Studios, 18 April, 2019.

Star Trek: Beyond. 2016. Directed by Justin Lin. Paramount Pictures.

'Into A Mirror Darkly'
Border Crossing and Imperial(ist) Feminism in
Star Trek: Discovery

Judith Rauscher

> Through all the good that we are now or could produce, or the evil that we may consciously or unconsciously tolerate, humanity yearns for revelations of itself. With the curiosity of the sentient, we are always fascinated by our reflection and SF provides mirrors that stretch to either end of our existence. (Kerslake, 2007, 1–2)

In this essay, I examine the faces of imperial(ist) feminism as imagined by the CBS series *Star Trek: Discovery* (*DSC*) (2017–ongoing). *DSC* represents several different manifestations of imperial feminism, each of them embodied by one of the show's primary female characters. In my analysis, I focus on the geographical border crossing in the series and the figurative border crossings it engenders. The most significant geographical border crossing occurs when, in the first season, the crew of the *U.S.S. Discovery* jumps to the so-called Mirror Universe, which is dominated by the fascist Terran Empire, and then returns to the Prime Universe, which in the meantime has been devastated by a war between the Federation and the Klingons. I argue that *DSC* is a feminist text, in which two very different post-feminist futures collide and eventually seep into each other, forcing the female characters to explore what they are willing to do to gain power and to ensure victory for their side. In the future represented by the Mirror Universe, the empowerment of women depends on their integration into totalitarian militaristic structures that rely on openly imperialist and racist ideologies. In the future represented by the Prime Universe, the position of every individual in the United Federation of Planets – regardless of gender or race – is determined by democratic ideals of universal liberty and equality, at least in principle. By contrasting these two possible futures and by intermingling them through instances of border crossing, *DSC* speaks to the idea, expressed by some transnational feminists, that promoting diversity without an explicitly anti-imperialist stance is not enough. What is more, through its complex treatment of gender politics together with questions of race and imperialism, the series responds to the changed social and political climate in the United States during its production. Specifically, it responds to the return to the mainstream political and cultural arena of discourses promoting ethnic nationalism and white supremacy.

Border Crossing and the Women of *Star Trek*'s Mirror Universe

Gene Roddenberry famously based the original *Star Trek* series (1966–1969) on ideals of equality, universal liberty, and peaceful collaboration.[1] Yet, as scholars have repeatedly pointed out, the franchise – with its premise of a 'Wagon Train to the Stars' led by Starfleet, the Federation's exploration and defense service – undeniably also carries imperialist undertones (cf. Inayatullah, 2003; Kanzler, 2004; Pounds, 2011; Hassler-Forrest, 2016; Cutler-Broyles, 2017). These imperialist undertones are inextricably linked to the recurring theme of geographical border crossing. Border crossing in *Star Trek* is a plot device that opens up new spheres of action for characters but also induces them to cross figurative borders, whether those drawn by official Federation regulations or by personal moral convictions. For female characters in previous *Star Trek* series border crossing has frequently constituted an ambiguous emancipatory gesture, the most famous example being Captain Janeway (Kate Mulgrew) of *Star Trek: Voyager* (1995–2001; cf. Roberts, 2000; Relke, 2006; Dove-Viehbahn, 2007). On the one hand, *U.S.S. Voyager*'s removal to the Delta Quadrant frees Janeway from Starfleet structures of command and by consequence from the patriarchal logic of earlier *Star Trek* series, situating her instead in what one might call with Teresa de Lauretis 'patriarchy's space-off' (Burnham, 1993, 65). At the same time, this 'space-off' literally and figuratively remains a space apart from the common *Star Trek* universe of the Alpha Quadrant. The Mirror Universe too constitutes such a space apart for female characters in *Star Trek*.

The function of the Mirror Universe in *Star Trek* is an ambiguous one, especially when it comes to spatialized representations of women's emancipation. First introduced in the episode 'Mirror, Mirror' of *The Original Series* (*TOS*) during the 1960s, the Mirror Universe is an alternative reality that exists in a parallel dimension relative to the

---

[1] For an examination of the ways in which *DSC* is connected to and influenced by the founding ideals and historical context of the *Star Trek* franchise, see Torsten Kathke's essay 'A *Star Trek* About Being *Star Trek*: History, Liberalism, and *Discovery*'s Cold War Roots' in this volume.

so-called Prime Universe, in which all the *Star Trek* series are set. Among all possible alternative universes, the Mirror Universe is special because references in mirror episodes such as *Deep Space Nine*'s (*DS9*) 'Shattered Mirror' or *DSC*'s 'Vaulting Ambition' to events from mirror episodes from earlier series indicate that a direct link exists between the Prime Universe and this particular alternative reality. The Mirror Universe is also unique because, as Steffen Hantke argues, 'at least in its conception,' it is the 'diametrical reversal' (2014, 562) of the Prime Universe. Whether in *TOS*'s 'Mirror, Mirror' or in the longer mirror storylines of *DS9* and *DSC*, this logic of reversal has not only provided writers with the opportunity to experiment with 'dark' versions of established Prime Universe characters (see the title of the two-part *ENT* episode 'In a Mirror Darkly' alluded to in the essay's title), it has also allowed them to contrast different political systems and ideologies along with the racial and gender politics underpinning them.

In contrast to the Prime Universe, the Mirror Universe is ruled by the Terran Empire, an ultra-violent, hyper-nationalist and racist totalitarian regime. Ever since *TOS*, representations of the Terran Empire have been Orientalizing and replete with allusions to antiquity as well as the Third Reich (Hantke, 2014, 566), featuring scenes of decadence and violence as well as set and costume design that would be familiar to fans of classical Hollywood sword-and-sandals films. The visual rhetoric of *DSC*'s Mirror Universe, too, borrows from these older filmic traditions. At the same time, it also references more recent depictions of empires on screen. The throne room on the Terran flag ship *I.S.S. Charon*, for example, was not only inspired by the futuristic Bund Finance Center in Shanghai, as noted on *After Trek* (1x12, 'Episode 12'), it also resembles the throne room of King's Landing from HBO's *Game of Thrones* (*GoT*) (2011–2019), creating a design that associates *DSC*'s Terran Empire with one of the U.S.'s greatest non-Western economic rivals as well as with pre-republican royalism. Another similarity between *DSC* and *GoT* is telling in the context of my argument about imperial(ist) feminism: in both shows powerful and outright ruthless women are at the forefront of their respective 'empires,' raising questions about female empowerment and the violence necessary to achieve and maintain it.[2]

---

[2] As Dan Hassler-Forrest suggests in his reading of the *Star Trek* franchise based on Hardt and Negri's notion of 'Empire' as the dominant form of global capitalism in the post-industrial era, *TNG* especially, but also the series afterward not only have imperialist undertones, they also 'illustrate larger tensions specific to capitalism's transition from imperialism to Empire' (49) by indulging in a 'fantasy of peaceful and benevolent imperialism' (50) that remains moored in a 'colonialist imperative and the "racist imaginary" it

Women in *Star Trek*'s Mirror Universe have always been depicted as hyper-sexualized versions of their Prime Universe counterparts, as manifested, for example, in the revealing uniforms of female Terran officers in *TOS* and *Star Trek: Enterprise* (*ENT*) (Cutler-Broyles 42; Hantke, 2014, 567). As problematic as such production choices are, representations of female empowerment in the mirror episodes have also helped to expand the repertoire of roles available to women in the franchise. While the only woman with a major role in *TOS*'s 'Mirror Mirror' is Marlena Moreau (Barbara Luna), Mirror Kirk's (William Shatner) mistress whose place in the empire's social and political hierarchy is largely determined by the logics of heteropatriarchy, the Mirror episodes of *ENT* and *DS9* depict female characters who are not merely 'captain's women' but female rulers. Both Terran Empress Hoshi Sato (Linda Park) of *ENT* and Bajoran Alliance Intendant Kira Nerys (Nana Visitor) of *DS9* use sex as well as murder to secure positions of power for themselves, pointing to the possibilities but also the limits of female agency in the Mirror Universe (Kanzler, 2004, 206–07). Mirror Hoshi – presented as a mixture of captain's woman and regular Terran officer – claims her title of empress after poisoning her lover Mirror Archer (Scott Bakula) in bed. Mirror Kira of *DS9* also attains and maintains power through a mixture of sexual(ized) manipulation and violence. Usually dressed in dominatrix-style outfits, openly bisexual, and aggressively assertive, she is representative for how non-heteronormative sexualities are deployed as signs of moral deviance in *Star Trek*'s mirror episodes (Cutler-Broyles, 2017, 42). This problematic conflation of female dominance with queerness, and of queerness with sadistic tendencies is also taken up in a brothel scene in *DSC* in which the leather-clad Terran Emperor Georgiou (Michelle Yeoh) is shown in bed with a male and a female Orion sex worker (1x15, 'Will You Take My Hand'). While discussing payments for services rendered, Mirror Georgiou suddenly knocks the male Orion unconscious, before choking his female companion at gun point in order to extort a piece of information that she is unlikely to possess. Like the other female rulers from the Mirror Universe, Emperor Georgiou not only relies on sex as a tool to advance her political goals, she mixes sex and violence in ways that cast her as a dubious role model for female empowerment. While the mirror episodes thus show independent and empowered women, these representations remain limited and limiting

articulates' (50, quoting Golumbia, 91). Although *DSC* engages with precisely these imperatives more critically than previous series, I would suggest, it cannot completely untangle itself from them, especially in its depictions of the Mirror Universe and the Klingons.

because they stigmatize non-heteronormative forms of sexuality (for example by conflating consensual BDSM practices with non-consensual inflictions of pain) and consistently sexualize female agency. In the case of Empress Hoshi Sato and Emperor Georgiou, two characters played by actors of Asian descent, such depictions are particularly problematic because even though the characters' sexual self-determination subverts Orientalist stereotypes of Asian women as passive sex objects, their hypersexualization perpetuates racist and indeed imperialist (feminist) fantasies prevalent in both science fiction and beyond.

Scholars discussing the politics of the Mirror Universe usually argue that it serves as a foil against which the defining values of the Prime Universe can be measured (Hantke, 2014, 562; Hassler-Forrest, 2016, 56; Cutler-Broyles, 2017, 42). If the Terran Empire is an ultra-violent, hyper-nationalist, militaristic, imperialist, sexist, and racist totalitarian regime, so the theory goes, the Federation should appear as non-violent, non-nationalist, non-militaristic, non-imperialist, non-sexist, non-racist, and democratic. Of course, things are more complicated in *Star Trek*, especially in the later series. In his essay on representations of militarism in selected Mirror episodes, Steffen Hantke writes: 'If *Star Trek* disavows, denies, or rejects militarism, then these episodes offer a space in which the rules of repression are temporarily suspended' (2014, 563). If we examine the Mirror Universe, he argues, U.S. militarism emerges as a recurring theme in the franchise at large (Hantke, 2014, 566). The same logic applies to the themes of imperialism and racism, or expansionist and ethnic nationalism, I argue. Because the Mirror Universe is overtly imperialist and racist, imperialism and racism also deserve close examination in the Prime Universe. This is especially true for *DSC*, which employs the theme of travel between the two universes as one of the main plot elements of season one and continues to examine the aftereffects of the characters' geographical and moral border crossings well into season two. Rather than keeping Prime and Mirror Universe strictly apart by promptly restoring all inter-dimensional border crossers to their original dimension – as previous series did – *DSC* intermingles the two universes more permanently. Because of this lasting entanglement and the positions the show's main female characters occupy in the two entangled universes, *DSC* invites investigation of the complex relationship between feminism, imperialism, and racism in the *Star Trek* universe and, by extension, in contemporary U.S. society and culture, from which the show draws and which it comments on.

Border Crossing and the Imperial(ist) Feminism(s) of *Star Trek: Discovery*

Feminist critics have long discussed social and cultural border crossing – along with theoretical and conceptual border crossing – as a means of rethinking and challenging structures of oppression and hierarchies of power. Sometimes, though not always, they have considered these figurative border crossings in relation to geographical border crossing. Chicana, post-colonial, and transnational feminists such as Gloria Anzaldúa (1987), Inderpal Grewal and Caren Kaplan (1994), or the feminist collaborative H.J. Kim-Puri (2005) suggest that the movements of people, goods, and ideas across literal and figurative borders – as well as blockages of such movements – raise important questions about the ways in which discourses on race and gender in the United States and elsewhere are shaped by (neo-)colonialist and imperialist ideologies and practices. Scholars such as Chandra Mohanty (2003) further suggest that analyses of border crossing and how it is policed reveal the complicity of mainstream Euro-American feminism with those political, economic, social, and cultural processes that perpetuate racial inequalities on a national as well as on a global scale. If it fails to address the complex relationships between imperialism, nationalism, global inequalities, and racial injustice, this scholarship suggests, the mainstream feminism practiced by many white, liberal, first-world feminists may be understood as a present-day manifestation of what black British feminists Valerie Amos and Pratibha Parmar describe as 'imperial feminism' (53).

In their 1984 essay 'Challenging Imperial Feminism,' Amos and Parmar denounce 'the ways in which a particular tradition, white Eurocentric and Western, has sought to establish itself as the only legitimate feminism' (3). They stress that '[t]he "herstory" which white women use to trace the roots of women's oppression ... is an *imperial history* rooted in the prejudices of colonial and neo-colonial periods' (5; emphasis added). Feminist analyses of imperial feminism and its legacies frequently concern the past, such as when Lora Wildenthal draws on Amos and Parmar to explicate the imperial feminism of German colonialist Frieda von Bülow, hinting at the historical continuities between the racist ideologies that fuel imperialist projects and the kind of ethnic nationalism that tends to form the basis of totalitarian and fascist regimes, whether in the past or today.[3] Referencing Grewal and

---

[3] For a more detailed description of the historical continuities between the racial politics of German imperialism and the genocidal politics of German fascism, continuities that are also implied in *DSC*, see Fatima El Tayeb's

Mohanty, among others, media scholar Deepa Kumar discusses the nature of 'imperialist feminism' in the twenty-first century. According to Kumar,

> the logic of imperialist feminism in the twenty-first century ... [is] shaped by the deeply racist framework of the 'clash of civilizations,' which is based on the idea that the West is a superior culture because it believes in democracy, human rights, secularism, women's rights, gay rights, freedom of speech, and a whole host of other liberal values, whereas the Global South is barbaric, misogynistic, driven by religion, and illiberal. (2006)

While the Mirror Universe storyline in *DSC* also allows for a discussion of imperial feminism in the traditional sense, the storyline surrounding the Klingon–Federation war and its aftermath evoke precisely the kind of 'clash of civilizations' Kumar references here. When she notes in her article that 'today, empire is still a masculine and sexist enterprise, but what has changed in the twenty-first century is that there is now a "place for women"' (2006), this is all the more true for the twenty-third century of *DSC*. More even, because the cast of the show is so racially diverse, an analysis of imperial(ist) feminism(s) in *DSC* must consider, as Kumar does, that 'even with women and people of color at the helm of empire, racism and sexism still remain central to the imperial mission.'

When discussing the link between imperialism and feminism in *DSC*, maybe the obvious place to start is the character of Terran Emperor Philippa Georgiou, a fierce and extremely dangerous woman who has ascended to the highest positions of power in the Mirror Universe by playing by its brutal rules. Known as 'her most Imperial Majesty, Mother of the Fatherland, Overlord of Vulcan, Dominus of Qo'noS, [and] Regina Andor' (1x12, 'Vaulting Ambition'), she mercilessly persecutes the enemies of the empire and grounds her right to rule in her own strength and ability to lead as well as in an ideology of Terran racial superiority. This ideology claims human supremacy over alien races, including the Vulcans, Klingons, and Andorians, whose home worlds the emperor controls. Notions of racial superiority govern everyday social relations in the Terran Empire, where all non-humans are barred from higher offices and where Kelpiens, a gentle and peaceful alien species, are either slaves or treated as animals of slaughter (1x12). Terran ideas of human supremacy and expansive nationalism also translate into direct

---

essay 'Dangerous Liaisons: Race, Nation, and German Identity' from the edited collection *Not so Plain as Black and White* (2010).

political action, as indicated by 'Terran General Order 4:' 'Any *exotic species* deemed a threat to the Imperial Supremacy will be extinguished without prejudice' (1x12; emphasis added). The Terran imperialism that Emperor Georgiou promotes specifically targets 'exotic species' and thus openly acknowledges the racist ideologies on which it is premised and the horrendous acts of violence it uses to enforce its goals.

The Terran Empire's expansionist ethnic nationalism is also addressed in a scene of episode 1x13 ('What's Past is Prologue'), in which Emperor Georgiou is confronted by her most dangerous competitor, Mirror Lorca (Jason Isaacs). In the middle of staging a coup, Mirror Lorca tries to convince the imperial troops to switch sides by taunting the emperor over the ship-wide comm system:

> Hello Philippa. I've watched for years; you let *alien races spill over the borders*, flourish in our backyard, then have the gall to incite rebellion. The Terrans need *a leader who will preserve* our way of life, *our race*. Try as you might, it's clearly not you. ... To all, I make this offer: renounce Georgiou. The Empire is dying in her hands. But you don't have to... [T]ogether [we] will make the Empire ...[pause]... glorious again! (1x13; emphasis added)

The rhetoric Mirror Lorca uses in this scene to describe the alien species rebelling against Terran rule has a variety of historical precedents. Yet, it also specifically alludes to the rising racist and anti-immigrant sentiments in the United States during the production of seasons one and two of *DSC*.[4] The last sentence of the quoted passage for instance echoes the infamous slogan of Trump's 2016 U.S. presidential campaign and subsequent presidency: 'Make America great again.' Indeed, the racist sentiment expressed by Mirror Lorca is not at all as far removed from the political rhetoric of the 45th president of the United States as one

---

[4] Jason Isaacs, who plays Mirror Lorca on the show, has repeatedly suggested that the Mirror Universe, as it is scripted in *DSC*, is 'an all too imaginable version of the present' (1x12, 'After Trek'). In an interview with *Inverse*, he elaborates on this idea, alluding specifically to his monologue in 'What's Past is Prologue': '[The Mirror Universe] is a world where some people believe in racial purity and are against immigration, and they think it's okay to lie to get what you want, and that in the end the weak should be treated harshly. Sadly, those views are prevalent in the world today, and in fact there are people in seats of power who espouse those views every day' (Britt, n.p.). For further analysis of Lorca and the imperialist and toxic masculinity he presents, see Sabrina Mittermeier and Jenny Volkmer's essay on questions of masculinity in their contribution to this volume.

would hope, given that the quoted *DSC* character is a Terran sociopath from a universe in which everybody in pursuit or positions of power is manifestly evil. I will come back to *DSC*'s commentary on the larger political context of its production at the end of this essay. For now, let me emphasize that the above scene depicts a direct confrontation between the female leader of a brutal imperialist regime and her most formidable male rival. If Emperor Georgiou has failed the empire, as her opponent alleges, it is not because she did not ruthlessly enforce Terran rule and its underlying ideals of human supremacy. After all, she is responsible for the destruction of the Klingon homeworld and thus for the near extermination of the empire's most formidable enemy. Mirror Georgiou has risen in the ranks of the Terran Empire because she has not only played by its rules but excelled in the game. The imperial feminism she represents is one in which women are willing to do whatever is necessary to gain a seat at the table. As suggested by her honorary title 'Mother of the Fatherland,' Emperor Georgiou's brand of imperial feminism is one in which women assume positions of power by exhibiting an imperialist femininity that rivals or even surpasses the imperialist and racist masculinity that informs all social relations and political structures in the Terran Empire.

All would be well according to the traditional logic of *Star Trek* if Emperor Georgiou remained in the Mirror Universe, serving as a concrete yet safely distant example of everything that Starfleet is supposed to fight and stand against. Yet, Mirror Georgiou crosses over into the Prime Universe with the help of Michael Burnham (Sonequa Martin-Green), where she remains, eventually joining Section 31, a Starfleet special operations organization that does not adhere to Federation principles.[5] Specialist Michael Burnham, the tortured hero of the series, travels to the Mirror Universe onboard the science vessel *U.S.S. Discovery*, which jumps there using an experimental spore drive that was developed by Starfleet in an effort to gain the upper hand in a gruesome war between the Federation and the Klingon Empire caused by Burnham. Arriving in the Mirror Universe, Burnham realizes not only that her mirror counterpart is presumed dead, she is also the adoptive daughter of Emperor Georgiou.[6] In an attempt to find information that

---

[5] Early in 2019, CBS announced a *DSC* spin-off focusing on Emperor Georgiou's work for Section 31, while also indicating that the Terran character would continue to appear in future *DSC* seasons.

[6] The *DSC* comic *Succession* (2018) reveals that Mirror Burnham is only in hiding, but returns to take her adoptive mother's place as Terran emperor once Mirror Georgiou has crossed over into the Prime Universe. According to the comic, Mirror Burnham dies, along with the entire Terran population

will allow the crew of the *Discovery* to return home, Prime Burnham is forced to pose as the emperor's lost daughter. Before she is invited to the imperial palace, however, Burnham has to go undercover on one of the flagships of the imperial Terran fleet. In a voice-over overlaying a series of scenes that show her daily routine as the captain of the *I.S.S. Shenzou*, Prime Burnham expresses concern that impersonating a high-ranking Terran officer will eventually destroy her. While the audience observes as Burnham is given a bath by the enslaved Mirror Saru (Doug Jones) or attending the execution of three crew members found 'guilty of malicious thoughts against [their] emperor' (Mirror Detmer (Emily Coutts), 'The Wolf Inside' 1x11), Burnham reflects:

> It's been two days. But they're already inside my head. Every moment is a test. Can you bury your heart? Can you hide your decency? Can you continue to pretend to be one of them? Even as, little by little, it kills the person you really are?... I've continued to study their ways, read all that I can. It's getting easier to pass. Which is exactly what I feared the most. (1x11)

Forced to watch Burnham participate in the horrible yet ordinary routines of a Terran captain and seeing her follow Terran laws and societal conventions, the audience is given a sense of the danger of the kind of habitual normalization that comes with long-term exposure to an elaborate system of oppression. Only the painfully controlled voice-over reminds viewers that what they are witnessing is Burnham's desperate struggle to maintain her identity and moral integrity. When she refuses to bomb a rebel camp against the emperor's explicit orders risking to be executed as a traitor, a parallel to *TOS*'s 'Mirror, Mirror,' she demonstrates that her struggle is successful and that she really believes that it is '[b]etter [to be] dead than one of them' (Burnham, 1x11). Burnham's tragic flaw, the series reveals, is not a lack of moral conviction; it is an excess of it and the consequent overwhelming desire to right past wrongs. Because Burnham feels guilty for the death of her mentor Captain Georgiou, she falls under the influence of Mirror Georgiou and takes the emperor along when the *Discovery* returns to its own dimension. While she thus resists her own integration into Terran imperialist structures, she helps a Terran cross over into the Prime Universe who is well versed in the practical implementation of imperialist ideologies. Although she eventually prevents Mirror Georgiou

> of the imperial capital, when the technologically enhanced Mirror Airiam releases a toxin targeting only human beings.

from committing yet another act of mass murder, Burnham represents a feminism that becomes temporarily complicit with the imperialist project. It is complicit because it fails to oppose imperialism's agents due to personal allegiances and because of a temporary overlap of goals (though not of means), here stopping the Federation's war with the Klingons.

Cadet Sylvia Tilly (Mary Wiseman), an ambitious young science officer stationed on the *Discovery*, represents a different version of this kind of feminism that becomes temporarily complicit with imperialist ideologies. Like Burnham, she has to impersonate her alter ego from the Mirror Universe in order to help her ship escape detection from Terran forces. Mirror Tilly, Terran records show, has 'gained the rank of captain by stabbing [her] previous superior in bed' and is known among the anti-Terran rebels as '[t]he Slayer of Sorna Prime' and '[t]he Witch of Wurna Minor' ('Despite Yourself,' 1x10). Facing herself in a mirror after she has changed into the Terran uniform, Prime Tilly is both 'terrified' and 'excited' (1x10) about the prospect of having to pose as the *Discovery*'s captain. Although Tilly assures Burnham that she is 'nothing like her [counterpart]' who is 'a twisted version of everything [she has] ever aspired to be' (1x10), being captain is precisely what Prime Tilly has always wanted. Indeed, during one of her first conversations with Burnham she tells her new roommate: 'Here's a thing most people don't know about me: I'm gonna be a captain someday' ('Context is for Kings' 1x03). Likely because she has imagined herself in the captain's chair countless times before, Tilly seems surprisingly at ease when she first takes over command, exchanging verbal blows with the captain of the Terran starship *Cooper*. While Burnham suffers immensely during her undercover operation on the *I.S.S. Shenzou*, Tilly – in her much safer position on the disguised *U.S.S Discovery* – enjoys her temporary promotion. She enjoys the (illusion of) power that the Mirror Universe offers a young woman like herself and thrives under the recognition she receives for playing her part convincingly. Back in the Prime Universe, she continues to crave this recognition and thus agrees to accompany Mirror Georgiou on her secret mission to Qo'noS, flattered by the potential the emperor sees in her. Although she, too, turns against the emperor as soon as she learns about Georgiou's plan to destroy Qo'noS, Tilly represents a feminism that is in constant danger of being seduced by the fantasies of individual superiority and promises of personal success that a racist system offers to those who feel presently disempowered, yet destined for greatness.

Ideas of collective rather than individual superiority and promises of collective rather than personal success are what lead Admiral Katrina

Cornwell (Jayne Brook) to embrace Terran ideologies and practices. Cornwell never crosses over into the Mirror Universe, but instead spends several weeks as a prisoner of the Klingon Empire before she is rescued by the crew of the *Discovery*. Deeply affected by this experience, she is willing to cross more and more figurative borders as the Federation-Klingon war begins to escalate. Witnessing the Klingon take-over of Federation space and devastating Klingon attacks on civilian Federation targets, the survivors of Starfleet command – represented in the series by Admiral Cornwell and Vulcan Ambassador Sarek (James Frain) – consider all means appropriate to protect Earth. When the *U.S.S. Discovery* returns to the Prime Universe with Mirror Georgiou on on board, they allow her to take the position of her prime counterpart, hoping that the emperor's experience in defeating the Klingons will give the Federation an advantage in the war. Here is how Cornwell explains the situation to the crew of the *Discovery* in the tellingly entitled episode 'The War Without, the War Within':

> We have all mourned the enormous loss of life due to this war. The acts of violence committed against us are the acts of *a foe without reason*, without honor. And they will not stop coming after us in the hopes of *destroying everything that we hold dear*. These are *desperate times* and they call on us to do more than merely protect our people, defend our borders. (1x14; emphasis added)

Using emotionally charged language reminiscent of the rhetoric used by the Bush administration after the attacks of 9/11 to justify the War on Terror, Cornwell demonizes the Klingons and argues that the Federation must temporarily abandon its principles, eventually ordering the *Discovery* to take the fight to the 'Klingon homeworld.' By helping to enlist Emperor Georgiou, Cornwell allows the Federation to enter into an alliance with a fascist leader and mass murderer who, at least in theory, represents everything that is antithetical to Starfleet's core values. Cornwell knows very well that Emperor Georgiou is not headed to Qo'noS 'to map its surface and isolate vulnerabilities and military targets' (1x14). In exchange for her freedom, the Terran Emperor has offered to destroy the Klingons' home planet just like she did in her own universe. By condoning Mirror Georgiou's integration into Starfleet (and later into Section 31), Cornwell also condones Terran ideologies and practices. If Mirror Georgiou's belief in human supremacy comes from elsewhere, Cornwell's brand of imperial feminism is decidedly home-grown. By making room for the emperor in the Prime Universe, rather than detaining her or returning her to the Mirror Universe,

Cornwell becomes representative of a feminism that tolerates and even embraces imperialist ideologies in a situation of crisis.

When Cornwell speaks about the Klingon–Federation war, she implies that the Klingons have been the aggressors, while the Federation has merely been trying to defend itself. Yet, *DSC* also suggests that the war may at least in part have been caused by the Federation's unacknowledged imperialist tendencies. Such an interpretation is suggested not only by T'Kuvma's (Chris Obi) opening monologue in 1x01 ('The Vulcan Hello'), in which he urges the Klingons to join forces against an ever-expanding Federation, but also by the conversation between Cornwell and another strong female character: L'Rell (Mary Chieffo), a female Klingon who is captured by/defects to the Federation. Visiting L'Rell in her holding cell on the *Discovery*, Cornwell is desperate to know why the Klingons 'target civilians, hospitals, [and] food convoys' and 'slaughter innocents' in their fight against the Federation, upon which L'Rell echoes T'Kuvma's speech by replying scornfully that her people 'fight to preserve Klingon identity' (1x14). Cornwell dismisses this explanation, claiming that '[n]o one is looking to destroy [Klingon] culture' because '[Federation] laws are founded in equality... freedom.' L'Rell once more objects, arguing instead that 'the Federation ... seeks universal homogenization and assimilation.' What becomes apparent in this scene is a clash of cultures. L'Rell hints at the fact that the war with the Federation is a desirable state for Klingons, while a peace treaty would be viewed as assimilation and thus as proof of the very loss of identity the Klingons try to prevent by fighting the war. For the Klingons fighting the Federation *is* preserving Klingon culture, regardless of the war's outcome. Cornwell's dismissal of L'Rell's argument is valid only from a human-centric perspective that presumes that the ideal of peaceful co-existence promoted by the Federation (if necessary by war) is a universally acknowledged value. Although the admiral's desire to end the bloodshed is understandable (from a human point of view), the assumption that Federation values are necessarily the ones by which all species in the Alpha Quadrant should live follows a logic of cultural imperialism. In the symbolic confrontations between Cornwell and L'Rell throughout season one of *DSC*, Cornwell can be said to embody a culturally imperialist power that insists on the superiority of its principles and seeks to enforce them by all means necessary. As a woman who holds one of the highest positions of power in the Federation, Cornwell represents a feminism that embraces cultural imperialism (turned imperialism), effectively discounting the values and thus to some extent the value of the racialized Other that the Klingons represent in the *Star Trek* universe.

Othering, Racialization, and Imperialist Feminism in *Star Trek: Discovery*

One of the reasons why a reading of the Federation as a (culturally) imperialist power suggests itself in *DSC* is because the series uses filmic strategies of (racial) Othering when depicting the Federation's enemies, whether in the Mirror or in the Prime Universe. Put differently, it inscribes into the show, at least initially, what film scholar E. Ann Kaplan in drawing from Laura Mulvey has famously described as an 'imperial gaze' (*Looking for the Other*, 1997), that is, a viewing position that reproduces a racist, colonial imagination in its depiction of the Other. Like its predecessors, *DSC* exoticizes Terrans and racializes Klingons, while at the same time using *Star Trek*'s potential for multilayered representations of cultural identity and race to call racial hierarchies and racialized notions of cultural difference into question. The highly diverse cast together with the Mirror Universe plot of *DSC* complicates the representation of female characters of color, exploring their place in the different imperialist projects depicted in the series, whether that of the Terran Empire, the Klingon Empire, or indeed that of the Federation.

Whether in the Prime Universe or the Mirror Universe, the word 'race' is only used in *DSC* to distinguish the human 'race' from other alien species, not in order to differentiate between and discriminate against certain individuals or groups based on skin color. Yet, the show's producers and writers also play with the fact that this second sense of the word 'race' has always operated as a subtext in conversations about different alien 'races' in *Star Trek* (cf. Bernardi, 1998; Roberts, 2000; Kanzler, 2004; Pounds, 2011; Scodari, 2012). In a notable exchange between Michael Burnham and Admiral Brett Anderson (Terry Serpico) during *DSC*'s first episode, the admiral admonishes Burnham for suggesting that the Klingons are 'relentlessly hostile' because it is 'in their nature' (1x01), suggesting that she should be 'the last person to make assumptions based on race' given her own 'background.'[7] Since humanity in the twenty-third century has abandoned the idea of multiple human 'races,' Anderson here refers to Burnham's adoption by a mixed Vulcan–Human couple. Yet, because Michael Burnham is played by black actress Sonequa Martin-Green and because Admiral Anderson's whiteness is particularly emphasized in this scene – he appears in it as a pale projection of light – their exchange does more than to insist that

---

[7] Whit Frazier Peterson also addresses this exchange in his essay 'The Cotton-Gin Effect: An Afrofuturist Reading of *Star Trek: Discovery*' published in this volume.

'it would be unwise to confuse race and culture' (1x01) when trying to understand the behavioral differences between humans and Klingons. The scene also reminds the audience that 'race' as a social category defined by skin color is not a matter of biology, but a cultural construct used to enforce power hierarchies and to legitimate oppression. As the series shows, racialized notions of cultural difference can be used to fuel imperialist ideologies. The concrete effects of such ideologies include both the extermination campaign the Terran Empire conducts against the non-human rebels in the Mirror Universe and the war the Federation wages against the Klingons in the Prime Universe.

Othering and racialization are most obviously at play in *DSC*'s depiction of the Klingons. From the moment the Klingons appear in the series, they are marked as 'racial others' who subscribe to utterly different values than the Federation. As indicated earlier, the audience first encounters the Klingons when T'Kuvma urges his fellow Klingons to take up arms against the Federation in the very first scene of the show. As the camera gradually zooms out from T'Kuvma's eye to his face and upper body, the viewers' attention is directed first at a fiery, yet human-looking eye, then at the Klingon's oily black skin, thick lips, and pointed teeth, and finally at his elongated, hairless head covered in bone-ridges. Like the other Klingon warriors surrounding him, T'Kuvma appears both monstrously human and exaggeratedly inhuman, a depiction that harks back to the racist representations of Klingons in earlier *Star Trek* series. Due to this history and the even longer Euro-American tradition of racializing enemies on screen, filmic clues such as dark skin, aggressive-sounding foreign speech, or scenes like the one later in the first episode, in which the Klingons gather around the open sarcophagus of a fallen warrior wrapped in cloth like an Egyptian mummy, remain powerful signifiers of racialized difference. Despite their changed design, then, the Klingons in *DSC* are still cast as racial Others.[8]

However, the Klingons are not only racialized; the show also relies on strategies of Othering and on a racialization of *cultural* difference to define Klingon identity and their relationship to the Federation. Indeed, T'Kuvma claims that the Federation does not merely endanger Klingon sovereignty and identity, but that '[Klingon] purity is a threat to them,' which is why '[t]hey wish to drag [the Klingon Empire] into the muck, where humans, Vulcans, Tellarites, and filthy Andorians mix' (1x02, 'Battle at the Binary Stars'). T'Kuvma's explicitly racist rhetoric of 'purity' in this speech betrays a biological understanding of 'race'

---

[8] Diana A. Mafe also makes this point in an interview published in this volume.

linked to the expansive 'Klingon supremacy' (1x02) he promotes. This is also why it is significant that L'Rell's comments about Klingon identity in her conversation with Cornwell refer primarily to an incompatibility of cultures (1x14). Distancing herself from T'Kuvma as well as from his successor, General Kol (Kenneth Mitchell), who – like the former – insists on expansive 'Klingon Supremacy' (T'Kuvma, 1x02, 'Battle at the Binary Stars'; Kol, 1x08,'Si Vis Pacem, Para Bellum'), L'Rell demonstrates why she becomes the Klingon leader who manages to unite the warring houses *and* make peace with the Federation in season two of the series. One could even go so far as to suggest that she succeeds because she abandons the racist ideologies of the Klingon Empire and becomes, by Klingon standards at least, a representative of anti-imperialist feminism.

Because of the narrative structure of the first season of *DSC*, the representation of the Klingon Empire shares certain similarities with that of the Terran Empire. Like the Klingons of the Prime Universe, Terrans are almost exclusively depicted infighting, torturing prisoners, attacking civilian settlements and rebel camps, preparing for war, or engaging in battle. Only a few Klingon and Terran characters, such as L'Rell, Voq, Emperor Georgiou, and Mirror Lorca, are shown in other social settings, allowing them to become more fully rounded, complex characters. While costume and set designs for the Mirror Universe have included Orientalist elements, the Terrans have never been racialized in the same ways as the Klingons. Still, the Terran Empire's brutal enforcement of human supremacy points to white supremacy as one of the pillars of Terran imperialist ideology. Its function as the Federation's mirror image consequently raises questions about *Star Trek*'s tendency to depict Starfleet as a predominantly (though never exclusively) human organization and human Starfleet officers as predominantly (though never exclusively) white. The fact that *DSC* features the most diverse cast as well as the most elaborate Mirror Universe plot in *Star Trek* history complicates its engagement with issues of race, gender, and imperialism. When the *Discovery* crosses over into the Mirror Universe, the show not only places several characters played by actors of color in an utterly xenophobic and racist society, it imagines some of them as very productive members of that society. For the purpose of this article, I will suggest what this means for the negotiation of the imperial(ist) feminisms of the three main female characters who cross from one universe into the other and end up impersonating their respective alter egos: Sylvia Tilly, Michael Burnham, and Emperor Georgiou.

From what the audience learns about her, Tilly arrives at her post on the *Discovery* armed with a nearly indestructible faith in the inherent goodness of people and the conviction that she will rise in the ranks of

Starfleet once she gets a chance to prove herself. The chance presents itself to her first when she has to impersonate 'Captain Killy' to protect her crew from the Terran forces and later when she joins Emperor Georgiou's secret mission to Qo'noS. While Tilly is certainly incredibly smart and works hard for her goals, she is also not burdened by the obstacles Burnham has had to confront since childhood. Put differently, Tilly begins her career in Starfleet from a position of privilege that is the result of her unquestionable (one might argue excessive) humanness/humanity, a humanness/humanity that is coded as whiteness in the *Star Trek* franchise. Although she critically reflects on the dangerous appeal of Terran (read human/white) supremacy, suggesting that 'the only way we can stop ourselves from becoming them is to understand the darkness within us and fight it' (1x14), she nonetheless profits from the possibilities the Terran Empire opens for her. Indeed, Tilly's flirtation with the imperial(ist) feminism of her Mirror Universe counterpart is only possible, I would argue, because of her humanness (whiteness). I do not mean to deny that Tilly is compassionate and brilliant. But, ultimately, the fact that she resists the temptation of becoming 'Killy' and rejects Emperor Georgiou as a role model after she uncovers her genocidal plans is enough to prove that she deserves a place in Starfleet's command training program and thus the chance of one day occupying one of the most powerful positions in the Federation. For other characters on the show, most notably Michael Burnham, the bar is set much higher.

In contrast to Tilly's experiences on the *Discovery*, Burnham's time in Starfleet is marked by an ongoing struggle to be(come) fully human. At first, she is an outsider because of her Vulcan upbringing, which keeps her from integrating into the primarily human crew of the *Shenzhou*. Then she loses her position, because her Vulcan upbringing together with the trauma of having been orphaned by a Klingon attack cause her to mutiny, a moment's decision with catastrophic longterm consequences. In order to be successful, Burnham must survive a series of harrowing trials, proving that she is human and can be, despite her Vulcan mindset and very human flaws, a worthy member of Starfleet. After her return from the Mirror Universe, her devotion to Starfleet's core principles is tested yet again, when she must oppose Starfleet command's plan to sacrifice Qo'noS to end the war with the Klingons. She even suggests a collaboration with L'Rell, effectively installing her as the new leader of the Klingons. Tilly learns from her time in the Mirror Universe that she can be what she has always hoped to be, but that rising in the ranks of Starfleet is only desirable if the organization and each officer in it, but especially the most privileged ones, continually work to resist the pull of a supremacist logic. Burnham learns that she can succeed to do so by embracing both her Vulcan upbringing and her humanity. Their brush with Terran racist ideologies and their ultimate rejection of these ideologies teaches both women valuable lessons. However, their very different learning processes also illustrate that some people have to work much harder to achieve what others are granted primarily by virtue of their birth. Anti-imperialist (and anti-racist) feminism has to account for these differences.

Because Emperor Georgiou is played by Chinese-Malaysian actress Michelle Yeoh, her role in *DSC* most drastically expresses the particular paradox of twenty-first century imperali(ist) feminism as Deepa Kumar describes it. Like Empress Sato before her, Mirror Georgiou is both an exoticized (human) Other and the ruler of a fascist empire that strives for complete domination of all racialized (alien) Others: she is literally a woman of color 'at the helm of empire' (Kumar, 2006). More than that, because she crosses over into the Prime Universe and remains there, she embodies the very real danger of a return of imperialist and racist ideologies to a society like the Federation that claims to reject imperialism and discrimination of all kinds and instead prides itself on defending individual freedom, liberty, and equality at all costs. This danger is further underlined by the fact that Mirror Georgiou becomes a leading figure in Section 31 precisely at the moment when this autonomous intelligence agency is increasingly at odds with Starfleet regulations and Federation values, eventually turning into an independent secret police that uses assassination, torture, and mass murder to protect the Federation (*DS9* 6x19, 'Inquisition'), tactics suspiciously similar to those employed in the Mirror Universe. Read as a comment on current political developments and debates, the figure of Emperor Georgiou, like that of Mirror Lorca who lives undetected in the Prime Universe for several months, is suggestive of the resurgence of racist, nationalist, and imperialist views in the United States before and during *DSC*'s production. Unlike Lorca, who, despite his Hispanic name, represents the kind of white masculinity commonly associated with imperialism, the figure of Emperor Georgiou draws attention to the active role of women in imperialist projects of the past and present. What is more, her character points to the fact that even women of color (in positions of power or privilege) can become complicit in the very structures of oppression that marginalize them. While *DSC* suggests that imperialism and the ideologies of imperial(ist) feminism will always be more seductive and immediately rewarding for white women like Tilly and Cornwell, it implies that women of color can become agents of empire, too. In the end, Michael Burnham is the show's hero because she challenges imperialist ideologies and the racist logic that accompanies them from within a system that puts her as a woman of color/human raised in a mixed-species household at considerable disadvantage. Even in a time of uttermost political and personal crisis, she resists the imperialist (feminist) worldview according to which the 'alien' Other is an enemy whose very nature justifies domination and destruction. Burnham resists this logic and so must we.

Conclusion

The Cold War *Star Trek* series presented Terran imperialism, hypernationalism, and racism as ideologies that could easily be contained and resisted as long as the crew members who crossed over into the Mirror Universe followed the example of the all-American hero Captain Kirk and as long as the crew members who remained in the Prime Universe could be trusted to recognize and neutralize the Terran intruders quickly. Fifty years later, *DSC* suggests that Terran ideologies can easily remain undetected (as with Mirror Lorca) or unopposed (as with Emperor Georgiou), if those in power and those following orders unquestioningly fail to speak up, because a temporary alliance with the enemy 'within' seems justified in order to defeat the enemy 'without.' In the end, the show can be read as a comment on contemporary (American) society at large, in which sexist, racist, nationalist, and imperialist tendencies have never been a matter of the past and have only ever, if at all, been pushed closer to the margins of political discourse. More specifically, *DSC* represents one feminist future in which racism and imperialism are an integral part of social and political structures (the Mirror Universe), and one feminist future in which racism and imperialism seem a relic of the past but make a forceful return as the story unfolds (the Prime Universe). Because it represents such a return, *DSC* can be read as a cautionary tale about what can happen if feminists think they can compromise on their anti-racist and anti-imperialist politics. When I speak of 'feminists' here, I mean to include everyone who considers themselves a feminist, but I primarily mean white European and American feminists; and when I suggest that feminists may think that they can compromise on their anti-racist and anti-imperialist politics, I mean to say that they should not.

Works Cited

Valerie Amos and Pratibha Parmar, 'Challenging Imperial Feminism', *One Chant: Black Feminist Perspectives, Feminist Review,* 17 (1984): 3–19.

Gloria Anzaldúa, *Borderlands/La Frontera: The New Mestiza* [1987], 2nd ed. (San Francisco, CA: Aunt Lute Books, 1999).

Daniel Bernardi, *'Star Trek' and History: Race-ing Toward a White Future* (Brunswick, ME: New Rutgers University Press, 1998).

Ryan Britt, 'Jason Isaacs Finally Explains Captain Lorca's Secret: The *Star Trek: Discovery* Captain Explains the Big Reveal', *Inverse,* 28 January (2018), www.inverse.com/article/40623-jason-isaacs-star-trek-discovery-interview.

Michelle Burnham, 'Loopholes of Resistance: Harriet Jacob's Slave Narrative and the Critique of Agency in Foucault', *Arizona Quarterly: A Journal of American Literature, Culture, and Theory,* 49.2 (Summer 1993): 53–73.

Teresa Cutler-Broyles, 'What We See When We Look in the Mirror: Star Trek's *Alternative Sexuality*', in Nadine Farghaly and Simon Bacon (eds.) *To Boldly Go: Essays on Gender and Identity in the Star Trek Universe* (Jefferson, MO: McFarland, 2017): 41–53.

Aviva Dove-Viebahn, 'Embodying Hybridity, (En)Gendering Community: Captain Janeway and the Enactment of a Feminist Heterotopia on *Star Trek: Voyager*', *Women's Studies,* 36 (2007): 597–618.

Fatima El-Tayeb, 'Dangerous Liaisons: Race, Nation, and German Identity', in Patricia Mazón and Reinhild Steingröver (eds.) *Not so Plain as Black and White: Afro-German Culture and History, 1890–2000* (Rochester, NY: University of Rochester Press, 2010): 27–60.

Inderpal Grewal and Caren Kaplan (eds.), *Scattered Hegemonies: Transnational Feminist Practices* (Minneapolis: University of Minnesota Press, 1994).

Steffen Hantke, 'Star Trek's Mirror Universe Episodes and US Military Culture through the Eyes of the Other', *Science Fiction Studies,* 41.3 (2014): 562–78.

Dan Hassler-Forrest, *Science Fiction, Fantasy, and Politics: Transmedia World-Building Beyond Capitalism* (London and New York: Rowman & Littlefield, 2016).

Naeem Inayatullah, 'Bumpy Space: Imperialism and Resistance in *Star Trek: The Next Generation*', in Jutta Weldes (ed.) *To Seek Out New Worlds: Science Fiction and World Politics* (New York: Palgrave, 2003): 53–75.

Katja Kanzler, *'Infinite Diversity in Infinite Combinations': The Multlicultural Evolution of Star Trek* (Heidelberg: Winter, 2004). *American Studies: A Monograph Series.*

E. Ann Kaplan, *Looking for the Other: Feminism, Film, and the Imperial Gaze* (New York: Routledge, 1997).

Patricia Kerslake, *Science Fiction and Empire* (Liverpool: Liverpool Univerity Press, 2007). *Liverpool Science Fiction Texts and Studies.*

Hyung Sook Kim, 'The Politics of Border Crossings: Black, Postcolonial, and Transnational Feminist Perspectives', in Sharlene Nagy Hesse-Biber (ed.) *Handbook of Feminist Research, Theory and Praxis* (Oaks: Sage, 2007): 107–22.

J.J. Kim-Puri, 'Conceptualizing Gender–Sexuality–State–Nation: An Introduction', *Gender & Society*, 19.2 (2005): 137–59.

Deepa Kumar, 'Imperialist Feminism', in *World Economy: The Return of Crisis, International Socialist Review*, 102 (2006): n.p., https://isreview.org/issue/102/imperialist-feminism.

Chandra Talpate Mohanty, *Feminism Without Borders: Decolonizing Theory, Practicing Solidarity* (Durham, NC: Duke University Press, 2003).

Michael Charles Pounds, '"Explorers": *Star Trek: Deep Space Nine*', in Sandra Jackson and Julie E. Moody-Freeman (eds.) *The Black Imagination: Science Fiction, Futurism and the Speculative* (Tübingen: Peter Lang, 2011): 47–80. *Black Studies & Critical Thinking*.

Diana M.A. Relke, *Drones, Clones and Alpha Babes: Retrofitting Star Trek's Humanism, Post-9/11* (Calgary: University of Calgary Press, 2006).

Robin A. Roberts, 'Science, Race, and Gender in *Star Trek: Voyager*', in Elyce Rae Helford (ed.) *Fantasy Girls: Gender in the New Universe of Science Fiction and Fantasy Television* (New York and London: Rowman & Littlefield, 2000): 203–21.

Christine Scodari, '"Nyota Uhura Is Not A White Girl": Gender, Intersectionality, and *Star Trek 2009*'s Alternate Romantic Universes', *Feminist Media Studies*, 12.3 (2012): 335–51.

Lora Wildenthal, '"When Men Are Weak": The Imperial Feminism of Frieda von Bülow', *Gender & History*, 10.1 (1998): 53–77.

Episodes Cited

'Mirror, Mirror.' *Star Trek: The Original Series*, written by Gene Roddenberry and Jerome Bixby, directed by Marc Daniels, Paramount Television, 6 October, 1967.

'Inquisition.' *Star Trek: Deep Space Nine*, written by Bradley Thompson and David Weddle, directed by Michael Dorn, Paramount Pictures, 8 April, 1998.

'Battle at the Binary Stars.' *Star Trek: Discovery*, written by Gretchen J. Berg and Aaron Harberts, directed by Adam Kane, CBS Television Studios, 24 September, 2017.

'The Vulcan Hello.' *Star Trek: Discovery*, written by Akiva Goldsman and Bryan Fuller, directed by David Semel, CBS Television Studios, 24 September, 2017.

'Context is for Kings.' *Star Trek: Discovery*, written by Gretchen J. Berg, Aaron Harberts, and Craig Sweeny, directed by Akiva Goldsman, CBS Television Studios, 2 October, 2017.

'Si Vis Pacem, Para Bellum.' *Star Trek: Discovery*, written by Kirsten Beyer, directed by John Scott, CBS Television Studios, 6 November, 2017.

'Despite Yourself.' *Star Trek: Discovery*, written by Sean Cochran, directed by Jonathan Frakes, CBS Television Studios, 8 January, 2018.

'The Wolf Inside.' *Star Trek: Discovery*, written by Lisa Randolph, directed by T.J. Scott, CBS Television Studios, 15 January, 2018.

'Vaulting Ambition.' *Star Trek: Discovery*, written by Jordon Nardino, directed by Hanelle M. Culpepper, CBS Television Studios, 22 January, 2018.

'Episode 12.' *After Trek*, hosted by Matt Mira, CBS Television Studios, 28 January, 2018.

'What's Past is Prologue.' *Star Trek: Discovery*, written by Ted Sullivan, directed by Olatunde Osunsanmi, CBS Television Studios, 29 January, 2018.

'The War Without, the War Within.' *Star Trek: Discovery*, written by Lisa Randolph, directed by David Solomon, CBS Television Studios, 5 February, 2018.

'Will You Take My Hand.' *Star Trek: Discovery*, written by Akiva Goldsman and Gretchen J. Berg, directed by Akiva Goldsman, CBS Television Studios, 11 February, 2018.

Interrogating Gender

Star Trek Discovers Women
Gender, Race, Science, and Michael Burnham

Amy C. Chambers

Introduction

Michael Burnham, and in turn Sonequa Martin-Green, brings women of color, and specifically black women, from the margins to the center of the narrative world of *Star Trek*,[1] by building upon the limited but often groundbreaking secondary character representation the *Star Trek* franchise has offered to women of color in its more than 50-year history. Women of color who have held significant roles in *Star Trek* include: Uhura (Nichelle Nichols *Star Trek: The Original Series*, 1966–1969);[2] Guinan (Whoopi Goldberg, *The Next Generation*, 1988–1993); Keiko O'Brien (Rosalind Chao, *The Next Generation*, 1991–1992 and *Deep Space Nine*, 1993–1999); Kasidy Yates-Sisko (Penny Johnson, *Deep Space Nine*, 1995–1999); B'Elanna Torres (Roxann Dawson, *Voyager*, 1995–2001); and Lily Sloane (Alfre Woodward, *First Contact*, 1996). Now in *Discovery*, Michael Burnham and Captain Phillippa Georgiou (Michelle Yeoh) place women at the center *alongside* a cast of secondary women of color characters including Dr. Gabrielle Burnham (Sonja Sohn), Joann Owosekun (Oyin Oladejo), Ellen Landry (Rekha Sharma), Dr. Pollard (Raven Dauda), May Ahearn (Bahia Watson/Claire Qute) and Queen

---

[1] The concept of drawing black women from the margin to center of narratives is taken from bell hooks' *Feminist Theory: From Margin to Center Feminist Theory: From Margin to Center* (Boston, MA: South End Press, 1984) (revised 2nd ed., 2000).

[2] The first *Star Trek* series has been retrospectively named (by fans and scholars) *Star Trek: The Original Series* to provide clarity and resist confusion between the different series found in the televisual *Star Trek* franchise storyworld. Individual *Star Trek* series will be referred to by their subtitles throughout this chapter, e.g. *Star Trek: The Original Series* is *The Original Series*; *Star Trek: Discovery* is referred to as *Discovery*; *Star Trek: Voyager* is *Voyager*; and so forth.

Me Hani Ika Hali Ka Po (Yadira Guevara-Prip). *Discovery* offers 'visible diversity' that goes 'beyond the surface level ... [expressing] depictions of science, technology and power, informed by complex and cogent backstories' (Keeler, 2019, 136). These women on the *U.S.S. Discovery* are not only part of a diverse crew, but also part of a community of women of color who have narrative agency and complexity – they are not presented as exceptions or anomalies but instead normalized as part of the wider demographics of the show.

Burnham is revolutionary in terms of the role she plays as a black woman scientist and a black woman protagonist in the *Star Trek* universe. Burnham and Captain Georgiou are introduced to viewers tracking across a desert-planet discussing their current mission with the science vessel *U.S.S. Shenzhou* to save an alien species from extinction. *Discovery* takes place in the *Star Trek* timeline prior the adventures of the crew of the *U.S.S. Enterprise* (*The Original Series*, 1966–1969) including Burnham's own adoptive brother Spock (played by Ethan Peck in season two). Burnham was adopted by the Vulcan ambassador to the United Federation of Planets Sarek (James Frain) and his human wife Amanda Grayson (Mia Kirshner) – Spock's biological parents – after Burnham's own parents are both believed to have been killed by Klingons. At the time of her graduation from the Vulcan Science Academy, Michael Burnham was the only human to have graduated from the institution – she graduates first in her class – but is rejected from the Vulcan Expeditionary Group because of her species (human). She instead joins Starfleet and trains in xenoanthropology – a bioscientific and anthropological specialism that defines her as an expert in first contact. Burnham's mutinous actions in the first two episodes of the first season shift the focus of the work of *Shenzhou* and later *Discovery* from science to war as all ships are made available to the war effort against the Klingons. Once seconded to the crew of the *Discovery* it is revealed that the captain of that ship, Gabriel Lorca (Jason Isaacs), engineered her arrival believing that he could use her advanced scientific knowledge to weaponize the technology onboard; rather than science for the advancement of knowledge, the *Discovery* becomes a science vessel for the advancement of war. Lorca manipulates Burnham, just as he does Starfleet and the crew of the *Discovery*, by explicitly rejecting the idea that his commitment to the spore drive research is militaristic in 'Context is for Kings' (1x03) – a lie that is rapidly exposed as the war continues. Throughout much of the first season Burnham acts as a bridge between the scientific ambitions of Paul Stamets (Anthony Rapp) and the military motivations of Lorca as she listens to both of their perspectives and negotiates the tension between scientists and the military. Although defined as a xenoanthropologist professionally, it is Burnham's extensive knowledge of both physics and biology that ultimately saves her from life imprisonment and progresses research on the spore drive that ultimately averts *Discovery*'s decimation at the hands of the Klingon fleet.

Stories about women scientists tend to focus on their relationship to/with/against men 'omitting any overt mention of race,' but the *Star Trek* franchise has offered a speculative space where the complexities of 'gender and race interact' (Roberts, 2000a, 205). *Voyager*'s Kathryn Janeway (Kate Mulgrew) was 'bestowed the ambiguous honor' of being the first woman captain on a titular vessel (Dove-Viebhan, 2007, 597), and also the first woman scientist to feature as a lead character. Janeway as a character must 'tread carefully between the possible indictment of mannishness on the one hand and the accusation of hyper-femininity on the other' in taking a role and a position in a franchise that had only been previously occupied by white men (597). She trained as a Starfleet science officer (speciality unknown) and built and worked with a team of women scientists including astrophysicist Seven of Nine (Jeri Ryan), and engineer B'Elanna Torres (Roxann Dawson). Roberts (2000a, 206) argues that both Torres and Seven of Nine are coded as 'bi-racial' because they are 'mixed-species female alien.' *Discovery* is Burnham's story but many of the major plot twists of season one are driven or shown to have been manipulated by a man: Captain Lorca. Nevertheless, with the introduction of Michael Burnham *Star Trek* places a black woman scientist at the center of the narrative world rather than at the margins of a(nother) white person's story.

Women scientists are often seen as anomalous exceptions and 'sidelined in subordinate roles' in the fictional (and indeed real) world of white, male-dominated scientific research (Simis et al., 2016, 93). Even in the supposedly race- and gender-blind future of *Star Trek*, a black woman science specialist is still considered groundbreaking. Yet, despite this unique positioning of a black woman in a major science fiction franchise, Burnham's representation as a scientist still sees her aligned with some of the limiting stereotypes repeatedly applied to women (fictional and non-). Her representation is complicated by including the hard/soft science binary where women scientists are affiliated with the biosciences; the presentation of women in science as almost impossibly brilliant polymaths while also being defective women (neither successful mothers or lovers); and approaching science from a gendered (feminine/caring/softer) perspective.

There is very little scholarship written on the representation of black women in science fiction – they do appear scattered across the history of moving image Anglo-American science fiction in part due to the unprecedented success and continuing receivership of Uhura/Nichols (O'Keeffe, 2013), but they have often been overlooked by (predominately white) scholars. Adilifu Nama's book *Black Space: Imagining Race in Science Fiction Film* (2008) constituted the first intervention into the scholarship surrounding Anglo-American science fiction cinema and its failure to consider the representation of race.[3] Nama (2008, 128) presents post-structuralist readings of science fiction exposing the 'black allegories' in 'white narratives,' claiming that the dearth of black faces 'signals a normalization of white supremacy in the future' and the perpetuation of institutionalized racism in these imagined futures (25). Despite the originality of Nama's monograph, the work does not fully consider the representation of black women as a doubly marginalized group, with the majority of examples analyzing male characters and male-centric narratives. Diana A. Mafe's *Where No Black Woman Has Gone Before: Subversive Portrayals in Speculative Film and TV* (2018) offers the first book-length analysis of black women in science fiction. Mafe argues that the lack of scholarship on an already massively underrepresented group 'speaks to the erasure of black women not only in the speculative genre but also in scholarship about the genre' (2018, 11). Women of color experience a double bind as they are often offered little representation onscreen and then even less attention in scholarship.

Black women have been historically analyzed either in terms of their race *or* their gender – but rarely if ever as a complex raced and gendered subject. As Mafe (2018a) notes, with reference to the work of Mary Anne Doane (1991), discussions of women in fiction are usually assumed to refer to white women and the term 'black' is almost exclusively aligned with black men. Doane (1991, 231) surmises that: 'What is lost in the process is the situation of the black woman. Her position becomes quite

---

[3] This lack of attention in scholarship is relatively specific to moving image media. Although Mafe and Nama's monographs are the only book-length studies to specifically deal with the representation of race in science fiction cinema, thus far, the question of race and science fiction literature has been the subject of several texts. Key texts include: Sharon DeGraw, *The Subject of Race in American Science Fiction* (London: Taylor & Francis, 2009); De Witt Douglas Kilgore, *Astrofuturism: Science, Race, and Visions of Utopia in Space* (Philadelphia: University of Pennsylvania Press, 2003); Isiah Lavender, *Race in American Science Fiction* (Bloomington: Indiana University Press, 2011); John Rieder, *Colonialism and the Emergence of Science Fiction* (Middleton, WI: Wesleyan University Press, 2008); Elisabeth Anne Leonard (ed.), *Into Darkness Peering: Race and Color in the Fantastic* (Westport, CT: Greenwood Press, 1997).

peculiar and oppressively unique: in terms of oppression, she is both black and a woman; in terms of theory she is neither.' Yet, with the recent popularity of black-led science-based fictions such *Hidden Figures* (2016), *Black Panther* (2018), and *Discovery*, black women are not only offered representation but firmly placed at the center of science-based narrative worlds. Spaces are opening up for future narratives and characterizations that do not require black women to be doubly oppressed by both creative and academic communities. Crucially, the critical and indeed financial success of these black-led science-based texts have shown that having a normalized black woman scientist as a main – if not *the* main, in the case of Michael Burnham – character does not constitute a barrier to financial or critical success.

Representing Science and Women Scientists in *Discovery*

Science and technology and their imagined futures provide a backdrop for the *Star Trek* universe. The theory and practice that gives the narrative a spectacular speculative frame is often perceived as neutral (or at least benevolent) as Starfleet explores the universe. As the series progresses and specifically across the arc of episodes that introduces the science of *Discovery*,[4] the series' key scientific fields are identified as biology and physics – the two in which Burnham has expertise. She is a professional xenoanthropologist (the study of extra-terrestrial cultures), but throughout the series there are multiple references to her knowledge of 'high-level physics' and 'quantum mechanics.' Her expertise across these two scientific fields, once she is able to combine them, make her invaluable to the crew and the narrative as it is revealed that *U.S.S. Discovery* travels using an organic propulsion network. The 'intergalactic ecosystem' of the mycelial network has the potential to offer an infinite number of interstellar pathways that allow for very accurate instantaneous travel across the known universe and all other quantum realities. But when Burnham is transported onto the *U.S.S. Discovery*, as fabricated by Lorca, it is not to in the service of the impartial altruistic science, as suggested in Burnham's initial introduction and Lorca's

---

[4] The 'science' that underpins the first series of *Discovery* is established across three episodes (episodes three, four, and five in season one). These episodes develop the concept of the spore drive, the series' focus on the relationship between biology and physics, and establishes the aptitude and scientific practice of the main character – Michael Burnham – as a woman of *many* sciences.

duplicitous proclamations (1x03), but rather one that uses her specific scientific expertise to gain a tactical advantage in combat and break into the Mirror Universe.

Historically, scientists have been represented in Anglo-American media as 'white, privileged American males' and, on the whole, this has not changed (Kirby, 2017, 292). There has been a recent wave of black women scientists appearing on both the small and silver screen, but *Black Panther*'s Shuri (Letitia Wright), NASA's *Hidden Figures* (Dorothy Vaughan (Octavia Spencer), Mary Jackson (Janelle Monáe), and Katherine Johnson (Taraji P. Henson)) and the Burnhams (both mother and daughter) on *Discovery* are still the minority in the small group of women scientists being offered as representation. Studies on women scientists in fictional media from key critics including Jocelyn Steinke (2005, 2010, 2018) and Eva Flicker (2003, 2008) have shown that women are underrepresented when compared to men. Diane A. Mafe has argued that even when women are offered space on science fiction screens they are predominately privileged white women who often work to reinforce 'white male authority' (2018a, 2). The paucity of women scientists on screen also emulates the dearth of women and specifically women of color in the sciences in reality. But representation is not simply about reflecting the problems of the present day: science fiction – as a speculative form – should allow for an imagining of alternatives that are not permeated with the trappings of existing institutionalized discrimination.

The current scholarship on women in science on screen is limited but has thus far almost exclusively focused on the role and provenance of white women. The black woman, as Doane (1991) notes, is often 'lost in the process' of analysis as she is both raced and gendered – so discussions of women scientists tend to focus on the white woman in part because of the bias that Doane identifies and moreover sadly because they are also rarely offered representation.[5] There have been other examples of fictional black women scientists in science fiction film and television including haematologist Dr. Karen Jenson (N'bushe Wright) in *Blade* (1998), medical doctor-in-training Martha Jones (Freema Agyeman) in *Doctor Who* (2007–2010), astronaut Molly Woods

---

[5] In Steinke and Tavarez's 2018 study of 42 films released between 2004 and 2012, 72 women scientists were identified in comparison to 142 men – which is particularly striking as this was not a study of *all* science-based films from the period of study but only those specifically with women in prominent speaking roles. The ratio of almost exactly 2:1 for male/female scientist speaking roles shows that, even in films with women scientists in central character roles, they are still outnumbered.

(Halle Berry) in *Extant* (2014–2015), the already mentioned tech-genius Shuri in *Black Panther*, astrophysicist Dr. Josie Radek (Tessa Thompson) in *Annihilation* (2018), engineer Ava Hamilton (Gugu Mbatha-Raw) in *The Cloverfield Paradox* (2018), and engineer Naomi Nagata (Dominique Tipper) in *The Expanse* (2015–). Despite these notable examples it is very 'rare' for black women scientists to be seen in science fiction, which makes analysis of black women scientists all the more important (Meyer, 2018, n.p.).

Star Trek idealizes science and the scientist but, throughout much of its history, the science future it imagines has been distinctly white, straight, and male. In *Discovery* Michael Burnham offers representation as not only a woman scientist but specifically as a black woman scientist, which makes her doubly rare in science fiction representation. Burnham notably works alongside a crew of (named) scientist characters who also further the show's diversity including: astromycologist (study of fungi in space) Paul Stamets and his partner – both romantic and professional – Dr. Hugh Culber (Wilson Cruz), another person of color.[6] Burnham is also not the only woman in the engineering lab as she appears alongside the red-headed theoretical engineer Cadet Sylvia Tilly (Mary Wiseman) working with the ship's organic propulsion system (the spore drive) and to rescue Burnham's adoptive Vulcan father Sarek (James Frain) with experimental neurological technology.[7]

---

[6] Previous characters have been read as queer in the *Star Trek* franchise, but Culber and Stamets' relationship is established and then normalized and placed in context alongside other romantic relationships within the series. For further analysis of LGBTQ representation in the *Star Trek* franchise in general and on *DSC* in particular, see Sabrina Mittermeier and Mareike Spychala's essay '"Never Hide Who You Are": Queer Representation and Actorvism in *Star Trek: Discovery*' published in this volume.

[7] The initial reception of Cadet Tilly raised questions about whether the character was intended to be interpreted as being on the autistic spectrum – her self-definition of having 'special needs' is not fully explained and left to speculation. Even though Wiseman has responded to these suggestions to say that her character was not intended to be read as autistic (Hatchett, 2018), the reception of Tilly as another instance of diversity and representation in the show is worth noting as it generated discussions of representing disability. See Teresa Jusino, 'Did *Star Trek: Discovery* Just Introduce a Recurring Character on the Autism Spectrum?', *The Mary Sue*, 2 October (2017), https://www.themarysue.com/cadet-sylvia-tilly-star-trek-discovery/, and Keisha Hatchett, 'Is Star Trek: Discovery's Tilly on the Autism Spectrum? [video interview with Mary Wiseman]', *TV Guide*, 7 February (2018), https://www.tvguide.com/news/is-star-trek-discoverys-tilly-on-the-autism-spectrum/.

Season two of *Discovery* sees the development of Tilly as a key woman scientist character, although Burnham remains the central character for the season and her scientific and emotional intelligence continues to underpin her actions. Burnham takes on the mission of saving her brother (Spock) and investigating the mysterious actions of the Red Angel. Once the identity of the time-traveler is revealed to be Burnham's mother – Gabrielle – *Discovery*, if only briefly, gains its first black woman astrophysicist and engineer. Dr. Gabrielle Burnham's expertise allows her to escape death and travel through time to warn her daughter of the universe's impending and complete depopulation. Dr. Burnham had been developing the Red Angel suit as a time-travel device for Section 31 prior to the Klingon attack where she used the suit to escape, but it later became a tool for jumping through time in attempts to prevent a newly sentient artificial intelligence (Control) from downloading the Sphere data, a key step in the destruction of all sentient beings.

The woman scientist that had been very much second to Burnham in the first season emerges as a key site of science in the second. Tilly is featured in several sequences in the first two episodes of season two, experimenting on a chunk of asteroid made of dark matter (or, as Tilly explains, 'not composed of non-baryonic matter'). The asteroid is strapped into *Discovery*'s hold with the support of a gravity simulator, but it is still volatile, as comedic scenes of Tilly working with the material attest. Tilly's tenacity sees her repeatedly return to the problem of the dark matter, its connection to the Red Angel, and how its power might be harnessed. Tilly is also frequently referred to for her expertise when on the bridge as a science officer – offering analysis of data and working with and attempting to manage and protect the Sphere data.

The encounter with the asteroid also brings Jett Reno (Tig Notaro) onto the ship – a woman engineer who survived the *U.S.S. Hiawatha*'s crash landing on the asteroid and sustained the lives of injured crew members before their rescue. Reno is introduced to the show via three drones that signal her need for help from *U.S.S. Discovery*, her characterization is founded in her problem solving and adept application of medical and engineering knowledge. Her addition to the crew adds another woman of science and also a queer woman. Reno's wife died in the Federation–Klingon War and she continues to wear her wedding ring in memoriam. Like Culber and Stamets, Reno's queerness is not hidden and, more importantly, is not revealed as being something that defines her as different or other – instead it is simply there.[8] Reno and

---

[8] The phrasing in this sentence is purposely drawn from a discussion of the campaigns surrounding the release of *Star Trek: Voyager* from LGBTQI fans

Tilly offer distinct images of women of science with their physicality suiting and amplifying their characterization and the message that it is competency that counts. Tilly offers a non-standard Hollywood aesthetic with an athletic rather than skinny build, and her long red curly hair, although neat in professional settings, is not as restrained as expected from fleet personnel. She has presence both physically and intellectually that is often expressed through loquacious energetic enthusiasm – but her ability is unquestioned by her peers and superiors even when her presentation is unconventional. Reno is represented as somewhat less traditionally feminine and recalls the androgyny of *Alien*'s Ellen Ripley (Sigourney Weaver). She seemingly aligns with Flicker's (2008) typology of the 'gruff woman's libber' or 'male woman,' but once placed within the wider context of the *Discovery* crew it is difficult to critique Reno as such because she is not the exception to a male majority.

The women scientist stereotypes that Flicker (2003, 2008) catalogued seem to be based upon the notion of the fictional woman scientist in isolation and as anomaly. By representing women as part of a diverse working environment – here, specifically, the science and engineering lab – the images of women that may have been considered limiting previously are less pronounced with women expressing themselves however they wish without fear of their appearance affecting the perception of their expertise. Reno, as a later addition to the *Discovery* crew and a humorous challenger to Stamets' sharp tongue and cantankerous demeanor, becomes part of the spectrum of the definition of who can be a scientist.

Whereas Reno is shown as a practical engineer and Tilly is identified specifically as a theoretical engineer, Burnham must take on the burden of being the impossibly polymathic woman scientist. Her focused high-level intelligence is in part attributed to her Vulcan upbringing – where she was educated to the highest standard surpassing the expectations of her adoptive family and species. But it is also due to a trend in science fiction films in which it is necessary for the woman scientist to be represented as a 'superstar' who sacrifices her femininity for science' (Elena, 1997, 270). As Eva Flicker (2003, 316–17) surmises: 'The portrayal of women scientists ... is orientated on their deficiency – either not a "real" woman or not a "proper" scientist – [which] contributes to the formation of myths about women scientists' lack of competence.'

---

such as the 'Voyager Visibility Project' that wanted the show to include characters for whom their 'queerness is neither hidden nor revealed *as difference*, but is simply there' (Pearson, 1999, 2). The inclusion and naturalization of queer characters is still quite unusual, with few appearing without coming-out narratives fixated upon their sexuality/gender identity.

Burnham must navigate this tension of not being a 'real' woman or a 'proper' scientist, alongside not being seen as entirely human (emotionally deficient) due to her Vulcan upbringing. In the time loop episode – 'Magic to Make the Sanest Man Go Mad' (1x07) – Stamets, who knows that he is repeating the same 30 minutes because of his genetic connection to the spore drive, needs a secret from Burnham that he can use to convince her in future loops that he is telling the truth about their predicament. Her secret is that she has never been in love. Despite her intelligence and successes Burnham has 'failed' to 'have it all' as a professional woman and needs time to practically stand still before she can progress into a heteronormative relationship (with Ash Tyler (Shazad Latif)).

'Representation in [a] fictional world' as Gerbner and Gross (1976, 182) argued 'signifies social existence' whereas 'absence means symbolic annihilation.' Women scientists and more acutely women scientists of color have been symbolically annihilated from both science fiction and the history of science. Gaye Tuchman (1979) specifically notes that in the media women are largely invisible and, when they are visible, they are marginalized or used as a symbolic representation of gender equality. It is not, as historian of science Patricia Fara (2008, 19) observes, that women scientists have been 'written out' but rather that they 'have never been written into these stories.' *Discovery* offers representation that has previously been missing – but this means that Burnham, and equally the actress Sonequa Martin-Green, carries a substantial 'burden of representation' as she is the first woman of color and the first active woman scientist to lead a *Star Trek* franchise production (Mercer, 1990). Burnham propels the representation of women scientists forward by placing them at the center rather than the margins of someone else's story. Any discussion of women scientists is often marred by this burden as these women (indeed both fictional and real) are not only critiqued for their scientific ability and their duty to represent and inspire their gender, but they must also be practically 'perfect' women (exceptionally successful as mothers, lovers, *and* scientists).

In the same way that black women are doubly underrepresented as both raced and gendered subjects, then, the burden of representation also weighs heavier upon them as they are made symbolic of two underrepresented groups and thus judged doubly as harshly as they are expected to 'speak *for* the entire community from which they come' because of their representational scarcity (Mercer, 1994, 214; original emphasis).

Women Scientists Practicing Science

Science is and has been traditionally framed as a 'value-neutral knowledge' practice that is *not* associated with understanding and studies of gender (Harding, 1995, 296). But as Sandra Harding argues '[science and technology] are not value neutral or outside culture' and instead 'fully embodied' into society (296). Harding (1991, 55) established the notion that science and technology industries have attempted to improve gender issues by *just adding women* 'without questioning the legitimacy of science's social hierarchy' and thus its mirroring of discriminatory practices found therein. Attempts historically (Harding was analyzing the 1980s and 1990s) and more recently to diversify scientific cultures – both real and imagined – result in recurrent issues that fail to address institutional and structural problems that continue to limit women's participation and representation in the sciences.

As a fictional woman in scientific research and practice, Michael Burnham can be seen to align with the existing problematic history of representation either where, as argued above, women are seemingly represented as polymathic 'super scientists' or conform to the restrictive stereotypes identified by Eva Flicker (2003, 2008). Flicker (2003, 317) argues that fictional women scientists have presented 'more of a stereotypical woman's role than the occupational role as a scientist,' which may have an impact on audience perceptions and frame these women as anomalous transgressors into the realms of science practice, which Robin Roberts (2000b, 278) identifies as 'the last [bastion] of male dominance.'[9] Although Michael Burnham deviates from the stereotype of the white woman scientist, her scientific practice is still allied to some of the restrictive expectations of women scientists on screen. She predominantly works in the biosciences and it is her empathy for and 'relationship' to/ with the large alien creature 'Ripper' that begins the journey to at least partially resolving issues with controlling the spore drive.

Ripper is an alien creature that strongly resembles a real-world microscopic creature called a tardigrade that displays a genetic symbiosis with the spores (from a specific alien fungus) and thus access to the

---

[9] Flicker (2003, 2008) identifies seven (the seventh was added in a 2008 chapter that revised the list) different types of fictional women scientists: the old maid; the gruff women's libber/male woman; the naïve expert; the evil vamp; the daughter or assistant; the lonely heroine; and the clever, digital beauty (added 2008). These limiting stereotypes tend to position women in relation to male scientist counterparts (mother, lover, assistant) or shame these women because of their failures to align with societal expectations concerning marriage, love, and childbearing.

mycelial network that allows the 'giant space tardigrade' and in turn the *U.S.S. Discovery*'s Displacement-Activated Spore Hub drive (spore drive/s-drive/DASH) to make expansive light-year jumps in a matter of seconds.[10] As Burnham explains in 'Choose Your Pain' (1x05): 'Like its microscopic cousins on Earth, the tardigrade is able to incorporate foreign DNA into its own genome via horizontal gene transfer. When Ripper borrows DNA from the mycelium, he's granted an all-access travel pass.' Ripper is retrieved from the *U.S.S. Glenn* in 'The Butcher's Knife Cares Not for the Lamb's Cry' (1x04) after *Discovery* responds to a distress call to discover the crew dead and the ship seemingly ravaged by this unknown alien. At first misunderstood as a violent alien (hence the moniker Ripper) that needs to be tortured to be controlled, Burnham uses her knowledge of xenoanthropology and biology to argue that: 'nothing in its biology suggests it would attack, except in self-defense.' Notably, Burnham chooses to investigate (as a scientist) rather than interrogate and dominate Ripper.

In her feminist critiques of science, Evelyn Fox Keller (1982, 1985, 1987) introduced the concept of gendered science and argues that science is one of the institutions of power that feminists should want to change and that there exists a possibility 'to make science a human, rather than masculine, project' (Oliver, 1989, 138) – 'a science less restrained by the impulse to dominate' (Keller, 1982, 39). Keller intimates that throughout the history of male-directed science, the discipline has been understood as 'the power to dominate nature' (1987, 47). In *Discovery*, Burnham is not only a raced and gendered Other, but also a scientific Other as she chooses to approach her subject as something to be empathized with rather than controlled. An approach that is not considered by her scientific colleagues and the security officer who is tasked with monitoring the mutineer. In her remark: 'understanding how it feels was not our mission,' security officer Ellen Landry, also a woman of color,[11] represents a traditional

---

[10] The spore drive and the representation of the tardigrade in *Discovery* as an advanced instantaneous form of interstellar transportation has been criticized by a number of scientists including Professor Steven Saltzberg (Professor of Biomedical Engineering, Computer Science, and Biostatistics, Johns Hopkins University). As Saltzberg (2017) remarks: 'using horizontally transferred DNA for space travel is so nutty, so bad, that it's not even wrong. Even if tardigrades could absorb foreign DNA (they can't), how the heck is this supposed to give them the ability to tap into the (wildly implausible) intergalactic spore network?'.

[11] Landry is also a further example of progressive casting, where the standard secondary white male character is instead a woman of color who aligns with previously established notions of the 'tough woman' (Inness, 2004). Landry

approach to science and also the tension the crew of science vessel *Discovery* face as their mission of exploratory science is replaced with one of weaponization. Whereas Stamets and Burnham focus their research on progressing science, albeit with different approaches, Lorca (with Landry as his emissary) is obsessed with using their expertise to create a spore-based biological weapon.

The opening of 'Choose Your Pain' (1x05) presents a vivid dream/nightmare sequence where Burnham sees herself taking the place and thus the pain of the tardigrade. Her sentimental connection to the creature is confirmed in a later sequence in the lab where a shot-reverse-shot between Ripper (showing his full alien body) and Burnham places the two characters in conversation, providing the audience once again with an insight into the effect the torture of Ripper has on Burnham. She is visibly emotional. This is a response that she has been taught to repress in her Vulcan upbringing but one that is shown here to give her the insight she needs to understand and then appropriately utilize the tardigrade. Burnham quite literally takes on the emotional labor of the scientific experiments – as a woman she is seen to be capable of not only understanding her subject but also accessing her emotions and empathy in order to do so. She has what Keller (1983) terms 'a feeling for the organism' that is unfathomable to the initially emotionally deficient Stamets who has no ethical issues with exploiting rather than understanding the tardigrade.[12] Burnham pleads with her colleague to release Ripper exclaiming: 'Making Ripper the critical component of the s-drive is unsustainable for the creature and your invention' (1x05). The animate co-pilot suffers immeasurably each time a jump is made, a feeling that is communicated to audiences via Burnham's own pained expressions. Once Stamets installs himself as the new co-pilot – which *is* raised as an ethical issue by First Officer Saru (Doug Jones) who remarks that 'eugenics experiments are forbidden' under Starfleet's science regulations (1x05) – Ripper is released back into the void of space. Burnham corresponds once again on behalf of the tardigrade as

---

transgresses traditional notions of a security officer's gender but does so in the relatively safe/acceptable body of a 'beautiful, slender, heterosexually desirable' woman (3).

[12] The concept of 'a feeling for the organism' was developed specifically in reference to Nobel Prize-winning scientist and cytogeneticist Barbara McClintock in Keller's 1983 biography of her. McClintock discovered genetic transposition and developed theories that explained the suppression and expression of genetic information. A specialism that aligns with the genetic research involved in accessing the mycelium network and its use (although scientifically inaccurate understanding) of horizontal gene transfer.

she surmises that: 'what makes it most happy is to be free' (1x05). Upon Ripper's release it is only the woman scientists who are present – Tilly and Burnham – and shown crying in response to tardigrade's release back into the wild and in recognition of their own scientific success with the spore drive.

Conclusion: Normalizing Women of Color/Science

Star Trek has historically given women space to be scientists, but *Discovery* goes further than previous entries into the mythos by having a black woman physicist/bioscientist protagonist. It imagines a future when neither race nor gender present a barrier. Michael Burnham is in many ways 'groundbreaking' as she 'fulfils the untapped potential of her famous predecessor' – the bridge-bound Uhura – by controlling much of the narrative of *Discovery* and driving it forward (Mafe, 2018b).

The majority of science fiction, and indeed film and television more generally, is predominantly produced by white male writers and directors, which lessens the likelihood of stories being written that explore alternative perspectives. It is 'endemic to white culture,' as Richard Dyer (1997, 2) has stated, that whiteness, and specifically male whiteness, is normalized and naturalized. Race (non-Caucasian) and gender (non-male) are used by writers and producers to define characters as Other and even anomalous – with 'black womanhood' historically signifying 'an ultimate Otherness' (Mafe, 2018a, 15). Diversity needs to happen not only on screen but across the industry – diverse stories not only offer representation but an opportunity to critique the flaws in the system. For a genre immersed in futurism, science fiction often fails women and people of color – and most definitely for those multiply marginalized at the intersections of gender, race, and sexuality.

Michael Burnham features in the first new *Star Trek* small screen fiction to appear since J.J. Abrams' reboot of the franchise beginning with *Star Trek* (2009).[13] Although the representation of women scientists, and specifically the representation of women of color, is beginning to change with the emergence of greater diversity of onscreen scientists and some key examples of women who are not immediately defined by

---

[13] The *Star Trek* film reboot that Abrams inaugurated exists, narratively, in an alternative timeframe – *the Kelvin Timeline*, named for the ship destroyed in the opening scene. *Discovery* exists in the same timeline as the other television series and the films that feature characters from the *Original* and *Next Generation* series.

their relationship to men and the family – these women are found more frequently in small screen fictions. Although there is 'not a plethora of examples' television has allowed 'for more ambiguity regarding who is' and can be 'the hero' with more opportunities for women characters to develop (Mafe, 2018a, 141, 125). Television series provide more spaces for women scientists of color and women scientists generally to exist – perhaps because of the platform's inherent opportunities for writers/producers to develop, drop, and introduce characters over a potentially long-term serial narrative. Films have extremely long production scales and are only one entity on which producers will be judged (critically and financially) – television has a different development and dissemination process where even a small but dedicated/repeat-viewing 'boutique audience' can be sufficient to make a series financially viable (Mittel, 2015, 34) – audiences that may well positively respond to the incorporation of unrepresented character types and narratives.

Series like *Orphan Black* (2013–2016), *Extant* (2014–2015), *Doctor Who* (2005–ongoing), and the *Star Trek* franchise (most recently *Discovery*) allow for women scientist characters to develop without a need to anchor them to male scientists or familial narratives, and also include characters who further diversify the representation of women. The bio-science fiction clone drama *Orphan Black* features several prominent LGBTQ characters including the women scientists Delphine Cormier (Évelyne Brochu) and her girlfriend Cosima Niehaus (Tatiana Maslany), who exclaims that her 'sexuality is not the most interesting thing about [her].' Similarly to Culber and Stamets in *Discovery*, it is their scientific acumen that defines them and their agency within the narrative and not their same-sex relationship, which is normalized rather than spectacularized. Queer scientist representation is even more limited than the representation of both men and women from racial and ethnic minorities, and the inclusion of Culber (alongside Stamets) in *Discovery* constitutes not only the first openly gay mixed-race couple but the first gay scientist of color to feature in the *Star Trek* universe.

Improving, increasing, and diversifying media representation is only one way of affecting change, but it is an important part of a long-term project to change the representation and perception of the sciences in a way that stops constraining people by their race, sexuality, ability, and gender. Michael Burnham, alongside an emerging number of black women scientists in both cinematic and small screen fictions, represents an opening up of the imagined future where not only race but also gender can be found at the forefront of the discovery of worlds and cultures where no one has gone before.

Works Cited

Sharon DeGraw, *The Subject of Race in American Science Fiction* (London: Taylor & Francis, 2009).

Mary Ann Doane, *Femme Fatales: Feminism, Film Theory, Psychoanalysis* (London: Routledge, 1991).

Aviva Dove-Viebhan, 'Embodying Hybridity, (En)gendering Community: Captain Janeway and the Enactment of a Feminist Heterotopia on *Star Trek: Voyager*', *Women's Studies: An Inter-disciplinary Journal*, 36.8 (2007): 597–618.

Richard Dyer, *White: Essays on Race and Culture* (Abingdon: Routledge, 1997).

Alberto Elena, 'Skirts in the Lab: Madame Curie and the Image of the Woman Scientist in the Feature Film', *Public Understanding of Science*, 6.2 (1997): 69–278.

Patricia Fara, *Pandora's Breeches: Women, Science and Power in the Enlightenment* (London: Pimlico, 2008).

Eva Flicker, 'Between Brains and Breasts – Women Scientists in Fiction Film: On the Marginalization and Sexualization of Scientific Competence', *Public Understanding of Science*, 12 (2003): 307–18.

—— 'Women Scientists in Mainstream Films: Social Role Models – a Contribution to the Public Understanding of Science from the Perspective of Film Sociology', in Bernd-Rüdiger Hüppauf and Peter Weingart (eds.) *Science Images and Popular Images of the Sciences* (New York: Routledge, 2008): 241–56.

George Gerbner and Larry Gross, 'Living with Television: The Violence Profile', *Journal of Communication*, 26.2 (1976): 172–99.

Susan Harding, 'Just Add Women and Stir?', in Gender Working Group, United Nations Commission on Science and Technology for Development (ed.) *Missing Links: Gender Equity in Science and Technology for Development* (New York: United Nations Development Fund for Women, 1995): 295–308.

—— *Whose Science? Whose Knowledge?: Thinking from Women's Lives* (Ithaca, NY: Cornell University Press, 1991).

Keisha Hatchett, 'Is Star Trek: Discovery's Tilly on the Autism Spectrum? [video interview with Mary Wiseman]', *TV Guide*, 7 February (2018), https://www.tvguide.com/news/is-star-trek-discoverys-tilly-on-the-autism-spectrum/.

bell hooks, *Feminist Theory: From Margin to Center* (Boston, MA: South End Press, 1984).

Sherrie A. Inness, '"Boxing Gloves and Bustiers": New Images of Tough Women', in Sherrie A. Inness (ed.) *Action Chicks: New Images of Tough Women in Popular Culture* (New York: Palgrave, 2004): 1–20.

Teresa Jusino, 'Did *Star Trek: Discovery* Just Introduce a Recurring Character on the Autism Spectrum?', *The Mary Sue*, 2 October (2017), https://www.themarysue.com/cadet-sylvia-tilly-star-trek-discovery/.

Amanda Keeler, 'Visible/Invisible: Female Astronauts and Technology in *Star Trek: Discovery* and National Geographic's *Mars*', *Science Fiction Film and Television*, 12.1 (2019): 127–50.

Evelyn Fox Keller, *A Feeling for The Organism: The Life and Works of Barbara McClintock* (New York: Freeman, 1983).

—— 'Feminism and Science' (1982), in Helen E. Longino and Evelyn Fox Keller (eds.) *Feminism and Science* (Oxford: Oxford University Press, 1996): 28–40.

—— 'The Gender/Science System: Or, Is Sex to Gender as Nature Is to Science?', *Hypatia*, 2.3 (1987): 37–49.

—— *Reflections on Gender and Science* (New Haven, CT: Yale University Press, 1985).

De Witt Douglas Kilgore, *Astrofuturism: Science, Race, and Visions of Utopia in Space* (Philadelphia: University of Pennsylvania Press, 2003).

David A. Kirby, 'The Changing Popular Image of Science', in Kathleen Hall Jamieson, Dan Kahan, and Dietram A. Scheufele (eds.) *The Oxford Handbook of the Science of Science Communication* (Oxford: Oxford University Press, 2017): 291–300.

Isiah Lavender, *Race in American Science Fiction* (Bloomington: Indianan University Press, 2011).

Elisabeth Anne Leonard (ed.), *Into Darkness Peering: Race and Color in the Fantastic* (Westport, CT: Greenwood Press, 1997).

Helen E. Longhino and Evelynn Hammonds, 'Conflicts and Tensions in the Feminist Study of Gender and Science', in Marianne Hirsch and Evelyn Fox Keller (eds.) *Conflicts in Feminism* (New York: Routledge, 1990): 164–83.

Diana A. Mafe, 'Normalising Black Women as Heroes: *Star Trek Discovery* as Groundbreaking', *Media Diversified*, 6 March (2018b), https://mediadiversified.org/2018/03/06/normalising-black-women-as-heroes-star-trek-discovery-as-groundbreaking/.

—— *Where No Black Woman Has Gone Before: Subversive Portrayals in Speculative Film and TV* (Austin: University of Texas Press, 2018a).

Kobena Mercer, 'Black Art and the Burden of Representation', *Third Text*, 4.10 (1990): 61–78.

—— *Welcome to the Jungle: New Positions in Black Cultural Studies* (London: Routledge, 1994).

Karlyn Ruth Meyer, 'Dr. Karen Jenson, Hematologist: How 1998's *Blade* Set the Stage for Black Women Scientists on Screen', *Lady Science* (2018), https://www.ladyscience.com/blog/dr-karen-jenson-hematologist-how-1998s-blade-set-the-stage-for-black-women-scientists-on-screen.

Jason Mittell, *Complex TV: The Poetics of Contemporary Television Storytelling* (New York: New York University Press, 2015).

Adilifu Nama, *Black Space: Imagining Race in Science Fiction Film* (Austin: University of Texas Press, 2008).

Moira O'Keeffe, 'Lieutenant Uhura and the Drench Hypothesis: Diversity and the Representation of STEM Careers', *International Journal of Gender, Science and Technology*, 5.1 (2013): 5–24.

Kelly Oliver, 'Keller's Gender/Science System: Is the Philosophy of Science to Science as Science Is to Nature?', *Hypatia*, 3.3 (1989): 137–48.

Petra Pansegrau, 'Stereotypes and Images of Scientists in Fiction Films', in Bernd-Rüdiger Hüppauf and Peter Weingart (eds.) *Science Images and Popular Images of the Sciences* (New York: Routledge, 2008): 257–66.
Wendy Pearson, 'Alien Cryptographies: The View from Queer', *Science Fiction Studies*, 26.1 (1999): 1–22.
Constance Penley, *NASA/Trek: Popular Science and Sex in America* (London: Verso, 1997).
John Rieder, *Colonialism and the Emergence of Science Fiction* (Middleton, WI: Wesleyan University Press, 2008).
Robin Roberts, 'Science, Race, and Gender in *Star Trek: Voyager*', in Elyce Rae Helford (ed.) *Fantasy Girls: Gender in the New Universe of Science Fiction and Fantasy Television* (Lanham, MD: Rowman & Littlefield, 2000a): 203–21.
—— 'The Woman Scientist in *Star Trek: Voyager*', in Marleen Barr (ed.) *Future Females, The Next Generation: New Voices and Velocities in Feminist Science Fiction Criticism* (Lanham, MD: Rowman & Littlefield Publishers, 2000b): 277–90.
Steven Saltzberg, 'New *Star Trek* Series Makes Massive Science Blunder', *Forbes*, 30 October (2017), https://www.forbes.com/sites/stevensalzberg/2017/10/30/new-star-trek-series-makes-massive-science-blunder/#11ce2591b377.
Molly J. Simis, Sara K. Yeo, Kathleen M. Rose, Dominique Brossard, Dietram A. Scheufele, Michael A. Xenos, and Barbara Kline, 'New Media Audiences' Perceptions of Male and Female Scientists in Two Sci-Fi Movies', *Bulletin of Science, Technology & Society*, 35.3/4 (2016): 93–103.
Jocelyn Steinke, 'Cultural Representations of Gender and Science: Portrayals of Female Scientists and Engineers in Popular Films', *Science Communication*, 27.1 (2005): 27–63.
—— 'Gender Representations of Scientists', in Susanna Hornig Priest (ed.) *Encyclopedia of Science and Technology Communication* (Thousand Oaks, CA: Sage, 2010): 323–25.
—— and Paola Maria Paniagua Tavarez, 'Cultural Representations of Gender and STEM: Portrayals of Female STEM Characters in Popular Films 2002–2014', *International Journal of Gender, Science and Technology*, 9.3 (2018): 245–76.
Gaye Tuchman, 'Women's Depiction by the Mass Media', *Signs: Journal of Women in Culture and Society*, 4.3 (1979): 528–42.

Episodes, Films, and Television Series Cited

'Context is for Kings.' *Star Trek: Discovery*, written by Gretchen J. Berg, Aaron Harberts, and Craig Sweeny, directed by Akiva Goldsman, CBS Television Studios, 1 October, 2017.
'The Butcher's Knife Cares Not for the Lamb's Cry.' *Star Trek: Discovery*, written by Jesse Alexander and Aron Eli Coleite, directed by Olatunde Osunsanmi, CBS Television Studios, 8 October, 2017.

'Choose Your Pain.' *Star Trek: Discovery*, written by Kemp Powers, story by Gretchen J. Berg, Aaron Harberts, and Kemp Powers, directed by Lee Rose, CBS Television Studios, 15 October, 2017.

'Magic to Make the Sanest Man Go Mad.' *Star Trek: Discovery*, written by Aron Eli Coleite and Jesse Alexander, directed by David M. Barrett, CBS Television Studios, 29 October, 2017.

Star Trek: First Contact. 1996. Directed by Jonathan Frakes. Paramount Pictures.
Blade. 1998. Directed by Stephen Norrington. New Line Cinema.
28 Days Later. 2002. Directed by Danny Boyle. Fox Searchlight Pictures.
AVP: Alien vs Predator. 2004. Directed by Paul W.S. Anderson. 20th Century Fox.
Star Trek. 2009. Directed by J.J. Abrams. Paramount Pictures.
Hidden Figures. 2016. Directed by Theodore Melfi. 20th Century Fox.
Annihilation. 2018. Directed by Alex Garland. Paramount Pictures.
Black Panther. 2018. Directed by Ryan Coogler. Marvel Studios.
The Cloverfield Paradox. 2018. Directed by Julius Onah. Paramount Pictures.

Star Trek: The Original Series. NBC: 1966–1969.
Star Trek: Next Generation. CBS: 1987–1994.
Star Trek: Deep Space Nine. CBS: 1993–1999.
Star Trek: Voyager. CBS: 1995–2001.
Doctor Who. BBC: 2005–ongoing.
Orphan Black. BBC America: 2013–2017.
Extant. CBS: 2014–2015.
The Expanse. Syfy: 2015–2018. Prime Video: 2018–ongoing.
Star Trek: Discovery. CBS: 2017–ongoing.

Not Your Daddy's *Star Trek*
Exploring Female Characters in
Star Trek: Discovery

Mareike Spychala

Introduction: *Star Trek: Discovery*'s Female Characters

Star Trek: Discovery, (2017–ongoing; *DSC*), one of the newest television instalments in the *Star Trek* franchise, has been notable for the prominence it affords its female characters and especially black female characters and female characters of color. Not only are the show's first and second seasons centered on First Officer (and later mutineer and ultimately Commander) Michael Burnham (Sonequa Martin-Green), the first African American woman to lead a *Star Trek* show, several other female characters and their relationships with each other take on prominent roles throughout the two seasons that have aired so far. Out of all the entries into the *Star Trek* canon, *DSC* is the show featuring the most female characters and also the one giving these characters the most to do. In addition to Burnham, there are 12 more named female characters, some of which, like Cadet Sylvia Tilly (Mary Wiseman) are part of the show's main cast, appearing in almost all episodes, while others, like Captain Georgiou (Michelle Yeoh) or Commander Jett Reno (Tig Notaro) recur in a few episodes. Among the Klingons the spy and later High Chancellor L'Rell (Mary Chieffo) takes on an increasingly prominent role, acting as a foil to Burnham throughout the first season. In season two, her struggle to unite the Klingon Empire and solidify her power allows for an interrogation of the patriarchal power structures in Klingon society that has seldom been featured in previous series. While there are also memorable and pivotal male characters – Lieutenant Commander Paul Stamets (Anthony Rapp) and Dr. Hugh Culber (Wilson Cruz), the franchise's first openly gay couple, Captain Gabriel Lorca (Jason Isaacs), the eventual villain of season one, as well as a young Lieutenant Spock (Ethan Peck) and Captain Christopher Pike (Anson Mount) in season two – it is the female characters who are instrumental in resolving the plots of both the first and the second season and carrying the show.[1] Most notably, in the finale of season two, almost all the risky and important actions required to defeat Control, a Section 31 A.I. gone rogue, are undertaken by female characters.

This is fairly new for the franchise. While *Star Trek: The Original Series* (1966–1969; *TOS*) made history by featuring a female lieutenant of Bantu origin on the bridge with the character of Nyota Uhura (Nichelle Nichols), the show remained firmly centered on its three white, male leads. Later *Star Trek* series like *The Next Generation* (1987–1994; *TNG*) continued featuring mostly white female characters in minor – and often stereotypical – roles. It was not until *Star Trek: Voyager* (1995–2001; *VOY*) that audiences got to follow a female captain in Kathryn Janeway (Kate Mulgrew). *Star Trek: Discovery*, through including of so many different and fully-fledged female characters, not only continues in the franchise's liberal tradition, it also explores new ways in which female characters can be represented in televised (American) science fiction series. This essay will argue that the show's female characters push against and sometimes transcend generic tropes that have limited characters like *TNG*'s Deanna Troi (Marina Sirtis) and Dr. Beverly Crusher (Gates McFadden), picking up on and contributing to contemporary debates about gender and gender identity.

Reframing Established Tropes: Female Characters and Femininity in *Star Trek: Discovery*

As Brian Attebery (2002) has pointed out with regard to literary science fiction, '[u]ntil the 1960s, gender was one of the elements most often transcribed unthinkingly into SF's hypothetical worlds' (5). He locates this conventionality in questions of gender representation in the mostly male audience of science fiction stories and notes the tension between commercial interests and their tendency towards 'predictability' (5) and the genres inherent trends towards modifications of basic building blocks of stories (5). Veronica Hollinger (2003) makes a similar point, observing that science fiction 'has been slow to note the historical contingency and cultural conventionality of many of our ideas about sexual identity and

[1] Sabrina Mittermeier and Jenny Volkmer's essay '"We Choose Our Own Pain. Mine Helps Me Remember": Gabriel Lorca, Ash Tyler, and the Question of Masculinity' explores two of the show's main male characters, while Sabrina Mittermeier and Mareike Spychala's essay '"Never Hide Who You Are": Queer Representation and Actorvism in *Star Trek: Discovery*' takes a closer look at the impact of the characters of Dr. Culber and Lieutenant Commander Stamets. Both of these essays are published in this volume.

desire, about gendered behavior and about the "natural" roles of women and men' (126).[2] While Attebery and Hollinger focus mostly on literary science fiction, their observations also hold for most science fiction films and television series, as becomes clear when one takes a closer look at the *Star Trek* franchise itself.

Thus, Mark Bould (2003) argues that 'TV sf relies on types of character interaction common to soap opera,' and that the medium's restrictions '[have] rendered it conventional and conservative' (94). A similar point about a shift of such television series, in this case specifically *TNG*, is made by Lynne Joyrich (1996, 61–84), who also notes *TNG*'s move towards the format of the soap opera in its plots (73–74), and critically reads female characters like Counselor Deanna Troi and Dr. Beverly Crusher. Troi, she notes, 'personifies the professionalization of femininity itself.' She further points out that '[h]ere femininity, defined precisely as a "receptive capacity," is (to reiterate Heath's words) both literally "universalized" – operative throughout distant galaxies – and "occupationalized" – constructed as a respected career' (Joyrich, 1996, 64). While this may be a step up from the female characters in the original *Star Trek*, it also allows the series to 'construct a "progressive" image of a twenty-fourth century career woman while still alleviating twentieth century anxieties about working girls' (64). This 'professionalization of femininity' (64) and the anxieties it addresses become even more apparent when one keeps in mind that the *Enterprise* initially featured a female chief of security in Lieutenant Tasha Yar (Denise Crosby) who presents as markedly less traditionally feminine than either Dr. Crusher or Counsellor Troi. Yar dies during *TNG*'s first season, after Crosby, who thought she was not used enough, asked to be written out of the show (Greenberger, 2015, 158). In this development, which Katja Kanzler has called 'symptomatic' (2004, 168), the show's writers missed creating a female character that pushed against gendered character tropes and presented an alternative femininity, and maybe even a female masculinity.

Still further development is visible when one looks at subsequent *Star Trek* shows. M. Keith Booker comments on the 'feminist orientation' of *VOY* (1995–2001) and interprets this as an indication of the successive growth of American society with regard to stances about the roles that should be obtainable for women (2018, 30). Featuring the franchise's

---

[2] A thorough overview over the changing treatment of gender in literary science fiction can be found in Helen Merrick's essay 'Gender in Science Fiction' (2003) while Mark Bould traces similar developments for television shows and films in his essay 'Film and Television' (2003).

first, fully developed and series-carrying female captain, as well as a half-human and half-Klingon female engineer, and, from season four onwards, a former Borg drone and scientist, marked VOY as different from preceding *Star Trek* series. Especially the inclusion of a woman of color in a major role in the character of B'Elanna Torres (Roxann Dawson) made VOY stand out when compared with the other series, which only included black women or women of color in recurring roles.

Despite these partially positive developments, characters like Captain Janeway also proved that there was still a way to go when it came to the representation of women in science fiction television in general and *Star Trek* in particular. Not only was there backlash against Janeway from some sections of the fanbase – a phenomenon that was to be repeated after the announcement of Michael Burnham as the lead character in *Discovery* – the show also did not always deliver on what it seemed to promise by putting a woman front and center. While Aviva Dove-Viebahn reads VOY as a 'feminist heterotopia' (2007, 599) and Janeway as '*both* "motherly" and "fatherly"' (2007, 605; original emphasis), Michèle A. Bowring notes that Janeway is gendered more and more in her depiction (2004, 392) as the series continues and argues that '*Endgame* refutes the notion that 20th century people can imagine a woman who is a leader and who does not fall into the prison created by 20th century dualisms regarding women and leadership' (2004, 384).[3] One reason for this might be the fact that Starfleet, despite its declared goal of discovery and diplomacy, is still a military organization and that this military tradition brings with it many assumptions and anticipations regarding gender roles (Korzeniowska, 1996, 24), traditions that the writers of all *Star Trek* series cannot quite disentangle themselves from.

Janeway's leadership style is not the only thing that seems influenced by the writers' perceptions of gender. Diana M.A. Relke comments on the differences between Janeway and the captains preceding her in the franchise by noting that 'the [sexual] freedoms both Picard and Kirk

---

[3] The 'feminization' that Bowring notes with regards to Janeway (2004, 392) is, from season four onwards, upstaged by the former Borg drone Seven of Nine (Jeri Ryan). It is notable how closely becoming human is connected to becoming hyper-feminine where this character is concerned. As Anne Cranny-Francis has pointed out, 'Seven of Nine is left to reconfigure herself as human, a process signified not by the reestablished authority of her mind (as with Picard [in the *TNG* two-parter 'Best of Both Worlds']), but by her production of a female body' (2000, 158). Seven of Nine, then, is another example of the ways in which the *Star Trek* franchise has struggled with longstanding gendered assumptions and dichotomies in its representation of female characters.

have enjoyed with impunity are denied to her' (2006, 25). To 'assert her "femininity" without impeaching her authority,' the show increasingly focuses on maternal relationships and Janeway's 'rechanneling [of] her libidinal energy into her maternalism' (2006, 26). Sherrie A. Innes makes a similar argument about the tempering of Janeway's initial representation as a tough woman (1999, 119). And, Relke argues, 'the show substitutes maternalism for the kind of intense friendship that sustains Janeway's counterpart Captain Kirk' (Relke, 2006, 28). *DSC* avoids some of these problems, not only because Michael Burnham, the show's lead, is not the titular ship's captain, but also because Burnham is surrounded by and forms strong friendships with other female characters and even enters into a romantic relationship with Lieutenant Ash Tyler (Shazad Latif) as the first season progresses.[4] In addition, season two expands on some of the show's minor characters, including a variety of different femininities and introducing deep friendships between, for example, Sylvia Tilly, Airiam (Sara Mitich; Hannah Cheesman), Joann Owosekun (Oyin Oladejo), and Keyla Detmer (Emily Coutts). Airiam a cybernetically augmented human, is ultimately killed off in 'Project Daedalus' (2x09), but not before Tilly helps her to temporarily break out of the control of the A.I. that has taken over Airiam's body by sending her memories of their friendship and asserting that Airiam is 'a great friend' (2x09). This representation of female friendships, however, is undercut somewhat by the fact that the relationships between these characters are mostly introduced in 2x09 rather than developed and referenced over a longer period.

Still, the friendships between these women are one of the most noteworthy ways in which *DSC* goes against established depictions of gender and gendered relations in *Star Trek* and science fiction more broadly. As Jon Wagner and Jan Lundeen point out in a passage that Relke also quotes (2006, 29), *Star Trek* has

---

[4] It needs to be noted however, that Burnham has been sentenced as a mutineer and stripped of rank by the time she enters into this relationship. By implication, then, this relationship only seems to be possible as long as Burnham is outside of Starfleet's power structure. What is more, the relationship with Tyler, who, while having a human consciousness and identity, is also the surgically altered Klingon Voq, is exceedingly tricky and viewers see Burnham and Tyler separate at the end of season one and again at the end of season two. Thus, it remains to be seen if future seasons will allow Commander Burnham to go beyond some of the same limitations that were placed on Janeway where romantic and sexual relationships are concerned.

failed to exploit the possibility of enhancing the mythos of friendship/Philia by developing deep friendships among women[.] After thirty years, there are still no female friendships that carry anything like the emotional depth or the elements of self-transcendence that one sees in male friendships. It is hard to offer any explanation other than the most painful one: that *Trek* has remained so wedded to patriarchal notions of the 'otherness' of women and their sexual (as opposed to social) nature that it has proven unable to take its own central mythos as far as it might. (1998, 115)

While Wagner and Lundeen's criticism holds true for previous *Star Trek* shows and the films that debuted between 2009 and 2013, *DSC* explicitly focuses on relationships between female characters and, in season one, especially on Michael Burnham's 'rediscovery' of her humanity via these relationships after her attempts to assimilate into Vulcan society during her childhood and teenage years. While this focus on her emotions does have deeply gendered undertones that harken back to those described about Deanna Troi, Burnham's role within Starfleet, first as first officer, and later as a science officer, does not represent the same 'professionalization of femininity' that Joyrich noted for the former (1996, 64).[5] In addition, while the women in earlier *Star Trek* shows are often characterized through their relationships with male characters, working 'to buttress and support the men, not to tell them what to do or to assume command roles' (Dupree, 2013, 283), Burnham has important personal and professional relationships with men and women. The show's first episode, for example, opens with Burnham and her captain, Philippa Georgiou, on an away mission; their relationship is marked by a deep, trusting friendship that is expressed through the banter the two women engage in – banter that is notably reminiscent of the relationship between *TOS*'s Kirk and Bones, for example. While Georgiou dies one episode later, in a recording of her last will, she lets Burnham know that she 'is as proud of [her] as if [she] were [her] own daughter' (1x03, 'Context is for Kings'). As noted above, Burnham develops deep friendships with several members of the crew, most importantly with Cadet (later Ensign) Sylvia Tilly and Lieutenant (later Lieutenant Commander) Paul Stamets once she is brought aboard the *U.S.S. Discovery* by Captain Lorca. What is more, season two explores not only Burnham's relationship with her

---

[5] For a critical exploration of the portrayal of Burnham as a black, female scientist, see Amy Chambers' essay '*Star Trek* Discovers Women: Gender, Race, Science, and Michael Burnham' in this volume.

foster-brother Spock, but also adds her mother, Dr. Gabrielle Burnham (Sonja Sohn) as a pivotal character.

The relationship between the reserved Burnham and the much more outgoing Tilly especially is one founded on friendship, mutual aid, and support. In season one, it becomes increasingly important during the *Discovery*'s time in the Mirror Universe. In episodes ten through 13 they rely on and help each other survive the hostile environment they find themselves in. When Tilly is apprehensive about pretending to be her alter ego 'Captain Killy' in an effort to allow the ship to blend in and take the place of the *I.S.S. Discovery*, Burnham reassures her by pointing out that 'Terran strength is born out of pure necessity because they live in constant fear, always looking for the next knife aimed at their back' and telling Tilly to draw strength from 'an entire crew that believes in [her]. That's what a real captain does' (1x10, 'Despite Yourself'). This reassurance does not only provide an instance of Burnham referencing Tilly's goal to become a captain and implying that she has the qualities needed for that position, it is also an important observation about the differences between the Prime and the Mirror Universe, one that affirms the collaborative nature of life in the United Federation of Planets and in Starfleet and contrasts it against the fascist dog-eat-dog mentality of the Mirror Universe.

Tilly's support of Burnham becomes most important after the ship has found its way back into the Prime Universe, when Burnham deals with the emotional consequences of Tyler's role as an unwitting double agent and his, or rather the Klingon Voq's, attempt on her life. While Burnham at first refuses any contact with Tyler after Voq's consciousness inside him has been killed, Tilly encourages her to talk to him: 'Say what you have to say, even if it's goodbye' (1x14, 'The War Without, the War Within'). Here, we see them switching their previous roles. This reciprocal support and Burnham's position as the protagonist avoid the pitfall of making Burnham, a black woman, be the character who props up a white character, a trope that the website *TV Tropes* refers to as the 'magical negro.'

In the first few episodes of season two, and especially in 'Saints of Imperfection' (2x05), Burnham and Tilly's friendship and mutual support is emphasized again. After Tilly's abduction into the mycelial network at the end of 'An Obol for Charon' (2x04), 2x05 opens with shots of a desperate Burnham and a voice-over narration that gestures towards the depth of their friendship by implicitly comparing the loss of Tilly to Stamets' loss of his partner and by noting that 'there is no word for the unique agony of uncertainty. I do not yet know the fate of my friend' (2x05). This and Burnham's 'I thought I'd lost you' upon finding Tilly in the network highlight their close friendship, as does Tilly's decision to remain onboard the ship with Burnham and some of the other crew members in 'Such Sweet Sorrow, Part One' (2x13) when it becomes clear that Burnham and the *Discovery* need to travel to the future. Beyond Tilly, Burnham is briefly shown to share friendships with other female characters, for example Airiam (2x09) and, if not a friendship then at least a relationship based in great mutual respect with the ship's new security chief Nhan (Rachael Ancheril; 2x10, 'The Red Angel'). This insistent focus on women's mutual support, while somewhat sidelined in the latter half of season two when the narrative focuses more on Burnham's relationship with her foster-brother Spock, is a marked shift for *Star Trek* and science fiction shows in general, especially because none of them are there to solely bolster and hold up male characters, as Dupree has pointed out for the female characters on *TNG* (2013, 283).

But Burnham and the other female characters on *DSC* are not only a contrast when compared to female characters on older *Star Trek* shows. The show also handles gender remarkably differently from more recent movies, like *Star Trek* (2009), written by Roberto Orci and Alex Kurtzman.[6] Especially the representation of Lieutenant Uhura in these movies, which center on familiar characters from *TOS*, but put them into an alternate timeline commonly referred to as 'Kelvin Universe,' has reaped criticism. Deborah Tudor and Eileen R. Meehan (2013, 133), for example, have noted that her mere presence 'should not be mistaken for feminist progressivism; in fact, Uhura signifies the way in which contemporary neoliberalism attempts to legitimate unequal gender representations as natural.' Diana A. Mafe even argues that the 2009 film 'signals a kind of retrograde for the character' (2018, 143). *DSC* on the other hand, explicitly works against unequal gender representations and pushes against gendered structures established by former entries into the *Star Trek* franchise. This is clearly visible in the centrality of female characters and the focus on their relationships with each other that I have explored above. In addition, the resolution of the Federation–Klingon War that dominates season one, and the ultimately successful outcome of the final battle of season two, crucially depends on the show's female characters.

The war in season one ends when Burnham and the Klingon L'Rell, T'Kuvma's (Chris Obi) and later Voq's right hand, reach a compromise

---

[6] The marked contrast between the 2009 movie and *DSC* is even more interesting because Alex Kurtzman has co-written three scripts for the latter and has been the sole showrunner for season two.

during 'Will You Take My Hand?' (1x15). After learning of Mirror Georgiou and Starfleet Command's plan to end the war by destroying all of Qo'noS, Burnham stands up to Cornwell, eventually prevailing due to her insistence that the Federation's principles 'are all we have.' Instead, they hand the detonator for the bomb intended to destroy the planet to L'Rell as 'an alternative' to continued war. As Burnham explains, 'Klingons respond to strength. Use the fate of Qo'noS to bend them to your will. Preserve your civilization rather than watch it be destroyed' (1x15). This scene once again exemplifies the centrality of female characters in *DSC*. What is more, by featuring Burnham and L'Rell as well as Cornwell and Mirror Georgiou as pivotal characters in the resolution of this conflict, the show represents viewers with a breadth of important, varied female characters, that earlier iterations of the franchise never achieved.

'Standing behind you I am free to move': Gender and Power in the Klingon Empire (L'Rell, 1x04, 'The Butcher's Knife Cares Not for the Lamb's Cry')

L'Rell, who is, in many ways, a foil for Burnham, warrants attention beyond this scene. In previous *Star Trek* series, Klingon culture has been presented as deeply patriarchal with 'male identity ... communicated through listing one's male progenitor' (Vande Berg, 1996, 62). Female Klingons have only been featured as one-off or recurring characters in previous shows, with the exception of the half-human, half-Klingon B'Elanna Torres in *VOY*, who, similar to *TNG*'s K'Ehleyr (Suzie Plakson), was characterized by deep anxieties about her mixed heritage and a continuing struggle with her Klingon character traits. L'Rell, on the other hand quickly becomes the central Klingon character on *DSC* and the driving force behind the first season's Klingon subplot. At the same time, she occupies a liminal position that is similar to Burnham's in season one.[7] Like Burnham, who is human but grew up on Vulcan, L'Rell stands between two heritages:

> My father was T'Kuvma's blood kin, but my mother was House Mo'Kai, the watcher clan, the deceivers, the weavers of lies. When

---

[7] Other Klingon or half-Klingon characters whose liminality is comparable to L'Rell's are Voq as well as Tyler, who struggles with his hybridity especially in 'Point of Light' (2x03), and Worf (Michael Dorn) in *TNG*. For a closer exploration of the latter's liminal status, see Leah R. Vande Berg (1996).

I was a child, she gave me a bat'leth and told me to cleave my own heart. To choose one house over the other. Instead I built a bridge to serve both. (1x04)

This not only foreshadows the later bridge-building Burnham and L'Rell engage in, it is also a glimpse into the structure of Klingon society and already represents somewhat of a rejection of its patriarchal structures because L'Rell steps outside of, or rather across, the usual male line of descent.

It also becomes clear early on that L'Rell and not Voq, T'Kuvma's chosen successor, is the better strategist of the two, convincing Voq to forego T'Kuvma's politics of Klingon purity to get a dilithium processor from the wrecked *U.S.S. Shenzhou* so the Sarcophagus ship can be made maneuverable again (1x04). In this conversation, she also tells him, 'I do not want the mantle of leadership. Standing behind you, I am free to move' (1x04). Her goal of furthering Klingon reunification, however, is put in jeopardy by dissenting voices like General Kol's (Kenneth Mitchell). The leader of House Kor quickly moves to undermine and exile Voq, making L'Rell's position even more unstable. Kol is the embodiment of the hypermasculine Klingon leader who, in contrast to L'Rell, is interested in leadership for the sake of enlarging his own power, not because of any larger political goal. In her negotiation of her position under Kol's leadership and the larger plot to disguise Voq and bring him aboard the *Discovery*, L'Rell's membership in House Mo'Kai becomes especially interesting.

It is the matriarchs of House Mo'Kai who perform the procedure that turns Voq into a copy of the human Starfleet officer Lieutenant Ash Tyler. The explicit reference to these matriarchs, combined with L'Rell's prominent role in the show is interesting because it suggests that women thrive and have a larger amount of influence in House Mo'Kai, which specializes in spycraft. I read this as a commentary on power structures in patriarchal societies like the Klingon Empire, which, dominated by ideals of hypermasculinity and strict honor codes, require women and other marginalized people to find ways to move within and around these structures. L'Rell, by admitting to navigating these power structures most effectively when she is standing in T'Kuvma's and Voq's shadows (1x04), is a direct example of this. Once she more openly assumes a position of power, the prejudices she faces as a female Klingon emerge with a vengeance. While I have noted similarities between L'Rell and Burnham where their liminality is concerned, they also act as foils for each other here. The Klingon Empire and the Federation are presented as embracing very different structures where gender and power are concerned, structures that become even clearer after L'Rell assumes the position of high chancellor at the end of season one (1x15).

These different structures are especially visible during the Klingon subplot in 'Point of Light' (2x03). The exchanges between Kol-Sha (Kenneth Mitchell), L'Rell, and Tyler that introduce this plot highlight L'Rell's precarious position as a female leader. The deceased Kol's father emerges as her main antagonist in this episode. This fact is, of course, highly symbolic. Here patriarchy, embodied by Kol-Sha, is quite literally trying to reassert itself. Kol-Sha's first challenge to L'Rell centers on Tyler's presence at a High Council meeting. He uses explicitly gendered and sexualized language: 'If you want whatever this is as your plaything, he belongs in your bed, not here' (2x03). By describing Tyler, a Human–Klingon hybrid, as 'whatever this is,' Kol-Sha demonstrates a rejection of him that is based on a belief in Klingon supremacy. At the same time, one can read this scene as a prime example for how misogyny operates in a patriarchal society. Feminist philosopher Kate Manne argues that 'misogyny should be understood as the "law enforcement" branch of a patriarchal order which has the overall function of *policing* and *enforcing* its governing ideology' (2018, 63; original emphasis). She goes on to explain that

> [m]isogyny attempts to force women back into [their place] or to punish them for desertion. Alternatively, it may punish women for taking men's place or trying to. It does so via hostile treatment enacted by individual agents as well as collective or group activity, and purely structural mechanisms. (84)

Kol-Sha's suggestion that Tyler is L'Rell's 'plaything' and that his place is in her bed (2x03), is exactly such an attempt at putting L'Rell back into a feminized place because she dares to fill a role that was previously only held by male Klingons. It is no surprise, then, that Kol-Sha's condescension towards Tyler and L'Rell are preparations for a longer speech in which he attacks the political agenda she is in the process of enacting.

Once viewers and later Kol-Sha learn about L'Rell and Voq's son, the latter turns out to be a point of weakness that further threatens her chancellorship. Kol-Sha uses the child as a bargaining chip to try and force L'Rell to turn her power over to him and is only stopped by the appearance of Mirror Georgiou, newly recruited into Starfleet's Section 31. The contrasts between Klingon and Federation society shown in 2x03, I argue, are new for the *Star Trek* franchise in so far as similar plots in previous shows usually invited readers to identify with the Federation and what was portrayed as its superior values,[8] affirming a feeling that the Federation – and by extension the viewers – had moved beyond gender inequality. Given the timing of *DSC*'s release, however, it is hard not to read L'Rell's situation as a comment on the misogynist backlash currently underway in U.S. society and thus see the events in 2x03 as an invitation to readers to identify with the Klingons in a departure of the usual positioning. In this reading, the Federation becomes a possible, idealized future that has not yet been reached in the twenty-first century.[9] After all, Michael Burnham's rise to power within Starfleet is presented as unimpeded by the kind of misogyny L'Rell faces.[10]

At the same time, this change of the usual identifications and Georgiou saving L'Rell can be read as connected to the Federation's – and ultimately *Star Trek*'s – imperialism. As Vande Berg has argued with regard to Worf's position 'cultural imperialism … is the dominant discursive position affirmed by *TNG*' (1996, 65). As she points out, Klingon culture '[is] presented as primitive in contrast to the Federation's civility' (1996, 62). This holds true in 2x03, too. Additionally, Georgiou's position as rescuer on behalf of the Federation evokes persistent, post-9/11 discourses that used the situation of women in the global South to argue for interventions by the United States and its Western allies.[11] Georgiou's explanation that '[w]e have to ensure that she stays in the chancellor's seat' (2x03) and thus the admission that the Federation is intervening in other species' internal affairs, but not out of genuine concerns for the advancement of gender equality, but rather to protect its own interests, only makes this clearer.[12]

---

[8] Vande Berg, for example, examines the way in which Worf's initial approach to paternity is portrayed 'as a primitive one' that needs to be 'replace[d] with those the dominant Federation culture accepts' (64).

[9] Similarly, Mary Chieffo, who plays L'Rell has noted that 'embodying this storyline is about reflecting a mirror to our society, like this is the extreme of where we could go, this is what we have to understand is kind of the extent of the female power' (Ulster, 2019) in interviews before the season premiere.

[10] 2x01 seems to highlight this tongue-in-cheek when Connolly (Sean Connolly Affleck), a science officer who repeatedly and without apparent reason questions Burnham's expertise, gets killed after ignoring her warnings during an action scene involving flying pods.

[11] For a multifaceted engagement with feminism and imperialism and the way in which feminist discourses and movements were (ab-)used in the aftermath of 9/11, see *Feminism and War: Confronting U.S. Imperialism* (2008) edited by Robin L. Riley, Chandra Talpade Mohanty, and Minnie Bruce Pratt.

[12] The Federation's imperial tendencies and especially the imperial feminism

In addition to these larger readings, it is also possible to compare L'Rell and Mirror Georgiou based on their position as rulers in patriarchal societies. Georgiou, looking at L'Rell and her son, comments on the inconvenience of children and how hers were looked after by someone else to ensure her effectiveness (2x03). She also cautions L'Rell against Tyler's continued presence: 'Every minute you remain here your councilors must reorganize their tiny male brains why it isn't them standing on the dais. They will assume that all your decisions are Tyler's' (2x03). Here, once again, *DSC* nods to the function of misogyny in patriarchal societies. As Manne points out, 'misogyny ... may manifest itself when women's capabilities become more salient and hence demoralizing and threatening' (2018, 101). We also see Georgiou asking whether L'Rell could kill Tyler and her son to preserve her power – and L'Rell's refusal. These scenes, then, imply both parallels between the patriarchal power structures in the Terran and the Klingon Empire, and different ways to negotiate them.

'She is my mother': Reframing Motherhood in *DSC* (Michael Burnham, 2x10)

In addition, the plot of 2x03 can also be read as an allegory on motherhood in contemporary culture and the question whether women can 'have it all,' i.e. a career, children, and a successful family life. Where L'Rell is concerned, *DSC* seems to answer this question with a resounding 'No.' However, it does so by highlighting that it is the patriarchal power structures of Klingon society that turn the child's and Tyler's presence into elements that can be used against her. This is not only driven home by L'Rell faking Tyler and the child's death and her declaration that she will have no more biological children, but also by the new title that L'Rell, in a shrewd political move, announces in the same breath: 'Do not refer to me as chancellor, for I deserve a fiercer title. From this point forth, you may call me Mother' (2x03). This title is also emphasized visually, through a darker, much less revealing outfit. This additional title hearkens back to the matriarchs of House Mo'Kai and reveals not only L'Rell's determination and cunning as a politician, but also, in conjunction with her new outfit, which female figures are allowed positions of power in patriarchal cultures. It also mirrors one

---

that is presented and examined in *Star Trek: Discovery* is examined in more depth in Judith Rauscher's essay '"Into A Mirror Darkly": Border Crossing and Imperial(ist) Feminism in *Star Trek: Discovery*' published in this volume.

of Emperor Georgiou's titles, 'Mother of the Fatherland' (1x12, 'Vaulting Ambition'), once again highlighting parallels in the power structures between these two empires and, through L'Rell's hiding Tyler and the child rather than killing them, the differences between these two rulers.

L'Rell and Georgiou are not the only mothers or mother figures who appear in *DSC*'s second season, however. Burnham's adoptive mother Amanda (Mia Kirshner), Ambassador Sarek's (James Frain) wife and Lieutenant Spock's mother, and Burnham's own mother, Dr. Gabrielle Burnham, also play important roles. While Amanda appears in 2x03 as another foil for L'Rell, especially in her determination to protect her son, Dr. Burnham, who is presumed dead, first features in the cliffhanger of episode 2x10, and then in 2x11 ('Perpetual Infinity'), which explores not only her connection to the larger plot of the season – the *Discovery*'s investigation of seven mysterious signals, a being called 'the Red Angel,' and the rogue A.I. Control – but also her relationship with Michael. Such a number of mothers, and especially the number of scenes in which their role as mothers is explored in connection to the overarching plot, is uncommon for science fiction television shows. While '[t]he topic of motherhood in general is a "media obsession"' (Timson quoted in Podnieks, 2012, 3), science fiction television 'appears committed to the absent mother' (Feasey, 2017, 233).

This absence of mothers or representations of motherhood has mostly been true for *Star Trek*, too, with Ericka Hoagland describing mothers as an '"absent presence" in the *Star Trek* universe' (2017, 127). While *TNG*'s Dr. Crusher raises her teenaged son aboard the *Enterprise-D*, her dual function as mother and ship's doctor is mostly left unexplored and 'her selfhood is contingent upon separating her from her identity as a mother.' At the same time, and paradoxically, Crusher's (and Troi's) official functions are based on their private roles (Kanzler, 2004, 168; Hoagland, 2017, 133). Other mothers, like *Deep Space Nine*'s Jennifer Sisko (Felecia M. Bell), are dead before the show even starts. Thus, Hoagland's point that, 'the narratives concerning femininity and, by extension, motherhood, in *Star Trek* are noteworthy for their conventionality, rather than their liberality' (2017, 126) holds. Dr. Gabrielle Burnham starts out as an absent mother with Burnham introduced as an orphan in season one. However, episode 2x11 reveals that Dr. Burnham escaped the Klingon attack that supposedly claimed her life by using an experimental time suit she was working on at the time and traveling 950 years to the future. The episode also stresses the similarities between Burnham and her mother, highlighting the fact that both women are dedicated to their work as scientists and the goals they set themselves. It is these goals that also make Dr. Burnham a different mother than the ones we usually encounter in *Star Trek*. Hoagland, drawing on Buchanan and the 'flattening effect' she describes (Buchanan, quoted in Hoagland, 2017, 130), points out that it 'manifests in two ways: one, by casting female characters in roles that are easily coded within the matrix of motherhood, and two, by generally diminishing the presence and significance of mothers through a reliance on stereotypes and outright expulsion' (2017, 130). Dr. Burnham's role, on the other hand, is at first not easily realigned with dominant ideas of motherhood. Not only is she connected to the 'Red Angel,' and thus central to season two's main plot, she has also, for the past 20 years, been attempting to stop Control, the rogue A.I. that emerges as a major foe in the second half of the season, from wiping out all sentient life. Specifically, she needs to stop Control from gaining access to the data that the *Discovery* collects from a dying alien sphere in 2x04, a mission that, ultimately, is transferred to her daughter and the *Discovery* crew after she gets pulled back into the future at the end of 2x11.[13]

This passing on of a vital mission from mother to daughter is uncommon in science fiction television shows, especially so for black women. It allows *DSC* to explore the relationship between Burnham and her mother in ways that is groundbreaking for the *Star Trek* franchise. Dr. Burnham at first keeps her distance from her daughter, requesting that only the captain beam down to the facility where she is being held, and later telling Burnham that their meeting 'is meaningless' (2x11). When Burnham insists that their reunion matters and that Dr. Burnham's video logs indicate that she was trying to reunite with her family, her mother replies: 'I don't know what you've been telling yourself all these years, but I let you go a long time ago. I had to' and '[t]here's only the bigger picture now. Nothing else' (2x11). Here, the narrative seems to be 'separating her from her identity as a mother' (Hoagland, 2017, 133). At first, then, Dr. Burnham remains, for all intents and purposes, an 'absent presence' (127), pushing her daughter away in favor of her self-appointed mission. As a scientist and in this exchange, she is different from Dr. Crusher or Troi, whose work '[is] written as part and mere extensions of their private existence' (Kanzler, 2004, 168). Her refusal to talk to Burnham, however, does not last. In a second, emotionally charged exchange, Dr. Burnham says:

---

[13] This episode also features an exchange between Dr. Burnham and Mirror Georgiou that would be interesting to look at with regards to depictions of motherhood in *Star Trek*, but that, for reasons of space, is not part of this essay.

I watched you. When you first beamed aboard the *Shenzhou* with Sarek, when you finally learned the Vulcan salute from Spock as a child, ... I was there when you read *Alice in Wonderland* out loud to yourself on your 11th birthday pretending to read it to your father and to me. I heard you, baby. I heard you. ... Seeing you reminded me of what I was fighting to save. (2x11)

This conversation occurs while Burnham and Stamets are attempting to send the sphere data into the future to protect it from Control while also keeping Dr. Burnham in the present. While, emotionality, as Lynne Joyrich has pointed out, is one of 'those traits considered most inherently "feminine"' (1996, 64), neither of the women are reduced to their emotions. Their relationship and their emotions neither sideline Burnham or her mother from the episode's larger arc, nor do they have to be disavowed. Instead, this scene allows them to own these feelings and reconnect, emphasizing their relationship, the impact it has on their identities, and their roles as scientists, a bold step forward from the position of other mothers in *Star Trek*. What is more, Dr. Burnham's assertion that she was present for the most important moments of Burnham's life, and the revelation that she intervened to save her daughter in some ways retroactively turns her from an absent into a present mother. Unfortunately, the episode somewhat undercuts these developments by the episode's end, when Dr. Burnham is pulled back to the future after the above exchange. As for Troi and Dr. Crusher, integrating her functions as a scientist and mother, and the passing on of her mission to her daughter, seem to 'validat[e] [her] exclusion from "tougher" jobs' (Kanzler, 2004, 169). It remains to be seen if and how season three will continue this exploration of motherhood in the *Star Trek* universe.

Still, as with the friendships between female characters, *DSC* also broadens the representation of mothers and of mother–daughter relationships shown in the *Star Trek* franchise. In addition, it represents a much wider range of different female characters and, by extension, different femininities, through its main and supporting cast and, as has been noted above, allows these characters to take on pivotal roles throughout its first two seasons and especially in the finale of season two. While Captain Pike and Commander Saru (Doug Jones) for the most part remain on the bridge of the *Enterprise* and the *Discovery* respectively during the final confrontation with Control in 'Such Sweet Sorrow, Part One and Two' (2x13, 2x14), it is the female characters who get in on the action, whether it is Burnham who uses a newly-built time suit to open a wormhole to the future and signal the *Discovery* where – or rather when – to jump to in order to get the sphere data out of Control's reach, Tilly who, with closed eyes, repairs a power conduit just in time to save the ship's shields, or Commander Reno, who exposes herself to the effects of the time crystal to ensure the time suit is operational when Burnham needs it. This focus on female characters, and female characters who present a spectrum of femininity, from the sarcastic, butch Reno to the bubbly, optimistic Tilly, is a large step away from the overwhelmingly male teams that dominate other *Star Trek* series and science fiction television shows in general.

New Directions for Women in Science Fiction Television

The first two seasons of *DSC* present a departure from earlier science fiction shows on American television where the portrayal of female characters is concerned. As this essay has shown, the show not only offers a wide variety of female characters from different racial and ethnic backgrounds and with different occupational specialties, it also allows these characters to take center stage, especially in pivotal moments for the show's plot, moments that in the science fiction genre usually go to male leads. In addition, *DSC* also focuses on the relationships, both familial and friendship-based, between these women, subverting, in some ways, established narrative choices like that of the absent mother. In doing so, it at some moments transcends the often essentialized and even conservative portrayals of female characters in earlier *Star Trek* shows. In addition, it uses L'Rell, a complex female Klingon, to interrogate patriarchal power structures and their impact on the personal and the societal level while also highlighting the cultural imperialism that is often part of the Federation's engagement with other species.

With the *Discovery*'s jump 930 years into the future at the end of season two, it will be interesting to see how these representational strategies, and especially the exploration of Burnham's relationship with her mother, continue in the third season. What is more, since the show no longer has to incorporate well-known – usually male – characters in an attempt to integrate it into the franchise's established timelines, it consequently has the chance to not only focus even more on its core crew, but also to go forward even more boldly in its portrayal of female characters.

Works Cited

Brian Attebery, *Decoding Gender in Science Fiction* (New York and London: Routledge, 2002).

M. Keith Booker, *Star Trek: A Cultural History* (Lanham, MD: Rowman & Littlefield, 2018).

Mark Bould, 'Film and Television', in Edward James and Farah Mendlesohn (eds.) *The Cambridge Companion to Science Fiction* (Cambridge: Cambridge University Press, 2003): 79–95.

Michèle A. Bowring, 'Reistance is *Not* Futile: Liberating Captain Janeway from the Masculine–Feminine Dualism of Leadership', *Gender, Work and Organization*, 11.4 (2004): 381–405.

Lindal Buchanan, *Rhetorics of Motherhood* (Carbondale: Southern Illinois University Press, 2013).

Anne Cranny-Francis, 'The Erotics of the (cy)Borg: Authority and Gender in the Sociocultural Imaginary', in Marleen S. Barr (ed.) *Future Female, The Next Generations: New Voices and Velocities in Feminist Science Fiction Criticism* (Lanham, MD: Rowman & Littlefield, 2000): 145–63.

Aviva Dove-Viebahn, 'Embodying Hybridity, (En)Gendering Community: Captain Janeway and the Enactment of a Feminist Heterotopia on *Star Trek Voyager*', *Women's Studies*, 36 (2007): 597–618.

M.G. Dupree, 'Alien Babes and Alternate Universes: The Women of *Star Trek*', in Nancy R. Reagan (ed.) *Star Trek and History* (Hoboken, NJ: Wiley, 2013): 280–94.

Rebeccah Feasey, 'Television and the Absent Mother: Why Girls and Young Women Struggle to Find the Maternal Role', in Berit Åström (ed.) *The Absent Mother in the Cultural Imagination* (Berlin: Springer Nature, 2017): 225–40.

Robert Greenberger, *Star Trek: The Complete Unauthorized History* (Minneapolis, MN: Voyageur Press, 2015).

Ericka Hoagland, 'Mothering the Universe on *Star Trek*', in Nadine Farghaly and Simon Bacon (eds.) *To Boldly Go: Essays on Gender Identity in the Star Trek Universe* (Jefferson, NC: McFarland, 2017): 126–42.

Veronica Hollinger, 'Feminist Theory and Science Fiction', in James and Farah Mendlesohn (eds.) *The Cambridge Companion to Science Fiction* (Cambridge: Cambridge University Press, 2003): 125–36.

Sherrie A. Innes, *Tough Girls: Women Warriors and Wonder Women in Popular Culture* (Philadelphia: University of Pennsylvania Press, 1999).

Lynne Joyrich, 'Feminist Enterprise? "Star Trek: The Next Generation" and the Occupation of Femininity', *Cinema Journal*, 35.2 (1996): 61–84.

Katja Kanzler, *'Infinite Diversity in Infinite Combinations': The Multicultural Evolution of Star Trek* (Heidelberg: Universitätsverlag Winter, 2004).

E. Ann Kaplan, *Motherhood and Representation: The Mother in Popular Culture and Melodrama* (New York: Routledge, 2013).

Victoria B. Korzeniowska, 'Engaging with Gender: *Star Trek*'s "Next Generation"', *Journal of Gender Studies*, 6.1 (1996): 19–25.

Diana A. Mafe, *Where No Black Woman Has Gone Before: Subversive Portrayals in Speculative Film and TV* (Austin: University of Texas Press, 2018).

'Magical Negro', *TV Tropes*, https://tvtropes.org/pmwiki/pmwiki.php/Main/MagicalNegro.

Kate Manne, *Down Girl: The Logic of Misogyny* (Oxford: Oxford University Press, 2018).

Helen Merrick, 'Gender in Science Fiction', in James and Farah Mendlesohn (eds.) *The Cambridge Companion to Science Fiction* (Cambridge: Cambridge University Press, 2003): 241–52.

Elizabeth Podnieks, 'Introduction: Popular Cultures Maternal Embrace', in Elizabeth Podnieks (ed.) *Mediating Moms: Mothers in Popular Culture* (Montreal: McGill-Queens University Press, 2012): 3–32.

Diana M.A. Relke, *Drones, Clones, and Alphababes: Retrofitting Star Trek's Liberal Humanism, Post 9/11* (Calgary: University of Calgary Press, 2006).

Robin L. Riley, Chandra Talpade Mohanty, and Minnie Bruce Pratt (eds.), *Feminism and War: Confronting U.S. Imperialism* (London and New York: Zed Books, 2008).

Deborah Tudor and Eileen R. Meehan, 'Demoting Women on the Screen and in the Board Room', *Cinema Journal*, 53.1 (2013): 130–36.

Laurie Ulster, 'Interview: Mary Chieffo On L'Rell's Sensuality, Power, And "Klingon Couture" In "Star Trek: Discovery"', *TrekMovie*, 22 January (2019), https://trekmovie.com/2019/01/22/interview-mary-chieffo-on-lrells-sensuality-power-and-klingon-couture-in-star-trek-discovery/.

Jon Wagner and Jan Lundeen, *Deep Space and Sacred Time: Star Trek and the American Mythos* (Westport, CT: Praeger, 1998).

Episodes and Films Cited

'Battle at the Binary Stars.' *Star Trek: Discovery*, written by Gretchen J. Berg and Aaron Harberts, directed by Adam Kane, CBS Television Studios, 24 September, 2017.

'Context is for Kings.' *Star Trek: Discovery*, written by Gretchen J. Berg, Aaron Harberts, and Craig Sweeny, directed by Akiva Goldsman, CBS Television Studios, 1 October, 2017.

'The Butcher's Knife Cares Not for the Lamb's Cry.' *Star Trek: Discovery*, written by Jesse Alexander and Aron Eli Coleite, directed by Olatunde Osunsanmi, CBS Television Studios, 8 October, 2017.

'Lethe.' *Star Trek: Discovery*, written by Joe Menosky and Alex Kurtzman, directed by Douglas Aarniokoski, CBS Television Studios, 22 October, 2017.

'Si Vis Pacem, Para Bellum.' *Star Trek: Discovery*, written by Kirsten Beyer, directed by John Scott, CBS Television Studios, 5 November, 2017.

'Despite Yourself.' *Star Trek: Discovery*, written by Sean Cochran, directed by Jonathan Frakes, CBS Television Studios, 7 January, 2018.

'The Wolf Inside.' *Star Trek: Discovery*, written by Lisa Randolph, directed by T.J. Scott, CBS Television Studios, 14 January, 2018.
'Vaulting Ambition.' *Star Trek: Discovery*, written by Jordon Nardino, directed by Hanelle M. Culpepper, CBS Television Studios, 21 January, 2018.
'The War Without, the War Within.' *Star Trek: Discovery*, written by Lisa Randolph, directed by David Solomon, CBS Television Studios, 4 February, 2018.
'Will You Take My Hand?' *Star Trek: Discovery*, written by Gretchen J. Berg and Aaron Harberts, directed by Akiva Goldsman, CBS Television Studios, 11 February, 2018.
'Brother.' *Star Trek: Discovery*, written by Gretchen J. Berg, Aaron Harberts, and Ted Sullivan, directed by Alex Kurtzman, CBS Television Studios, 17 January, 2019.
'Point of Light.' *Star Trek: Discovery*, written by Andrew Colville, directed by Olatunde Osunsanmi, CBS Television Studios, 31 January, 2019.
'An Obol for Charon.' *Star Trek: Discovery*, written by Alan McElroy and Andrew Colville, directed by Lee Rose, CBS Television Studios, 7 February, 2019.
'Saints of Imperfection.' *Star Trek: Discovery*, written by Kirsten Beyer, directed by David Barrett, CBS Television Studios, 14 February, 2019.
'Project Daedalus.' *Star Trek: Discovery*, written by Michelle Paradise, directed by Jonathan Frakes, CBS Television Studios, 14 March, 2019.
'The Red Angel.' *Star Trek: Discovery*, written by Chris Silvestri and Anthony Maranville, directed by Hanelle M. Culpepper, CBS Television Studios, 21 March, 2019.
'Perpetual Infinity.' *Star Trek: Discovery*, written by Alan McElroy and Brandon Schultz, directed by Maja Vrvilo, CBS Television Studios, 28 March, 2019.
'Such Sweet Sorrow, Part One and Two.' *Star Trek: Discovery*, written by Michelle Paradise, Jenny Lumet, and Alex Kurtzman, directed by Olatunde Osunsanmi, CBS Television Studios, 11/18 April, 2019.

Star Trek. 2009. Directed by J.J. Abrams. Written by Roberto Orci and Alex Kurtzmann. Spyglass Entertainment and Bad Robot Productions.

'We Choose Our Own Pain. Mine Helps Me Remember'
Gabriel Lorca, Ash Tyler, and the Question of Masculinity

Sabrina Mittermeier and Jennifer Volkmer

This chapter wants to discuss how *Star Trek: Discovery* (*DSC*) depicts masculinity by taking a closer look at the characters of Captain Gabriel Lorca (Jason Isaacs) and Lieutenant Ash Tyler (Shazad Latif) as the prime examples the show offers of both hegemonic and potentially alternative (heterosexual) masculinities in its first season, and will also address the character of Captain Christopher Pike (Anson Mount) that was integrated in its second season, but has roots in *The Original Series*.[1] We argue that with its original characters, *DSC* directly engages with and subverts existing tropes of post-network television generally, as well as the science fiction and action genres, and the *Star Trek* franchise in particular. To do so, we will discuss several concepts of masculinity, most importantly hegemonic masculinity and toxic masculinity. While there are as many masculinities as there are men, hegemonic masculinity encompasses the ideas of a certain society about what traits a man should possess. In *Discovery*, so we will argue, this is embodied by Lorca – something that the show only reveals gradually, playing with tropes that have become ingrained in post-network television. Additionally, toxic masculinity is the current term to describe certain traits that are often part of hegemonic masculinity, but as an ideal to aspire to are ultimately detrimental to men and the societies they live in, such as physical

---

[1] While Lorca, Tyler and Pike are of course not the only central male characters, the fact that Paul Stamets (Anthony Rapp) is a homosexual man (who is discussed in another chapter in this book) and also not trained in Starfleet provides an alternative here, but since we specifically want to engage with military and hegemonic straight masculinities, we choose not to discuss him here in more detail. Saru (Doug Jones) is also left out since his different species would warrant a much more in-depth look than this chapter could offer scope-wise, the same is true for the Klingon Kol (Kenneth Mitchell).

strength and violent tendencies.[2] We will engage with these models throughout, and also place them in a context of military masculinities, as Starfleet is a quasi-militaristic organization, and the first season of *DSC* is set in a war context, shaping both Lorca's and Tyler's journeys – and to a lesser extent, also Pike's in the second season.

'Rules are for admirals in back offices' (1x06, Lethe)

Television scholar Shawn Shimpach has argued that while the action heroes of the post-network era are now performing competitive masculinities, and are

> facing cultural and textual threats to their claims of universal signification, these heroes still very much represent normative white masculinity. Each of these heroes evinces plentiful masculine heroic traits such as rough physicality, short patience for bureaucratic impediments, detailed knowledge of obscure subjects, and easy aptitude with weapons and technology. (2010, 44)

Discovery's Captain Lorca is the embodiment of this type. His lack of patience for bureaucracy is highlighted time and time again over the course of season one, sometimes humorously, like his indifference to the gormagander's fate in 'Magic to Make the Sanest Man Go Mad' (1x07), most often, however, in more serious scenes, for example when he clashes with Starfleet Command over *Discovery*'s missions. His repeated disregard for Admiral Terral's (Conrad Coates) orders might, in hindsight, stem from the fact that the latter is Vulcan, but he is equally exasperated with Admiral Cornwell (Jayne Brook), to whom he declares that 'rules are for admirals in back offices' in 'Lethe' (1x06). His rough physicality is contrasted with that of other males on the ship, particularly scientist Paul Stamets (Anthony Rapp). In 'Choose Your Pain' (1x05), Lorca is held as a prisoner of war and beaten and bloodied, something that is echoed later when he breaks his own nose as part of a cover up for the backstory he concocts to infiltrate Emperor Georgiou's (Michelle Yeoh) palace ship in 'Despite Yourself' (1x10).

He also has all the skills Shimpach mentions: he keeps his own laboratory on the *Discovery* containing not only an assortment of weapons

---

[2] What constitutes toxic masculinity and its negative effects on men and people surrounding them is discussed, among others, by Terry Kupers (2005).

(such as a Klingon *bat'leth*), but also dead and preserved creatures, such as the newly-caught tardigrade that he also wishes to weaponize (1x04, 'The Butcher's Knife Cares Not for the Lamb's Cry'). Over the first half of the season, he also acquires enough knowledge about the spore drive and collects the data from the jumps to eventually successfully override the computer and complete his journey back to his home dimension. Before he is revealed as a Terran, his behavior is continuously chalked up to his identity as a military man (one that potentially suffers from PTSD) and his status as the captain of the *Discovery* that has become Starfleet's most powerful weapon in the war effort. While he clashes with Command more than once, most of his unusual actions (including the sanctioning of Stamets' self-inflicted eugenics experiments) are possible because he was seemingly given a carte blanche by them in order to win the war. As he informs Stamets in episode 1x04, the *Discovery* is no longer a science vessel, but a warship, and he eventually prides himself on turning his crew into 'fierce warriors' (1x09, 'Into the Forest'). The show also draws a direct connection between him and Captain Benjamin Sisko (Avery Brooks), the only other wartime captain, who in *Star Trek: Deep Space Nine*'s (1993–1999) aptly-titled 'Favor the Bold' (6x05) leads the *U.S.S. Defiant* into battle during the Dominion War, quoting an old saying: 'Fortune favors the bold.' Lorca says the exact same words to Cornwell in 'Lethe' when he sends her off to meet with the Klingons, eventually leaving her to die – thus making the scene much more sinister in hindsight, and putting a spin on this echo of Sisko.

The impression of Lorca as a salty military man that 'gets the job done' is further heightened by his Southern US accent, which actor Jason Isaacs chose deliberately in order to play into this trope, roughly basing it on military officers that he worked with on a previous project (FedCon, 2018). The accent emerges more strongly in scenes where he is in his element as a military leader, for example when he tells his first officer Saru (Doug Jones) to 'get us the hell outta dodge' in episode 1x04, or greets him and the ship with 'the cavalry showed up' one episode later. Audiences are used to this type of character, not just from action movies, but also particularly from the war genre, and the ideas of masculinity that come with it. As Eberwein (2007) has argued, 'war film originates in a gendered context that valorizes masculinity at a time of war' (6). Higate and Hopton (2005) have further elaborated on the inherent ties between military men and hegemonic ideas of masculinity:

> Traditionally, the casual sexism, competitiveness, and celebration of aggression and the domination of others that are characteristic of hegemonic masculinity have been explicitly and unambiguously

reflected in military culture. ... Similarly, militarism (i.e., the celebration of military culture in national politics and popular culture) has represented an affirmation of the legitimacy of hegemonic masculinity. (14–15)

As the viewer, then, it is easy to excuse Lorca's behavior as it is rooted in such a long tradition of mediated images of both military officers and men in general that get away with breaking the rules and their attitude that 'sometimes, the ends justify terrible means,' as Lorca points out to Michael Burnham (Sonequa Martin-Green) (1x11, 'The Wolf Inside'). Mittell has argued that white male anti-heroes, characters he also calls 'hideous men,' have become a staple of twenty-first century American television (2015, 142–43). Some of these 'stretch a rebellious member of a typically upright organization to its moral limits' (143), which is exactly what Lorca does to the members of his crew, and particularly to Burnham, who, however, remains firmly rooted in her Starfleet values – something he fails to understand and that ultimately contributes to his downfall.

The prevalence of these anti-heroes has also led to what Mittell terms 'fictionalized Stockholm Syndrome, in which time spent with hideous characters engenders our sympathy as we start to see things from their perspective' (2015, 144). In the case of Lorca, this is also aided by the audience's expectation to identify with the Starfleet captain as the protagonist, as will be discussed further below. The tendency of viewers to excuse what is essentially abusive behavior on an anti-hero's/Lorca's part is also connected to charisma that 'largely stems from an actor's performance and physicality but is also cued by how other characters treat the antiheroes' (144). Isaacs delivers a very charismatic performance (one that is also aided by his accent) and while characters like Stamets are continuously opposed to Lorca's actions, Burnham, the protagonist, is much more sympathetic towards him, as is Ash Tyler, who is, thus, additionally guiding the viewers' perception and judgment.[3]

---

[3] The way other main characters treat a character is essential to the audience's perception of that character; if a character is supposed to be read as the villain, other main characters that are framed as the heroes cannot treat them like a friend if we are to understand that they are adversaries. Additionally, here the opposition of Lorca and Stamets also plays into the American anti-intellectualism propagated especially in action movies where the (military) hero's brute force often is the only working answer as opposed to scientists' more intricately thought-out solutions that are usually less extreme.

'Gettin' outta here was always a two-men job. I just waited till I found the right man' (1x05, 'Choose Your Pain')

Lorca's relationship with Ash Tyler is equally rooted in his status as a military man. They meet as prisoners of war on the Klingon prison ship, and Lorca immediately addresses Tyler as 'soldier' (1x05). They bond over their shared fate in the prison, particularly their shared loss and pain. Tyler recalls having been captured at the Battle of the Binary Stars, the event that began the war, and Lorca relates his story of having to sacrifice his whole crew on the *U.S.S. Buran* to save them from torture and slow death at the hands of the Klingons. Tyler admits to having suffered not only torture, but also sexual abuse from their captor L'Rell (Mary Chieffo), while Lorca claims his light sensitivity is a direct consequence of the *Buran*'s explosion. Both of the stories are revealed to be false by the end of the season, but at this moment, it furthers the narrative of a war-ridden Starfleet and creates sympathy for both characters (and for each other), culminating in the scene after their successful escape when Lorca remarks: 'We choose our own pain. Mine helps me remember' (1x05). The next episode, 'Lethe,' (1x06) then sees them building on this homosocial bond when they participate in a shooting simulation, a scene visibly recreating action hero tropes. Consequently, Lorca appoints Tyler as his new chief of security. This type of bond then is clearly rooted in their military prowess, but also Tyler's willingness to subordinate himself to Lorca, a willingness that, as Isaacs has clarified, directly fuels Lorca's interest in Tyler (*Destination Star Trek*, 2018).

Over the course of the series, then, Lorca is revealed as a textbook abuser, including in his relationship with Tyler. The type of homosocial, militaristic bond between the two is something Lorca had previously shared only with Landry (Rekha Sharma), the former chief of security on the *Discovery*. Yet, the reveal that he is actually a Terran and, thus, a fascist, as well as Tyler's vulnerability in his relationship to Burnham and his hybrid identity throw their characterization as military men into sharp relief, and consequently criticize prevailing ideas of hegemonic masculinity.

While Lorca's status as a wartime leader differentiates him from previous Starfleet captains, he still fits the mold – he is a white, middle-aged, presumably heterosexual[4] man. While *Deep Space Nine*

---

[4] It is unclear whether Mirror Georgiou's comments in 2x10 that everyone in the Mirror Universe is pansexual is merely a taunt or meant to be serious, but we only ever see or hear about Lorca engaging in sexual relationships

(*DS9*) had an African-American man in the lead with the aforementioned Captain Sisko and also dealt with war, the series was structured differently because of its setting on a starbase rather than a ship, as well as the fact that Sisko is a commander for the first few seasons and only becomes a captain later. *Star Trek: Voyager* (*VOY*) (1995–2001) was the first series to put a woman in the captain's chair with Kathryn Janeway (Kate Mulgrew), but this choice received backlash from fans early on and, despite its long run, never gained quite the cult status that earlier shows had (Booker, 2018, 28). Thus, the epitome of the Starfleet captain remains the one in charge of the *Enterprise*: be it James T. Kirk (William Shatner) in *The Original Series* (*TOS*) (1966–1969), or his successor, Jean-Luc Picard (Patrick Stewart) in *The Next Generation* (*TNG*) (1987–1994), or even, besides it being a relative critical flop, Jonathan Archer (Scott Bakula) in *Enterprise* (*ENT*) (2001–2005). It is an archetype that also transcends audiences of the franchise, as characters like Kirk or Picard have become recognizable to non-Trekkies as well, not least of all because of internet meme culture.

It is thus a curious choice that in its second season, *DSC* opts to install Christopher Pike as the ship's new captain. The character stems from the original pilot for *TOS*, 'The Cage' and the two-parter 'The Menagerie,' (*TOS*, 1x11; 1x12) and is the captain of the *U.S.S. Enterprise* before Kirk takes the helm. Pike becomes the temporary captain of the *Discovery* within the second season's premiere and remains in this position until the ship's jump into an unknown future at the season finale. He also seemingly establishes himself as a contrast to Lorca in that he is transparent about his background and reveals that he sat out the war with the Klingons on the sidelines (2x01, 'Brother'). Yet, he also rebuffs Michael and establishes his authority more than once, and his actions remain somewhat unclear over particularly the first half of the season (possibly due to the mid-season showrunner change). Instead his arc is brought into full circle with the events in *TOS* when he has to face what is framed as his fate, being physically disfigured and injured due to a training accident and having to rely on a support chair (2x12 'Through the Valley of Shadows'). The narrative explanation of this as a form of destiny then, is interesting in light of Lorca's own claims that he is 'living proof that fate is real,' (1x13, 'What's Past is Prologue') and his understanding of his rightful place to rule the Terran Empire that is quickly shown to be nothing but white, male hubris. Pike's claims seem to dismantle this idea somewhat, even if they might have possibly been

with women, despite his chemistry with Mirror Stamets that has sparked at least a few slash fics.

intended to be a deliberate contrast, as he accepts a gruesome personal fate to save Starfleet (and franchise canon), whereas Lorca only cares for himself. His choice to live with this future is further explained to be made precisely because he is a Starfleet captain and, for him, that means believing in 'service, sacrifice, compassion, and love' (2x12), another contrast to Lorca, who never filled any of these criteria. This is also hinted at in 'Choose Your Pain' (1x05), when Saru pulls up a list of the most decorated Starfleet captains, which features Pike, and further cemented when Cornwell declares him 'the best of Starfleet' (2x09). While this perpetuates the idea that Lorca does not embody this ideal, it is arguably problematic in that the show now presents us with yet another straight, white male as something to aspire to, and thus seems to return to the franchise's initial framing of its humanist values as only to be embodied by straight white males like Picard and Kirk.[5] While the character of Lorca in many ways served as an implicit criticism of the trope of the Starfleet captain, Pike seems to reconfirm it – even if his behavior otherwise can be classified as non-toxic masculine.

The captain is also usually the character that narratives across *Star Trek* shows center on, often framing the narrative of individual episodes through their captain's logs. This choice was apparently made early on for *TOS* so as not to 'confuse' the audience, in spite of Gene Roddenberry's personal wishes to focus on the whole crew of the *Enterprise* (Pearson and Davies, 2014, 114). *DSC* on the other hand is centered around Michael Burnham, an African American woman – and yet, audiences are conditioned, we argue, to turn towards the captain for guidance. This was, for instance, noticeable in the media's reactions to the show that focused a great deal on Jason Isaacs over Martin-Green, and even in CBS's official promos for each episode that usually featured Lorca's dialogue as voice over rather than Burnham's. Such audience expectations and the network's deliberate positioning of Lorca as a narrative center in these promos then further contribute to the normalization of Lorca's actions, the above discussed 'fictionalized Stockholm syndrome' (Mittell, 2015, 144). In this context, it is also interesting to note that the character of Pike received a very positive echo in the press as well as with the fanbase – as the second season has concluded, there is a seemingly ever-growing group of fans that would

---

[5] This is especially confusing since Burnham was shown as the embodiment of Starfleet's core (humanist) values at the end of season one, directly opposing Command to protect these values and Starfleet's integrity, while Pike is only said to embody them, but never truly put to the test up until 2x12.

like to see a Pike-centric spin-off focusing on a pre-*TOS Enterprise*, which would de facto be a step back for a franchise that, as season three of *DSC* has been greenlit, still is helmed by a black woman. Despite such fan wishes, the showrunners however continue with Martin-Green at the helm, since Anson Mount is not slated to return, and the *Discovery* jumped into an uncertain future at the end of season two without the *TOS*-based characters on board. Nevertheless, the introduction of Pike has only further enforced the existing archetype of the Starfleet captain instead of continuing to dismantle it.

'No matter how deep in space you are, I always feel like you can see home' (1x03, 'Context is for Kings')

This archetype, as Stefan Rabitsch has argued, is modelled on the romanticized British naval officer/hero in the vein of Horatio Hornblower. Ultimately, Lorca emerges as a perverted version of that ideal. While he remains a 'man alone' (Rabitsch, 2018, 124), he does not, as previous captains, lead by 'judicious example' and also does not form 'an archetypal Nelsonian "band of brothers (and sisters)"' with his officers (Rabitsch, 2018, 123), regularly seeking their advice. Pike, however, is shown to do so over the course of the second season, further cementing the trope, if providing an alternative to Lorca, who, as his first officer Saru points out, 'keeps his own counsel' (1x04). Lorca's story mirrors (pun intended) that of *'naval pathfinder'* (Rabitsch, 2018, 118; original emphasis) Kathryn Janeway, who ends up stranded on the other side of the galaxy and has to go back home to the Alpha Quadrant. When we first meet him in 'Context is for Kings,' (1x03) Lorca is seen gazing out at the stars that reflect in his eyes and remarks: 'No matter how deep in space you are, I always feel like you can see home.' He refers to 'home' several times over the course of the following episodes, most notably in 'Into the Forest I Go' (1x09), before he secretly overrides the console to jump back to his dimension with the words 'Let's go home!' Yet while Janeway always looks out for her crew and is hellbent on bringing all of them home safely, Lorca only cares about himself, and even endangers his crew to get back to the Mirror Universe. In addition to this first scene, he is frequently seen looking outside into space, be it in his ready room, his quarters or on the bridge – an acting choice apparently made by Isaacs, who wanted to convey that Lorca did not want to be where he was and was constantly keeping his eye on the goal to return to rule the Terran Empire (FedCon, 2018).

E. Leigh McKagen, however, rightly argues that *VOY*'s dealings with the Delta Quadrant follow in the problematic footsteps of nineteenth century adventure narratives and their inherent imperialist ideology. Janeway and her crew are shown mapping and naming the 'uncharted' territory – '"uncharted," of course, only to the Federation' (2018, 7) – and so the show contributes to a normalization and legitimization of empire (2018, 4). Lorca is seen in engaging in similar tactics by using the data from the spore drive jumps to chart his own way back via the mycelial network. Aside from this being another case of him mentioning 'home' as an anchor point to return to, the Terrans are imperialist rulers that either wipe out or oppress all other species that they consider racially inferior, a fact that is foreshadowed by Lorca's laboratory, which is essentially a colonial trophy room. The fact that Lorca passes so easily in the Federation structure, then, can be seen, so we argue, as an inherent criticism of '*Star Trek*'s ... continuous retelling of Anglocentric sagas of colonialism and imperialism' (Rabitsch, 2018, 176).[6] Additionally, while all Terrans, including the female Emperor Georgiou, adhere to these ideals, there are well-researched ties between ideas of hegemonic masculinity and colonialism – and adventure narratives have similarly been categorized as an inherently masculine genre (Connell, 2005, 76), further tying Lorca's character back to previously discussed tropes.

The Terrans' ideals, which are clearly rooted in present-day white supremacy, are also reflected in Lorca's Southern accent. While still in the Prime Universe, the accent only shines through in moments when he feels most in his element as a military leader (as discussed above) or when he drops his guise because he is agitated. In 'Choose Your Pain' (1x04), for example, there is a notable moment when L'Rell tortures him. She comments on his eyes, which, as it later turns out, are a genetic marker from the Mirror Universe (1x12, 'Vaulting Ambition'), and he quips: 'Oh we all got somethin', honey.' He proceeds to taunt her about her sexual relationship to Tyler on racist grounds, pointing out that humans 'don't even have the right number of organs' for Klingons, suggesting his disdain for what he perceives as miscegenation. Isaacs, who improvised some of these lines (*Destination Star Trek*, 2018), thus draws a clear connection between these racist (and sexist) undertones and the use of the Southern accent. The racist implications of this accent are then even further stressed by the fact that, as soon as Lorca enters his home dimension, and particularly when his true identity is

---

[6] Judith Rauscher's chapter in this volume on '"Into A Mirror Darkly": Border Crossing and Imperial(ist) Feminism in *Star Trek: Discovery*' further addresses *Star Trek*'s inherent ties to imperialism.

finally revealed in 1x12, the accent becomes much more pronounced throughout.

Yet, Lorca's reveal as a fascist, also exhibiting what Mittell has termed 'Machiavellian intelligence' (2015, 145), does not only subvert televised tropes of masculinity (or rather takes them to their most extreme conclusion), it also emerges as a zeitgeisty plea to recognize the wolves among us. As Isaacs adds in regard to the Mirror Universe, it is depicted as

> a world where some people believe in racial purity and are against immigration, and they think it's okay to lie to get what you want, and that in the end the weak should be treated harshly. Sadly, those views are prevalent in the world today, and in fact there are people in seats of power who espouse those views every day. It's not a coincidence that I [Lorca] was sort of encouraging my followers to make the Empire Great Again. (*Inverse*, 2018)

As white supremacist ideals never vanished, but rather lay largely dormant for decades, and are now moving back to the forefront, the narrative surrounding his character thus indeed strikes a nerve.

'There were so many women. It's good to be the Captain' (1x12, 'Vaulting Ambition')

Isaacs, while admitting that he 'reverse engineered' the character of Lorca, since he 'had to be unlike any other Captain' (*Telegraph*, 2017) due to his Terran heritage, has said that he has also played him as a 'subtle tribute to Kirk,' (*ET*, 2017) when it comes to his relationships with women:

> I think in this tradition of Star Trek captains and these alpha males who rise to the top, he's got a taste for the good life and he's got an eye for his female officers. ... It was clear Captain Kirk had his way with any member of the micro-skirted crew members he wanted. (*ET* 2017)

While Kirk is notorious for being a ladies' man, Picard has had his fair share of dalliances too. Besides the often hinted at flirtation with the unavailable Dr. Beverly Crusher (Gates McFadden), he is also given backstory with several other female officers, usually admirals that visit the *Enterprise* for the duration of one episode. Much of the appeal of the

Starfleet captain thus lies in his sexual prowess – tying the archetype back to the trope of the action hero and military man. After all, as Higate and Hopton (2007) state, 'there are clear links between militaristic attitudes, male self-esteem, and sexual charisma' (14–15). Lorca's Southern accent also plays a role in this context, as Isaacs had partially chosen it because Lorca can be 'immensely charming' (quoted in Miller, 2017). Indeed, the captain is shown to be mostly courteous towards Burnham throughout the first half of the season, yet his actual intentions are much more sinister, as his treatment of other women indicates. With his first appearance in 'Context is for Kings' (1x03), he is established right away to have a problematic sexual relationship with his subordinate Commander Landry. While it is never made explicit, both actors have confirmed this,[7] and it is heavily implied in the subtext: 'Anything, anytime, Captain,' Landry suggestively tells Lorca (1x03). He also goes on to seduce Admiral Cornwell in order to distract her from the fact that he does not remember the history she shares with his Prime Universe alter ego in the aptly titled 'Lethe' (1x06). Both characters are also revealed to have relationships with him in his home universe – Mirror Landry is his loyal right-hand woman (1x13) while Cornwell so far has only appeared in the comics but seems to be loyal to him there as well (Beyer and Johnson, 2018). In 1x12, Lorca is also revealed to have mistreated another woman named Ava, until 'something better came along.' For him, people, but particularly women, are interchangeable, as Whit Frazier Peterson also argues in his chapter of this book, and Lorca says earlier in the same episode: 'There were so many women. It's good to be the Captain.' Lorca's toxic masculinity is thus not only put in line with those of right-wing movements currently reemerging in the Western world, but also implicitly criticizes the sexist undertones of previous Starfleet captains, particularly *TOS*'s Kirk.[8]

In addition to these women, Lorca also has a troubling relationship with Burnham. He is revealed to have been her lover in the Mirror Universe, but with a stomach-churning twist: Emperor Georgiou, who

---

[7] Originally, there had been a scene shot that would have made this relationship much more sexually explicit, something Rekha Sharma described as #MeToo related on a panel on *Star Trek: The Cruise III* in 2019.

[8] Pike is in this context hard to pinpoint – his slightly flirtatious demeanor with Tilly in the second season's premiere made at least the authors of this chapter slightly uneasy, but since he is not shown to enter any inappropriate sexual relationships with crew members over the course of his arc, his character at least does not reconfirm these traits of the trope. The only romantic, if not sexual, relationship he is shown in with is Vina (Melissa George), another character from 'The Cage.'

served as a maternal figure to Burnham, explains that Lorca was her *ersatz* father, until she came of age, and that he 'groomed' her (1x12), a term usually reserved for sexual predators preying on underage children. His relationship with her in his home dimension is also why he seeks her out once he crosses into the Prime Universe, since he believes in destiny across universes, and that, consequently, the Michael Burnham we have come to know will eventually rule beside him. This entitlement is what also leads to his downfall, because in contrast to what he tells her in 'Context is for Kings,' he does in fact not know her at all. He is incapable of understanding Michael as a person, her morals and, in turn, those of Starfleet, as for the Terrans, their ideals of equality are but an experiment doomed to fail. Lorca fails because of his white male privilege, his entitlement, and he dies at the hands of the women he betrayed, giving his character a rather satisfying ending.

'You are my tether. You bring me back' (1x11, 'The Wolf Inside')

In contrast to Lorca and his purely sexual affairs, Ash Tyler enters into an actual romantic and sexual relationship with Michael Burnham. For instance, Tyler freely shares his feelings and childhood memories with Burnham, such as stories of him and his father fishing (1x08, 'Si Vis Pacem Para Bellum'). As Plummer argues 'it is in the creation of new stories, narratives, and dialogues regarding men's different sexual lives that we can start to glimpse the potential for changing the hegemony' (Plummer, 2005, 192). Unlike the extremely secretive Lorca, Tyler thus offers Burnham a look at his true self and creates room for her to safely share her own thoughts, memories and emotions. This creates the basis for an equal partnership, thus showing a different distribution of emotional labor than the usual representation of heterosexual relationships on screen.

The trained psychiatrist Cornwell alerts Lorca to the necessity of psychological evaluation and treatment of Tyler, before he can resume his duty. Lorca, however, denies this, again emphasizing his prioritization of military duties over mental and emotional health for himself and his crew (1x06). When Tyler starts to experience flashbacks, he initially tries to cover up these lapses, even when directly confronted about them by Burnham (1x10). This behavior shows how alike Tyler and Lorca can be and how much Tyler looks up and tries to emulate him; however, it is Tyler that ultimately subverts the captain's toxic ideals of masculinity. Actor Shazad Latif has commented that 'what could you see in the first few episodes [of Tyler], it's just a classic American action hero,' but that as the first season progresses, this idea is 'flipped on its head' (*Okay Player*, 2018). There was a conscious decision on behalf of the actor, and the writers, to interrogate this trope:

> I just wanted to do something that, one, wasn't boring, and two, that's progressive and of its time. ... With all this going on right now [such as #metoo], especially, any character who adheres to the classic male action hero just seems outdated. It needs to be deeper than that. Otherwise, it's just going to fall by the wayside when you're watching it, and I just become another boring male character running around shooting stuff. (Latif, *The Verge*, 2018)

Tyler's willingness to be vulnerable is one of the most visible markers of this subversion, and it is most apparent in his relationship with Burnham. While he initially tries to hide his problems arising from his split personality (or rather, personhood), he does share them eventually, but they are framed in a context of PTSD – drawing another parallel between him and Lorca, though he initially makes Burnham his co-conspirator, as already discussed above: Tyler is forging bonds and Lorca is failing to do so, if not actively avoiding it. While Lorca engages in sexual relationships with various women, we also know that he knows none of them intimately; instead, he is projecting his own ideology and fantasies onto them. Lorca's interactions with Cornwell prior to sleeping with her are a direct contrast to Tyler and Burnham's established bond before they sleep with each other.

DSC also clearly frames this attitude as positive and as a contrast to Lorca. While Lorca continuously tries to bring Burnham to his side, expecting her to join him until his death because he is completely blinded by his own delusions, Tyler respects her choice to walk away from him, even though he sees her as his tether to humanity (1x14, 'The War Without, the War Within') and eventually even chooses to stay on Qo'noS to act as a go-between for the Federation and the Klingons (1x15, 'Will You Take My Hand'). In season two, when we first meet him again in episode three, 'Point of Light,' he still serves as an advisor to L'Rell, but his presence is severely contested by her paternalistic political opponents, and thus ultimately ends up serving for the top-secret Federation agency Section 31. By the end of the season, he is even made head of the organization, as his 'worldview is uniquely suited to the dualities intrinsic to Section 31' (2x14, 'Such Sweet Sorrow, Part Two'). His hybridity between human and Klingon ultimately makes him an asset to Starfleet, but so does his moral compass, his 'tether'

Michael Burnham, who he continues to follow when he suspects Section 31 is acting out of their own volition and is potentially destroying the Federation from within. Their genuine love and respect for each other thus continues to shape his character beyond their initial relationship – a type of relationship that Lorca neither values nor understands.

'You get to live your life, the way you deserve to. Not at war. But at peace' (1x09, 'Into the Forest I Go')

When Tyler develops genuine romantic and sexual interest in Burnham it also leads to him having to confront the experiences he made as a POW on the Klingon prison ship. He also opens up about having repeatedly been raped by his Klingon captor (1x09). This conversation is preceded by several short flashbacks showing the rape, as well as Tyler confiding in Lorca that the success of his survival was ensured by a Klingon taking a 'special interest' in him (1x05). The viewer is thus aware of what was done to Tyler before Burnham is. The fact that Tyler talks about his trauma at all is significant, as *DSC* thus features a man who embodies the classical image of a good soldier on screen, but upends stereotypes by actually addressing his trauma. Additionally, while it is not unusual for soldiers' trauma to be depicted on screen, it is normally physical trauma, further emphasizing the focus on the bodies of male soldiers rather than their psyche.

Yet Tyler is also a survivor of rape.[9] This makes him a male protagonist that suffers from trauma that is not only usually not addressed in the context of soldiers, but also only experienced by female characters – another important deviation from conventional depictions on American television. Tyler confides in Burnham about the rape and his feelings about it, confessing to feeling guilt and shame because he 'encouraged

---

[9] We are aware that this narrative has been troubled by the fact that, presumably, for Voq, the sex with L'Rell was consensual, yet for Tyler it was experienced as assault, and this is the way he remembers it. Shazad Latif has also commented on this: 'It's interesting because in reality Voq was just having sex. And they're in love, and that's what's technically happening, but obviously in Tyler's mind, because he is in my head, he was a real guy and his memories are real and he's still a real person, he's just coming through in someone else's core being. In his mind, it's sexual assault. So, to play it both is very weird and interesting because you don't normally get to do that. But to explore adds another layer for an actor and for the story line. Especially in times like now, with what's going on, it's a very, very interesting thing to explore' (*Vulture*, 2018).

it' in order to survive, and explains that he has had nightmares about it (1x09). Therefore, the effects of the sexual abuse on Tyler are verbally stated by him during his conversation with Burnham, and they are also shown twice visually, first by his viscerally violent reaction to L'Rell upon escaping the Klingon ship with Lorca in 1x05 and secondly by his freezing up upon seeing her again in 1x09. It is thus made explicit during several episodes that Tyler is emotionally traumatized by the rape. It is also made explicit that Burnham believes him – he receives emotional support from her, as well as physical comfort and, additionally, Burnham is also not repulsed by him or shown in any other way deterred from continuing their relationship by this revelation. The kiss they share after the conversation demonstrates that she is still romantically and sexually interested in him. All of this further avoids tropes of how rape is usually handled on television.

Having a male rape survivor is still a rarity on screen. Having one that is shown to be emotionally traumatized by it is even rarer. While there is little research about real-life male sexual assault survivors, Heather Hlavka identifies dominant ideas of masculinity as stigmatizing 'male victims of sexual assault ... as having failed in their masculine duty to protect themselves' (2016, 485). By almost exclusively making women the target of sexual violence in mainstream media, and not even acknowledging rape when done to a man by a woman – this stigma is further perpetuated, sometimes even to the point of 'belief that male sexual assault is not possible' (Hlavka, 2016, 486). *DSC*, however, counteracts this narrative, and even does so by depicting a capable soldier as rape survivor. Tyler thus represents an alternative masculinity to American television audiences, and one that also directly contrasts the one displayed by Lorca. Tyler, as discussed, is shown as vulnerable because of his trauma, and the show is willing to explore this vulnerability. Actor Shazad Latif has also commented on how he and his scene partners, Sonequa Martin-Green and Mary Chieffo, worked on upending the underlying gender dynamics of this: 'The thing I love about Tyler is that the women that he's with in the scene are stronger than him, usually, when we see him in pain, in the med bay, or just being cradled by either L'Rell or Michael' (*Okay Player*, 2018). Tyler is also seen crying in several of these scenes, something that Latif also was adamant about being depicted (*The Verge*, 2018).

Yet, Tyler also makes mistakes and exploits Burnham's feelings and their relationship to avoid any kind of treatment, assessment, or removal from active duty, even when it is clear he needs help and is not fit to perform his assigned tasks (1x10). His refusal to allow help not only endangers himself, it endangers others, and *Discovery* makes this clear – after all, it is Tyler/Voq that kills the medical officer Dr. Culber (Wilson Cruz) when he tries to help Tyler and finds out what is wrong with him in 1x10. Latif has also argued that this shows the larger consequences of rape and the resulting trauma: 'there's a bigger picture to sexual assault that doesn't just include the victim – it affects everyone around him, including friends, loved ones and that's something that needs to be addressed in our society' (*Trek Core*, 2018). In 2x03, when he still serves under L'Rell and she kisses him, he admits that her touch still feels 'like violation' to him, further highlighting that the trauma he endured remains part of his identity, even as he by then is seemingly coping better and it is no longer interfering with his work.

His relationship with L'Rell is, however, further complicated by the fact that it is revealed in the same episode that she and Voq had a child born *ex utero* that she kept secret from anyone outside of her house, Mo'Kai. As the baby becomes a target for her political opponents, Tyler is tasked with hiding him in the monastery of Boreth, despite his intent to be a father to his son. When the location and existence of his son have to be disclosed later in the season (2x12), he does not fall back into old habits and instead immediately shares crucial information with Michael (and later on Pike), further showing both his growth and his continued willingness to be emotionally vulnerable.

Just like Lorca, Tyler initially, literally, soldiers on through any pain to get the mission done as their successful escape in 1x05 shows. However, the show makes it very clear that emotional and mental trauma cannot just be willed away. And although there is an entirely different issue underlying this story as well with the Voq/Tyler switch, the message about this kind of trauma is still clear: it needs treatment. And it further sends the message that it is not only acceptable and necessary to seek help, it is also okay to be vulnerable – regardless of gender.

'The side I've chosen, is ... where it is possible to feel compassion and sympathy for your enemy' (1x15, 'Will You Take My Hand')

The initial homosocial military bond Lorca and Tyler share is narratively broken up when Tyler's hybrid identity as a Klingon sleeper agent and Lorca's villainous plan are revealed, but it is also done metaphorically when Tilly makes the conscious effort to reintegrate Tyler into the crew by sitting down at his table in the mess hall in 1x14. When they are joined by Lieutenant Detmer (Emily Coutts) and Lieutenant Bryce (Ronnie Rowe Jr.), he is officially reinstated into the *Discovery*'s crew, a stark contrast to the individual, preferential status that Lorca gave him and that was clearly meant to make him loyal to Lorca rather than the crew as a whole. Starfleet's values of unity and acceptance thus effectively trump Lorca's militaristic, hegemonic and, eventually, toxic masculine ideals. By differentiating himself from Lorca and, most importantly, by actively deciding to do so, Tyler is also eventually saved and can function as an important conduit between the Federation and the Klingons.

His respect for Burnham, another direct contrast to Lorca's possessive attitude, also leads to them parting on good terms – mutual understanding thus lays the foundation of a peaceful Klingon–Human relationship and possibly even reconciliation that is also shown in the season two finale, when Klingon ships under L'Rell's command come to help the *Discovery* and the *Enterprise* in their battle against Control. His alternative masculinity thus also has larger positive consequences for the war effort, and potentially shapes the future of the Federation. While the introduction of Christopher Pike has somewhat rebuilt the archetype of the Starfleet captain that Lorca's character had at least chipped at, it is also Ash Tyler and the non-toxic masculinity he stands for that are realigned with the ideals of Starfleet and the Federation, while Lorca's toxic behavior is actively attributed to that of the fascist Terrans. This is not coincidental. Ted Sullivan, executive producer and writer on the show, has said that he and the whole team working on *Discovery* 'felt we had a unique opportunity to talk about what is going on in the world right now. That is what *Star Trek* is supposed to do' (*Trek Movie*, 2018). By actively interrogating what it means to be a man not only in the twenty-third, but more importantly, in the twenty-first century, they have successfully done so.

Works Cited

Angelica Jade Bastién, Interview with Shazad Latif, 'Star Trek: Discovery's Shazad Latif on Lieutenant Ash Tyler's Vulnerability, Sexual Assault, and That Twist', *Vulture*, 1 February (2018), https://www.vulture.com/2018/02/star-trek-shazad-latif-lt-ash-tyler-that-twist.html.

Kirsten Beyer, Mike Johnson, and Angel Hernandez, *Star Trek: Discovery: Succession Part 4* (San Diego, CA: IDW Publishing, 2018).

Keith Booker, *Star Trek: A Cultural History* (London: Rowman and Littlefield, 2018).

Ryan Britt, Interview with Jason Isaacs, 'Jason Isaacs Finally Explains Lorca's Secret-', *Inverse*, 28 January (2018), https://www.inverse.com/article/40623-jason-isaacs-star-trek-discovery-interview.

R.W. Connell, 'Globalization, Imperialism, and Masculinities', in Michael Kimmel, Jeff Hearn, and R.W. Connell (eds.) *Handbook of Studies on Men and Masculinities* (Thousand Oaks: Sage Publishers, 2005): 71–89.

Robert Eberwein, *Armed Forces – Masculinity and Sexuality in the American War Film* (Rutherford, NJ: Rutgers University Press, 2007).

Heather R. Hlavka, 'Speaking of Stigma and the Silence of Shame: Young Men and Sexual Victimization', *Men and Masculinities*, 20.4 (2016): 482–505.

Paul Higate and John Hopton, 'War, Militarism and Masculinities', in Michael Kimmel, Jeff Hearn, and R.W. Connell (eds.) *Handbook of Studies on Men and Masculinities* (Thousand Oaks: Sage Publishers, 2005): 432–46.

Jason Isaacs, FedCon, 19 May, 2018, Maritim Hotel Bonn, Germany. Convention Panel.

—— 'Man in the Mirror', *Destination Star Trek*, 27 October, 2018, NEC, Birmingham, England. Convention Panel.

Terry Kupers, 'Toxic Masculinity as a Barrier to Mental Health Treatment in Prison', *Journal of Clinical Psychology*, 61.6 (2005): 713–24.

Devon Maloney, Interview with Shazad Latif, 'Star Trek: Discovery's Shazad Latif explains why Ash Tyler is more than an "outdated classic male action hero"', *The Verge*, 9 February (2018), https://www.theverge.com/2018/2/9/16993328/star-trek-discovery-shazad-latif-ash-tyler-klingon-vulnerability-voq-reveal-spoilers.

E. Leigh McKagen, 'Imperial Worlding: Adventure Narratives, Empire, and Brave New Worlds in Star Trek: Voyager', *Worlding SF* Conference, 8 December, 2018, University of Graz, Austria. Conference Paper.

Liz Shannon Miller, Interview with Jason Isaacs, '"Star Trek: Discovery": Why Jason Isaacs First Said No to Becoming the New Captain, and His Controversial Tribble Stance', *Indiewire*, 2 October (2017), https://www.indiewire.com/2017/10/star-trek-discovery-jason-isaacs-interview-tribbles-1201882465/.

Jason Mittell, *Complex TV: The Poetics of Contemporary Television Storytelling* (New York: New York University Press, 2015).

Roberta Pearson and Maire Messenger Davies, *Star Trek and American Television* (Berkeley: University of California Press, 2014).

Ken Plummer, 'Male Sexualities', in Michael Kimmel, Jeff Hearn, and R.W. Connell (eds.) *Handbook of Studies on Men and Masculinities* (Thousand Oaks: Sage Publishers, 2005): 178–94.

Philiana Ng, Interview with Jason Isaacs, '"Star Trek: Discovery's" Jason Isaacs on Captain Lorca's Debut and His "Subtle" Shatner Tribute', *ET*, 1 October (2017), https://www.etonline.com/exclusive-star-trek-discoverys-jason-isaacs-captain-lorcas-debut-and-his-subtle-shatner-tribute.

Stefan Rabitsch, Star Trek *and the British Age of Sail: The Maritime Influence Throughout Series and Films* (Jefferson, NC: McFarland and Company, 2018).

Tristam Fane Saunders, Interview with Jason Isaacs, 'Jason Isaacs on Twitter Bullies, Being Trolled by William Shatner, and Anthony Rapp's Bravery: "What he did was heroic"', *The Telegraph*, 13 November (2017), https://www.telegraph.co.uk/on-demand/0/jason-isaacs-twitter-bullies-trolled-william-shatner-anthony/.

Danielle A. Scruggs, Interview with Shazad Latif, 'Shazad Latif of "Star Trek: Discovery" Explains How His Role Challenges Masculinity', *Okay Player* (2018), https://www.okayplayer.com/interviews/shazad-latif-star-trek-discovery-interview.html.

Shawn Shimpach, *Television in Transition: The Life and Afterlife of the Narrative Action Hero* (New York: Wiley Blackwell, 2010).

Trek Movie Staff, Interview with Ted Sullivan, 'Jason Isaacs And "Star Trek: Discovery" Producers Talk Prime Lorca, Emperor's Future And More', *Trek Movie*, 29 January (2018), https://trekmovie.com/2018/01/29/jason-isaacs-and-star-trek-discovery-producers-talk-prime-lorca-emperors-future-and-more/.

Episodes Cited

'The Menagerie: Part One and Two.' *Star Trek*, written by Gene Roddenberry, directed by Marc Daniels, Desilu Productions, 17/24 November, 1966.

'The Cage.' *Star Trek*, written by Gene Roddenberry, directed by Robert Butler, Desilu Productions, 27 November, 1988.

'Favor the Bold.' *Star Trek: Deep Space Nine*, written by Ira Steven Behr and Hans Beimler, directed by Winrich Kolbe, Paramount Television, 6 June, 1998.

'Context is for Kings.' *Star Trek: Discovery*, written by Gretchen J. Berg, Aaron Harberts, and Craig Sweeny, directed by Akiva Goldsman, CBS Television Studios, 1 October, 2017.

'The Butcher's Knife Cares Not for the Lamb's Cry.' *Star Trek: Discovery*, written by Jesse Alexander and Aron Eli Coleite, directed by Olatunde Osunsanmi, CBS Television Studios, 8 October, 2017.

'Choose Your Pain.' *Star Trek: Discovery*, written by Kemp Powers, directed by Lee Rose, CBS Television Studios, 16 October, 2017.

'Lethe.' *Star Trek: Discovery*, written by Joe Menosky and Alex Kurtzman, directed by Douglas Aarniokoski, CBS Television Studios, 22 October, 2017.

'Magic to Make the Sanest Man Go Mad.' *Star Trek: Discovery*, written by Jesse Alexander and Aaron Eli Coleite, directed by David Barrett, CBS Television Studios, 30 October, 2017.

'Si Vis Pacem, Para Bellum.' *Star Trek: Discovery*, written by Kirsten Beyer, directed by John Scott, CBS Television Studios, 5 November, 2017.

'Into the Forest I Go.' *Star Trek: Discovery*, written by Bo Yeon Kim and Erika Lippoldt, directed by Christopher J. Byrne, CBS Television Studios, 12 November, 2017.

'Despite Yourself.' *Star Trek: Discovery*, written by Sean Cochran, directed by Jonathan Frakes, CBS Television Studios, 7 January, 2018.

'The Wolf Inside.' *Star Trek: Discovery*, written by Lisa Randolph, directed by T.J. Scott, CBS Television Studios, 14 January, 2018.

'Vaulting Ambition.' *Star Trek: Discovery*, written by Jordon Nardino, directed by Hanelle M. Culpepper, CBS Television Studios, 21 January, 2018.

'What's Past is Prologue.' *Star Trek: Discovery*, written by Ted Sullivan, directed by Olatunde Osunsanmi, CBS Television Studios, 28 January, 2018.

'The War Without, the War Within.' *Star Trek: Discovery*, written by Lisa Randolph, directed by David Solomon, CBS Television Studios, 4 February, 2018.

'Will You Take My Hand?' *Star Trek: Discovery*, written by Gretchen J. Berg and Aaron Harberts, directed by Akiva Goldsman, CBS Television Studios, 11 February, 2018.

'Brother.' *Star Trek: Discovery*, written by Gretchen J. Berg, Aaron Harberts, and Ted Sullivan, directed by Alex Kurtzman, CBS Television Studios, 17 January, 2019.

'Point of Light.' *Star Trek: Discovery*, written by Andrew Colville, directed by Olatunde Osunsami, CBS Television Studios, 31 January, 2019.

'An Obol for Charon.' *Star Trek: Discovery*, written by Alan B. McElory and Andrew Colville, directed by Lee Rose, CBS Television Studios, 7 February, 2019.

'The Sound of Thunder.' *Star Trek: Discovery*, written by Bo Yeon Kim and Erika Lippoldt, directed by Douglas Aarnioski, CBS Television Studios, 21 February, 2019.

'Through the Valley of Shadows.' *Star Trek: Discovery*, written by Bo Yeon Kim and Erika Lippoldt, directed by Douglas Aarnioski, CBS Television Studios, 4 April, 2019.

'Such Sweet Sorrow: Part Two.' *Star Trek: Discovery*, written by Michelle Paradise, Jenny Lumet, and Alex Kurtzman, directed by Olatunde Osunsanmi, CBS Television Studios, 18 April, 2019.

Queering *Star Trek*

'Never Hide Who You Are'
Queer Representation and Actorvism in *Star Trek: Discovery*
Sabrina Mittermeier and Mareike Spychala

A Utopian Future, But for Whom?

The lack of LGBTQ representation in the *Star Trek* franchise has long cast a shadow over the utopian, inclusive future it claims to represent. While creator Gene Roddenberry had said he would be willing to add a gay character to *The Next Generation* (*TNG*) as early as 1986, by his death in 1991 this change had not been implemented (Jenkins, 2004, 195). The later series *Deep Space Nine* (*DS9*; 1993–1999), *Voyager* (*VOY*; 1995–2001), and *Enterprise* (*ENT*; 2001–2005) similarly failed to include LGBTQ characters and only a handful of stand-alone episodes over the years would even dare to address the subject, and those that did produced rather mixed results, as we will discuss. As Katja Kanzler had summed up in 2004, long before *Discovery* was on the horizon: '*Star Trek*-the-media-text is rather characterized by its queer absences; it is the text's recreations by some of its fans that do queer *Star Trek*' (223).

Fanart and fanfiction featuring queer versions of established characters do indeed have a long tradition in *Star Trek* fandom. Famously, slash fanfiction 'originated as a genre of fan writing within *Star Trek* fandom in the early 1970s' (Jenkins, 2004, 192) with stories focusing on Kirk and Spock as a romantic pairing first appearing in fanzines from the 1970s (Verba, 2003, 19) onwards. The term 'slash' points to the practice of using an oblique stroke to mark a homosexual relationship (Jenkins, 2004, 192). This convention has since been more widely adapted and is also used to indicate heterosexual pairings appearing in fanfiction.

Hence, there is an established tradition of queer readings and fan productions that tapped into what could be called the queer subtexts of the *Star Trek* franchise. With *Star Trek: Discovery* (*DSC*; 2017–ongoing), the newest addition to this franchise, this queer subtext is finally being translated into the main text via the characters of Lieutenant Commander Paul Stamets (Anthony Rapp) and Dr. Hugh Culber (Wilson Cruz), who live together on the eponymous starship and whose status as a couple is known to their crewmates. As we will argue in this paper, throughout the first and second seasons of the show, the narrative not only expands on the love story between Stamets and Culber and establishes them as one of the show's main couples. Through continuous citations of and references to earlier *Star Trek* shows and especially *The Original Series* (*TOS*), *DSC* also makes LGBTQ relationships that were only potential subtexts before explicit.

Moreover, by casting Anthony Rapp and Wilson Cruz, two openly gay actors, who have long been advocating for LGBTQ rights and visibility, the show did not only commit to representation on screen, but also off screen. Therefore, this chapter will also focus on the actors' involvement in activism and the importance of representation for the LGBTQ community.

A Long Time Coming: Queer Representation in *Star Trek*

The fundamental values of *Star Trek*, the idea of 'infinite diversity in infinite combinations,' were in many ways betrayed from the beginning. Although the make-up of the cast of *TOS* was groundbreaking for American television in the tumultuous and Cold War-riddled 1960s, with its African female officer Nyota Uhura (Nichelle Nichols), the Japanese Hikaru Sulu (George Takei), or the Russian Pavel Chekov (Walter Koenig), there was never any doubt about who constituted the main cast of the show: the three white, straight men whose names were the only ones featured in the series' opening credits: William Shatner, Leonard Nimoy, and DeForest Kelley. Pointing this out does not intend to diminish the legacy of Gene Roddenberry and the many others who brought this franchise to life, but simply to address the limits of the show's cultural context of production. There is a well-known story of Martin Luther King Jr. approaching Nichelle Nichols and convincing her to stay on the show when she intended to quit because of the quality of the work she was getting to do. It speaks volumes, as in the times of the Civil Rights movement, it was her mere visibility that mattered. Likewise, it would have been more than surprising, basically impossible, to have an openly queer character featured on the bridge of the *Enterprise*, or even on a distant planet – back in 1966, network television was the true final frontier to be conquered. As Henry Jenkins has put it:

Nobody had expected the original *Star Trek* series, released in a pre-Stonewall society, to address directly the concerns of gay, lesbian, and bisexual fans. They had taken it on faith that its vision of a United Federation of Planets, of intergalactic cooperation and acceptance, included them as vital partners. (2004, 194)

But, times change, and the franchise was expected to change with it. Thus, 'when *Star Trek: The Next Generation* appeared, at a time when queer characters had appeared on many American series, they hoped for something more, to be there on the screen, an explicit presence in its twenty-fourth century' (Jenkins, 2004, 194). It was all the more disappointing when it did not.

Indeed, much had changed in the American television landscape between the end of *TOS* in 1969 and the premiere of *TNG* in 1987 but, as the saying goes, the more it changed the more it stayed the same. While the first positive representations of gay men found their way to the screen as early as the 1970s (trailblazers include the 1971 *All in The Family* episode 'Judging Books by Covers' (1x05) or *M*A*S*H*'s 'George' (2x22) from 1974), the majority of the few existing gay characters at the time were either bad, effeminate stereotypes or portrayed as outright sociopaths. Unsurprisingly, the 1980s were marked by the AIDS crisis, whether that meant sympathetic representations that tried to do political advocacy (such as *Designing Women*'s 1987 episode 'Killing All the Right People' (2x04) that was nominated for two Emmy awards) or much more negative portrayals, furthering the idea of gay men as degenerate perpetrators of disease. Lesbians generally featured even less, as did bisexual and transgender people (both groups would not see more meaningful representation until well into the 2000s, if not 2010s, while non-binary people are only scarcely portrayed even today).

Yet, while still fraught, queer representation was here to stay and, understandably, *Star Trek* fans expected to be included in its utopian future. Gene Roddenberry, then still at the helm of the budding franchise, sent mixed messages to the queer fans advocating for inclusion. As early as 1986, even before the premiere of *TNG*, he admitted at a fan gathering that the issue needed to be addressed eventually (Jenkins, 2004, 195), and raised it at a staff meeting for the show in late 1987 (Drushel, 2013, 32). Out of this meeting came a pitch for a script dealing with queer issues – the now infamous 'Blood and Fire' by veteran writer David Gerrold (the author of *TOS*'s 'The Trouble Wih Tribbles,' 2x15), in which he tackled AIDS through a metaphorical storyline. Gerrold had intended it as a tribute to Michael 'Mike' Minor, an illustrator on *Star Trek: The Motion Picture* (1979) and the art director of *The Wrath of Khan*

(1982), who was already too sick to join the *TNG* production team and died from AIDS-related complications on May 4, 1987. However, the script was never filmed: initially it underwent multiple revisions (Gerrold had originally intended for there to be a gay couple in the episode, the first thing to go), and finally, was vetoed altogether by producer Rick Berman, resulting in Gerrold angrily leaving the show and making his story public (Jenkins, 2004, 198; Drushel, 2015, 32). Berman was afraid of an audience backlash against the episode (Jenkins, 2004, 198), which was a valid concern at the time. After all, when drama series *Thirtysomething* (1987–1991) showed two men waking up next to each other in bed in the 1989 episode 'Strangers' (3x06) a public outcry led to regular sponsors pulling out, costing ABC about $1.5 million in advertising revenue, which also prompted them to remove the episode from reruns. Nonetheless, such concerns were never discussed publicly by *Star Trek*'s producers – possibly because they would have in turn had to deal with fans' anger at them placing more importance on the capitalist concerns of the television network over promoting what they perceived as *Star Trek*'s core values. Ironically, the producers also framed their continued exclusion of queer lives as part of their ideology, aided by Roddenberry himself stating in an interview with gay magazine *The Advocate*: 'I've never found it necessary to do a special homosexual-theme story because people in the time line of The Next Generation, the 24th century, will not be labeled' (quoted in Jenkins, 2004, 197). Roddenberry passed away in 1991, the same year of the interview, and the remaining producers, showrunners Michael Piller and Jeri Taylor, and most notably, executive producer Rick Berman, continued to hide behind this 'circular logic' (Jenkins, 2004, 197).

Nevertheless, *TNG* aired an episode with at least a queer subtext not much later: 'The Host' (4x23), at the end of season four, which introduced the species of the Trill that consist of a symbiont and a host. In it, Dr. Beverly Crusher (Gates McFadden) falls in love with the Trill Odan who has a male host (Franc Luz). However, when his host sustains injuries, the symbiont is temporarily transferred to Will Riker's (Jonathan Frakes) body – a choice that ultimately does not deter Beverly from pursuing the romance, even though Will is her colleague and friend (something Robin Roberts has also pointed out, 1999, 116). Yet when, by the end of the episode, Odan joins with a female host, Kareel (Nicole Orth-Pallavicini), Beverly decides to break off the relationship and admits that it may be a 'human failing,' but that she cannot 'keep up' with 'these kinds of changes.' She suggests that 'perhaps, someday, our ability to love won't be so limited,' and Odan/Kareel kisses the inside of her wrist (as they used to), leaving Beverly with a questioning look on her face as the credits roll. While this ending remains somewhat ambivalent, it is a curious choice to blame Beverly's inability to be attracted to another woman's body on the human condition instead of her presumed heterosexuality – heteronormativity seems to be a firm constant in the twenty-fourth century, a far cry from Roddenberry's claims of a simple lack of labels. Or as Katja Kanzler (2004) has put it, within what we see of Starfleet, '[t]he mere lack of alternatives most forcefully installs heteronormativity' (205). Dr. Crusher's disavowal of Odan's new host body can further be read as transphobic,[1] something that would also become even more important when the Trill Jadzia Dax was introduced as a central character on *DS9*. Despite all of this, as McFadden reports, 'some people were outraged at any hint of homosexuality in this episode' (quoted in *Memory Alpha*).

Cries for queer representation grew even louder as the show progressed, leading to a 'conscious response' (Jenkins and Tulloch, 1995, 252) in the form of the episode 'The Outcast' (5x17), that first aired on March 16, 1992, towards the end of show's fifth season. The episode has received much attention from scholars and fans over the years, most of it negative – its main flaw is a conflated understanding of sex and gender, as well as sexual attraction. In the episode, Will Riker falls for Soren (Melinda Culea), a member of the J'naii, a species that once had two sexes but evolved into having just one – yet Soren reveals that she identifies as a woman, a fact that makes her the titular outcast in her own society, where this is viewed as a criminal perversion to be medically treated. Nonetheless, the script wanted to address homosexuality, as well as conversion therapy, more than engage with trans issues, a fact confirmed by writer Jeri Taylor who called it a 'gay rights story' (quoted in Jenkins and Tulloch, 1995, 255). Indeed, Soren's delivery of what reads like a pride speech at her tribunal thus remains powerful in its own right. Roberts (1999) has pointed out that the scene casts her in favorable and sympathetic light (119) – yet there is a danger that it might only resonate with queer people and could have gone over straight audiences' heads, as Jenkins and Tulloch's (1995) research suggests (257). The conflation of sex and gender, and the apparent favoritism towards a binary conception of gender in the end, also more than muddles the message. While Will's sincere feelings for Soren and his fight for her are another high point of the episode (much owed to Jonathan Frakes' heartfelt delivery), its advocacy for gay rights would

---

[1] For more on this issue, see Si Sophie Pages Whybrew's chapter titled '"I Never Met a Female Michael Before": *Star Trek: Discovery* between Trans Potentiality and Cis Anxiety' in this book.

have hit home harder and likely made the episode's message more clear, had Soren been portrayed by a male actor – something that apparently was vetoed by Rick Berman who argued that 'having Riker engaged in passionate kisses with a male actor might have been a little unpalatable to viewers' (quoted in Tremeer, 2019). Frakes however, who after all would have been the one doing the kissing, apparently found it much more 'palatable' – he continued to advocate for this casting (Jenkins and Tulloch, 1995, 285), and has publicly criticized the decision ever since, even recently calling the casting choice 'bizarre' (Tremeer, 2019).

The other big issue with this episode ultimately is that Soren's forced conversion therapy is seemingly successful, although this in the end quick solution to the plot is likely owed to the episodic nature of *TNG*'s storytelling – had Soren remained free to express her love and attraction to Riker, she would have had to remain on the *Enterprise*. It also seems to play into the trope of the tragic queer character, something much more prevalent in the television landscape of the 1990s, when queer characters were scarcely ever allowed any happy endings. Although 'The Outcast' remains decidedly mixed in its messages and impact, the fact that anything outside the boundaries of heteronormativity again falls to alien species is possibly the biggest disappointment. This is another issue that could have been addressed had Riker fallen for a female-identified character played by a male actor, since then Riker also might have been seen as queer – but, even in this case, it would have enforced cisnormativity. Ultimately, both 'The Host' and 'The Outcast' 'treat queer lifestyles as alien rather than familiar aspects of the Federation culture' (Jenkins, 2004, 190) and signify that queerness is not part of humanity in the twenty-fourth century – suggesting the conclusion that queer people either remained 'closeted or that they had ceased to exist' (Jenkins, 2004, 196).

The franchise continued to go strong all through the 1990s, with *DS9* running from 1993 to 1999 and *VOY* from 1995 to 2001, but queer representation was almost nowhere to be found on either show – there had been rumors of a minor character on the feature film *Star Trek: First Contact* (1996), Lieutenant Hawk (Neal McDonough), being gay, but they were quickly refuted by, again, Rick Berman (Drushel, 2013, 37). Tellingly, Hawk only was presented as explicitly gay when he made an appearance in the novel *Section 31: Rogue*, a much more niche product than the cinematic release. Meanwhile, the depiction of queer characters made great strides elsewhere on American television – while cable TV channels such as HBO were trailblazers, network television also followed suit, with Ellen DeGeneres' coming out both on and off screen in 1997 seen by many as a watershed moment. More and more shows of all genres added gay or lesbian supporting or even main characters during this time, and so *Star Trek* seemed continuously out of step with the zeitgeist. While *DS9* seemed most steeped in queer subtext (less graciously read as 'queerbaiting'), none of it was ever made explicit: neither the homoerotic undertones of Garak (Andrew Robinson) and Dr. Bashir's (Alexander Siddig) relationship, or the coming out of Major Kira Nerys (Nana Visitor) many fans would have liked to see. Garak's character is particularly of interest here, as actor Andrew Robinson has since confirmed that he intentionally played his interest in Bashir as queer and has always viewed his character as pansexual or, as he calls it, 'inclusive' (quoted in Sourbut, n.dat.), something he also insinuated in *A Stitch in Time* (2000), a *DS9* novel he wrote. Kira meanwhile is revealed to be bi- or pansexual only in the Mirrorverse, playing into the previous oversexualization of female characters in this other dimension – something *DSC* also took up, and which will be addressed below. The only more explicitly queer representation on screen was explored through the aforementioned Trill Jadzia Dax, whose whole species could have served for a more nuanced portrayal of trans issues but always failed to do so – in many ways, the biggest missed opportunity in all of *DS9*. The fact that she shared a same-sex kiss on screen in 'Rejoined' (4x06) was lauded by many, and still caused quite the controversy at the time, with a Southern affiliate even censoring the kiss ('Rejoined (episode),' *Memory Alpha*) and conservative viewers fielding angry calls to Paramount (Tremeer). Yet in many ways, it was not more than a sweep's week ploy, seemingly playing into the 'voyeuristic gratification with which scenes of lesbian love apparently provide heterosexual men' (Kanzler, 2004, 215). After all, it took another 22 years (!) for *Star Trek* to feature another same-sex kiss. And despite writer and producer Moore being 'proud of the fact that nowhere in the episode does anyone even blink at the fact that these are two women' ('Rejoined (episode),' *Memory Alpha*), Ira Steven Behr's comment that 'we're not doing a show about lesbians, we're doing a show about Trills' ('Rejoined (episode),' *Memory Alpha*) speaks volumes. Jadzia's romantic interest, Dr. Lenara Khan (Susanna Thompson), is another Trill, so their love for each other is in many ways framed by heteronormativity, since the symbionts had originally been in a heterosexual relationship. Also, Jadzia later goes on to marry Worf and, aside from this brief encounter, is thus mostly coded as a straight, cis woman – and any hints at queerness are ascribed to her alienness, and yet again not part of the Federation's humanity.

Noticeably, any explicit queerness is completely absent from *VOY*, despite behind-the-scenes advocacy to finally introduce a gay character to the franchise. Indeed, Kate Mulgrew who portrayed Captain Kathryn

Janeway, has been outspoken about wanting to see representation on her crew over the years and expressed regret for not being able to effect change. She approached Rick Berman about the issue multiple times, only to be rebutted with the claim it would be dealt with 'in due time' (quoted in Scahill, 2002). Yet, for Berman, who remained at the helm even for *ENT* (2001–2005), the time apparently had still not come in the early 2000s, when other television shows had begun to feature a variety of queer characters and to tackle issues way beyond homophobia. There are only two episodes on *ENT* that qualify as even having any queer subtext, and the whole show is far from any meaningful representation – in many ways, after *DS9* and *VOY*, it seemed to be a step back on a number of issues.

The 2003 episode 'Stigma' (2x14) finally made good on the chance passed up with 'Blood and Fire' over 15 years earlier, by addressing AIDS – it was explicitly commissioned as part of UPN's efforts to raise awareness for the KNOW HIV/AIDS campaign co-ordinated by its parent company Viacom (*KHN*, 2003). This is perhaps also why it comes off as a bit heavy-handed. Written by Brannon Braga and Rick Berman, the episode uses the stand-in Pa'nar Syndrome, a disease only contracted by Vulcans able to perform mind-melds. This minority is shunned on Vulcan and forced to live in secret and, as it transpires, the Vulcan doctors that the *Enterprise*'s Dr. Phlox (John Billingsley) consults with have no interest in curing the disease since it only affects the marginalized, drawing a parallel to the Reagan administration's handling of the AIDS crisis. However, despite not being part of the 'minority' herself, T'Pol (Jolene Blalock) contracts the disease when another Vulcan forces himself on her. Although the script takes great pains to make this fact clear, and ultimately handles the rape narrative well (and ties in with a previous episode, 'Fusion,' 1x17), the circumstances of her infection further remove all of this 'stigma' from any Starfleet character, even the non-human. Furthermore, Captain Archer (Scott Bakula) who advocates for her and criticizes the Vulcans for their bigotry declares that humanity has long overcome such ostracization, and thus falls back on the implicit superiority of humanity (or, more explicitly, those in Starfleet) that seems inherent to *Star Trek*. The fact that queerness remains something that only alien races inhabit is again repeated here, even in the episode's subplot, that explores the polyamorous nature of Dr. Phlox's species, the Denobulans, and Trip Tucker's (Connor Trineer) discomfort with it. David Gerrold, the writer of 'Blood and Fire,' when asked about *Star Trek*'s eventual treatment of AIDS, rightly pointed out that it 'could have made a greater impact in 1987 when the stigmatization was greater, no treatments were available, and blood shortages exacerbated by AIDS hysteria were critical' (Drushel, 2015, 34). Despite its efforts then, 'Stigma' ultimately feels strangely out of place in the television landscape of 2003.

Only a few episodes later, 'Cogenitor,' (2x22) at first glance is *ENT*'s answer to 'The Outcast,' introducing a three-gender species – yet the episode seems to deal more with class and race issues, since the mistreated members of the third gender serve as slaves for the rest of the species, as Greven has pointed out (2009, 43). Even in the new millennium then, *Star Trek* still had not answered its queer fans' rightful calls for representation in a future touting utopian equality and diversity. When in 2016's *Star Trek: Beyond*, the Kelvin timeline's Hikaru Sulu (John Cho) reunited with his husband and daughter in a blink-or-miss it moment, fans rejoiced, but even the original Sulu, George Takei, an out gay man, did not approve, as he believed it to be a retcon of Gene Roddenberry's work (Abramovitch, 2016). The scene was also edited, and thus the first same-sex kiss of the franchise was left on the cutting-room floor (Cross and Joannou, 2018). It ultimately would take until 2017, and most importantly, a new team of producers, to finally make good on its never fulfilled premise of 'infinite diversity' on the small screen.

Queering the Canon: Slash Fanfiction and Fan Activism

As mentioned in the introduction to this essay, *TOS*, and more specifically the fanfiction written about *TOS*, has long been credited as being influential in the invention of so-called 'slash' fanfiction, or fan-written stories that focus on queer relationships between canonical characters, and often narrowly on explicitly sexual interactions within such relationships. Early scholarship on fandom and fanfiction has focused on the ways in which these stories rewrite and add to the canon established by a television show or other cultural products. Thus, Henry Jenkins (1992, 2005) has argued that 'slash turns that subtext into the dominant focus of new texts' (1992, 210). More recent scholarship on slash fiction, for example by Robin Reid, has further criticized the 'unquestioned assumptions about the connection between gender roles and bodies, and thus between bodies and reading/writing preferences' (2009, 480). Judith May Fatallah (2017) also traces the development of fan studies including the changing views on the significance and influence of slash fanfiction and adds additional questions about 'the resistant or subversive nature of slash: firstly, do slash writers subversively create a queer subtext in the source, by way of a resistant reading, or are they making latent [sic] what is already there' (31)?

In addition to slash fanfiction and its introduction of LGBTQ relationships and issues into the *Star Trek* universe, fan activism has long been important in criticizing and holding the franchise's powers that be accountable. Bruce E. Drushel traces the efforts made by fan activists, for example, the Gaylactic Network, members of which 'confronted *Star Trek* creator Gene Roddenberry and writer David Gerrold at a fan convention either in 1986 and 1987' (2013, 31) and participated in a sustained letter-writing campaign arguing for LGBTQ representation (33). Jenkins also addresses The Gaylactic Network, noting that 'fans already exercise a form of grassroots cultural politics which powerfully reflects their interests in the media and their own ideological stakes' (1995, 239).

After the appearance of Sulu's husband in *Star Trek: Beyond* mentioned above, queer fans 'created a multi-city, cross country futuristic equality celebration tour called... GAAAYS IN SPAAACE' (*GAAAYS IN SPAAACE*; original emphasis). To date, GAAAYS IN SPACE has organized events across several major American cities, during *Star Trek: Las Vegas*, one of the largest *Star Trek* conventions in the United States, and during *Star Trek: The Cruise III* in January 2019, making the large number of queer *Star Trek* fans clearly visible. What is more, the group's website notes that '[e]ach and every GAAAYS IN SPAAACE event is a celebration of historic importance for LGBTQ Trekkies and all of our straight allies who have forever maintained that this day would eventually arrive' (*GAAAYS IN SPAAACE*; original emphasis), emphasizing not only how long it took for the *Star Trek* franchise to show even the smallest bit of LGBTQ representation, but also the community's continuing hope for it. With the arrival of *DSC* and the characters of Lieutenant Commander Stamets and Dr. Culber, some of that need has been met. At the same time, the representation of an out, canon gay couple in a *Star Trek* show has implications not only for the franchise itself but also for the fan productions focusing on *DSC* or these characters in particular. While this essay will provide a first analysis of the importance of Culber and Stamets and read the way they have been represented as a retroactive addition of LGBTQ identities into the canon, the latter considerations about fanworks lie outside of its focus.[2]

---

[2] For an exploration of how the canon representation of LGBTQ relationships affects fanfiction and especially the long-held belief that fanfiction is necessarily subversive, see Kerstin-Anja Münderlein's essay '"To Boldly Discuss": Socio-Political Discourses in *Star Trek: Discovery* Fanfiction' published in this volume.

'Hugh and I fell in love after I told him to get lost:' Queer Representation on *Star Trek: Discovery* (1x07, 'Magic to Make the Sanest Man Go Mad')

After the franchise's failure to include sustained and meaningful LGBTQ representation in the successive *Star Trek* shows or movies, *DSC* is the first series to feature a gay couple as part of its main cast, with characters that are, to differing extents, involved in and important to the larger narrative arcs in the first two seasons. Additionally, Stamets and Culber are introduced first in their professional capacities aboard the ship in episode 1x03 ('Context is for Kings') and only revealed to be a couple in an instantly iconic toothbrushing scene in 1x05 ('Choose Your Pain'). Commenting on this introduction to the characters and their relationship, Anthony Rapp explains:

> [W]hat I'm really proud of is, like everything with *Star Trek*'s diversity, there are no arrows pointing to it, no big neon sign flashing, no story line about what it's like to be a gay character on the ship. It just *is*. That, to me, is part of the evolution as well. (Russell, 2017; original emphasis)

This is important as it represents a normalization of LGBTQ characters and relationships. Stamets and Culber are part of the social world on board the *U.S.S. Discovery* and neither this scene nor the later plots involving their relationship focus on them as a 'special issue,' like the episodes discussed above. And, by featuring two human Starfleet officers as the first openly gay couple, *DSC* avoids projecting LGBTQ identities and sexualities onto alien species while implicitly reaffirming heterosexuality as the human norm. By making the characters central to the ship's return from the Mirror Universe in the first season, and by continuing to explore their relationship in season two after Culber's resurrection, the showrunners and writers made sure to present them as integral members of the crew whose love for each other is vital to the story, without reducing them to their sexual orientation.

While Culber's death in 1x10 was criticized by some as another instance of the 'Bury Your Gays' trope, which has been defined as 'the presentation of deaths of LGBT characters where these characters are nominally able to be viewed as *more expendable* than their heteronormative counterparts' ('Bury Your Gays'; original emphasis), the fact that Culber and Stamets' 'gay love ... not only saved the world but saved the universe,' to quote Wilson Cruz (Brown, 2018), and has continued beyond that, seems to subvert the trope to some extent. In the second season, the show also highlights Stamets' grief over the death of his partner and the trauma and PTSD Culber experiences after being trapped in the mycelial network for months. In several interviews, Cruz has noted that his inspirations for portraying this trauma lie in the HIV/AIDS crisis and specifically the moment when drugs that substantially prolonged life were introduced in the late 1990s: 'I thought a lot about what that must have felt like. ... if you're given a second chance at life, what do you do with that? Do you continue to live the life that you had been living or do you make new choices?' (*The Ready Room*, 2019). This is born out in the second half of season two, when Stamets and Culber briefly separate due to Culber's struggles with his trauma – a new development for *Star Trek*, where, due to the episodic nature of earlier shows, trauma was often not explored in more detail.

Cruz is not the only one who makes these connections to real-world history. The final scenes of 'Saints of Imperfection' show Stamets waiting in sickbay as Culber is being examined, despite the fact that they are not married, as Cruz asserted in an interview shortly before the episode aired (BUILDSeries, 2019). Stamets' presence can be seen as a further connection back to the AIDS epidemic and the fight for marriage equality it sparked. This is an aspect of the way the couple is represented in the show that was also picked up on by fans who have lived through the epidemic. On *Twitter*, user @luminousfinn points to the AIDS crisis in a thread after episode 2x14 ('Such Sweet Sorrow, Pt. 2') aired and notes that the episode shows '[t]hat we, in the 23rd century, have got to a point where we no longer have to fight this fight. Where our relationships are recognized as a matter of fact' (2019). Here, then, *DSC* evokes important stepping stones in the fight for LGBTQ equality, all while showing a possible, positive future that these fights might culminate in.

In addition to Culber and Stamets, *DSC* has also featured LGBTQ people among its recurring characters and in background shots, the latter most notably during the party scenes of 'Magic to Make the Sanest Man Go Mad' (1x07) where one can see a lesbian couple dancing and laughing together. In addition, the Terran Emperor Philippa Georgiou (Michelle Yeoh), who is brought into the so-called Prime Universe by Michael Burnham towards the end of season one, is revealed to be pansexual in 'Will You Take My Hand?' (1x15) when she first takes two Orion sex workers to bed and then extracts information from them. While this, and her claims about other Mirror Universe characters' pansexuality in 'The Red Angel' (2x10), can be seen as further representation, it also plays into longstanding stereotypes about bi- and pansexual characters in general, as well as an existing correlation between LGBTQ identities and moral ambiguity within the *Star Trek* franchise. As Teresa Cutler-Broyles, focusing on the fact that it is usually female Mirror Universe characters who are coded as bisexual, puts it: 'in a moral universe, female power is problematic, and distinctly separate from sexuality. And when it occurs, the logic of storyline and culture tells us that it will be eradicated/ reabsorbed back into the traditional trappings of power' (2017, 47). Kanzler has similarly noted that the portrayal of Mirror Kira Nerys is 'a queer imagery [that] stands for an alterity coded in a distinctly threatening way' (Kanzler, 2004, 207). While this is not necessarily true for *DSC* as a whole, it does seem to apply to Georgiou in this instance, especially when one keeps in mind the 'depraved bisexual' trope that Tremeer (2019) has also pointed out.[3] The fact that LGBTQ people are shown to exist in both universes somewhat breaks with the negative implications in earlier shows but, as it does so, it 'sets a bi woman against two gay men' (Tremeer, 2019) – this perception is heightened because we have so far not gotten confirmation that Georgiou's prime counterpart, who is killed in the show's pilot, also identified as pansexual.

Season two of *DSC* also introduces Commander Jett Reno, played by lesbian stand-up comedian Tig Notaro. As with Culber and Stamets, audiences first meet Reno fulfilling her duty as a Starfleet officer on the damaged *U.S.S. Hiawatha* in 'Brother' (2x01), before her relationship and her wife are introduced later in the season. This continues the show's representation of LGBTQ characters as full and accepted members of Federation society. Reno's relationship with her wife, a Soyousian, comes up in 'Through the Valley of Shadows' (2x12) when she mentions her during an exchange with Culber. This conversation between two openly queer characters about their respective relationships marks another first for the *Star Trek* franchise.

At the same time, this scene, and the inclusion of LGBTQ characters in *DSC* as a whole, have shown how spurious many of the previous showrunners' claims about the impossibility of representation were. Jenkins provides a whole list of reasons Roddenberry and studio representatives gave for not representing LGBTQ people in reaction to the Gaylaxians' letter-writing campaign. Among others, they insisted that '[t]he representation of homosexuality on Star Trek would necessarily become the site of some form of dramatic conflict' (Jenkins, 2004, 197) or that explicit sexual content would be needed to depict LGBTQ characters. As *DSC* has shown, none of these claims actually hold any

---

[3] Further resources examining the almost exclusively negative representation of bisexual characters (and overwhelmingly bisexual women) are Spencer Kornhaber's article 'The Trope of the Evil Television Bisexual' (2015) and Maria San Filippo's *The B Word: Bisexuality in Contemporary Film and Television* (2013).

water if, rather than making LGBTQ representation into a 'special' issue, showrunners, writers, and actors are dedicated to representing LGBTQ people in the same way heterosexual people have been represented in the franchise and wider media – as part of the normal fabric of life.

The enthusiastic reaction of LGBTQ fans to the introduction of Stamets and Culber bears out how important representation is and how long it took for *Star Trek* to reach this point. What is more, it is precisely in a science fiction show dedicated to showing a positive future that this representation might have the biggest impact. As Judith Butler has pointed out,

> [t]he critical promise of fantasy, when and where it exists, is to challenge the contingent limits of what will and will not be called reality. Fantasy is what allows us to imagine ourselves and others otherwise; it establishes the possible in excess of the real; it points elsewhere, and when it is embodied, it brings the elsewhere home. (2004, 29)

DSC, then, has '[brought] the elsewhere home' into the *Star Trek* canon and brought the franchise into alignment with recent societal progress.

Bringing Queer Subtext into the Limelight: Lieutenant Stamets, Dr. Culber, and *Star Trek* Canon

The introduction of both Lieutenant (later Lieutenant Commander) Stamets and Dr. Culber in season one is not only important because of how it is handled, but also because it evokes characters and dynamics familiar to *Star Trek* audiences since *TOS*. When we first see Culber and Stamets in sickbay, Dr. Culber has to fix Stamets' broken nose after a failed spore drive jump. When Culber mentions that Stamets almost injured his frontal cortex, the latter replies: 'The frontal lobe is overrated. It only contains memory and emotional expression. It's completely unnecessary.' Culber counters: 'Well, I'll save it. You know, just in case you might wanna have a feeling one day' (1x04, 'The Butcher's Knife Cares Not For the Lambs Cry'). This interaction, among others, and the sarcastic tones in which it is delivered by the actors, can be read as clear allusion to interactions between Dr. McCoy and Commander Spock in *TOS*, who are generally depicted as sharing a deep friendship, but also clash in this manner over their differences.

These allusions to *TOS* are further strengthened by the fact that Captain Lorca (Jason Isaacs) interrupts them during the sickbay scene in 1x04, addressing them as 'Gentlemen,' an address Kirk often uses to interrupt

McCoy's and Spock's arguments. The fact that these dynamics are so clearly alluded to in the interactions between Stamets and Culber can be interpreted as the show taking a possible queer subtext of *TOS* that has been explored in the fanon – the *TOS* characters most often shipped in fanworks are Spock and Kirk, but there are also a number fan works that ship Spock and McCoy or all three of the original show's main characters – and making it canon, further affirming that there is a space for LGBTQ people in *Star Trek*'s utopian future. One could argue with Fatallah here and say that 'fandom's discursive transformations [are] making industrial impact, and impacting the broader cultural sphere' (2017, 193). Through these allusions to *TOS*, the show seems to gesture backwards in time to the franchise's history, validating not only fans' queer rereadings of the show, but also highlighting, in a way, the prior absence of LGBTQ representation. This last point is further driven home in the scene in 2x08 mentioned above when the Terran emperor insinuates that the Mirror counterparts of Stamets and Culber are pansexual, leading to Stamets asserting: 'Well, in this universe, and in every other universe I can possibly imagine, I'm gay. And so is he' (2x08). This assertion of the characters' homosexuality does not only seem to be a way for *DSC* to rectify, to some degree, the missed opportunities of representation in the franchise as a whole, but also a direct rebuke to some fans' (and internet trolls') criticism of the introduction of a gay couple.

While *DSC*'s portrayal of LGBTQ couples such as Stamets and Culber is groundbreaking in many ways, it remains rather homonormative. It risks affirming marriage and monogamy as the frame that is applied to measure the validity or truth of romantic relationships, while those that act outside these norms, like Georgiou, still suffer from rather trope-heavy characterization. However, there is some potential to read this relationship as a subtle interrogation of the heteronormative assumptions that underlie earlier entries into the *Star Trek* canon and, of course, science fiction narratives and popular culture in general. In 'Saints of Imperfection' (2x05), Stamets is identified as 'widower' in Michael Burnham's (Sonequa Martin-Green) opening monologue. The use of this term seems even more deliberate in light of the fact that the characters are not married. Using 'widower' to describe Stamets once again emphasizes the depth of the love shared between him and Culber, as well as the extent of his grief after Culber's death. While this further normalizes and legitimizes their relationship, putting them on the same level as the countless heterosexual couples featured in the *Star Trek* franchise before them, it can potentially push viewers to take another look at ingrained assumptions surrounding romantic relationships and the cultural constraints and classifications that enclose them. As Butler has argued, 'it is crucial to expand our notions of kinship beyond the heterosexual frame' (2004, 26) because 'those who live outside the conjugal frame or maintain modes of social organization for sexuality that are neither monogamous nor quasi-marital are more and more considered unreal, and their loves and losses less than "true" loves and "true" losses' (2004, 26–27). Naming the unmarried Stamets a 'widower' makes his loss true and gestures at precisely this unreality that is often attached to unmarried couples especially unmarried LGBTQ couples. Thus, while *DSC* becomes 'part of the articulation of the possible' (Butler, 2004, 29) in some respects, there are also aspects of LGBTQ representation that could be improved on.

Representation On and Off Screen: Actorvism and Advocacy

DSC is a prime example for how much representation behind the camera matters to what we see on screen. While the franchise has two out gay actors with George Takei and Zachary Quinto, Takei came out decades after his role and has even disapproved of Sulu being reframed as queer in the Kelvin timeline (see above), and Quinto is relatively private about his life and his Spock is in a heterosexual relationship with Zoe Saldana's Uhura. With the casting of Wilson Cruz and Anthony Rapp, however, the showrunners made sure that the franchise's first queer main characters would be depicted by someone aware of the responsibility that came with this. Cruz came out the age of 19 and made history as being the first out gay man playing an out gay character on American network television in the short-lived teen drama *My So-Called Life* (1994–1995), while Rapp has been out since 1997. In 1995, they starred together briefly in the popular Broadway musical *RENT*, that also deals with queer lives, establishing themselves as household names in queer circles. Cruz has also worked for GLAAD, an organization monitoring LGBT content in the media, and describes himself as an 'actorvist' – a moniker that Rapp has also since taken on. Talking about their casting in *DSC* in gay magazine *Attitude*, Rapp clarified that they were aware of the significance, calling the first male–male kiss on the show 'historic,' but that since they 'have been in the public eye as out activists and actors for so long, it didn't feel like pressure but more like an opportunity' (quoted in Cross and Joannou, 2018, 48). He also mentions that they had discussions with the producers early on whether intimacy was going to be shown, but they were adamant on making it happen; in fact, season one showrunner Aaron Harberts, himself an out gay man, had been the one advocating for their casting in the first place (Cross and Joannou, 2018, 52) and Bryan Fuller, who had originally been attached to the show, had announced the inclusion of a gay character in 2016 (Trendacosta). Harberts, Rapp, and Cruz were, however, also diligent at delivering a non-sexualized representation of their gay characters and otherwise avoiding tropes.

While Stamets and Culber remain indeed non-sexualized and their love story is touching, both the showrunners and the actors came under fire for what many fans perceived as 'Bury Your Gays,' as discussed above. In an unusual move given the secrecy CBS had shown surrounding any other plot in today's spoiler culture, the producers and actors were granted permission to speak openly in the media about the fact that Cruz would return to the show and that Culber would be resurrected. This was done immediately following the episode in the companion show *After Trek*, as well as by Cruz and Rapp via their social media channels, yet the outrage remained understandably huge. Season two has made good on the promise of resurrecting the doctor and has even promoted Cruz to a series regular, yet the show has since been criticized for bestowing further hardship on the characters. Nonetheless, Cruz and Rapp both remain vocal spokespeople, reassuring and engaging with fans on a daily basis, particularly on *Twitter*, taking seriously their roles as actorvists.

Conclusion: 'Gay love saved the universe'

After a long and fraught history with queer representation, the *Star Trek* franchise has finally acknowledged that LGBTQ people are part of its humanist, egalitarian future – a fact that fans had long imagined for themselves, through queer readings, writing slash fic, and other transformative works. *DSC*, however, is the first instalment that truly represents queer lives, on screen as much as behind it – which has made all the difference. And yet the treatment of its main queer characters has not always satisfied fans, who have viewed some of it as still falling into the traps of old tropes, despite the actors' continued activism and avid engagement with them. Further, while gay male representation is now finally part of the *Star Trek* story world, and lesbian lives have found some recognition on the sidelines, with explicit connections to *Star Trek* canon and decades of fanon and queer readings even suggesting that *DSC* may be consciously rewriting canon or at least acknowledging the possibility that characters in former shows may have been members of the LGBTQ community, the representation for everyone existing outside of clear sexual or gender binaries is still lacking. The pansexual Mirror Georgiou repeats many harmful stereotypes of bi and pan people, whereas genderqueer and trans characters still do not seem to be a part of the Federation's humanity in the twenty-third century and beyond. While

Aaron Harberts had voiced plans for a trans character (Cross and Joannou, 2018, 52), he is no longer one of *DSC*'s showrunners and, at the time of writing, nothing further on queer representation has been announced for the greenlit season three of the show. While *DSC* then has made many strides for queer representation, it still has not quite caught up with the realities of American life, nor other current television, where more and more bisexual, transgender and also, if cautiously, genderqueer characters have found a home over the recent years. The franchise that has always branded itself on 'infinite diversity in infinite combination,' then, still has a lot of work to do – work that is currently still mostly done by its fans.

Works Cited

Seth Abramovitch, 'George Takei Reacts to Gay Sulu News: "I Think It's Really Unfortunate"', *The Hollywood Reporter*, 7 July (2016), https://www.hollywoodreporter.com/news/george-takei-reacts-gay-sulu-909154.

Tracy Brown, '"Star Trek Discovery" Stars Anthony Rapp and Wilson Cruz on How Gay Love Saved the Universe', *LA Times*, 21 July (2018), https://www.latimes.com/entertainment/herocomplex/la-et-hc-star-trek-discovery-love-20180721-story.html.

'Bury Your Gays', *TVTropes*, https://tvtropes.org/pmwiki/pmwiki.php/Main/BuryYourGays.

Judith Butler, *Undoing Gender* (Oxfordshire: Taylor and Francis, 2004).

David Cross and Cliff Joannou, 'Where No Gay Man Has Gone Before', *Attitude*, February (2018).

'Wilson Cruz talks Season 2 of CBS' "Star Trek: Discovery"', *BUILDSeries*, YouTube, 13 February (2019), https://www.youtube.com/watch?v=FMxclzeEJHY&t=982s.

Teresa Cutler-Broyles, 'What We See When We Look in the Mirror: Star Trek's *Alternative Sexuality*', in Nadine Farghaly and Simon Bacon (eds.) *To Boldly Go: Essays on Gender and Identity in the Star Trek Universe* (Jefferson, NC: McFarland, 2017): 41–53.

Bruce E. Drushel, 'A Utopia Denied: Star Trek and its Queer Fans', in Bruce E. Drushel (ed.) *Fan Phenomena: Star Trek* (Bristol: Intellect, 2013): 30–41.

Judith May Fatallah, *Fanfiction and the Author: How Fanfiction Changes Popular Cultural Texts* (Amsterdam: Amsterdam University Press, 2017).

'Genesis of "GIS"', *GAAAYS In SPAAACE*, https://www.gaaaysinspaaace.org/about.

David Greven, *Gender and Sexuality in Star Trek: Allegories of Desire in the Television Series and Films* (Jefferson, NC: McFarland, 2009).

'The Host (episode)', *Memory Alpha*, https://memory-alpha.fandom.com/wiki/The_Host_(episode).

Henry Jenkins, '"Out of the Closet and Into the Universe:" Queers and Star Trek', in Harry Benshoff and Sean Griffin (eds.) *Queer Cinema – The Film Reader* (New York: Routledge, 2004): 189–207.

—— '"Out of the Closet and Into the Universe:" Queers and Star Trek', in John Tulloch and Henry Jenkins (eds.) *Science Fiction Audiences: Watching Doctor Who and Star Trek* (New York: Routledge, 1995): 237–65.

—— *Textual Poachers: Television Fans and Participatory Culture* (New York: Routledge, 1992).

Katja Kanzler, *'Infinite Diversity in Infinite Combinations' – The Multicultural Evolution of Star Trek* (Heidelberg: Winter Verlag, 2004).

Spencer Kornhaber, 'The Trope of the Evil Television Bisexual', *The Atlantic*, 28 October (2015), https://www.theatlantic.com/entertainment/archive/2015/10/tvs-evil-bisexuals-still-live/412786/.

@luminousfinn, 'And it left this weeks episode in sickbay with another layer of depths too…', *Twitter*, 19 April, 2019, 05:18 p.m., https://twitter.com/luminousfinn/status/1119258895770431488.

—— 'What most younger lgbt people doesn't seem to know…', *Twitter*, 19 April, 2019, 05:18 p.m., https://twitter.com/luminousfinn/status/1119258885137813504.

'The Outcast (episode)', *Memory Alpha*, https://memory-alpha.fandom.com/wiki/The_Outcast_(episode).

'The Ready Room with Wilson Cruz', *The Ready Room*, Facebook, https://www.facebook.com/watch/?v=817244965296381.

Robin Reid, 'Thrusts in the Dark: Slashers' Queer Practices', *Extrapolation*, 50.3 (2009): 463–83.

'Rejoined (episode)', *Memory Alpha*, https://memory-alpha.fandom.com/wiki/Rejoined_(episode).

Robin Roberts, *Sexual Generations:* 'Star Trek: The Next Generation' *and Gender* (Champaign: University of Illinois Press, 1999).

John Russell, '*Star Trek: Discovery*'s Anthony Rapp on Playing the Shows First Openly Gay Character', *Out*, 5 October (2017), https://www.out.com/entertainment/2017/10/05/star-trek-discoverys-anthony-rapp-playing-shows-first-openly-gay-character.

Maria San Filippo, *The B Word: Bisexuality in Contemporary Film and Television* (Bloomington: Indiana University Press, 2013).

Andy Scahill, 'A Brand New Voyage', 8 August (2002), http://www.totallykate.com/teafive/outiname.html.

Liz Sourbut, 'Tailor Made', *Amazon.co.uk*, https://www.amazon.co.uk/gp/feature.html?ie=UTF8&docId=53485.

Eleanor Tremeer, 'How Queer Is Star Trek?', *io9*, 25 April (2019), https://io9.gizmodo.com/how-queer-is-star-trek-1834241022.

Katharine Trendacosta, 'Star Trek: Discovery Will Likely Have a Female Lead', *io9*, 10 August (2016), https://io9.gizmodo.com/star-trek-discovery-will-likely-have-a-female-lead-1785119736.

Joan Marie Verba, *Boldly Writing: A Trekker Fan and Zine History, 1967–1987*, 2nd ed. (Minneapolis, MN: FTL Publications, 2003).

'Viacom, Kaiser Family Foundation Launch 'KNOW HIV/AIDS' PSA Campaign', 6 January (2003), https://khn.org/morning-breakout/dr00015328/.

Episodes Cited

'The Trouble with Tribbles.' *Star Trek*, written by David Gerrold, directed by Joseph Pevney, Desilu Studios, 29 December, 1967.
'Judging Books by Covers.' *All in the Family*, written by Burt Styler and Norman Lear, directed by John Rich, Tandem Productions, 9 February, 1971.
'George.' *M*A*S*H*, written by Gary Markowitz and John W. Regier, directed by Gene Reynolds, 20th Century Fox Television, 16 February, 1974.
'Killing All the Right People.' *Designing Women*, written by Linda Bloodworth-Thomason, directed by Harry Thomason, Columbia Pictures Television, 5 October, 1987.
'The Host.' *Star Trek: The Next Generation*, written by Michel Horvat, directed by Marvin V. Rush, Paramount Studios, 11 May, 1991.
'The Outcast.' *Star Trek: Next Generation*, written by Jeri Taylor, directed by Robert Scheerer, Paramount Studios, 14 March, 1992.
'Rejoined.' *Star Trek: Deep Space Nine*, written by Ronald D. Moore and René Echevarria, directed by Avery Brooks, Paramount Television, 30 October, 1995.
'Stigma.' *Star Trek: Enterprise*, written by Rick Berman and Brannon Braga, directed by David Livingston, Paramount Television, 5 February, 2003.
'Congenitor.' *Star Trek: Enterprise*, written by Rick Berman and Brannon Braga, directed by LeVar Burton, Paramount Television, 30 April, 2003.
'Context is for Kings.' *Star Trek: Discovery*, written by Gretchen J. Berg, Aaron Harberts, and Craig Sweeny, directed by Akiva Goldsman, Roddenberry Entertainment, 1 October, 2017.
'Choose Your Pain.' *Star Trek: Discovery*, written by Kemp Powers, directed by Lee Rose, Roddenberry Entertainment, 15 October, 2017.
'Brother.' *Star Trek: Discovery*, written by Ted Sullivan, Gretchen J. Berg, and Aaron Harberts, directed by Alex Kurtzman, CBS Television Studios, 17 January, 2019.
'Saints of Imperfection.' *Star Trek: Discovery*, written by Kirsten Beyer, directed by David Barrett, CBS Television Studios, 14 February, 2019.
'If Memory Serves.' *Star Trek: Discovery*, written by Dan Dworkin and Jay Beattie, directed by T.J. Scott, CBS Television Studios, 7 March, 2019.
'The Red Angel.' *Star Trek: Discovery*, written by Chris Silvestri and Anthony Maranville, directed by Hanelle M. Culpepper, CBS Television Studios, 21 March, 2019.
'Through the Valley of Shadows.' *Star Trek: Discovery*, written by Bo Yeon Kim and Erika Lippoldt, CBS Television Studios, 4 April, 2019.
'Such Sweet Sorrow, Part Two.' *Star Trek: Discovery*, written by Michelle Paradise, Jenny Lumet, and Alex Kurtzman, directed by Olatunde Osunsanmi, CBS Television Studios, 18 April, 2019.

'I Never Met a Female Michael Before'
Star Trek: Discovery between Trans Potentiality and Cis Anxiety

Si Sophie Pages Whybrew

Ein Gespenst geht um in Europa – das Gespenst des Kommunismus. Alle Mächte des alten Europa haben sich zu einer heiligen Hetzjagd gegen dies Gespenst verbündet, der Papst und der Zar, Metternich und Guizot, französische Radikale und deutsche Polizisten. (Marx and Engels, 2005, 19)[1]

Star Trek and the Specter of Trans Potentiality[2]

In 1847, Karl Marx and Friedrich Engels wrote the above words in their introduction of *The Communist Manifesto*. In the English translation 'das Gespenst des Kommunismus' turns into the 'spectre of Communism' that is 'haunting Europe' and is in return being hunted by an alliance of nineteenth century European powers who seek to 'exorcise' it from their realm and arguably from memory (Marx and Engels, 1978, 473). Of course, I will be the first to admit that these words have nothing to do with either *Star Trek* or transgender identity. Nevertheless, I do feel they can be usefully employed to highlight the franchise's incessant obsession

---

[1] In the English translation from Robert C. Tucker's *The Marx–Engels Reader*, this passage reads: 'A spectre is haunting Europe – the spectre of Communism. All the Powers of old Europe have entered into a holy alliance to exorcise this spectre: Pope and Czar, Metternich and Guizot, French Radicals and German police-spies' (Marx and Engels, 1978, 473).

[2] I want to express my gratitude to the two remarkable editors of this collection, Sabrina Mittermeier and Mareike Spychala. Without their input, dedication, hard work, and expertise, this essay would not have come about. I am thankful for the opportunity to work with them on this project, for our friendship, and the time we spent together at various conferences and events.

with, and simultaneous anxiety about, transgender identification. Indeed, it is useful to highlight the *Star Trek* franchise's embeddedness within the larger, often violent and most importantly continuous Eurocentric legacy of trans erasure. When I refer to Eurocentric cultures, I follow Derek Gregory's definition of Eurocentrism as '[a] world-view that places "Europe" at the centre of human history' and is based on 'the assumption that it provides the model and master-narrative of world history: that its histories … are the norm and the rule, from which others learn or deviate' (2009, 220). This entails the conviction that 'its cultural and political systems act as the bearers of a universal Reason that maps out the ideal course of all human history' (2009, 220). According to Gregory, Eurocentrism is 'closely entwined with the projects of colonialism and imperialism' and thus 'cannot be confined to the continent of Europe. Thus, it is 'a global ideology' (2009, 221).[3] Hence, I would like to propose that, similar to the specter of communism, the mere potential of trans identification has haunted Eurocentric cultures both in their colonization efforts and at home and that *Star Trek* as a quintessential Eurocentric narrative reflects this legacy. Similarly, just as Marx and Engels assert for the specter of communism, the specter of trans potentiality has been under constant and often violent threat of eradication in Eurocentric cultures particularly since the emergence our modern gender binary in the eighteenth century.[4]

---

[3] This also includes the United States as an outgrowth of European colonialism. In fact, we might see *Star Trek* not only as an expression of Eurocentrism but also of 'Anglocentrism' in that it reflects an outlook based on 'the superiority of knowledge produced in Anglo-American contexts' and is indicative of a 'supposed neutrality of concepts and categories […] and] tend[s] to conceal the partiality and local character of Anglo-American theoretical [and in this case cultural] production and reproduce[s] it as "unlimited", "universal" or at least "transferable"' (Simonsen, 2009, 28–29).

[4] In his book *Making Sex: Body and Gender From Greeks to Freud*, Thomas Laqueur argues that the late eighteenth century saw a shift from a view of 'sexual difference as a matter of degree, gradations of one basic male type' to an understanding that 'articulate[d] sharp corporeal distinctions' between two clearly distinguished types (men and women) who were seen as 'different in every conceivable aspect of body and soul' a view supposedly based on 'discoverable biological distinctions' (2003, 5). According to Laqueur, unlike its precursor, this two-sex model sought the truth of gender in 'the stable, ahistorical, sexed body' that was used to make 'prescriptive claims about the social order' (Laqueur, 2003, 6). As Laqueur makes clear, this 'shift in the interpretation' (2003, 9) was the result of an epistemological shift in scientific thought from a focus on 'resemblances' towards difference and 'certain political circumstances' (Laqueur, 2003, 10, 11). Consequently,

As Susan Stryker points out for the United States, this anxiety about gender transgression is reflected in the proliferation of anti-cross-dressing laws that accompanied urbanization and the resulting formation of early queer communities and first wave feminist's efforts at dress reform in the nineteenth and twentieth centuries (2008, 32–35).[5] We can interpret these efforts and their contemporary counterparts as elements of a larger project to uphold the untenable, hegemonic belief in Eurocentric societies that there are, always have been, and always will be only two genders and that these genders are based on a stable, unchangeable biological truth, i.e. cisnormativity (Bauer et al., 2009, 356). Cherokee two-spirit scholar Qwo-Li Driskill connects this trend to the project of the European colonization of North America:

> Colonization has always used our genders and sexualities as a reason to attack, enslave, or 'civilize' us. ... 'Gender' is a logic, and a structural system of oppression. ... It is a wholly colonial imposition. This doesn't mean I think that our identities as men, as women, as Two-Spirit and trans people are some kind of false colonial consciousness. I do think, though, that 'gender' is a weapon to force us into clear Eurocentric categories, keep us contained in there, ensure we monitor each other's behavior, and, then, while we are distracted, take our lands. (2016, 167)

Therefore, I assert that Eurocentric societies and their associated cultural products (including science fiction) are always already marked by cisnormative anxiety about their inherent trans potentiality. As Robert Phillips points out, 'The anxiety at the root of this unease with transgender subjectivity can be traced back, in part, to a fear of the ambiguous' (2014, 20). For, as Susan Stryker makes clear, 'To encounter the transsexual

---

Laqueur emphasizes that 'Sex, in both the one sex and the two-sex worlds, is situational, it is explicable only within the context of battles over gender and power' (2003, 11).

[5] Of course, it bears mentioning that this anxiety arguably finds one of its most dramatic expressions in the surgical alteration and erasure of intersex children (Fausto-Sterling, 1993, 23; Fausto-Sterling, 2000, 8; Preves, 2003, 20; Holmes, 2009, ix–x). However, as intersexuality is not a gender identity, but rather 'an umbrella term that describes incongruity between external genitalia, internal reproductive anatomy, hormonal levels, and chromosomes,' grouping the violation of intersex children's bodily autonomy under the umbrella of trans potentiality and anxiety would be reductive even if the latter can be considered to be an outgrowth of cisnormativity (Reis, 2011, 373).

body, to apprehend a transgendered consciousness articulating itself, is to risk a revelation of the constructedness of the natural order' (2006, 254).

In the case of *Star Trek*, the franchise's ambivalent and contradictory relationship towards divergent gender identities and expressions, and the possibility of trans identification, is well documented both in scholarship and fan discussions. For example, Victoria B. Korzeniowska notes that *Star Trek: The Next Generation* (*TNG*) (1987–1994) was marked by 'obvious moves towards androgyny and sexual equality in career function' but the show ultimately 'perpetuates the prescriptive notion of gender-stereotyped behavior' in that it only allows 'minor figures to deviate from these paradigms' (1996, 19). As Jack Fennell points out, one of these deviations can be seen in the *TNG* pilot episode 'Encounter at Farpoint' in which as he puts it 'two physiologically male crewmembers can be seen wearing short-sleeved mini-dress uniforms (also called "skants") similar to those worn by Deanna Troi and various other female crewmembers' (2017, 72). Although Katharina Andres points out that these 'male dresses' also find their expression in the dress uniforms worn by central male characters such as Captain Jean-Luc Picard, she makes clear these uniforms only appear in 'very few episodes' and 'either disappear after a short time or, in case of the dress uniforms, are replaced by a less dress-like uniform consisting of a long jacket and black pants' (2013, 645).

Another example of how the show addresses the potential of divergent gender identities is through the allegory of alien species. Ironically, although the franchise might try to suggest the possibility of alternative gender identities through this strategy, it ultimately serves to reinforce cisnormativity in that it juxtaposes a human cisgender crew with alien societies that diverge from this norm and thus seems to suggest that all humans are cis, whereas trans or gender non-conforming identities are something alien to humanity. In other words, by choosing to address divergence of gender identity through the allegorical allusion of alien species, *Star Trek* ultimately places them outside the realm of intelligibility (Butler, 2004, 57). This is significant because being placed outside of the realm of intelligibility means that they 'fail to be protected by the law' (Butler, 2009, ii). Thus, this lack of intelligibility puts trans individuals in a precarious position and 'at heightened risk for harassment and violence' (2009, ii).

One of the most prominently evoked instances of this theme are the symbiotic Trill. Susan J. Wolfe (2006) describes the Trill as 'an alien race in which humanoids "join with" symbionts, slug-like creatures each of which lives in the abdominal cavity of its host, with whom it then shares a single fused consciousness.' In fact, Fennell identifies the Trill as one of 'three broad tropes' with which the franchise addresses the idea of a change in 'gender presentation or biological sex' (2017, 77). However, while 'a symbiont dwells alternatively inside males and females, the hosts are chosen for their 'suitability for joining, not his/her gender' (Wolfe, 2006). This stands in stark contrast to trans experience in which transitioning is the result of an incongruity between gender identity and gender assignment at birth (Stryker, 2008, 1). The first appearance of the Trill on *TNG* involves a romance between the doctor of the *U.S.S. Enterprise* Dr. Beverly Crusher (Gates McFadden) and a Trill ambassador named Odan. Tellingly, this romance ends abruptly when Odan's male host (Franc Luz) is killed, and the symbiont is transferred to a female host (Wolfe, 2005). Strikingly, Dr. Crusher, who had no problem continuing their relationship when Odan temporarily shared the body of her long-term friend Commander William Riker (Jonathan Frakes), ends the relationship at this point by telling Odan:

> Perhaps it is a human failing, but we are not accustomed to these kinds of changes. I can't keep up. How long will you have this host? What would the next one be? I can't live with that kind of uncertainty. Perhaps, someday, our ability to love won't be so limited. ('The Host,' 4x23)

This not only betrays the show's reluctance to address same-sex desire and love (Bernardi, 1998, 116–17; Wolfe, 2005), but also Dr. Crushers and arguably the show's unease about the possibility of gender fluidity and transition.

The franchise revisits the species on *Deep Space Nine* (*DS9*) in the form of the recurring character Jadzia Dax (Terry Farrell) – later Ezri Dax (Nicole de Boer). Interestingly, despite the troubled introduction of the Trill on *TNG*, both Jadzia and Ezri became thoroughly linked to trans identification and experience, both in academic discourse and the fandom more broadly. For example, Kathy E. Ferguson argues 'while each host is categorizable within the gender binary, the overall subject position proliferates outside of those terms' (2002, 186). Likewise, Lauren Coates of the website *The Mary Sue* writes: "Though it may not have been intentional, many fans of *Deep Space Nice* have come to view the Trill as coded representation for the transgender community" (2019). This development was likely helped by the fact that the show explored all nine, differently gendered hosts of the Dax symbiont and their relationships to one another (Ferguson, 2002, 184). As Ferguson notes, '[e]ach of the hosts, and sometimes their friends as well, plays with the gender slippage of their embodied situation' (2002, 185). Importantly, the fact that Dax was a recurring character allowed the show to explore 'the way she's treated by other characters,' which in turn offered many points of identification for 'transgender Trekkies' (Coates, 2019). For example, in an article entitled 'When I Transitioned, I Looked to Dax' on the website *Women at Warp*, Elissa Harris writes: 'She [Dax] may not be explicitly trans, but in terms of the stories that get told through her – about gender, personal change, social discomfort and assumptions based on appearances... she is very much trans' (2017). Strikingly, Harris writes of her experience with the character:

> When I saw Dax as a kid, I saw someone who had done what I wished I could do, and to my absolute shock when I finally did it myself, I discovered that Star Trek had, without me even realizing, given me a basis for at least beginning to understand what this might be like. (2017)

However, as Coates points out, 'the comparison [with trans experience] is hardly a perfect one,' but rather the identification can be seen as a result of 'a community that has seen little to no genuine representation for decades' (2019). Likewise, in an article entitled 'How *Deep Space Nine* Almost Didn't Fail Me' in *Uncanny Magazine*, David J. Schwartz notes:

> *DS9* deals with Dax's own identity conflicts on numerous occasions, but these are presented as problems of many faces, of perceptions, or of suppressed memories. Never once are we shown that Dax experiences dysphoria or agonizes over a disconnect between body and mind. (2017)

Another and arguably one of the most telling examples of this allegorical approach to alternative gender identities in *Star Trek* before *Discovery* stems from the *TNG* episode 'The Outcast' (5x17) and its presentation of the alien species of the J'naii. As Stephen Kerry describes them, the J'naii are an androgynous alien species and more importantly a society that has 'outlawed' any gender identity and forcibly corrects those among them who exhibit any signs of binary gender identification (2009, 704). Originally conceived as an allegorical attempt at presenting a gay rights argument, the episode centers on a romantic encounter between Commander Riker and a J'naii named Soren (Kerry, 2009, 704). As Kerry points out, the fact that Soren 'is played by a female actor makes the claims that this is a "gay" episode ludicrous"[6] (2009, 704–05). Instead, the episode accidentally addresses the question of gender identity and normativity when Soren reveals to Riker that she identifies as a woman (Fennell, 2017, 86). As a result of the ensuing relationship, Soren is discovered, tried, and, despite Riker's attempts to save her, forced to undergo conversion therapy (Fennell, 2017, 86).[7] While the episode might have functioned as an important critique of both conversion therapy and cisnormativity the fact that the show constructs a fictional scenario in which a gender non-conforming society oppresses those among them who identify with a binary gender (i.e. the reverse of cisnormativity) turns reality on its head and seems to suggest that non-binary individuals are a threat to binary people or aim to erase them. Thus, 'The Outcast' clearly reveals the *Star Trek* franchise's unease with trans identification. As these examples show, the *Star Trek* franchise has exhibited a continuing unease about gender non-conformity and the prospect of gender transition throughout its many iterations.[8]

---

[6] As Kerry also points out, Jonathan Frakes had originally advocated for Soren to be played by a male actor (Kerry, 2009, 205).
[7] For more on these two episodes and a general discussion of queer representation in *Star Trek*, see Sabrina Mittermeier and Mareike Spychala's essay on '"Never Hide Who You Are": Queer Representation and Actorvism in *Star Trek: Discovery*' in this volume.
[8] In addition to the examples discussed above, Stephen Kerry identifies and discusses two examples of the trope of 'the pregnant male' on *Star Trek* (2009, 706–07). It is also worth mentioning that the term 'transgender' (although in its grammatically and politically incorrect variant) appears for the first and only time in a wedding toast delivered by Lieutenant Commander Data in the movie *Star Trek: Nemesis*. Here, Data addresses the wedding party with the words 'Ladies, gentlemen, and invited transgendered species.' It should be noted that its use is not just grammatically incorrect, but also completely nonsensical. Viewers are left to ponder what 'transgendered species' might be. Are they species that always fail to identify with their assigned gender and, if so, why do they assign gender at birth despite its apparently universal fallaciousness? Or are they just species that do not fit within the purview of the apparently still universal human conception of binary gender and, if so, is it not speciecist of Data to label them as such? All we know is that they are certainly not 'ladies' or 'gentlemen' who apparently do not need to be identified according to species.

'A Surprising Name' or the Peculiar Reception of *Star Trek: Discovery*

I will now explore how the previously mentioned themes of trans potentiality and cis anxiety found their reflection in the initial reception of *Discovery*. As I will show, *Discovery*'s reviewers initially struggled to come to terms with its nascent trans potentiality. In fact, when it was announced that the show's female protagonist would bear the name 'Michael Burnham,' speculation and worry emerged among online commentators about the prospect that Michael might be *Star Trek*'s first transgender character. On the day of the announcement, *CNET*'s Amanda Kooser titled her story '"Star Trek: Discovery" Lead Gets a Surprising Character Name' and offered two explanations for this 'intriguing choice.' First, she raised the question of whether 'Michael [is] a more common woman's name in the future?' Second, she asked, 'Could the character possibly be transgender' (2017)? Likewise, *LGBTQ Nation*'s Dawn Ennis acknowledged that there thus far had been no explanation for the choice of name, but that it 'might be an awesome step in gender-neutral characters, or perhaps it's a pronunciation thing' (2017). Andrew Whalen of the website *Player.One* wondered about the 'main character with a mysterious name' and remarked that 'Michael isn't exactly known as a gender-neutral name,' but while he also suggested the possibility of a trans character, he concluded 'the most likely explanation is that Michael Burnham is part of the long *Star Trek* tradition of breaking apart traditional categorical norms' and thus chalked the name choice up to '*Star Trek*'s internationalist future, where the erasure of national boundaries has also meant the intermingling of labels and cultural signifiers' (2017). Others were far less careful in their pronouncements. The *Daily Star*'s Peter Dyke boldly asserted 'Star Trek Discovery: Netflix show to have its first ever transgender character' only to backtrack at the end of the article by pointing out: 'The transgender speculation is just a rumour' (2017). However, there were also more worried tones. On one side of the political spectrum, Michael Bedford of the website *Monkeys Fighting Robots*, while also indulging in speculations about a possible trans character, worried about the prospect of this character being portrayed by a cis actor 'yet again' (2017). On the more conservative side, a commentator on the blog *Fansided* named Ketwolski warned that 'If the writers are indeed creating our first transgender Trek character, they need to do so with caution. Put too much light on her sexuality and it becomes an SJW [social justice warrior] issue; alienating your baby-boomer crowd' (2017). The same user expressed his worries more directly in the accompanying YouTube video remarking:

> I don't mind the gay, I don't mind the bi, I don't mind the lesbian, I don't mind the transgender, I don't mind any of that stuff, but in this time period those lifestyles, those, those you know sexual orientations they are not important, none of its important. ... It's just a natural part of life, it's just there, that's just it. ... So as long as she wants to play a transgender character, that's great, but I don't want a scene where they look at the camera and they are like 'we got transgender characters, look how cool we are.' ... That's not *Star Trek* to me. (Ketwolski, 2017)

On the far right, the host of the self-titled *Dave Cullen Show* expressed outright frustration at *Discovery* having chosen the name Michael for a woman and worried about the 'infestation of *Star Trek* by social justice warriors and feminist ideology' (Cullen, 2017). Manu Saadia probably best summed up this last group of responses in the title of his article in *The New Yorker*: 'For Alt-Right Trolls, "Star Trek: Discovery" Is an Unsafe Space.' In it, Saadia, remarks that 'Many commenters ... were clearly appalled by the absence of white men in command positions' and points out that one even 'dubbed the show "Star Trek: Feminist Lesbian Edition."' Sadly, Saadia's article fails to observe the outrage over Michael Burnham's name but, importantly for this chapter, he does highlight the 'complete absence of ... even mildly gender-fluid characters in Starfleet uniforms' (2017).

As these responses reveal, the choice of the show's main character's name was troubling enough to trigger a diverse range of anxious responses. In the end, most of these speculations and worries turned out to be unfounded when Michael Burnham was revealed to be a cisgender woman who just happened to go by the name Michael. Nevertheless, later articles offered several different explanations to alleviate the seemingly ongoing mystification. In an article on *ComicBook.com*, Jamie Lovett highlights that choosing male-sounding names for female lead characters is a hallmark of the show's co-creator Bryan Fuller. Sonequa Martin-Green – the actress who plays Michael – is also quoted as saying: 'I appreciated the statement it makes all on its own to have this woman with this male name, just speaking of the amelioration of how we see men and women in the future.' Furthermore, she suggests: 'I also just decided for my creation and for my background and whatnot that I was named after my father'[9] (Lovett, 2017). Nevertheless, the fact that the name provoked so much worry and speculation and evidently demanded this much clarification is very telling, and as I will show also finds its expression on *Star Trek: Discovery* itself.

---

[9] The show's second season confirms that Michael was named after her father.

Trans Potentiality and Cis Anxiety on *Star Trek: Discovery*

'I never met a female Michael before' (1x03, 'Context is for Kings')

Interestingly enough, *Discovery* does not address the name directly in its first two episodes. In these episodes, we primarily see Michael interact with the crew of her old ship, the *U.S.S. Shenzhou*. As a result, although Michael's name might puzzle viewers given the fact that she is otherwise clearly presented and addressed as a woman, it is of little significance to the onscreen crew and thus does not merit any discussion (1x01, 'The Vulcan Hello'; 1x02, 'Battle of the Binary Stars'). This only changes when Michael arrives on the *U.S.S. Discovery* and meets her new roommate Cadet Sylvia Tilly (Mary Wiseman). In a rather comic scene, an overexcited Tilly reflects the audience's unease discussed above when she, upon hearing Michael's name, chuckles, rolls her eyes and responds 'I never met a female Michael before' and to top it off even remarks 'do you think that suits you?' Only to answer the question herself by blurting out 'I'll call you Mickey. I think that's a little more approachable.' However, her enthusiasm at resolving her own discomfort is quickly dampened when Michael drily and clearly annoyed responds, 'No, you won't.' At which Tilly shyly remarks to herself 'Oh yeah, no I won't' and observes 'the only other female Michael that I have ever heard of was Michael Burnham the mutineer. You're not her, are you?' At this, Michael slowly turns her head towards Tilly and stares at her with a serious and challenging expression (1x03).

Not only does the scene disprove the notion that gender is a non-issue or that gendered terms and names have lost their normative power in the future of *Star Trek*. More importantly, it offers the most obvious avenue of identification and recognition to trans viewers in all of the first season of *Discovery*. Although Tilly's response to Michael's name might be interpreted as a reassuring gesture towards a presumed cisgender audience in the sense of a comforting 'you are not alone in your cis anxiety,' the scene will also be familiar to trans viewers. Not only will the experience of having someone question your name or pronouns ring true with many trans folx, but the way in which Tilly tries to resolve her own discomfort by declaring 'I'll call you Mickey. I think that's a little more approachable' will be painfully familiar to them, too. Here, the 'more approachable' can be seen as a veiled demand for a more feminine gender presentation, which should also find its expression in the more playful and as such 'more feminine' name. On the other hand, Michael's clear rebuke of Tilly's imposition of identity will likely provide a point of identification and validation to trans viewers. Ultimately, this remains the only scene in which Michael's name is directly addressed throughout the first season of *Discovery*. At the same time, the show leaves no doubt about the fact that Michael seemingly has no issue with being addressed and identified as a woman. Throughout the first season, Michael is continuously addressed with female pronouns, called a 'daughter' on many occasions and neither protests nor seems to experience any discomfort at this. Also, thanks to numerous flashbacks, viewers get to witness Michael at various stages throughout her life without any radical changes in either gender identity or expression. Consequently, the show puts to rest any speculation with regards to Michael being the franchise's first human transgender character. However, as I will discuss below, this does not mark the end of *Discovery*'s apprehension towards trans potentiality.

The Tyler/Voq Story: *Star Trek: Discovery* meets the *Transsexual Empire*

Although the scene between Tilly and Michael is the most obvious example of trans potentiality and cis anxiety during the first season of *Star Trek: Discovery*, it is certainly not the most glaring display of the latter. This questionable honor belongs to a narrative arc that I will call 'the Tyler/Voq Story' or '*Star Trek: Discovery* meets the *Transsexual Empire*.' As the name indicates, this story revolves around two characters – namely, Lieutenant Ash Tyler (Shazad Latif), the chief of security aboard the *USS Discovery*, and a Klingon named Voq, who was originally the designated leader of the Klingon Empire but was deposed and forced into hiding (1x06, 'Lethe'; 1x02, 'Battle at the Binary Stars'; 1x04, 'The Butcher Cares Not for the Lamb's Cry').

When the viewers last see Voq, he is talking to L'Rell (Mary Chieffo) aboard the *U.S.S. Shenzhou* after having been abandoned there by his rival Kol (Kenneth Mitchell). In this scene, L'Rell tells him that he has lost his followers to Kol and that they will now 'have to strategize on a grander scale.' Moreover, she informs him that 'In order to convince the 24 houses to follow T'Kuvma's teachings, you must win this war.' When Voq inquires what her plan is she tells him that she will take him 'to the home of the Mo'Kai' where she will leave him 'with the matriarchs, who will expose you to things you never knew possible.' However, L'Rell warns Voq that this 'comes at a cost,' to which he inquires 'What must I sacrifice?' To this L'Rell responds with an ominous 'Everything' that is further underscored by foreboding music in the background as the camera zooms into Voq's face (1x04). This is the last that the audience sees of Voq for much of the first season.

The audience is first introduced to Tyler in the subsequent episode. Here, Tyler is a prisoner aboard a Klingon prison ship where he was tortured and raped[10] by L'Rell, his captor (1x05, 'Choose Your Pain'). After being freed by the captain of the *U.S.S. Discovery*, Tyler quickly becomes an integral part of its crew (1x05; 1x06). That is until he encounters L'Rell again during a mission to infiltrate and destroy the Klingon flagship, at which point his carefully kept facade falls apart as his memories of what happened to him are triggered causing him to have a severe panic attack (1x09, 'Into the Forest I Go'). Initially, this is explained to the audience as a result of torture-induced PTSD (1x09). This narrative begins to show cracks in the following episode that is suggestively titled 'Despite Yourself' (1x10). Here, Tyler actively seeks out L'Rell in the ship's brig to ask her what was done to him. In the ensuing scene, Tyler lowers the forcefield and the two move closer, as if they are about to kiss. However, instead, Tyler grips L'Rell by the throat in a gesture that evokes a similar scene between Voq and L'Rell aboard the *U.S.S. Shenzhou* (1x10; 1x04). When Tyler relaxes his grip on her, L'Rell begins to recite a Klingon prayer, Tyler's face twitches, and he begins to recite it with her. Not only does this scene establish a clear if troubled bond between Tyler and L'Rell, but the fact that Tyler recites the prayer with her and his reaction to it suggest that he is clearly not only suffering from PTSD but might actually be a Klingon sleeper agent that L'Rell is trying to activate (1x10).

Tyler continues to have further blackouts throughout the episode and seeks out Dr. Hugh Culber (Wilson Cruz) for help. However, rather than offering relief, the latter nervously tells him: 'it appears that the Klingons have transformed you both mentally and physically' and refuses to clear him for duty. At this, Tyler starts hearing the Klingon voice of L'Rell and breaks Dr. Culber's neck. This establishes Tyler not just as a Klingon infiltrator (Voq) disguised in a human body and hidden behind a human identity, but a dangerous infiltrator at that – a conclusion that is further underscored by Lieutenant Stamets' ghostly remark: 'The enemy is here' (1x10).

[10] I purposely use the term rape here as it reflects Tyler's remembered experience of the events. Although it may be argued that Tyler remembers consensual sexual encounters between L'Rell and her lover Voq – with whom Tyler unbeknownst shares both consciousness and body – I feel it is vital to center Tyler's experience of these memories. In fact, even if, as the show seems to suggest, Voq actively and willingly participated in these encounters, Tyler certainly did not. Indeed, Tyler himself asserts this when he confronts L'Rell in the brig and tells her, 'You forced me' (1x10, 'Despite Yourself').

Tyler is seemingly unaware of these events when he joins Michael on a mission to infiltrate the Mirror Universe's *I.S.S. Shenzhou*. In fact, he tells her, 'Whatever happens to you or me. However we change. I am here to protect you.' Nevertheless, in the next and equally suggestively entitled episode 'The Wolf Inside,' it becomes obvious that Tyler will not be able to fulfill this promise (1x11). During a mission, Tyler/Voq starts having flashbacks of T'Kuvma (Chris Obi) speaking and attacks Voq's double from the Mirror Universe. After they return to the ship, a distraught Michael confronts Tyler about his erratic and dangerous actions. During this conversation, Tyler/Voq tells her:

> I remember it all. We needed to infiltrate your ship. Learn your secrets. You were willing to betray your captain to protect your people. I sacrificed my body and mind to protect mine. I have the human's face now, but inside I remain Klingon. I remain Voq, son of none. The torchbearer. (1x11)

In response, Michael tries to reassure Tyler that Dr. Culber will find a way to help him but, to her horror, Voq replies, 'Dr. Culber saw past this feeble body into the heart and mind of a warrior, which is why I killed him.' (1x11) When Michael draws her phaser to defend herself, Voq tries to kill her but is stopped by Mirror Universe Saru (Doug Jones) and arrested. As this scene reveals, Tyler was Voq all along – even if the former was not aware of it – and used his disguise to infiltrate the *Discovery*. Further, it shows that Voq is extremely dangerous and will stop at nothing to avenge T'Kuvma or win the war. However, it also suggests an additional conclusion. Namely, that Voq unwittingly through the actions of Tyler also invaded Michael's heart and body. This latter aspect will be of particular significance for the remainder of my analysis.

At first glance, none of this has anything to do with trans identity – that is, until *Discovery* actively suggests this link in a scene from episode 1x14, which is tellingly entitled: 'The War Without, the War Within.' At this point, Voq's personality has been removed from the mind he shared with Tyler after Saru successfully convinced L'Rell to perform the removal procedure by arguing that both Voq and Tyler would die otherwise. As Saru is informed by the doctor, 'By all assessments, the patient now presents as Ash Tyler… I find no remaining evidence of Klingon aggression or muscular stamina.' When Saru inquires whether Tyler is 'Human or Klingon' now the doctor responds 'Neither, both? We can't be sure not without understanding the science behind the reassignment procedure' and suggests that they ask Tyler about it. In this context, several elements suggest an implicit connection to (outdated) medical terminology viewers may connect to discussions about trans identification. First, the fact that the doctor remarks, 'the patient now presents as Ash Tyler' may evoke this association. More importantly, the term 'reassignment procedure' is particularly problematic. In fact, it becomes even more problematic when Tyler explains the process in the following words: 'The Mo'Kai call it a choH'a.' Species reassignment protocol. Specifically designed to infiltrate classified Starfleet intelligence' (1x11). As the blogger Benny Vimes observes in a post on the website *The Orbit*, Tyler's description of the process Voq underwent as 'a species reassignment protocol' is eerily similar to the medical term 'sexual reassignment surgery.' This creates a troubling link between the Tyler/Voq invasion narrative and trans identity. Although the latter term has at this point been largely superseded by the terms 'gender affirming surgery' or 'gender confirmation surgery,' this association will likely still be evoked with many trans- as well as cisgender viewers. Hence, as Vimes points out, a potentially valuable discussion of PTSD is replaced with a narrative that 'seems to intentionally compare the experience Tyler/Voq has undergone to the experience of transgender people.' This is particularly troublesome considering all we learn about this process. As Vimes remarks:

> Voq didn't undergo this process because he deeply identified as a human. He stole the appearance, memories, and personality of a non-consenting human prisoner in order to infiltrate a group of people he wanted to harm. His identity as a Klingon never changed, nor did his values. He only underwent this process in order to trick Starfleet into thinking of him as one of them. (Vimes, 2018)

Moreover, the fact that Voq kills Dr. Culber further establishes him as a violent and dangerous intruder. As Vimes makes clear, 'Voq's behavior is exactly what those who oppose transgender people believe we do. They believe that trans women are men pretending to be women in order to infiltrate cis women's spaces and do them harm.' Hence, although the Tyler/Voq story is reflective of the general science fiction trope of alien invasion or infiltration, it is also indicative of another invasion fantasy that is explicitly transphobic. Namely, it brings to mind the transphobic fantasies about trans women invading cis women's bodies and spaces by trans exclusionary radical feminists like Mary Delay, Janice Raymond, Germaine Greer, and, most recently, Sheila Jeffreys. As my space in this chapter is limited, I will limit myself to a brief examination of the similarities between the Tyler/Voq arc and Janice Raymond's transphobic diatribes from her 1979 book *The Transsexual Empire*. As Raymond writes here,

> All transsexuals rape women's bodies by reducing the real female form to an artifact, appropriating this body for themselves. ... Rape, although it is usually done by force, can also be accomplished by deception. It is significant that in the case of the transsexually constructed lesbian-feminist, often he [sic] is able to gain entrance and a dominant position in women's spaces because the women involved do not know he [sic] is a transsexual. (Raymond, 1994, 104)

In the pages that follow this remarkable display of paranoid transphobia, Raymond attempts to establish a connection between trans women and the historical figure of the eunuch and argues that trans women similar to them function as '"keepers" of woman-identified women' in that they infiltrate their spaces and exert patriarchal control over them in order to 'rise in the Kingdoms of the Fathers' (1994, 105–06). Consequently, in Raymond's opinion, trans women only transition in order to invade cis women's spaces and exert violent control upon their unexpecting occupants. Gender-affirming medical care is portrayed as a means of deception to perpetrate violent actions. It is this image that the Tyler/Voq story invokes, regardless of whether consciously or unconsciously. In fact, although the show mainly focuses on the invasion of a seemingly safe space,[11] as I pointed out above, the show also suggests the former in that Voq, through the actions of an unaware Tyler, also invades Michael's heart and body and even tries to kill her in her own personal safe space – her quarters. This violation of her safe space and the trust she felt towards Tyler is made even worse by the fact that Michael had to be on constant guard as she interacts with the Mirror Universe crew of the *I.S.S. Shenzhou* and only found respite from this dangerous situation in her quarters and the safety she felt with Tyler. This means that *Discovery*'s horror story of the 'species reassignment protocol' just like its gothic and radical feminist precursors is indicative of an anxious fear at the realization that our 'cultural constructions of what is "natural" and "normal" are in fact illusory and fragile' (Haefele-Thomas, 2018, 111). For, as Patricia Elliot and Lawrence Lyons point out, 'The trans

---

[11] Here, the invasion of a Starfleet ship and the violation of the safety, communality, and commonality within by a Klingon in disguise can be seen as analogous to Raymond's narrative of trans women gaining access to cis women's spaces through 'deception.'

project ... makes the presumably natural unnatural, and the presumably essential merely contingent' (2017, 363). Ultimately, the way *Discovery* chooses to confront this troubling realization is particularly frustrating considering that, as Vimes suggests:

> [The writers] could have called it a 'species overlay process' or a 'body and memory swap' or any one of many other options. They chose instead to use a phrase that calls to mind the medical procedures that make so many people in our current culture deeply uncomfortable, and to amplify rather than decrease that discomfort. (2018)

Thus, whether wittingly or through lack of awareness, *Discovery* reiterates the paranoid fantasies of trans exclusionary radical feminists or radical lesbian feminist (RLF) and gives them a new lease on life, if only by association. As Elliot and Lyons make clear, in this discourse trans people must appear as dangerous because they represent 'transgressive boundary crosser[s] who undermine ... the clear boundaries marking the fixed categories of sex that are necessary for the identity of the RLF community' (2017, 362). This community is based on a discourse that identifies 'the Tyranny of masculine power' as a threat that it seeks to escape through 'the community of the feminine, defined in opposition to it' (2017, 362) a seemingly utopian vision based on the premise that 'the body itself is a natural signifier of sexual identity' (2017, 363).

A New Hope?

At this point in this chapter, I have discussed how *Star Trek: Discovery* is both indicative of trans potentiality in that it offers potential points of identification for trans viewers, but that it also invokes a transphobic legacy – due to an unfortunate choice of words – and thus reflects Eurocentric anxieties about the possibility of trans identification.

Nonetheless, this does not mean that *Discovery* is bound to continue on this troubling journey. As I see it, the ideal way for *Discovery* to maneuver itself out of this situation is to finally acknowledge humanity's inherent transness. This could be done by introducing compelling trans characters. In doing so, *Discovery* might offer a positive counter-narrative to the troubling associations evoked by the Tyler/Voq story. That being said, in its second season *Discovery* has chosen a different path. Rather than introducing trans characters, the show's writers decided to refocus the Tyler/Voq narrative on Tyler's traumatic experience. As a result, viewers see Tyler grapple with his trauma and hybrid identity as he negotiates his relationship with L'Rell, the Klingon Empire, and the Federation (2x03, 'Point of Light'). In fact, the show continues to have a strong focus on the issues of hybridity and transformation. For example, these themes also find their expression in the transformative experience of Saru (2x04, 'An Obol for Charon'), and Dr. Culber's experience of returning from the dead (2x05, 'Saints of Imperfection'). This shift away from the most troubling aspects of the Tyler/Voq narrative towards the exploration of trauma and hybrid identity offers interesting possibilities. However, the fact that *Discovery* continues to avoid any discussion of trans identities seems to be indicative of continued anxiety towards representing them on *Star Trek*.

Nevertheless, it seems important to point out that representation alone is a deeply flawed and imperfect solution. For as Reina Gosset, Eric A Stanley, and Johanna Burton remark in the introduction to their 2017 book *Trap Door: Trans Cultural Production and the Politics of Visibility*:

> while representation is often viewed as a "teaching tool" that allows those outside our immediate social worlds and identities to glimpse some notion of a shared humanity [... we] must also grapple and reckon with radical incongruities—as when, for example, our 'transgender tipping point' comes to pass at the same political moment when ... trans women of color ... are experiencing markedly increased instances of physical violence. (Gosset et al., 2017, xvi)

Consequently, I would like to end with the words of Che Gossett from the same collection. Gossett points out that trans visibility is often 'premised on invisibility' in that, in order to 'bring a select few into view,' it tends to make other less desirable subjects 'disappear into the background' and thus 'reinforces oppression.' This causes Gosset to conclude that

> The violence of colonialism and racial slavery, through which Black, queer, and/or trans identities have been forged, cannot be addressed through the politics of 'trans visibility' as these are based on 'respectability politics' that not only obfuscate liberatory trans politics ..., but ultimately offer little recourse to those of us most targeted by the prison regime and white supremacy under the guise of feminism. (2017, 183–84)

As Gossett's words illustrate, trans visibility can only ever be a small part of a much greater political struggle, and we need to interrogate it for the exclusionary norms it reproduces. Ultimately, this means that whatever form of trans representation the future of *Star Trek* may offer, it will have to be further questioned for the exclusions it creates.

Works Cited

Katharina Andres, '"Fashion's Final Frontier": The Correlation of Gender Roles and Fashion in Star Trek', *Culture Unbound*, 5 (2013): 639–49.

Greta R. Bauer, R. Hammond, R. Travers, M. Kaay, K.M. Hohenadel, and M. Boyce, '"I Don't Think This Is Theoretical; This Is Our Lives": How Erasure Impacts Health Care for Transgender People', *Journal of the Association of Nurses in AIDS Care*, 20.5, September (2009): 348–61. *PubMed. gov*, doi:10.1016/j.jana.2009.07.004.

Michael Bedford, '*Star Trek: Discovery* – Sonequa Martin-Green Finally Confirmed [SPOILERS]', *Monkeys Fighting Robots*, 6 April (2017), https://www.monkeysfightingrobots.co/star-trek-discovery-sonequa-martin-green/amp/.

Daniel Bernardi, *Star Trek and History: Race-Ing toward a White Future* (New Brunswick, NJ: Rutgers University Press, 1998).

Judith Butler, 'Performativity, Precarity and Sexual Politics', *AIBR. Revista de Antropología Iberoamericana*, 4.3 (2009): i–xiii, doi:10.11156/aibr.040303.

—— *Undoing Gender* (New York: Routledge, 2004).

Lauren Coates, 'How Transgender Star Trek Fans Came to View Jadzia Dax as Their Own', *The Mary Sue*, 9 April (2019), https://www.themarysue.com/jadzia-dax-transgender-star-trek-fans/.

Dave Cullen, *Star Trek: Discovery Is Truly God Awful (Spoilers)*, 27 September (2017), https://www.youtube.com/watch?v=aBb0hyuIfYQ.

Qwo-Li Driskill, *Asegi Stories: Cherokee Queer and Two-Spirit Memory* (Tucson: University of Arizona Press, 2016).

Peter Dyke, '*Star Trek Discovery:* Netflix Show to Have Its First Ever Transgender Character', *Daily Star*, 27 July (2017), https://www.dailystar.co.uk/showbiz-tv/hot-tv/633146/Star-Trek-Discovery-UK-Netflix-trailer-cast-Michael-Burnham-Sonequa-Martin-Green/amp.

Patricia Elliot and Lawrence Lyons, 'Transphobia as Symptom: Fear of the "Unwoman"', *TSQ: Transgender Studies Quarterly*, 4.3–4, (2017): 358–83. Duke University Press, doi:10.1215/23289252–4189874.

Dawn Ennis, 'Why Did "Star Trek" Name "Walking Dead" Star's Character 'Michael?', *LGBTQ Nation*, 3 April (2017), https://www.lgbtqnation.com/2017/04/star-trek-name-walking-dead-stars-character-michael/.

Anne Fausto-Sterling, 'The Five Sexes: Why Male and Female Are Not Enough', *The Sciences*, 33.2 (1993): 20–24. *The New York Academy of Sciences*, doi:10.1002/j.2326–1951.1993.tb03081.x.

—— *Sexing the Body: Gender Politics and the Construction of Sexuality* (New York: Basic Books, 2000).

Jack Fennell, 'Infinite Diversity in Infinite Combinations: The Representation of Transgender Identities in Star Trek', in Nadine Farghaly and Simon Bacon (eds.) *To Boldly Go: Essays on Gender and Identity in the Star Trek Universe* (Jefferson, NC: McFarland, 2017): 72–89.

Kathy E. Ferguson, "This Species Which Is Not One: Identity Practices in *Star Trek: Deep Space Nine*." *Strategies: Journal of Theory, Culture & Politics*, 15.2, November (2002): 181–95, doi:10.1080/1040213022000013894.

Che Gossett, 'Blackness and the Trouble of Trans Visibility', in Reina Gossett et al. (eds.) *Trap Door: Trans Cultural Production and the Politics of Visibility* (Cambridge, MA: MIT Press, 2017): 183–90.

Reina Gossett et al., 'Known Unknowns: An Introduction to Trap Door,' in Reina Gossett et al. (eds.) *Trap Door: Trans Cultural Production and the Politics of Visibility* (Cambridge, MA: MIT Press, 2017): xv–xxvi.

Derek Gregory, 'Eurocentrism', in Derek Gregory et al. (eds.) *The Dictionary of Human Geography*, 5th ed. (Malden: Wiley-Blackwell, 2009): 220–22.

Ardel Haefele-Thomas, 'That Dreadful Thing That Looked Like A Beautiful Girl: Trans Anxiety/Trans Possibility in Three Late Victorian Werewolf Tales', in Jolene Zigarovich (ed.) *TransGothic in Literature and Culture* (New York: Routledge, 2018): 97–115.

Elissa Harris, 'When I Transitioned, I Looked to Dax', *Women at Warp: A Roddenberry Star Trek Podcast*, 4 April (2017), http://www.womenatwarp.com/dax-trans/.

Morgan Holmes, *Critical Intersex* (Farnham: Ashgate, 2009).

Stephen Kerry, '"There's Genderqueers on the Starboard Bow": The Pregnant Male in *Star Trek*', *The Journal of Popular Culture*, 42.4 (2009): 699–714. *Wiley Online Library*, doi:10.1111/j.1540-5931.2009.00703.x.

Ketwolski, 'Is the "Star Trek: Discovery" Lead Transgender?', *Fansided*, 14 April (2017), https://redshirtsalwaysdie.com/2017/04/13/star-trek-discovery-lead-transgender/amp/.

Amanda Kooser, '"Star Trek: Discovery" Lead Gets Surprising Character Name', *CNET*, 3 April (2017), https://www.cnet.com/news/star-trek-discovery-sonequa-martin-green-michael-burnham/.

Victoria B. Korzeniowska, 'Engaging with Gender: Star Trek's "*Next Generation*"', *Journal of Gender Studies*, 5.1 (1996): 19–25. doi:10.1080/09589236.1996.9960626. *Taylor & Francis Online*.

Thomas Laqueur, *Making Sex: Body and Gender from the Greeks to Freud* (Cambridge, MA: Harvard University Press, 2003).

Jamie Lovett, 'How "Star Trek: Discovery" Lead Character Michael Burnham Was Named', *ComicBook.Com*, 23 September (2017), https://comicbook.com/startrek/2017/09/23/star-trek-discovery-michael-burnham-name/.

Karl Marx and Friedrich Engels, *Manifest Der Kommunistischen Partei* (Stuttgart: Reclam, 2005).

—— 'Manifesto of the Communist Party', in Robert C. Tucker (ed.) *The Marx–Engels Reader*, 2nd ed. (New York: Norton, 1978): 469–500.

Robert Phillips, 'Abjection', *TSQ: Transgender Studies Quarterly*, 1.1–2 (2014): 19–21. *Duke University Press*, doi:10.1215/23289252-2399470.

Sharon E. Preves, *Intersex and Identity: The Contested Self* (New Brunswick, NJ: Rutgers University Press, 2003).

Janice G. Raymond, *The Transsexual Empire: The Making of the She-Male* (New York: Teachers College Press, 1994).

Elizabeth Reis, 'Coming of Age with Intersex: XXY', in Henri G. Colt et al. (eds.) *The Picture of Health: Medical Ethics and the Movies* (Cary, NC: Oxford University Press, 2011): 372–76.

Manu Saadia, 'For Alt-Right Trolls, "Star Trek: Discovery" Is an Unsafe Space', *The New Yorker*, 26 May (2017), https://www.newyorker.com/tech/annals-of-technology/for-alt-right-trolls-star-trek-discovery-is-an-unsafe-space.

David J. Schwartz, 'How *Deep Space Nine* Almost Didn't Fail Me', *Uncanny: A Magazine of Science Fiction and Fantasy*, (2017), https://uncannymagazine.com/article/deep-space-nine-almost-didnt-fail/.

Kirsten Simonsen, 'Anglocentrism', in Derek Gregory et al. (eds.) *The Dictionary of Human Geography*, 5th ed. (Malden: Wiley-Blackwell, 2009): 28–29.

Susan Stryker, 'My Words to Victor Frankenstein above the Village of Chamounix: Performing Transgender Rage', in Susan Stryker and Stephen Whittle (eds.) *The Transgender Studies Reader*, vol. 1 (London: Routledge, 2006): 244–65.

—— *Transgender History*. (Berkeley, CA: Seal Press, 2008).

Benny Vimes, 'Trans Antagonism in Star Trek: Discovery', *The Orbit*, 8 February (2018), https://the-orbit.net/scrappy/2018/02/08/trans-antagonism-star-trek-discovery/.

Andrew Whalen, '"Star Trek: Discovery" Casts Main Character with a Mysterious Name', *Player.One*, 3 April (2017), https://www.player.one/star-trek-discovery-casts-main-character-mysterious-name-592132?amp=1.

Susan J. Wolfe, 'The Trouble with Trills: Gender and Consciousness in Star Trek', *Reconstruction*, 5.4 (2005), https://web.archive.org/web/20080614074221/https://reconstruction.eserver.org/054/wolfe.shtml. Internet Archive.

Episodes Cited

'The Host.' *Star Trek: The Next Generation*, written by Michel Horvat, directed by Marvin V. Rush, Paramount Television, 13 May, 1991.

'The Outcast.' *Star Trek: The Next Generation*, written by Jeri Taylor, directed by Robert Scheerer, Paramount Television, 14 March, 1992.

'The Vulcan Hello.' *Star Trek: Discovery*, written by Bryan Fuller and Alex Kurtzman, directed by David Semel, CBS Television, 24 September, 2017.

'Battle at the Binary Stars.' *Star Trek: Discovery*, written by Bryan Fuller, directed by Adam Kane, CBS Television, 24 September, 2017.

'Context is for Kings.' *Star Trek: Discovery*, written by Bryan Fuller, Gretchen J. Berg, and Aaron Harberts, directed by Akiva Goldsman, CBS Television, 1 October, 2017.

'The Butcher's Knife Cares Not for the Lamb's Cry.' *Star Trek: Discovery*, written by Jesse Alexander and Aron Eli Coleite, directed by Olatunde Osunsanmi, CBS Television, 8 October, 2017.

'Choose Your Pain.' *Star Trek: Discovery*, written by Gretchen J. Berg et al., directed by Lee Rose, CBS Television, 15 October, 2017.

'Lethe.' *Star Trek: Discovery*, written by Joe Menosky and Ted Sullivan, directed by Douglas Aaniokoski, CBS Television, 22 October, 2017.

'Into the Forest I Go.' *Star Trek: Discovery*, written by Bo Yeon Kim and Erika Lippoldt, directed by Chris Byrne, CBS Television, 12 November, 2017.

'Despite Yourself.' *Star Trek: Discovery*, written by Sean Cochran, directed by Jonathan Frakes, CBS Television, 7 January, 2018.

'The Wolf Inside.' *Star Trek: Discovery*, written by Lisa Randolph, directed by T.J. Scott, CBS Television, 14 January, 2018.

'The War Without, the War Within.' *Star Trek: Discovery*, written by Lisa Randolph, directed by T.J. Scott, CBS Television, 4 February, 2018.

'Point of Light.' *Star Trek: Discovery*, written by Andrew Colville, directed by Olatunde Osunsanmi, CBS Television, 31 January, 2019.

'Obol for Charon.' *Star Trek: Discovery*, written by Jordon Nardino, Gretchen J. Berg, and Aaron Harberts, directed by Lee Rose, CBS Television, 7 February, 2019.

'Saints of Imperfection.' *Star Trek: Discovery*, written by Kirsten Beyer, directed by David Barrett, CBS Television, 14 February, 2019.

Veins and Muscles of the Universe
Posthumanism and Connectivity in
Star Trek: Discovery

Lisa Meinecke

Star Trek: Discovery does not just take us back to the time of the Klingon Wars; it also introduces us to a never before seen class of spaceships, the *Crossfield* class. The *U.S.S. Discovery*, NCC-1031, is Starfleet's state-of-the-art science vessel, with the capacity for a complement of 136 officers (1x05, 'Choose Your Pain') and 300 science projects at top clearance level. As many of the experiments conducted onboard are top secret or black ops, the *Discovery* is heavily armed and secured by Starfleet's intelligence forces. The ship's scientific endeavors are applied science; while the *Discovery* is deployed to explore the universe, the research conducted here aims to develop technologies for Starfleet's military branch (1x03, 'Context is for Kings'). The main, and most secret, research project is the displacement-activated spore hub drive: an experimental propulsion system installed in addition to the typical warp and impulse drives. Both spaceships of the *Crossfield* class, the *Discovery* and her sister ship, the *U.S.S. Glenn*, are equipped with this technology, enabling and employing the research of *Discovery*'s astromycologist Lieutenant Paul Stamets (Anthony Rapp) and Straal (Saad Siddiqui), his counterpart on the *Glenn*. Stamets' and Straal's research centers on a species of fungus called *prototaxites stellaviatori*, whose root network is spread over a subspace domain covering the entire universe. As Stamets explains, the spores of *prototaxites stellaviatori* are the 'progenitors of panspermia,' 'the building blocks of energy across the universe' (1x03). Its mycelium comprises the 'veins and muscles that hold our galaxies together' (1x03). The mycelium is a biophysical organic structure that enables quantum entanglements and thus connects all organisms of the universe across spacetime. The astromycologists have discovered that the mycelium can function as a network of pathways, which can be accessed by the fungal spores, 'an infinite number of roads, leading everywhere' (1x03), and developed an experimental drive system in order to travel the mycelium with the help of the spores, the aforementioned spore drive.

***

As this spore drive takes a pivotal role in many of the show's narratives, literally driving the plot along over the course of the first season, this essay aims to set a spotlight on this system, to analyze its entanglements with the multiverse, the ship, and the crew. Furthermore, the spore drive will be contextualized in the canon of the franchise, tracing reconfigurations and new imaginations of older narratives at the core of *Star Trek*. The drive system and its entanglements will be juxtaposed with *The Next Generation*'s (*TNG*) Data and the Borg. This will enable analysis of *Discovery*'s reimagination of connectivity and embedded cybernetic embodiment, opening up new spaces for an overarching posthumanist critique of the franchise.

As all fungal root networks, *Star Trek: Discovery*'s mycelium is rhizomatic in nature, and I will turn to the work of French philosophers Gilles Deleuze and Félix Guattari to grasp the multiplicities of mycelial interconnections and entanglements. Deleuze and Guattari employ the concept of fungal roots to express an ontology of radical, anti-hierarchical, de-centralized connectivity. The aim of this analysis is not to equate the fictional mushroom of *Star Trek: Discovery* with this imagery simply for the convenience of relating one mushroom root to another, but the rhizome appears useful as an inherently chaotic ontology: 'any point of a rhizome can be connected to anything other, and must be' (Deleuze and Guattari, 2008, 7). The rhizome is therefore not only an objection to any kind of ontological (or epistemological, for that matter) hierarchy or structural order, but also the idea of radically de-centralized connectivity that creates meaning, that is in a constant state of flux (Deleuze and Guattari, 2008, 21).

The second figuration in this essay's analysis is Donna Haraway's seminal cyborg, 'a cybernetic organism, a hybrid of machine and organism, a creature of social reality as well as a creature of fiction' (1991, 145). The cyborg will help us shed light on posthumanist narratives in *Star Trek: Discovery*, on the blurring of boundaries between organism and machines, on the connection between the drive and the mycelium, and the way human and non-human agencies are constituted in relation to that boundary. However, the cyborg, as understood by Haraway, is also a metaphor for a radical social and feminist politics, and we would do well to remember that:

> Cyborg feminists have to argue that 'we' do not want any more natural matrix of unity and that no construction is whole. Innocence, and the corollary insistence on victimhood as the only

ground for insight, has done enough damage. But the constructed revolutionary subject must give late-twentieth-century people pause as well. In the fraying of identities and in the reflexive strategies for constructing them, the possibility opens up for weaving something other than a shroud for the day after the apocalypse that so prophetically ends salvation history. (Haraway, 1991, 157–58)

The story of the spore drive and Stamets' entanglements with it is not merely about a new spaceship propulsion system troubling the narrative conventions of a well-established franchise, but also a political statement about cosmic ecology and a deconstruction of the discursive binaries between machine and organism, nature and technology, individual subjectivity and collective embeddedness. Rosi Braidotti describes posthuman knowledge as an epistemology that 'enacts a fundamental aspiration to principles of community bonding, while avoiding the twin pitfalls of conservative nostalgia and neo-liberal euphoria' (Braidotti, 2013, 11). Working with the cyborg and Braidotti's critical posthumanism, which is, not incidentally, strongly influenced by Deleuzian nomadic thought, means to engage with a problematization of the autonomous subject and also with a wholehearted declaration for and affirmation of the subjectivities of the Other.

This frame is, however, troubled by Haraway's rejection of Deleuzian concepts. Linda Williams points out that

> Haraway's critical dispute with Deleuze and Guattari is essentially founded on questions of degree in measuring the relations of interdependence between the human and the non-human world, along with differing perspectives on the most effective means to develop awareness of such processes of interdependence. (Williams, 2009, 44)

Haraway's conceptualization of interspecies companionship has little consideration for Deleuze and Guattari's disdain towards domestication in favor of the pack: 'The dumb subject who, for Deleuze and Guattari appears to represent "the masses," for Haraway is a subject that communicates quite regularly with non-human alterity, if only in daily conversations with the family pet' (Williams, 2009, 49). While both sides argue against a strict binary and power hierarchy between humans and non-human animals, the point of contention is in the perspective on interspecies entanglements. For this analysis it is important to point out that Haraway's ontologies are grounded in materialism, unlike Deleuzian becomings, which constitute 'a becoming conscious, and a becoming active in human relations with a non-human world conceived as a perpetual process of interaction, flux and communication' (Williams, 2009, 50).

***

While *Star Trek* has always been known for its staunchly enlightened liberal humanism, *Discovery* allows for the potential to take a step further by introducing the mycelium. Universal liberal humanism (commonly attributed to franchise creator Gene Roddenberry) is a mindset that centers on the inherent goodness and rationality of mankind and rests on a linear teleology of progress. According to Braidotti, '[f]aith in the unique, self-regulating and intrinsically moral powers of human reason forms an integral part of this high-humanistic creed' (Braidotti, 2013, 13). In *Star Trek*, humanity has progressed to a bright, enlightened future, all social hardships and struggles have been transcended. Mankind has joined together as one and endeavors to explore the galaxy, driven by inherent curiosity and thirst for adventure (*TNG*, 1x26, 'The Neutral Zone'). Here, human connection is created on the basis of rationality and humanist values. Alien species encountered throughout the galaxy are held to these standards of humanity, and, if they are able to share these value systems, can be enfolded into the Federation, and thus human society. What lies at the heart of the utopian vision of the *Star Trek* franchise are the strengths of liberal humanism: an ever-optimistic trust in mankind, grounded in belief in equality, rationality, and human dignity.

However, liberal humanism has increasingly come to be criticized for lacking consideration for the lived realities of society as well as for the consequences of structural imbalances of power. Humanism has little space for diverse perspectives and, at its worst, is ignorant to the struggles of marginalized people due to its central focus on universalist values. Braidotti explains:

> Central to this universalistic posture and its binary logic is the notion of 'difference' as pejoration. Subjectivity is equated with consciousness, universal rationality, and self-regulating ethical behaviour, whereas Otherness is defined as its negative and specular counterpart. In so far as difference spells inferiority, it acquires both essentialist and lethal connotations for people who get branded as 'others'. These are the sexualized, racialized, and naturalized others, who are reduced to the less than human status of disposable

bodies. We are all humans, but some of us are just more mortal than others. (2013, 15)

Steering away from older Trek traditions, *Discovery* allows us to imagine a different vision of the future, which values and celebrates the intricacies of living in a pluralistic society. The mycelium establishes a network of common threads connecting and balancing all living things in the multiverse, no matter how different. *Discovery*'s mission succeeds not because of humanity's intrinsic potential for progress, but specifically by allowing space for difference, for a multitude of perspectives, and by taking the Other seriously. As Anna Tsing states in her seminal work about the (non-fictional) matsutake mushroom, '[f]ungi are thus world builders, shaping environments for themselves and others' (2015, 138). The mycelium's purpose is exactly this: connecting and balancing the universe and all living things; the nature of the universe can thus be considered organic. Tsing also explains the rhizomatic properties of fungal roots:

> Mycorrhizas form an infrastructure of interspecies interconnection, carrying information across the forest. They also have some of the characteristics of a highway system. Soil microbes that would otherwise stay in the same place are able to travel in the channels and linkages of mycorrhizal interconnection. Some of these microbes are important for environmental remediation. Mycorrhizal networks allow forests to respond to threats. (2015, 139)

The spore drive makes use of this highway function of the mycelium of *prototaxites stellaviatori*. Straal and Stamets were able to develop a propulsion system that enables a starship to travel the mycelium in small 'jumps' (1x03). At the beginning of the series, both the *Discovery* and the *Glenn* have been able to employ their experimental spore drives in this way. However, the system is highly unstable and volatile as the ship computers are unable to select, secure, and navigate single *hyphae* of the mycelium to reach a specific, predetermined location in the universe. Stamets on the *Discovery* is cautious in the face of this danger as well as cautious of Starfleet's goal of using his research in the war against the Klingons; he keeps his jump attempts limited. This is an ongoing source of tension between himself and Captain Lorca (Jason Isaacs) who, as we find out over the course of the season, intends to use the spore drive technology to transfer back to his home, the alternative Mirror Universe. Stamets' colleague, however, is less restrained and attempts progressively longer jumps over further distances, resulting in an accident with catastrophic consequences, killing the entire crew, including Straal himself (1x03).

Investigating the ruins of the *Glenn*, the *Discovery*'s away team discovers an aggressive and monstrous alien creature, which has killed an entire Klingon landing party, obviously in pain and distress. The creature is transferred to the *Discovery* for the purpose of investigating its role in the *Glenn*'s accident. Specialist Michael Burnham (Sonequa Martin-Green), who is a xenoanthropologist by training and experienced in studying alien life, is tasked with examining the still raging creature. Despite the alien's aggressive panicked rage, which results in the death of security chief Ellen Landry (Rekha Sharma), Burnham realizes that it is, in fact, not merely a predator, but that it lives in symbiosis with the fungus and its spores. In fact, the alien resembles a gigantic tardigrade and shares some of the properties of this earth animal, its physical resilience to extreme environmental conditions and, most interestingly, the capacity to incorporate the DNA of the fungus into its own genetic makeup via a process of horizontal gene transfer (Arakawa and Blaxter, 2018, 17). By sharing DNA with the fungus, the animal gains access to the mycelial network and is able to travel the universe with the help of the spores, a natural spore drive (1x04, 'The Butchers Knife Cares Not for the Lambs Cry'; 1x05, 'Choose Your Pain').

***

Jon Wagner and Jan Lundeen frame the role of DNA in the storytelling traditions of *Star Trek* as a regularly used plot device that functions twofold; to invoke notions of scientific rationality on the one hand, but also to 'stand in for the antique metaphysics of teleological predestination and invisible essences' on the other: 'throughout all of Trek's post-1960s corpus, DNA is used in a mystical sense, in which these humble replicating proteins take on cosmic metaphysical role as the keepers of the sacred essence and destiny of a person, race or species' (Wagner and Lundeen, 1998, 153).

Star Trek: Discovery relies clearly on these narrative traditions when it comes to the relationship between the tardigrade and the mycelium. By incorporating the foreign DNA of the fungus, the tardigrade is not merely in symbiosis with the network, it takes part in it and shares some of its basic substance (in the Aristotelian sense; see Wagner and Lundeen, 1998, 151). Here, as indicated by Wagner and Lundeen, the incorporation of the fungal DNA by the alien tardigrade is ostensibly grounded in scientific reality, but also the somewhat mystical impetus of what Deleuze and Guattari call a becoming: an intimate connection between organisms, an entanglement that creates a new multiplicity and changes all participants involved in symbiosis on a substantial level (Deleuze and Guattari, 2008, 238–39) and ties together all life. 'Each multiplicity is symbiotic; its becoming ties together animals, plants, microorganisms, mad particles, a whole galaxy' (250) and 'each multiplicity is already composed of heterogeneous terms in symbiosis, and that a multiplicity is continually transforming itself into a string of other multiplicities, according to its thresholds and doors' (249). Deleuze and Guattari point out that these multiplicities are defined and shaped by their borders and that the borderline is constituted by the Outsider or Anomalous, who secures the stability of the processes of becoming and sets the course for the lines of flight, for the pathways of the rhizome:

> Each multiplicity is defined by a borderline functioning as Anomalous, but there is a string of borderlines, a continuous line of borderlines (fiber) following which the multiplicity changes. And at each threshold or door, a new pact? A fiber stretches from a human to an animal, from a human or an animal to molecules, from molecules to particles, and so on to the imperceptible. Every fiber is a Universe fiber. A fiber strung across borderlines constitutes a line of flight or of deterritorialization. It is evident that the Anomalous, the Outsider, has several functions: not only does it border each multiplicity, of which it determines the temporary or local stability (with the highest number of dimensions possible under the circumstances), not only is it the precondition for the alliance necessary to becoming, but it also carries the transformations of becoming or crossings of multiplicities always farther down the line of flight. (Deleuze and Guattari, 2008, 249)

Stamets and Burnham realize that the missing element necessary to stabilize the *Discovery*'s spore drive system is exactly the tardigrade, anchoring it in the position of the Outsider in the multiplicities that come into existence when the drive is connected to the mycelium. The animal can be employed as a living computer, functioning as navigator for the drive and therefore granting safe passage through the mycelium. They also realize that Straal had started to work on interface technology in order to connect the tardigrade to the drive system (1x04). According to the Federation's central ideological principles, the animal needs to be a willing participant in the navigation process. However the insistence of Burnham, Stamets, and medical officer Dr. Culber (Wilson Cruz) on protecting the tardigrade's dignity is contested by Starfleet's desire to build more spore drives and capture more tardigrades, in order to replicate *Discovery*'s propulsion system beyond the prototype (1x05). For Starfleet, the tardigrade is a working animal, more of a material resource and logistical support than a sentient participant in a complex collaboration (Braidotti, 2013, 70).

***

Since Burnham and Stamets are unable to communicate with the animal directly, and it seems to suffer under the conditions of the jumps, Stamets proposes an alternative plan: a human volunteer could be genetically manipulated with the tardigrade's DNA, in order to take its place in symbiosis with the mycelium and to function as human computer in the navigation system of the drive. This plan is rejected instantly by Acting Captain Saru (Doug Jones), who has taken command after Captain Lorca was kidnapped by the Klingons, reminding us that genetic engineering is illegal in the Federation (as are all eugenic experiments). Saru, enacting his interpretation of Lorca's authoritarian style of command, decides to integrate the tardigrade into the system without its explicit consent, reasoning that the physical resilience of the animal will ensure it comes to no harm (1x05).

The drive connects the ship to the mycelium, which is connected to the tardigrade at the interface, creating a complex cybernetic multispecies assemblage. *Discovery* can use the animal's mind to create a star map to the mycelium and is therefore now able to jump across the known universe in an instant. Deleuze and Guattari also use the image of a map to describe the rhizome:

> The map is open and connectable in all of its dimensions; it is detachable, reversible, susceptible to constant modification. It can be torn, reversed, adapted to any kind of mounting, reworked by an individual, group, or social formation. It can be drawn on a wall, conceived of as a work of art, constructed as a political action or as a meditation. Perhaps one of the most important characteristics of the rhizome is that it always has multiple entryways. (2008, 12)

The rhizome of the mycelium includes the *Discovery* on its jumps, they are connected to the tardigrade and the fungus in a symbiotic process of becoming-with. *Discovery* now has access to the multiplicities of possible pathways across the universe, to an infinite number of possible entrances, but also to an equally infinite number of exits. The computing power of the tardigrade's mind, embedded in the mycelium, enables secure jumps over extremely large distances. *Discovery* now has the ability to travel any place in the known universe in an instant.

However, the activation of the spore drive comes at considerable cost. While the tardigrade is capable of coping with the extreme physical strain of having to navigate the ship through the mycelium, the animal still seems to suffer. The technology scavenged from the *Glenn* is not designed for being particularly gentle to the navigator: interfacing the tardigrade with the drive involves two big robotic arms with large needles piercing the body of the animal to connect to its neural networks (1x04, 1x05). Burnham notes that the animal seems 'incredibly regenerative, but with each jump *Discovery* makes, it cries out. And the last 48 hours, it seems sluggish. Depressed.' (1x05). Acting Captain Saru rejects Burnham's concerns and orders her to keep the drive system running as, due to the animal's extreme physical strength and resilience, there are no clear harmful impacts measurable. The tardigrade's mental state deteriorates more and more with every jump and, in a crucial moment, when the *Discovery* is threatened by a Klingon ship, the animal goes into stasis. Saru is willing to act against the Federation's principle and orders Stamets to revive the tardigrade, even though Dr. Culber cautions that this will likely cause its death. Unwilling to be responsible for the creature's continued suffering, Stamets injects himself with the tardigrade's DNA and takes its place as the ship's navigator, against Saru's orders and the laws of the Federation (1x05).

***

Unlike the tardigrade – which is freed and released into space to travel the mycelium – Stamets is a willing, and in fact enthusiastic participant as navigator of the drive system. Dr. Culber creates small implants for Stamets' forearms for the drive to be plugged into and redesigns the interface technology to enable a minimally invasive connection to the ship's system (1x07, 'Magic to Make the Sanest Man Go Mad'), since Stamets' human body does not have the same physical strength and regenerative properties as the tardigrade's. Still, the procedure changes Stamets. He is in a process of becoming-with the tardigrade and the mycelium, intensified by the physical demands of the drive. While integrated into the drive, Stamets becomes part of the multiplicities of the mycelium. This process is continuous and transformative. Integrated into the drive system, Stamets steps apart from *Discovery* and allies himself to the mycelium and the tardigrade: in his liminal position between the ship and the network, he receives the ability to cross these boundaries and gain access to new pathways.

Stamets takes on the tardigrade's position in the drive system and thus the ability to navigate through and thus communicate with the network, he commits to an alliance with the mycelium. His mind and, in fact, his body are quite literally opened to another plane of existence. This manifests at first in a state of somewhat uncharacteristic euphoria and affection towards his friends and colleagues; after all, Stamets just connected to all living things in a profoundly spiritual, transcendent experience (1x07). However, he slowly starts to slip, because his consciousness is not equipped to sustain a prolonged state of entanglement with all cosmic life. The side-effects of being entangled with the spore drive include existing simultaneously in the *Discovery*'s original dimension and the mycelial plane, which allows Stamets to remain outside of Harry Mudd's (Rainn Wilson) time loop (1x07), but Stamets' mind also slips deeper into the mycelium and he starts to have flashes of an alternative reality (1x08, 'Si Vis Pacem, Para Bellum').

Later in the season, the spore drive and Stamets' connection becomes integral to Lorca's betrayal of his crew and the ships' voyage to and back from the alternative Mirror Universe (1x09, 'Into the Forest I Go'; 1x13 'What's Past Is Prologue'). Stamets gets stuck in the mycelium and loses his ability to cross the borderline back to *Discovery* due to manipulations by his Mirror Universe counterpart, who has worked to create a massive reactor, not only providing power to a huge spaceship, but also to a weapon capable of destroying entire planets. The network cannot sustain this draining of mycelial energy and starts to collapse due to the imbalance, threatening all life in the multiverse. Stamets also meets his newly deceased partner Dr. Culber in the network and their relationship strengthens Stamets' connection to the mycelium. Culber also warns Stamets of the deterioration of the network caused by its weaponization in the Mirror Universe (1x12, 'Vaulting Ambition'). Secure in his entanglements with the network and with the help of Ensign Tilly's efforts to save him, he is able to return to the *Discovery* and, having fully leaned into his connection with the network, gains the ability to use the spore drive securely and without the threat of losing himself in the network. This ultimately allows him to guide *Discovery* back to its home universe (1x13).

However, the fungus – and thus the spore supply for the drive – on *Discovery* have already been corrupted and died. Stamets realizes that he has to destroy the *I.S.S. Charon*'s reactor in order to allow the mycelium to regenerate, but the only option is to use the entire remaining spore supplies on *Discovery*, load them into torpedoes and shoot them into the reactor core. *Discovery* is able to coast home on the shock wave of mycelial energy, navigated by Stamets plugging back into the drive system. Navigating the regenerating rhizome almost causes him to lose his way, but he is successfully able to balance his connections to the drive and the network by relying on his relationship with Culber and his advice to find the 'clearing in the forest' (1x13). He is able to lead *Discovery* home, but overshoots, arriving nine months in the future, when the war with the Klingons has already been lost.

***

The mycelial network is a multispecies rhizome, entangling and empowering all life. Stamets' drive technology is an extremely powerful transhumanist cybernetic biotechnology at the interface to this network. As such, these narratives are not unknown to *Star Trek*; *Discovery* here takes a new spin on stories that have been told in earlier incarnations of the franchise. The question of the ethics of using the tardigrade as a navigator to the detriment of the creature is strongly reminiscent of *Star Trek: Voyager's* double episode 'Equinox' (5x26, 6x01). In this episode the *Voyager* encounters another Starfleet ship, the *Equinox*, which has also been displaced to the Delta Quadrant. It turns out that the *Equinox* crew have been killing aliens from a different dimension to boost their warp drive capacity. Similar to *Discovery*'s decision to plug the tardigrade into the spore drive, this was originally a crisis decision. Unlike *Voyager*, *Equinox* had not been able to make friends or allies in the Delta Quadrant and had been in a constant struggle with hostile aliens and perpetually threatened by a lack of resources to keep going. The alien species starts to attack *Equinox* in self-defense, which further alienates the ship's crew from the idea that these beings are lifeforms that should be respected. They are now a hostile enemy species and killing them may be morally wrong, but also considered to be necessary to be able to travel through the inhospitable Delta Quadrant towards the Federation's safe havens.

Saru's decision to employ the tardigrade as navigator is motivated by a similarly existential anxiety: just like the *Equinox*, he has to cope with the loss of a stable command structure and feels constantly threatened by his environment. The difference: as soon as *Voyager* finds out about what is happening on the *Equinox*, Captain Janeway (Kate Mulgrew) tries everything in her power to curtail further use of the aliens for fuel. She is acting within the ethical framework of the Federation's principles, which requires her to protect the alien life forms. She is, simply put, not having any of it. Lorca, however, has no particular qualms about harming an alien life form and orders Stamets, Culber, and Burnham to disregard any signs that the creature is suffering, thus proving his speciesism and foreshadowing the later revelation of his fascist character. Saru's role in this is slightly more complex due to his anxious disposition. As indicated above, and shown in episode 1x08 in full consequence, Saru always feels threatened and is always in crisis. He explains early on:

> Your world has food chains. Mine does not. Our species map is binary; we are either predator or prey. My people were hunted, bred, farmed ... we are your lifestock of old. We were biologically determined for one purpose, and one purpose alone – to sense the coming of death. (1x01, 'The Vulcan Hello')

This is instrumentalized by Lorca, whose aggressive military actions further heighten the Kelpien's sense of continuous danger. After the creature goes into stasis, he tells Burnham to 'pry it open if you have to' (1x05). In crisis mode, and under pressure to recover the kidnapped Captain Lorca, Saru does not stop to consider the possible ethical ramifications of his actions and he is also willing to accept the consequences of causing harm to a creature for the benefit of his crew. He rejects not only Burnham's advice, because he considers her a threat, blaming her for starting the Klingon war and the death of Captain Georgiou (Michelle Yeoh), but he refuses to communicate with his crew about the best possible strategy to ensure Lorca's safe return. Instead he decides to mirror Lorca's militaristic authoritarianism and decides that harming the tardigrade is an acceptable means to the end of saving the captain. He almost seems resentful of the creature for its physical resilience. In his crisis, he shows little sympathy to a being very different from himself: for the Kelpien, who is by nature easily hurt and defenseless, the tardigrade's physical power and strength must seem extremely alienating.

In *Star Trek*, there is a tradition of employing imaginations of the posthuman to sharpen the liberal humanism at the core of the franchise. In *TNG* (1987–1994), the android Data is on a quest to become more human, precisely to illustrate what makes us human: 'The Next Generation's depiction of identity centers on the liberal production of the human self as one driven by becoming. Becoming is, of course, the context in which subjectivity is constituted as an ongoing and never-complete process of performances' (Cover, 2011, 209). Data's story exemplifies this idea of what being human means in *Star Trek*. He is one of the arguably few characters in *TNG* who undergoes a significant character development over the course of the show, because the franchise's core ideology requires him to try to perform 'being human' in progressively complex ways: his personal rights are a matter of ongoing debates (*TNG*, 2x09, 'Measure of a Man'; *TNG*, 3x16 'The Offspring'), he tries his hand in various creative activities ranging from painting to poetry, keeps a pet, and cultivates strong friendships with the *Enterprise*'s crew. For the android character, this is about fitting into the cultural and social environment of the *Enterprise*, his quest to become as human as possible is as much about the ideal of enlightened humanism as it is about a marginalized character trying to pass in a hegemonic culture. Data himself states: 'If being human is not simply a matter of being born flesh and blood, if it is instead a way of thinking, acting and... feeling, then I am hopeful that one day I will discover my own humanity' (*TNG*, 4x11, 'Data's Day'). Data facing everyday social life on the *Enterprise* therefore defines what humanness means on the ship and on the show. The show's humanist core shines particularly brightly when Data struggles or makes mistakes, in instances where he enacts his becoming-person.

The android's story is both framed and contested by the introduction of the posthuman other in a number of different incarnations. On the planet on which he was originally found, the *Enterprise* crew discovers the dismembered parts of Data's 'brother' Lore (*TNG*, 1x12, 'Datalore'), an android of the same model, but with a crucial addition: a computer chip that allows Lore to express human emotion, which Data himself lacks. However, despite his apparent superior skill set, Lore proves to be erratic, ruthless, violent, and unwilling to adapt to Starfleet's cultural norms. Where Data tries to integrate into Federation society, Lore considers himself inherently logically and physically superior to humankind and thus rejects the show's anthropocentric ideology by striving for posthuman supremacy, a conflict at the heart of many narratives about the technicized other. Data's process of becoming is highlighted through the lens of his potential to become posthuman, which is then further problematized by the Borg.

***

The Borg collective became arguably the most iconic antagonists of the entire franchise, precisely because they stand fundamentally and diametrically opposed to Starfleet's (and, specifically, Picard's) liberal humanism. They are a hivemind of cybernetic drones without any personal identity in search of control, order, and perfection, which they aim to achieve by relentlessly conquering other species and integrating them into their collective, assimilating them. The assimilation process requires the members of the species to become Borg. They are not only integrated into the hive, but their bodies are also altered substantially in order to turn them into drones. Arms, eyes, and other body parts are crudely replaced by technology and physical functions are partly replaced by interfaces to the collective; Borg drones do not need food or sleep. In *TNG*'s production context, their mindless totalitarianism serves as a compelling representation of Cold War socio-politics and technology. Robert Tindol points out:

> The Borg ... are a state of mind and a "bad idea" rather than a racial or perhaps even an ethnic identity. Seemingly paralleling anti-Communism in its most paranoid manifestations, the fear of the Borg is the fear of a dire fate to which death is decidedly preferable. "Better morgue than Borg" may not have quite the ring that "better dead than red" possessed, but a tempting assumption is that the creation of the Borg for the 1980s *Star Trek: The Next Generation* television series was in keeping with the longstanding employment of movie and television genres as metaphoric encounters with the Soviet Union. (Tindol, 2012, 152)

The Borg thus signify the opposite of the core values of the Federation. Their collective rhizomatic hivemind stands opposed to the franchise's focus on the autonomous subject: the Borg are neither autonomous, nor subjects. Therefore, they are a danger to everything Starfleet values, from personal identity to cultural pluralism and diplomacy, but they also serve as a mirror narrative to problematize *Star Trek*'s ideological set up. Daniel Bernardi points this out in his influential book *Star Trek and History: Race-ing Toward a White Future*:

> Bent on assimilating civilization into its mechanistic way of life, the Borg actually start with the Enterprise – a small city itself. They then proceed to 'assimilate' the Enterprise crew in hopes of changing the past to dominate the future. The result is a multiracial mass that threatens the humanistic world of the democratic Federation and its all-too-white heroes. (1998, 87–88)

Both Starfleet and the Borg share progressivist and imperialist politics which are in many ways quite similar. Starfleet strives to create a better society through political union with other species and integrating them into a *Leitkultur* consistently dominated by human and Vulcan cultures, the Borg aim for perfection through order and homogeneity through a radicalized concept of sameness. Considering this, the Borg are not only iconic enemies in a show that does not usually go for 'dark' or 'edgy' content, but also open up space for a possible critical reading of *Star Trek*'s ideology. This furthermore enables a critical examination of liberal humanism itself, an idea that has come to be increasingly contested particularly in academic humanities and cultural studies. Mia Consalvo argues for the Borg:

> Putting aside their conquering tendencies, the Borg live as one – all voices are equal, all work is shared. Isolation is not an option, discord is unknown. For human society struggling with increasing alienation, rage and fear, this way of life may be tempting, at least on some levels. The Borg offer another way of doing things. (2004, 197)

Here, the Borg have come to be considered not only a mirror narrative contesting the Federation's humanism, but also a genuinely desirable political alternative. Whether or not one is assimilated into the collective or not almost seems to come down to a personal lifestyle choice.

***

To summarize, the cybernetic Borg collective is commonly read as cyborgs as introduced in Haraway's cyborg manifesto. In some ways this interpretation is an obvious one, since the Borg are, well, cyborgs. They lack a clear origin story, they are both technological and organic, a collective lacking race or gender, and they are direct descendants from the Cold War military industrial complex. However, as explained above, Haraway's cyborgs are as much about science fiction as they are about a material reality (Haraway, 1991, 150), they are a social metaphor for a radically emancipatory politics of hybridity that transcends dichotomies between nature and culture, male and female, productive and reproductive work. Cynthia Fuchs reads *TNG* 4x01 ('The Best of Both Worlds, Part Two') through the lens of Haraway's cyborg:

> Profoundly challenging the notion of an embodied and discrete masculine identity, this image of a penetrated, ungendered and unfamiliar Picard collapses conventional binary terms of difference: self and other, desire and repulsion, culture and nature, death and life. Simultaneously absorbing and punctured by multiple inorganic

implants, Picard's is a white male body in crisis, contestable, without desire or agency, and spectacularly incorporated. (1995, 282)

This is where a reading of the Borg through the lens of the *Manifesto* fails: as cyborg collectives go, the crude assemblages of bulky technology and violated organism are simply not particularly hybrid. There are no liminalities between their organic and their machinic parts; part of what makes the Borg an effective body is that their bodies are roughly pieced together and lack cohesion. Their totalitarianism reterritorializes the rhizome of their hive mind, their potential for connectivity and new multiplicities are curtailed by their desire for radical sameness and total normativity. While the monstrosity of the drone bodies does just barely problematize human masculinity by means of the penetrative surgeries required in assimilation, the drones as well as Picard-as-Locutus (*TNG*, 4x01) retain their gender by default. And Consalvo errs in attesting egalitarianism to the Borg – all voices are *not* equal in the collective, mostly because there is merely a single, static, hive and all individual subjectivities have been violently dissolved into the hive. Resistance is, after all, futile.

Situating *Discovery*'s mycelial network, the spore drive, the tardigrade, and Stamets' interface in the context of *TNG* allows us to reframe the overarching narrative tradition of posthumanism in *Star Trek*. I argue that the mycelial network reframes well-established narratives about rhizomatic cyborg connectivity. In many ways, the story of the spore drive echoes the Borg: both are giant rhizomatic structures, multispecies assemblages, concerned with balance for all life in the universe. Like the Borg, the mycelium problematizes notions of personal identity and autonomous subjectivities in Stamets' multispecies becomings. The mycelium takes up the mantle from the Borg collective in a reimagination of everything that appears politically desirable about the Borg in contemporary progressive politics and updates the narrative to include not only indications of connectivity and egalitarian pluralism, but also an ecology of sustainability and resilience. In this, Stamets is much more a Cyborg in Haraway's sense than the Borg ever were, with all the emancipatory potential for a new, critically posthumanist ontology. At the end of the first season[1] his cybernetic becomings create true, balanced hybridity on a radically open map to the multiverse.

---

[1] This essay mainly focuses on reading *Star Trek: Discovery* season one through the lens of *Star Trek: The Next Generation*. A broader comparative analysis with the rest of the franchise (i.e. *Star Trek: First Contact* (1996, dir. Jonathan

Works Cited

Kazuharu Arakawa and Mark Blaxter, 'Tardigrades in Space', *The Biologist*, 65.1 (2018): 14–17.
Daniel Bernardi, *Star Trek and History: Race-Ing Toward a White Future* (New Brunswick, NJ: Rutgers University Press, 1998).
Rosi Braidotti, *The Posthuman* (Cambridge: Polity Press, 2013).
Mia Consalvo, 'Borg Babes, Drones, and the Collective: Reading Gender and the Body in *Star Trek*', *Women's Studies in Communication*, 27.2 (2004): 177–203.
Rob Cover, 'Generating the Self: The Biopolitics of Security and Selfhood in *Star Trek: The Next Generation*', *Science Fiction Film & Television*, 4.2 (2011): 205–24.
Gilles Deleuze and Félix Guattari, *A Thousand Plateaus: Capitalism and Schizophrenia*, translated by Brian Massumi (London and New York: Continuum, 2008).
Cynthia J. Fuchs, '"Death Is Irrelevant": Cyborgs, Reproduction, and the Future of Male Hysteria', in Chris Hables Gray (ed.) *The Cyborg Handbook* (New York and London: Routledge, 1995): 281–300.
Donna J. Haraway, 'A Cyborg Manifesto: Science, Technology, and Socialist-Feminism in the Late Twentieth Century', in Donna J. Haraway (ed.) *Simians, Cyborgs, and Women: The Reinvention of Nature* (New York and London: Routledge, 1991): 149–81.
Robert Tindol, 'The Star-Trek Borg as an All-American Captivity Narrative', *Brno Studies in English*, 38.1 (2012): 151–58.
Anna Lowenhaupt Tsing, *The Mushroom at the End of the World: On the Possibility of Life in Capitalist Ruins* (Princeton, NJ: Princeton University Press, 2015).
Jon G. Wagner and Jan Lundeen, *Deep Space and Sacred Time: Star Trek in the American Mythos* (Westport, CT: Praeger, 1998).
Linda Williams, 'Haraway Contra Deleuze and Guattari: The Question of the Animals', *Communications, Politics, and Culture*, 49.1 (2009): 42–54.

Episodes and Films Cited

'Datalore.' *Star Trek: The Next Generation*, written by Robert Lewin and Maurice Hurley, directed by Rob Bowman, Paramount Domestic Television, 18 January, 1988.
'The Neutral Zone.' *Star Trek: The Next Generation*, written by Deborah McIntyre and Mona Clee, directed by James L. Conway, Paramount Domestic Television, 16 May, 1988.

Frakes)), especially in light of the introduction of the JahSepp and the Control A.I. in *Star Trek: Discovery*'s second season, merits further research.

'The Measure of a Man.' *Star Trek: The Next Generation*, written by Melinda M. Snodgrass, directed by Robert Scheerer, Paramount Domestic Television, 13 February, 1989.

'The Offspring.' *Star Trek: The Next Generation*, written by René Echevarria, directed by Jonathan Frakes, Paramount Domestic Television, 12 March, 1990.

'The Best of Both Worlds, Part Two.' *Star Trek: The Next Generation*, written by Michael Piller, directed by Cliff Bole, Paramount Domestic Television, 24 September, 1990.

'Data's Day.' *Star Trek: The Next Generation*, written by Harold Apter, directed by Robert Wiemer, Paramount Domestic Television, 7 January, 1991.

'Equinox, Part One and Two.' *Star Trek: Voyager*, written by Rick Berman, Brannon Braga, and Joe Menosky, directed by David Livingston, Paramount Television, 26 May/22 September, 1999.

'The Vulcan Hello.' *Star Trek: Discovery*, written by Akiva Goldsman and Bryan Fuller, directed by David Semel, CBS Television Studios, 24 September, 2017.

'Context is for Kings.' *Star Trek: Discovery*, written by Bryan Fuller, Gretchen J. Berg, and Aaron Harberts, directed by Akiva Goldsman, CBS Television Studios, 1 October, 2017.

'The Butcher's Knife Cares Not for the Lamb's Cry.' *Star Trek: Discovery*, written by Jesse Alexander and Aron Eli Coleite, directed by Olatunde Osunsanmi, CBS Television Studios, 8 October, 2017.

'Choose Your Pain.' *Star Trek: Discovery*, written by Gretchen J. Berg, Aaron Harberts, and Kemp Powers, directed by Lee Rose, CBS Television Studios, 15 October, 2017.

'Magic to Make the Sanest Man Go Mad.' *Star Trek: Discovery*, written by Aron Eli Coleite and Jesse Alexander, directed by David M. Barrett, CBS Television Studios, 29 October, 2017.

'Si Vis Pacem, Para Bellum.' *Star Trek: Discovery*, written by Kirsten Beyer, directed by John S. Scott, CBS Television Studios, 5 November, 2017.

'Vaulting Ambition.' *Star Trek: Discovery*, written by Jordon Nardino, directed by Hanelle M. Culpepper, CBS Television Studios, 21 January, 2018.

'What's Past is Prologue.' *Star Trek: Discovery*, written by Ted Sullivan, directed by Olatunde Osunsanmi, CBS Television Studios, 28 January, 2018.

Star Trek: First Contact. 1996. Directed by Jonathan Frakes. Paramount Pictures.

Coda
Star Trek and the Fight for the Future
Sabrina Mittermeier and Mareike Spychala

Several of the essays in this collection analyze how *Star Trek: Discovery*'s (*DSC*; 2017–ongoing) first two seasons, set as they were ten years before *The Original Series* (*TOS*; 1966–1969), grapple with, nod to, and extend the existing canon of the *Star Trek* franchise. While this situation within the timelines of the franchise's fictional universe allowed *DSC* to comment on and interrogate established storytelling patterns and tropes, it also put limitations on the worldbuilding and narratives that could be told and necessitated a number of explanations to make any pretense at continuity within the universe feasible. In the first season, the *U.S.S. Discovery*'s sojourn in the Mirror Universe had to be classified and kept secret from the rest of Starfleet and the remaining Federation to explain why the crew of the *Enterprise–A* in *TOS* had never heard of it when some of them cross over accidentally in 'Mirror, Mirror' (2x04). Now, at the end of season two, it seems as if all of the Starfleet records on the *Discovery* will end up expunged – or at least highly classified. The ship itself has jumped over 900 years into the future, effectively erasing itself from the timeline, raising intriguing questions about the show itself and the topics it has touched upon in its first two seasons.

One way to read this development would be as a remake within the show itself. This move into an even farther future, one that has never been seen in any *Star Trek* television series or films, allows for the show to both keep established characters and continue telling stories about the effects of the events seen in the previous two seasons, while also providing it with a 'fresh start.' Not only does this disentangle it from established canon, it also impacts the worldbuilding of the show, transforming the *Discovery* from one of the newest, most advanced ships in Starfleet into what, barring any catastrophic future events, would be a hopelessly outdated model. It further has the potential to shake up the character constellations we have seen in *DSC* so far. At the same time, it runs the risk of reading as a cop out, or even an admission of defeat after two years of criticism heaped on the show from some parts of the fanbase as well as some media outlets. However, as *DSC* effectively reanimated a whole franchise that is now also one officially (CBS launched the Star Trek Global Franchise Group in May 2019), it might also simply open up new ways for transmedia storytelling and crossovers with all the other properties being launched, such as *Star Trek: Picard*, which is slated to be released in early 2020.

There is yet another way of looking at the end of *DSC*'s season two that is closely related to the one laid out above. The show, especially its second season, draws on *Star Trek*'s potential for nostalgia inherent in a decades-old franchise. This potential is not only evident in the ways the first season probes questions of how the Federation comes to be the organization seen in other *Star Trek* shows, but also in iconic characters, such as Captain Pike (Anson Mount) being added in season two and asserting that '[w]e are always in a fight for the future' (2x07). The fact that the *Discovery* leaves these characters behind in the past at the end of 'Such Sweet Sorrow, Part Two' (2x14) can thus also be read as an indication for the showrunners' commitment to one of the innovations *DSC* has dedicated itself to since season one: the focus on a character, namely Michael Burnham (Sonequa Martin-Green), who is not only a black woman, but also not the captain of a starship, and thus to move beyond the established *Star Trek* canon and narrative tropes, character constellations, and casting choices. It will be interesting to see how the third season will deal with the vacuum that an empty captain's chair seems to form in a franchise that has always so centrally depended on the figure of the (mostly male, mostly white) captain as its leader and moral arbiter. Indeed, the archetypal white, male leader, Captain Pike, is now again, seemingly, left behind in the past, while the more diverse crew of the *U.S.S. Discovery* is going forward into the future, potentially indicating a further move away from some of *Star Trek*'s established conventions and a wish to explore less well-trodden paths.

Certainly, *DSC*'s and the larger franchise's future remains wide open at this point. While the parameters of this future are unclear at the time of writing, the fact that there even *is* a future, due to the collective efforts of the *Discovery*'s crew and their allies at the end of season two, seems to indicate an inherently positive outlook in keeping with the older *Star Trek* series. On the meta level, there seems to be a similar optimism for the still expanding franchise and its ever-growing and continually diversifying (and sometimes divided) fandom. Regardless of what the future holds, after a 50-year long history, *DSC* still insists it is one worth fighting for.

Notes on Contributors

Ina Batzke is a post-doctoral researcher and lecturer in American Studies at the University of Augsburg and the University of Münster. Her most recent publication, *Undocumented Migrants in the United States. Life Narratives and Self-representations* (Routledge, 2019), summarizes her latest research interests in Life Writing and Critical Refugee Studies. In her new project, she explores the intersections between reproduction, biotechnology and feminism in U.S. American and Canadian novels, films, and television series.

Sarah Böhlau studied German Literature and History at the Otto-Friedrich-Universität in Bamberg and the National University of Ireland in Galway. She joined the graduate program of the medieval literature studies in Bamberg and recently finished her thesis titled: 'Unterwegs ins Mittelalter – Zeitreisen in der deutschsprachigen Jugendliteratur des 21. Jahrhunderts' ('Off to the Middle Ages – Time Travel in German Young Adult Literature of the 21st Century'). Her academic research focuses on medievalism in contemporary popular culture, with a special interest for the unconventional storytelling devices (like time travel) that science fiction and fantasy narratives offer aplenty. Her love for *Star Trek* predates her education as a literary scholar by a decade, but she keeps getting pleasantly surprised how deeply the two areas are intertwined.

Amy C. Chambers is a senior lecturer in Film and Media Studies at Manchester School of Art, Manchester Metropolitan University, UK. Her research examines the intersection of science and entertainment media with specific focus on women and science, and discourses surrounding science and religion on screen. Amy's scholarship also explores post-classical Hollywood filmmaking; science fiction film/television (1968–1977); women in speculative fiction; narratives of women's science expertise in the media; transmedia storytelling; and medicalized horror. Twitter: @AmyCChambers/Website: https://amycchambers.com/.

Sharing his birthday with Leonard Nimoy, **John Andreas Fuchs** seems to be meant for boldly exploring strange new worlds – both real and fantastic. And that is what he does teaching EFL, Social Studies, Religious Education, and Art at Oberschule im Park in Bremen. He holds an MA (Magister Artium) in contemporary history, American literature and didactics of history as well as both the Erstes and Zweites Staatsexamen (Lehramt Gymnasium). He was Assistant Professor with the Chair of School Pedagogy at Katholische Universität Eichstätt-Ingolstadt (KU) where he taught courses on Educational Science, the History of Education, and Religious Education. He also taught courses on American History and American Literature both at KU and Ludwig-Maximilians-Universität München (LMU). He is working on a doctoral thesis on Catholicism and anti-Catholicism in American TV-series with the American Institute at LMU (Professor Michael Hochgeschwender). And, yes, he likes *Star Trek*.

Torsten Kathke received his doctorate in American Cultural History from Ludwig-Maximilians-Universität, Munich in 2013. He is the author of *Wires That Bind: Nation, Region and Technology in the American Southwest, 1854–1920* (transcript, 2017), a study of the effects improved communication had on power relations among local elites in Arizona and New Mexico. His current research project analyzes the market for popular non-fiction books in the United States and West Germany during the 1970s and 1980s. He is currently a lecturer at the Obama Institute for Transnational American Studies of Johannes Gutenberg University in Mainz, Germany and specializes in the history of the United States and Germany during the nineteenth and twentieth centuries, including the history of the U.S. West, Media History, and the History of Popular Culture.

Diana A. Mafe is Associate Professor of English, Black Studies, International Studies, and Women's and Gender Studies at Denison University and the author of *Where No Black Woman Has Gone Before – Subversive Portrayals in Speculative Film and TV* (University of Texas Press, 2018) and *Mixed Race Stereotypes in South African and American Literature: Coloring Outside the (Black and White) Lines* (Palgrave Macmillan, 2013).

Lisa Meinecke is a doctoral candidate at the America-Institute of Ludwig-Maximilians-Universität in Munich, Germany. Her dissertation project with the working title 'Degrees of Freedom: Becoming-Person and the Technicised Other in American Popular Culture' analyzes popular depictions of artificial intelligence, with special focus on the boundaries between personhood and technology. Her research interests include the History of Science and Technology, Popular Culture Studies, and the Histories of Religion and Social Reform. Lisa also used to be a research manager at Technical University Munich and has had the privilege to work with the EU robotics project ECHORD++ and the Munich Center for Technology in Society, before returning to the America-Institute in 2018. Her paper on *Star Trek: Discovery* was first presented at PCAACA 2019 and received the PCASFF Student Paper Award 2019.

Sabrina Mittermeier holds a doctorate in American Cultural History from Ludwig-Maximilians-Universität in Munich, Germany, and is currently a lecturer and post-doctoral researcher at the University of Augsburg. She is the author of a forthcoming monograph under the working title *Middle Class Kingdoms – A Cultural History of Disneyland 1955–2016* (Intellect, 2020), as well as the co-editor of the *Routledge Handbook to Star Trek* (2021), and the volume *Here You Leave Today – Time and Temporality in Theme Parks* (Wehrhahn, 2017). She has also taught and published on other diverse topics of American popular culture and history, such as the intersection of video games and theme parks, historical film, LGBT representation on American television, or musical theater. Her post-doc projects deals with LGBT public history in the United States and West Germany and are eagerly awaiting funding. Twitter: @S_Mittermeier.

Kerstin-Anja Münderlein is a research assistant for English Literature at the Otto-Friedrich-Universität Bamberg. After her MA in English and American Studies in Bamberg, she pursued a PhD in English Literature (degree awarded in March 2019). Her dissertation traces the relationship of genre, reception, and frames with the help of Gothic parodies of the late eighteenth and early nineteenth centuries. She has published on the poetry of the First World War and eighteenth century Gothic. Currently, she is preparing her post-doc project on literary forms in social media as compared to traditional forms of literature. Besides the aforementioned, her research interest include Fan Studies, Elizabethan and Jacobean Drama, and Nineteenth Century and Golden Age Crime Fiction. Contact: kerstin-anja.muenderlein@uni-bamberg.de.

Whit Frazier Peterson is a lecturer, research associate and PhD candidate at the University of Stuttgart in Stuttgart, Germany, with interests in African American Literature, Modernism, Surrealism, Afrofuturism and Black Speculative Fiction. Although he now lives with his wife and two daughters in Europe, somehow, surreally, he also grew up in the Washington DC area, lived for 12 years in New York, and has self-published two novels: the first about Zora Neale Hurston and Langston Hughes, and the second set during the 2008 election cycle. He is currently at work on a dissertation about literary anthologies and canon formation, and is writing a historical novel set in the future.

Judith Rauscher is a lecturer and post-doctoral researcher in American Studies at the University of Bamberg, where she received her PhD with a dissertation on 'Poetic Place-Making: Nature and Mobility in Contemporary American Poetry' in 2018. She holds an MA in Comparative Literature from Dartmouth College (2010) and an MA in English and American Studies from the University of Bamberg (2012). Judith Rauscher has published articles on Canadian petro-poetry, U.S. American multiethnic poetry, the environmental imaginaries of poetry about air travel, and ecopoetics. Her current research project focuses on late nineteenth- and early twentieth century speculative fiction and is tentatively entitled 'Revisions of the American Eve: Gender, Community, and the Technoscientific Imagination in U.S. Popular Culture (1860–1930).'

Michael G. Robinson is a professor of communication studies at the University of Lynchburg. Mike received his PhD in American Culture Studies from Bowling Green State University. His scholarly interests include Audience Research, Genre Studies, Media Criticism, Media History, Superheroes and, of course, Science Fiction. He enjoys discussing popular culture topics and has appeared in local and national media broadcasts. He published an article about Doctor Who for *Time Travel Television* (2015). A fan *in utero* thanks to his mother's science fiction television interests, Mike is thrilled to be joining a collection of articles about *Star Trek*.

Henrik Schillinger is a researcher at the Institute of Political Science at the University of Duisburg-Essen. His publications and research interests include Norm Contestation in International Relations, the Politics of Popular Culture, and Post-structuralist Theories. Email: henrik.schillinger@uni-due.de.

Arne Sönnichsen is a researcher at the chair of International Relations and Development Policy at University of Duisburg-Essen. His publications and research interests encompass Outer Space Governance, Science and Technology Studies and the Politics of Popular Culture. Email: arne. soennichsen@uni-due.de.

Mareike Spychala is a PhD candidate, research assistant, and lecturer at the University of Bamberg's American Studies department. Her PhD project focuses on autobiographies by female veterans of the Iraq War and especially on the varied intersections of gender and imperialism in these narratives. She has taught on a variety of topics, among others on American War Literature, the Western in German and American Culture, and African American and Afro German Literature and Culture In 2018/19, she co-edited the conference proceedings for an international conference on the topic *War and Trauma in Past and Present* (to be published with Wissenschaftsverlag Trier) that she co-organized at the University of Bamberg in March 2018 in addition to the present volume. She earned her BA from the University of Salzburg and her European joint master's degree from the University of Bamberg and the Université Paris Diderot – Paris 7.

Will Tattersdill is Senior Lecturer in Popular Literature at the University of Birmingham, UK. His *Science, Fiction, and the Fin-de-Siècle Periodical Press* (Cambridge University Press) was published in 2016; he is currently working on an examination of dinosaurs in popular culture.

Jennifer Volkmer is a PhD student at Ludwig-Maximilians-Universität (LMU) Munich's Amerika Institut. Her thesis focuses on the depiction of motorcyclists in US-American Movies and Television from 1953 to 2017, especially on the therein constructed masculinities. She has given several talks, about topics such as *Death of Stalin* (2018) and the Continued Relevance of Historical Film; Motorcycle Riding and the Modern-day Pilgrimage; US Politics and Television Audiences; and *Thelma and Louise* (1991) revisited in the MeToo context. She earned her BA in Political Science, as well as her MA in American History, Society and Culture from LMU Munich.

Andrea Whitacre holds a doctorate in Medieval Literature from Indiana University, where she teaches courses on Medievalism, Science Fiction, and Fantasy. In addition to articles on medieval writers Gerald of Wales and Marie de France, she has previously published on gender in the *Star Trek* reboot films in *The Kelvin Timeline of Star Trek: Essays on J.J. Abrams' Final Frontier*. Her current project, titled 'Change and Identity: The Medieval Werewolf and the Layered Body,' examines the literary werewolf figure and conceptions of the transforming body in the high to late Middle Ages.

Si Sophie Pages Whybrew is a PhD candidate at the University of Graz in Austria and is employed as a research associate at the University of Graz and the University of Saarbrücken. Si is working on a dissertation project entitled 'Transitioning into the Future? Trans Potentialities in North American Science Fiction from 1993 to 2018.' Si has published articles on Djuna Barnes' *Nightwood*, the representation of intersexuality in American medical dramas, and on recognition and affects of trans belonging in contemporary trans authored science fiction.

Acknowledgments

Our thanks as editors, first and foremost, go to our authors, who delivered insightful, well-researched, often funny analyses on *Discovery*, but also *Star Trek* more broadly. We could not be prouder to bring together so many different approaches and analytical viewpoints for this collection. We also owe a debt of gratitude to two amazing women and science fiction scholars: Diana A. Mafe, whose perspective in her research and in the interview included in this collection has been more than inspiring, and Sherryl Vint, who so kindly agreed to write a preface long before we even had a final line-up, and whose support has also led us to secure publication with Liverpool University Press. We would also like to thank Liverpool University Press, specifically our editors, Jenny Howard, and later Christabel Scaife, who helped us develop this project and bring it over the finish line. And last, but not least, our amazing cover artist, Steffi Hochriegl for visualizing both *Discovery* and this collection so beautifully.

Mareike would like to thank her co-editor for together dreaming up and then realizing this project. Further thanks are due for her decision to run with me and co-write a previously unplanned article about Culber, Stamets, and LGBTQ representation when I went: 'Culber and Stamets are like Bones and McCoy, they're making subtext, text! In this paper I will….' Working on this collection, traveling together, and getting up to all other kinds of nerdy shenanigans with you has been an amazing experience – thank you! I would also like to thank my family for always supporting me, even if they do not quite understand my love for all things SFF. Further thanks are due to my supervisor at the English and American Studies Institute, Professor Dr. Christine Gerhardt, for her words of support and to my colleagues, Dr. Judith Rauscher and Dr. Kerstin-Anja Münderlein, for the writing sessions, lending open ears, and for always giving the best advice. Thank you, too, to the U.S.S. Spaceboos Discord for all the fanworks, speculation, and yelling. And last, but certainly not least, I owe a debt of gratitude to the writers and cast of *Discovery*. I did not know how much I needed this show until it had made its way onto my screen. Special thanks go to Sonequa Martin-Green for her incomparable, inspiring performance as Michael Burnham, Mary Chieffo (nothing but respect for my High Chancellor!) for her incredible kindness and enthusiasm, and Anthony Rapp and Wilson Cruz who, every day, are torchbearers lighting the way towards a better future. Your interest in and excitement about this book has meant the world to me.

Sabrina would like to thank her co-editor Mareike for embarking on this project with her, boldly nerding – who could have known where it would lead us and the doors it would open? I will forever be grateful to you for this and your friendship, that in many ways was built on both this show and this book. I would also like to thank my co-author Jenny Volkmer who has since become a partner in crime much beyond our shared love for Lorca! Lorca! and his tribble – it truly is the right timeline. Thanks are also due to my parents, for supporting me on this journey, and specifically my dad, who sat me down in front of *Voyager* when I was about six years old and made me a Trekkie for life. My never-ending gratitude also goes out to the whole cast of *Discovery* who, on multiple occasions, have shared their excitement and interest in this book, and whose support has given me life beyond just this project. Specifically mentioned here should be my favorite Klingons in the galaxy, the incomparable Mary Chieffo, Kenneth 'Prime Lorca' Mitchell and Shazad Latif; the first two gay men to boldly go where no gay man had gone before, Anthony Rapp and Wilson Cruz; Rekha Sharma, whose light shines so brightly always; and Jason Isaacs, who will forever be a true captain to me. Hello.

Index

9/11 8, 12, 15, 52, 106, 123, 204, 225, 254, 298

actorvism 14, 346–48
Afrofuturism 13, 201–19
afronaut 213
American diplomacy *see* diplomacy
anti-hero 310
archetype 13, 93, 312–17, 323

Berg, Gretchen J. 12, 88, 90
Berman, Rick 74, 90, 334–38
binary 12, 170, 226, 269, 333–35, 352–57, 376, 384, 387
Black Mirror 10, 81, 83, 93–96
border crossing 13, 243–61, 376
Borg, the 46–47, 52, 74–75, 170, 290, 374, 385–88
Braga, Brannon 92, 112, 128, 338
Brook, Jayne 25, 54, 72, 114, 211, 253, 308
Brooks, Avery 6, 47, 76, 88, 309
Burnham, Gabrielle 138, 267, 274, 293, 300
Burnham, Michael 1–2, 6, 8, 10, 13, 21–36, 43, 53–54, 62, 72, 88–89, 97, 113–21, 131–40, 146, 154, 167, 170–72, 177–80, 191–98, 202–06, 210, 226–35, 244, 251–61, 267–81, 287–303, 310–23, 342, 345, 358–60, 378–92, 400
'Bury Your Gays' 32, 341, 347

canon 2–10, 23, 28–29, 32, 42, 53–56, 62, 76, 97, 106, 149, 166–69, 173–82, 193–94, 202, 217, 287, 313, 339–40, 344–47, 374, 391–92
captaincy 6–7, 22, 25–31, 35, 47, 53–55, 70, 114, 118–21, 181, 192–94, 233, 253, 290–93, 307–18, 323, 381–84
CBS 30, 53, 61–62, 85–89, 92, 105, 243, 251, 313, 347, 392
CBS *All Access* 28, 53, 86–87, 105, 113, 157
Chieffo, Mary 67, 121, 194, 227, 255, 287, 298, 311, 321, 361, 400
cisnormativity 336, 353–57
Cold War 3, 10–11, 41–59, 210, 224–25, 244, 261, 332, 386–87
colonialism 48, 192, 223, 245, 248, 256, 315, 352–53, 367
Control 12, 64, 274, 288, 300–03, 323
Cornwell, Katrina 8, 25, 27, 29, 54, 72, 114–15, 120–21, 177–80, 203, 211–12, 253–55, 258, 260, 295, 308–09, 313, 317–19
Cruz, Wilson 12, 22, 33, 44, 67, 115, 133, 160, 171, 213, 273, 287, 322, 341–42, 346–48, 362, 379, 400
Culber, Hugh 12, 22, 31–33, 36, 44, 66, 75, 115, 117, 133–39,

401

160, 171, 176, 213, 273–74, 281, 287–88, 322, 332, 340–47, 362–67, 379–84, 399
cyborg 52, 374–75, 387–88

diplomacy 5, 13, 41, 221–37, 290, 386
  mytho-diplomacy 225, 229–32
  U.S. exceptionalism 42, 50, 227, 229–31
diversity 2, 6, 11–14, 26–27, 34, 37, 41, 44, 46, 53, 56, 83–84, 88, 96, 165–66, 203–07, 213, 217, 227, 243, 268, 273, 280, 332, 339, 341, 348
dystopia 6, 8–9, 23, 36, 54, 107, 112, 118, 209

Emperor Georgiou *see* Georgiou, Philippa
empire *see* imperialism
empowerment 193, 243–46
Enlightenment 42, 50–51, 213
episodic structure 148, 158
  see also seriality
estrangement 221–38
Eurocentrism 248, 352–53, 366
exploration 2, 8, 29, 31, 36, 41, 52, 64, 70, 81–83, 96, 204, 221, 226, 233, 244, 302–03

fans 1, 5–8, 14–15, 24, 30, 33–34, 53–56, 61–63, 75, 82–87, 93–96, 148, 156–58, 166–73, 182, 196, 245, 267, 274, 312–13, 331–48, 355, 358
  fanbase 6, 152, 165–66, 290, 313, 392
  fanfiction 156, 165–85, 331, 339–40
  fanon 10, 166, 169, 175, 345, 347
  slash 175–76, 312, 331, 340, 347
Federation 1–5, 8, 24–26, 30, 33–36, 42–48, 52–54, 83, 93, 97, 108–11, 116–22, 158, 170, 177–78, 180, 197–98, 202–10, 218, 224–37, 243–60, 268, 274, 293–98, 303, 315, 319–20, 323, 333, 336–37, 343, 347, 367, 376, 379–87, 391–92
Federation–Klingon War 33, 118, 166, 170, 249, 255, 274, 294, 384
femininity 13, 27, 251, 269, 275, 288–92, 300, 303
feminism 13, 27, 194–95, 218, 243–63, 267, 278, 289–90, 294, 297–99, 353, 359, 364–67, 374
  imperial feminism 243–63
foreign policy 204, 222–37
Frain, James 43, 89, 95, 120, 134, 194, 204, 254, 268, 273, 300
Frakes, Jonathan 72, 90, 98, 129, 334–36, 355–57
franchise 2–15, 21–37, 42, 52, 55–56, 61–65, 72, 76, 81–98, 117, 127, 147–48, 152, 158, 165–67, 182, 191, 203, 207, 213, 217, 222–23, 237, 244–47, 259, 267–69, 273, 276, 280–81, 287–97, 301–03, 307, 312–14, 331–57, 361, 374–76, 383–92
frontier 41–43, 48–52, 65, 69–71, 221–23, 229, 231, 332
Fuller, Bryan 53, 87–89, 205, 217, 346, 359

gender 3, 5, 11–14, 31, 45, 50, 175, 191, 197, 244–45, 248, 258, 267–81, 289, 291–98, 309, 321–22, 333–35, 339, 347–48, 352–68, 387–88
Georgiou, Philippa 1–2, 9, 21–22, 25–27, 36, 43, 55, 64, 72–73, 76, 89, 106, 113, 116–23, 158, 177, 194–95, 198, 206, 210–11, 226–29, 233, 246–61, 267–68, 287, 292, 297–301, 308, 311, 315–17, 342–47, 384
Gerrold, David 12, 71, 333–34, 338–40

Grayson, Amanda 62, 89, 194, 268, 300
Groundhog Day episode 127–40, 145–47
 see also time loop

Harberts, Aaron 12, 88–90, 346–48
heteronormativity 32, 246–47, 276, 335–37, 345
homonormativity 345
homophobia 7, 338
homosexuality 31, 67, 307, 331, 334–35, 343–45
humanism *see* liberal humanism
hybridity 234, 295–97, 311, 319, 322, 367, 374, 387–88

imperialism 2, 13, 50, 225, 243–61, 298–99, 303, 315, 352, 386
Isaacs, Jason 2, 7, 25, 30, 43, 54, 61, 113, 131, 158, 167, 193, 202, 233, 250, 268, 287, 307–17, 344, 377, 400

Janeway, Kathryn 6, 88, 244, 269, 288, 290–91, 312–15, 338, 383
Jones, Doug 9, 25, 54, 120, 228, 252, 279, 302, 307–09, 380

Kelley, DeForest 63, 332
Kelvin timeline 85, 147, 280, 294, 339, 346
Kirk, James T. 5, 22–31, 44–46, 62–70, 73, 85, 97, 106–09, 246, 261, 290–92, 312–17, 331, 344–45
Kirshner, Mia 62, 89, 194, 268, 300
Klingon 1–2, 6, 8, 12, 21, 33, 43, 46, 48, 54, 56, 67, 70–71, 74, 113, 116, 120–22, 137–39, 166, 170, 176–79, 194, 197–98, 204, 221, 226–37, 243, 246, 251–59, 268–69, 274, 287, 290–93, 295–300, 303, 307, 309, 311–12, 315, 319–23, 361–65, 377–83, 400
 Klingon Empire 5, 21, 43, 251, 257–59, 287, 296, 361, 367
Kol, General 258, 296, 307, 361
Kol-Sha 297
Kurtzman, Alex 12, 61, 89, 97, 294

Landry, Ellen 29–30, 211, 267, 278–79, 311, 317, 378
Latif, Shazad 3, 12, 116, 131, 158, 170, 194, 213, 234, 276, 291, 307, 318–22, 361, 400
LGBTQ 7, 12, 32, 171, 274, 281, 331–32, 340–47, 358, 399
liberal humanism 3, 9, 11–13, 26–29, 34–36, 83, 202–04, 210, 217–18, 313, 347, 376, 384–87
Lorca, Gabriel 2, 7, 13, 25–31, 43, 47, 54–56, 61, 67, 75, 113–23, 127, 131–39, 158, 160, 167, 172, 180–81, 193, 202–03, 206–13, 218, 233, 250, 258, 260–61, 268–71, 279, 287, 292, 307–23, 344, 377, 380–84, 400
L'Rell 67, 69, 121, 170, 179, 194–98, 227, 234–35, 255, 258–59, 287, 294–303, 311, 315, 319–23, 361–63, 367

marginalization 23, 30, 35–36, 56, 169, 193, 222, 236, 260, 270, 276, 280, 296, 376, 385
Martin-Green, Sonequa 1, 6, 21, 34, 43, 53, 62, 88, 113, 132, 146, 167, 191, 202, 205, 226, 251, 256, 267, 276, 287, 310, 313–14, 321, 345, 359, 378, 392, 400
masculinity 14, 43, 251, 260, 289, 296, 307–23, 388
 hegemonic masculinity 309–11
 toxic masculinity 94, 317–18
militarism 22, 29, 62, 72, 223,

232, 243, 247, 268, 308, 310–11, 317, 323, 384
military 2, 22, 23, 25, 29, 30, 35, 47–50, 61–63, 70, 72, 120, 254, 268–69, 290, 307–11, 315–18, 322, 373, 384, 387
Mirror Universe 2, 6–10, 21–36, 54–55, 75, 105–23, 166, 195, 202, 206–07, 210–12, 216–18, 232–34, 243–61, 272, 293, 311, 314–17, 341–47, 363–65, 377, 382, 387, 391
misogyny 7, 44, 249, 297–99
Mitchell, Kenneth 258, 296–97, 307, 361, 400
Moore, Ronald D. 3, 128, 150, 337
mother 62, 119, 138, 155, 194, 209, 249, 251, 269, 272–76, 290, 293, 295, 299–305
motherhood *see* mother
Mount, Anson 9, 27, 54, 61, 97, 287, 307, 314, 392
Mudd, Harry 65, 130–40, 146, 382
mycelial network 14, 25, 33, 117, 145, 154, 216, 271, 278–79, 293, 315, 342, 373–83, 388
mycelium *see* mycelial network
myth *see* mythology
  frontier myth *see* frontier
mytho diplomacy *see* diplomacy
mythology 1, 49, 56, 81–84, 96, 98, 113, 127, 201, 215, 223, 225, 230–32, 236, 275, 280, 292

nationalism 43, 224, 248–49
  ethnic nationalism 244, 247, 250
Netflix 28, 53, 86, 128, 149, 151, 153, 157, 358
Nimoy, Leonard 1, 25, 46, 50, 62, 65, 89, 109, 332
normalization 191–98, 235–37, 252, 268, 270–73, 280–81, 313, 315, 341, 345
nostalgia 9–10, 47, 81, 96, 375, 392

Notaro, Tig 12, 33, 75, 274, 287, 343
Number One 1, 9

orientalist 11, 44, 247, 258
Other 12–14, 170, 218, 228, 256, 375, 377, 378
Othering 256–58

Paramount 84–85, 337
patriarchy 192, 297
  patriarchal 244, 292, 295–99, 365
  patriarchal power structures 287, 303
Peck, Ethan 6, 61, 89, 97, 193, 204, 268, 287
Periodicals 10, 145, 151, 153
  periodical publishing 148
  periodical rhythm 152, 159
Pike, Christopher 9–10, 27–30, 54–55, 61–62, 97, 287, 302, 307–08, 312–14, 317, 323, 392
posthuman 27, 29, 375, 384–85
post-network era 3, 10, 122, 308
  see also post-network series
  see also post-network television
post-network series 105–07, 117, 123
post-network television 307
post-racial 44, 203, 215
power structure 29, 34, 287, 291, 300
  see also patriarchal power structures
prequel 5, 7, 24, 29, 48, 159
prime directive 1, 46, 109, 226
Prime Universe 25, 27, 30, 32, 75, 107–13, 116–23
progress 202, 213, 215, 218
PTSD 74, 114, 138, 179, 212, 309, 319, 342, 362–64

queer
  queer characters 338, 343, 346, 347

queer representation 31, 337, 347–48
queer subtext 337–39, 345
queerbaiting 337
queerness 31–32, 246, 274, 336–38

race 3, 5, 11, 13, 26, 45, 50, 192, 197, 201–02, 205, 213, 215, 243–44, 248, 256–58, 269–72, 276, 280–81, 339, 378, 387
see also cotton-gin effect
racism 43–44, 50–51, 192, 247, 249, 257, 261, 270
racialization 3, 257
rape 67, 69, 73, 214, 320–22, 338, 362, 365
Rapp, Anthony 12, 22, 44, 61, 115, 130, 145, 171, 268, 287, 307–08, 332, 341, 346, 373, 400
Red Angel 3, 5, 97, 138, 274, 300–01
Reno, Jett 12, 33, 274–75, 287, 303, 343
representation 13–14, 119, 175–76, 179, 217, 224, 256, 267, 269–73, 276–77, 280–81, 288, 290–91, 294, 302, 355–56, 367, 386
of diplomacy 227–28, 230–31, 234–37
see also queer representation
retcon 81, 85, 159, 339
rhizome 14, 374, 379–80, 383, 386, 388
Roddenberry, Gene 3, 7, 9, 26–27, 31, 34, 41, 47–48, 50, 65–68, 70, 71–72, 74–75, 83–84, 87, 90, 92, 96, 109, 157, 165, 227, 244, 313, 331–35, 339–40, 343, 376
Romijn, Rebecca 9

Sarek 43, 89, 134, 194, 204, 254, 268, 273, 302
Saru 9, 25, 27–29, 54, 120–21, 181, 228, 252, 279, 302, 307, 313–14, 363, 367, 380–81, 383–84
science fiction 8, 10, 12–13, 33, 51–52, 63, 65, 70–71, 81, 94, 114, 138, 148, 150–51, 154, 202, 222, 247, 269–70, 272–73, 275–76, 280–81, 288–91, 294, 303, 307, 344–45, 353, 364, 387
black women in science fiction 269–70, 272–73, 276
science fiction television 84, 96, 153, 196, 289, 300–01, 303
Section 31 97, 122, 251, 254, 260, 274, 288, 297, 319–20, 336
seriality 105–06, 110, 117, 148, 150, 153, 157–58
extended seriality 105–06
serial 81, 105–07, 113, 117, 123, 148–60, 281
Victorian serial 149
series
difference from serial 105
see also television series
sexual assault
see also rape
sexuality 3, 31–32, 75, 175, 195–96, 198, 247, 280–81, 335, 341–46, 353, 358
see also homosexuality
sexualization 23, 195–96, 247, 337
Sharma, Rekha 29–30, 211, 267, 311, 378, 400
Shatner, William 24, 46, 62–63, 95, 108, 246, 312, 332
Sisko, Benjamin 6, 47, 53, 55, 76, 88, 110, 119, 309, 312
Social Justice Warrior 53, 358–59
Sohn, Sonja 138, 267, 293
soldier 22, 122, 204, 228, 311, 320–22
species reassignment protocol 364–65
Spock 1, 5–6, 9, 25, 28, 43, 46, 50, 52, 61–62, 64–65, 68–69, 73, 89, 97, 108–09, 155, 193–94,

204, 268, 274, 287, 293–94,
300, 302, 331, 344–46
spore drive 22, 33, 67, 116, 132,
134–35, 138, 154, 166, 171,
206, 216, 233, 251, 268–69,
271, 273, 276–78, 280, 309,
315, 344, 373–75, 377–83, 388
Stamets, Paul 12, 14, 22, 25, 29,
32–33, 44, 61, 66–67, 75, 115,
117, 130–40, 145–47, 150,
171–72, 176, 216, 268, 273–76,
279, 281, 287, 292–93, 302,
307–10, 312, 332, 340–47, 362,
373, 375, 377, 379–84, 388, 399
Star Trek films
Star Trek 5, 31, 62, 85, 280, 294
Star Trek: Beyond 5, 12, 31–32,
167, 229, 339–40
Star Trek: The Final Frontier 52
Star Trek: First Contact 74,
110–11, 267, 336
Star Trek: Into Darkness 5, 61
Star Trek: Nemesis 73, 357
Star Trek: The Search for Spock
46, 52
*Star Trek: The Undiscovered
Country* 52, 71, 73
Star Trek: The Voyage Home 52
Star Trek: The Wrath of Khan 6,
46, 52, 63, 70, 165, 333
Star Trek series
Star Trek: The Animated Series
61–62
Star Trek: Deep Space Nine 2,
6, 9, 29, 42, 47, 52–53, 55,
72, 83–84, 88, 91, 95, 107,
109–10, 112, 119, 122, 150,
245, 267, 300, 309, 311, 331,
355
Star Trek: Enterprise 5, 9, 24, 26,
52, 72, 73, 84–85, 92, 107,
110–12, 122, 147, 149, 246,
312, 331
Star Trek: The Next Generation 9,
11, 23, 26–27, 31, 41, 52, 63,
66, 70–74, 83, 85, 92, 105,
111–12, 128, 130, 145, 147,
152, 154, 159, 173, 217, 245,
267, 288–89, 294, 298, 312,
331, 333–34, 354–56, 374,
376, 384–85, 386–88
Star Trek: The Original Series 2, 5,
23, 43, 105, 107–10, 111–13,
122, 147, 156, 165, 170, 244,
267–68, 288, 307, 312, 332,
391
Star Trek: Picard 10, 392
Star Trek: Voyager 2, 6, 9, 11, 27,
52–53, 67, 72, 74, 83–85, 88,
112, 145, 244, 267, 269, 274,
288–90, 295, 312, 315, 331,
336–38, 383, 400
Starfleet 6–8, 2–3, 25–27, 29,
34–36, 43, 46, 48, 54–55, 61,
64, 70–74, 89–90, 108, 111,
113–16, 118, 12–13, 133, 140,
146, 148, 170, 172, 174, 180–81,
204, 208, 211, 213, 216–17,
226, 228, 233, 235, 244, 251,
254, 258–60, 268–69, 271,
279, 290–93, 295–98, 307–14,
317–19, 323, 335, 338, 341, 342,
359, 364–65, 373, 377, 380,
383, 385–86, 391
Starfleet captain
see also captain
stereotype 168, 194, 198, 247, 269,
275, 277, 301, 320, 333, 342,
347, 354
storytelling 3, 5, 7, 13, 51, 53, 64,
81, 93, 127–28, 150, 152–53,
157, 159, 336, 378, 391–92
serialized storytelling 10, 153
Straal, Justin 373, 377–79
streaming 14, 55
streaming service 10, 53, 85–87,
97, 105, 153, 157
strong female character 68, 167,
195–96, 255
subtext 14, 134, 256, 317, 331–32,
334, 337–39, 344–45, 399
Sullivan, Ted 5, 323

tardigrade 14, 67, 131, 171, 181, 216, 277–80, 309, 378–84, 388
television 3, 6, 10–12, 14, 22, 32–33, 44, 50–55, 63, 66, 69, 71, 74, 82, 85–86, 89, 92–93, 96, 107, 128–29, 145, 165, 168, 193, 202–03, 206–07, 213, 217, 236, 272, 287, 290, 300–01, 303, 307–08, 310, 320–21, 332–36, 338–39, 343, 346, 348, 386, 391
   prestige television 150
   television series 24, 48, 81, 84, 105–06, 112, 147, 154, 156, 202, 280–81, 289, 386, 391
Terran Empire 7, 23–24, 108, 111, 116, 118–19, 170, 206, 210, 216, 232–33, 243, 245, 247, 249–51, 256–59, 312, 314
   Terran Emperor *see also* Emperor Georgiou
The Orville 9–10, 81, 83, 91–93, 96–97, 147
Tilly, Sylvia 27, 33, 67, 72, 116–17, 121, 132–34, 172, 179, 194–95, 253, 258–60, 273–75, 280, 287, 291–94, 303, 317, 322, 360–61
time crystal 137, 139–40, 303
time loop 10, 127–33, 136–40
   computer game as narrative influence 129–30, 137
   paradox of 129–30
   recursive time loop 127
   (time) looper 127–31, 134, 139–40
time travel 127–29, 138
   as storytelling device 127–28
toxic masculinity 94, 307–08, 317, 323
trans potentiality 351–53, 358, 360–61, 366
transgender 14, 333, 348, 351–61, 364, 367
transhumanism 14, 383

transphobia 335, 364–66
Transsexual Empire 361, 365
trauma *see also* PTSD
   traumatic memory 138
Trekker 86, 92, 168
Trekkie 30, 145, 156, 168, 312, 340, 356, 400
trope 6, 12–14, 23–24, 41, 95, 127–30, 145, 152, 202, 205, 207–09, 215, 231, 233, 236, 288–89, 293, 307, 309, 311, 313–17, 319, 321, 336, 347, 355, 357, 364, 391–92
   see also 'Bury Your Gays'; depraved bisexual; magical negro
Tyler, Ash 3, 12–13, 116, 121–22, 131–33, 135–40, 158, 170, 172, 177–80, 195–96, 198, 213, 234–35, 276, 291, 293, 296–97, 299–300, 307–08, 310–11, 315, 318–23, 361–67

United Federation of Planets 5, 36, 42, 46, 93, 108, 243, 268, 293, 333
U.S. exceptionalism 224, 230–31
   exceptionalist foreign policy 225
U.S.S. Buran 114, 311
"U.S.S. Callister" (tv episode) 10, 81, 83, 93–95
U.S.S. Discovery 6, 22, 27, 113, 116, 120, 170, 172, 204, 206, 232–33, 243, 251, 254, 268, 271, 274, 278, 292, 302, 323, 341, 360, 362, 373, 391–92
U.S.S. Enterprise 6, 9–10, 27–28, 47–48, 61–62, 64–65, 68, 70–74, 81, 89, 97, 109, 268, 302, 312–14, 316, 323, 332, 336, 338, 355, 385–86, 391
U.S.S. Shenzhou 27, 113, 118, 120, 204, 205, 268, 289, 296, 300, 360–62
U.S.S. Voyager 244

utopia 2–3, 5, 7–9, 11, 21–23, 35, 41–42, 90, 108, 111–12, 118, 122, 165–66, 171, 175, 181, 227, 231, 235, 270, 331, 333, 339, 345, 366, 376

Viacom 85, 338
Vulcan 2, 27, 43–44, 62, 68, 73, 88, 110, 115–16, 165, 171, 177, 194–95, 204, 213, 221, 226, 228, 232, 249, 254–57, 259, 260, 268, 273, 275–76, 279, 292, 295, 302, 308, 338, 360, 384, 386

war 2, 6, 8, 11, 25, 36, 49–50, 52–54, 56, 61, 64, 69, 75, 91, 108, 111, 170, 172, 175, 177, 179–80, 182, 211, 307–09
 see also Cold War
 Klingon and Federation war 5, 12, 33, 43, 48, 55, 115, 118, 120–22, 166, 170–71, 181, 197, 231–33, 235, 243, 249, 251, 253–55, 257, 259, 268, 274, 294–95, 311–12, 323, 361, 363, 373, 377, 383–84
war on terror 8, 106, 225
Western (film) 43, 48, 51, 65
white supremacy 244, 258–59, 270, 315, 367
whiteness 2, 41, 202, 215, 217, 256, 259, 280
Wilson, Rainn 130, 146, 382
Wiseman, Mary 27, 72, 121, 132, 172, 194, 253, 273, 287, 360
women scientists 13, 269, 271–73, 275–77, 280–81
worldbuilding 106, 109, 112, 116, 123, 148, 158, 391

Yeoh, Michelle 1–2, 9, 21, 43, 64, 89, 116, 158, 194, 206, 226, 246, 260, 267, 287, 308, 342, 384